Ex Líbrís

# Ordeal of the Union

Defender of the Union: DANIEL WEBSTER

# Ordeal of the Union

VOLUME II...

## A HOUSE DIVIDING

1852 · 1857

## by ALLAN NEVINS

"*Political history, to be intelligible and just,
must be based on social history in its largest sense*"
LETTERS OF JOHN RICHARD GREEN

New York · *CHARLES SCRIBNER'S SONS* · London

# CONTENTS

# ILLUSTRATIONS

vii

# Ordeal of the Union

# 1

## Enter the Pleasant Mr. Pierce

THAT GREAT NATIONAL LOTTERY, the Presidential campaign, in which so much of the gambling instinct of Americans finds satisfaction, involves a varying equation between personalities and issues. It was obvious as 1852 opened that personalities and party loyalty, not questions of public policy, would decide the coming contest. The country was enjoying a prosperous lull after the storm, and any mandate it gave would be for a continuance of the truce. Business interests had decreed that the recent compromise must stand, and with business was aligned the great mass of farmers, workmen, and professional folk. No man could be elected who was not regarded by the whole country, and particularly the uneasy South, as distinctly "safe." As for tariff policy, the banking system, internal improvements and foreign affairs, the old landmarks had not been disturbed during the Fillmore Administration, and these questions were not regarded as clear-cut campaign issues.

It was to be a Democratic year; so nearly everybody agreed. Four years earlier Taylor had been elected by martial fame and strategic position. Now he was dead, his colorless successor commanded no enthusiasm, and the Whig Party, without ideas or commanding new leaders, and with a deep inner schism between Sewardites and South, held a forlorn position.

### [ I ]

The fear of Democratic leaders was that the lingering cleavage between friends and foes of the Compromise might ruin their chances of victory. The resentful freesoil Democrats of the North and State Rights Democrats of the South, each side sure that it had been cheated, must be won back to the party banner. Such observers as Buchanan, peering from his Wheatland retirement as a fox peers from his burrow, believed that Massachusetts, New York, and Ohio were all precarious. Nevertheless, if Democrats could carry the South, Pennsylvania, and the Northwest, they could regain control of all three branches of the government. The conviction grew that a conservative pro-

3

Compromise Northerner for President, and a mild Southern Rights man for Vice-President, would make an ideal ticket.[1]

Every step in party management was taken with an eye to harmony. It became necessary early in 1851 to find a new editor for the Washington Union, for the venerable Thomas Ritchie had fallen into financial embarrassment. Arrangements were made by which Father Ritchie transferred this central Democratic organ to Andrew Jackson Donelson as editor, with Robert Armstrong his business partner.[2] As nephew, secretary, and confidential adviser to Jackson, and as loyal helper of Polk, Donelson had gained a wide public experience. A big, portly man, with a huge head wreathed in curling hair, a broad forehead, and a firm mouth, he possessed ample personal force. It was true that extravagance, a large family, and planting debts had thrown his finances into disorder, so that he owed money, among others, to Van Buren. But friends assured him that if he took over the Union he would get the contract to print the census returns of 1850, and could make one or two hundred thousand dollars out of it. A staunch upholder of the Compromise, he was nevertheless acceptable to many Southern Rights men, who knew that although a Tennesseean he had a large plantation and stock of slaves in Mississippi.[3]

Of tactful temper, Donelson took care to consult men of varying opinions. When his salutatory editorial appeared on April 15, 1851, he expressed a hope that it would irritate nobody. In particular, he had tried to please both Buchanan and Robert J. Walker on the tariff; a difficult matter, for one favored and the other opposed an increase in duties on railroad iron. It was understood that while the Union would resist any tampering with the Compromise, it would not go out of its way to attack the Rhetts and Quitmans. It was also understood that it would play no favorites among aspirants for the Democratic nomination. Perhaps the editor's best asset was his passionate faith in the party his uncle had done so much to recreate. The one cure for all existing evils, he wrote Buchanan, was the election of a Democratic President. "If this is not done I do not see how the Union can be preserved. The Whigs can never exert strong measures in order to secure the execution of the laws." [4]

1   See the sheaf of letters to Howell Cobb from various Southerners in February-June, 1852, U. B. Phillips, ed., Toombs, Stephens, Cobb Corr., 284-301. For the curious and absurd movement to nominate a Union ticket of Clay and Cass, see Henry S. Foote, Casket of Reminiscences, 83ff.

2   Robert M. McLane, March 31, 1851, to Buchanan; Buchanan Papers.

3   Buchanan to Cave Johnson, March 22, 1851; and see Cave Johnson to Buchanan, November 18, 1851. Buchanan Papers.

4   June 30, 1851; Buchanan Papers. For the disgust of John B. Lamar, a Union Democrat of Georgia, with the disposition of Buchanan and Donelson to assert that since the finality of the Compromise was conceded, any expression to that effect was supererogation, see his letter of March 8, 1852; Toombs, Stephens, Cobb Corr., 287, 288.

Every effort was made to suppress Democratic squabbling in the various States. In New York the partial harmony attained in the fall of 1851 was sedulously preserved, with the resourceful William L. Marcy, erstwhile foe of the Barnburners, now turning to them for support in his dream of the White House.[5] In Ohio the old quarrels slept. A battle between the pro-slavery and freesoil wings of the Indiana party, led respectively by the pugnacious Jesse D. Bright and the gentlemanly Joseph A. Wright, shook the party there to its foundations, but early in 1851 Bright won a decisive victory. He resided in Madison on the Ohio, where Southern feeling was so strong that any opponent of slavery became a political outcast; and he owned lands and slaves in Kentucky. Able, alert, and harshly domineering, he had made himself master of the southern part of the State. Like Oliver P. Morton later, he was too imperious to brook any opposition; and terming Wright—actually a man of high character, born in Pennsylvania and educated in what later became the Indiana State University at Bloomington—a political gambler and scoundrel, he used every weapon to defeat him. With William H. English and other capable lieutenants fighting at his side, Bright not only secured his reëlection to the Senate, but cemented his general control over Indiana politics.[6]

This was an event destined to have national significance. Stephen A. Douglas, watching the contest from Chicago, would rue the day when the hot-tempered slaveholder, a boon companion of Southern Senators and Representatives in Washington, thus gained his additional six years in the upper chamber. But the struggle once over, and Bright satisfied with his victory, Indiana Democrats turned to the national battle with a fair degree of unity.

The upheaval in Missouri which early in 1851 had cruelly turned Thomas Hart Benton out of the Senate, giving his seat to a Whig lawyer of St. Louis named Henry S. Geyer, had naturally left rankling memories behind it. Benton himself, toiling in shirt sleeves on that *Thirty Years' View* which he hoped would become a political Bible, read in every home, was full of proud and disdainful wrath. He wrote Hannibal Hamlin that he did not let his literary work debar him from that vital task, "the redemption of the State of Missouri from the Whigs and nullifiers." [7] Though Benton was equally opposed to Geyer, the stiff politician who catered to railroad promoters and slavery interests, and Atchison, the rough "disunionist" Senator, he of course abominated Atchison's principles the more deeply. A large constituency in St. Louis was always ready

5 The skilful hand of Horatio Seymour brought a majority of the New York delegates behind Marcy; Alexander, *Political History New York*, II, 170. If he could not have the presidency, his friends wanted him in the next Cabinet.

6 William S. Gerber, "A Chapter in the Early History of Journalism in Indiana," MS, Indiana State Library.

7 Meigs, *Benton*, 423.

to support the old Roman, as his successful run for the House in the fall of 1852 was to demonstrate. Nearly everybody, however, regarded the Compromise battle as a closed chapter, and the party marched into the presidential canvass with fairly cohesive ranks. Meanwhile, the divisions in Pennsylvania, where the crafty Simon Cameron was stealthily trying to undermine Buchanan, and had seduced Richard Brodhead, the new Senator, to assist him in that enterprise, aroused great local animosity, but would not endanger any national ticket so long as no Pennsylvanian headed it. In Massachusetts alone did the Democratic quarrels portend possible disaster. The schism between the conservative wing under B. F. Hallett and his aides, and the freesoil Democrats of Rantoul's stripe, would be hard to close.[8]

[ II ]

But when it came to the choice of a Democratic candidate, intense rivalries developed. The principal aspirants were three Senators, Cass, Douglas, and Sam Houston; James Buchanan and W. L. Marcy, both with long public records; and W. O. Butler of Kentucky, a Mexican War major-general who "looked well on a horse" but was best remembered as a Jacksonian protégé and candidate for Vice-President in 1848. It could not be said that the party lacked men of sage experience. All these figures except Douglas were old or elderly, and had been in public affairs for at least thirty years. Cass, Marcy, Butler, and Houston had actually been officers in the War of 1812, and Buchanan a private. However ripely experienced, they seemed to belong to the past rather than the future. Indeed, Cass, if elected, would be seventy before his inauguration, and Marcy sixty-six.

It was natural that the party element which called itself Young America should turn to Douglas, who was young in years, bold in temper, and pugnacious in spirit. The determination and enterprise of Disraeli and Bentinck in the previous decade had made the Young England party famous, and Douglas's followers represented a not dissimilar combination of economic conservatism and political aggressiveness. As Young England had used Disraeli's vision, interest in lower-class welfare, and witty eloquence to revivify the Tory party of the younger Pitt and Canning, so Young America hoped to use Douglas's brains, energy, and combativeness to revivify the Democracy of Jackson. They wished the United States to follow a more trenchant set of policies: to drive forward the settlement of the West; to drop the quarrel over slavery in favor of a realistic development of national power; to help the oppressed democrats and radicals in

8  Gideon Welles, September 18, 1851, to John M. Niles; Welles Papers.

Europe; and to adopt a bold expansionist programme in the Caribbean.[9] They counted on the support of cotton-planters, Northern merchants, railroad-builders, land-speculators, and the German and Irish immigrants. Douglas, still too young to be widely popular or to possess a powerful machine, now set himself to create a following and build up an organization; and he was abetted by men who had more drive than discretion.[10]

For a time in the summer and fall of 1851 the dynamic Illinoisan was sanguine of success. Travelling extensively, speaking at commencements, agricultural fairs, and other tempting occasions, conferring with politicians, he seemed to make astonishing progress. What he and his supporters called The Ticket—Douglas and R. M. T. Hunter—would just suit the general demand for a Compromise Northerner and a mildly anti-Compromise Southerner. George N. Sanders of the Patent Office was the Johannes Factotum of the movement, importuning editors, buttonholing politicians, and pulling every string. That veteran German-American newspaperman, Francis J. Grund, used his entrée to the columns of the Philadelphia *Ledger* and New York *Herald* for all it was worth. "Douglas is going it with a rush," he wrote.[11] David L. Yulee enthusiastically brought little Florida into line. Beverley Tucker—not the novelist, but a nephew of plausible and boisterous manners who had built up a claim-agent business in Washington, and who dabbled in politics—threw himself into the crusade with pen and voice. Visiting New York in the spring of 1851, he helped whip up sentiment for Douglas among the Democrats of that city, whose brothy bhoys recognized in the Illinoisan a kindred spirit. A practised lobbyist, Tucker thought he could prove himself a match for the regular party leaders. "*Young America* is to speak out and is to be *heard* and *heeded* too at the coming election, and we intend to prove to you that it is not necessary to be professional men in *politics* or *science* to be felt in the country," he assured Hunter.[12] In New England various machine politicians took up the Little Giant, whose dignity was enhanced by an honorary degree this summer from Middlebury College in his native Vermont.

"Everything looks well—much better than either of us had a right to expect," Douglas jubilantly confided to Hunter on May 6, 1851. He was then in New York. "In this state I think both divisions of the party will come together

9 What many Young Americans had in mind was expressed by an Arkansas leader who wrote that triumph was certain "with Douglas and Cuba inscribed on our party flag, as in 1844 we had Polk, Dallas, and Texas." *National Intelligencer*, April 13, 1852.

10 Douglas's friends, John A. Dix wrote Gideon Welles in the autumn of 1851, "have been very busy everywhere"; Welles Papers.

11 March 20, 1851; R. M. T. Hunter Papers, Univ. of Va. Douglas told the farmers of upstate New York this fall that planting and farming were mutual allies, and that the protective tariff system was inimical to both. N. Y. *Weekly Tribune*, September 27, 1851.

12 April 5, 1851; Hunter Papers, Univ. of Va.

upon the basis of *entire silence on the slavery question* and support the Ticket. This is the opinion of our best-informed friends. I have declined the Public Dinner tendered me. Mr. Sanders will send you the correspondence when published. I leave for Chicago today. I have seen the invitation for a Public Dinner to you. All the great business houses have signed it and a better list of names cannot be selected in this city. Our friends are unanimous that you should accept and will urge you to do so. My opinion however is that you should decline in a well-considered and judicious letter, but at the same time notifying them that you intend to visit the city in a quiet way during the hot weather and perhaps some of the northern watering places where you will be pleased to meet them in the social circle, etc., etc. I think you should come here this summer and remain some time, but I doubt the policy of a public demonstration. All looks exceeding well in N' Carolina. Of Virginia you can judge better than I can, altho I believe the Compromise men will cheerfully unite on you for the sake of harmony. At least many of them tell me they would do so. Write me at Chicago, fully but confidentially, and I shall read your letters and *instantly burn them.*" This characteristic letter showed the impetuosity of his ambition. His friends were working so hard that by the close of 1851 the New York *Tribune* thought him leading the field.[13] When Congress met, he seized the opportunity offered by Kossuth's visit to hurl defiance at the crowned heads of Europe—and called for the annexation of Cuba.

But in pushing so early and relentlessly, Douglas was sure to raise up enemies. Moreover, their weapon was at hand—the cry that he represented predatory special interests. The freebooter crusade led by that little whipster, Senator William R. King wrote Buchanan on March 6, 1852, was shocking. "Every vulture that would prey upon the public carcass, and every creature who expects the reward of office, are moving heaven and earth in his behalf. To his elevation they look with confidence for the realization of all their base projects, and should the country be cursed with his rule, I have no doubt, from my knowledge of the man, that they will be able to thrust their dirty hands into the Treasury up to the shoulders."[14] Gideon Welles took the same view. "The vicious influences of the party," the Connecticut editor told a friend, "the jobbers for claims, the plunderers of the national domain, are urging Douglas, as well as those who go for internal improvements, ocean steamers,

---

13  Hunter Papers, Univ. of Va. Greeley's journal had a low opinion of Douglas. Noting in the spring of 1851 that he "is dining and speechifying at Richmond in the most approved style," and seeking "to make capital" there, it added: "It is not a little curious that when a Northern man marries in the South and acquires slave property (which of course he don't own, his wife taking that responsibility), he immediately begins to fancy himself a fit candidate for the Presidency." N. Y. *Weekly Tribune*, April 12, 1851. Douglas in 1847 had married Martha Denny Martin of North Carolina.

14  Buchanan Papers.

and so on."[15] When the Douglas men in Louisiana allied themselves with the theatrical State Rights enthusiast, Senator Pierre Soulé, the Frenchman's old-time rival John Slidell became a venomous opponent, and caught up the hue and cry. The Douglas-Soulé partisans, who had bought the New Orleans *Delta* and four country papers, were base politicians and adventurers, declared Slidell. If they could nominate Douglas for President, "I should despair of the republic, and although I should be cautious in expressing such an opinion, no consideration could induce me to support him."[16]

It was quite true that an industrious bevy of lobbyists and privilege-hunters were supporting Douglas. Besides Beverley Tucker, they included the notorious George Law, a burly, whiskery, self-reliant contractor and promoter, who had long been active in railroading and Hudson River steamboating, and who had become the principal figure in the United States Mail Steamship Company, which held a lucrative contract for a bi-weekly mail service from New York to Havana and the Isthmus; Knox Walker, a politician sometimes called the prince of lobbyists; and the before-mentioned John Louis O'Sullivan, who loved filibustering and tropical annexations.[17] Several Western land speculators played their part. Indeed, Douglas, who since his settlement in Chicago in 1847 had made a good deal of money in real estate, was something of a Western land speculator himself. But the movement had its very respectable side. That sober Penobscot Democrat, Hannibal Hamlin, who had been about Washington almost ten years, first in the House and then the Senate, was interested in it. The Little Giant had a devoted Illinois lieutenant in William A. Richardson, soldier, lawyer, and Representative from the Quincy district. Reputable newspapers had "hoisted" Douglas's name: the Chicago *Democrat*, the Springfield (Ill.) *State Register*, the Memphis *Express*, the Louisville *Democrat*, and many lesser sheets. While Douglas had his brassy side and was no moral paragon, his public integrity was never impugned, and he grew steadily toward statesmanship.

As 1852 began, the Senator was busy scattering notes of encouragement. "I need not assure you," he wrote William H. English, "that I feel grateful for your efforts in my behalf, nor that I am also grateful at the prospect that Indiana will be for me with Illinois when the day of trial arrives."[18] "My prospects improve every day," he informed a friend on February 25. "If two or three Western States will speak out in my favor the battle is over." But the elder politicians were confident that his candidacy would prove a flash in the pan. Buchanan predicted that it would break down utterly unless Knox Walker,

15  Welles, February 25, March 19, 1852; Welles Papers.
16  Sears, *Slidell*, 87ff.
17  Robert G. Albion, *Rise of New York Port*, 158, 365; *Dictionary of American Biography*.
18  December 29, 1851; English Papers, Indiana State Library.

who was going to Tennessee to offer General Pillow the bait of a vice-presidential nomination which had already been dangled before Hunter, should somehow get the delegates from Jackson's State. Before 1852 was five weeks old Buchanan was exultant: "Douglas is, undoubtedly, sinking fast." [19]

He wrote with reason, for a heavy calamity befell Douglas. Raising some money, late in 1851 George N. Sanders purchased O'Sullivan's attempt to do for American Democracy what *Blackwood's* did for British Toryism, the *Democratic Review*. An irascible, hotheaded man, he determined to throw it into the thick of the battle. Sanders would ruin any man he joined, one observer acridly remarked [20]—and he was right. The January issue bloomed out with a sensational article called "Eighteen-Fifty-Two and the Presidency." Assailing timid Quaker policies, it announced that a new generation of American leaders had appeared; men not trammelled by the "anterior era," who would bring not only "young blood" but "young ideas" to the party. "The statesmen of a previous generation, with their personal antipathies and their personal claims, with personal greatness or personal inefficiency, must get out of the way." A chorus of dismay arose. Douglas seemed making war against the elder statesmen, and the "old fogies" at once united against the "young rogues."

But Sanders was just beginning. Irritated by the New York *Evening Post's* description of Douglas as Law's steamboat candidate, he prepared a hotter article. "Don't be scared," he wrote Douglas, "it will not be thunder, but it shall be an earthquake." [21] Declaring the party needed a candidate with a policy, this peppery essay excoriated W. O. Butler as typical of numerous aspirants without convictions, an assault which hurt the more because it was true. Southern friends of Butler boiled with anger, and on March 3 John C. Breckinridge rose in the House to attack Douglas as responsible for the cut-and-thrust, knock-down and drag-out course of the magazine. In that month's issue Sanders answered with a still more outrageous article, denouncing Breckinridge, Marcy, and the old fogies generally, and declaring emphatically for Douglas's nomination. With a nest of hornets about his head, he was striking out blindly.

Distressed and alarmed, Douglas hastily besought Sanders to adopt a milder policy—but in vain. The April issue of the *Review* declared that a vicious conspiracy was being developed. It was a conspiracy to misrepresent and vilify Douglas, simply because "he was not so old in years or ideas that his friends or his enemies could fairly include him in the category of imbeciles we have delineated." Douglas explained to other Democrats that he had no connection

19  To Cave Johnson, December 3, 1851, and to Henry A. Wise, February 4, 1852; Buchanan Papers.
20  E. Lynch, July 24, 1852, to Franklin Pierce; Pierce Papers.
21  February 3, 1852; Douglas Papers.

with or control over the *Review*. He had approved of Sanders' acquisition of the magazine, had helped induce certain men to contribute, and had signed a testimonial after the first offending issue had appeared—but that was all.[22] He now assured the old "charlatans" and "fogies" that he venerated them and prized their wisdom. But the editor had given conservative leaders their opportunity. Already highly irritated by Douglas's whirlwind campaign for delegates, they turned upon him savagely. Representative William H. Polk of Tennessee and others abruptly deserted the champion of Young America. The ill-feeling made any compromise or bargain with the older men impossible, and his chances rapidly dwindled. When he stepped up to sage old Francis P. Blair one spring day to demand, "Now that Butler is used up you will support me?" Blair coolly said that he would not.[23]

Any man less self-confident and aggressive than Douglas would have felt crushed. Buchanan's supporters half-contemptuously offered him the second place on their ticket if he would join them.[24] The gossip now current about him was summed up in a graphic letter of Andrew Johnson's. He was the candidate of the cormorants, a hothouse product brought forward by a set of plunderers who, if successful, would "disembowel the treasury, disgrace the country and damn the party to all eternity." These men threw their arms about his neck on the street; they read complimentary pieces to him in oyster cellars and sent them off to subsidized sheets; they stood beside him in barrooms to laugh, drink, and discuss some swindling claim on the government. The whole concern were miserable banditti, "much fitter to occupy cells in the penitentiary than places of state." [25]

Douglas, in fact, had raised up an implacable league of enemies. His loose personal habits—though, as one journalist remarked, he was often tight; his ill-chosen associates; his humble origin and self-made Western career, exciting the scorn of Eastern and Southern aristocrats; his unorthodox ways, shocking his jealous elders; even his transcendent abilities, grudgingly acknowledged—these all counted against him. But with characteristic tenacity he kept on fighting. Far too resilient of spirit, too sanguine of temper, too able and masterful, to give up, he maintained a Washington headquarters which became famous for its whiskey and cigars, was full of Western visitors, and coined daily epigrams about "ten cent Jimmy Buchanan" and "Cass whose reputation was beyond the C."

22  Douglas Papers, December–April, 1851–52.
23  Blair to Van Buren, April 30, 1852; Van Buren Papers.
24  Cave Johnson, May 6, 1852, Buchanan Papers; Milton, *Eve of Conflict*, 89; "Reminiscences of Washington," *Atlantic Monthly*, May, 1880, p. 663ff.
25  April 4, 1852; Roy F. Nichols, *Democratic Machine*, 117, 118.

## [ III ]

Equally sad were the reverses which befell Buchanan's hopes. This white-haired, dignified, benevolent-looking gentleman, who with many vacillations and timidities stealthily edged himself toward the presidency, had collected an army of powerful supporters. Strongly Southern in weight, they included his messmate of early Washington days, that spare, prim old bachelor, William R. King of Alabama, commonly known as Miss Nancy King; Henry A. Wise of Virginia and Cave Johnson of Tennessee, also old friends; Isaac Toucey of Connecticut; John Slidell of Louisiana; and Slidell's nephew by marriage, the wealthy, pushing August Belmont of New York. Though Cass had aspirations of his own, he preferred Buchanan to anybody but himself, and let Buchanan know it.[26] For a time it was hoped that William L. Marcy of New York would join the group. But the self-contained, saturnine Marcy refused to commit himself. An experienced politician, he had a strongly marked face, with shaggy eyebrows which half concealed his piercing and observant glance, so that his expression was cunningly masked while he studied the thought and feeling of others. Gifted with a dry sense of humor, he had a way of laughing silently while he shook like a bowlful of jelly. He was never averse to playing his own game while gently smiling on (and at) others.[27]

Slidell in the spring of 1851 urged Buchanan to overcome his "dread of locomotion" and visit Saratoga, the prime resort of politicians, in an effort to reach an understanding with Marcy and others. When Buchanan, to whom positive action was always distasteful, declined, Slidell hastened northward to his native State. At the Springs and in the metropolis he explored the situation. He found Robert J. Walker professing the friendliest sentiments—but he distrusted the Mississippian. Talking with Marcy, he met such noncommittal friendliness that he urged Buchanan to offer him strong inducements for support. "I consider his advocacy of your nomination all-important," he wrote.[28]

In repeated conferences with Belmont and others, Slidell also developed a scheme for establishing a powerful New York daily, edited on the conservative principles of the London *Times*. Since Bryant's *Evening Post* had become belligerently freesoil, a thick-and-thin Democratic journal seemed much needed. It could be made the leading commercial paper, Slidell believed, and given a profitable circulation. Perhaps Caleb Cushing would consent to direct it, but Buchanan's friend John W. Forney should be political editor, and it must of course support Buchanan for the presidency. The industrious Forney, who was

26  George Plitt, April 4, 1852; Buchanan Papers.
27  Wise, *Seven Decades of the Union*, 234–236.
28  August 8, 1851, Buchanan Papers.

working day and night for Buchanan, carrying on the Harrisburg *Pennsylvanian*, writing the address and resolutions of the Pennsylvania State convention, helping to nab delegates, and doing all kinds of disagreeable odd jobs, certainly merited such a place.[29] Much of the needed money was rapidly subscribed by Democratic merchants, bankers, and lawyers who felt that Buchanan, Slidell, and Belmont would make a trustworthy group in managing the government.[30]

But just as success seemed imminent the combination broke up. "At this propitious moment," as Buchanan lamented to Cave Johnson, "the Van Burens began to tickle Marcy with the idea of being President himself. His leading friends Cutting, O'Conor, Sedgwick, and others who were to support me hauled off; and backed out from the paper, unless it should remain perfectly neutral on the subject of the presidency. This they did after an interview with the Governor [Marcy]. . . . The whole concern fell through; because my friends had the most money." Belmont, the largest single subscriber, clung staunchly to Buchanan. There was some talk of compromising on a paper committed to nobody, with some other editor than Forney, but this proved impossible.[31] Bitterly disappointed, Slidell wrote Buchanan that the selfish Marcy might yet see the light and help turn the scales in the proper direction, but the chances were that he would cling to ambitions until too late. This was an astute view, for Marcy was an even more active candidate than he let Slidell suppose. His lieutenants in the spring of 1852 were seeking support in Louisiana itself.[32]

In other States also Buchanan met disappointment—though for a time his hopes ran high. As 1851 closed his friends were hard at work in New York, he had received pleasing assurances from Maine and Connecticut, he had some chance in the rest of New England, and he was stronger in Pennsylvania than ever before. Christmas found him certain that his prospects were bright, and if he could believe assurances from Washington, were steadily improving. "This strength," he correctly remarked, "is in great part derived from the

---

29 Cf. George Plitt, May 21, 1851, on Forney; Buchanan Papers.

30 Buchanan's prime articles of faith were two in number: a restricted central government, doing as little and spending as little as possible, and an administration of that government which stood firmly against freesoil movements and was fair to the South. These tenets were expressed over and over again in his confidential letters. Writing early in 1852 to C. Neale, for example, he testified his admiration for Virginia: "An Administration of the Federal Government founded upon her ancient principles of 1798 and 1799 can alone save the country from a latitudenous (*sic*) construction of the Constitution and a wasteful and extravagant expenditure of public money." Auchampaugh, *Robert Tyler*, 50, 51. And in a letter to a political aide he burst out: "I would tremble for the fate of my country should Scott be elected President by a Northern and Northwestern sectional vote." To C. L. Ward, July 14, 1851; Buchanan Papers. The fate of the nation might have been different had Buchanan not been hag-ridden by this fear of a Southern revolt against Northern policies.

31 Belmont, December 6, 1851, to Buchanan; Buchanan Papers.

32 Cf. Sears, *Slidell*, 85-95.

general impression that I am strong with all branches of the Southern Democracy." [33] Sentiment in Tennessee was divided between himself and Cass, with some voters favoring Houston. By early February he was writing Henry A. Wise in complacent vein: "From the information which I daily receive, I am convinced you are right in supposing that Virginia is with me, and I shall be nominated. Unless greatly mistaken in the signs of the times, they point more and more to this result." He cheered on his Virginia friends, pointing out that the Old Dominion's delegates might determine his fate. The noisy but insignificant Cameron faction in Pennsylvania would send emissaries to Richmond, he warned, and scatter their guerrilla sheets broadcast in an effort to prove that he could not carry his own State. "This is simply ridiculous." [34]

But Virginia did not pronounce for Buchanan with the unanimity for which he had hoped. Despite all Wise's efforts, the convention there followed precedent in leaving the delegates unbound, and while a majority were certainly for Buchanan, a minority seemed to favor Douglas. New Jersey, where the monopolistic Camden & Amboy Railroad was somehow popularly identified with Buchanan's fortunes, revolted and chose a set of delegates who, though uninstructed, supported Cass. California and Maryland were lost. More disappointing still was the result in Louisiana. Here the personal hostility between Soulé and Slidell was extremely bitter; it was impossible for the one to obtain a Douglas delegation or the other a Buchanan delegation; and a group of Cass men was sent to the national convention. This was the best arrangement that Slidell could make.[35] Such reverses were discouraging, for the Northwest was fairly sure to support Cass or Douglas.

In the end Buchanan, still a formidable aspirant, was left with Pennsylvania (where the State convention in March required explicit pledges of every delegate) and a Southern block his main support. To be sure, at home Simon Cameron still pursued him with unrelenting hostility. The two men lived in the same section, had many interests in common, and did not as yet differ radically in opinions. But personal dislike and jealous ambition for control made them sworn enemies. To the last, Cameron supported Cass. He had banking, railroad, and newspaper interests; many of his political friendships dated back thirty years; and he and his firm ally Senator Richard Brodhead exercised wide influence and held some counties in the palm of their hands. As an ironmaster he had been irritated by the low-tariff views of those Southerners whom Buchanan so assiduously courted, and other manufacturers agreed with him. Most parts of the Quaker commonwealth, however, took pride in the idea of a

33  To Cave Johnson, December 3, 22, 1851; Buchanan Papers.
34  To Wise, February 4, March 18, 1852; Buchanan Papers.
35  William R. King, March 24, 1852; Buchanan Papers.

son in the White House, and Buchanan could count on the general loyalty of the delegation. He could count, too, on a fairly compact body of cotton men and Virginians.

Of the other aspirants, Marcy was a man of fine qualities, liked even by political opponents. An unprejudiced umpire would possibly have pronounced him the best fitted of all the aspirants to be President. Of old Yankee stock, a graduate of Brown, a good lawyer and forcible writer, he placed an individual stamp on all his activities. No one could deny that this protégé of Van Buren and the old Albany Regency had been an efficient governor (his support of a geological survey resulted in giving his name to the highest mountain of the State), and a highly competent Secretary of War. His geniality, honesty, and administrative grasp commanded respect. "He has enough of the witchery of mischievous fun and tact to make him racy as a politician and delightful as an acquaintance," wrote a friend. "He is as piquantly mischievous as Mephistopheles himself. This may be the reason that he has been, comparatively with other public men, much underrated." [36] But he was involved in the unhappy broils of feud-ridden New York. Daniel S. Dickinson, convinced that the Barnburners (now successfully courting Marcy) were responsible for the party defeats of '48, had determined to do everything in his power to see Cass renominated. The New York delegation was split, twenty-four for Marcy and eleven for Cass. Moreover, the bhoys of New York city preferred Douglas. The strategy of Marcy's followers was to have him selected as second choice by as many delegations as possible, but at no time did he muster genuine strength.

The venerable Cass, with his pompous, surly manner, unique talent for straddling difficult issues, and very real abilities, was a more formidable figure. But in the West, where his principal strength lay, he met a sharp rivalry from Douglas. Moreover, he was unpopular with Southern Rights men, for he was an intense lover of the Union and hater of secession talk. Some thought that even if nominated he would find it difficult to obtain Southern support. [37] Above all, he was handicapped by the memory of his defeat four years earlier. As for W. O. Butler, he lacked distinction. Then, too, it was reported that Sumner, John Van Buren, and F. P. Blair, Sr., favored him, and half the South would not touch with a ten-foot pole any man who bore the least taint of Free-Soilism. [38] If Cass was risky, he was worse! Conversely, such men as Dallas of Pennsylvania and Dickinson of New York were too much committed to the Southern standpoint to be strong in vital parts of the North.

36  F. Byrdsall, December 1, 1851; Buchanan Papers.
37  William R. King, December 12, 1851; Buchanan Papers.
38  Edmund Burke to Pierce, April 9, 1852, Pierce Papers; John A. Dix, December 6, 1851, Welles Papers.

## [ IV ]

Obviously, the leading candidates were busy trying to kill each other's chances, and by the spring of 1852 they had so nearly accomplished this that politicians were peering about for a dark horse. A New England group had been magnifying the name of Levi Woodbury, the puritanical, conservative jurist whom Polk had appointed to Story's seat on the Supreme Court. Caleb Cushing, Hannibal Hamlin, and Benjamin F. Butler were enlisted, and in due time Benton and even the reluctant Blair ("a sad nostrum," he wrote) moved to join the combination—for they saw in Woodbury a fellow-Jacksonian. But when the judge died in September, 1851, it became necessary to find a successor. Various New Englanders then turned to Franklin Pierce, a younger man of the Jacksonian school, who had gained some reputation as a brigadier-general in Scott's army during the march on Mexico City. A mass convention which met in New Hampshire early in 1852 to select a candidate for governor was skilfully induced to recommend Pierce to the Baltimore Convention, though whether for the presidency or vice-presidency was not stated. Pierce then stunned his friends by publishing a letter declaring that the use of his name at Baltimore would be "utterly repugnant" to him.[39] But they were confident that they could persuade him to take a more amiable attitude; the Concord Regency Democrats organized a movement; and two politicians, Edmund Burke and B. B. French, brought all their influence to bear.

Burke, a friend of Pierce who had been Congressman, commissioner of patents, and co-editor with Ritchie of the Washington *Union*, but who had now resumed legal practise, journeyed to the capital in March, 1852. His ostensible business was patents; his real errand was politics. He was shortly writing Pierce that he had carefully analyzed the situation. The three most prominent candidates were Cass, Buchanan, and Douglas, but Buchanan would have such scanty support outside Pennsylvania that the real battle would probably be between the other two. "The old experienced politicians here are of the opinion that it will result in the defeat of both." The convention would then turn to the lesser candidates: to Marcy, Dickinson, Butler, or Linn Boyd.

"Now," ran Burke's counsel, "in my judgment if at the proper time—at the Convention—you will allow your name to be used as a compromise candidate, you stand as good a chance for the nomination as any man I can think of. In casual conversation I have asked Southern gentlemen how you would suit the South, and they have invariably replied most favorably." John S. Barbour of Virginia, destined to be prominent in the coming national convention, had told Burke that a majority of his State convention did not really want Buchanan,

39 Roy F. Nichols, *Franklin Pierce*, 193.

Cass, or Douglas, but would warmly support Pierce. Representative John G. Floyd of Long Island had declared that both New York factions would do the same. "Hence I believe you are among the very probable candidates for the Presidency. . . ." [40] B. B. French also wrote Pierce, plying him with arguments.

And Pierce, as expected, quickly consented to let his name be used. His divisional commander in Mexico, General Gideon Pillow, joined the New England group, first working in Tennessee and then visiting various seaboard cities. He hoped to be chosen for Vice-President on Pierce's ticket. Letters were introduced into the Baltimore *Sun* and Philadelphia *Public Ledger* urging Pierce's availability. Meanwhile, Burke established friendly contacts with leaders in the Cass, Douglas, and Marcy camps. While part of the Massachusetts delegates, led by Caleb Cushing, were for Pierce, others under B. F. Hallett were for Cass; and visiting Boston, Burke induced Hallett to agree that if Cass were put out of the running, the delegation would unite on the New Hampshire leader. Maine and New Hampshire were thoroughly safe. [41]

It was agreed by Pierce's adherents that, as he desired, his name should not be presented on the first ballots, but his followers should scatter their votes among the other leaders, quietly letting it be known that they thought him the best man to "harmonize" the convention if it went into a long deadlock. It was also agreed that he must divest himself of all taint of Free-Soilism. Early in January he had been heckled at a public meeting into admitting that he disliked the Fugitive Slave Act and thought it inhuman! An opportunity to rectify his position was offered by a letter which Robert G. Scott, a Virginia editor who was understood to be a mouthpiece for some of the strongest Southern leaders, addressed on May 17 to all candidates. [42] Scott asked each man whether he would sustain the Compromise, would discountenance all attempts to amend the Fugitive Slave Act, and if a bill for that purpose passed, would veto it. Pierce, at the prompting of his managers, ignored the letter, but sent one of the Maine delegates a candid statement. He declared that he and his friends, having fought the battle in New Hampshire for the fugitive slave law upon the ground of constitutional right, held that the various compromise measures must be "substantially and firmly maintained." [43]

The last weeks before the Democratic convention demonstrated the uneasiness of the sectional truce. The House in April adopted resolutions offered by two Georgians, Jackson and Hillyer, one asserting the "binding efficacy" of

40 April 9, 1852, Pierce Papers.
41 Fuess, *Caleb Cushing*, II, 118ff; Nichols, *Democratic Machine*, 122–127. Fuess quotes a law student in Pierce's office as having said the day the New Hampshire delegation left for Baltimore that the Mexican War generals had "fixed up all the arrangements to make Frank Pierce the Democratic nominee for President."
42 Harry Hibbard, May 29, 1852, Pierce Papers.
43 N. Y. *Evening Post*, June 12, 1852.

the compromise bills, including the fugitive slave law; the other declaring that the compromise laws were to be regarded as a permanent adjustment of the questions they embraced. But the vote was only 101 to 64 for the former, 100 to 65 for the latter.[44] The weightiest opposition came from Northern Whigs and Northern Democrats who could not accept the fugitive slave law as a finality. So heavy an adverse vote shocked many Union men. Nor could it escape notice that many State conventions of both parties neglected to mention the Compromise. Another straw in the wind was Andrew Jackson Donelson's sudden resignation (May 12) of his editorship of the *Union*.[45] The radical free-soilers and radical States Rights men had joined hands to withhold from this loyal Unionist the public printing contracts on which he had counted. Leaving the capital, Donelson pronounced a curse on both their houses. Such Southern extremists as Soulé, and such Northern radicals as Rantoul, he wrote, would never tolerate an honest editor who condemned secessionist agitation on the one side and the nullification of Federal law on the other.[46]

## [ V ]

The Democratic convention, meeting in Baltimore June 1st, organized itself with John W. Davis of Indiana as president. Every candidate had his lieutenants on hand. For Buchanan, the faithful Cave Johnson, Henry A. Wise, John W. Forney, and J. C. Van Dyke were indefatigably busy. Marcy, unaware that Caleb Cushing had deserted to the Pierce forces, wrote him that his attendance was a matter of the first importance! [47] Dickinson, Cameron, and Jesse D. Bright of Indiana took charge of the interests of Cass, who seemed stronger than anybody else. Edmund Burke and other members of the Pierce group were quietly at work. The noisiest element, naturally, were the Douglasites. From New York and other large cities came what disgusted conservatives called a series of "rowdy gangs," who filled hotel lobbies, purlieus of the convention hall, and galleries.[48] They did the Illinoisan little good. "The associations of Douglas and his active supporters, jobbers, and so on, lost him ground every day for two weeks before the convention—and had they secured his nomination I could not have voted the ticket," declared Cave Johnson. Marcy likewise

44  Nichols, *Democratic Machine*, 39, 40.
45  Cave Johnson, a friend of Donelson's, was deeply disturbed by the events which forced that man from his editorial chair, and sent Pierce a plaintive letter. With the great body of Compromise men, who were at least four-fifths of the Southern voters, he thought Donelson thoroughly congenial. It was the dissatisfaction and hostility of "the extreme Southern members" of Congress which had led to his ejection. June 10, 1852, Pierce Papers.
46  July 26, 1852, Pierce Papers.
47  May 21, 1852, Cushing Papers.
48  F. Byrdsall, November 15, 1852, Buchanan Papers.

left his testimony that the disreputable agents for Young America aroused great alarm.[49]

Balloting began on Thursday, June 3. The delegates present numbered 288, and to the accompaniment of a wild yell of joy from Smith Van Buren, who detested Cass and Buchanan, the two-thirds rule was adopted. On the first ballot the vote stood 116 for Cass, 93 for Buchanan, 20 for Douglas, and 31 for half a dozen other men.[50] That day and the next the convention took one fruitless ballot after another, reaching the thirty-third before adjournment on Friday evening. On the twenty-second ballot Buchanan's vote rose to 104. Had Marcy then come to his aid, he would probably have been named, but the New Yorker held coldly aloof. Buchanan's vote immediately fell, and that of Douglas rose to a high mark of 93. His enemies, to prevent his nomination, forthwith threw sufficient votes to Cass to give that leader 133 on the thirty-third ballot. At this point the Buchanan forces, determined for various good reasons never to let Cass enter the White House, forced an adjournment, and called an evening council of war at Carroll Hall.[51] One reason was that they did not want to let Simon Cameron boast of victory!

At this conference Pennsylvania and five Southern States supporting Buchanan—Virginia, North Carolina, Georgia, Alabama, and Mississippi—were represented. A variety of interests appeared. Many Southerners were anxious to have the future of their section safeguarded, which meant that they wished to defeat Cass and Douglas as champions of popular sovereignty. By virtue of the two-thirds rule, the South held a clear veto. The North and West might possess a strong numerical majority, but while the South could not, and did not wish to, impose its own man on the party, it could block any man whom it considered dangerous. Many other delegates were genuinely anxious to see Buchanan carry off the prize. A plan was worked out which pleased all groups. It was decided that if they could prove to the adherents of several minor candidates that their favorites had no chance, then a successful rally about Buchanan might be arranged. Three States, Pennsylvania, Georgia, and Alabama, were directed to cling to Buchanan as staunchly as the Old Guard, dying but never surrendering; the remaining three were to experiment with other men. Plainly, the scheme held many risks, for one of the experiments might prove only too successful! It seemed the only possible expedient, however, and if a good man did win, no

49 Johnson July 23, Marcy June 6, 1852; Buchanan Papers.
50 Much bitterness had developed between some elements of the Cass and Buchanan forces. One observer called them fierce as tigers. Certain Buchanan men never forgave Marcy for not letting his delegates go to their leader. Van Dyke to Buchanan, June 8, 1852, Buchanan Papers. But Marcy later assured Buchanan that he dared not release them, for if he had done so many would instantly have voted for Douglas. It appears that Marcy had no real hope of the nomination once the convention opened; Fuess, *Cushing*, II, 124.
51 Nichols, *Democratic Machine*, 137, 138.

great harm was done. For whom should they vote? "We settled unanimously on Marcy, Pierce, and Butler," writes Henry A. Wise.[52] But some Virginia delegates resolved also to give Dickinson a run for his money.

On Saturday morning, in pursance of this plan, the Virginia delegation suddenly switched its vote to Dickinson. But he refused to countenance the movement, declaring that as Cass's manager he could not stand for the nomination. The North Carolina and Mississippi delegations thereupon swung to Marcy, who continued to gain until on the forty-sixth ballot he had ninety-eight votes. Then the Cass and Buchanan men refused to let him go further, and he dropped back. The time had now come to experiment with a third candidate, proving that he too could not win. On the forty-seventh ballot a number of delegates turned to Pierce, who had been slowly gaining ground. His managers had conferred with both wings of the New York delegation, assuring them that he supported the Compromise as a final settlement, and was uncommitted as to the patronage, which he would presumably distribute among all who backed him, without regard to factional divisions.[53] Similar assurances had been given to other States. On the forty-eighth ballot more delegates moved into the Pierce column.

Then, on the forty-ninth, Dobbin of North Carolina announced with an eloquent flourish that his State was voting for Pierce, and the slipping delegations became an avalanche. State after State swung into line until the final result stood Pierce 282, Cass 2, Douglas 2, and Houston 1. Buchanan's sponsors were aghast. They could do nothing but explain to their chieftain that the best-laid plans gang aft agley. The turn toward Pierce, ruefully wrote Alfred Gilmore, was a move that got out of hand. "The intention was to return to you on the fiftieth ballot. The experiment was carried too far." And Cave Johnson made a similar statement. The delegates had wished only to give Pierce "a chance of being voted for, and to show he had no chance, and finally to fall back on yourself." Yet he was not regretful. "The movement operated like an electric spark, and the result seems satisfactory in every quarter, and will perhaps secure us more votes than any other nomination." [54]

This was the second time in party history that a dark horse had raced through to the goal, and just as after Polk's nomination, disappointed groups were loud in denouncing the convention system. William R. King, despite the fact that he received the vice-presidential nomination, expressed utter disgust. He thought it plain that, conventions being mere unruly mobs, no hope existed

52  To Pierce, June 22, 1852; Pierce Papers.
53  Harry Hibbard to Pierce, June 24, 1852; Pierce Papers. For a thoroughgoing attack on Dickinson's sincerity and a charge of gross duplicity in the convention proceedings, see Washington Union, December 4, 1853.
54  June 6, 8, to Buchanan; Buchanan Papers.

for the selection of a man of high abilities and ripe experience. The glittering prize would always bring forward a crowd of applicants who, though possessing few qualifications, would still have friends to battle for them; and they would unite to destroy the eminent leaders of the party in the hope of winning. Anticipating Bryce, he declared that it was the logical tendency of the system to place inferior men in the White House. Glancy Jones indulged in the same melancholy reflection—nobody could be nominated who in the public eye was equal to the station. Characteristically, Cave Johnson made a proposal for reform. He knew of no system better than conventions, but they must be disciplined. "The mode of selecting the delegates must be improved and the laws of the convention changed, so that after a certain number of ballots the lowest should be dropped and the number of votes given be adjusted to the Democratic strength of each State." [55]

But a majority of the party accepted the new leader joyously. Since he had not been sufficiently in public life to make enemies and his deeper convictions were a mystery, every faction and section felt that it could gamble on him. Even King declared that next to Buchanan he was more acceptable to the South than any other man, for he was a gentleman, a conservative Democrat, and quite respectable for talents and information. Herschel Johnson of Georgia was equally pleased. "For thirty-nine ballotings," he wrote, "we interposed Buchanan successfully against others less acceptable to our people. . . . Hence General Pierce, although a Northern man, is, in truth, the candidate of the South." [56] Indeed, Pierce had a host of Southern friends, dating from his old senatorial days, who hastened to congratulate him. P. G. T. Beauregard, a regular New Orleans correspondent, bubbled over with delight; so did ex-Senator C. C. Clay of Alabama, recalling their long and intimate acquaintance; and so did George W. G. Brown of Virginia. [57] Buchanan characteristically accepted Pierce with the anticipation that he would cast aside all the scurvy New England influences for those of the Old Dominion and her noble Southern sisters. "The South are entitled to very great influence with him, and I hope will assert their rights in a proper manner. I shall aid them all in my power."

And while the South thus purred, most freesoilers of the North and moderates of the border showed great contentment. Francis P. Blair led a group of

55  June 12, 16, July 23, 1852, to Buchanan; Buchanan Papers.
56  P. S. Flippin, *Herschel Johnson*, 48ff. "Frank Pierce never made an *effort* in public life that can be recalled without an *effort*," remarked the N. Y. *Courier and Enquirer*; June 8, 1852.
57  June 9, 15, 1852; Pierce Papers. Even South Carolina secessionists hastened to come into camp. Milledge L. Bonham wrote Pierce that, "although a Secession member of our State convention," he was going to support him for the presidency. "A nomination so favorable to the south had not been anticipated." He spoke also for Pickens, who was "very much gratified at your nomination." June 7, 1852. Pierce Papers.

Northern friends into Carroll Hall to say they were delighted with the nomination. The two factions in New York, happy to have defeated each other, were glad to unite on a neutral leader. The historian Bancroft, who years before had called Pierce the fittest candidate that New England could offer, reiterated his praises. John A. Dix wrote in the same vein, saying that the nomination had relieved the party from an immensity of embarrassment in his State. When a friend asked "Prince" John Van Buren what he thought of the choice, he responded that Pierce was a "fine, talented young man, and a first-rate good fellow." Marcy was delighted, and believed the ticket would receive the united support of the party.[58]

Indeed, the nomination seemed to inspire a general love-feast. That smutchy Massachusetts politician B. F. Hallett found in it evidence of the purity of the organization. And, he unctuously added, "it came from Virginia and the magnanimous South, as a peace-offering of union and brotherly concord to the North." [59] The Democratic press teemed with references to the enthusiasm of the rank and file. In one sense, Young America had come out with flying colors, for Pierce was not quite forty-eight, and if he possessed any ideas they might prove new. But the old fogies had the satisfaction of checkmating Douglas; if we had named *him*, exulted Cave Johnson, "we would have been dishonored and disgraced." [60] Everybody could weave pleasing fancies about the nominee, as Bancroft did in writing that he owed his victory to that moderation of spirit and mind which had kept him aloof from all political intrigue, and had left in his public career nothing to efface or explain.[61]

The platform, hurriedly read before a tired, dwindling convention and voted without debate, rehearsed the historic principles of the Democratic party. On the central issue of the day it was explicit. It declared that the party "will abide by and adhere to a faithful execution of the acts known as the compromise measures settled by the last Congress—the act for reclaiming fugitives from service or labor included; which act, being designed to carry out an express provision of the Constitution, cannot with fidelity thereto be repealed nor so changed as to destroy or impair its efficiency." It also pledged resistance to all efforts to revive the slavery agitation in Congress or outside, under whatever shape or color the attempt might be made. The ink on the declaration was to

58 June 5, 6, 12, to Pierce, Pierce Papers. "The democratic party is now thoroughly united," wrote Horatio Seymour, who was elected governor of New York this fall, "and every action that recognizes old divisions must be deemed treason to the principles we profess. I am aware that some feelings of distrust remain in some quarters, but they will yield to fair and impartial treatment." To George R. Herrick, September 24, 1852; Hunter Papers, Univ. of Va.

59 June 5, 1852, Pierce Papers. For much interesting material on B. F. Hallett's political record, see Russell B. Nye, *George Bancroft: Brahmin Rebel*, 90–136.

60 June 8, 1852; Buchanan Papers.

61 June 7, 1852; Pierce Papers.

fade early in 1854! To Northern Democrats who believed that the fugitive slave law ought to be sharply revised, such language was a bitter pill. "The platform," wrote Preston King, "is mischievous in its present and future consequences upon the party and upon the country. There is however imperishable life in the principles of Democracy and the party will fight through in spite of all evil." Even the radical freesoiler Robert Rantoul, a talented man, full of life, hope, and ambition, who was snatched to his grave this summer, for the sake of the party supported the platform. So, with private interpretations of their own, did Dix, Preston King, and Bryant in New York, Wilmot in Pennsylvania, and John Wentworth in Illinois.[62]

[ VI ]

On the Whig side, drama was lent the pre-convention campaign by the pathetic efforts of Daniel Webster to win the nomination. Henry Clay lay on his deathbed in the National Hotel in Washington. But Webster, his ambition flaring up in a last fierce effervescence, still followed the will-of-the-wisp that had so long beguiled both men. Flattering advisers induced him to take an exaggerated view of his chances. Robert C. Winthrop wrote when the chapter was ended: "Alas! that so many indiscreet friends should have involved him in so much of doubtful conduct at the very close of his career! . . . Everett, and Choate, and the Curtises, ought never to have suffered him to be made the tool of a set of unworthy parasites and flatterers." [63] Throughout 1851 and the early months of 1852, the orator strove pertinaciously to advance his political fortunes. He appealed to Henry W. Hilliard of Alabama, for example, not to accept appointment as minister to St. Petersburg because he would need Hilliard's services in the convention, and if all went well, in the campaign. You need not fear, he promised, but that, if we succeed, you will obtain a far pleasanter situation than one amid the snows of Russia. A considerable group of New England papers, led by the Boston *Courier*, fell in behind the Secretary.[64]

Webster's hope was that, Fillmore giving way, he might be carried into the presidency as a representative of the great idea of Union, the paladin who had done so much to defeat the extremists of both sections. As Secretary of State

62 Obviously, the platform did not approve of the Compromise; it merely stated acquiescence in it. It did not term it a finality; it merely promised a faithful execution of it. The *Evening Post* declared that it was not obligatory in any moral or political sense. According to the Washington *Union*, this platform was the result of earnest and repeated consultations between Democrats who entertained widely different views as to the merits of the compromise measures. It was impossible either to disapprove or approve the Compromise in express terms. Had this been done, a bolt and party defeat would have ensued. Union was imperative—and the two wings of the party united, characteristically, on an equivocation.
63 October 23, 1852, Kennedy Papers.
64 C. H. Van Tyne, *Letters of Daniel Webster*, 463.

he was far from unwilling to strengthen the rally about national principles by a spirited and even bumptious foreign policy. Controversy with Austria gave him an opportunity to present the United States as a world champion of democracy. The Austrian representative, Chevalier Hülsemann, having presented a protest against President Taylor's intention of recognizing the independence of Hungary if a strong de facto government were set up by her revolutionists, Webster stepped forward with a reply which has remained justly celebrated. No bolder vindication of the historic American policy of sympathy with struggling democracy has ever been penned. Indeed, he himself admitted that this Hülsemann letter, which appeared in the press in the opening days of 1852, was somewhat rough and boastful.

His object, as he confessed to George Ticknor, was twofold: first, to "tell the people of Europe who and what we are, and awaken them to a just sense of the unparalleled growth of this country"; and second, to "touch the national pride, and make a man feel *sheepish* and look *silly* who should speak of disunion." [65] The paper not only vindicated the American rule with respect to the recognition of revolutionary *de facto* governments, but by implication spoke up for the worldwide expansion of liberty and democratic self-government, and bombastically declared that America's course was never to be lightly questioned. Citizens rubbed their hands with delight over his ringing sentence: "The power of this republic at the present moment is spread over a region one of the richest and most fertile on the globe, and of an extent in comparison with which the possessions of the house of Hapsburg are but as a patch on the earth's surface." [66] This was stump-speech diplomacy. So, too, was Webster's declaration that America, giving the world a successful example of free government, stood as the natural inspiration of republican movements in Europe. A truer note was struck in his remark that Americans would express their opinions freely and fully upon political events in other lands, would rejoice to find their own principles of civil liberty planted elsewhere, and would hope to see them flourish in Austria herself.

The letter gave men the more pleasure because it appeared just as Kossuth was beginning his tour, and just as Louis Napoleon had carried out the *coup d'état* which subverted the republican liberties of France. Webster enforced its main ideas in his before-mentioned speech at the Kossuth banquet. America should make her moral influence felt for freedom, he said, as Chatham and Burke had made theirs felt in 1775. Of the two giants wrestling for world dominion, the autocratic power supported by arms and the popular power sustained by the aspirations of the masses, the former constantly declined and the

65 Curtis, *Webster*, II, 537.
66 Thirty-first Cong., 2d sess., Senate Exec. Doc. No. 9.

latter irresistibly grew. "The part we shall have to act in all this great drama is to show ourselves in favor of those rights, to uphold our ascendency, and to carry it on until we shall see it culminate in the highest heaven over our heads." [67] Within limits, this doctrine has seldom failed to appeal to true Americans.

But the weakness of Webster's political hopes lay in three brutal facts: that Fillmore refused to give way, that the country, as internal calm settled upon it, declined to think about perils to the Union, and that the fever for Kossuth and European revolutions proved a fire of damp straw, quickly burning out in places and refusing to burn at all in others. Though Fillmore had but a slender chance —for nobody thought him a strong man, the hostility of the Seward faction made it impossible for him to carry New York, and his enforcement of the fugitive slave law had turned much of New England and the Northwest against him—*his* friends had aroused his ambition, too. Conferring with him in January, they persuaded him not to carry out his original intention of declining, but let matters take their course; and the Whig Convention in Kentucky promptly endorsed him for the presidency.[68] After all, he had justly earned a renomination. The disappointment of Webster was patent. Though Wall Street men subscribed funds generously for his battle, he lost half his strength the moment he failed to become the Administration candidate. As for riding the Union cause, Greeley correctly called that a dead horse, for even South Carolina had now repudiated disunionism.[69]

Webster's ultimate strength, sadly enough, was thus confined to New England. He made some vain attemps to obtain delegates elsewhere. Ben Wade, writing to his wife, chronicled one of them. The orator had brought down a great unnamed politician from New York, Wade related under date of February 8, 1852. This man's first mission was to Seward, to learn on what terms he might be induced to support Webster, and then he came to Wade with a promise of magnificent gifts if Ohio could be brought into line. "This was something like the promise of the kingdoms of the earth, by another discontented gentleman in the olden time. I told him in pretty considerable plain terms what Ohio thought of the Secretary of State, and that I was of the same opinion." [70] The story may be taken with a grain of salt, for Seward, Weed, and Wade all

67 Curtis, *Webster*, II, 573–576.
68 When Fillmore had first succeeded to the presidency he made it clear that he did not expect to stand for a nomination, but his friends protested. As late as December, 1851, he had fairly decided to make no run, and Crittenden wished him to announce this decision. Stuart urged him to remain on the course. Later his friends decided that he should make no public statement pro or con and await events. Joseph C. G. Kennedy, December 10, 1851, to Clayton; Clayton Papers.
69 N. Y. *Weekly Tribune*, January 24, 31, February 28, March 30, 1852.
70 Wade Papers.

notoriously condemned Webster's position on the Compromise and notoriously favored Winfield Scott's nomination. But the Secretary was pulling what wires he could, and pulling them without effect.

It was a bleak spring for Webster. His health had grown infirm; he looked haggard and careworn; and visiting Marshfield in May, he was thrown with such violence from a phaeton that he remained in bed for ten days. Indeed, his life was probably shortened by the shock to his nervous system.[71] Summer brought on that complaint of hay-fever and asthma (he called it catarrh) which was so distressing to him. Talk of his resignation (and he himself had talked of it a good deal) died away; but, as a member of the State Department staff wrote, he had not strength to withstand the shocks he could throw off in palmier days. He somehow found time for those scholarly avocations which had always given breadth and elasticity to his mind, and in February delivered an admirable address before the New York Historical Society on historical literature. Pointing out the inadequacy of purely political history, he emphasized the importance of attention to artistic and cultural progress, and to changes in occupations and manners. A good social history of Greece, of Rome, and of Great Britain, he correctly stated, remained to be written. His paper contained discriminating passages of criticism, showing that he had read attentively not only the ancient historians, but Niebuhr, Arnold, and Merivale, Hallam, Lingard, and Macaulay; and it deserved the publication in full which the New York press gave it. No other candidate could have come anywhere near bending such a bow.[72]

In the political field, however, he made little progress. As he told a wildly cheering crowd in Faneuil Hall in May, he had no platform but the platform of his life and character, and he needed none beyond his devotion to the Union and Constitution. But while with his impressive figure, his swelling brow, his piercing eyes, his rich mind and magical eloquence, he could entrance any audience before which he appeared in person, he was weak in far-distant communities, which thought of his pomposities, his aristocratic connections, his fleshly frailties, and his age. President Fillmore, with the national patronage, and Scott, with his military renown, held the advantage. "I have had eno' of cheering prospects and sickening results," he wrote his son Fletcher in May.[73]

"I suppose we must run Scott for President, and I hate it," Greeley confided to Colfax.[74] As leaders in both parties (Buchanan for one) shrewdly foresaw,

71  Fuess, *Webster*, II, 284.
72  Webster remarked that the day after this display of classical learning, people in Broadway would accost him: "Good morning, Mr. Webster. Recently from Greece, I understand; how did you leave *Mr. Pericles* and *Mr. Aristopanes?*" Charles Lanman, *Private Life of Daniel Webster*, 98.
73  *Works*, National Edition, XVI, 643.
74  February 12, 1851; Greeley-Colfax Corr.

Scott was the predestined candidate of a party which had never won save with a general for nominee. Of Virginia birth, forty years' service in the army, and acknowledged integrity and ability, Scott (like Pierce) had the advantage of being without political record or commitments. His candidacy was in the hands of John M. Clayton, who formally launched it at a public dinner on November 16, 1851. Washington headquarters were presently opened by James S. Pike, whose attacks on Fillmore were so red-hot that Seward compared them to a series of sermons he had once heard: "Hell—more Hell—still more Hell." [75] Scott was primarily the man of the Northern Whigs, and not least of Seward and Weed in New York, thirsting for revenge upon Fillmore and detesting Webster. But he also possessed the support of a few Southerners like Senator Mangum of North Carolina.

In Congress an attempt was made to conquer old animosities in his behalf. "The trouble has been to settle the question whether General Scott should come out with a platform indorsing the Compromise," Ben Wade informed his wife.[76] "The South insist upon it, and the North were divided. Our Click acts for the Whigs of the North, who agree to abide by our decision. And last night, for the first time, I brought our Click to a final and irrevocable decision, that the South should take Scott as he is, without sectional pledges. . . . And I know now the victory is won. Our men are bound now to present a united front, and I have no fears for the South. They dare not go against us." He was half right. The staunchest Southern Whigs would take Scott; doubtful Southern voters would not.

Though far from taciturn, Scott had made but one or two recorded utterances upon the slavery question. One was the safe statement that Congress could touch slavery within the Federal District, but not within a State. He had also written, far back in 1843, that it was a high moral obligation of masters and of slaveholding States "to employ all means, not incompatible with the safety of both colors, to ameliorate slavery, even to extermination." All efforts to force him to add to these remarks failed. In the past he had shown an alarming penchant for letter-writing on all possible occasions, but under pressure he now promised a discreet silence.[77]

The fact was that the party drifted to Scott as the Democrats had finally drifted to Pierce, because he seemed neutral, colorless, and safe, with a good war record. Most Southern Whigs distrusted him because of Seward's backing.

75  C. W. Elliott, *Winfield Scott*, 610; Pike's MS Autobiography, Pike Papers.
76  February 8, 1852; Wade Papers.
77  Wade, December 10, 1851, to his wife; Wade Papers. Wade boasted to his wife that he had muzzled Scott. He called on him and said that he was the only man who could carry Ohio, but that he "must write no more *South* letters"; "the old man was highly pleased and promised to keep his mouth shut." December 10, 1851, Wade Papers.

They had seen Taylor under Seward's thumb; they did not want another military chieftain under the same control. The conventions of Tennessee, Virginia, Mississippi, and North Carolina passed resolutions expressing a clear preference for good Millard Fillmore. Texas took the same stand, and the South Carolina convention voiced its admiration for both Fillmore and Webster without choosing between them.[78] But the Whig party had no two-thirds rule to enable the South to veto an undesired man. Representative Christopher Williams of Tennessee told the House that the Southern Whigs did not object to Scott in himself, but did object to electing with him Northern abolitionism, a Northern abolition cabinet, and a Northern attempt to repeal or hamstring the fugitive slave law. "Now, these sentiments of Kit Williams," remarked the well-informed correspondent of the New York *Express*, "are nearly if not quite universal in every Southern State." [79] Edward Stanly of North Carolina and Edward C. Cabell of Florida promptly informed the public that Williams need not worry, for Scott would support the Compromise and repudiate all abolitionists; but this statement failed to reassure many.[80]

## [ VII ]

The Whig convention, opening in Baltimore on June 16th, heard a pious exhortation from John G. Chapman as its president; they were all brothers, and there was no North or South, East or West. The platform was quickly adopted, 227 to 66, asserting that the Compromise acts, including the fugitive slave law, were accepted as a final settlement, in principle and substance, of the dangerous questions which they embraced. This was a triumph of the moderate majority over the violent anti-slavery wing; and Henry J. Raymond of the New York *Times* at once charged that party managers had made a bargain by which the North would give way on the platform, and the South would accept Scott as a candidate. His statement excited the rage of Southern leaders. "A lie!" they shouted, and vainly tried to expel Raymond from his seat. The radical anti-slavery men remained deeply resentful.

There being 396 delegates, 149 votes were essential to a choice. On the initial ballot Fillmore received 133, Scott 131, and Webster 29, and for fifty subsequent ballots this alignment was very nearly maintained. Webster's vote never went above 32. It was obvious that the combined Fillmore-Webster vote would suffice to defeat Scott, but it was not clear that either man could deliver a sufficient number of his votes to the other. Fillmore had indeed prepared a letter of withdrawal, but it was found that if he dropped out only 106 followers

78  *National Intelligencer*, February 9, March 27, April 17, May 15, May 20, 1852.
79  Washington correspondence dated April 2, 1852.
80  See Stanly's letter, *National Intelligencer*, April 8, 1852.

could be relied upon to vote for Webster. As it was also found that Webster could not make sure of 41 votes of his own, the President's managers thought it useless to recede. Even a dinner by Webster's backers to the Southwestern delegates, at which Rufus Choate, rising from a sickbed, made an impassioned speech, accomplished nothing.[81]

Though Fillmore would have been the soundest choice, there was but one way out of the deadlock, and on the fifty-third ballot, a break by Pennsylvania delegates to Scott resulted in the general's nomination. Henry Wilson hated Webster. He saw the final result with glee. Suiting the gesture to the word, he exclaimed: "We have dirked him! We have dirked him!" [82] Some Southern delegates, taking heart from the platform endorsement of the Compromise, had swung over to Scott. Perhaps there *had* been a bargain! William A. Graham of North Carolina was thereupon nominated for Vice-President, and after passing resolutions complimenting Fillmore and Webster, the convention adjourned.

If Pierce's nomination had produced general Democratic jubilation, Scott's but enhanced the heartburning and gloom among the Whigs. The sturdy soldier had brains, character, and strong Union principles. But he was completely destitute of civil experience, his fussy vanity was sufficient to burst the White House, and his personal idiosyncrasies made him an easy butt of ridicule. Greeley thought that his nativist leanings, aristocratic habits, and lack of winning qualities were fatal handicaps. He had shown great elation over the mere prospect of his selection, and had made some absurd statements, assuring Edward Everett's son-in-law that he "respected the presidency more than he desired it." While Southern Whigs were only half-placated by the platform and Graham's nomination, such Northern organs as the New York *Tribune* made a wry face. The resolutions, said Greeley's journal, were forced upon an unwilling minority. They "were driven through by the argument of menace and terror—were rammed down by the potent intimation, 'Swallow in silence or we bolt.' " [83]

81 Fuess, *Webster*, II, 286–288.

82 Washington *Union*, March 12, 1857; some notes on Webster. Of course Scott's "hasty plate of soup" and "fire upon my rear" letters of Mexican War days were endlessly satirized.

83 Henry A. Wise (Everett's son-in-law), April 4, 1851; Everett Papers. N. Y. *Tribune*, June 22, 1852. The anger among the Silver Grays was more intense. They had hoped to the last for the nomination of Fillmore or Webster, and they regarded the outcome as a triumph for Seward. They knew that as Fillmore had proscribed all Seward's friends, so Seward, if he came into power, would be relentless in his persecution of Fillmore's adherents. A stern determination possessed many of them not to submit to annihilation from that quarter. But, said one Democratic onlooker, they would not bolt the Scott ticket; they knew a surer way to kill. Samuel D. Partridge, June 29, 1852, Pierce Papers. In Boston, State Street was wrapped in Stygian darkness. "Taller cursing and swearing I think you could never have heard," wrote Edmund Quincy. He added that the *Transcript* wept, the *Courier* blubbered, and the *Post*, a Democratic sheet, lifted a voice of indignant sympathy. June 28, 1852, Quincy Papers.

On receiving the news of the nomination, Webster contented himself with the caustic query, "How will this look in history?" That evening a party of Whigs serenaded Fillmore, and then trooped to the Secretary's door. Their band had to play several spirited airs before Webster appeared on his steps, wrapped in a long dressing-gown and an air of sad weariness. He spoke briefly without once mentioning Scott. When in conclusion he said that he would sleep soundly and rise with the lark, and bade the crowd a sombre good night, they departed as if they had heard a funeral sermon.[84]

Webster's disappointment and disillusionment were profound. His last chance for the presidency had been lost. But keener than this sense of failure was his grief that his vote was so humiliating; that Henry Clay had advised Southern delegates to support Fillmore; and that despite his courageous Seventh of March speech, not a single Southerner had come to his side. His despondency made his Washington residence, usually so bright, seem a house of mourning. To his friend Blatchford he wrote that the convention's performance had been deplorable: "It shows a great deal of folly and a great deal of infidelity."

Turning northward, he tarried briefly at the Astor House, whose manager, Charles A. Stetson, a close friend who always kept a special suite for Webster, thought him feeble and unwell. Coming upon him standing alone in a corridor, Stetson sympathetically placed his hand upon Webster's breast with the remark, "I hope all is right here." The reply came fervently: "Yes, sir, I am too near God to have a single heartburning against a human creature, but I have a chagrin as profound as my nature; and it is that, after having performed my duty to my Southern brethren, they had neither the courage nor kindness to place me on the record of that Convention. I do not say I did not want the nomination, but I would rather have had *their record* than the nomination."[85] Retiring to his Marshfield farm, he spoke of the Whig party as moribund, and went to the unhappy extreme of advising his friends to vote for Franklin Pierce, whom he had known and liked almost from boyhood.[86]

Nor did Webster's wide army of New England friends feel less keenly. Two July meetings were held in Faneuil Hall to protest against the Baltimore nominations and urge an independent vote for Webster. At the first, Hubbard Winslow made an effective speech. He quoted Robert Toombs as saying that all real control of the nomination of a President had been taken out of the hands of the people and placed in those of unauthorized juntas. He described the poignant grief of Boston when Scott's triumph was announced. "But we shall

---

84  "Reminiscences of Washington," *Atlantic Monthly*, May, 1880.
85  *National Intelligencer*, June 22, 1854; Washington *Union*, March 14, 1857.
86  Curtis, *Webster*, II, ch. 38; Charles Lanman, October 19, 1852, Pierce Papers.

not soon forget the thronging multitudes of State Street, awaiting with an almost breathless solicitude the repeated throbbings of those impassioned wires; nor the deep gloom that settled upon all faces, and seemed to pervade the entire city and country around us, when the final announcement came. The shock of an earthquake would not have been more appalling." While Scott was doubtless a great general, what would men think of placing Webster in charge of the armies? He echoed the mayor of Boston, who had said that no other living man had been so shamefully slandered as Webster. The second meeting presented Webster to the people as an independent candidate. This was no mere gesture, for on September 15 a Webster Union Whig Convention met in the same hall, with Henry Lyman of Watertown as chairman, and with many delegates present from towns outside Boston. A ticket of electors was approved, an executive committee appointed, and an address to the nation issued.[87]

All this was a touching illustration of Bay State devotion to Webster; nor were other demonstrations wanting. When he reached Boston on July 9th the shops and offices closed; an immense concourse, swelled by every arriving train and boat, filled the city; and, heralded by bells and cannon, and escorted by troops, he rode from Roxbury down beflagged streets to the Common, where a multitude of eager admirers awaited him. When he proceeded to Marshfield, the whole countryside turned out in another tumultuous welcome. In a sense, the State knew that it was bidding him farewell. Whether he lived months or years, his resplendent public career was ended.

Clay, if in full manhood vigor, might have done much to heal the Whig dissensions and infuse a fighting spirit into the party. But he was lying mortally stricken in his rooms in Washington, attended by devoted friends and two of his sons. Thin, frail, and suffering from a dry, hacking cough, he steadily lost strength. He was gratified by the seal of approval which both conventions had placed on his Compromise. But the nomination of Scott grieved him, and like Webster, he had a clear premonition of the approaching collapse of his party. On June 29, at eleven in the morning, he died. The Senate met only to adjourn, almost every house in the city hung out crepe, and minute guns were fired and bells tolled throughout the afternoon. From Washington the mourning spread across the country, for few American statesmen have been more widely beloved than "Harry of the West." On July 1st, his body was impressively escorted to the Senate chamber, where, in the presence of Fillmore, the Cabinet, the two houses, and military and diplomatic officers, the funeral was held. A thousand-mile tribute of respect followed, as the remains were taken by way of Baltimore, Philadelphia, New York, Albany, Rochester, Buffalo, Cleveland, Cincinnati, and Louisville to his Lexington home.[88]

[ VIII ]

Astute political leaders felt little doubt that Pierce would win. Webster was sure of it. Our government, Robert C. Winthrop had prophesied long before the campaign opened, is as certain to go into Democratic hands in November as the seasons are to roll round. The Democratic canvass was managed with great energy. B. B. French hurriedly penned a campaign biography of the nominee, and Hawthorne wrote a better one. "I am taking your life as fast as I can—murdering and mangling you," the novelist wrote Pierce on July 27.[89] Great pains were taken to stir up the foreign-born voters. August Belmont spent time and money generously in rallying the German leaders and news-papers of New York and Pennsylvania, boasted that from the Staats-Zeitung down the press was all on the right side, and later declared that the German population to a man had gone to the polls for Pierce. A delicate game had to be played with Kossuth, for while the Southerners were generally hostile to his mission, nearly all German-Americans and many Irish heartily sympathized with the revolutionary cause that he represented. Pierre Soulé called upon him, buttered him with compliments, explained why the Democratic platform had been silent on the Hungarian question, and protested that the Whigs would play him false. The mercurial Louisianian left convinced that Kossuth was heart and soul with the Democrats.[90] As for the Irish, such leaders as Charles O'Conor, James T. Brady, and Robert Emmet, with the three-year-old New York Irish-American, urged them into line.

But the main reason for Democratic exuberance was that the party had patched up its slavery quarrels, while the Whigs had not. Everybody lent a hand in the battle. Martin Van Buren, in one of the shortest letters he ever wrote, said that he earnestly desired Pierce's election. Cass and Buchanan were busy in their respective States. Marcy made a tour to western New York and came back delighted at the prospect. When a history of the two parties was suggested, George Bancroft eagerly caught up his pen. Gideon Welles bubbled over with good advice to the nominee; the great error of previous candidates, he pointed out, was that they had insisted on writing letters, and Pierce should lie low. Everybody knew he was a Democrat of the strict-construction, State Rights school; let him not go into further particulars. Sanders was blazing

88  New York and Washington newspapers, June 30 et seq.; G. G. Van Deusen, Henry Clay.
89  Pierce Papers.
90  June 30, 1852, Pierce Papers.

away in his *Democratic Review* like a frigate delivering broadsides; Bryant's *Evening Post* had again become a pillar of the party. Nor was the Little Giant missing. B. B. French, convinced that the idol of the Western pioneers and the bhoys of New York and Boston could win a multitude of votes, called upon Douglas in Washington and was delighted at his reception. He wrote Pierce: [91]

> He agrees with me, and says he is ready at *any* sacrifice of time and means— at any personal inconvenience, to go anywhere, and do any honorable thing to effect your election; and whatever you and your friends advise and desire, *that* he will do. He added he was not personally acquainted with you—I think he said that he had seen you—and that he had no ulterior views or wishes beyond your election, that he told his friends, when they saw fit to leave him . . . that he was rejoiced at your nomination, that he should support you with all his soul, and that his impression *now* was, that he should not only support you for *this* term, but for a reëlection, and added, "but as to this nothing certain can be said, let us get him elected now, as he will be, and let the future take care of itself."

The Democrats ramped and roared with monster ratification meetings at Tammany Hall, at Pierce's Hillsborough, N. H., birthplace, and at other strategic points. They got out fifty thousand extra copies at a time of the *Democratic Review*. They besought Archbishop John Hughes for an endorsement which he warily refused. On the tariff and on Andrew Johnson's Homestead Bill (Johnson was "a little cracked" on that subject, wrote one Democrat) Pierce maintained a discreet silence. "Young America," slavery men, former Free-Soilers (though not of course Sumner or Chase), and popular-sovereignty men were all kept united.

By comparison the Whig campaign seemed dispirited and listless. Impending defeat hung over it like a black cloud. Webster's defection, Fillmore's frigidity, Clay's death, and the cutting hostility of New York's Silver Grays, whose hatred for Seward knew no bounds, were all sorry handicaps. The party had no cohesion, for it no longer had strong principles or dominating personalities. How deeply it was torn by factions became plain when two rival bodies of irreconcilables broke away, one Northern and one Southern.

The Free Soil radicals, spurning Scott, held a convention at Pittsburgh in August, where they nominated John P. Hale and George W. Julian. Attracting a large attendance from New York, Pennsylvania, and the Northwest, they drew up a platform which militantly denounced the Compromise, opposed any more slave States or Territories, called for popular election of all public

91 June 27, 1852, Pierce Papers. French was national treasurer, Robert McLane national chairman. W. M. Gwin headed an efficient Washington committee.

officers, and demanded cheap postage and free homesteads.[92] Prominent in the party were Giddings, Chase, Sumner, Horace Mann, and Henry Wilson. At the other extreme, a body of leading Southern Whigs abruptly bolted Scott. That candidate, in his well-written letter of acceptance, had made no explicit comment upon the Compromise, merely saying that he took the nomination "with the resolutions annexed." In high wrath over his chilly silence, seven Southern Representatives, led by Toombs and Stephens of Georgia, Charles J. Faulkner of Virginia, and Alexander White of Alabama, drew up resolutions of rejection. Two Tennessee Representatives issued a subsidiary statement of similar tenor. The manifesto declared that Scott seemed to have studiously avoided any endorsement of the Compromise; that nothing in his career indicated that he had favored its principles; that in at least one public letter he had expressed hostility to slavery; and that he was obviously the favorite of anti-slavery Democrats.[93]

In effect, this was a declaration that many Southern Whigs refused to trust Seward and feared he would dominate Scott. It was a silly gesture, for Scott was actually a man of strong Union convictions, and far too independent to be controlled by Seward. John A. Quitman, who knew his staunch qualities from service under him in Mexico, pronounced the idea "stuff." Moreover, Scott had ardently supported the Compromise. Secretary Graham, who lodged at the same hotel with Scott in the summer of 1850, has left his testimony that no man was more the advocate of the Compromise bills, none exerted himself more actively to procure votes in Congress, and none rejoiced more heartily over the final victory.[94] But the revolt was not the less important for being ill-founded. It and the Free Soil defection, in which lay one germ of the future Republican Party, practically ensured Scott's defeat—and also sealed the ultimate fate of the party.

Yet even with their ranks distracted and partly mutinous, the Whigs fought gallantly to the end. "We are getting out about a million of the life of Genl Scott," Ben Wade informed his wife as the canvass opened.[95] This was written by James S. Pike of the New York *Tribune* staff on a week's notice, and more than a million copies were used. Henry C. Carey issued a flock of pamphlets

92 *National Intelligencer*, August 12, 14, 1852. Bryant's refusal to support the Free Soil ticket was a heavy blow. Martin Van Buren, in one of the shortest letters he ever wrote, stated that he hoped for Pierce's election, and David Wilmot announced his adherence to Pierce. The Free Soil ticket drew more heavily from the Whigs than from the Democrats; see the *National Intelligencer*, June 12, July 10, August 7, 1852.

93 The other Representatives signing the statement were James Johnson of Georgia, W. Brooke of Mississippi, and James Abercrombie of Alabama. The two Tennesseans were M. P. Gentry and C. H. Williams. See *National Intelligencer*, July 3, 1852; Henry Cleveland, *Alexander H. Stephens*, 79; U. B. Phillips, *Toombs*, 109, 110.

94 Graham to John Barnett, July 6, 1852; Graham Papers, Univ. of North Carolina.

95 July 2, 1852, Wade Papers.

for workingmen which held up protection as the brazen serpent in the wilderness. Such publications counted, for as Buchanan admitted, the tariff issue was now making Pennsylvania—a State of about five hundred iron works, with thirty thousand employees—uncomfortably close in elections.[96] Before election day Carey printed a million copies of his brochures, one of which was entitled *Ireland's Miseries*. "If they have converted only *one per cent* of the readers," he boasted, "they could settle our question for us." He thought that Scott would get the mass of the Irish vote in Pennsylvania, and if he did, would carry the State by twenty thousand votes. His *Letter to a Farmer of Ohio* was specially directed toward the Northwest, and Greeley believed that it might be used there with overpowering effect. The Whigs paid their own special attentions to the German-American vote, and a German-language life of Scott was scattered broadcast; while the party tried to produce the impression that it was much more cordial toward Kossuth than were the Democrats.[97]

Scott, for all his capable record in two wars, his patriotism and high-minded integrity, and his eagerness to please, was too stiff and pompous to appeal to the popular heart. His self-confident egotism betrayed him into impulsive blunders. The country chuckled when, journeying into the Middle West, he tried to flatter the voters by clumsy compliments to the "rich old Irish brogue" and the "German foreign accent." That his speeches were genuinely able and honest too often escaped notice. Bad party management and Scott's own temporary illness made a fiasco of the great mass meeting arranged at Buffalo, as near as American crowds could come to the site of his victory (if such it could be called) at Lundy's Lane. Everything in his past that could be embarrassing was dragged out. There was no denying that he had once written a letter expressing sympathy with nativist aims. "I admit the fact," declared Greeley, "and plead [his] repentance."[98] Indeed, after asking in 1845 for stricter naturalization laws, Scott three years later had manfully confessed his error. It was now emphasized, however, in all German and Irish districts.

Toward the end the campaign degenerated on both sides into irresponsible mud-slinging. So violent were the attacks upon Scott that according to one observer, thousands of people by election day looked upon him "as one of the most dishonest men in the world, and d—d mean at that!"[99] Newspaper articles stigmatized Pierce as a drunkard—and indeed as Senator he had been addicted to liquor, but had conquered the habit. They attacked his war record; a Southern lady travelling to Concord heard a train-boy selling a pamphlet "all about General Pierce falling off his horse in Mexico at the sight of blood."

96 To Cave Johnson, December 22, 1851; John Bassett Moore, ed., *Works*, VIII, 430.
97 Carey Papers, September-November, 1852, Huntington Library; Greeley-Colfax Corr.
98 July 15, 1852, Greeley-Colfax Corr.; Elliott, *Winfield Scott*, ch. 45.
99 R. P. Letcher, December 18, 1852, to Crittenden; Crittenden Papers.

The Whigs assailed his alleged acquiescence in a clause of the New Hampshire Constitution disqualifying Catholics from office, which he had really opposed, and ran advertisements in the press headed, "To Your Tents, Catholics!" Such charges had special effect in Pennsylvania, where the well-known attorney James Campbell had been defeated for supreme court justice the previous year because of religious prejudice.[100] Buchanan delivered a carefully-considered speech touching upon the Catholic issue, of which August Belmont alone distributed two thousand copies, while Campbell loyally threw his influence behind Pierce. Scott, too, was accused of anti-Catholic feeling, and hastened to write a letter to the Boston *Pilot* in self-defence, placing an order for a large edition to be given away.[101] Simultaneously, other Democratic critics assailed him (a devout Episcopalian) because one of his daughters had become a nun!

Certain as all politicians were of the outcome, Pierce's victory over Scott was more crushing than men had anticipated. The Whigs carried only four of the thirty-one States—Kentucky and Tennessee on the border and Massachusetts and Vermont in New England—with but 42 electoral votes against Pierce's 254. If we may believe Cave Johnson, even Tennessee went for Scott in error. The voters assumed that since he was from the South all his feelings were identified with slavery, whereas since Pierce was from the North he must be abolitionist at heart. Some even professed great fear of emancipation under Pierce![102] In any event, the defeat was so overwhelming that many Whigs agreed with the novelist John P. Kennedy, now Secretary of the Navy, that it was almost ludicrous.[103] It was so complete that shrewd observers wondered whether the party could ever recover. Shattered into discordant sectional elements by the slavery question, and further broken into jealous local groups by the ambition of numerous chieftains, its fragments might at an earlier date have been reknit into a living body by Webster and Clay; but their reign was over.

"The Whig Party seems almost annihilated by the recent elections," Schuyler Colfax confided to Tom Corwin. Thurlow Weed admitted, "There may be no political future for us. . . ."[104] While Seward was more hopeful, assuring Sumner that the organization would endure, both the New York *Times* and *Tribune* declared that Whiggism had received its death blow, and awaited only the undertaker.

And though both Colfax and Weed hoped that the party might revive, for

100　Isaac Y. McKinley, June 7, 1852; Pierce Papers. Some good observers denied this, terming Campbell unfit, and his defeat warranted.
101　George F. Emery, June 26, 1852; Pierce Papers; Elliot, *Winfield Scott*, 642.
102　November 13, 1852; Buchanan Papers.
103　November 29, 1852, Kennedy Papers.
104　November 18, 1852, Corwin Papers; Bancroft, *Seward*, I, 310, 311.

the nation needed a strong Opposition, many former Whigs of extreme views rejoiced in the idea of its permanent downfall. Anti-slavery men believed the way would now open for a strong freesoil party. In the Deep South multitudes held that any further alliance with the hateful Seward-Weed element was totally impossible. "The Presidential election went very much as I hoped and expected except in Tennessee and Kentucky," wrote the grimly exultant Toombs. "We can never have peace and security with Seward.

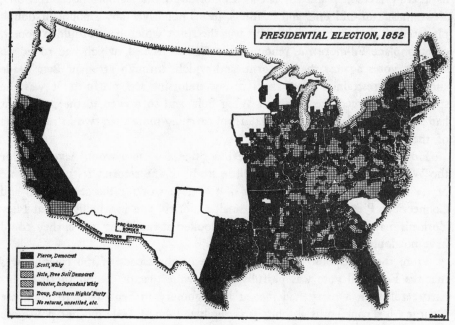

PRESIDENTIAL ELECTION, 1852

■ Pierce, Democrat
▥ Scott, Whig
▨ Hale, Free Soil Democrat
▧ Webster, Independent Whig
▩ Troup, Southern Rights Party
☐ No returns, unsettled, etc.

POST-GADSDEN BORDER
PRE-GADSDEN BORDER

The Popular Vote Stood Pierce 1,601,274; Scott, 1,386,580.

Greeley & Co. in the ascendency in our national councils, and we can better purchase them by the destruction of the Whig Party than of the Union. If the Whig Party is incapable of rising to the same standard of nationality as the motley crew which offers it under the name of Democracy it is entitled to no resurrection.—It will have none." [105]

It was a national misfortune that the great party which in its best days had done so much for Hamilton's principle of a strong national government, for internal improvements, and for industrial development; which by its patrician tone had lifted politics to a higher level; and which, above all, had been so nobly devoted under Clay and Webster to the idea of national unity, should thus lie dismembered and moribund. Had the Seward-Weed group permitted

105  December 5, 1852, Crittenden Papers

the renomination of Fillmore, the party would have lost the election, but its strength would have been conserved. The head and front of Fillmore's offending was simply that, under the solemn obligation of his oath, he had maintained the fugitive slave law as an expression of a clear constitutional requirement. Democrats North and South had subordinated their special demands to party unity, but the Seward-Weed-Greeley school simply refused to be reconciled to the Compromise. If we must have a platform, wrote Greeley privately, let us insert a freesoil plank to "act as a chloride to the Compromise infection"; if we must run Old Fuss and Feathers, let us not have "any amount of dough plastered all over his face." [106] This was the spirit which had forbidden honest, commonplace Fillmore the renomination he had earned; which had rolled up sixty-six votes against the platform; and which, through arrogant Ben Wade and others, restrained Scott from firmly endorsing the platform. It was the spirit which forced the Southern Whig bolt, and so prevented the party that had swept eight slave States in 1848 from carrying more than two in 1852—one of these perhaps in error.

How much a few personal and local sacrifices for unity would have done for the Whig Party is evident from a little study of the returns. Its popular vote of 1,386,580 was not far below that of 1,601,274 cast for Pierce; in Ohio and Connecticut Pierce won only by a small majority, and in Michigan and New York his majority was not large. As men looked at the Whig grave, they could have no doubt as to who had dug it.

From the standpoint of the Union, the bright aspect of the election was that the Free Soil vote was pitifully small, while that of the Southern Rights party (for such a party had met at Montgomery in September to nominate George M. Troup) was absolutely negligible. John P. Hale did not poll quite 156,000 votes, and Troup received only about 3,500. In Mississippi that recent disunionist leader, Jefferson Davis, quietly accepted Pierce and the platform, while both his State and contumacious little South Carolina supported the regular Democratic ticket. Beyond question, Pierce's election signified that the country was anxious for an end of the sectional contest; for peace, harmony, and good will. The voters trusted the Democratic promise to resist all attempts at renewing in Congress, or out of it, the agitation of the slavery question.

Yet those who looked beneath the surface could perceive that the determination of many Northerners to reject a practical application of the fugitive slave law was matched by the equal determination of many Southerners to resist any such challenge. Two letters which had been written to Pierce on the same day, July 13th, show what divergent expectations were pinned to him. One,

106  January 13, February 12, 1852; Greeley-Colfax Corr.

from Representative John Letcher of Virginia, declared that he confidently trusted Pierce to protect the South. "I am entirely satisfied of the soundness of your position on the slavery question, from an examination of your course while in the two Houses of Congress, and will use all honorable effort to secure your election." The other, from David Wilmot, also pledged support, but declared that he fully expected Pierce to check the South. "I am jealous of the *power* of the South. I see in the *mighty interests* of slavery, a power hostile to the rights of the people, and dangerous to the institutions of the country." [107]

The abolitionists and radical freesoilers were not receding one inch. On the other side, the secessionist elements of South Carolina still had their secret committees and secret circulars, and Rhett had by no means given up his disunion plans.[108] The Southern Rights Association in Alabama, meeting at Montgomery early in 1852 with Yancey as its most prominent figure, had declared that while its members would no longer press the issue of secession as a cure for the Compromise evils, they would guard against future aggressions.[109] I know well, wrote Calhoun's disciple and literary executor, R. K. Crallé, that the great cause of *immediate* disunion has been defeated. "But woe to the memory of those through whose baseness and treachery it was lost. The time cannot be far distant, when the evils of consolidation shall develop themselves to a much abused and betrayed people; and then will come the day of retribution—the day of reckoning. If I do not much mistake the signs of the times a very few years will be sufficient to make us fully realize the folly and madness of that policy which the Southern States have been seduced to adopt." [110]

And the campaign evoked from John A. Quitman a letter in which he enunciated once more the portentous thesis that any citizen holding slaves had a right to carry them into any Territory, where the national power must shield and foster them. It is the duty of Congress, he wrote, "to pass such laws as may be necessary to protect such property as well as any other. When the common government refuses such protection, it would disregard the object which called it into existence." Preposterous and horrifying as this demand must have seemed to any freesoiler whose eye fell upon it, time was to prove that it had to be taken seriously.[111] It was the thin end of a wedge which, driven deeper year by year, was in 1860 to rive the Democratic Party and the Union asunder.

107 Pierce Papers.
108 Anderson Court House, S. C., *Southern Rights Advocate*, March 31, 1852.
109 *National Intelligencer*, March 9, 15, 16, 1852.
110 To John A. Quitman, September 3, 1852; Claiborne Papers, Miss. Dept. of Archives and History.
111 September 5, 1852; copy of letter in De Leon Scrapbook, South Caroliniana Library.

[ IX ]

Daniel Webster's life ebbed away with that of his party. Returning to Marshfield from a final Washington sojourn early in September, he found himself suffering from a complication of ailments: catarrh, diarrhoea, general debility, and failing eyesight.[112] From the beginning of October he knew that his end was near. Characteristically, he ordered that his sailboat, with the stars and stripes nailed to its masthead, should be so moored that he could see the flag from his bed, and that at night a ship's lantern should be hung near enough to cast its rays on the waving banner. He breathed his last just before dawn of a bright Sunday morning, October 24th. Ralph Waldo Emerson, staying at Plymouth, faintly heard the tolling bells of Marshfield. Though the whole country felt the shock, Massachusetts, a great part of whose people had for many years almost idolized the statesman, specially manifested its grief. Boston on that Monday and Tuesday transacted no business that was not indispensable. Buildings were swathed in black; pendent mourning draped the Bunker Hill monument. The memorial meeting in Faneuil Hall was the most impressive that living men had ever witnessed. Though it was held at noonday, the windows were darkened, and the lamps solemnly lighted. The three thousand people who crowded the building sat in the deepest silence, every man looking as if he were at the funeral of his father. George S. Hillard, one of the speakers, could hardly articulate; as he proceeded he saw men weeping all about him; and when he turned to Healy's picture of Webster delivering the reply to Hayne, an audible shiver ran through the audience. Edward Everett delivered a eulogy exquisite in diction, tender and melting in sentiment.

The President proposed that the government should take charge of the funeral, but Webster had left instructions for a more fitting ceremony. The final scene enacted by the seaside, under a rich October sun, was august in its simplicity. "I went down to the funeral on Friday last," wrote one of Webster's closest friends. "The day was as lovely as if heaven had been mindful of the wishes of the people, and although as you know Marshfield is an out-of-the-way and not easily accessible place, yet there were ten or twelve thousand persons present. The body was on a sort of bier or case, entirely exposed to view from head to foot, and draped as when alive in a blue coat and white trousers. It lay under an aspen whose yellow leaves stirred as with grief. The face had begun to be a little changed with time, but the brow looked noble and majestic as ever. There were two files of persons on either hand passing up, looking at the face, and then defiling off to the right and left, and many hard Yankee faces with water standing in their eyes. The arrangements of the funeral

112 Curtis, *Webster*, II, 660, 661.

were conducted with very good taste. He was buried not as a great man, but as farmer and householder of Marshfield. My heart swelled when I saw the eminent men all passed by, and six plain men of Marshfield called out to be pallbearers. Was not that beautiful? The procession moved through the fields about a mile to the tomb, which is on a hill, and there the body was laid down and again exposed to view, and then with a short prayer committed to its last repose." [113]

From the graveside of the defender of the Union, and from the seeming grave of the Whig Party which under Webster and Clay had been a phalanx of strength to the national idea, men could turn—to what? To an unknown party future, to unguessed but certain sectional broils, and to an unknown leader. "Threatened Renewal of the Slavery Agitation"—such was the caption of a widely-reprinted editorial of the Philadelphia *North American* which appeared at the height of the campaign, calling attention to obvious omens of a new sectional clash. Who would meet such a renewal? Toombs had written of the situation with somewhat excessive asperity. "The nation with singular unanimity has determined to take a man without claims or qualifications, surrounded by as dishonest and dirty a set of political gamesters as even Catiline ever assembled, rather than the canting hypocrites who brought out General Scott." [114] Yet there was an element of truth in what he said. The great triumvirate, Calhoun, Clay, Webster, were gone. Old party lines were breaking. The slavery quarrel, temporarily muted, might burst forth at any moment. And where in the new Administration could be found men of clear vision, statesmanlike temper, and courageous devotion to the Union above all other objects?

The character of the new President would have offered a curious study to Thackeray or Turgenev. He was one of the quickest, most gracefully attractive, and withal weakest, of the men who have held his high office. It is a revealing fact that the news of his nomination filled his wife and closest friend with alarm. Mrs. Pierce, whose nervous anxiety was plain to callers, was thinking primarily of the intemperate habits which had played a part in his resignation from the Senate years earlier. The Whig press had called him the hero of many a well fought *bottle*. Nathaniel Hawthorne, who with an expression of sympathetic woe exclaimed, "Frank, I pity you—Indeed I do, from the bottom of my heart!" was thinking of public burdens and perplexities. [115] Yet wife and friend shared a deeper cause for anxiety.

Frank, as his intimates called him, was gay, loquacious, bubbling over with kindness, and beguilingly demonstrative. In private life his quick sympathies

113 November 2, 1852, to Lieber; Lieber Papers, Huntington Library.
114 December 5, 1852, to Crittenden; Crittenden Papers.
115 M. B. Field, *Memories*, 156-160.

and affections made him a highly engaging person. He carried into the White House many effervescent, boyish traits which pleased all his associates—until they discovered how superficial was the good will which underlay his offhand invitations to lunch or dinner. He cordially threw his arm over the shoulders of his acquaintances. An innocent vanity mingled with his merry, friendly qualities. Conscious of his handsome head and fine bearing, he liked to appear even in the executive offices in garb more striking than dignified; for a time in a dazzling dressing-gown lined with cherry-colored silk. He took obvious delight, during the early months, in his dignities and powers as President. But though not without serious qualities, including religious fervor, strong family affections, and a genuine loyalty to strict-construction principles of government, he was on the whole a man of shallow nature. No depth of conviction, no powerful force of will, underlay his bright surface qualities. This charming, pliable, vacillating executive, surrounded by men of stronger intellect and greater determination, was to yield first to one and then to another; and while borrowing something from W. L. Marcy and something from James Guthrie, he was to be swayed most of all by the two dominating personalities of his Cabinet, Jefferson Davis and Caleb Cushing—two men who took the same general views of politics.[116]

116  Cf. Field, *Memories*, 155–174, for a revealing view of Pierce; Nichols, *Franklin Pierce, passim*; "Reminiscences of Washington," *Atlantic Monthly*, May, 1880.

# 2

# *Weak President: Rending Factions*

PIERCE, taking up the reins of office in 1853, had a clear choice between two lines of policy and unhesitatingly took the weaker and more convenient. He could assert that the Compromise constituted an irrevocable settlement of the slavery issue; could point out that there was not a square foot of territory under the American flag whose status as to slavery was not settled; could insist that no man would be given important office who did not make his adherence to the Compromise clear; and could declare that he would tolerate no dissension on this issue. He could show, that is, that he meant to have a strong Administration and to place it on a high ground of principle. The alternative course was to try to please all the factions; to attempt to conciliate every section and group by a catholic distribution of offices; to be bland, conciliatory, and yielding; and by concessions, trades, and blandishments, to strive to unite the recently warring elements. The first course would require courage. It would bring Pierce into frontal conflict with the formidable Southern Rights extremists and the no less implacable freesoil Democrats of the North. The second course was easy and seemed to offer a bright promise of party harmony. A man of sterner temper and keener perception than Pierce would have seen that party unity is never bought by offices and smiles, but only by a determined fight for principle; and that something greater than party harmony was at stake—the safety of the nation.[1]

Trying to woo all party charioteers and please all factions, Pierce went into office with an inharmonious Cabinet, representing a medley of views. He scattered gifts to groups which, remaining bitterly antagonistic, were quick to forget their benefits and stubbornly venomous over the concessions to their enemies. In dealing with the major party chieftains, he placed himself in a

1 Late in November the governor of South Carolina, sending the legislature his annual message, referred to previous Northern aggressions; stated his belief that the recent cessation from hostile acts against Southern institutions would be brief; and expressed a hope that on the recurrence of aggression, which was certain, the Southern States would rise in their majesty and strength, and either force their rights to be respected inside the Union, or take their place among the nations of the globe as a free Southern Confederacy. *National Intelligencer*, November 27, 1852.

position not of mastery, but of subservience. As soon as the offices were all gone, he had ten critics or enemies for every friend. And when a brilliant young Alcibiades grasped at the leadership that Nicias did not exercise, Pierce had to fall in behind a chariot that was being driven headlong toward the ruin of the Administration.

## [ I ]

It was no Jackson, it was not even a Polk, this "Young Hickory" who took the oath as President on March 4, 1853, and for the first time in the country's history pronounced an inaugural address without manuscript or notes. For days Washington had been filling with hungry politicians and curious tourists. It was estimated that by the evening of the third, twenty thousand had arrived, jamming all the hotels and boarding-houses, and spilling over into the halls of public buildings, where many napped that night. "It seems as if a resurrection had brought to life all our rotten, fishy politicians," wrote a Pennsylvanian.[2] One man only was conspicuous by his absence. Vice-President-elect William R. King, dying of tuberculosis, was in Cuba, where a special act of Congress permitted him to take the oath of office.

Early in the morning drums throbbed and brass instruments resounded in all parts of the city. The adjacent counties were pouring their population into the District by foot, horse, and carriage, while the Potomac boats were jammed. By noon, with seventy or eighty thousand people on hand, Pennsylvania Avenue was lined with expectant spectators, Lafayette Square held a throng admiring the new statue of Jackson by Clark Mills, and another crowd swirled about the Capitol. A raw northeasterly wind brought gusts of snow, melting as it fell, but near noon the skies began to clear and the sun became wanly visible. Brightly uniformed lines of regulars and militia, fire companies in red shirts and shining helmets, political clubs, and brass bands formed in resplendent column before the city hall. As the clock struck twelve, the music pealed forth, commands echoed along the line, and the procession marched down Louisiana Avenue to Willard's Hotel, where it closed about a barouche containing Fillmore, Pierce, and their official escorts, Jesse D. Bright and Hannibal Hamlin.

As soon as Chief Justice Taney administered the oath, Pierce stepped forward and with energetic gestures delivered his address in a clear, strong voice which reached most of the fifteen thousand people before him. He was loudly cheered. Then, returning with Fillmore to the White House, he received the congratulations of the people who swept through the mansion. It was

2  Henry Welsh, March 2, 1853; Buchanan Papers.

a triumphal day—though grief for his son, the only surviving child, recently killed before his eyes in a railway accident, left a stamp of sadness upon his countenance.[3]

The President's address, though not without a decorous note of humility, breathed firm self-confidence, and showed that he neither recognized any grave problem before the nation nor proposed any policy that would create new issues. Speaking in Jeffersonian vein of the dangers of a concentration of power, he declared that the national government should confine itself to the exercise of authority "clearly granted by the Constitution." He laid stress on the importance of integrity and economy in the public service. He announced his belief that the Compromise measures were strictly constitutional and must be unhesitatingly carried into effect, giving special advertence to "the rights of the South in this respect." Plainly, he would lend himself to an energetic enforcement of the fugitive slave law. Not less pleasing to the slavery wing of the party was his declaration that he would not shirk from territorial expansion—the expansion that Jefferson, Monroe, and Polk had made a party tradition.

"Indeed," he said, "it is not to be disguised that our attitude as a nation and our position on the globe render the acquisition of certain possessions not within our jurisdiction eminently important for our protection, if not in the future essential for the preservation of the rights of commerce and the peace of the world. Should they be obtained, it will be through no grasping spirit, but with a view to obvious national interest and security, and in a manner entirely consistent with the strictest observance of national faith." [4]

## [ II ]

The Cabinet, a highly ill-assorted body of able men, had been made up by a prolonged and painful process of shoving, hauling, and bargaining. Beset by the claims of Unionists and Southern Rights men in the South, radical free-soilers and Compromise men in the North, Pierce had talked with them all and given each group high expectations. One of his first steps after election had been to call William L. Marcy into conference and to ask Jefferson Davis to come up from Mississippi for the same purpose.[5] In political convictions two Democrats could hardly be further apart than these men. Marcy, a rugged, sagacious old Jacksonian now identified with the Barnburners, loved the Union with passionate devotion and was loath to see slavery extended by an inch; while the cold, proud Mississippian had lately been ready to break up the

3 *National Intelligencer*, N. Y. *Herald*, March 5, 1853.
4 Richardson, ed., *Messages and Papers*, V, 197–203.
5 To Davis, December 7, 1852, Pierce Papers. Family illness kept Davis at home.

nation if slavery were not left free to widen its control of land and wealth. That Pierce should make both his confidants showed that he was trying to carry water on both shoulders. Meanwhile, he was hounded from morn to midnight by rival groups, and his mail was swollen by letters of entreaty.

Old Francis P. Blair, for the freesoil Democrats, urged his son Montgomery for the attorney-generalship, and Pierce's boyhood friend, John A. Dix of New York, for the Secretaryship of State.[6] The Douglas Democrats in the West wanted one of their men in the Cabinet; say Henry B. Payne of Ohio as head of the Interior Department.[7] A large body of New York conservatives or Hunkers, led by Charles O'Conor, signed a memorial for the appointment of Daniel S. Dickinson to Cabinet office.[8] Many Southerners and Pennsylvanians were anxious to see Buchanan again in the State Department, and he longed for the place. Pierce punctured his hopes by writing him that he had resolved to offer no former Cabinet member a place in his Administration; a decision which drew from Buchanan the curt comment that the new President might well make some use of the great talents that Polk had given employment. At the same time, Pierce rendered it plain that he would lend no encouragement to Buchanan's enemy Simon Cameron, who slyly called on him just before the inauguration and was sent away with dusty answers.[9] Southern Rights men advocated the inclusion of Jefferson Davis in the Cabinet. Well-tried Unionists like Alexander H. Stephens and Henry S. Foote found the thought gall and wormwood, to which rumors that Caleb Cushing of Massachusetts might become Attorney-General added a drop of vitriol.

For weeks the excitement remained at fever heat. New York was the most explosive spot, a veritable powder magazine. Marcy's Northern friends had the aid of the moderate Unionists of the South in urging that he be given the State Department or Treasury, and he was willing to accept either place. Not only was he attacked by Dickinson's bigoted Hunkers, but he was more quietly opposed by John A. Dix's freesoil phalanx. To please the old Jacksonians and Barnburners, Pierce, when Dix paid a visit to Concord, offered him the Secretaryship of State, but the Hunkers raised such a commotion that he sent for his old

6 W. E. Smith, *The Francis Preston Blair Family in Politics*, II, 286, 287.
7 H. V. Willson, November 18, 1852, after an interview with Pierce, to Douglas; Douglas Papers .
8 E. C. West, January 18, 1853, to Douglas; Douglas Papers.
9 Pennsylvania Democrats had been acrimoniously divided by the rivalry of Cass and Buchanan for the nomination at Baltimore. "The hostility there engendered still remains in full force," wrote F. M. Wynkoop from Pottsville, Pa., on November 14, 1852, "and both parties are straining to weaken each other in the estimation of the President: Brodhead with a majority of the delegation in Congress on the one side, and Buchanan with his host of friends aided by the prestige of our late state convention on the other." Caleb Cushing Papers. It was Buchanan's greatest piece of luck that he did not go into the Cabinet.

friend again, explained the situation, and received Dix's gracious withdrawal.[10] In fact, there was such general turmoil that for a time it was thought that Pierce might cut the knot by making no appointment from New York at all, or by naming some highly neutral person.[11] "If Dix is in," wrote one vexed observer, "then Blair, Benton, and Van Buren are in. If Marcy, then the Albany clique. If Dickinson, then the devil knows who." [12] The President-elect did offer the State Department to R. M. T. Hunter of Virginia, who for various reasons—a desire to stay in the Senate, a fear that acceptance would impair his presidential chances, and family opposition—declined it.[13]

In the end Pierce, cautiously balancing group against group, dealt with the New York factions by making Marcy his Secretary of State, offering to send Dix to Paris, and giving the Hunkers control of the customhouse by naming G. C. Bronson as collector of the port. He conciliated Buchanan and his powerful following by offering him the ministership to England (a position which enemies of the sage old politician thought would safely shelve him, but which instead kept him out of harm's way during a period of dangerous domestic turmoil), and by naming Buchanan's adherent, James Campbell, as Postmaster-General. The Cameron clique filed an impassioned protest against this latter choice, but Pierce quietly replied: "I have fixed my Cabinet; and if I find that I have made a mistake, I will correct it." [14] Incidentally, Campbell was a Catholic, and the appointment pleased his church. The border States were given a representative in bluff, able James Guthrie, who became Secretary of the Treasury; a successful Louisville lawyer, much interested in railroads and banking, and president of the latest constitutional convention of Kentucky. The Northwest also had its representative in Robert McClelland of Michigan, given the Interior Department. But these two last-named men played no rôle in national politics; they were administrators and nothing more.[15]

If pliability marked Pierce's dealings with the Northern factions, downright flabbiness characterized his relations with those of the South. The Union Democrats who, fighting so hard for the Compromise, believed they had saved the country, were ignored. Their arch-enemy, the Mississippi leader who since

10  Morgan Dix, *John A. Dix*, I, 271, 272.
11  August Belmont, November 30, 1852; Buchanan Papers.
12  E. C. West, January 18, 1853; Douglas Papers.
13  H. H. Simms, *Robert M. T. Hunter*, 78, 79.
14  Glancy Jones, Washington, February 25, 1853, to Buchanan; Buchanan Papers.
15  R. S. Cotterill, "James Guthrie, Kentuckian," *Ky. State Hist. Soc. Reg.*, September, 1922. There is a brief sketch of McClelland in the *Collections* of the Pioneer Society of Michigan, IV, 454ff. Cotterill's characterization of Guthrie in the *Dictionary of American Biography* is worth quoting: "uncouth and unprepossessing . . . lame for life from a wound received in a personal encounter . . . a man of many eccentricities, of a domineering and arrogant personality, and wholly lacking in the usual graces of the politician." A biography of Guthrie is much needed.

Calhoun's death had best represented the idea of secession, was raised to Pierce's right hand as Secretary of War. "As for Jefferson Davis," wrote Francis J. Grund, "the very mention of his name causes the bristling up of such men as Cass, Gwin, Clemens, Cobb, Foote, and a host of others. Be assured that such a nomination, unheard of as the thing may be, stands a chance of *rejection in the Senate*. . . . There are those who say that the Administration would, in such a case, start with a minority in one or the other House. . . . This would . . . destroy the vital principle of Pierce's popularity . . . Foote and Cobb will raise such a howl that its echo will be heard even in the mountains of Vermont." [16] Davis tells us in his memoirs that he was happy in the peaceful pursuits of a planter, improving his land, raising livestock, and erecting buildings. Then, going to Washington to attend the inauguration, he was persuaded to enter the Cabinet; Pierce, after all, was an old army friend—and Davis knew that as Secretary of War he could do good service for Southern interests.

Had Pierce been a man of stern principle, he would never have given so important a place to one of the chief enemies of the Compromise. The fact was that the Southern extremists had greater power to injure him than the moderates, and he yielded too much to them. Even the unimportant James C. Dobbin of North Carolina, made Secretary of the Navy, was regarded as leaning to the Southern Rights side.[17]

As for the diplomatic appointees, they were remarkable not only for their strong Southern sympathies, but for their even stronger expansionism. A number of them were bound to make energetic efforts to widen the American domain. James Gadsden of South Carolina was sent to Mexico, under Southern propulsion, to obtain a fat slice of that republic. Pierre Soulé went to Spain with the annexation of Cuba in view. Under Southern demands Pierce finally substituted John Y. Mason of Virginia, another ardent expansionist, for Dix as Minister to France; and he named Solon Borland of Arkansas, a fellow-veteran of the Mexican War, as minister to Nicaragua.[18] In vain did Marcy protest against the choice of the secessionist Soulé. Pierce slighted the Unionists in the South because he thought them largely Whig, and he did nothing for moderate Democrats like Clemens and Cobb.

As if to reinforce the more radical Southern element, Pierce appointed Caleb Cushing his Attorney-General. To such sober, freedom-loving New England Democrats as Gideon Welles, this was a sore blow. Fifty-three this year, Cushing in his varied career had amply displayed his high abilities, im-

16  January 1, 1853, Cushing Papers.
17  U. B. Phillips, ed., *Toombs, Stephens, Cobb Corr.*, 328.
18  Borland, a Senator, 1848–53, was also made Minister to the other Central American states. His temper is indicated by the fact that before the secession convention of Arkansas took final action in 1861, he led a militia company to demand the surrender of Fort Smith

mense erudition, and general want of principle. After four years in Congress as a Whig, he had joined the Democrats, had headed with Henry A. Wise what Clay called the corporal's guard of President Tyler's friends in Congress, had been honored by that unpopular leader with a Cabinet nomination which the Senate refused to confirm, and had made a brilliant record as the first American minister to China. Returning to the United States, he had advocated vigorous prosecution of the Mexican War, led a regiment to the front, and became brigadier-general. His industry, address, and versatility were astonishing. He could negotiate a treaty, lead a charge, write a book, and, though never a truly great lawyer, present luminously all the facts bearing on any legal issue.

Yet Cushing never commanded the trust of discriminating observers. When in 1851 Governor Boutwell appointed him to the supreme bench of Massachusetts, the State was shocked; for, writes George Frisbie Hoar, most people regarded him as a man without moral convictions and as utterly subservient to the slave power. His friendliness to Southern extremists was in due time to be amply demonstrated, for as Pierce's Attorney-General, he soon wrote a letter declaring that the anti-slavery movement must be "crushed," while later still, in the crisis of the Democratic convention of 1860 and incipient secession, his partnership with the leaders of the Lower South deserved the word sinister.[19] Political observers in 1853 at once concluded that Jefferson Davis and Cushing would establish their ascendency over Pierce—and this view proved well-founded.

By withholding the announcement of his Cabinet to the last moment, Pierce measurably avoided the storm of censure that would otherwise have fallen upon Davis and Cushing. One of Cushing's political backers frankly warned him that his own appointment would have to be a *fait accompli* or it would meet a perfect typhoon of wrath.[20] A week before the inauguration, few politicians knew just who the Cabinet members would be. Cass was reported to be angry because he had not been consulted. So was Douglas. Foote and other Southern Unionists were deeply incensed. F. P. Blair, cut to his very soul to learn that the Jacksonians had been passed over and Southern radicals favored, bearded Pierce near the end of February at a dinner aboard the steamboat *Ericsson*. "I told him," he informed Martin Van Buren, "that he had put in his Cabinet his enemies—men who felt his nomination a blow to their ambitions and who certainly would avenge it on him unless he complied with their wishes in

19 Hoar, *Autobiography*, I, 173. Already Cushing was hated by thousands of New Englanders as the "crusher of abolitionists"; William S. Robinson, *"Warrington" Pen Portraits*, 205. At a later date the war governor of Massachusetts was to refuse his proffered military services because he did not trust Cushing's loyalty; Fuess, *Cushing*, II, 277.
20 F. J. Grund, January 1, 1853, Cushing Papers.

avenging it upon those honest men whose affections had been with him from his youth upwards. . . ." [21]

The Administration quickly fell into routine efficiency. Astute onlookers did not find Pierce difficult to assay, and they knew that he would try to cling to beaten paths. "He is shrewd, keen, and penetrating," wrote a sharp Pennsylvanian after a half-hour chat. "A well-balanced mind, but not of the first order. Has a good knowledge of men, and is extremely well satisfied with his present position." This self-complacency included, as Buchanan noted on a late spring visit to the capital, a strong desire to arrange matters for a second term. [22] At first Pierce took his duties lightly. During June his old friend, B. B. French, signing land patents at the White House, saw him almost hourly. "He is, to me, exactly the same free and easy, laughing and joking Frank Pierce that he always was, and I love him just as well as if he were not President!" That he proved an efficient moderator of Cabinet meetings is well attested— and it is also clear that he was nothing more than a moderator. When he visited New York on July Fourth to open the Crystal Palace Exhibition and speak to a great concourse, his brisk, self-confident, and jaunty manner almost concealed the fact that he had nothing to say.

The four ablest members of the Cabinet, Davis, Marcy, Cushing, and Guthrie, were all conspicuously hardworking. Lights burned late in their offices as they dealt with patronage, met daily problems, and mapped out reforms. Davis was prompt in planning genuinely constructive measures for the army— a concentration of the scattered Western troops into larger bodies among the Indians; better pay and promotion to encourage recruiting; and the addition of two regiments of riflemen and other forces to the establishment. [23] Cushing managed the legal work of the government with trenchant mastery.

As for blunt, humorous Marcy, preoccupied with his duties, he was socially a favorite of the other Cabinet members, though they thrust him into a corner in political matters, excluding him from their secret councils. His diplomatic papers were models of forcible argument, for he had formed a direct style in writing editorials for the Albany *Argus*. Many of these papers were composed at home, where, sitting in his library of five thousand volumes, he would work in his dressing gown, with his faded red handkerchief on the table before him, until noon. A gentleman of the old school, not averse to a glass of wine and a pinch of snuff, he could be delightful in chatting upon the scholarly topics he loved; he could be briskly efficient on points of diplomacy—the Mexican Minister remarked that he transacted more business in ten minutes with Marcy

21  Smith, *Blair Family*, II, 289.
22  June 1, 1853, to Henry A. Wise; Buchanan Papers.
23  *Annual Report Secretary of War*, 1853, 1854.

than in an hour with anybody else. But he was frigid and even bearish to office-hunting politicians, turning his back on them. The fact that he was author of the maxim, "To the victor belong the spoils," is evidence of his epigrammatic powers rather than of any leaning toward the worst side of politics. A lover of the best in British, American, and French literature, he delighted to make presents of such books as Burton's *Anatomy*, Milton's prose, and Sir Thomas Browne's *Urn Burial*—and when he came to die it was with an open copy of Bacon's essays lying by his side. He was in many ways the brightest adornment of an Administration whose principal measures he profoundly disapproved.[24]

But it was not a well-controlled Administration. August Belmont wrote Buchanan that the President's choice of his principal officers would not tend to harmony, and that a particularly severe opposition to the Administration might be expected from all who had stood by the Union during the Compromise fight. He believed that what he called the mosaic portion of the Cabinet could not long withstand the rough handling it would receive.[25] The disharmony was soon evident. But that was not the worst of the situation. Benton, who always prided himself upon knowing the *inside* story of affairs, declared that when the Administration ended, it ought not really to be termed the Pierce Administration—for Pierce had not directed it. It was "an Administration in which he was inoperative, and in which nullifiers, disunionists, and renegades used his name and his power for their own audacious and criminal purposes."[26]

[ III ]

The summer and autumn of 1853 found life in Washington more placidly enjoyable than it would be for many a long year to come. The capital city was growing rapidly, with new streets, many new buildings, and so much fashion that quiet people complained of the social whirl. In some respects its habits still had a bucolic side. A typical bureaucrat, B. B. French, who was successively clerk of the House, secretary to President Pierce, and commissioner of public buildings, kept a cow and horse at his place on East Capitol Street and

24 See the sketch in the N. Y. *Evening Post*, quoted in the *National Intelligencer*, July 23, 1857; the *National Intelligencer*, May 14, July 9, 1857; John Bassett Moore, "A Great Secretary of State: William L. Marcy," *Pol. Sci. Quarterly*, September, 1915; William Gorham Rice, "The Appointment of Governor Marcy as Secretary of State," *Mag. of Hist.*, Feb.–March, 1912, January, 1913. Marcy's "Diary and Memoranda" are printed in the *Am. Hist. Review*, April–July, 1919.
25 March 5, 1853; Buchanan Papers.
26 To George Robertson, November 1, 1857, *National Intelligencer*, November 26, 1857.

grew fruit and vegetables. He was fond of fowling in the vicinity of Washington and once within two hours killed a hundred ortolans on the Patuxent River.[27] But the northern part of the city in particular was rapidly filling up with new brick and stone buildings, some very handsome. The cost of living was rising. Servants were still cheap—when William A. Graham had come to the city to join Fillmore's Cabinet, he had engaged a cook, formerly Dolly Madison's, at $8 a month, a manservant belonging to Robert E. Lee at $12, and a coachman at $15 [28]—but rents and food were so high that government clerks had difficulty in making ends meet. Brown's Hotel now made a regular charge of $75 a week for room and board to a Congressman and his wife.[29] It was later said that in the first half-dozen years of the 1850's, the value of Washington real estate quadrupled.[30]

In a city still ill-adorned, the unveiling of Clark Mills's statue of Jackson in Lafayette Square early in January had been an impressive event. Members of both houses, led by the Speaker, had marched up with a procession of soldiers, marines, and militia troops; the President, Cabinet, and General Scott, with numerous official guests, attended; and Stephen A. Douglas delivered an oration. Less critical than subsequent generations, most people pronounced the statue truly beautiful.[31] The White House had been newly painted, new walks had been laid in the grounds, and large gas lamps had been placed at all the entrances. During the spring of 1853 the eastern wing of the Patent Office, so handsome an edifice that the Secretary of the Interior promptly removed himself and his clerks thither, was completed, with the western wing well under way. With gaslights, hot-air heat, and hot and cold water in these additions, the building was counted the best-equipped in the city.[32] This spring, too, saw the new hall of the Library of Congress opened, a chamber ninety-one feet long and thirty-four feet wide, beautifully finished. "At first view of this enchanting room," exclaimed a reporter, "thousands will experience, as we did, a glow of rapturous delight, not unmixed with something of a selfish sentiment of congratulation

27 French Papers. French notes that a friend killed forty eight dozen ortolans—that is, bobolinks—in a week's shooting. His diary describes what was presumably a typical Washington breakfast: dip toast, cold corned beef, boiled eggs, and coffee.
28 Graham to his wife, August 13, 1850; Graham Papers, U. of N. C.
29 J. S. Williams, November 26, 1852, to Gideon Welles; Welles Papers.
30 N. Y. Commercial Advertiser, November 26, 1856. For a view of bureaucratic underpayment, written slightly later but applicable to this time, see James Parton, "Uncle Sam's Treatment of his Servants," Topics of the Time (1871).
31 National Intelligencer, January 11, 1853. Mills, who had begun life as a drifting daylaborer, was befriended by John S. Preston of South Carolina, and William C. Preston, who paid his expenses in art study. It was not until 1847, on his way north to begin his studies, that he saw in Richmond his first statue, Houdon's Washington. When asked to design the equestrian monument of Jackson, he had not seen either Jackson or an equestrian statue. Charles E. Fairman, Art and Artists of the Capital.
32 National Intelligencer, April 21, 1853.

that as citizens of Washington we are endowed with so great a privilege as the library affords." [33] This was in the western extension of the Capitol. The huge white obelisk of the Washington Monument, as yet only about 120 feet high, looked like a particularly squat and ugly lighthouse; still, it was moving slowly upward and promised to be a great future landmark. Plans were being made for the new dome of the Capitol, for which in two years more the scaffolding would rise.

A much-needed contribution to the health and comfort of the city, the aqueduct to the great falls of the Potomac, was initiated with suitable ceremony in the fall of 1853. A steamer full of official guests ran up to the falls. President Pierce, with appropriate words, lifted the first spadeful of turf; Jefferson Davis, with a short address, the second; and Douglas, with an invocation of the Constitution, the third. Then they and two hundred others sat down to a collation.[34] The cost of this conduit, running sixteen miles from the falls to a reservoir in Georgetown, was met partly by Congress and partly by the city. Captain Montgomery C. Meigs, supervisor of many of the national works of the period, was in charge, his skill and energy being expected to complete it in 1857. Till then the city depended on wells, and the White House had water from an unfenced spring in Franklin Square.[35]

Yet although the city was improving, its general aspect remained that of a shambling, dilapidated, ill-planned town set off by a few fine buildings and squares. Pennsylvania Avenue, partly gravelled, needed much repair; most other streets were alternately dust and mud. The "Tiber" canal running down to the Potomac remained almost an open sewer. The Center Market-House on the Avenue, where Webster had bought his ducks and shad, was an unsightly old edifice, and on market days country wagons often filled the Avenue from Seventh to Eleventh Street with filth and litter. The bridges across the Potomac were in such bad condition as to be positively unsafe. The Mall, the principal open reservation of the city, remained neglected and unkempt save for the space occupied by the Smithsonian Institution. Congress had made a trifling appropriation in 1850 for bettering one section of it, and this had been expended in doing heavy damage to the excellent natural surface of the plat between Twelfth and Fourteenth Streets. The aspect of Judiciary Square, in the center of the city, was ruined by the frowning jail, which had been repeatedly con-

---

33  *Idem,* August 16, 1853.
34  Bryan, *History of the National Capital,* II; W. Tindall, *Standard History of the City of Washington; National Intelligencer,* November 10, 1853.
35  *Report Commissioner of Public Buildings and Grounds* (Dr. Blake), 1856; printed in *National Intelligencer,* February 19, 1856. Dr. Blake wanted a railing put about the square. "Even with an ample supply of water from the Potomac," he wrote, "when the waterworks shall have been completed, this spring ought to be preserved for the pureness of its water." He also wished to have Center Market-House removed.

demned by grand juries as unsanitary and unsafe. Certain localities near the Potomac were still the seat of malarial fever.[36]

Washington's social life was focussed, as always, in two main centers, one official, one the old aristocracy (sometimes not so old) of the city; and the tone of the two circles was very different. The White House, where the President and his wife felt their bereavement sorely, was not a place of gaiety. Mrs. Pierce did not make her first appearance in public till near the close of 1853, emerging in black velvet and diamonds, so worn and pallid that she awakened universal sympathy.[37] All dinners and receptions at the White House were marked by great simplicity, the only remarkable features of the entertainments, to one visitor, being the gold spoons that dated from Monroe's time and the stiff bouquets from the government greenhouse.[38] Jefferson Davis' house was also visited by death, for in the second year of the Administration he lost his infant son. For many months afterward, writes his wife, the grief-stricken man "walked half the night and worked fiercely all day." Secretary Marcy entertained little, though visitors found his unpretentious house notable for a fine collection of German paintings made by his wife's sister while traveling. But the daughters of Secretary Guthrie vied with other Southern hostesses, such as Mrs. Toombs and Mrs. Howell Cobb, in the originality of their entertainments.[39]

Southerners, indeed, easily carried off the palm among the entertainments given by political figures. William Aiken of South Carolina, Representative and former Governor, with a fortune built on planting, delighted in balls and receptions at his imposing house, to which came figures of distinction—the historian Bancroft, the ethnologist Schoolcraft, the philanthropist George Peabody. The illuminated and garlanded staircase was often crowded with belles,

36 National Intelligencer, September 22, November 30, 1852, April 21, 26, 1853; Report Commissioner of Public Buildings and Grounds, 1853. The city had no sewage system worthy of the name. Excrement was deposited in above-ground boxes in each yard, which were regularly emptied. "Now, what becomes of it?" asked a writer in the National Intelligencer. "Instead of being sent to the proper localities, it is carried to the poudrette factories. Next, let us see where these are located: one on Fifteenth Street, about nine squares north of the official residence of the President of the United States; the other on the high land touching on Boundary Street, near Seventh Street. If a chemist desired to seek on a grand scale an arrangement for the pouring of heavy gases from one level to another, he would choose exactly these localities." October 15, 1855.

37 Mrs. Clement C. Clay, A Belle of the Fifties, 27.

38 Idem, 29; Cf. Hiram Fuller, Belle Brittan on a Tour, Letters 1-5.

39 Davis, Jefferson Davis, I, 534, 535; National Intelligencer, July 23, 1857, for the Marcy paintings. The MS diary of John V. L. Pruyn (New York State Archives) describes a brilliant ball by the Brazilian Minister in honor of the birthday of his empress, and other social affairs. On December 31, 1853, he dined with President Pierce at four. Mrs. Pierce was still grief-stricken over the death of her boy. "I succeeded in engaging her in conversation, almost the whole time, and one of the gentlemen said to me after leaving, that he believed that I had accomplished more in that way than had been done since Mr. P. had been in Washington. . . . But one wine was served, and the President did not take any."

military and naval officers, and diplomats. Aiken had added a ballroom to his residence, and here an orchestra, on a platform half hidden by laurel and ever-green, poured forth the waltzes and polkas. Secretary Guthrie, personally in-different to society, entertained on a lavish scale as a matter of public duty—his ballroom as large as a public hall. So did Judge John A. Campbell of the Supreme Court. To evening gatherings many of the women wore Paris gowns, set off with ostrich-feather fan, lace scarf, and diamond cross or brooch. The supper tables presented a splendid vista of napery and silver, with cornucopias and pyramids of bon-bons and candied fruit. Gautier, the fashionable caterer, did his work with a flourish; and all the dinners, receptions, or fetes included a grand semi-military movement of ebony waiters, for black servants, perfectly drilled, were employed in scores. At all of them punch and wines flowed freely, and at the large dinners the terrapin, roast turkey, lobster, and hothouse fruits were of the finest quality and in overpowering quantity.[40]

Among old Washingtonians the most prominent figure was the tall, hand-some W. W. Corcoran, who had been reared in Georgetown, had been prominent in the city's banking life since 1830, and with his partner George W. Riggs had handled most of the government's loans during the Mexican War. His house was famous for his fine paintings, and for Powers's Greek Slave, effectively installed in a guarded alcove. It was the center not only of frequent receptions and evening dances, but of much philanthropic activity, for Corcoran was a generous giver to churches, colleges, and public charities. He made his large weekly dinners almost an institution. Once when genial Howell Cobb had been dining there, he accosted Senator C. C. Clay in front of the Treasury. "Ah, Clay," he said, with an air of satisfaction. "Been to Corcoran's. Johannisberger and *terrapin*, sir! I wish"—and giving his waist-coat a tug, he glanced at the great stone building beside him—"I wish the Treasury were as full as I am!" [41] Riggs also had a handsome house, where he welcomed many guests; and when Patti made her Washington debut in "Traviata," Mrs. Riggs invited a select company to meet the operatic troupe after the performance.[42] Another of the notable hostesses was Mrs. A. S. Parker, who presided over a costly residence, with spacious parlors, ballroom, and conservatories, and who especially liked to gather the young people about her. Mrs. Ogle Tayloe, a New Yorker by birth who had married a Virginian, had a mansion filled with treasures. Her sympathies were pointedly with the South, and antislavery leaders were not welcome at her parties.

Social lines were strictly drawn among the old aristocracy, where family

40 Alexander Mackay, *The Western World*, I, chs. 9, 10; Marcy C. Ames, *Ten Years in Washington*, 231ff.
41 Mrs. Clay, *A Belle of the Fifties*, 121, 122.
42 MS Recollections of Mrs. Clay, Duke Library.

counted for much more than wealth or rank. The beautiful Adele Cutts, for example, won her entry into Washington society through her relationship to Dolly Madison, her grandaunt. The daughter of an ill-paid departmental clerk, she was once heard to complain of the cost of gloves; but she was welcomed at the best houses, and when later she married Senator Douglas, many felt that, for all his position and reputed wealth, she had condescended to him. A natural affinity bound the old families, their connections ramifying through the old South, with the more polished members of the diplomatic corps. Matrimonial alliances between the two groups were not uncommon. Baron de Bodisco, Russian Minister from the time of Van Buren, had married the youthful Harriet Williams, called the most beautiful girl in Georgetown, while his successor, the discerning Baron de Stoeckl, also took an American wife. One of Senator Benton's daughters, Mme. Boileau, was the wife of a French attaché. At the British legation, the Bulwers early in the 1850's entertained lavishly and delighted in many of the Washington folk; the next Minister, Crampton, was a bachelor and lived more quietly; but Lord and Lady Napier, who followed, played a central rôle in the social life of the capital.[43]

Yet in the round of dinners, balls, concerts, and receptions, it was impossible to avoid a good deal of what Senator C. C. Clay's wife called promiscuity. Not only did Senators, Representatives, and military and naval officers of varied backgrounds have to be asked freely, but when important "constituents" came to Washington they also expected courtesies. Rough Ben Wade of Ohio, when his wife wondered how she would fare if she visited the city, reassured her; there was no snobbery, he wrote. "There are a great many females, here, from every part of the Union. . . . But the fashionables are of the real upper crust, and no copying of it. And you know enough of the world to have observed that anyone may get along much better with these than with their counterfeits in our busy villages. Here once admitted to their society and all is easy and agreeable, no stiffness, no turning up the nose, as among the bastard aristocracy." [44] In another letter he remarked that society was too heterogeneous to become stratified, and that any peculiarity would not be criticized with half the severity it would meet in Ashtabula.

43 But plain Washingtonians like B. B. French, seeing little of the dinners and balls, lived (or might live) a more intellectual life. French records the general delight in Dickens and Tennyson, both constantly read and quoted; he tells of the curiosity aroused by Coventry Patmore's "The Angel in the House"; he writes admiringly of Peg Woffington and Christie Johnston, "by an author named Read." Lectures were constantly being given at the Smithsonian Institution by leading scientists and litterateurs of the day. French Papers. In the general lack of picture galleries, the paintings filling the panels of the Capitol rotunda attracted more attention than they deserved. Washingtonians flocked eagerly in 1853 to see the eighth and last, Powell's "Discovery of the Mississippi by De Soto in 1542."
44 January 22, 1852; Wade Papers.

Wade himself went to the pains of buying a book on Washington etiquette, reading it, and sending it home. But, calling himself a backwoodsman as ignorant of social usage as a Comanche Indian, he refused to be impressed by any of the splendors. At a White House dinner he took nothing but a little bread and wine and gazed curiously at his partner, Mrs. Curtis—"she is among the reigning belles of the place, and her hair was filled with gay flowers and diamonds, and her dress low in the neck"—until she put him at ease by talking about spiritualism.[45] At Winfield Scott's house on a night cold as Greenland, he saw the general's daughter and another girl depart for a ball. "Their bosoms and throats and arms were entirely bare down as low as I dare mention," commented the Ohioan. "And they wore no bonnets, nor anything, on their heads, but ribbons and jewels in their hair, and with a little light silk thrown over their shoulders they stepped into the coach, to ride about half a mile. . . ." Going to see an English actor, Brook, in *Othello,* Wade was shocked by the play. The language made him blush—some of it was worthy of a house of ill fame; "and then, after the obscenity, they must all be butchered before your eyes, in a manner as cruel as they butcher hogs in Cincinnati." To tell the truth concluded Wade, "Shakespeare was a coarse, vulgar barbarian, with very little wit." [46] There were many Wades in Washington.

An important part of the Washington world were the hotels and boarding-houses, and the "messes" formed in them. Much the largest of the hotels was the National, a rambling, capacious old cluster of buildings, now growing so dingy that it had to be completely renovated in 1855, with new furniture, hangings, rugs, chandeliers, china, glassware, and silver. Its cuisine, managed by three French chefs with the aid of a famous Virginia Negro cook, became the special pride of its proprietors. Brown's Hotel, with a capacity for 450 guests as against the National's 800, had a history that went back to the early years of Washington, when it was called the Indian Queen's Tavern. Since 1821 it had been conducted by the Browns, father and sons, who made it a special rendezvous for Southern Congressmen. For many years it possessed a great bell which admonished the whole city of the hour of breakfast, dinner, and supper; and this was replaced for a time by a gong as loud as the ram's horn which brought down the walls of Jericho. As Pierce's Administration opened, the old brick structure gave way to a larger marble edifice. Willard's Hotel, at the corner of Pennsylvania Avenue and Fourteenth, was another old hostelry, which had steadily expanded and was soon to swallow up the neighboring Mansion House. Then there were a dozen smaller places—Gadsby's, long kept by a Boniface popular with every politician, but soon to become the Washing-

45 Cf. Mary G. Windle, *Life in Washington,* 249ff.
46 February 14, 1852; Wade Papers.

ton, under new management; the Exchange Hotel, resort of a large number of respectable farmers and shopkeepers from the neighboring Virginia counties—a house just refitted with velvet carpets, brocade curtains, large mirrors, and other indications of the growing luxury of the time; the Kirkwood, and others. Some visitors complained that the hotels put too much money into the display of the ornate parlors, and too little into the comfort of the rooms upstairs.[47]

Residents at the hotels could largely choose their own associates, and sectional lines were more and more strictly drawn. Senator C. C. Clay and his wife, taking up their residence at Brown's, ate at the same table with Orr of South Carolina, Taylor of Louisiana, J. L. M. Curry of Alabama, L. Q. C. Lamar of Mississippi, and other Southerners—the strongly pro-slavery Pugh of Ohio being the only Northerner. "We keep free-soilers, Black Republicans, and Bloomers on the other side of the street," Mrs. Clay was later to write. "They are afraid even to inquire for board at this house."[48] The boarding-houses were much drearier places than the hotels. "The only activity is among the flies," one Congressman complained. "The table is literally black with them, and no one pretends to brush them off."[49] Here, too, the growing tension of the sectional struggle caused men to choose their associates carefully, so that confidential subjects might be frankly discussed, and the Mississippian or Georgian seldom had an opportunity to exchange informal views with the Illinoisan or New Yorker of opposite party. The gambling houses plentifully strewing the north side of Pennsylvania Avenue, and the lottery offices which shouldered them, were places of more catholic resort.

[ IV ]

Public attention till Congress met in December, 1853, was divided between foreign affairs and the factional quarrels of the Democrats, both of which had qualities of opera bouffe. By midsummer, Cushing, who had taken over the old Interior Department building opposite the Treasury, with an audience chamber there which was said to be more crowded than the White House anterooms, was called the Richelieu of the Administration. He took pains to talk with everybody of importance who came to Washington. Jefferson Davis and he not only held the controlling hand in domestic affairs, but against Marcy's opposition strove to keep the tiller even in foreign relations.[50]

47  See National Intelligencer, October 18, 1855, for long article on Washington hotels; but cf. Frederick Law Olmsted, Journey in the Seaboard Slave States, 1–5, for their discomfort.
48  A Belle of the Fifties, Ch. 3.
49  Letters of L. O. Branch, N. C. Hist. Review, X, 47ff.
50  Fuess, Cushing, II, 136, 137.

For a time the cautious Buchanan, complaining of Pierce's discourtesy, hesitated to accept the mission to England. Issues of grave importance—the fisheries, Canadian reciprocity, the modification of the Clayton-Bulwer treaty— were to be discussed, and if he were exiled, Buchanan wished the honor of any settlement to be mainly his. As a former Secretary of State, he would object to seeing weighty negotiations conducted in Washington by Marcy while he twiddled his thumbs and attended London dinner-parties. He made this entirely clear to Pierce when he accepted his post. When a little later Marcy suggested that his powers might after all be limited, he threatened to resign unless the British negotiations were carried on in London; and Marcy agreed in so far as the Clayton-Bulwer treaty was concerned. Before leaving, Buchanan dined with several of the Cabinet. The ascendency of Davis and Cushing was perfectly clear to him, and he jocularly remarked that old fogies like himself and Marcy might well retire and give younger men an opportunity for preference; a statement so agreeable that Davis and Dobbin escorted him to his hotel arm-in-arm.[51]

Meanwhile, John Y. Mason, an old-school Virginian of commanding presence, kindly heart, and good head, but chock-full of prejudices and highly emotional, betook himself to Paris with little thought of *haute politique*. With six daughters to educate, he had long used official position (including Cabinet posts under Tyler and Polk) to supplement his income from land and slaves. He found Louis Napoleon just settling himself as Emperor of the French. The despot liked to hear him discourse eloquently in favor of free trade, but Mason's chief preoccupation seemed to be to make sure of an adequate supply of Virginia hams, Virginia tobacco—and good drinkables.[52]

A teapot tempest arose when Marcy, a man of Jeffersonian simplicity, issued a circular urging all the nation's representatives to appear on court occasions in the ordinary dress of an American gentleman. Theretofore the conventional costume of American diplomats had been a plain blue uniform adorned with gold lace and embroidery, with a white waistcoat. Franklin had made a dress that was plain to the point of oddity respected and admired at the French court. In its general purpose Marcy's circular was entirely sensible. Plain dress augmented rather than diminished the distinction of Americans; for once it was understood that the American minister would appear amid a crowd of laced, gilded, and bespangled figures in a black coat, that became as distinct a uniform as if he wore the Yankee stars on his breast and the stripes on his trousers.[53] But Marcy erred in leaving the adoption of the plain costume to the discretion of diplomatic officers.

51 Curtis, *Buchanan*, II, ch. 3.
52 M. B. Field, *Memories*, 57–74. "Fat, ruddy, and fifty-five" was the Richmond *Whig's* characterization of Mason; November 6, 1850.
53 W. H. Trescot, *National Intelligencer*, October 5, 1853.

What the Secretary should have done was to issue a specific and peremptory order, making the issue—if one arose—between government and government, not between diplomat and foreign court. As the order ran, many American representatives were placed between two embarrassing pressures. In Paris, London, and other capitals they would displease court officials unless they wore a special and more or less resplendent uniform; while if they donned this, they would displease Marcy. August Belmont, who had been sent to the Hague, felt the dilemma keenly. When he applied to the Foreign Minister for his audience with the king, saying that in compliance with instructions he would wear a citizen's ordinary dress, he met sharp objection. The king, rejoined the Foreign Minister, would much prefer the use of a uniform; while Belmont, he added, could easily wear one, for Marcy's order left the decision discretionary, and word had just come from Berlin that the American Minister there, after some dispute, had agreed to put on a uniform. Belmont, however, insisted on being presented in the plainest garb, declaring that the instructions were emphatic, had received the approbation of the American people, and coincided with his own view of the proprieties.[54]

The minister to Prussia whose example was thus cited did not fare so well. Peter D. Vroom, a former governor of New Jersey, was practically coerced into wearing a uniform, because the sovereign would not receive him without it. The Berlin court, decidedly hostile to the American republic anyway, and permitting the *Kreuzzeitung* to publish articles on the United States full of the foulest abuse, was apparently glad to inconvenience the minister. A different spirit ruled in London and Paris, where Victoria and Napoleon were friendly. But the etiquette of the French was strict, and Mason decided that he had discretion to put on court dress.[55] With Mason's advice, Buchanan at St. James's also followed his own judgment. He insisted upon wearing black coat and trousers and white waistcoat, but added a plain black-hilted sword as a concession to court officials and to distinguish himself from the upper servants! He was received, he wrote home, with the utmost kindness. "Having yielded, they did not do things by halves. As I approached the Queen, an arch but benevolent smile lit up her countenance—as much as to say, you are the first man who ever appeared before me in court in such a dress. I must confess that I never felt more proud of being an American than when I stood in that brilliant circle in the simple dress of an American citizen." [56]

54  Belmont, November 15, 1853, to Douglas; Douglas Papers. See Amos A. Ettinger, *Pierre Soulé's Mission to Spain*, for the course followed by that diplomat.
55  Mason, March 5, 1854, to Buchanan; Buchanan Papers.
56  February 24, 1854, to Harriet Lane; Buchanan Papers. It may be noted here that Benjamin Moran, clerk and secretary under Buchanan, disliked the "butler's dress," and rejoiced when in 1861 Charles Francis Adams returned to full diplomatic costume; a naval

Marcy, whose presidential ambitions were unconcealed, had possibly a political motive in his circular on diplomatic dress, and perhaps one also in his treatment of the Koszta affair. Martin Koszta, a Hungarian refugee who had lived for about two years in the United States and had declared his intention of becoming a citizen, was seized at Smyrna, Turkey, and haled aboard an Austrian warship. He stood in dire peril of execution. Captain D. N. Ingraham of the sloop *St. Louis*, a spare, sharp-spoken, straightforward, "salt marsh" South Carolinian, instructed by the American chargé at Constantinople that Koszta was entitled to protection, demanded his surrender, and in the face of very superior forces, cleared ship for action. A naval battle seemed imminent when it was agreed that the French consul should take care of Koszta until the dispute was settled. While the country rang with applause of Ingraham, Marcy came forward to justify that officer's conduct; and in a calm but firm note to the Austrian charge in Washington, Hülsemann, maintained that Koszta, having obtained a domicile in the United States, was properly shielded by its strong arm. What was more, he characterized the Austrian kidnapping as a lawless act, "an atrocious outrage." Stating a good legal case, this note pleased the bumptious temper of the masses and delighted all immigrants who had fled from the tyrannies of Central Europe. Even the Whigs liked it, Fillmore giving it partial approval, and the New York *Tribune* declaring that America should not worry about Vattel and Grotius, but make a few precedents of her own. Americans generally agreed that no matter how poor, how friendless or how struggling an adopted citizen might be, he ought to be protected against all the powers of the Old World. The stirring episode aroused the jealousy of some of Marcy's colleagues.[57]

The expansionist policy which Pierce had announced in his inaugural was pursued as vigorously as circumstances permitted. Caleb Cushing, accompanying the President to the Crystal Palace Exhibition, told a Newark crowd that "we are now the men of modern Rome," and that Rome "conquered" and "went on annexing." [58] One territorial gain was easily secured. In 1853 Santa Anna rose to power again in Mexico; he needed money; and James Gadsden, the former aide-de-camp of Jackson who had been sent to Mexico City, found him receptive to a bargain. As the year closed he and Gadsden signed a treaty

---

blue coat with gold embroidered standing collar, gold eagle buttons, white kerseymere waistcoat and breeches, white silk stockings, gold knee-buckles, black shoes with gold buckles, and a fine gilt eagle-headed sword. Victoria was also pleased, remarking: "I am thankful we shall have no more American funerals." Moran's MS Diary, July 19, 1861.

57 Full text of the dispatch is in the *National Intelligencer*, October 1, 1853. For a note on the jealousy of Marcy, see Buchanan, *Works*, IX, 17. The *Tribune's* statement is in the issue of September 26, 1853. See S. F. Bemis, ed., *American Secretaries of State,* VI, 268-273.

58 Text of speech, *National Intelligencer*, May 2, 1857.

which gave the United States a broad strip south of the Gila for fifteen millions. An indignant Senate minority attacked the treaty as a scheme promoted by greedy slaveholders and railroad speculators; and Benton, declaring the land worthless, quoted Kit Carson as saying that not even a wolf could pick up a living from it. In the end, however, the treaty was ratified after some boundary alterations which made the area ceded about 45,535 square miles, and after a reduction of the purchase price to ten millions. Time disclosed values in the

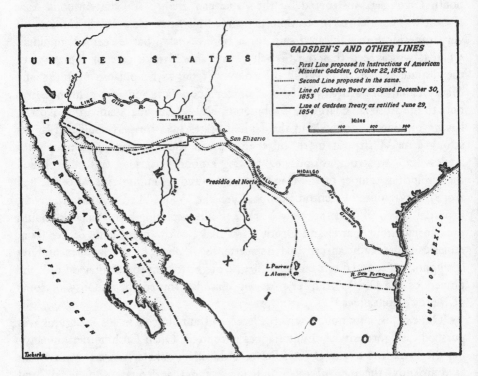

GADSDEN'S AND OTHER LINES
First Line proposed in Instructions of American Minister Gadsden, October 22, 1853.
Second Line proposed in the same.
Line of Gadsden Treaty as signed December 30, 1853
Line of Gadsden Treaty as ratified June 29, 1854

land which Carson had not seen; but the immediate milk in the coconut was an improved route for a southern railroad to the Pacific. Gadsden, much disappointed that he failed to gain room for a port on the Gulf of California, felt that the South had missed an opportunity to establish a new Trieste there, and wrote the Charleston *Courier* that it had gained something but not enough.[59]

Cuba, however, the object of ardent desire on the part of Pierce, Davis, and Cushing, of a host of Southerners, and of considerable knots of Northern speculators, was a more difficult prize. The efforts of the filibusters of 1849–51, culminating in the ill-starred Lopez expedition, had achieved nothing except

59  P. N. Garber, *The Gadsden Treaty, passim.*

to fire Castilian pride, strengthen the determination of Madrid to hold the island, and arouse the apprehensions of Britain and France. The British in particular, condemning the piratical arrogance of Yankee filibusters, had no wish to see the Caribbean closed; while the London *Times* voiced a fear that if the Southern States took Cuba, the North would demand Canada as a balance.[60] Yet in some ways the pear seemed to be ripening. Year by year the discontent of the Cubans became more glaring, the nerveless incompetence and corruption of the Spaniards more shocking. Harriet Martineau, writing in the London *Daily News* as Fillmore's Administration closed, had warned Spain that she must act at once to improve her administration, stop the slave trade, remedy complaints, and make her case fair before the world, if she were to command much sympathy in resisting American pressures.[61]

The fact was that the existing state of Cuba, as many a critic pointed out, constituted an outrage upon the name of Christian civilization. Spanish laws, the most conspicuous relic of mercantilism anywhere on the globe, mercilessly exploited the island. The Spanish officials were a swarm of robbers; justice was sold to the highest bidder; most of the clergy were idle reactionaries; public works were neglected; not one free child in ten was taught to read. But this was not the worst of it. Within the previous decade the production of the "ingenios" or sugar estates, without any marked increase of free laborers, had been doubled. How? Everyone knew the answer. Though Spain had pledged herself to stop the slave trade, thousand of Negroes were annually run in from Africa. Competent observers estimated that in 1849 about 8,700 slaves were landed, and in 1853 (to be sure, an unusual year) no fewer than 12,500.[62] Conditions aboard the ships which thus slipped through the Anglo-American cordon were horrible even for the slave trade.

On many great plantations the sad blacks fared little better than on the slave-ships. Twelve, sixteen, and even eighteen hours of toil a day, under the burning sun, were extorted from the Negroes by the lash. At night they were huddled together, often without respect to sex, in barracoons hardly fit for cattle. They were fed on salt fish, dried junk, and ill-cooked vegetables. Little or no regard was paid to family life; all instruction was denied; holidays there were none. Many planters regarded their hands as machines to be worked to exhaustion, and the death-rate was appalling. To supplement the African importations, raids had been made on the shores of Yucatan, from which many Indians were carried off to servitude. Bad as slavery was in parts of the lower South, it was

60 September 9, 1851.
61 Quoted in *National Intelligencer*, January 20, 1853.
62 W. L. Mathieson, *Great Britain and the Slave Trade, 1839–1865*, 142, 143.

paradise compared with Cuban slavery. To guard the unhappy island Spain maintained an army of 25,000 and a fleet of thirty or forty ships.[63]

Yet it was not, alas! for humanitarian reasons that Americans thought of loosing the Spanish yoke. To Southern leaders and to the Administration organ, the Washington *Union*, the idea of slave emancipation in Cuba was a horrifying bogey. Throughout 1853 the *Union* raised the cry that Britain was about to persuade Spain to substitute an apprenticeship system, or voluntary labor, for slavery.[64] If British emancipation in Jamaica had encouraged the Northern abolitionists and struck at the foundations of Southern slavery, what would not the British-inspired emancipation of Cubans do? One object in acquiring Cuba would be to make sure that it remained slave; another, to use it for slave-breeding and slave-buying. Beyond these considerations, it had obvious strategic value. It was a Northern Secretary of State, and no less a statesman than Edward Everett, who in 1852 had brusquely rejected the Anglo-French proposal of a tripartite convention guaranteeing the existing status of the island. As we have seen, he emphasized considerations of national safety and commercial freedom. Since Cuba could be used by any hostile occupant to cut off the commerce of the Gulf States, blockade the Mississippi, and impede communication with California, American policy toward the island must not be straitjacketed forever. Everett always thought Cuba a natural appendage of America; and deeply aroused, he wrote this rejection in an hour, standing at his sideboard in Willard's Hotel. While both parties and almost unanimous public feeling applauded the sharp independence of the note, Southern Democrats were especially happy.[65]

One of the Democratic leaders most anxious to achieve annexation was the financier August Belmont—and he thought he knew how to manage it. No sooner was Pierce elected than he began laying his plans by artful letters to Buchanan and others. While he did not doubt that if stern necessity required it, the American people would take the island by force, he much preferred a peaceful acquisition; and he believed that an adroit negotiation would end in purchase. In order to bring the proud Castilians to listen to overtures, the United States should on the one hand keep up the Spanish apprehensions of invasion, thus compelling the maintenance of costly forces in the island; and on the other, make use of the dissatisfaction in European financial circles which an exhaustion of the Spanish treasury must produce. Not only should the bankers of Paris, Brussels, Amsterdam, and London be enlisted, but powerful

63  Richard H. Dana, *To Cuba and Back: A Vacation Ramble;* Antonio Gallenga, *The Pearl of the Antilles;* J. I. Rodrigues, *Estudio histórico sobre . . . la idea de la anexión de la isla de Cuba a los Estados Unidos de América.*
64  See editorial, December 1, 1853.
65  Thirty-second Cong., Second Sess., Sen. Exec. Doc., 13.

agents must be found in Spain itself, so that the pressure of public opinion there might eventually force the Ministry to come to terms. This task could hardly be executed by the envoy to Madrid, whose official position would impede his movements; it must rather be left to the Ministers in London and Paris, and the chargé in Naples.[66]

These three agents, declared Belmont, could cleverly draw into line the large and powerful financial interest of the numerous holders of Spanish bonds. In London and Paris the Ministers could approach the great banking houses of Huth, Baring, and Rothschild. From Naples the chargé could bring influence to bear upon the Queen Mother of Spain. Thus by pressure, maneuvering, and cajolery, the ripe pear might be jarred loose without any such direct overtures as had failed in 1848. Buchanan transmitted the plan to Pierce, adding an idea of his own. "Besides," he wrote, "Queen Christina, who is avaricious and exercises great influence over her daughter, the Queen of Spain, and her court, has very large possessions in the islands, the value of which would be greatly enhanced by its cession to the United States." [67]

Belmont hoped that he himself would be made chargé at Naples, for he had resided in the city some twenty years earlier and knew its people; and when this post was denied him, he asked for Brussels. This, he pointed out, was close to London, Paris, and Amsterdam, upon which Spain relied to bolster her rotten treasury. "Knowing most of the leading financiers in these places, I could from there induce them directly and indirectly to withdraw their funds from the Spanish finances and convince them how perfectly ruinous for Spain would in time become the maintenance of Cuba by sheer force of arms and at an expense which absorbs all the revenues of the Island, even under the present outrageous system of taxation." [68] Financial pressure he regarded as not merely the most efficient but perhaps the sole way of bringing her to her senses.

For a time this intrigue made progress. There is evidence that Pierce, with Davis and Cushing in the background, supported it. Belmont was sent to the Hague, an even better place than Brussels for his machinations. Buchanan from London kept in sympathetic touch with him. For secretary of legation Buchanan took over Daniel E. Sickles, a warm friend and constant correspondent of Belmont. Now thirty years of age, the handsome, dashing, and utterly unscrupulous Sickles, sprung from an old New York family, was already notorious as a city politician and an Albany legislative leader. In fact, he was so well known for rascality as well as energy and adroitness, that judicious

66  November 22, 30, 1852, Buchanan Papers.
67  December 11, 1852; Buchanan, *Works*, VIII, 493–499.
68  April 22, 1853; Buchanan Papers.

people held up their hands at his appointment. It was said that Marcy refused to sign the commission, this finally being done by a subordinate.[69] Before the secretary left, Pierce gave him an encouraging talk. "Mr. Sickles," he said, "our foreign appointments have been too carelessly made—men have been selected without reference to their fitness for diplomacy or the particular place to which they have been accredited. In this matter I mean to take great pains to secure the services of gentlemen who, like Mr. Belmont, possess the confidence of discerning men and who have the qualifications which he possesses to serve the country abroad." [70] At the Hague, Belmont kept himself ready for quiet, unofficial trips to London, Paris, and even Madrid, where he might all unsuspected gather powerful friends for his scheme. With patience, time (he talked of four years), and unity of action at the chief European capitals, Cuba would be won.[71]

At home a group of Democratic journalists, meanwhile, continued their efforts to whip up sentiment for annexation. A brief but important debate on Cuban-American relations had taken place in the Senate ten weeks before Pierce was inaugurated.[72] From the office of the *Democratic Review* promptly appeared a pamphlet ridiculing the more conservative opinions expressed in the discussion; opinions that the United States should be content to let Spain hold Cuba for the present, not interfering unless other governments tried to grasp the island, or it achieved its own independence. The pamphlet ridiculed these "stale and wornout doctrines," declared that "the whole race of statesmen who have thus far been in place are about to disappear before the flood of progress and improvement," and wound up with the flat declaration: "Our people want Cuba and will have it; it is idle for politicians to name the cases in which they will give their consent to its acquisition." The measures to be taken, said the *Review* article, were simple; the country should follow Cromwell in praying God and keeping its powder dry—and it should at once give the next President a credit of several millions in case of need.

Six weeks before Pierce took office, the House emphatically voted down a proposition to place at his discretion ten million dollars.[73] But the *Democratic Review*, the Washington *Union*, and the New York *Herald*, with lesser journals, continued to mutter of war. They harped upon the idea that Britain and France intended to bring about emancipation in Cuba. The *Union* talked of secret conventions; of large preparations; of a desire to destroy the republic by using Cuba to set the North and South against each other.[74] These utter-

69 Constance Robertson, *Salute to the Hero*, 23; M. B. Field, *Memories*, 171, 172.
70 Reported by Belmont March 7, 1853; Buchanan Papers.
71 See his letter of August 5, 1853, to Buchanan; Buchanan Papers.
72 *Cong. Globe*, 32d Cong., 2d sess., 139 ff., December 23, 1852.
73 See *National Intelligencer*, January 25, 1853, for caustic comment.
74 December 1, 1853.

ances made some impression. If emancipation were forced, wrote Cave Johnson, war would follow. "There will be no dissenting voice in this part of the country, though we know our tobacco and cotton crop would be ruined thereby, and though we know that we should have another crop of heroes to fill all the offices for the next half-century, and perhaps ultimately change the character of the government itself." [75]

But Belmont's scheme met unexpected difficulties. The courtly, spasmodic Mason in Paris was willing to lend himself to it; but Mason was proverbial for his easy good nature and want of firmness—Benton had somewhat unfairly said that he "only wants his belly full of oysters and his hands full of cards." [76] He was none too reliable. Still more, Belmont correctly distrusted Soulé, the new Minister to Spain; a preposterous choice, brought about primarily to get the man out of Slidell's political path in Louisiana. [77] Actually, it was this hot-tempered Sir Lucius O'Trigger who, from the moment he reached Madrid, constituted the gravest obstacle. The Louisianian had some good qualities, for he was a cultivated gentleman of fine manners and conversational charm, endowed with reckless courage. But he had been so closely connected with old filibustering schemes that his appointment was almost an affront to Spain. He was preceded by his reputation not only as a bellicose expansionist, but as a fierce sympathizer with European radicalism—a man who, as he put it in a spreadeagle speech on the eve of his departure, had his ear attuned "to the throes of anguish which move the downtrodden people of the Old World." This speech was delivered to a crowd of Democrats and "Cuban liberators" in

75 November 20, 1853, Buchanan Papers. It should be noted that the events following the defeat of Lopez and the execution of "the gallant fifty-one" had resulted in a great deal of war talk in Spain. The riotous outbreaks in New Orleans, Mobile, and Key West, accompanied by the sacking of a Spanish consulate in the first-named city, had aroused deep resentment. Many influential journals in the peninsula had talked of sending the United States an ultimatum. This would result in war, of course; but countless Spaniards thought that they would not come off second-best in a conflict. They talked of a world-wide system of privateering, conducted from the Spanish stations in the Canaries, Puerto Rico, Cuba, the Philippines, and the homeland, against the huge and very rich merchant marine of the republic. Swarms of corsairs would be loosed in every sea. As Spain had no merchant shipping of consequence, she would suffer little. Meanwhile, if driven to the last extremity, Spain could save Cuba from the United States by emancipating all Negroes in the island, and arming them against anybody who tried to reenslave them. On the reception of the news from New Orleans, it was reported, "the cry for war came up from every province of the monarchy, and the whole nation seemed to rise like one man and call upon the government to exact immediate reparation or permit them to avenge the wrong." No people were prouder than the Spaniards. Madrid letter, dated December 5, 1851, in *National Intelligencer*, January 6, 1852.
76 Mason, partly through inertia and partly through Secretary Marcy's neglect, was also ignorant of the government's full intentions. More than a year after the Pierce Administration began, he confessed to Buchanan that he had not talked with the foreign office about Cuba because he was ashamed to admit that he did not know the facts! May 31, 1854; Buchanan Papers.
77 Slidell took Soulé's seat in the Senate; cf. Nichols, *Democratic Machine*, 193.

New York, who saw him off with a noisy procession carrying banners and transparencies, one of which read:

The Antilles flower, the true key of the Gulf,
Must be plucked from the crown of the old Spanish wolf. (!)

His discourse also contained the minatory sentiment that, with Europe balancing on the verge of war, a whisper from America might decide the fate of the Old World Powers more potently than the decrees of emperors.

It would have required great tact and prudence, precisely the qualities Soulé lacked, to overcome the well-founded prejudice against him. The London *Times*, indeed, expressed astonishment that after what was known of Soulé and after his valedictory speech, the Spanish Court should submit to receive a declared enemy in the guise of a foreign envoy, adding that if the Cabinet of Madrid were not sunk to the very dregs of political life, such an outrage could not be committed.[78] He was soon in hot water. The French Ambassador, M. de Turgot, felt the keenest dislike for him as a political radical who had fled France in youth, and had ever since attacked French monarchism; and he lost few opportunities to slight the Minister. On November 15, 1853, he gave a grand ball which all the diplomatic corps attended. Mrs. Soulé appeared so richly dressed that she became the cynosure of attention, and the wife of the French Ambassador, who was a sister of the French Empress, made cutting remarks. One of the Spanish grandees, the Duke of Alba, took up the snickering raillery, and as Mrs. Soulé passed, murmured, "Look at Margaret of Burgundy!" —with obvious reference both to her costume and her corpulence. The younger Soulé, who had read *Tour de Nesle*, caught the insult, and let out an angry "Polisson!" When Soulé heard the story, he marched up to Alba at the refreshment buffet, caught him by the elbow, and glared into his face! This defiance so nonplused the grandee that he hastily retired to an adjacent room, where he remained *perdu* the rest of the evening.[79]

All this was opera bouffe, and so were the duels which followed. The younger Soulé challenged the reluctant Alba, and they crossed swords. The elder Soulé then challenged de Turgot, they exchanged two shots on a December Sunday, and de Turgot fell with a bullet in his leg.[80] All fashionable Madrid rushed to the French embassy to express its sympathy; and Soulé was relegated to a social Coventry, where his principal associates became intriguing

78 August 26, 1853. Cf. Anonymous, *The Attaché in Madrid; or, Sketches of the Court of Isabella II* (1856).
79 Full account by F. Gaillardet, dated Paris, December 22, 1853; in *Courrier des Etats-Unis*.
80 See the long account by the Paris correspondent of the *National Intelligencer*, January 21, 1854.

members of various opposition parties. An American visitor presently found that every night, between ten and two, visitors cloaked to defy recognition were ushered through Soulé's darkened door for secret conferences.[81] Essentially, his diplomatic usefulness was at an end, and his secretary of legation, Perry, later made a fairly well-based claim for the credit of whatever real diplomatic work was done during his incumbency. The Minister used to talk by the hour to Dowager-Queen Christina about the purchase of Cuba, and foolishly thought that he was making progress—for the shrewd Christina was not easily misled.[82]

But there were other difficulties than Soulé's follies in Belmont's way. He himself was soon under attack for promoting his private business along with his diplomatic duties;[83] while the events leading to the Crimean War gave European bankers graver problems to study than the fate of Cuba.

The other international areas saw equally little accomplished during Pierce's first year. In London, Buchanan was pleased to find that Lord Clarendon, the foreign secretary, was a man of experience, talents, and amiable deportment, and to discover in the country at large a feeling of marked good will toward America. He kept Marcy faithfully informed of British views, tried to explain to him the Clayton-Bulwer treaty, which Marcy thought as enigmatic as a Delphic oracle, and kept close watch on British attitudes toward Central America and Cuba. But as yet no foreign stroke reflected either discredit or glory on the Administration.

[ V ]

If drama failed in foreign affairs, it was amply provided by the tooth-and-nail fighting of the Democratic factions. All spring and summer Washington was crowded with office-seekers. It was the familiar story; thousands infected by a mania worse than any fever, thronging from all parts of the Union, and in many instances spending every dollar they had—with not one in five hundred

81  M. B. Field, *Memories*, 82, 83.
82  Horatio J. Perry's long dispatch (really a report) on Soulé's failure as minister dated Madrid, September 6, 1854, was sent to Marcy; a copy is in the Buchanan Papers. For the public controversy between Perry and Soulé as to diplomatic events, see the Washington *Union* for September–October, 1855. Before Soulé was appointed, Perry had written to President-elect Pierce, January 10, 1853, warning him against a policy of threats and irritations. "Spain will defend the island of Cuba with the last effort of her power," he stated. "France is her ally, and in case of war will enter the contest with her against the government of the United States. There is no doubt that communications to this effect have taken place, and the Emperor Napoleon has guaranteed the possession of Cuba to Spain against the supposed aggressive policy of the American republic. . . . Communications of the most satisfactory character to Spain in this question have certainly been made by Napoleon III."
83  See N. Y. *Tribune*, September 7, 1854, for the attack on Belmont's probity.

successful.[84] Removals of Whigs were incessant. The place of the ousted was supplied by Democrats chosen on Pierce's principle of a sop to every faction, with special favor to the two extremes. It is notorious, growled one editor, "that the out-and-out Union men have been overslaughed all over the country, and that secessionists and freesoilers have been richly rewarded for their opposition to the Compromise." [85] Some called it a Chinese policy, for in China sedition was bought off by a general amnesty and the promotion of the chief rebels to be high mandarins. It was certain that it did nothing to sustain a principle.

Nor did it do anything to maintain party unity. Discontent simmered among the Compromise Democrats of New England and the Union Democrats of the South. Resentment spurted up into open rebellion in New York.

To say that in that State of complicated politics the Democrats were split into two wings, Hunkers and Barnburners, is to oversimplify the position. It is more realistic to distinguish three groups: the Barnburner Democrats, led by John A. Dix and "Prince" John Van Buren; the Softshell or conciliatory Hunker Democrats, led by Marcy, Governor Horatio Seymour, Samuel J. Tilden, and John Cochrane; and the conservative Hunkers led by Daniel S. Dickinson. Factional zones faded into unidentifiable hues at the margins, and the Softshell Democrats and Barnburners in particular were rapidly merging their forces. Some leaders veered from side to side as the winds of ambition impelled them; both Seymour and Marcy, for example, had once been counted Hunkers. The superficial character of the party changed completely between 1847-48, when the Free Soil secession brought the State and national tickets to defeat, and 1851, when nominal reunion took place; it changed again between 1851 and the middle of 1854. But the three groups named could be clearly identified in Pierce's first year.[86]

Pierce, in his policy of smiling on everybody but specially favoring both ends against the middle, slighted the Hardshell Hunkers. It was as bitter as death to Dickinson to see Marcy, who had done so much in 1852 to defeat Dickinson's favorites for the presidential and gubernatorial nominations, Cass

---

84 Cf. Ben Wade to his wife, January 24, 1852, on his disgust with office-hunting. Pierce's papers are full of letters on trifling patronage problems. For example, he writes a party lieutenant in Concord: "The U. S. Mail Agency on the route between the City of New York and Boston via Stonington is vacant. Salary, 800 per annum. Do you know any active, capable, meritorious man, sound and honest in his politics, and in all other respects upon whom you would be glad to see the appointment conferred? Write me immediately." Again: "The change in the postoffice at Derry was made last week. My attention has been called to the case. . . . An examination of the case has satisfied me that the change ought not to have been made." September 24, 1853. It was for such work that the American people elected a President.

85 Unnamed journal quoted in *National Intelligencer*, April 30, 1853.

86 Alexander, *Political History New York*, II, 180-190; N. Y. *Express*, quoted in *National Intelligencer*, November 24, 1853; Marcy Papers, 1853. The Softshells valued party unity and wished to reunite with the Barnburners; the Hardshells were intransigent.

and John P. Beekman, lifted to the Secretaryship of State. It was equally painful to see Dix offered the ministership to France. Getting no better reward than the collectorship of the port, the Hunkers were told that even in the New York customhouse a due share of appointments must go to the Barnburners. They bided their time to show their resentment.

The opportunity came with the State convention at Syracuse in September, 1853. On its eve the supposed voice of the Administration, the Washington *Union*, published an article assailing Dickinson; an article which, if not instigated by the unrelenting Marcy, was written to please him. When the convention opened thirty-six seats were contested, and on them rested the question whether the Hunkers or Barnburners would control the organization. A wild crowd poured into the hall. Each faction nominated a chairman, elected him, and put him on the platform. Yells, hisses, and songs drowned out the voices of both. For a time violence was with difficulty averted. When Hunker spokesmen declared that they had been threatened with axes and guns, their enemies dubbed them the "terrified." In the end the convention split asunder, drew up two platforms, and named two tickets for the minor offices at stake.

This party schism in New York was a heavy blow to Pierce. It advertised the failure of his ends-against-the-middle policy. To the last he had played an equivocal game. While the *Union* was attacking Dickinson, he was quoted as supporting Dickinson's Hunkers—"They may denounce and abuse me, but they cannot drive me from their and my principles" [87]—and making remarks complimentary to Dickinson himself. The New York *Tribune* had predicted that if the convention endorsed Dickinson, Pierce would be quick to repudiate the attack by the Administration organ and to hail Dickinson's ascendency. "The President has in fact talked on one side, let the *Union* write on the other. He is playing both ends. He can shift at the end to be with the winner, no matter who he is." And behold, there was really no winner—only a grievous division!

A Kilkenny battle ensued in New York, the Hardshells and Softshells assailing each other far more viciously than they fought the Whigs. Such epithets as "seceders," "traitors," and "bullies" were hotly exchanged. Dickinson, stumping the larger cities, expressed a scorching disdain for Governor Seymour, and promised that he would not long hold his place. To Dickinson's side rallied the two principal Federal officeholders among the Hunkers. Collector Bronson used withering rhetoric in a letter declining to attend a Barnburner meeting in Tammany Hall. As a lover of honesty, he declared, he could not approve of nominations brought about by fraud and violence. "Those who introduce convicts and bullies into our conventions for the purpose of controlling events must not expect their proceedings will be sanctioned by me." Charles

[87] N. Y. *Tribune*, September 10, 1852.

O'Conor, the Federal Attorney, seconded him in a letter which arraigned the Barnburners as chronic troublemakers and enemies of national union. At a great Hunker ratification meeting in New York on the night of September 26, which mustered four thousand people, with firing cannon, soaring rockets, and vociferous cheering, James T. Brady went to bolder lengths still. He denounced Secretary Marcy as "a selfish, scheming, and vindictive politician, whose Van Buren education has not been extirpated," and promised that at the next national convention, they would "cleanse the party from the effects of a leprous association."

In this unhappy quarrel, the Administration had no need to take sides, and should prudently have stood aloof. The Hunker bolt was generally regarded as a move against Marcy personally and not a demonstration of hostility to the Administration; after all, Dickinson had a very old score against the Secretary. Moreover, the Administration had increasing reason to pursue a cautious course. Criticism of Pierce as a commonplace man of willowy backbone, and of the Cabinet as ragged, inharmonious, and ineffective, was growing. A caustic article in *Putnam's* on "Our New President" expressed a widening distrust of his capacities. Congress would soon meet with no great measures of public policy before it, for Pierce had shown no ability to originate any. In view of the lack of tried leaders in either chamber, now that the dominating influence of Clay, Calhoun, and Webster had been removed, all the forces of sectional discord might break loose. Men did not have to go as far as the New York *Tribune*, which declared that Pierce was the weakest and most uncertain executive in the history of the government, to believe that he could not control events.[88] Rumors were afloat that in order to improve the prestige of the Administration, a new journal would be established in New York, with Forney as editor, and the President himself, his friend Pierce Butler, and a wealthy friend of Attorney-General Cushing among the stockholders.[89]

Yet the Administration projected itself into the very midst of the battle. Secretary Guthrie, after delivering an oral rebuke to Collector Bronson, sent him a letter of castigation which was immediately published.[90] The President, he wrote, was anxious to have the offices distributed among all party groups; Bronson had instead made nearly all appointments from the Hunkers; and he must now mend his ways. In effect, the letter blamed the Hunkers for the schism, which Guthrie wrote could and ought to have been prevented. Bronson replied with asperity, accusing Guthrie of meddling with matters beyond his province, intimating that he wished factious men put into office, and

88  Washington correspondence, September 20, 1853.
89  N. Y. *Tribune*, September 13, 1853.
90  Dated October 3; text in *National Intelligencer*, October 11, 1853.

declaring that some customhouse appointments were properly to be made on his own authority. Guthrie then wrote a second letter of chastisement; and just before election day it was announced that Pierce had appointed a new collector of the port, H. J. Redfield, and a new naval officer. The anger of the Hunkers knew no bounds.[91]

A movement was at once instituted to make Bronson the Hunker candidate for governor the following year. Charles O'Conor, after waiting a decent interval, sent in his resignation. The *National Democrat*, declaring that the customhouse was being made a mere tool of the Administration, tartly added that the party had been "cheated in the man it has placed at the head of the nation." [92] Not even among the Barnburners did Pierce meet any gratitude, for Bryant's *Evening Post* stigmatized Guthrie's rule of adherence to the hastily-adopted Baltimore platform as "disgracefully illiberal." [93]

In fact, the Administration was universally censured. The *National Intelligencer* declared that everyone blamed Guthrie for a foolish letter and Pierce for an unnecessary quarrel. "Nothing could have been more silly," a keen observer wrote Buchanan, "than the war on Dickinson, which has become a war with a powerful party. I was in Washington at its commencement. All was quiet—except a little local conflict in New York about local policy. The Bolters of 1848 claimed *par excellence* to be the Administration favorites. The old line controverted the fact, and the very contest was strengthening the Administration. Dickinson himself, who had been entirely passed by, was quietly practising law—his name was not even mentioned in the newspapers. He was just in the line of safe precedence to oblivion. He was literally politically dead—but Marcy wanted him deader. So one of his tools published a malignant and bitter epitaph in the *Union*, and in an instant the dead sprang to life—to the utter confusion of the pursuers." [94]

Nor was the situation improved when Attorney-General Cushing on October 29 threw the Administration into the Massachusetts contest. An inveterate enemy of the old Democratic-Free Soil coalition in his State, he had been angered by the nomination of several county coalition tickets for the

91  D. L. Seymour of Troy presently wrote Douglas: "I have from the first hoped that the President would retrace his steps, and by his *acts* show the country that he intended to correct the prejudices which Gov. Marcy had led him to excite in the minds of the National Democrats of this State. But if he will not do this—if on the contrary he will under the guidance of Marcy and his free soil allies in the State continue the course of policy which has wounded the feelings of his friends and already alienated the minds of many, then must it be expected that this entire section of the party will cease to regard him as their friend and will look elsewhere for a friend and defender." May 8, 1854; Douglas Papers.
92  Quoted in *National Intelligencer*, October 27, 1853; cf. Alexander, II, 157.
93  Quoted in *National Intelligencer*, October 29, 1853.
94  J. B. Bowlin, January 11, 1854; Buchanan Papers.

senate. In a dictatorial letter, later dubbed "Cushing's Ukase," he harshly condemned these alliances and read out of the party all concerned in them.[95] The President, he declared, was determined to exterminate "the dangerous element of Abolitionism, under whatever guise or form it may present itself." This whip-cracking epistle aroused deep resentment. At a meeting in Faneuil Hall, Charles Francis Adams held a copy aloft, and terming it the most monstrous manifesto ever presented to a free people, declared that if he knew the Democrats of Boston, they would spurn it, hiss it, and spew it out of their mouths. It cost the Administration votes and prestige. Moreover, a new State constitution was to be voted upon this fall—one decidedly more favorable to the Democratic Party than the old; and Cushing's letter was instantly pronounced a death blow to the instrument. Had the Democrats played their cards well, they might have kept their control of Massachusetts—but Cushing had ruined their hopes.[96]

The sequel may be briefly stated. The Whigs swept New York by an average plurality of 66,000; and the Hunkers, although the influence of the Administration, of Tammany, and of the greater part of the press was thrown against them, ran neck and neck with the Barnburners for second place. A caricature represented Pierce and Marcy as Louis XVI and his Minister. "Why, this is revolt!" exclaims Pierce, and "No, sire, it is revolution!" responds Marcy. In Massachusetts the voters rejected the constitution written by a Democratic-Free Soil convention and chose a Whig governor. In other States—Pennsylvania, Ohio, New Jersey, California, and various border and Southern States—the Democrats fared well; but all eyes were fixed upon New York and Massachusetts, lost by Administration follies. Dickinson now boldly took the offensive against Pierce. The Hunkers held a congratulatory meeting in the metropolis; open insults were hurled at the President; and when Commodore Stockton tried to defend him, he was howled down. "The cloven foot has appeared," warned the Washington *Union*.[97] What was worse, Dickinson could assert that he represented the *real* Democracy in New York. The vote of the Hunkers, wrote J. Glancy Jones to Buchanan, "gives the death blow to the Administration policy," and he added: "This will produce a reaction South, and Pierce is gone." [98]

Party discontents were rapidly spreading. In Missouri the forces led by Benton, who hoped to regain his place in the Senate, refused in a public meeting to endorse the Administration. The opposing faction led by Senator Atchison was infuriated by the President's attempt to make an anti-slavery

95  Text in Fuess, *Cushing*, II, 139–140.
96  H. F. French, November 3, 1853, French Papers; N. Y. *Tribune*, September 30, 1853.
97  December 4, 1853.
98  November 12, 1853; Buchanan Papers.

man postmaster of St. Louis. Old-line Democrats of Ohio and Illinois grumbled that the patronage had nearly all gone to the freesoil Democrats. James B. Bowlin, one of Douglas's friends, blamed Pierce savagely for his maladroit handling of the patronage. "His efforts have entirely failed to unite the party," Bowlin wrote Buchanan. "It is torn into shreds and tatters." [99] The vote of all the sound-thinking Democrats he estimated at 1,500,000, while the two extreme wings, the Southern Rights men and radical freesoilers, could not in their best days muster more than 300,000; yet "they have nearly all the offices." Another correspondent of Buchanan's declared that in view of the discordant Cabinet and the unwarrantable interference in State elections, Pierce's Administration would be viewed by future historians as a nonentity.[100]

Even Pierce's old friend Edmund Burke, who had done so much to get him elected, was attacking the Administration, which he said had rewarded the party traitors and proscribed the true party leaders. The Washington *Union*, he added, had been intolerably insolent and dictatorial.[101]

Finally, when Congress opened, the low prestige of the Administration was advertised by a signal defeat. It had put forward Robert Armstrong, the financially distressed proprietor of the *Union*, as its candidate for printer to the Senate. Indeed, it had given out that his election was a *sine qua non*, and that the last vestige of hostility to Marcy and Guthrie must be crushed. Senators Cass and Douglas had been persuaded to support Armstrong. But the badly-edited "organ" had made many enemies; and when the vote was taken, Beverley Tucker of the Washington *Sentinel*, a violent pro-slavery, pro-Southern, pro-expansionist daily which commenced publication September 24, 1853, received twenty-six votes against Armstrong's seventeen. The *Union* itself admitted: "The Senate has been laying down the law to the Administration, in an act so direct and emphatic as to preclude all possibility of a misconstruction." [102] It is not surprising that men who saw Pierce in mid-December found him looking wretchedly.

The informed verdict upon Pierce by the end of the year was stated by a hundred observers who had wished him well. Bennett's New York *Herald* had turned against him; Francis J. Grund, Washington correspondent of the Balti-

99 January 16, 1854; Buchanan Papers.
100 L. P. Clover, June 15, 1854; Buchanan Papers.
101 January 9, 1854; Douglas Papers.
102 December 15, 1853. Charles Eames and Roger A. Pryor edited the *Union* for a time; then A. O. P. Nicholson. It did the Adminstration more harm than good, for it was highly erratic. John W. Forney and Attorney-General Cushing sometimes contributed. Pierce's understanding of public opinion was defective and his secretary, Sidney Webster, did little to enlighten him. Indeed, Webster's complacent pamphlet history entitled "Franklin Pierce and his Administration," written partly in 1869 and partly in 1892, shows that he had no comprehension of the forces of the time.

more *Sun* and Philadelphia *Public Ledger*, was a severe critic; and even the London *Times* printed harsh articles. "If he does not prove a Tyler," wrote Gideon Welles, "I shall be thankful. I had permitted my anticipations to run too far when he was nominated, and I was convinced of this in his first act. No wise man or sound Democrat would have taken to his bosom Caleb Cushing . . ." [103] Pierce had no knowledge of men and no self-reliance, concluded Welles. So close a friend of the President as B. B. French was equally severe. He had instantly declared Guthrie's letter a blunder, and Cushing's a still greater stupidity. "It has been intimated to me that Guthrie's letter was sent out under the especial advice of the President—if so, he is not quite so cute in politics as I had thought he was . . ." [104] In far-off Tennessee sagacious old Cave Johnson took a gloomy view. After reviewing the Administration's errors, with special emphasis on its failure to stand by all Compromise men, he declared: "The effect of these things will probably be to prevent a renomination of the President or any member of the Cabinet." Looking ahead, he foresaw stormy waters. "The difficulties which the Administration has encountered in the distribution of offices," he predicted, "will be increased upon the meeting of Congress, when the Pacific Railroad, the disposition of the surplus, and other questions connected with it are brought up for discussion." [105]

In still more distant Louisiana, John Slidell declared ten months after Pierce took office that he had run a very weak course. He thought Administration meddling in State politics regrettable under any circumstances, but particularly inept when exercised in behalf of the wrong side! The Cabinet was weak; yet discordant as it was, its strongest members controlled the President, who had fallen into disrepute. "There is probably not a member of the Senate," wrote Slidell, "who does not consider his own individual opinion in every other respect entitled to quite as much consideration as that of the President. In other words he is the *de jure* not the *de facto* head of the party." [106] Albert G. Brown of Mississippi, soon to exchange his seat in the House for one in the Senate, returned the same verdict. It was not long before he was writing home from Washington that, much as he desired the success of Pierce, who had shown him every courtesy, he anticipated a failure; for he found a good deal of bitterness among the Democrats, and what was worse, a too common disposition to speak slightingly of the President. A little later he was adding that the more he saw of the Administration, the more he was satisfied that it would shackle down to nothing. "It has not vitality enough in both houses of Congress to lift it above the sneers and scoffs and ridicule of the veriest dolt that chooses to

103 No date, but probably October, 1853; Welles Papers.
104 To H. F. French, November 6, 1853; French Papers.
105 November 20, 1853; Buchanan Papers.
106 Sears. *Slidell*, 96ff.

assail it. . . . By and bye, unless they mount the Cuban war and ride it in triumph, the whole country will be ready to write *to let* on the door of the White House." [107]

To most Americans, as Congress met in the closing weeks of 1853, the national situation carried no anxieties. The country was prosperous; its foreign relations were placid. If the President was nerveless and the Administration inert, the nation had often before drifted without meeting any harm. Few men saw, as Cave Johnson partially did, that three interlocking factors, the lack of a strong hand at the helm, the practical certainty that a new President would have to be chosen in 1856, and the death of the great Senatorial triumvirate, leaving the upper chamber undisciplined and unawed, created a strong temptation for dramatic action by some ambitious Congressional leader. Pierce lacked a policy. The party was torn by dissension because it had not been lifted to any solid ground of principle. The leader who could open up a new path of national effort, lifting the people's eyes to fresh goals, might impose himself upon the country as the hero of a better era. But what if the action were too dramatic, the new policy too risky?

107 March 1, April 4, 1854; Claiborne Papers, Miss. State Archives.

# 3

# *Disaster: 1854*

LINCOLN'S "HOUSE DIVIDED" speech is justly famous. But more than six years earlier, on March 25, 1852, the abolitionist Edmund Quincy had used the same Biblical quotation to point the same prediction. "It was said more than eighteen hundred years ago that a house divided against itself cannot stand, and the truth of the saying is written on every page of history, antecedent and subsequent. It is not unlikely that the history of our own country may furnish fresh and pregnant examples, by which philosophy may teach the same truth to future ages." When Quincy wrote this Pierce had just just been seated in the presidential chair; men talked of the Compromise as a finality; the waters of public sentiment, recently so stormy, lapped gently on a peaceful strand. But Quincy declared that either slavery must be abolished or its increasing pressure would "at last make a fissure that will shatter into heaps the proud structure upon the heads of those that put their trust into it." He felt a deep sea-swell in the South toward secession, partly for autonomy, partly for revenge. The secessionists might soon grow sufficiently strong and desperate to break away from their Northern brethren. "It is not unlikely; for men's passions, in revolutionary times, overpower their cooler reason. And these are such times." [1]

At first glance it might seem that Quincy was entirely wrong. Men could retort with that other Biblical quotation about the angel in the myrtle tree, who said that he had passed to and fro, "and behold, all the earth sitteth still and is at rest." The angry disputes precipitated by the Mexican War had been closed by an honorable adjustment. Extremists both North and South had just been routed in their main strongholds. The new Administration had approximately two-thirds of both House and Senate behind it. An overflowing Treasury, general domestic prosperity, and peaceful foreign relations augured well for the future. Nevertheless, the abolitionist editor was right.

The slavery question was in fact irrepressible. Men spoke softly not to rouse

1  Quincy's letter in *Anti-Slavery Standard;* copy in Quincy Papers.

78

the sleeping tiger, but in his sleep he stirred and growled. Dispatches which denoted the underlying stresses frequently cropped into the newspapers. Now it was the news in 1852 that the California legislature, after warm debate, had given everyone who had brought slaves into the State prior to the acceptance of the constitution a year to remove them; the news in 1853 that it had extended the law a twelvemonth; the news in 1854 of an additional extension—an indulgence, growled Greeley's newspaper, that established slavery in California as thoroughly as anybody could wish.[2] Now it was a tiny item announcing that the supreme court of Missouri had just tried a suit involving the rights of a Negro named Dred Scott, once the property of an army surgeon named Dr. John Emerson. The slave had been carried into Illinois and Wisconsin Territory for a residence of about five years, and claimed his freedom on that ground. But the court, overruling a lower tribunal, decided that by voluntarily returning to a slave State, Scott had lost whatever title he possessed to liberty.[8] Now the item dealt with a New York decision under which the slaves of a Virginian travelling to Texas were freed from his custody; a decision which aroused great indignation in the South, public contributions being raised to indemnify the owner.[4] Now it was some atrocious cruelty to a slave which broke into the prints; now some flagrant instance of resistance to the fugitive slave law.

The thinness of the crust which the Compromise had laid over the erupting lava of 1849–50 was occasionally demonstrated by a minor political explosion. Early in January, 1854, the Ohio Democrats held a convention in Columbus. A platform was reported reaffirming that adopted the previous year; whereupon a delegate moved that an express endorsement of the Baltimore platform of 1852, which had so explicitly called for maintenance of the fugitive slave law, be added. The effect was like casting a firebrand into a powder-keg. Slavery and anti-slavery forces sprang into disorderly lines. Shouts of dissent and approval made a bedlam of the hall. The chairman, after calling for order until he was hoarse, sat down and let the tumult rage. Delegates leaped to their benches; only men with stentorian lungs could make themselves heard. Some shouted, "Dodging is disgraceful!"; others retorted, "We don't want your New York politics here!" The Cincinnati delegation was fierce for the Baltimore endorsement, and the Western Reserve vehement against it. Finally the vote was taken by counties. When the motion passed by a heavy majority, groans and hisses broke out; a substitute set of resolutions was at once moved; and the storm raged more fiercely than ever. The endorsement forces finally

2 N. Y. *Tribune,* June 13, 1854.
3 *National Intelligencer,* April 8, 1852.
4 *Idem,* January 18, 1853.

triumphed, but only amid fervent threats of a revolt by the freesoil Democrats.[5]

It was a time for discretion, and most political leaders were ready to act with studied conservatism. But in the absence of a strong Administration grip and of the old parliamentary giants, two or three rash men could unchain the captive Samson.

## [ I ]

At the beginning of November, 1853, Stephen A. Douglas was back in Washington from a tour which had carried him from London to St. Petersburg, the Crimea, and Syria. If the trip had not altered his strong nationalistic prejudices in foreign affairs, it had solaced him for the recent loss of his adored young wife, Martha Martin, had refreshed him, and had quickened his already lusty ambitions. Everyone knew he was ready for a greater role in public affairs than ever. He was keenly interested not only in his future chances for the presidency, but in the development of the West, the growth of Chicago, where he had large real-estate investments, and the various plans for a Pacific Railroad. He was in good spirits, for the European scene had given him interesting new ideas and impressions. Friends who gathered about him in Washington found him "chock full of anecdotes, adventure, and a perfect knowledge of the people" among whom he had travelled. They were pleased that his Americanism had not suffered; that he had upheld the dignity of his country "in the midst of crowns and coronets." He began to entertain largely. A caterer's bill for a party on December 28th covered beef, tongue, duck, pheasants, pigeons, and other comestibles to a total of $62.11.[6]

His admirers were of course eager to make him Pierce's successor. But he saw that the party dissensions presented perils as well as opportunities, and having burned his fingers by too hasty action in 1852, was now circumspect. It was generally assumed that his hopes of the great prize had risen in proportion as it became evident that Pierce was a deplorably weak executive. Such had been the verdict of one of Buchanan's videttes, C. L. Ward, after a tour of the West and South and a sojourn in Washington the previous spring.[7] It had likewise been the conclusion of his enemies, who were already trying to form combinations against him. William Hale, attorney-general of Michigan,

5 *Idem*, January 14, 1854. "Old Line Democrats" and "Independent Democrats" were the two names used; see the material on Ohio politics in *Diary and Correspondence of Salmon P. Chase*, 248–254.

6 N. Y. *Herald*, Washington *Union*, November 30–December 6, 1853; Isaac R. Diller, December 22, 1853, to Douglas; other miscellaneous material in Douglas Papers.

7 April 5, 1853; Buchanan Papers.

was a hostile plotter; so was Thomas Hoyne, the federal attorney in Chicago.[8] Senator Bright of Indiana was urging Buchanan to help him defeat Douglas's requests for political appointments.[9] Meanwhile the Little Giant's lieutenants were busy laying ambitious plans. Several of them urged him to pay a flying visit to the West to make capital there before Congress opened, and they assured him that Cass was already behind his candidacy.[10]

Unquestionably the omens upon Douglas's political future were auspicious. The devoted Senator Yulee summed them up, at the same time urging him to consolidate his strength in the Northwest. The Baltimore Convention, wrote the Floridian, had turned the eyes of the country fully upon him. "In the very cradle of your national popularity you had strength to crush all the old combinations and organizations, and to open the way to the dynasty of a new generation." His course since then had been masterly, warming the heart of the Democratic party; and his friends had multiplied everywhere, for he stood well with the State Rights men, the South, New England, and the general organization. Had not the Northwest always been true to the party, and had she not effectively allied herself with the South? "The N.W. is powerful in numbers and wealth and becoming more so. The N.W. has never had a President. Her weight in the Union, her services to the party, her fidelity to the Constitution and the country, her friendly bearing toward the South, her connection with the North, the good terms she is on with all sections, will give her strong, and if well presented, *insuperable claims* to the Presidency next term. If the Northwest unites upon *you*, and asks *your nomination*, the standing you have now with the party everywhere, will bring an instant and acclamatory nomination." [11] Yulee was an ardent railway promoter.

But Douglas had learned that the aspirant who raised his head too early became a target for every club. In a confidential letter of November 11th to the editors of the *State Register* in Springfield he deprecated all newspaper talk of him up for the presidency. "I do not wish to occupy that position. I do not think I will be willing to have my name used. I think such a state of things will exist that I shall not desire the nomination." He wished to remain "entirely non-committal." This was a shrewd policy. The paramount duty of all, he declared, was to strengthen the party. "The party is in a distracted condition, and it requires all our wisdom, prudence and energy to consolidate its power and perpetuate its principles. Let us leave the Presidency out of view for at least two years to come." [12]

8  Lanphier, November 21, 1853; Douglas Papers.
9  April 20, 1853; Buchanan Papers.
10  Andrew Harvie, Isaac Cook, and others, November 14–30; Douglas Papers.
11  January 28, 1853; Douglas Papers.
12  Full text in P. O. Ray, *Repeal of the Missouri Compromise*, 185, 186.

The distracted party—that was very much in Douglas's mind, for Democrats were fearful that under Pierce it would lose all morale and unity. He told the editors that three main questions must be boldly faced by the Administration. One was the surplus revenue, which threatened to accumulate in the Treasury until it caused a disastrous monetary stringency, and which should be reduced by lowering the tariff to a legitimate revenue standard. The second was the improvement of rivers and harbors, which could best be financed by a well-devised system of tonnage duties. The third was the Pacific Railroad, which should be built not by any money grant from the government, but by a gift of alternate sections of land.

Letters often conceal as much as they disclose, but the frank tone of this epistle leaves no doubt of two facts: that Douglas wished to postpone talk of his presidential candidacy for two years, and that he thought the ensuing session would have before it no major problems beyond a slight tariff revision, a rivers-and-harbors plan, and Pacific Railroad legislation. He believed all three easily soluble, and soluble by steps equally agreeable to the Northwest and South. Though chairman of the Senate Committee on Territories, he did not refer to any territorial question whatever.[18]

[ II ]

The Pacific Railroad question indeed seemed to be coming to a head. First opened in practical fashion by Asa Whitney in 1844, it had engaged the eager attention of promoters and politicians until dozens of schemes were in the air. Whitney, a Connecticut merchant and enterpriser who believed he looked like Napoleon Bonaparte, was still laboring indefatigably for a line from Lake Michigan by way of South Pass to San Francisco or the mouth of the Oregon, to be built with the aid of a huge government land grant. In 1851–52 he was in England seeking support.[14] Senator Gwin of California had another scheme which had now been before Congress for two sessions. His plan contemplated a western terminus in San Francisco; a trunk following some undetermined route; and a whole series of eastern branches—one to Matagorda Bay in Texas, one to New Orleans, one to Memphis, one to St. Louis, and one to Dubuque. To finance it he proposed a combination of Federal land grants and cash subsidies. During the summer of 1853 two members of the Cabinet came out in favor of Gwin's scheme. Many expected to see it pushed hard.[15] While leaving the trunk route undecided, Gwin frankly preferred a line from Memphis through

13 Allen Johnson, *Douglas*, 226–228; Milton, *Eve of Conflict*, 97–99.
14 N. H. Loomis, "Asa Whitney, Father of Pacific Railroads," *Miss. Valley Hist. Assn. Proc.*, VI; *National Intelligencer*, February 3, 1854.

Fort Smith, Santa Fé, Albuquerque, and on westward by Walker's route to Los Angeles and San Francisco. Farther south, Senator Rusk of Texas had a grandiose plan for a railway through El Paso to San Diego.[16] Thomas Hart Benton, equally condemning Whitney's northern route and an extreme southern route, was advocating what he called "a great central national highway" from St. Louis westward.[17] Missouri interests, Chicago interests, Memphis interests, New Orleans interests, were all anxiously alert.

Easily the most striking scheme was that of the organizers of the Atlantic & Pacific Railroad Company, a New York corporation with aggressive Southern backing. In the winter session of 1852–53 Senator Brooke of Mississippi brought forward a bill proposing that the United States pledge the payment of $30,000,000 for construction of its line. The company was to be allowed to select its own route, and everybody knew that the Memphis-Little Rock-Fulton-El Paso-San Diego line was contemplated.[18] Senator Rusk's plan could obviously be integrated with this larger scheme. The road, which A. B. Gray was to survey, would run through the Gadsden Purchase. Its cost, according to Brooke, could be easily met by the Federal credit (which would be repaid) and supplementary land grants. This Southern project seemed even more formidable than Gwin's.

"Stories are circulating freely in the West," Cave Johnson reported to Buchanan late in 1853, "that the N. Y. Company, with a capital of one hundred millions, will lobby for the road and distribute stocks among the members [of Congress] and influential agents, and pass it over even a Presidential veto. R. J. W[alker] who is said to have subscribed ten millions is the chief manager in Washington—Law at New York—Foulkes of the Memphis Bank, takes a million, cum multiis aliis, of no more means and less character. There is said

15 See *Cong. Globe*, 32d Cong., 2d sess., 314ff., January 17, 1853, for full debate. Cf. Frank Hodder, "The Railroad Background of the Kansas-Nebraska Act," *Miss. Vall. Hist. Review*, XII; the *National Intelligencer*, December 6, 1853, describes Cabinet support.

16 Rusk lobbied actively at Austin for a land grant, giving a great dinner December 5, 1853, for legislators and prominent citizens. A bill was brought into the legislature to give the railroad sixteen sections for every mile built through Texas. *National Intelligencer*, December 29, 1853.

17 Meigs, *Benton*, 418. The Pacific Railway Company received its franchise from Missouri in 1849, and ran its first train on December 2, 1852, between St. Louis and Cheltenham, five miles. On May 6, 1853, the line was opened as far as Kirkwood, fourteen miles. Kirkwood was specially organized as the first railroad town west of the Mississippi, and was named in honor of the engineer of the Pacific road, James P. Kirkwood, late of the Erie. The ultimate destination was Kansas City and the Missouri River, but it was not reached until 1865. See Railway Envelope in Missouri Historical Society; also railroad matter in the Gratz Papers there. A Federal land grant had been made in 1852 for a railroad from Hannibal to St. Joseph in Missouri, which ultimately proved a feeder to the greatness of Chicago rather than St. Louis. Another Federal land grant had been made in 1853 for a projected railroad from Little Rock, Ark., to the Texas boundary and to Fort Smith.

18 *Cong. Globe*, January 17, 1853, *ut supra*. See N. Y. *Courier*, September 14, October 20, December 2, 1853; February 1, 1854.

to be a provision in their agreement, that *at no time is there a call to be made for more than one-fourth of one per cent*—the work is to be accomplished out of the public land and the surplus money—what a stupendous project!! The Yazoo speculation will be thrown into the shade by this stupendous scheme, and the frauds perpetrated in it will be molehills beside the mountain when contrasted with the corruption and frauds which that scheme will introduce into our country; but this is not all, several Presidents, Vice Presidents, ambassadors, and so on are to be made by it, and all the old fogies such as yourself, Cass, etc., are to be thrown overboard." [19]

Cave Johnson was not the only opponent of this Atlantic & Pacific Company. Its speculative character, aroma of corruption, and ultra-Southern character raised up numerous enemies. Many believed that it was secretly involved with schemes of filibustering and Southern expansion. It was well known that Secretary Jefferson Davis favored the southernmost route, and had been chiefly instrumental in getting Pierce and Marcy to undertake the Gadsden Purchase to furnish a direct line along the Gila Valley. Reports got into the newspapers that Gadsden might have obtained most of Sonora and all Lower California but for Robert J. Walker's indiscreet talk. Walker had let it be known in Washington that he expected his railroad to run through the area which Gadsden was empowered to buy, and had chattered too freely of Gadsden's instructions and authority. Hearing of this through its Minister, the Mexican government raised the price and reduced the area of the cession. Thomas Hart Benton violently denounced the Walker project, declaring again that a wolf could not keep alive in the deserts the line would traverse, and accusing the backers of schemes of annexation and slavery-domination in Cuba and Mexico. The St. Louis *Democrat* and New York *Tribune* joined in the bombardment, asserting that it "viciously sectionalized" what should be a great national undertaking. Douglas's declaration against any direct Federal money grant was in all probability aimed at the proposal. [20]

The only action taken by Congress in 1853 was to authorize Secretary

19 November 20, 1853; Buchanan Papers.

20 Meigs, *Benton*, 418-422; N. Y. *Tribune*, September 13, 1853, January 24, 1854; St. Louis *Democrat*, September–December, 1853. When a special committee of the Senate reported a bill for a road leaving the route to be fixed later, Shields of Illinois, apparently instigated by Douglas and Cass, offered an amendment prohibiting expenditure of any of the appropriated funds within the borders of a State. This was a blow at the proposals for railroad building with Federal funds in Arkansas, Texas, and California, and also an ingenious effort by Douglas to curry favor with Southern State Rights men. See Milton, *The Eve of Conflict*, 101. But the Texas railroad project remained very much alive, and a constant worry to Douglas and other Northern men. Early in 1854 a well-known Albany attorney, John V. L. Pruyn, visited Washington and talked with backers of the Atlantic & Pacific Railroad project. He then examined a bill that Rusk had drawn, revised it, and delivered it to him in improved shape. MS Diary, March 25, 1854. New York State Archives.

Jefferson Davis to expend $150,000 in surveying possible routes to the Pacific. Under this appropriation four main expeditions were fitted out: a northernmost under Governor Isaac I. Stevens of Washington Territory, who was to explore westward from the headwaters of the upper Missouri tributaries, seeking some eligible pass in the Rockies; another under Captain Gunnison along the thirty-eighth parallel; a third under Lieutenant Whipple along the thirty-fifth parallel; and a fourth under Major Emory through Texas and along the Gila, following the general line of the thirty-second parallel. Speaking very roughly, the first might be called the St. Paul-Seattle route; the second the Chicago or St. Louis-San Francisco route; the third the Memphis-San Francisco route; and the fourth the New Orleans-San Diego route. Secretary Davis of course tacitly favored the last-named, partly because it would benefit the South, partly because he had an exaggerated idea of the barrenness of the "arid" belt so long denominated the Great American Desert, partly because it would cross the mountains easily and be least impeded by snow. Then, too, it alone would have the benefit of a continuous belt of organized States and Territories, Texas, New Mexico, and California, through which to run.[21]

Though of the various routes the northernmost attracted the least public attention, strong efforts were made to interest Douglas in it. Isaac I. Stevens, a capable, hardheaded West Pointer of Yankee birth, thoroughly trained as an engineer, took care to keep the Senator constantly informed of the exploration of the St. Paul-Puget Sound line. "I have not forgotten," he wrote in the late summer of 1853 from Fort Benton, "the deep interest you took in Washington in the explorations for routes of a railroad from the Mississippi to the Pacific, nor the special solicitude you evinced for the one placed in my charge. You may be certain it has dwelt upon my mind. . . . Our success in exploring the regions we have passed through and in establishing friendly relations with all the Indian tribes had been unprecedented as it has been unexpected. A line had already been surveyed from the Dalles on the Columbia to the headwaters of the Mississippi. I know from personal observation that not only one but several good, easy, cheap routes can be pursued from the Mississippi to this point, all connecting by easy roads with the Yellowstone at Fort Union and with the falls of the Missouri twenty-odd miles above this point." [22]

He went on to inform Douglas of two passes that delighted him; Cadot's Pass, three thousand feet lower than the South Pass, and farther to the north, the Marias Pass, which he was sanguine would prove even better. Steamers

21 G. L. Albright, *Official Explorations for Pacific Railroads; Report,* Secretary of War, 1853; Davis, *Works,* III, 410–460.
22 September 18, 1853; Douglas Papers.

drawing eighteen inches could reach the falls of the Missouri, and once a steamboat line was established it would become a great emigrant route. Just west of the Rockies lay fertile and beautiful valleys, with mild climate and nutritious grass. "I often think of it. The emigrant on leaving the steamer in six days reaches the home he has longed and toiled for."

When Stevens arrived at Fort Vancouver he struck a still more triumphant note. The feasibility of a railroad to the Pacific "is no longer a matter of doubt, but is a fixed fact." The route was practicable; each of the mountain ranges afforded two good passes; timber and stone for building abounded; the country was admirably adapted to settlement and cultivation; and fine harbors were available on Puget Sound for terminals. He was sending Secretary Davis the fullest information, "sufficient for the purposes of Congress that winter." [23] Douglas was also besieged by Henry M. Rice, Minnesota's new Territorial delegate in Congress, who urged him to take immediate steps to throw the Illinois Central northward into Minnesota, thus completing one of the greatest transportation lines in the world.

"Its political, commercial, and social bearings will be unparalleled," wrote Rice. "You were the originator of this great work—you have advanced it with the extension of settlements northwest: you can send the iron horse through to the Great Lakes and thus cement the people of the States by ties of intimacy that will develop interests mutually beneficial to all. Will you do it? You can, comparatively, with little labor—the route, the country, its resources, in fact all points having bearings upon the subject you have in your head. You know the men to call to your aid in procuring the grant—you know the men to build the road. . . ." [24]

Douglas replied to these overtures encouragingly and even enthusiastically. Full of faith in the future of the West, he believed that four Pacific railroads could be built as easily as one, and that no cash subsidy would be needed. So much was he fascinated by Minnesota that in 1853 he organized a syndicate for large-scale speculation in northwestern lands, his special object being the natural terminus of a northern transcontinental railroad at the tip of Lake Superior. Employing an agent named D. A. Robertson, whom he cautioned to be silent as the grave, he gained title to six thousand acres, and had the town of Superior City laid out. It grew and thrived. As soon as the Sault Ste. Marie Canal was opened, land values shot upward. Douglas made a handsome profit— which he shared with John W. Forney and others—even without a railroad. But in 1853 he had a direct pocket interest of no small magnitude in both a central and a northern railway to the Pacific. Both were important to him, to

23  Olympia, W. T., December 5, 1853; Douglas Papers.
24  Washington, December 8, 1853; Douglas Papers.

his State, and to his Northwestern section; both, he felt, could quickly be built if the routes were cleared of Indians and if settlement in the Missouri Valley were facilitated.[25]

Discussing his plans with many interested friends, Douglas was ready to act as soon as the Pacific Railroad Committee of the Senate began debating the subject in the opening days of 1854. His own scheme was placed before that body on January 19. He proposed laying out provisionally a northern, central, and southern route, each with connecting branches on the east. The government should then offer alternate sections of public land in a strip twenty miles wide through in the States, and forty miles wide through the Territories, sealed competitive bids being invited for the construction. This, noted one committeeman, Edward Everett, in his diary, "is a plan to unite in a great effort the entire interest felt in the project in any part of the country."[26] As a good American, a good Democrat, and a good friend of the South, Douglas seemed avoiding sectional views, and proffering a program equally fair to St. Paul and Rock Island, Chicago and St. Louis, Memphis and New Orleans. His main object was to see the trans-Mississippi West rapidly developed. But the cost of a great triple work with three broad land-grant belts daunted his colleagues. After six weeks of animated discussion, the committee decided on March 2 upon a single railroad.[27]

The West, regarding Douglas as its champion, continued to shower him with appeals. "Friend Douglas," wrote Brigham Young, "what are you going to do about a railroad to the Pacific? Will you advocate the Route by the Box Elder Basin, the Black Hills, Bridger's Pass in the Rocky Mountains, Timpanogos or Provo Canyon, etc., as the best line for the first Railway to be built from the Missouri to the Pacific, or what do you think of it? You need not be shy in expressing your views on the subject, for rest assured that whatever route that Road takes it will be the very best one for the interests of Utah, and precisely where we would rather have it."[28]

25 A considerable body of letters in the Douglas Papers, 1853–55, bear on the Senator's Minnesota speculations. George Fort Milton in *Eve of Conflict*, 105, treats the offer to Forney as pure generosity. It was doubtless an effort to win the influence of that active Pennsylvania politician and editor, then a firm lieutenant of Buchanan and friend of many powerful Democrats. Forney was to divide his $2,500 share with a Southern leader whom he identifies only as "one of the best of the future Confederates." How many shares Douglas scattered judiciously in Washington it is impossible to say. Forney, *Anecdotes of Public Men*, I, 18–20.

26 January 19, 1854. Pierce in his long-winded annual message of December, 1853, had said that the government could well content itself with building military roads and naval harbors, leaving general communications to the energy of the people. But of course a transcontinental railroad could be defined as a military necessity.

27 Everett, MS Diary, March 2, 3, 1854.

28 April 29, 1854; Douglas Papers.

## [ III ]

As chairman of the Senate Committee on Territories Douglas had meanwhile to consider the now fairly exigent question of the territorial organization of the huge Nebraska country; a region falling into two sections, the Platte River district and the Kansas River district—the former roughly west of Iowa, the latter west of Missouri. Population was beginning to press upon the borders of this area, and the opening of its fertile lands to settlement seemed to some observers overdue. In the fall of 1853 two groups, one representing chiefly Missouri elements settled in and about Fort Leavenworth, with some Indians and missionaries, the other representing Iowans who lived along the river near Council Bluffs, elected two delegates to Congress. The Missourians and their friends chose the Rev. Thomas Johnson, a supporter of Senator Atchison, a slaveholder, and a staunch advocate of slavery; the Iowans chose Hadley D. Johnson, a freesoiler. Both elections were quite irregular and extra-legal. But they testified to the eagerness of the frontier population for the erection of a territorial government, the opening of settlement, and the building of a Pacific Railroad. [29]

Repeatedly, beginning as early as 1844, Douglas had proposed a territorial government for this wild Nebraska region. His third bill, in 1852, had embodied some curious features dictated by the needs of the heavy overland emigration to California. A volunteer military corps was to be sent out to construct forts along a government telegraph and mail line, and to maintain itself by agriculture. After three years of service each military farmer was to be rewarded with a section of land on the route.

But the normally easy task of setting up a territorial government was obstructed in Nebraska by half a dozen factors. These were the occupation of the region by powerful Indian tribes; the demand of many Southerners, holding the Missouri Compromise unconstitutional, that they be allowed to take slaves into this new area when organized; the dislike of most Southerners for the admission of strong new freesoil States; the special hostility of slaveholding Missourians to the creation of a great new free commonwealth on their western borders; and the sectional rivalries pinned to the various Pacific railroad schemes. Backers of the extreme Southern railroad route were quite willing to see the barrier maintained against a central line—unless they were paid a

29 See W. E. Connelley, "Provisional Government of Nebraska Territory," *Neb. State Hist. Soc. Proc. and Colls.*, Second Series, III. Hadley D. Johnson was an enthusiastic believer in the Pacific railroad project, and had settled at Council Bluffs in the sage conviction that it must be the eastern terminus of the line. Meetings to discuss and promote a Pacific railway were now becoming common in both Iowa and Missouri. The N. Y. *Times*, November 24, 1853, has an article on Hadley D. Johnson's selection.

generous price. Douglas's bill was stopped dead early in 1852 by objections that he regarded as dishonest and unjust. They show, he told the Senate with manifest irritation, "that we are to expect no protection at all; they evince direct, open hostility to that section of the country." He demanded that the Senators meet this broad question—"and if they are opposed to open a communication between the Atlantic and Pacific, if they are in favor of disunion, let them declare it." [30]

At the second session of the 32d Congress, in the winter of 1852–53, the usual petitions for territorial organization came in, but no action was taken until February. Then Representative Willard P. Hall of Missouri brought into the House a bill organizing the Territory of Platte, and Chairman William A. Richardson of the Committee on Territories (Douglas's close friend from the Quincy, Ill., district) reported it as a bill to organize the Territory of Nebraska, the area covered being the same. Based on the Missouri Compromise, it assumed the exclusion of slavery. It encountered a fierce Southern resistance. Nevertheless, it passed the House 98 to 43, by a majority of strongly sectional character. Of the 98 affirmative votes, 80 were Northern, while of the 43 negative votes, 30 were Southern.

In the Senate the Southern opposition was plainly more formidable still. Douglas reported the measure on February 17, 1853, without amendment. The session had only a fortnight to run; the calendar was crowded; and not until the last day was the bill reached. It then failed, primarily for lack of time, the vote on two efforts to bring it up being 25 to 20, and 23 to 17. Every Southern Senator except the two from Missouri voted for tabling it. On each trial five Northern Senators also voted against the bill, because they thought it premature or a violation of treaty stipulation with the Indians.[31]

Atchison of Missouri made the principal speech on the measure. Now forty-five, this Kentucky-born attorney had been in politics for twenty years as legislator, judge, and since Tyler's day Senator. A truculent, rough-mannered, explosive man, hardworking, persistent, and according to his lights sincere, he was one of the noisiest leaders of the slavery forces in Washington.[32] Indeed, he was more belligerent than most Southerners, for slavery in Missouri stood in dire peril and needed stern champions. It was he who had headed the the bi-party pack which had doomed Benton to destruction, and implacably hunted down that leader. He had helped to elect a pro-slavery majority in the legislature, which had drafted resolutions based on Calhoun's doctrine, demanding that slavery be admitted into all Territories, and calling upon Missouri's senators to

30  *Cong. Globe,* 32d Cong., 1st sess., 1762.
31  See *Cong. Globe,* 33d Cong., 1st sess., App., 168ff., February 10, 11, 1854, for various analyses of motive.
32  N. Y. *Tribune,* October 10, 1854.

vote for such admittance.[33] He had then presented these resolutions in the Senate, where Benton with characteristic courage had denounced them as treasonable, morally outrageous, and contrary to the true sentiments of Missourians. He had taken charge of the pro-slavery forces in the ensuing contest to dominate the legislature, and had engineered the bi-partisan combination that had put the insignificant Geyer into Benton's seat. Now, with the slavery forces, State and national, behind him, he was determined to defeat Benton for reëlection either to Senate or House, and to defend his own place—for Benton was a candidate to succeed him in 1855.

As the session expired, Atchison set forth two partial objections to the bill for organizing Nebraska Territory. One was that the Indian title to nearly the whole region remained unextinguished; the other that the Missouri Compromise still applied to the region, would be enforced unless specially rescinded, and though in Atchison's view unconstitutional, would do its work of excluding slaveholders accompanied by slaves. Speaking rapidly and excitedly, he said that he had investigated the situation the previous year. "I found there was no prospect, no hope of a repeal of the Missouri Compromise, excluding slavery from that Territory. Now, sir, I am free to admit that at this moment, at this hour, and for all time to come I should oppose the organization or the settlement of the Territory, unless my constituents and the constituents of the whole South, of the slave States of the Union, could go into it upon the same footing, with equal rights and equal privileges, carrying that species of property with them . . ."

But, continued Atchison, he had no hope that the restriction would ever be repealed. Gravely improper as the Northwest Ordinance and Missouri Compromise were, they were both irremediable. "There is no remedy for them. We must submit to them. I am prepared to do it. So far as that question is concerned, we might as well agree to the admission of this Terirtory now as next year, or five or ten years hence." He had concluded that it was time to organize the Territory. The necessary treaties with the Indians could be made at once. Organization was inevitable, and should be accomplished before speculators thronged to the area, complicating land titles and rendering settlement costly. He and Geyer both voted for consideration of the bill. Douglas, speaking at some length, never contradicted Atchison's statement that the Missouri Compromise was irrepealable, and never said a word about popular sovereignty.[34] Many students of the situation always maintained with Lincoln that the territorial bill had come so close to passage in 1853 that a determined effort would have carried it unchanged in 1854.

33  Meigs, *Benton*, 409, 410; Roosevelt, *Benton*, National Edition, 218, 219.
34  The whole debate is in the *Cong. Globe*, March 3, 1853; 32d Cong., 2d sess., 1111-1117.

But that effort was never made. Why? Here we meet one of the most arresting enigmas in all American history. For nearly ten years Douglas had pressed for organizing a Nebraska Territory in conformity with the Missouri Compromise. Atchison had at last consented to such organization. Why, holding these views in March, 1853, did they not maintain them in December, 1853? During the summer the obstruction presented by the Indians was largely removed. President Pierce sent George Manypenny, Commissioner of Indian Affairs, to negotiate with the tribes of the region. He held more or less formal conferences with eighteen Indian nations, impressing them by a cool, resolute hostility to any exorbitant and devious bargaining. As a consequence, treaties were shortly concluded with the main tribes north of Kansas River (the Otoe, Iowa, Kickapoo, Delaware, and others), under which about 11,500,000 acres were ceded to the United States; most of this land being unconditionally transferred and therefore subject to preëmption, but 634,500 acres being given up on condition that the government pay the proceeds of sales to the tribes. Treaties were also presently written with tribes south of the Kansas ceding slightly more than 2,000,000 acres, all but about 208,000 acres of which were subject to preemption. It remained only for the Senate to ratify these treaties, and for the Indian Office to take steps to have reservations and selections of land made for the Indian.[35]

The question of Territorial organization was thus left more urgent than ever. Settlers were eager to enter the region; indeed, some had already pushed into it. Manypenny declared on leaving for the West that the subject had worried Pierce and the Cabinet more than all the Cuban and Koszta difficulties put together. When he reached the Nebraska frontier he had found the whites impatient and excited, but quieted them with assurances that they could safely await the early action of the government. He took effective steps to break up unlawful settlements.[36] With the Indian impediment that had led Houston, Bell, Underwood, Fish, and others to vote against the bill removed, why should it not be taken up in its old form and swiftly passed?

One reason was that Atchison's conversion proved but temporary. He con-

---

35 *Report*, Indian Commissioner, 1853; *National Intelligencer*, November 4, 1853; April 22, July 29, 1854. Salmon P. Chase tells us that "I like Manypenny very much and have great confidence in his ability and honesty both." *Diary and Corr.*, 250. Nevertheless, Manypenny had previously shown that he was an active partisan of Senator Atchison (Johnson, *Douglas*, 239), and he was destined in the future to manifest a strong anti-freesoil bias in Kansas. He became an ally of George Pugh, who entered the Senate as a pro-slavery Democrat in 1855. Just what relation his summer's work in 1853 had to the plans of Atchison and Douglas it would be interesting to know. His official papers in the National Archives prove him a keen, hardworking official, vigilant against land speculators; yet he was very much a party man, with his own ambitions for the Senate.
36 Letters to McClelland, November 9, 1853, March 1, 1854; National Archives. Captain Seth Eastman's map is filed with Manypenny's reports.

fessed at the time, amid Senatorial laughter, that he had said too much. His personal habits being what they were, and the Senate's last-night mellowness being what it was, he was probably flown with wine. Returning to Missouri, he came under intense pressure to resume his hostility to the Missouri Compromise restriction. Slavery was at a virtual standstill there while the general population was rapidly growing. North and east stretched free boundaries; if Nebraska were organized under the restriction, free soil would also hem in the west. On every hand slaves would be running away, and anti-slavery sentiment rilling through the dam. If a transcontinental railroad were built, it would extend from free Illinois through slave Missouri into a free Kansas-Nebraska, and every train whistle would be a salute to freedom. Missouri slaveholders found the thought of all this intolerable. They knew that as soon as it became certain that Missouri was on the road to freesoil, Northern immigration would rise faster than ever, Southern immigration would dwindle, the prices of slaves fall, and many Negroes be sold southward; in short, a social revolution would be upon them. Exclaimed the St. Louis *Republican*:[37]

"If Nebraska be made a free Territory then will Missouri be surrounded on three sides by free territory, where there will always be men and means to assist in the escape of our slaves. . . . With the emissaries of abolitionists around us, and the facilities of escape so enlarged, this species of property would become insecure, if not valueless, in Missouri. The Free-Soilers and Abolitionists look to this result, and calculate upon the facilities which will be offered by the incorporation of this Territory with a provision against slavery, as a means of abolishing slavery in Missouri. This is the more evident from a pamphlet recently issued in New York, thousands of which have been scattered over this State, urging the incorporation of Nebraska Territory, with a provision against the introduction of slave property into it; and in the same pamphlet the reëlection of Col. Benton to the United States Senate is urged with the understanding that he would support such a measure. . . . If this scheme be accomplished, then it is not too much to say that six millions of property will be rendered valueless by this single act of legislation."

Telling various men that he wanted the Missouri Compromise restriction repealed, Atchison sounded the sentiment of the western Missouri counties. He found Benton riding his Pacific Railroad hobby hard. He found keen rivalry developing between advocates of the Platte Valley route through what is now Nebraska, and the Kansas Valley route through what is now Kansas. The people of western Iowa were eager to see the

---

37 Quoted in N. Y. *Tribune*, January 30, 1854. A census of Missouri taken in 1856 showed the white population of the State had increased since 1850 by 224,453, or 38 per cent, and the slave population by 1,823, or just over two per cent. See *National Intelligencer*, February 17, 1858, for comment.

Platte Valley line chosen. They encouraged the quite extra-legal choice of a Nebraska delegate to Congress, for one of his duties would be to keep the Platte Valley railroad scheme before members of Congress. A meeting at Wyandotte Council House in Nebraska on July 26, which impudently elected "provisional officers" for the Territory-to-be, endorsed Benton's plans for a Pacific railway. Missourians, meanwhile, were ardently interested in the Pacific Railway Company, which had now begun to build westward from St. Louis toward the Kansas River valley, and which, making steady progress, was destined to reach Jefferson City, the capital, early in 1856. Built through the most thickly settled section of the State, with both Federal land-grant and State aid, it seemed full of promise; an iron arm to clamp the future transcontinental line to St. Louis.

It is not strange that Atchison violently repudiated his midnight readiness to accept Nebraska Territory with a slavery restriction. Speaking at the border town of Weston on June 11, he declared for immediate organization provided that all citizens of all States, slave or free, might settle on equal terms. He would see Nebraska "sink in hell" before he would vote for her organization on a freesoil basis. Meanwhile, he assailed Benton's railway plans with terrific ferocity. "Of all the humbugs the old sinner has ever mounted," he wrote in a private letter, "of all the lame blind windbroken and spavined policies the old villain ever bestrode he has now mounted the shabbiest." [38] At Weston, attacking the nigger-stealers and vermin of the North, he came out for a Pacific road with Kansas City or St. Joseph as its starting point; that is, a Kansas Valley road. [39] Another wild, blustering speech was delivered at Platte City, his home. Under his incitements the Missouri slaveholders were growing bellicose. One meeting, roundly denouncing the Missouri Compromise, declared that "if the Territory shall be opened to settlement, we pledge ourselves to each other to extend the institutions of Missouri over the Territory at whatever sacrifice of blood or treasure." [40]

[ IV ]

The Thirty-third Congress opened in December, 1853, with an overwhelming Democratic majority in both chambers. Linn Boyd of Kentucky was elected Speaker of the House, while Atchison was president of the Senate. It is uncer-

38  May 29, 1853; Judge Samuel Treat Papers, *Mo. Hist. Soc.*
39  St. Louis *Republican*, June 13, 1853; editorial comment, June 13, 14.
40  See the review by Senator Doolittle, *Cong. Globe*, 35th Cong., 1st sess., 986ff. "Lyncens," in *Letters for the Present Crisis* (St. Louis, 1853), wrote that Atchison in his summer speeches was demanding that Nebraska "shall come in as a slave Territory, or, at least, with the question left open and all done to foster slavery that is possible."

tain whether the changes in membership had increased or lessened the chances for the Nebraska bill which had so nearly passed that previous spring. It is uncertain how much or little a strong presidential pressure for that bill could have accomplished. What is certain is that no test of strength occurred. The measure that had passed one chamber in March was now abandoned. If a Southern cabal to resist it had been formed, it was not challenged. Instead, a new bill was introduced which surrendered to the South in advance, repealed the Missouri Compromise restriction, and outraged the freesoil North.

The steps by which this was done may be briefly summarized. Senator Dodge of Iowa promptly introduced the very bill that had passed the House the previous session.[41] It was referred to the Senate Committee on Territories, completely dominated by Douglas. On January 4, 1854, after Douglas had consulted with Jesse D. Bright, the slaveholding Indianian, and another unidentified Northwestern Senator, he reported what was essentially a new measure. But this famous Kansas-Nebraska bill, as it came to be called, was not in perfected form, and rapidly passed through three stages before it was ready for final enactment.

In its first form the bill simply organized a Nebraska Territory with no statement regarding slavery, pro or con, except a clause reading: "And when admitted as a State or States, the said Territory, or any portion of the same, shall be received into the Union, with or without slavery, as their constitution may prescribe at the time of their admission." This language was identical with that of the Utah-New Mexico Acts. The accompanying report stated that opinions differed whether slavery was prohibited in the Nebraska country by *valid* enactment, the constitutionality of the Missouri Compromise being questioned; and that the committee were not prepared to recommend either an affirmation or repeal of the slavery-exclusion clause of that compromise. The vital question was thus left cloudy and uncertain. Was slavery excluded or not? Most men would infer that it was until the courts decided otherwise.[42] For several days Douglas himself seemed to assume that the Missouri Compromise restriction would remain in force unless the courts pronounced it invalid. Unhappily, the ambiguity irritated Southern leaders and gave Whig politicians an opening.

41 *Cong. Globe*, December 14, 1853. Dodge, now forty-two years old, was a native of Missouri, a self-schooled man, of considerable force of character and intellectual ability. After six years as delegate for Iowa Territory, he had been chosen in 1848 the State's first Senator. His early life had given him a strong sympathy for the South. He detested "the sickly sentimentality about slavery," felt no objection to the spread of the institution, and hoped for the day when Canada, Cuba, and northern Mexico would be added to the United States—the annexed areas becoming free or slave as their inhabitants wished. Cf. his speech on the Nebraska Bill, *Cong. Globe*, February 25, 1854; Louis Pelzer, *Augustus Caesar Dodge;* Beveridge, *Lincoln*, II, 175.

42 In this form the bill was instantly and fiercely attacked by the N. Y. *Tribune*, and instantly and heartily endorsed by the Washington *Union;* see issues of these papers, January 5-8, 1854. For the rally of the Democratic press in commendation, see Beveridge, *Lincoln*, II, 179.

Studying this bill, Atchison, who had apparently thus far been imperfectly consulted, felt outraged, for he regarded it as a breach of recent pledges given him by Douglas. According to a speech he made the next year, he threatened to force Douglas off the Committee on Territories, to take the chairmanship himself, and to report a bill repealing the slavery restriction. "I gave Douglas twenty-four hours to decide," he said. Atchison was member of a Senatorial "mess" which included A. P. Butler of South Carolina and J. M. Mason and R. M. T. Hunter of Virginia, and which exercised stern power on the slavery side. Under its pressure Douglas moved forward to give the bill its second form.

On January 10th the measure was reprinted by the Washington *Sentinel* with an additional twenty-first section which, Douglas explained, had been omitted in the first published version through "clerical error." [43] This significant section gave it an entirely new meaning. The power to decide for or against slavery in the new Territory was explicitly transferred from Congress to the people of that Territory. The new section declared that the true intent and meaning of the bill was to carry into practical operation three principles established by the Compromise of 1850; one being that fugitive slaves were recoverable in all Territories as in all States, one that the Supreme Court had an appellate jurisdiction upon questions of personal freedom and the title to slaves, and one, by far the most important, "that all questions pertaining to slavery in the Territories, and in the new States to be formed therefrom, are to be left to the people residing therein, through their appropriate representatives." In short, it enacted the popular sovereignty principle. The plain implication was that the Missouri Compromise restriction was dead.

This was a mighty gain for those Southerners who had so long protested against the restriction; it held out to them the promise of recovering all that they had lost in 1820; but it did not satisfy certain of their leaders. Clay's Whig successor in the Senate, Archibald Dixon, a clean-shaven, hard-mouthed, bleak-faced lawyer-planter of precise mind, pointed out the flaw. Unless the Missouri Compromise restriction were explicitly repealed, it would remain in force until the people had acted to end it. No slaveholder could emigrate to the Territory with slaves until after the people living therein had met, and through their representatives passed affirmatively on the question whether slavery could exist or not. This being so, argued Dixon, the decision would certainly go against slavery; for the laws up to that point would exclude all slaveholders while admitting freesoilers, abolitionists, Britons, Germans, and others opposed to the

43 Obviously a very curious clerical error. Allen Johnson searched out the original document. "Attached to the original draft, now in the custody of the Secretary of the Senate, is a sheet of blue paper, in Douglas's handwriting containing the crucial article. All evidence points to the conclusion that Douglas added this hastily, after the bill had been twice read in the Senate and ordered to be printed; but whether it was carelessly omitted by the copyist or appended by Douglas as an afterthought, it is impossible to say," *Douglas,* 223. For Atchison's speech see Lawrence *Free State,* November 19, 1855.

peculiar institution.[44] The bill as it stood promised the South equality but gave it a dismal inequality.

On the evening of Sunday, January 15th, therefore, Dixon bade his wife get pen and paper, and pacing his room, dictated an amendment for the repeal of as much of the Missouri Compromise as prohibited slavery north of 36° 30'. In the morning he showed it to at least one close friend. Then he rose in the Senate to give notice of his proposal. The Kentucky delegation were enthusiastic. "Governor," said Representative John C. Breckinridge, "why did none of us think of this before?" All Southern Democrats were instantly put on their mettle. They could not do less for slavery than the Southern Whigs were doing.[45]

But Douglas was taken completely aback by the Dixon amendment. He had unquestionably hoped that the meaning of the bill might be left equivocal, and the bold move of the slavery Senators (a cohort being ready to rally behind Dixon) startled him. It seemed to him not only that the amendment was too brutally explicit, but that it came too close to being a positive legislation of slavery into the Territory; for under it slaves could certainly be held there until a popular vote excluded them. He remonstrated with Dixon; he had the bill sent back to committee; and he spent a day or two in anxious pondering upon possible consequences. Well might he hesitate, for already the North was beginning to blaze with excitement and wrath. Then, taking Dixon for a drive, he listened to his arguments, and if we may believe Mrs. Dixon, finally assented to the amendment, exclaiming: "By God, sir, you are right, and I will incorporate it in my bill, though I know it will raise the hell of a storm." [46]

At the same time a second important modification of Douglas's original bill was forced upon him by pressure from another quarter; a change which made of the Nebraska area two Territories, not one. From the beginning men had talked of some division. The well-informed Washington correspondent of the *Missouri Republican*, in a letter dated January 6, spoke of *three* possible Territories, one including the country now Oklahoma. After noting the instant anger and agitation aroused by the bill, he went on:

"It is obviously the plan adopted by the Atchison party to this dispute

44 See Dixon's letter to the Louisville *Times*, quoted in *National Intelligencer*, January 31, 1854.

45 Mrs. Archibald Dixon, *True History of the Missouri Compromise and Its Repeal*, 442–444. In the House, Representative Philip Phillips of Alabama, a State Rights man of South Carolina origin, and a member of the Committee on Territories, took the same view as Dixon. He spoke to Senator R. M. T. Hunter the day after the original bill was introduced; Hunter spoke to Atchison; and Atchison brought about a meeting with Douglas. When Phillips argued that "repeal by implication" was improper, and that it should be "by express words," Douglas was impressed. Other conferences followed. H. B. Learned, "Relation of Philip Phillips to the Repeal of the Missouri Compromise," *Miss. Vall. Hist. Review*, VIII, 303–317. Douglas felt he had to yield to the Southern Democrats.

46 *Idem*, 444, 445; Clingman, *Speeches and Writings*, 335; Johnson, *Douglas*, 235, 236.

because Atchison and Douglas are inseparable friends, and because no definite action has yet been taken in Richardson's Committee of the House on the subject. Richardson is a long-tried and ardent personal friend of Douglas, and perhaps hates Benton as cordially as either that Senator or Atchison. I infer from these relations between the parties that it has been arranged to let the whole matter be settled in the Senate, and that Richardson will report no bill, or at least withhold any that may be formed, until the fate of Douglas's shall have

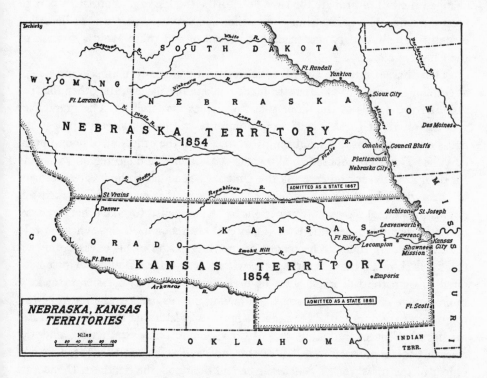

been virtually decided. It is well known to be the fact that the project of three Territories, instead of one, was suggested and discussed at Douglas's house, and after a good deal of anxious consideration, was given up because certain parties of influence could not be reconciled to the ejectment of the southern Indians in the country west of Arkansas." Such a project would have made a new slave State certain.

But if there could not be three, there could be two—and Iowans insisted that this be arranged. They had gained the impression that Commissioner Manypenny, while carefully extinguishing the claims of Indians lying west of Missouri, had left untouched those of some tribes lying west of Iowa. The inference was drawn that Manypenny, as Atchison's intimate, was favoring the railroad interests of Missouri as against those of Iowa. Hadley Johnson, the "delegate" elected by Iowa votes, was full of resentful suspicion. He infected Senator Dodge with his apprehensions, and together the two sought out Douglas. They pointed out that if only a single Territory were organized, its capital would lie far down on the Missouri, and all settlement and travel would follow the Kansas Valley; while creation of another Territory would give the Platte Valley an equal chance of development. Thomas Johnson, the Missouri-elected "delegate," reluctantly assented. After due consideration, Douglas changed the bill to provide for two Territories, the larger and northern part to keep the name Nebraska, while the smaller and southern part was to be called Kansas.[47] The boundary was made 37° instead of 36° 30' to avoid a division of the Cheokee country.

This division into the two Territories was temporarily unimportant except as seeming to many Missourians to mark out one for slavery, the other for free soil; and the details of the other successive steps matter little. The grand fact was the repeal of the Missouri Compromise restriction on slavery. It was the first step toward this that had been decisive, and all the others were bound up in it. When Douglas proposed to allow the settlers in this huge region to decide for or against slavery on entering the Union, he repudiated the great enactment of 1820 which had "forever prohibited" slavery in that area. Having taken this momentous initial move, he was certain to be compelled to take others by way of clarification and definitions of his intent. He recognized this when he told Dixon, "You are right." The record of the three stages of his bill is significant chiefly as showing that even the quickwitted, iron-willed Douglas at first hesitated to own the full implication of his action. It is always easier to make a radical move in two or three steps; but having put his hand to the plow, he had to go on. He correctly told the Senate a few weeks later that the original bill had the legal effect of repealing the Missouri Compromise restriction, and the amendment simply removed "all doubt and cavil as to the true meaning and object of the measure." [48] Whenever he had hesitated, the Southern Democrats had pushed him forward.

It was imperative for Douglas, immediately after his agreement with Dixon, to take action to bring the Administration behind his measure. Monday the 16th of January was the day that Dixon rose in the Senate with his motion; Wednesday the 18th was probably the day on which Douglas took his drive

47 St. Louis *Missouri Republican*, January 13, 1854; Beveridge, *Lincoln*, II, 179–182; Johnson, *Douglas*, 228–236; Bancroft, *Seward*, I, 334–338; Hadley D. Johnson, "How the Kansas-Nebraska Line was Established," *Neb. State Hist. Soc. Transactions*, II, 85ff. Action was also taken in the House looking toward a division. The Washington correspondent of the *Missouri Republican* reported under date of January 23 that "Major Richardson is about to report a bill from the House committee on territories, essentially different from Douglas's. It will provide for the organization of *two territories*, to be called Nebraska and Kansas."
48 *Cong. Globe*, 33d Cong., 1st sess., App., 325–338, March 3, 1854, for Douglas's full explanation.

with Dixon and announced his conversion. Conferences of the Senate and House Territorial committees, and meetings of Democratic leaders, filled the ensuing days. By the end of the week the committees were ready to report. It seemed important for the Senate committee to do so on Monday, the stated day for reports. This decision was reached late Saturday night. According to Secretary Jefferson Davis's account as written long afterward, early on Sunday Douglas, with a number of Senators and Representatives, called at the Secretary's house to explain the situation. They must see the President at once, he said. Davis demurred that Pierce did not receive on Sunday. But Douglas insisted, and Davis finally accompanied the deputation to the White House.[49]

Here Davis left the party in the reception rooms, gained access to Pierce's private apartments, and explained the situation to the docile President. If Pierce had read that morning's Washington *Union*, not much explanation was needed. As late as Friday the *Union* had attacked Dixon's repeal clause, but somebody had reached it, and the Sabbath issue contained a long editorial arguing for repeal. The President came out, shook hands, and listened as the bill was read and further expounded. He immediately gave his emphatic assent, remarking: "I consider the bill based upon a sound principle, which the compromise of 1820 infringed upon, and to which we have now returned."

This, we say, was Jefferson Davis's story as published in 1881, and any story written after nearly thirty years is open to question. The weathercock change of the Washington *Union* between Friday and Sunday indicates that Douglas and his allies had laid down the law to the editor sometime Saturday. In fact, a great deal certainly happened on Saturday. The well-informed correspondent of the New York *Herald* declares that the Cabinet held protracted sessions that day. He states that Secretaries Davis and Dobbin fought hard for the Dixon amendment, that other members resisted, that an amendment referring the issue to the Supreme Court was written and taken to Douglas, and that when Atchison, Mason, Hunter, and other slavery men rejected it, the Dixon amendment prevailed. If this is even partially correct, the Sunday morning call on Pierce was made not to convert him, but to force a final acceptance. Other evidence shows that Douglas, Atchison, Mason, Hunter, Phillips, and Breckinridge faced a chilly, reluctant President and made him toe the line. All Pierce's own policies required harmony with the Senate.[50]

While details elude us, certain broad facts are plain. It is clear that Douglas was crowded forward from an equivocal position to an extreme bill; Atchison pressed him, Phillips pressed him, Dixon pressed him—and above all the logic of his original stand pressed him. It is clear that a small group of men made the bill.

49  Mrs. Dixon, *True History*, 457, 458; cf. Nichols, *Franklin Pierce*, 319-324.
50  Davis, *Rise and Fall of the Confederate Government*, I, 28; Mrs. Dixon, *True History*, 457, 458; Washington *Sentinel*, January 24, 31, 1854; N. Y. *Herald*, January 15-23, 1854.

Cass, for example, was not consulted, although he was the ranking Democratic Senator, the father of popular sovereignty, a friend of Douglas, and a power in the Northwest. He told Chase that although he was decidedly against a renewal of the agitation, he must vote for the bill. It is clear that Pierce all too weakly accepted a measure destined to ruin his Administration. Even if he was secretly as worried as the New York *Express* said he was, he felt that he had to follow the Senate leaders; for his foreign policy depended on their support.[51]

The measure in its final form was reported to the Senate on Monday, January 23, 1854.

## [ V ]

One essential question of fact was raised by Douglas's bill and the accompanying report. Had Congress, applying in 1850 the popular sovereignty principle to the newly conquered and peculiar region of New Mexico and Utah, really intended universal application of that principle to *all* areas not yet organized? Had it intended a repeal of the long-revered, the supposedly inviolable, Missouri Compromise? If it had, then most members of Congress in 1850 had grossly deceived themselves. Douglas had not once hinted during the debates of 1850 that the new Compromise altered the position of the huge unorganized area of the Missouri Valley. Webster had repeatedly declared in the Compromise debates that the territories held before the Mexican acquisitions had "a fixed and settled character" as to slavery or non-slavery.[52] Not one man in the Senate, Edward Everett now wrote in his diary, had thought in 1850 of a supersession of the Missouri Compromise, and Robert Toombs privately acknowledged to him that there had been no idea that year of a repeal.[53] Oh, for one hour of Clay to confront Douglas! one hour of Dandolo! sighed scores of Congressmen.

And back of this essential question of fact lay great mountain-vistas of principle. Even granted that the time-hallowed compact was to be scrapped, at what point in the development of the Territory were the people to decide the momentous slavery issue? When the population reached five thousand, or thirty or fifty thousand?—or when the Territory applied for Statehood? How were angry and perhaps bloody dissensions among the settlers to be avoided? If they occurred, could the North and South be expected to gaze indifferently on the contest? And was it not the true principle that the *nation* had a far greater stake in the decision than the crude settlements which voted it?—that thirty millions were more to be considered than thirty thousand? Since the whole tendency of

51 Chase, *Diary and Corr.*, 256; N. Y. *Express*, April 24, 1854.
52 *Cong. Globe*, March 7, June 3, 1850.
53 Everett, MS Diary, February 6, 9, 1854.

the age ran counter to slavery, did not true principle demand that the nation save as much of its virgin territory as possible for freedom?

Each of these questions was of cardinal importance. Supporters of the bill were themselves bitterly divided as to the point at which popular sovereignty was to be applied. Douglas and others believed that the settlers should make their decision at an early stage and the popular will should constantly rule; most Southerners held that the settlers could make no decision till the Territory was ready for admission—slavery meanwhile entering freely. Only by a sharp suppression of debate on this vital point was unity maintained. Again, the fact that Congress was enacting civil strife on the Kansas plains was clearly foreseen. Extremists on both sides pointed it out before the bill passed, and some exulted in the prospect. They saw in the bill a gage of sectional battle. Passions rose at the prospect. As for the idea that the issue of slavery extension, pregnant with good or ill for the whole nation, should be decided by a handful of first-comers in the Kansas Valley, it appalled men who believed with Lincoln that the institutions of the country should be kept under the control of its whole people.

Robert Winthrop had this in mind when he burst out to the novelist Kennedy: "But slavery is, after all, such a devil of a thing to experiment upon, that where one has it fairly out of a Territory, it seems almost like a *provocatio coeli* to let it in!" He went on: "We are guardians of the infant commonwealths which lie cradled in these new Territories. We must do to them, as we would be done by. If I thank God that Massachusetts is not a slave State, how then can I turn round and let Nebraska or Kansas become one by refusing to interpose for their protection?" [54]

Against Douglas, as his opponents showed, could be quoted his own words. Less than five years earlier, addressing his constituents at Springfield on October 23, 1849, he had eulogized the Missouri Compromise as perdurable.[55] It had been in practical operation for a quarter of a century, he said; it had received the approbation of all parties and sections; it had tranquillized the whole country; it had given Clay his proud title of pacificator. Its origin, he went on, was "akin to that of the Constitution of the United States, governed in the same spirit of fraternal affection." All the evidences of public opinion indicated that it had "become canonized in the hearts of the American people as a sacred thing, which no ruthless hand would ever be reckless enough to disturb." And now his was the ruthless hand! His excuse, of course, was that the Compromise of 1850 had superseded that of 1820—though actually it had merely supplemented the earlier enactment.

The thinness of Douglas's arguments of precedence, the obvious shiftiness

54 February 27, 1854; Kennedy Papers.
55 *Illinois State Register*, November 8, 1849; Representative Cullom in *Cong. Globe*, April 11, 1854.

and subterfuge of his course, inspired instant question of his motives. The secret history of the measure remains an enigma. It was easy to accuse Douglas of offering the South a bribe to elevate him to the presidency. Edward Bates, veteran Whig leader of Missouri, who accepted Atchison's claims to authorship, shortly asserted: "He went to Douglas and declared, 'Introduce this bill; you are strong at the North; this will give you the South, and you will be President.' . . . It was a pure electioneering trick." [56] But such partisan accusations carry no weight. Ambitious as Douglas was, his motivation was at once more complicated and more elevated than this view suggests. He had just discouraged any talk of the presidency for the next two years, and certainly the bill was no electioneering trick. We may safely assume that it grew out of earnest conferences of a small number of Democratic leaders, that it had a variety of motives, and that it was intended to achieve a number of objects. We may also safely assume that Douglas was, as he always maintained, its primary author, though Atchison may have played a large role, and that he found counsellors in Atchison, Bright, and a select squad of other border and Southern Senators.[57]

The most favorable interpretation of Douglas's action suggests that he inevitably had in mind all the complex elements of the situation then existing. He had to think of the disorganized, discontented state of the Democratic party, lacking both leader and policy; [58] the obligation resting upon "Young America" for bold, trenchant action; his own legitimate ambition to become President; the demand of the Northwest for a Pacific Railroad, with the consequent necessity for settling the Kansas-Nebraska country to furnish its future path; the fear of Missouri slaveholders lest they be surrounded on three sides by freesoil territory; Atchison's stubborn assertion that he would let Nebraska "sink in hell" before he would see it organized on a basis excluding slaveholders with their property; and Atchison's ability to rally a solid block of Southern Senators behind him. Douglas knew that, as the Washington *Union* remarked on January 5, 1854, "this subject had been looked to with serious apprehensions, in consequence of the supposition that it might fearfully revive the slavery agitation." But he believed, with Webster, that nature had closed this whole region to

56  Speech to Whig convention, *National Intelligencer*, September 20, 1856. Cf. Allen Johnson, *Douglas*, 235: "The regrettable aspect of Douglas's course is his attempt to nullify the Missouri Compromise by subtle indirection. This was the device of a shifty politician, trying to avert suspicion and public alarm by clever ambiguities." The view of Beveridge (*Lincoln*, II, 176ff.) is that Douglas began by "feeling his way, testing the depth and direction of senatorial sentiment," and that his quick shifts of position were those of a "skillful parliamentary tactician." This difference of opinion rests upon a difference of standards. The question is whether we apply to Douglas the tests of political cleverness, or the tests of statesmanship.
57  These Senators certainly included Dixon, Hunter, and Dodge of Iowa. On the rôle of the last, see J. Sterling Morton and Albert Watkins, *History of Nebraska*, 129.
58  Here, writes Beveridge in his sympathetic analysis, "was a heaven-sent opportunity to rehabilitate the Democratic Party"; *Lincoln*, II, 176.

slavery.[59] He recalled how easily Congress, in dealing with New Mexico and Utah in 1850, had evaded the slavery issue by leaving it to the future determination of the inhabitants. As chairman of the Committee on Territories, he had to move immediately, and to move in a way that would maintain Democratic unity.

What solution, then, would hold the party together; enable Atchison, so hard pressed by Benton, to keep his promise to his constituents; open Nebraska to settlement with a rapidity that would encourage railway-building; and at the same time give freesoilers their full chance to hold the region? It seemed to him the most practical policy, and perhaps the fairest, to abrogate the Missouri Compromise, throw the area wide to slaveholder and Northerner alike, and let the popular will decide.

Efforts of subsequent students to overemphasize one element or another in this complex of motives are not convincing. One school has interpreted the bill exclusively in the light of the Missouri political situation. Atchison, they hold, eager for reëlection in 1855, had to incorporate a pro-slavery plan for the organization of the Kansas-Nebraska country in his platform; Douglas was Atchison's close friend, disliking Benton to the point of personal enmity; he realized the importance of consolidating the Democratic Party in Missouri; and he swung to Atchison's position.[60] But this explanation is not satisfactory. No direct proof exists, the thesis resting on inference alone; Douglas was never disposed to interfere in the politics of neighboring States; Atchison never showed any special gratitude to him; and we have seen that Atchison gave another explanation of the origin of the bill. It may be added that the passage of the Kansas-Nebraska bill proved of no political benefit to Atchison, who lost his battle for reëlection.

Another school has interpreted the bill almost exclusively in the light of Western railroad expansion. According to this theory, Douglas, embodying the restless, expansive spirit of the West, was eager to promote the growth of the

59 So, it may be noted, did Senator Dodge of Iowa. "Now, what will be the practical operation of this bill?" he presently asked in debate. "The owners of property everywhere are timid upon the point of its loss. You rarely find a man, the owner of slaves, ready to dash in among a new community like that which will people Kansas and Nebraska. There will be quite an emigration from Missouri and Arkansas to these Territories, but in the main it will be of that class of citizens who are in needy circumstances, and own no slaves. There may be a few persons in those States owning slaves who will emigrate to the proposed Territories, taking family servants to whom they are attached; nothing, however, but a splendid town site or water privilege can induce such to do so. They will probably be taken, under an arrangement with their owners, to serve a given number of years and receive their freedom; when, from the cheapness of land, these blacks may become owners of small tracts, upon which they may raise enough to carry themselves or their posterity to Africa, where alone they can live on terms of social equality." *Cong. Globe*, February 25, 1854; 33rd Cong., 1st sess., App., p. 381.
60 P. O. Ray, "Genesis of the Kansas-Nebraska Act," *Am. Hist. Assn. Report*, 1914, I, 259-280; Ray, *Repeal of the Missouri Compromise, passim.*

Northwest, was keenly interested in a Pacific railroad, and was ambitious to see Chicago its chief beneficiary. His Illinois Central land-grant had bound Southern Illinois to Chicago instead of St. Louis. In 1850 the organization of New Mexico Territory gave advocates of a New Orleans-Memphis-El Paso route a signal advantage, and made the organization of Nebraska imperative as an answer. Iowa was as deeply concerned as northern Illinois. Rapid action was possible only if the South were placated.[61] And Douglas, according to this theory, was the readier to make concessions to the South because he had to make concessions to southern Illinois. "Egypt," where he had long been a favorite, would perceive that his territorial bill gave northern Illinois special advantages; and he therefore had to cloak his intention of strengthening Chicago by a sweeping gesture in the direction of slaveholders and their southern Illinois friends.

But while this theory possesses some force as a partial clue to Douglas's action, it falls far short of providing a full explanation. A whole set of objections may be urged against it. (1) It did not suggest itself at the time to anybody of importance, whether Northerner or Southerner. It is impossible to find any direct and explicit statement of such an interpretation in the Congressional debates or the press. This is the more remarkable in that any suggestion of sectional railroad designs would have told heavily against the bill, and Douglas's enemies would have pounced on the idea had they thought it tenable. (2) Precipitate action to clear the way for a central route was not imperative. Douglas was the dominating personality in the Senate railroad committee, and could block the passage of a bill until Nebraska was organized even if this took years. (3) Since his syndicate operations at Superior City, Douglas's most direct pocket interest was in a northern and not a central route. (4) If railroad development was his motive, he failed completely. He never got any railroad bill passed— much less a bill looking toward Chicago as the eastern terminal. (5) Southern Illinois was too warmly attached to Douglas to need special favors to cement its loyalty, and its voters, who held no slaves, had no interest in a repeal of the Missouri Compromise and never indicated any demand for it. (6) As Douglas's

61 This railroad interpretation has been most fully elaborated by Frank H. Hodder in "Genesis of the Kansas-Nebraska Act," *Wis. State Hist. Society Bulletin*, No. 60 (1912); "The Railroad Background of the Kansas-Nebraska Act," *Miss. Vall. Hist. Rev.*, XII. It was first stated, however, by Douglas's close friend, James W. Sheahan, in his eulogy on Douglas, pronounced July 3, 1861; *Fergus Historical Series*, 1881, XV, 120–125. Sheahan pointed to the indispensability of a road to the Pacific, to the fact that the unorganized Nebraska area "like an immense block . . . barred the natural pathway," to the Southern demand for a transcontinental line terminating in Memphis, and to Douglas's desire for "a fair chance to have that railroad lead from the North, where it could have fine communication through Chicago to the Atlantic." He said flatly: "That was the motive for organizing these Territories—a motive having its origin in the desire to benefit the whole nation, and especially to give the Northwest a fair opportunity to compete for the commerce of the great East." But it was a Missouri Representative, J. J. Lindley, and not an Illinoisan, who said in the House debates that his State wished the immediate settlement of the Territory to bring about the construction of "that great enterprise of the age, the Pacific Railroad."

railroad bill of 1854 demonstrated, he believed that it would be equitable and practicable to build three lines, northern, central, and southern, at the same time and on the same terms. It would have been logical for him to attempt a sectional bargain, or rather sectional union, on this basis rather than on the repeal of the Missouri Compromise line.[62]

Atchison himself furnished evidence that competitive anxiety to make Chicago the sole terminus of a Pacific Railroad could hardly have actuated Douglas; for in an address to the people of Missouri, dated at Washington June 5, 1854, and published in the Washington *Sentinel*, he explained just what his own motives had been. A large portion of his constituents were slaveholders. He had told them at Parkville in 1853 that he would never vote to organize a Territory from which they would be excluded. In addition, however, he had been anxious to promote the railway enterprises of Missouri. The North, he stated, wished its railroads to Chicago extended westward on a line north of Missouri; the Southerners wanted a railroad to the Pacific far southward of Missouri. Under these circumstances, Missouri had to play her cards carefully. After careful consideration, her delegation in Congress had obtained land grants of sufficient value to ensure the construction of two roads across the State, one on each side of the Missouri River; and the State had then granted aid to a third road midway between the two. "We hope (and as our plan is honest we have no desire to conceal it), to be able to procure for Kansas Territory what we procured for Missouri—lands to aid in the extension of the St. Joseph road, northeasterly, up the valley of the Platte; lands to aid in the extension of the Springfield road across the Neosho and Arkansas rivers in the direction of Albuquerque. These grants will insure the extension of our three roads five hundred or six hundred miles each, toward California. . . ." Nothing in Atchison's breast was a secret to Douglas. Chicago stood in the long run to profit from the peopling of the Western plains, but as Atchison pointed out, in the short run St. Louis had most to gain.

Men's motives are seldom simple, seldom completely logical, and seldom

---

62 Hodder has stated the obvious reason why Douglas himself could never have mentioned his supposed railroad motivation. "If he emphasized the importance of the northern, or rather the central, route, he antagonized his friends in the South. If he favored a Chicago terminal, he sacrificed the interests of his constituents in southern Illinois and laid himself open to the charge of favoring his own private interest. If he favored a St. Louis terminal he sacrificed his own interests and those of his Northern Illinois constituents." *Dial*, September 1, 1909, quoted in Beveridge, *Lincoln*, II, 171. This, however, does not explain why neither his Northern nor Southern opponents failed to mention his presumed railroad motivation; why no neutral press commentator mentioned it; why it was in fact not mentioned at all until much later, when a rationalization of his conduct became necessary. Beveridge (*Lincoln*, II, 170) says that the success of a railroad to the Pacific, "the nation's dream and the nation's passionate desire . . . was inextricably interwoven with the organization of Nebraska," unless a Southern route were chosen. But it was by no means impossible without repeal of the Missouri Compromise. Time proved that such repeal did not facilitate it; it delayed it. It was even said in the Congressional debates of 1854 that it would delay it.

quite clear even to themselves. Douglas, his mind in Shakespeare's phrase a very opal, was a leader of extroverted personality, of rapid decisions and headlong action, and of pronounced love of combat. He was never disposed to give prolonged meditation to the complexities of a situation, or to undertake a careful weighing of forces and futurities. He did not think before he acted; he thought while acting. And what time did he have for thinking? He was just back from Europe; he labored under a press of accumulated business, public and private; he entertained and was entertained so incessantly that men like Forney wondered that he had leisure to read at all.[63] Relying upon a brain teeming with points and a marvelous memory, he was always quick to improvise. In this particular situation, pure impulse doubtless played a large part in his course.

For the rest, as we have said, he acted under a multiplicity of motives. He was certainly aware of his friend Atchison's political plight, certainly conscious of the stake of Chicago and northern Illinois in a transcontinental line, and certainly ambitious for a larger role in national leadership. But other considerations must have been equally in his mind. He was proud of his part in solving the New Mexico-Utah difficulty in 1850 and of the formula then used. He thought (as his first draft showed) that the Missouri Compromise restriction might well be left in dubiety, the North meanwhile taking the substance of a free Kansas and the South contenting itself with a verbal shadow. He was eager to clear the way for the operation of natural forces in the Nebraska country, which (contemptuous of mere moral and sentimental considerations) he believed the only real forces. He was proud of his record in supervising the organization of new Western Territories, a role which had become almost a mania or passion.[64]

Not least of all, he knew that the Administration lay rolling water-logged in doldrums from which its rescue was urgent. That shrewd border Senator, John Bell, commented forthwith: "The whole movement by Douglas from the first was to get up some counter excitement to call off the public attention from the conduct of the Administration." [65] And this was the view of Representative Cullom of Tennessee, who, picturing the Pierce regime as weak, tottering, and discredited, declared: "Some new and exciting movement was necessary to divert the public attention from the conduct of the Administration." [66] Thus a whole broad complex of reasons, half-reasons, and quarter-reasons reinforced his first impulsiveness.

63  *Anecdotes of Public Men*, I, 21.
64  *Cong. Globe*, 33rd Cong., 1st sess., 407ff.
65  S. F. Ordway, "John Bell," *Gulf States Hist. Mag.*, II, No. 1, 41, 42; Bell's letter of April 21, 1854.
66  *Cong. Globe*, 33d Cong., 1st sess., 538ff.; April 11, 1854. He denounced "this attempt to advance individual and party interests, under the flimsy pretext of doing justice to the South." The N. Y. *Herald* took the same view. Because of "evidences of public sentiment daily accumulating against the free-soil and secession spoils coalition," the bill was a bold move "to repair damages and to recover lost ground." January 25, 1854.

And once Douglas had struck the first blow, his blood was up. He would fight it out. When Atchison and Dixon showed that the South would *not* content itself with a verbal shadow, an ambiguity, he was momentarily shocked. Taken aback, he realized for the first time the momentous nature of his step; he saw that his whole career had been put to the touch. Under the pressure of the Southern phalanx he came to the inevitable decision. Gifted with a mighty *gaudium certaminis,* he roused himself like a tiger; he never thought of yielding; and he fought with terrible energy for the kill.[67]

## [ VI ]

What remains mysterious, in even the most sympathetic view of his motives, is his attitude toward free-soil opinion; an attitude curiously blind and callous, a mixture of incomprehension and indifference. For thirty-three years the Missouri Compromise had truly been enshrined in Northern hearts. Did he not realize that any sudden attempt to overthrow it would raise the greatest storm of the generation? Of course he did; he told Dixon that he would be assailed by demagogues and fanatics, showered with opprobrious epithets and hanged in effigy.[68] Knowing this, did he believe that the storm would be confined to radical circles and hence prove short-lived? Or, comprehending the depth of free-soil sentiment, did he hold the tempest in contempt because he thought he could master it? Beyond doubt he partly underestimated the force of Northern indignation, and partly despised it whatever its intensity.

He underestimated it because, feeling himself no moral repugnance to slavery, he could not imagine other men's anger at the idea of its admission to a domain hitherto inviolate. His biographers have found in all his speeches and letters only one or two statements intimating a dislike of slavery. A hundred can be found which show that, as he once said, he did not care whether it was voted up or down. He remarked on one occasion: "Slavery may be very essential in one climate, and totally useless in another. If I were a citizen of Louisiana, I would vote for retaining and maintaining slavery, because I believe

67 Both Beveridge and George Fort Milton, rejecting a monistic interpretation of Douglas's action, suggest (though less emphatically than I have done) the interplay of numerous motives. Beveridge, *Lincoln,* II, 176ff.; Milton, *Eve of Conflict,* 152–154. Cf. Randall, *Civil War and Reconstruction,* 132, who broadly emphasizes "circumstances associated with the inevitable development of the West." But none of these writers appreciates the chaotic condition into which Pierce had let the Democratic Party sink, and the mingled need for and temptation to Douglas's thrust toward leadership which this quarreling turmoil presented. Nor does any of these writers give proper weight to Douglas's heedless impulsiveness; Beveridge, indeed, treating his whole course as foreseen and planned from the outset, when it is plain from the three stages through which the bill passed, and from Mrs. Dixon's graphic account of his dismay and hesitation when he stood on the brink of the second, that he took his first step without due forethought of the inevitable sequels.

68 Mrs. Dixon, *True History,* 445, 447.

the good of that people would require it." [69] He said again: "We in Illinois tried slavery while we were a Territory, and found it was not profitable; and *hence* we turned philanthropists and abolished it." [70] And on still another occasion: "Whenever a territory has a climate, soil, and productions making it the *interest* of the inhabitants to encourage slave property, they will pass a slave code and give it encouragement. Whenever the climate, soil, and productions preclude the possibility of slavery being profitable, they will not permit it. You come right back to the principle of dollars and cents." [71] His attitude toward slavery was completely and exclusively materialistic. When it paid it was good and when it did not pay it was bad. His statement in 1850 that many looked forward with confidence to the time when the five border States, with probably North Carolina and Tennessee as well, would adopt gradual emancipation, was based on this ledger outlook.[72]

The slave himself he did not consider, nor did he regard a slaveholding society as one whit inferior to a free society. Again and again he made it plain that he shared the Southern conviction upon the natural and permanent inferiority of the Negro. "The civilized world," he said, "have always held that when any race of men have shown themselves so degraded by ignorance, superstition, cruelty, and barbarism as to be utterly incapable of governing themselves, they must, in the nature of things, be governed by others, by such laws as are deemed applicable to their condition." [73]

It was impossible for such a man to comprehend the fervent emotion with which millions of freedom-loving Northerners regarded the possibility that half the great West might become a land of slaves—for devote Kansas to slavery, and Colorado, New Mexico, and Arizona (to use present-day names) might all conceivably follow. When indignation welled up like the ocean lashed by a hurricane he was amazed. The fact that the irresistible tidal forces in history are moral forces always escapes a man of dim moral perceptions. Douglas did not realize that far more important than the early settlement of Nebraska and the definition of its railroad routes was the question whether its ultimate institutions would be beneficent or pernicious; an issue on which no avoidable risks were to be tolerated. He did not comprehend that far more important than the unity of the Democratic Party was the unity of the American people. He did not remember that it is the essence of democratic government that a temporary majority shall not abuse its power, nor shall cardinal changes be forced in national policy except after full and free discussion, and by emphatic assent

69  January 23, 1860; *Cong. Globe*, 36th Cong., 1st sess., 559.
70  February 29, 1860; *Cong. Globe*, 36th Cong., 1st sess., 915.
71  Memphis speech, November 29, 1858; Memphis *Avalanche*, November 30.
72  *Cong. Globe*, March 13, 1850; 31st Cong., 1st sess., 369.
73  Chicago speech, October 23, 1850; Sheahan, *Douglas*, 184.

of the people. These were all at bottom moral considerations, and his apprehension of them was cloudy and limited.

What he saw was the immediate problem, and he drove ahead with what he thought a practical, businesslike, and very adroit solution, disregarding the fact that it involved what half the North would regard as a perfidious and insulting breach of a solemn compact; disregarding, too, the possibility that his step might give a vicious, crippling institution a broad new foothold. The elder Blair, who declared with Jacksonian passion that he would devote the rest of his life to the opposition, voiced the widespread sense of outrage over the sudden and arbitrary presentation of this legislation. "Among us," he said, "extraordinary changes affecting large interests and reaching the feelings, the prejudices, the religious and political principles of men, as well as the political power of the States, had hitherto always been preceded or attended by every mode of forming and eliciting the public opinion, which is the vital movement in a republican government." But in this transaction, slashing brutally into the most anxious of all national questions, "not a whisper of the design was permitted to reach the public ear until its success was sealed by the private arrangements of the politicians in Congress, in conjunction with the President." [74] And when the measure was presented, added Blair, its object was first veiled, then half-unveiled, and when at last fully disclosed was justified by the assertion that the Compromise of 1850 had done what nobody who debated it has said it would do! The same protest against sharp practise came from ex-Senator Clemens of Alabama: [75]

"The bill states in substance that the Compromise of 1820 was repealed by the Compromise of 1850. Now, this is either true or it is not. If true, where is the necessity of repealing it over again? It is an anomaly in legislation to repeal a statute which is already repealed. . . . If it is not true, then the bill ought not to pass, because it bears a falsehood upon its face. The value of any compromise depends upon its *finality*. If when one party has the power it may repeal the part which is distasteful to them, when the other party has the strength why may they not also repeal that part which is disagreeable to themselves? . . . I hold it to be a good rule that we ought to be very careful how we make compacts, but once made to abide by them firmly, fairly, and honestly."

## [ VII ]

Pierce hastened to throw a certain amount of presidential support behind the measure. Though Jefferson Davis and Caleb Cushing were enthusiastically for it, several of their colleagues hesitated: Marcy's frowning silence showed

74 Speech at Republican organizing convention, February 22, 1856.
75 Letter of February 25, 1854, to Nicholas Davis; *National Intelligencer*, April 6, 1854.

plainly his disapprobation, and others were reported to acquiesce reluctantly.[76] But to make certain that the President was irrevocably committed, Douglas and Atchison had induced Pierce to write out the section which repealed the Compromise of 1820, declaring it superseded by the Compromise of 1850 and "inoperative."[77] The Washington *Union*, after first assailing the Dixon amendment as an attempt to destroy a sound piece of legislation by invoking sectional dissension, now turned about so completely that it declared that the leaders would rightly regard loyalty to the bill as a test of Democratic fidelity.[78] Politicians rallied to the measure. Before January ended Senator Bright was advising his Indiana protégé, Representative William H. English, that he should refuse to make any committals in caucus or outside against the territorial legislation.[79] The Administration press fell into militant line. Before the Dixon amendment had been incorporated, the Boston *Post* and Albany *Argus* had praised Douglas's proposal as admirable.[80] They took the same view after the bill was rewritten. A long list of other Democratic organs rushed to the breastworks: the New York *Journal of Commerce* and *Day Book*, the Washington *Sentinel*, the Trenton *True American*, the New Haven *Register*, the New Hampshire *Patriot*, the Binghamton *Democrat*, the Harrisburg *Pennsylvanian*, the Detroit *Free Press*, the Columbus *Statesman*, and *Illinois State Register*.

It is certain that Pierce had not the faintest idea that such a bill would be introduced when, in his annual message the previous month, he had spoken complacently of the general good-will, and declared emphatically that "this repose is to suffer no shock during my official term, if I have power to avert it." Neither had any of these editors. Yet the bill suddenly became the touchstone of true Democracy.

The party was thus shakily committed to Douglas's measure by the precipitate action of a small Senatorial group whose swift maneuver made the half-comprehending Pierce their confederate. "The President did not consult with scarcely any of the Compromise men of 1850, of either House or Senate, but plunged into it, I mean the Nebraska question," Representative John Robbins of Philadelphia wrote Buchanan from Washington.[81] "He has a few men with whom he is intimate, and to all others he bows most politely, but keeps at a respectful distance." If Douglas's motives were debatable, Pierce's were not. He was afraid of the strong men of the Senate, heavily influenced by Davis and

76 *Diary and Corr. of S. P. Chase*, 256, 257. According to the Washington *National Democrat*, Davis would have resigned had the Administration not adopted the bill, while Cushing was outspoken in his distaste for Marcy; quoted in N. Y. *Express*, March 21, 1854.
77 Ray, *Repeal of the Missouri Compromise*, 214; Beveridge, *Lincoln*, II, 182, 183.
78 January 22–31, 1854; cf. Nichols, *Franklin Pierce*, 324.
79 January 31, 1854; English Papers, W. H. Smith Memorial Library, Indianapolis.
80 Both quoted in Washington *Union*, January 10, 1854.
81 March 13, 1854; Buchanan Papers.

Cushing in the Cabinet, and ready to play a hazardous game for the retention of power. Everybody knew that a host of Northern Democrats would revolt. But the die was cast.

As it was cast, two interconnected battles began to rage, one in Congress and one in the country at large; each fought with a pertinacity, bitterness, and rancor unknown even in Wilmot Proviso days. It seemed certain from the beginning that the freesoilers would lose the Congressional struggle. The Democrats had large majorities in both houses; party discipline was powerful; Douglas was a ferocious fighter, the fiercest, most ruthless, and most unscrupulous that Congress had perhaps ever known; important groups were anxious to obtain Territorial organization at almost any price; and the popular sovereignty principle could be given a specious appeal to many who thought the voice of the people (even a frontier fragment) the voice of God. But in the country as a whole the freesoilers might win a moral victory. Highly significant was the quick response of the New York *Times*, than which no journal in the world was more moderate. As conducted by Henry J. Raymond, its quiet conservatism, courtesy, and scrupulous fairness had won it general respect. During 1853 it had frequently praised Pierce. But the moment the final text of the Nebraska bill became available, it declared that passage of the measure would root out from the Northern mind the last vestiges of confidence in the advocates of slavery, "and create a deep-seated, intense, and ineradicable hatred of the institution which will crush its political power, at all hazards, and at any cost." [82]

The immediate danger, as it seemed to Chase, Sumner, and other freesoilers, was that the bill would be hurried through Congress without proper debate and before public sentiment could be aroused. On January 24, the day after the bill was reported to the Senate in final form, therefore, an impassioned invocation of Northern opinion appeared in the press entitled "Appeal of the Independent Democrats in Congress to the People of the United States," or more briefly "Address to the People." [83] Though partially based on a draft by Joshua Giddings, the document was from the pen of Chase, who later boasted of it as the most valuable of his works. At first the two men, probably with J. Q. Adams's "Appeal Against the Annexation of Texas" in 1842 in mind, had planned merely an address of Ohio members of all parties to their constituents. [84] But Senator Sumner and Representative Alexander De Witt of Massachusetts, with Representative Gerrit Smith of New York, were enlisted

82  January 24, 1854.
83  The latter title used in the N. Y. *Times*, the former in the Washington *National Era*, January 24, 1854.
84  The N. Y. *Times*, January 24, 1854, gives it in that form, dated January 19; cf. *Cong. Globe*, 33d Cong., 1st sess., 281, 282.

as well. Chase had talked with Benton, who denounced the bill, and with Hamilton Fish, who had heard Mason of Virginia say that he did not want it. His Appeal was charged with a voltage of emotion which gave its language searing intensity.

"We arraign this bill," it declared, "as a gross violation of a sacred pledge; as a criminal betrayal of precious rights; as part and parcel of an atrocious plot to exclude from a vast unoccupied region immigrants from the Old World and free laborers from our own States, and convert it into a dreary region of despotism, inhabited by masters and slaves. . . ."

The phraseology of the Appeal was in fact grossly exaggerated, and the wisdom of its hasty publication was open to serious question. It accused the slave States of Punic faith. It arraigned them for a "monstrous plot" whose object was to spread servitude over a broad belt stretching from the Gulf to the Canadian boundary, and ultimately in the States and Territories bordering the Pacific, so as to "permanently subjugate the whole country to the yoke of a slaveholding despotism." This was obviously absurd. It warned the country against "servile demagogues" who held that the Union could be preserved only by truckling to slavery. It imputed base motives to Douglas: "Will the people permit their dearest interests to be thus made the mere hazards of a presidential game, and destroyed by false facts and false inferences?" Do not submit, it urged readers, "to become agents in extending legalized oppression and systematized injustice." Hurriedly penned, the Appeal contained historical inaccuracies upon which Douglas was quick to fasten.[85] The haste with which it was issued, involving an unhappy misunderstanding as to its sponsorship, was unfortunate. The fact that only six men signed it, all abolitionists or freesoilers verging on abolitionism, robbed it of much of its weight. But above all, its vitriolic and insulting phraseology, arousing resentment throughout the Southern membership of Congress, did much to consolidate their vote behind Douglas.

Haste was unnecessary, for Douglas consented on January 24th to postpone debate until the 30th. A carefully-weighed address, employing more argument and less denunciation, would have found numerous moderate signers; men like Robert C. Winthrop, who regarded the Nebraska bill as a great and grievous wrong, but had no desire to revile the Southern leaders. Most important of all, a reasoned and judicious approach might have won not a few Southern votes that went instead into Douglas's pocket. Could the bill have been defeated by such votes—no utter impossibility with better management— the cause of national union would have received an immense gain.[86]

Nor was the Appeal necessary to rally the North. The mere text of the bill,

85  *Cong. Globe*, 33d Cong., 1st sess., 275–280; January 30, 1854.
86  Cf. Winthrop, October 15, 1855, June 24, 1856, to W. C. Rives; Rives Papers.

with the editorials already appearing in the freesoil press, the speeches already coming from anti-slavery leaders, the sermons already being written, sufficed to set the section in a blaze. No such blast was needed to arouse Greeley, Raymond, Bryant, Bowles, Schouler, Horace White, and the thousand lesser freesoil editors of the North; to awaken Theodore Parker, Henry W. Bellows, or Henry Ward Beecher; or to call into action the New York, Boston, and Philadelphia merchants whose angry protest came in swift series of thunderclaps. It was true that the Appeal was widely circulated and generally read. It was true that some German and other foreign-language newspapers, to which it addressed a special plea, levied on it for ammunition; that countless ministers, whom it adjured to interpose in the name of humanity, quoted it from the pulpit. But why? Not because of the force of its arguments, or the scorching power of its invective. Because millions of Northerners, the moment they saw the final text of the bill, felt themselves betrayed and outraged, and seized on whatever missiles were within reach. Before the Appeal reached the North, men were drafting resolutions for the New York legislature; editors had begun to pen condemnations of the bill as emphatic as Raymond's—"Its very success will sow the seeds of a future contest which will admit of no compromise"; [87] merchants and professional men were indignantly consulting together.

[ VIII ]

Douglas immediately sprang forward to meet the attack. As he later told his brother-in-law Cutts, his Senate speeches contained the whole argument for the Kansas-Nebraska bill. "I passed the Kansas-Nebraska Act myself. I had the authority and power of a dictator throughout the whole controversy in both houses. The speeches were nothing. It was the marshalling and directing of men and guarding from attacks and with a ceaseless vigilance preventing surprise." He deeply resented Chase's attack. It seemed to him a dastardly blow because it accused him of selling his honor for the hope of the presidency; because it stigmatized him as a cheat and liar; because Chase, after writing it, had come to him with friendly mien and requested him to postpone the Senate debate so that he might study the question, when his real reason (said Douglas) was that he wished time to circulate his slanderous attack. His own first word of the Appeal was a copy that came by mail from Ohio. To his dying day he believed that Chase and Sumner had sought by fraud to forestall public opinion, and by lies to mislead it. Quivering with rage, he rose in the Senate on January 30th to open the formal debate.[88]

87  N. Y. *Times*, January 24, 1854.
88  J. Madison Cutts, *Constitutional and Party Questions*, 96; *Cong. Globe*, 33d Cong., 1st sess., 275ff.

The chamber was jammed, so many Representatives crowding in that the House had no quorum; the galleries were packed; press correspondents were scribbling eagerly. Two views could be taken of Douglas's effort. "He spoke," wrote the *Union* reporter, "under great excitement, and with an energy and power which made an impression that was manifested in a very unusual way in the Senate . . . in terms neither mild nor soft he laid bare the wickedness of the plot." [89] "The Senator from Illinois lost his temper before he began, and lost with it much of the respect of his audience," commented the New York *Times* correspondent. This, it added, he could ill afford, "for the vulgarity and vehemence of the abuse which he poured out upon Senator Chase and his fellow-signers" were highly discreditable. [90] The speech was in fact an adroit combination of argument and arraignment, and a skilful appeal to various prejudices. Chase and Sumner, said Douglas, were "the pure, unadulterated representatives of Abolitionism, Free Soilism, Niggerism in the Congress of the United States"—and he labored amain to cast odium on the opposition by representing it as purely abolitionist. At one point he was amazingly brazen. He attacked the "conspirators" for composing their Address on the Sabbath, a sacred day when others were at church; the fact being that the dating of the paper in some versions (not all) on Sunday was an error, that Chase was as strict in his churchgoing as Douglas was loose, and that on this particular Sunday Douglas and his deputation were busy entangling Pierce at the White House and perfecting their amendments!

Douglas was at his best in defending his motives and objects in the proposed legislation. He and his committee, he said, had been guided by the basic principle of local self-government in the Compromise of 1850, under which men fixed their own domestic institutions, "instead of having them determined by an arbitrary or geographical line." The true history of the two compromises, he averred, was totally different from that given in the Appeal. The government had long attempted to separate slavery and freedom by a geographical line. The Ordinance of 1787 confirmed those laws of climate, production, and other natural forces which made slavery desirable south of it, unprofitable north of it. Later the Missouri Compromise drew another geographical line through all the territory then owned by the nation. The principles of the Ordinance and Missouri Compromise required that when fresh territory was acquired to the westward, the general line should be extended to the Pacific. For several years he had labored to effect this extension, but his efforts had been defeated. By whom? The freesoilers in 1848 had blocked the projection of the line. The very men who now insisted that the compromise was a solemn com-

89 January 31, 1854.
90 February 1, 1854.

pact "are the men who successfully violated it, repudiated it, and caused it to be superseded by the compromise measures of 1850."

When the "abolitionists" denied that the new compromise really constituted a supersession, Douglas continued, they ignored a plain fact: that it abandoned the old principle of geographical limitation to set up a new principle of Congressional non-intervention and popular self-determination. This principle was not for New Mexico and Utah alone, but was of universal application. Part of New Mexico lay north of the 36° 30′ line, yet the rule of popular sovereignty was just as valid, under the compromise of 1850, above this line as below it. The Appeal declared that the Compromise of 1850 applied only to territory acquired from Mexico, but this was untrue, for part of the region with which it dealt had been acquired from France. The new adjustment had tried to "establish certain great principles, which would avoid the slavery agitation for all time to come. Was it our object simply to provide for a temporary evil? Was it our object simply to heal over an old sore, and leave it to break out again?" If men but acquiesced in the popular-sovereignty principle, then the slavery agitation would be dead forever.

Moreover, pursued Douglas, it was the only principle which could offer an effective settlement of the slavery issue. Congressional enactments had never excluded slavery from an inch of Northern soil; the enactments of nature alone had done that. The people of Illinois, he argued, disregarding the Northwest Ordinance, had long maintained slavery, and the State had finally abolished it by her own will and act. Iowa and California had made their own decision; so would Kansas and Nebraska. He had no doubt of the outcome. "In that climate, with its productions, it is worse than folly to think of its being a slaveholding country. I do not believe there is a man in Congress who thinks it could permanently be a slaveholding country."

While Douglas's intentions were doubtless patriotic, his leading arguments rested on unsound foundations or were streaked with half-truth. It was not a fact that in laying down a certain line the Missouri Compromise had established a "geographical principle" which should later have been applied to the area wrested from Mexico; the 36° 30′ boundary was simply the best that could be used in solving a specific problem. Far from representing a principle, it was disregarded in the Compromise itself by the admission of Missouri as a slave State north of the line. The Missouri Compromise embodied other vital elements, such as the balanced entry of Missouri and Maine, but nobody spoke of this balance as a principle, and in fact more free than slave States had since been admitted. As for Douglas's statement that the Utah-New Mexico legislation in the Compromise of 1850 had established a new "principle" which must be extended to all other Territories, this was simply dishonest. Nothing had been said in the debates of 1850 on any such principle; nobody had declared that the special rule applied to Utah-New Mexico must later apply to the Platte country; Webster had in fact made the very opposite statement. Though Douglas had had the ultimate organization of Nebraska in view as early as 1844, and certainly had it in mind in 1850, he then said not a word about the applicability of the Utah-New Mexico rule to the Nebraska region. Indeed, when the Nebraska bill of 1853 passed the House and almost passed the Senate, it kept the Missouri Compromise intact. If the alleged "principle" of 1850 had existed, would no allusion have been made to it in 1853? Douglas made none; Dixon, Atchison, and Stephens never breathed a word about this alleged perpetual principle. Nobody discovered it till 1854!

It was true that in organizing Utah the so-called Middle Park region north of the headwaters of the Arkansas River was cut off from the Louisiana Purchase and placed within the limits of Utah Territory. But it was also true that the Compromise of 1850 had actually recognized the continuing validity of the Missouri Compromise in that it had maintained the 36° 30′ line in that part of Texas which was cut off to be made part of the nation's unorganized territory. It reaffirmed section two, article three of the Texas annexation resolution, which in turn reaffirmed the Missouri Compromise prohibition. The obvious fact was that, as Representative Etheridge of Tennessee said later, if the Compromise of 1850 had been regarded as repealing the Missouri Compromise, it would have been defeated.[91]

Nor was the principle of the Missouri Compromise "violated," as Douglas said, when Congress refused to apply it to California. No moral obligation rested on Congress thus to apply it. The Missouri Compromise had not contained any positive establishment of slavery in the area south of that line; but Calhoun and others had demanded such a positive application in California. The moral obligation resting upon Congress might be defined in quite another light. Congress had decided in reaffirming the Ordinance of 1787, and in passing the Missouri Compromise prohibition, that it should "forever" close as much of the national domain as was practicable to slavery.

Finally, it was by no means self-evident, as Douglas maintained, that climate, soil, and other physiographic conditions made Kansas an impossible ground for slavery. Parts of it were not manifestly less suited to a slave economy than Delaware, Maryland, Kentucky, or Missouri, where slavery existed. While cotton would not grow there, hemp and tobacco might. Within the previous fifteen years many Kentucky hemp-growers had removed to the western borders of Missouri. They had succeeded so well that by the mid-fifties Missouri, with a thousand planters, grew more hemp than Kentucky; and in both States slave labor was deemed essential to the crop. During 1853 about

91 *Cong. Globe*, February 21, 1857.

63,000 bales of hemp were received at St. Louis, an increase of 14,000 bales over the previous year, and the price rose from $75 a bale in January, 1852, to $130 in December, 1853. The hemp areas of Missouri were precisely the areas where slaves were most numerous; more slaves in that State were held north of the Missouri River than south of it; and Platte County, organized only in 1845, which easily led in hemp-culture, by 1850 had 2,798 slaves.[92] A single Missourian within an hour's ride of the Kansas line was credited with more slaves than the five hundred of Randolph of Roanoke. And when Douglas said he supposed no man in Congress believed that Kansas could be made permanently slave soil, he gave an erroneous view of the facts.

The fact was that many so believed. Senator Hunter of Virginia was one. He later testified that there were few men with whom he conversed who did not hold that the future State would take its place with those cherishing slavery. They had every reason for believing so, for without mentioning Arkansas, adjoining Missouri had nearly a hundred thousand slaves, held largely in the border counties. "The proximity of its population, with the attractions of new fertile, and cheap land, I believed would lead the slaveholders of Missouri to diffuse themselves speedily over Kansas." [93] Jefferson Davis later declared that he had believed that natural causes would result in the introduction of slaves into Kansas, though he was not sure their footing could be maintained.[94] Frederick Stanton, who represented the Memphis district, believed that Kansas would probably not become a slave area but frankly hoped that it might. J. H. Stringfellow, the Missourian who soon became so prominent in slave-colonization projects in Kansas, subsequently told a Congressional committee that in his State the Kansas-Nebraska bill was understood as yielding Kansas to slavery, and that only the determined exertions of the North placed the matter in any doubt.[95] Representative F. K. Zollicoffer, a State Rights Whig of Tennessee, avowed a strong faith that slavery would triumph.

92 See articles on Missouri hemp in N. Y. *Tribune*, October 8, 1856; *National Intelligencer*, December 2, 1857.

93 Letter dated July 22, 1857, in Richmond *South*.

94 *Cong. Globe*, 35th Cong., 1st sess., 619; February 8, 1858. Beverley Tucker's Washington *Sentinel*, representing the ultra South, hoped to see Kansas enter as a slave State and thus "restore the equilibrium of the South in the federal government," September 27, 1854.

95 34th Cong., 1st sess., House Report No. 200, p. 925ff. Dr. Stringfellow testified: "At the time of the passage of that bill, and prior to that time, I never heard any man in my section of Missouri express a doubt about the nature of the institutions which would be established here provided the Missouri restriction was removed. . . . The conviction was general that it would be a slave State. The settlers who came over from Missouri after the passage of the bill, so far as I know, generally believed that Kansas would be a slave State." Much similar testimony may be found in the same report. Amos Rees testified: "Upon the passage of that bill it was generally understood that Kansas would become a slave State, as we intended to do all we could, legally, to make it so. When the two Territories were organized, under the same bill, it seemed to be a tacit understanding, universal among our [Missouri] people, that Kansas was to be a slave State and Nebraska a free State." P. 929.

And behind all the other dubieties of Douglas's bill and argument lay the equivocal character of popular sovereignty itself. The legislation for Utah and New Mexico had by no means provided for full self-government. As long as they remained in the status of Territories, no laws passed by their legislatures were to become valid until approved by a governor appointed by the President; while any law was subject to annulment by Congress. This was a very limited kind of self-government.[96] The decision as to slavery was not to be made until the States formed their constitutions for admission. But the Kansas-Nebraska Act left all matters pertaining to slavery to the people or their representatives without saying *when;* and the question whether this decision could be made prior to the writing of a State constitution would not down. Robert Toombs and others said it could not.[97] A number of leading Southern newspapers— the Montgomery *Journal*, the Charleston *News*, the Richmond *Enquirer*—said it could. They deplored the fact, though the *Enquirer* still supported the bill as wiping out the odious line of 1820.[98] But the meaning of the bill on this vital point remained hazy.

## [ IX ]

The great debate in Congress, thus opened by Douglas, was destined to run through four months. No man questioned its transcendent importance. "We are on the eve of a great national transaction," said Seward; "a transaction that will close a cycle in the history of our country." No giants of the stature of the leaders in the last grand forensic contest gave majesty to the discussion. No scenes were so dramatically thrilling as that in which Calhoun had risen from his deathbed to hear his last address read, or in which Webster had stood up to defy freesoil sentiment in his Seventh of March speech. Yet the debate riveted the attention of the whole country.

On the side of the new legislation Douglas was the soul of the struggle, the Roderick Dhu leading the van of every charge. With a nerveless Administration behind him, he rallied the party majority in both chambers and drilled them into an unyielding phalanx. From Pierce, whose attitude grew more and more lukewarm until just before the final vote the *Union* came out in the name of the Administration to deny that the bill would be made a party test, he obtained no aid after the first weeks worthy of the name.[99] As Northern anger burst into fever heat, and the clangor of arms from the Capitol resounded

96  Senator Truman Smith in *Cong. Globe*, 33d Cong., 1st sess., App., 168ff, February 11, 1854.
97  Pleasants A. Stovall, *Toombs*, 146–150.
98  March 9, 1854.
99  Cf. J. B. Bowlin's comment to Buchanan, April 21, 1854; Buchanan Papers.

ever more fiercely, the feeble executive fell back upon a curious religiosity. Everybody, he wrote Buchanan on Washington's Birthday, was discussing the Nebraska bill and the prospective war in Europe. "To my mind, nothing can be more apparent than that an Over Ruling Power is and has been controlling in the destinies of men and nations, nor can anything be more idle than to attempt to foresee or grasp the consequences. All we can do is to act with a wise and comprehensive view of what may be seen and what ought with the exercise of judgment and vigilance to be anticipated." [100] He suffered a good deal from "indisposition" and still more from that routine business "which it would seem is to never cease to accumulate." [101] Distressed by the excitement over the measure, he longed for its early passage. But he did not lend that active assistance in the manipulation of patronage and tightening of party cords which had been anticipated, nor did his Cabinet. Marcy's distaste never abated—indeed, some thought that one motive behind the bill had been Douglas's wish to brush Marcy out of his path for the nomination in 1856.

But Douglas rushed forward, as a friend put it, like a locomotive, scattering obstruction and commanding admiration even from men who abominated his measure. "How the *Little Giant* came to put his head in such a halter is matter for much speculation," J. C. Bowlin of St. Louis wrote Buchanan after a visit to Washington. "The North account for it readily by the luring prospects held out to him by the South for the Presidency—if that was the case, it was certainly a political blunder. . . . However he got into it, or from whatever motive, he has borne himself so nobly in the contest, has stood so firm and unflinching, amidst treachery and duplicity, that his strength would give dignity even to error. He has not yielded to the storm, but has braved it nobly, whilst his allies in the measure have been tossed about like leaves before an October blast." Robert C. Winthrop informed Douglas that although he vigorously disagreed with him, and had always done so, he admired the force of his speeches. "The effigy-burners do not seem to have consumed you as yet; or, if they have, your friends may say of you, in the words of Gray's elegy, 'E'en in your *ashes* burn their wonted fires.' " [102]

The Illinoisan was cheered on, too, by a host of champions. S. S. Cox, editor of the *Ohio Statesman*, waged a stirring fight for the bill in a closely divided State. "You have made cords of friends here," he wrote Douglas, "notwithstanding all that is said. More than one-half the opposition to the bill came from men who didn't like you *á priori*, without regard to the principles of the bill." Allen was one of these, and they had beaten Allen for the United States Senatorship. The sentiment of the States, he declared, was misrepresented:

100 Buchanan Papers.
101 March 13, 1854; Buchanan Papers.
102 Boston, April 17, 1854; Douglas Papers.

the Democrats had kept the party in line despite much opposition, and could at any time defeat the freesoil crew.[103]

Horatio Seymour assured Douglas that his closing speech on the Nebraska bill was splendid. "The argument is conclusive, and the objections upon every point are admirably answered." He wished a copy could be distributed through every Northern school district. "While the wire-pullers have succeeded in exciting at the north the blind prejudices of those who have no inclination to examine the subject, reflecting, considerate men can have no doubt as to the correctness of the position of the advocates of the measure." But Seymour was full of complaints against the Administration. The Democratic freesoilers would have died out a year before but for Pierce's gifts of patronage; his appointments had given the faction vitality; and they were now in "full operation vigorously and effectively against the bill." Now the old-line Democracy had to sustain the battle. They would cling to their principles, but they had small inducement to fight hard "when by so doing they encounter on one side the assaults of freesoilers at home, and are met upon the other by the crushing out process of a Nat'l Executive of their own choice."[104]

While Douglas thus proved himself the Roland of popular sovereignty, fighting with sledge-hammer blows, with sneer and sarcasm, with coarse personal invective, with arguments both foul and fair, what of the opposition leaders?

Here a triumvirate, a group representing the best mettle that Ohio, New York, and Massachusetts could muster to meet the onset, took the field. There was no mistaking the D'Artagnan of this trio. Seward and Sumner were spokesmen of power and courage, but the experience, resiliency, and intellectual and physical energy of Chase marked him as the leader. He had been much longer in political life and knew far more of its rough give and take than Sumner; he had a rude force that the subtle Seward lacked. Moreover, as a freesoil Democrat he was more unfettered than Seward, who was the leader of the Whig party and widely regarded as probably its next nominee. But if he was chieftain in the fight, he was ably seconded by the others. And all three knew that they had two battles to win; that if they lost in Congress, they could still carry off victory on the more important field of national opinion. On the very day that Douglas's bill was introduced in its first form, January 4, Seward wrote that he was heartsick. "I look around me in the Senate and find all demoralized. Maine, New Hampshire, Connecticut, Rhode Island, Vermont!!! All, all in the hands of the slaveholders; and even New York, ready to howl at my heels if I were only to name the name of freedom." This was

103 Columbus, C     ~h 2, 1854; Douglas Papers.
104 Buffalo, Ap          Douglas Papers.

attitudinizing, and Seward knew it. The three set themselves to speak to their fellow-Senators, and beyond the Senate, to all fairminded Northerners. Even Seward had faith, as they began their work, that Ohio, New York, and Massachusetts would yet show "an undivided hostility" to repeal.[105]

Behind the triumvirate a determined band of Congressional supporters was already rallying. Sam Houston, Truman Smith of Connecticut, Ben Wade, and others were ready to open fire in the Senate at once. Clayton, sadly confessing that his sentiments were at variance with those of some of his most valued friends, was about to explain his opposition. Debate quickly began to rage in the House, where New Englanders and spokesmen for the Lower South found it difficult to moderate their tongues. "Never," wrote the Washington correspondent of the *Missouri Republican* as early as January 31, "have I witnessed a more bitter feeling in Congress." Back of the battlers in the Washington arena the press of the country had fallen into two hostile ranks. Particularly in the free States, public sentiment had quickly turned from astonishment into indignation and then into stern determination. "The unanimous sentiment of the North is indignant resistance," stated the New York *Tribune* of March 2. "The whole population are full of it. The feeling in 1848 was far inferior to this in strength and universality." The three Blairs, so powerful in Maryland and Missouri, were all in arms.[106]

Within three weeks after Douglas's final bill had been reported, what a change in the whole national scene! Dark stormclouds hung over it, and livid lightning shook a portentous finger across the recently smiling landscape. Douglas had asserted that he wished to mollify the sectional conflict and give direction and unity to his party. Instead, he had torn open all the wounds of 1848–50, and reawakened the pain, fear, and anger of the fearful struggle of those years; he had split the Democratic Party asunder; he had completed the destruction of the Whig Party, so recently, under Clay, Crittenden, and Webster, a potent force for union; and he had set the scene for the entrance of a powerful new sectional party. It could be said that circumstances rather than Douglas were at fault. At any rate, between them they had thrown the nation into turmoil, and unleashed forces which no man knew how to control.

105  Bancroft, *Seward*, I, 343, 344; F. W. Seward, *Seward*, II, 218.
106  St. Louis *Missouri Republican*, February 8, 1854; Dix, *John A. Dix*, I, 284.

# 4

# *Fountains of the Great Deep*

TO COMPREHEND the anger with which the freesoil North rose against the Kansas bill, we must keep in mind a variety of considerations. The widespread conviction that pro-slavery influences represented by Jefferson Davis and Caleb Cushing ruled Pierce's councils; the allegation that Southern leaders had encouraged Gadsden to seek enough of the Mexican domains to make several new Territories, furnishing a broad theatre for the doctrine of Congressional non-intervention while settlers brought in slaves; Benton's assertion that Davis would soon renew the movement; the Administration's confessed ambition to bring Cuba under the stars and stripes—all this aroused fears of a large-scale expansion of slavery. With one hand the South would seize the Caribbean, with the other the Western plains. Many Northerners had long believed that they were paying too heavily for the Compromise of 1850 by accepting the Fugitive Slave Act. Now they learned that this was not half of it; that they had also bartered away the Missouri Compromise restriction. Assuredly this was an egregious price! [1]

And by no means least, to many Northerners the tactics of Douglas savored of chicanery and deceit. Throughout 1851, throughout 1852, throughout 1853, nobody had asserted that the line of 36° 30′ was wiped out. During two Congressional elections and one Presidential canvass, no such idea had been even hinted. But when the Democrats obtained overwhelming control of Congress, and when a pliable executive sat in the White House, Douglas

---

[1] Benton alleged that Gadsden had offered fifty millions for a broad strip including Sonora and Lower California, and asserted that in 1848 Jefferson Davis, then Senator, had labored to effect the annexation of this wide area. The plan of the Pierce Administration, declared Benton, was now to obtain this region. Soulé meanwhile was to offer Spain "two hundred and fifty millions for Cuba, and a rumpus kicked up if the island is not got." Time proved Benton correct as to most of this, though the sum he named was approximately double that ultimately authorized by the Administration. *National Intelligencer*, June 3, 1854. James S. Pike wrote the N. Y. *Tribune* from Washington that one of the most stupendous conspiracies ever hatched was under way. "It proposes no less an achievement than the forcible seizure of Mexico, Central America, and Cuba during the approaching struggle in Europe, and their conversion into slave States. . . . It is said that some of the first men of the republic are implicated. . . ." March 7, 1854.

suddenly brought out his measure; a measure resting on assumptions never approved by the voters and erecting a principle they had never endorsed. The North had helped seat that Congress because it wished the status quo, and it got instead a violent disruption of the status quo! This seemed a gross misuse of a transient majority, a flagrant perversion of deputed power.[2]

True democracy works in a different fashion. Had Douglas busied himself in 1850–53 battling for a clear understanding and acceptance of popular sovereignty, as Gladstone battled in the eighties for home rule and Theodore Roosevelt early in the new century for railway regulation, and had he consistently asserted that the restriction of 1820 was dead, his course would have been unexceptionable. But to seize victory for his "principle" by a sudden coup when circumstances favored it appeared to many Americans indefensible. It was the more outrageous because no tremendous crisis demanded action. Population was pressing toward the Nebraska area—yes; but that area in the fall of 1853 had only three white residents apart from those in government employ.[3] As Cass presently remarked, "Here are two Territories, organized with institutions, possessing almost unbounded powers of self-government, and yet there is not to this day a single white man who owns an acre of land in either of them." [4] For land-hungry settlers ample cheap land was available elsewhere. No urgent necessity demanded the passage of this legislation without full national discussion and explicit majority consent.

Northern freesoilers objected, too, because they foresaw economic and social injury. Particularly was this true of those prairie dwellers who had always assumed that slavery would never debar their westward march. Richard Yates, a Whig Representative from the Springfield district in Illinois, was quick to protest.[5] "If slaveholders are permitted to take their slaves into Nebraska and Kansas," he told the House, "the inequality and injury are to the free white men of the North and South who go there without slaves. . . . The effect of slave labor is always to cheapen, degrade, and exclude free labor. . . . The citizen of the North has a right to object, on the ground that the introduction of slaves will retard the prosperity of the state. Slave labor converts the richest soil into barrenness; free labor causes fertility and vegetation to spring from the very rock." And a greater Springfield Whig, Abraham Lincoln, was soon to stand up in the State House to expound, among other arguments, this very thesis.[6]

2 Representative John L. Taylor of Ohio, recalling that Pierce's popular majority over Scott had been only about 200,000, asked: "Does any man believe that, if General Scott had been President, this attempt would have been made to break down the Compromise of 1850?" *Cong. Globe*, 33d Cong., 1st sess., Appendix, 543ff.
3 *Report*, Commissioner of Indian Affairs, 1853.
4 Detroit speech, November 4, 1854; *National Intelligencer*, November 16, 1854.
5 *Cong. Globe*, 33d Cong., 1st sess., Appendix, 447.
6 Beveridge, *Lincoln*, II, 249ff.

On the Southern side the vigor with which many espoused Douglas's position also sprang from a complex of motives. The Missouri Compromise restriction had long been regarded as insulting and degrading by a multitude of Southerners. Apprehension that Missouri, if once surrounded on three sides by free States, would soon be lost as a bastion of slavery, was widely felt. If Kansas could be secured, then the Southwest could probably be secured with it; slavery would rule from Kansas City to Santa Fé and Tucson. But most important of all, not a few perceptive men saw a deeper possibility. By rapid action under Douglas's plan they could powerfully bulwark the old combination of South and Northwest.[7] If Kansas speedily became slave territory, then the Missouri-Kansas salient, allied to the South, would have a profound effect on the orientation of the whole trans-Mississippi and trans-Missouri region. Its trade would flow down the Missouri-Mississippi channel to New Orleans, not eastward to Chicago. Everybody knew that lower Illinois and Indiana were full of Southern migrants, and that Iowa and Minnesota were hopeful prospects for the Democratic Party. If the agricultural alliance of cotton and corn could be cemented, industrial New England and New York would be foiled in their efforts to wave their sceptre over the Northwest.

The one stubborn impediment to this plan for using slavery influence in Missouri and Kansas (with Democratic party strength there and roundabout) to cement the old entente of South and Northwest, lay in the convictions of most Northwestern people. They increasingly disliked slavery. They abominated its expansion. Indeed, a distinct and double cleavage in the Democratic Party itself was rapidly becoming visible. Many Southern Democrats accepted the Nebraska bill because it repealed the Missouri Compromise, although they loathed the doctrine of popular sovereignty. Many Northwestern Democrats accepted it because they liked popular sovereignty although they loathed the repeal of the Missouri Compromise. The two groups swallowed it, but each gagged over the part that pleased the other. At the same time, a multitude of Northern Democrats indignantly rejected the bill. Those who understood the importance of this double cleavage did not rate highly the prospects for continued Democratic unity.[8]

7 Robert Y. Hayne in his project for a Charleston-Cincinnati Railroad had wished to link the South and Northwest, and the dream had never died. T. D. Jervey, *Robert Y. Hayne and his Time*. For the thesis that slavery by 1850 had extended about as far as it could go, see C. W. Ramsdell, "The Natural Limits of Slavery Expansion," *Miss. Valley Hist. Rev.*, XVI, 151–171. He argues that slavery could not expand into western Texas for lack of fencing and transportation facilities, that the soil and climate of New Mexico were unfriendly, that the Ozarks limited it in Arkansas, and that Kansas was unsuitable.

8 *National Intelligencer*, September 28, 1854.

## [ I ]

The tremendous storm sweeping the North seemed to gather new force every week. City after city witnessed great massmeetings, to which flocked men theretofore reckoned highly conservative. Business interests which had always deplored the anti-slavery agitation were incensed by the reckless way

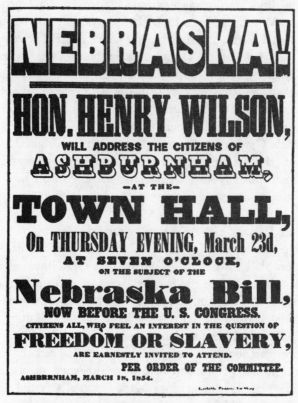

A Massachusetts Town Rises Against Douglas.

in which Douglas had reopened the quarrel and by the possibility that slavery would invade a great new fertile domain. The Northern clergy for the first time united in a mighty effort to arouse public feeling. Beside the clergy marched a vast body of professional men; lawyers, physicians, architects, lecturers, authors—the cultivated and reflective backbone of society. And all-pervasive in influence, tireless in iteration, powerful in utterance, the freesoil press of the North spoke with an energy for which the history of American journalism had no parallel.

In New York, wrote Greeley, the merchants were the first to protest, then the mechanics, and then the clergy.[9] Unquestionably no groups showed more activity against the "Nebraska infamy" than the businessmen of the larger cities. Boston merchants and others met in Faneuil Hall on February 23d, a crowd of fully three thousand of the "solid men" of the city.[10] Samuel A. Eliot, who had so valiantly defended the Compromise of 1850, presided; George Hillard, Robert C. Winthrop, Abbott Lawrence, and even the venerable Josiah Quincy, now eighty-three, made earnest addresses. "The North had got its back up," wrote Winthrop, "and I am pretty afraid that it will stay up, even after the question is settled." Already, on January 30th, a tremendous mass-meeting had been held at the Tabernacle in New York. Shepherd Knapp, head of the Mechanics' Bank, was president, while the vice-presidents numbered such distinguished businessmen as William F. Havemeyer, Moses Taylor, Wilson G. Hunt, Robert B. Minturn, James Suydam, and Moses H. Grinnell. The principal speakers were Democrats, and James W. Gerard recalled how he had gone to Castle Garden in 1850 to fight for Southern rights. Its temper calm but determined, the meeting adopted resolutions of remonstrance, not de-nunciation. That brilliant young Democratic leader Samuel J. Tilden, close to the moneyed community, was opposing the bill at much sacrifice of party friends.[11]

Cleveland on January 28th witnessed a remarkable outpouring of citizens, who passed resolutions declaring that the Nebraska proposal had startled Ohio and filled her people with horror. "You may set Ohio down as a *unit* against the treasonable scheme before the Senate," wrote a correspondent to the New York *Tribune*.[12] No Congressman, he added, would dare vote for the bill; "he would be hunted from the State as a wild beast or a mad dog, and politically destroyed." Chicago had her first large meeting in South Market Hall early in February. More than four hundred leading citizens signed the call; ex-Mayor James Curtiss, who had presided in 1850 over a meeting to sustain Douglas on the Compromise, was chairman; Judge Mark Skinner, a friend of Douglas and in his own words an Old Hunker Democrat, made the principal speech; and other Democrats were conspicuous in the proceedings.[13] Philadelphia held a vociferous meeting, presided over by Mayor Charles Gilpin, which protested against the bill and authorized the circulation of an address to the people of the State. In Cincinnati a thousand "unquestioned and adamantine" Democrats helped sign a call for an anti-Nebraska gathering.

From countless smaller cities and towns came reports of impassioned gather-

9   N. Y. *Tribune*, March 8, 1854.
10  Boston *Daily Advertiser*, February 23, 1854.
11  Winthrop to J. P. Kennedy, February 27, 1854, Kennedy Papers; Cook, *Tilden*, 78.
12  N. Y. *Tribune*, February 2, 1854.
13  N. Y. *Tribune*, February 13, 1854.

ings. In New Haven, where a meeting was addressed by businessmen, divines, and Yale professors, the aged Benjamin Silliman made the first political speech of his life. He had been born in the midst of the Revolution, he said; he had observed all the capital events of American history since that era; and for the first time he was filled with fears for the future of the country.[14] A meeting in Columbus, O., attracted attention for the eminence of its speakers—Jacob Brinkerhoff, Salmon P. Chase, and Judge J. R. Swan. Week after week, during February, March, and April, every newspaper chronicled gatherings, speeches, and resolutions.[15] A single number of the *Tribune* recorded seven in upper New York, four in Ohio, two in Pennsylvania, half a dozen in other States. When friends of Douglas tried to hold a meeting in Chicago with Dr. B. McVicker as chairman, the anti-Nebraska men turned out in strength, citizen after citizen rising to say that he had supported Douglas but could do so no longer, and voted down the resolutions proposed.[16] At Quincy, Ill., the opposition similarly took over a Douglas meeting, and passed resolutions indicting the Senator for the agitation then raging.[17]

With every week the vehemence of the movement increased. Its rising intensity was illustrated by New York. When the resolutions of the Tabernacle gathering, presented in the Senate by Hamilton Fish, were denied a reading, the indignation of the merchants was roused, and a new call was issued. Declaring that the citizens did not intend to see themselves defrauded of territory which was theirs by compact, nor yield to slavery a soil which their fathers had consecrated to liberty, it announced that they were determined that "this crime shall not be consummated, that despite corruption, bribery, and treachery, Nebraska, the heart of our continent, shall forever continue free." Moses H. Grinnell called the assemblage to order. By unanimous vote resolutions were passed asserting that although the New York merchants had always been firm friends of Southern rights, they would not yield a single foot of free soil to slavery. Machinery was set up for raising money, circulating petitions, arranging coöperation with other anti-Nebraska organizations, and arousing the electorate. An address was issued calling for erection in every town of committees of correspondence like those of the Revolutionary era, "when plots less treasonable were rife against our liberties." And finally, a monster massmeeting was arranged for May 13th in City Hall Park; a gathering at which five thousand people cheered the defiant utterances of Daniel Lord, Benjamin F. Butler, and other distinguished men.[18]

14 *National Intelligencer*, March 28, 1854.
15 N. Y. *Times, Herald; National Intelligencer*, February–April, 1854.
16 Indianapolis *Morning Journal*, February 20, 1854.
17 N. Y. *Tribune*, March 10, 1854. For an English account of the agitation against the bill, see the London *Times*, April 14, p. 8, May 30, p. 11, 1854.
18 N. Y. *Tribune*, March 13, 14, May 15; N. Y. *Herald*, March 14; Foner, *Business and Slavery*, 93–97.

The action of the New York, Boston, and other merchants was profoundly significant. Most of these businessmen had stood a Macedonian phalanx behind the Compromise of 1850; they had been strenuous for the election of Pierce; they had done everything they could to manifest sympathy with the rights of the South, contempt for the abolitionists. Yet they were now arraigning Douglas and the slave power in the sternest terms. In part their attitude might be attributed to dismay and resentment over the reopening of the sectional battle. But in the main it arose from hot indignation over what they held a perfidious act, and grim resolution that the West should be kept free. With the merchants stood a host of mechanics and laborers, who held their own meeting in New York in mid-February.

Very striking also was the feeling displayed by the German-Americans who since the mass migration begun in 1848 had usually acted with the Democrats, but who now broke away in thousands. Fully two thousand flocked to a New York meeting where Erhard Richter and others made speeches. While the *Staats-Zeitung* was frigid toward the Nebraska bill, the *Abend-Zeitung* actively belabored it.[19] The Germans of Pittsburgh, Cleveland, Indianapolis, and Chicago all met in protest. Some of their resolutions assailed the "Africanizing" of the West; they meant to settle it thickly themselves, and did not want Negroes there—much less slaves.[20]

The knowledge that Germans and other immigrant stocks, particularly the British, would vote against slavery in Kansas, led the Senate to adopt the Clayton amendment excluding aliens from the ballot or from office in the new Territories. No such exclusion had been applied to Illinois, Wisconsin, Iowa, or Michigan in the territorial stage. It produced an indignation which was expressed by many German-American journalists, including Douglas's warm friend Francis J. Grund. Another and younger German, Carl Schurz, was drawn to Washington, sat in the galleries, and formed some unforgettable impressions of the cascading debates. He studied Douglas, low, broad-shouldered, and big-chested, a deep frown knitting his brow, the incarnation of forceful combativeness; Seward, of the slim, wiry figure, the thin, sallow face, the overhanging eyebrows, and the dull, muffled voice; Chase, whose tall, erect frame, chiseled and powerful features, and broad, high forehead, made him a picture of intelligence, courage, and dignity; Sumner, with his distinguished bearing, air of refinement, and charming smile; Toombs, whose large, strong-featured head, massive figure, boisterous speech, and hearty, infectious laugh gave him a wonderful vitality and sparkle; and Mason of Virginia, whose face seemed

19 N. Y. *Tribune*, March 3, 4, 1854; the *Staats-Zeitung* finally came to unenthusiastic support.
20 Indianapolis *Morning Journal*, March 7, 10, 1854.

dull, attitude supercilious, and utterances pompous. But above all, Schurz formed a sharp impression of the battle that he saw developing:[21]

"I had seen the slave power officially represented by some of its foremost champions—overbearing, defiant, dictatorial. . . . I had seen in alliance with the slave power, not only far-reaching material interests and a sincere but easily intimidated conservatism, but a selfish party spirit and an artful and unscrupulous demagogy making a tremendous effort to obfuscate the moral sense of the North. I had seen standing against this tremendous array of forces a small handful of anti-slavery men faithfully fighting the battle of freedom and civilization. I saw the decisive contest rapidly approaching. . . ."

For the first time, too, the clergy of the North spoke almost as with one voice. Characteristically, the American clergy were timid rather than bold. Contrary to what some historians have said, they had been by no means united in opposition to the Fugitive Slave Act, nor as a body conspicuous against it. Most of them had acquiesced in it.[22] But at the outset of this contest the principal religious periodicals began exhorting them to arouse the people. These journals had never been so militant. The *Independent*, with Beecher a regular contributor, led the way. An equal spirit animated the *Congregationalist*, the *Christian Inquirer*, the *Christian Register*, the *Trumpet and Universalist Magazine*, the *Christian Freeman*, and the *Christian Ambassador*, which reached great ministerial groups.[23] Religious bodies began to pass resolutions. From scores of sources came suggestions for a clerical protest. At the beginning of March, 151 New York clergymen sent Congress a petition against the bill. On the 14th a memorial from 3,050 New England ministers, solemnly protesting "in the name of Almighty God" against the measure, was laid before the Senate. Douglas, stung to the heart by so searching a rebuke, assailed the churches for trying to coerce Congress and sneered at ministers who posed as spokesmen for the Almighty. In his own city of Chicago the clergy of all denominations then assembled; the form of the New England protest, though without the invocation of God, was adopted; a committee was appointed to gather signatures all over the Northwest; and as April ended the document, with more than five hundred names, went to Washington.[24]

Throughout the spring the Northern pulpits resounded with indignant

21 Schurz, *Reminiscences*, II, 30–37.
22 For a critical account of earlier church attitudes, see J. G. Birney, *The American Churches the Bulwarks of American Slavery;* W. Goodell, *Slavery and Anti-Slavery;* the Rev. Albert Barnes, *The Church and Slavery;* and Samuel J. May, *Recollections of the Anti-Slavery Conflict*, 329ff.
23 See article on the religious protest, N. Y. *Tribune*, June 19, 1854.
24 Letter by N. H. Eggleston, a Chicago clergyman, N. Y. *Tribune*, May 12, 1854, describes the Chicago protest. The Washington *Sentinel* on April 11 began publishing the names and addresses of the 3,050 New England clergymen. Saying that it was sure many of the names were spurious, it asked Yankee friends to pick out the false signatures.

appeals. Sermons by Theodore Parker, James Freeman Clarke, O. B. Frothingham, Thomas Starr King, and even the conservative Ezra Stiles Gannett were widely summarized and echoed. Some clergymen gave public addresses; many graced the platforms of anti-Nebraska meetings; not a few wrote for the press. Dr. Leonard Bacon's open letter to Senator Isaac Toucey of Connecticut, a noted Democratic wheel-horse, produced a special sensation.[25] The mild Horace Bushnell delivered a discourse in Hartford, later circulated as a pamphlet, which bore the significant title "The Northern Iron," and which cast ridicule on the idea of Southern secession. Even minor pastors burst into print with exhortations which were all too often intemperate stump speeches. One ranting utterance, the sermon of Rev. Dr. Heman Humphrey in the Baptist church of Pittsfield, Mass., on February 26th, began with a brief history of "aggression by our Southern masters"; declared that if the bill passed, it would open to the South "immense new breeding grounds . . . for raising black and grizzled livestock for the Southern shambles"; painted a picture of the 480,000 square miles of Kansas and Nebraska laboring under the bloody code of laws, the handcuffs, the scourges, the hounds, the licentiousness, and the brutal ignorance of slavery; and predicted that if the bill passed, it would kindle a flame which the waters of the Mississippi could not extinguish.[26]

With justice, Douglas pointed out that the shrill intemperance of many of these appeals did not befit the gown, and that it was unfair for ecclesiastics to deliver electioneering speeches against the Nebraska Bill on a day and in places where no reply could be made. He penned a tremendous broadside letter, filling seven newspaper columns, to the Chicago clergy. But Northern sentiment rejected his assertion that the church should not concern itself with such political issues. The ethical import of the question, the moral challenge offered by a reopening of the upper Louisiana Purchase to servile institutions, made clerical interposition proper. Though no scales exist to weigh such influences, the authority of the clergy was at this time probably greater than ever before or since. Protestantism had more princes of learning and eloquence; rural traditions of piety were still strong; materialistic and laodicean corrosions had made little progress; and in thousands of communities the minister's word was almost as potent as in old Cotton Mather's Massachusetts Bay.[27]

25 Bacon was chief editor of the *Independent,* a Congregational leader of power, and author of a book, *Slavery Discussed in Occasional Essays* (1846), which made a marked impression upon Lincoln. See Theodore Davenport Bacon, *Leonard Bacon, A Statesman in the Church,* 386, 387.
26 The Rev. Heman Humphrey, D.D., *The Missouri Compromise* (pvt., Huntington Library).
27 The N. Y. *Christian Inquirer,* founded by the able Unitarian minister, Henry W. Bellows, with James Freeman Clarke in these years its Boston correspondent (he signed his articles "Shawmut"), is as valuable as the *Independent* in suggesting the force and scope of clerical influence. Douglas's letter is in the Washington *Sentinel,* April 11, 1854.

The press, too, was a surging force, and the revolt of numerous Democratic editors in the North was as significant as the defection of Democratic merchants. Bryant's *Evening Post* led out the column. It shared Benton's and Greeley's erroneous belief that the Nebraska bill had been planned as the first act in a new Southern drama, and would be followed by the wresting of Cuba from Spain to make several additional slave States, the annexation of yet more land for slavery in northern Mexico, and the reopening of the African slave trade. News as well as editorial columns were efficiently used. The *Post's* Washington correspondent, visiting the White House on a February reception day, drew a scornful picture of Pierce: "whitened out to the true complexion of a parlor knight—pale and soft looking"; "meek in appearance," as the tail of Douglas's kite should be; full of inner vanity over his high position; and quite unaware that "his mad and wicked adhesion to the Nebraska perfidy" would ruin him.[28] Gideon Welles, the *Evening Post's* best New England correspondent, an old Jacksonian officeholder, vibrated with anger. The whole idea of squatter sovereignty he termed a dangerous absurdity. "For Congress to throw away the jurisdiction and supervisory control of that vast region of country, as yet unseeled and unsurveyed—a region more extensive than that of all the old thirteen States—to part with it to adventurers and intruders—is a species of reckless infidelity on the part of those members of Congress who resort to it, that is in perfect character and keeping with the violated faith involved in abrogating the Missouri Compromise." Most Democratic journals hewed to the party line, but the Buffalo *Republic* and others bolted—while such stand-pat sheets as the Cleveland *Plain Dealer* and Detroit *Free Press* were obviously unhappy.[29]

In New York city the *Herald* and *Journal of Commerce* were the only important newspapers adhering to the measure; the *Times* and *Courier and Enquirer* were as invincibly opposed as the *Tribune* and *Evening Post*. In Washington, the pontifical gravity and moderation of Gales and Seaton's *National Intelligencer* made its condemnation of the bill especially weighty. The Chicago *Democrat*, controlled by Douglas's oldtime friend John Wentworth, turned sharply against him; the Chicago *Press and Tribune* labored amain in the opposition. So did the Cincinnati *Gazette*, one of the oldest journals in the Ohio Valley; Walter N. Haldeman's Louisville *Courier;* and John D. Defrees's Indianapolis *Morning Journal*, which called Douglas "the little barroom politician." The Buffalo *Republic*, an old Democratic organ, angrily

28 Nevins, *Evening Post*, 248–250.
29 Welles, March, no day or addressee, 1854; Welles Papers. The Albany *Argus* of February 8, 1854, listed twenty-six Democratic papers of New York which supported the bill. But it also listed Albany *Atlas*, Buffalo *Republic*, Troy *Times*, Rochester *Union*, N. Y. *Evening Post*, and five other Democratic sheets as opposing it.

denounced the measure. But the van of the battle was led by the great editorial triumvirate Greeley, Bryant, and Bowles. The three men were in very different fashions masters of controversial journalism, Greeley excelling in forcible, hard-hitting Saxon prose such as Cobbett wrote, Bryant in swelling eloquence, and Bowles in logical power and slashing wit. They scattered their weekly and semi-weekly editions all over the North and West, and every page was a fragment from an incendiary bomb.[30]

[ II ]

While the North thus pulsed with massmeetings, burnings in effigy, and every other form of public expression, what of the South?

Not a little evidence can be cited for the view that the prevalent Southern mood, even as the bill approached enactment, was indifference. To be sure, Stephens of Georgia later wrote that never was an act of Congress so generally and unanimously hailed with delight at the South.[31] But Stephens moved in a special atmosphere. In the busy city of New Orleans, the *Bulletin* and the *Bee* united by mid-March in declaring that not a scintilla of excitement existed. Let the bill be rejected forthwith, said the *Bee*, and the South would sleep as sound of nights as before. "With the exception of the Washington *Union* and a very limited number of journals that seem to foster Mr. Douglas's ambitious designs . . . the entire Southern press is occupied with Nebraska no further than as a somewhat interesting topic of controversy in the national legislature." The Nashville *Advertiser*, which fairly spoke for Tennessee, remarked that two months of Congressional thundering had produced about as great a ripple in the State as a buckshot dropped into the Tennessee River. "The fact is, our people are a sensible, practical people . . . and they see and know that no good can result to them or to the country from the passage of the Nebraska Bill, and hence they care nothing about it." [32] In Georgia, the Macon *Messenger* felt it necessary to explain the lethargy of the section by the popular doubt whether the bill conferred any real benefit. Even in South Carolina the Charles-

---

30  Merriam, *Bowles*, I, 110ff.; John Bigelow, *Retrospections of an Active Life*, I, 136ff.; Greeley, *Recollections of an Active Life*, 291ff. The bill was Macbeth's voice, said Greeley: "Sleep no more!" Said the Chicago *Tribune*, then edited by Henry Fowler: "We will give no quarter to traitors, but follow to his political grave every man who betrays freedom." Philip Kinsley, *The Chicago Tribune: Its First Hundred Years*, 23. The bill aroused Joseph Medill in Ohio to begin a crusade for a new party, and caused Charles H. Ray of the Galena *Jeffersonian* to forsake the Democratic party; both future editors of the Chicago *Tribune*.
31  Johnston and Browne, *Stephens*, 360.
32  Quoted in *National Intelligencer*, March 18, April 13, 1854.

ton *News* and the Columbia *South Carolinian* proclaimed that nobody cared very much about it.[33]

But actually it would be misleading to call the South indifferent. Available indices of sentiment suggest rather that the vast majority of Southerners approved the bill, that this approbation was sincere though never heated or eager, and that a few areas were generally stirred. "It is absurd," remarked the Richmond *Enquirer* on March 3, "to say the South feels no concern about the issue of the Nebraska controversy in face of the fact that the Southern people are unanimous in support of the measure." This was an overstatement, for nothing like unanimity existed. But it is true that nearly all Democratic newspapers and other exponents of Democratic opinion cordially supported the bill, while the much smaller body of Whig journals ranged from lukewarmness to hostility. This division of opinion was manifest at the outset, and debate merely tended to confirm it. Such exceptions as presented themselves were found mainly in the Whig column, and portended that dissolution of the Whig Party which was soon an accomplished fact.

On the Democratic side the Richmond *Enquirer*, St. Louis *Missouri Republican*, and Mobile *Register* were all effective spokesmen. The bill had no sooner been introduced than the *Enquirer* said that Douglas's report gave him an additional claim to the confidence of the South and the gratitude of the country. All Democratic Senators and Representatives, it declared, should muster behind his leadership. As the weeks passed the *Enquirer's* advocacy grew more bellicose.[34] For Missouri Democrats the *Republican* confidently predicted that slavery would make a permanent conquest of Kansas. Indeed, both this spring and later it asserted that Kansas must be a slave State because "it is suited and adapted only to slave labor," and because "we have both the numerical and moral strength to make it so." [35] The Mobile *Register* was the more emphatic in support of the bill because the *Advertiser* in the same city held it up to public reprobation. Throughout the South the Washington *Union*, whose advocacy continued after changes which placed A. O. P. Nicholson and John W. Forney in control, had a very real party influence. It and the Democratic chieftains did their utmost to bring all the lesser newspapers into line. Howell Cobb, sending Douglas his hearty congratulations, struck a note that others took up. "I regard it as a crisis in the national democratic party," he wrote, "and he who dallies is a dastard and he who doubts is damned." [36]

33 All quoted in *National Intelligencer*, June 7, 1854. This paper, under the heading "Southern Sentiment," collected whole columns of indifferent, semihostile, and hostile comment.
34 January 31, February 3, 7, etc.
35 March 24, 1855.
36 Douglas Papers.

Some Whig papers, too, particularly in the Lower South, supported the bill with great pertinacity; while others, like the Richmond *Whig*, mildly took its side. The measure, said the Macon *Messenger*, is simply an effort to resist encroachments upon our rights, and establish the just principle of non-intervention.[37]

Outright hostility to the bill, on the other hand, was by no means infrequent in the South, and grave dubiety more common still. The leading commercial journal of the section, the New Orleans *Bulletin*, opposed it as inexpedient, impolitic, and calculated to do general harm. "We verily believe," it said as the contest drew to an end, "that if the struggle on the Nebraska bill could be continued two or three months longer, the real sentiment of the Southern people would become so unmistakably known that most of their Representatives would drop the demagogical abortion as a thing not fit to be touched. We find, by looking over our Southern exchanges, that the opposition to this measure is spreading and becoming more powerful every day." It would do the South no practical good; it would only feed a wild agitation inimical to both sections. The Louisville *Times*, the principal Whig organ of the Western border, grew bitter in its denunciation. It declared that the frightful demon of sectional antagonism had been wantonly unchained, and all the fruits of the late Compromise lost. The ablest Whig organ of the Eastern border, the Baltimore *Patriot*, took a similar view, accusing Douglas of maneuvering to secure the presidency. Various Texas papers, like the Houston *Telegraph*, assailed the measure; and while its friends essayed to explain this away on the ground that Texas interests wanted population to flow to their State rather than Kansas, this was hardly convincing. The Louisville *Journal* declared early in April that public sentiment was rapidly developing against the bill, and "if it were submitted to a vote of the Southern people tomorrow we doubt whether it would receive the support of a respectable minority." [38]

Particularly was Douglas's step attacked by editors hostile to the popular sovereignty principle. The section had long battled for the doctrine that neither Congress nor a Territorial legislature, which was its creature, should have the right to interdict slavery in any Territory. Would it now barter away this contention for a meagre mess of pottage? The Montgomery *Journal* pointed out that the Utah and New Mexico bills had been sound enough; they had prohibited action against slavery by the Territorial legislatures until the people were ready to form their State Constitutions. Now this high ground was being lost. The South, argued the Charleston *Evening News*, had no real stake in the passage of the bill. It simply gave up Congressional for popular interven-

---

37  Quoted in *National Intelligencer*, June 7, 1854.
38  Quoted in *National Intelligencer*, January 31, June 1, June 27, 1854.

tion. "What is here gained? One usurpation of power for another; one violation of the Constitution replaced by a greater and more flagrant." The Tallahassee *Sentinel* agreed. So did the Georgia *Union*, the Charleston *Mercury*, and other papers. We have our doubts and fears of the bill, said the Warrenton (Va.) *Flag*. "To us it appears a surrender of the very grounds for which the South fought and contended in 1850"—and the Alexandria *Gazette* approvingly quoted the article.[39]

A bold knot of Southern and border leaders stood up against the bill. Senator John Bell of Tennessee struggled against it from beginning to end; so did Houston of Texas; and so of course did Benton. The Blair family was implacable in its wrath. Theodore G. Hunt of Louisiana, a lawyer, a judge, a colonel in the Mexican War, and a man of high principle, asserted that the South did not really want Kansas, and would gain nothing for slavery from it; that the Compromise of 1850 in no wise superseded that of 1820; and that moderation, wisdom, and honor called upon Southerners to stand by their plighted faith, and resist a renewal of sectional prejudice and fanaticism.[40] Ex-Senator Jeremiah Clemens found no such elevated pedestal, objecting primarily to the popular sovereignty principle, but he was emphatic in his verdict: "The South must be the loser." [41]

Altogether, the contrast between the Northern and the Southern scene was arresting. It was well summed up by the Charleston *Mercury*. "In the former," it commented, "we find society convulsed, all the slumbering elements of sectional bitterness aroused, and the slavery agitation awake again. . . . Never before has the Northern sky portended such a storm. Never before have the Northern press approached so near to unanimity in the cause of Abolition." How was it in the South? "All is calm and easy indifference. The thunders which come rolling from the North die away before they reach our latitude, or if heard at all, are scarcely heeded." Nothing was more fatuous than the idea that Douglas's bill was a piece of Southern aggression. "By many it is regarded with indifference; by some openly opposed; while the mass look upon it as a thing of so little practical good that it is certainly not worth the labor of an active struggle to maintain it." [42] On the one side of the border was the most intense hostility to the Kansas-Nebraska Bill, while on the other no compact and decided sentiment was discoverable at all.

39 Quoted in *National Intelligencer*, April 8, 11, 25, 1854.
40 *Cong. Globe*, 33d Cong., 1st sess., App., 434ff.
41 Letter to Pierce, March 24, in *National Intelligencer*, March 28, 1854.
42 June 21, 1854.

## [ III ]

For once public opinion had singularly little direct effect upon Washington. Democratic leaders had decreed that the bill must pass, and Democratic regulars fell into line. Northerners like Toucey of Connecticut and Shields of Illinois defied the more or less obvious will of their States. It might seem that the South had a golden opportunity to demonstrate its generosity of temper and loyalty to the Union by defeating the bill. With John Minor Botts of Virginia exclaiming that he would "like to see this misshapen and ill-begotten monster killed"; with Clemens condemning it as an attempt to build "the funeral pyre of the republic"; with even the Washington *Union* admitting that "the South looks on unmoved," while the New Orleans *True Delta* spoke of the measure as "the Nebraska bore," why did not a sufficient group of Southerners join the Northern opponents in voting it down? A veteran North Carolina Whig, complimenting the *National Intelligencer* on its opposition, sagely asserted: "In my opinion the South had never had so glorious an opportunity of uniting in a common cause for its own good and that of the whole country as she has let pass unimproved. If she had, as one man, and at the very outset, rejected that Pandora box, she had secured more quiet on the subject of slavery than the passage of a dozen such bills could confer." But the Chase-Sumner Address had done its fell work of repelling many Southerners; the delusive hope of sectional gain was strong; and the party whip was plied with effect.[43]

In the Senate nearly all Democrats, whether Northern or Southern, lent Douglas their assistance. Brodhead of Pennsylvania, recalling that his advocacy of popular sovereignty went back to 1848, accepted the bill. Cass, claiming a still earlier espousal of "the doctrine of our revolutionary fathers," did the same.[44] Dodge and Jones of Iowa came up to the party mark. So did Gwin of California. Four Southern Democrats, Hunter of Virginia, Butler of South Carolina, and Brown and Adams of Mississippi, were conspicuous in the debates, while C. C. Clay of Alabama threw himself earnestly into the struggle. On the Whig side of the chamber, only two members ultimately failed to

43 Botts wrote that he was satisfied that this was "the most mischievous and pernicious measure" ever introduced into Congress; *Letters of J. M. Botts,* 3. Clemens thought the future dark. "We of the South ask nothing more than to be let alone. We have not moved in the matter, but it is we who must suffer, unless Northern men, who see and appreciate our position, will do justice." *National Intelligencer,* February 11, 1854. Francis Lieber, believing that the bill would be injurious to the North if it passed, still more injurious if it failed, lamented that "the South flies to it as a moth to the candle." *Life and Letters,* edited by T. S. Perry, 267ff. A useful survey by B. H. Langston, *The South and the Kansas-Nebraska Bill,* is in MS in the University of Texas Library.

44 *Cong. Globe,* 33d Cong., 1st sess., 690.

vote for the measure, Bell of Tennessee and Clayton of Delaware. The one dissenting Southern Democrat was Sam Houston, who declared that the Missouri Compromise had been a solemn compact between North and South, that when Texas was admitted into the Union it formed what might be termed part of her Constitution, and that so far as Texas was concerned, it was sacred.[45]

It was noteworthy that most Whig Senators from the slave area showed but a lukewarm adherence. Dixon of Kentucky, of course, evinced genuine zeal for the bill which he had helped to write. But Clayton was highly dubious. "I did not ask for it," he said of the measure. "I would not have proposed it; and I may regret that it was offered, because I do not believe it will repay us for the agitation and irritation it has cost. But can a Senator, whose constituents hold slaves, be expected to resist and refuse what the North thus freely offers as a measure due to us?" He might well have hesitated, for opinion in Delaware was chilly. Thirty-eight of his personal and political friends in February signed a petition begging him to oppose the bill, "odious in principle, uncalled for by any political agency, and if passed, opening the floodgates" to sectional conflict; to ward off this "foul public wrong." [46] In the end he turned against the measure because the popular sovereignty feature was a complete abandonment of non-intervention. Though absent on the final ballot, he announced that he would have voted nay.

His colleague James A. Bayard, an old Jacksonian Democrat, hesitated which path to take; in principle he favored the repeal of the Missouri Compromise restriction, but as a practical matter he feared that it would lead to a frenzy of sectional discord. In the end he very reluctantly voted for the bill. Badger of North Carolina, a Whig of nationalist convictions who had done much to get the Compromise of 1850 passed, made a dramatic volte-face. He first assailed the bill on the ground that no need existed for immediate organization of the Territory and that it threatened a grave injustice to the Indians. When the second objection was removed he took its side, but said that he expected the South to gain nothing from it—and in later years declared that his support had been the gravest political error of his life.[47]

And John Bell of Tennessee, after some initial hesitation, fought the bill at every step. For several weeks he weighed the conflicting arguments carefully. "When I saw all the South going headlong into the support of the measure, and some of my colleagues as zealous as any others, however strange and unaccountable as it was to me, I was really desirous of not breaking the ranks,"

45 *Idem.*, Appendix, 201ff.
46 N. Y. *Herald*, March 1, 1854.
47 A. C. Cole, *The Whig Party in the South;* W. A. Graham, *Discourse in Memory of George E. Badger.*

he confessed in a letter. But finding three of his Whig colleagues in the House adverse, he resolved to obey the dictates of his judgment and join them. "Most foolish and mischievous," was his measured judgment upon the bill. Douglas, he believed, had originated it to rescue the Administration from weakness and quarrelling; many were pushing it heedlessly; and some fire-eating secessionists rejoiced in the idea that the furor it aroused might end in the rupture of the Union. Bell's great final speech attacked the bill as premature and unnecessary, unfair to the Indians, certain to arouse a violent sectional quarrel, of no practical benefit to the South, and dangerous as a treatment of the prickly question of non-intervention. In private conferences some of his friends had told him that any Southerner who rejected the bill would be a traitor to Southern interests; but he saw no certainty that it forbade further Congressional interference.[48]

Though no question existed that the bill would easily pass the Senate, the debate nevertheless had its moments of drama. Because they were fighting a hopeless defensive battle, the opponents furnished the more striking spectacle. Chase, looking every inch a majestic statesman, fired the first heavy gun on February 3d. "Sir," he began, after explaining that he spoke without personal rancor, "these crowded galleries, these thronged lobbies, this full attendance of the Senate, prove the deep, transcendent interest of the theme." He applied himself primarily to the question whether the Compromise of 1850 really superseded the earlier compromise; and in dealing with it, he took up Douglas's assertion that the legislation of 1850 dealt with other land than that acquired from Mexico. "He says that part of it was acquired from Texas. But this very territory which he says was acquired from Texas was acquired first from Mexico. After Mexico ceded it to the United States, Texas claimed that that cession inured to her benefit. This claim, only, was relinquished to the United States." Douglas also said that the Middle Park district of the Louisiana Purchase had been included in Utah Territory. But this district, answered Chase, was a tiny pinpoint on the map, a secluded little valley without a single inhabitant. "The summit of the Rocky Mountains was assigned as the eastern limit of Utah. That limit, in consequence of the curvature of the mountain range, happened to include this valley. Nobody here, at the time of the passage of the Utah bill, adverted to that fact . . . nobody ever dreamed that the adoption of that range as the eastern boundary of Utah would abrogate to the Missouri prohibition. The Senator reported that boundary line. Did he tell the Senate or the country that its establishment would have that effect? No, sir, never." By still other arguments Chase riddled the idea of supersedure.

48 S. F. Ordway, *Gulf States Hist. Magazine*, II, *Cong. Globe*, 33d Cong., 1st sess., Appendix, 407ff. Bell had been absent from the city when the bill was first reported from the Committee on Territories, of which he was a member.

In his second major speech, on March 2, Chase offered an amendment designed to test the popular sovereignty principle. It declared distinctly that the people of the Territories, through their appropriate representatives, might if they saw fit prohibit slavery therein. Without such assertion, as Chase said, the veto power of governor and judges appointed by the President might make mincemeat of popular sovereignty. To this Cass, Douglas, and others replied that the bill gave the legislature power both to prohibit or establish slavery, subject to limitations of the Constitution; that Chase's amendment gave it power only to prohibit; and that the right of the Federal courts to pass on both powers would not be affected in the least by Chase's amendment. By a vote of 36 to 10, the amendment was defeated—as was his proposal to let the people elect their territorial officers.[49]

Sumner's chief speech, studded with quotations from Shakespeare and Milton, heavy with erudition gleaned from old state papers, and full of his rasping moral dogmatism, was a characteristic production. It smelled of the closet and the lamp. Yet in its plea for a return to the principles of those fathers who had condemned slavery and set limits to its bounds, its fervent expression of a hope that slavery would yet be regarded as sectional and freedom national, and its apostrophe to national unity, it was touched with eloquence. A crash of applause from the galleries greeted one sentence which was universally taken as applicable to Douglas: [50]

"Alas! too often those principles which give consistency, individuality, and form to the Northern character, which render it staunch, strong, and seaworthy, which bind it together as with iron, are drawn out, one by one, like the bolts of the ill-fated vessel, and from the miserable, loosened fragments is formed that human anomaly—a *Northern man with Southern principles*. Sir, no such man can speak for the North."

It was a happy fact, said Sumner, that the old materialistic questions of the bank, the sub-treasury, and the public lands, filled for the most part with the odor of the dollar, had been pushed to one side by the far grander question of slavery. It was of timeless and universal significance. "To every man in the land, it says with clear, penetrating voice, 'Are you for freedom or are you for slavery?' And every man in the land must answer this question when he votes." Edward Everett was not pleased by the opprobrious phrase about Northern men with Southern principles. It had apparent boldness; but when Douglas pressed Sumner to admit or deny that the allusion was to him, Sumner sat silent—and Douglas pointed out that the phrase had been most conspicuously applied to Van Buren, who was Sumner's own candidate for the Presidency in

---

49 *Cong. Globe*, 33d Cong., 1st sess., App., 133ff., 280ff.
50 *Idem*, App., 262ff. Sumner called his speech "The Landmark of Freedom."

1848. Yet on the whole, Everett was impressed by Sumner's speech. If some passages were grossly offensive to the South, others were "extremely pertinent and conclusive." The bitterness of the discussion appalled Everett. "Whenever the subject of slavery comes in it completely breaks down all party ties," he wrote. And he entered in his diary: [51]

"Every day's experience convinces me that matters are approaching a crisis in this country on the subject of slavery. The differences, not of interest but of opinion and feeling, are irreconcilable; the extension of our territory and settle-- ments require that the question should be met, and when met in the present temper of the two sections it admits of no amicable solution."

Though Seward said he made no long speeches, he delivered on February 17th an address of nearly three hours which Everett termed magnificent. About the thin, quiet little man, with his puckered face, shaggy brows, and sepulchral voice, clung an atmosphere of the uncanny; something derived from his Welsh ancestors which suggested that he controlled occult powers. At first glance he looked insignificant, yet his quick mind, ready flow of language, broad philo- sophical outlook, and oracular tone fascinated his listeners. Unlike Sumner, he was on cordial personal terms with the Southern leaders. Indeed, he told the shocked Montgomery Blair that he was the man who had put Dixon up to moving his repeal amendment.[52] This speech was notable for the force with which it denied that the Compromise of 1850 had abrogated that of 1820. If it had, he demanded, why did the Nashville Convention so angrily condemn it? The speech was also remarkable as an anticipation of Seward's subsequent utterance on the irrepressible conflict. You buried the Wilmot Proviso in 1850, he told his opponents, and here it is again stalking these halls clad in complete steel. "You will not cease to cherish slavery. Do you see any signs that we are becoming indifferent to freedom? On the contrary, that old, traditional, hereditary sentiment of the North is more profound and more universal now than it ever was before. The slavery agitation you deprecate so much is an eternal struggle between conservatism and progress, between truth and error, between right and wrong." It was an address, wrote Everett, which took a much more thorough and comprehensive view of the subject than mine.[53]

Yet Everett's briefer speech, delivered ten days earlier, had special force because he represented the conservative Whigs who had made the passage of the last compromise possible. It was purely argumentative, containing not one

51 MS Diary, February 4, 21, March 2, April 6, 1854.
52 So says Gideon Welles, *Lincoln and Seward*, 68; but Blair perhaps misunderstood him, for the statement is preposterous.
53 *Cong. Globe*, 33d Cong., 1st sess., Appendix, 150ff.; Everett's MS Diary, same date. A pamphlet edition of Seward's speech was soon being scattered widely at 12½ cents a copy. Another pamphlet, "The Nebraska Question," with much historical matter and speeches by Douglas, Chase, Everett, Seward, Badger, and Sumner, sold for a quarter.

word of reproach or denunciation. When he declared that, inquiring carefully in 1850 into the purport of the omnibus measures, he had never received a single intimation that they applied to any territory outside New Mexico and Utah, he was heard with attention; for nobody had better right to say what was in Webster's mind at that time. Congressional non-intervention in the territories he pronounced an anomaly; popular sovereignty an absurdity. Even under this bill there was not a law which the Territories might pass which could not be disallowed next day by Congress—and this was a power which Congress in other areas had exercised again and again.[54]

In some respects the most remarkable of all the arguments against the bill came from rough-spoken Sam Houston. An impromptu address delivered without notes as the debate closed, it was desultory and unpolished, but it made a few points with great emphasis. The fact that this popular-sovereignty principle had never been invoked for a long list of early Territories; the conviction of Texans that the Missouri Compromise could not be repealed without dishonor; the inutility of the measure to the South; the certainty that its passage would convulse the country from Maine to the Rio Grande— all this he set forth. Upon the decision of Congress, he said, "must depend *union or disunion.*" Houston regarded this as the best speech of his life. Had he not been absent at the beginning of the contest, he told friends, he could have changed the course of at least five or six Southern Senators; but when he returned they were committed and it was too late. They would have been glad to rally to his side had they known in time the course he would take. His desk was inundated by letters of appreciation from the West and North.[55]

While these opponents delivered blow after blow, Douglas obviously chafed with impatience. Certain of the bill's passage in the Senate, he feared that the tempest of Northern wrath would daunt the Democrats in the House unless quick action were taken. At every juncture he labored for haste. At every point, too, he insisted that his Northern colleagues must take an unequivocal stand beside him. "Douglas had found out," wrote a keen-eyed Washington correspondent, "that he has caught more than he bargained for. He sees that the Northern Senators, in voting for his bill, had just as well gather up their coffin nails. Being so far committed to it as to have no chance of a back-out, and fully alive to the consequences, he is determined to play the blind

54 *Cong. Globe*, 33d Cong., 1st sess., Appendix, 158ff. Everett told his Southern friends that the bill might well be called a measure "to annihilate all conservative sentiment in the non-slaveholding States." Letter dated October 31, 1857, in *National Intelligencer*, May 15, 1858. Tom Ewing's son, sitting hot with indignation in the gallery, found the moderation of the speech exasperating. "It was cool, passionless, mechanical, elegant—without a spark of the indignant spirit of the North which blazed in the hearts of the people." Undated memorandum, Ewing Papers.
55 *Cong. Globe*, 33d Cong., 1st sess., App., 325ff; F. L. Burr, March 6, Welles Papers.

Samson, and shake down the pillars of the temple. He will force every Senator to the scratch—allow no dodging. Douglas is tolerably deep, after all. He has seen that in every Democratic convention, the South has controlled the nomination, and hence, if he can arouse the sympathies of the South in his behalf, he will stand a better chance for the next nomination." [56] Whatever his views as to the Presidency, he certainly meant to make every Democrat from Pierce down face the music.

Day after day Douglas was in his seat when the session began, and still there when it ended. Week in and week out, his quick, piercing eyes watched every move with tigerish intentness. Whenever a stroke was needed, he was on his feet, tossing his mass of dark hair like a lion's mane and scowling at his enemies. Toombs, in his two set speeches and his numerous rapid-fire deliverances, combined indomitable energy with striking fire and impetuosity. He, too, had a bold front, an imperious demeanor, a command of raking invective. But Douglas, whose manner of speaking, as men remarked, harmonized with his forceful and combative appearance, was far more effective. He was doubtless the most formidable legislative pugilist in all our history. His clear-cut, direct, positive sentences "went straight to the mark like bullets, and sometimes like cannon-balls, crashing and tearing." [57] When in the right, he could present a statement of surpassing clarity; when in the wrong, he could skilfully twist logic or cloud the subject with irrelevancies; and at all times, he could rend an opponent with unscrupulous savagery. Chase correctly remarked that while to himself the last word was unimportant, to Douglas it was essential—for Douglas always wished to quit any field of defeat with an air of victory. His scornful visage, his insolent gestures, his insulting epithets, threw his opponents into hot but utterly helpless dudgeon.

As he said, Douglas gloried in facing the storm. "Sit down," he once told Weller of California, "don't mix in, this is my fight." [58] It was well that he was a host in himself, for half his Northern colleagues were chilly and all except his loyal colleague Shields and the crass Indiana slaveholder Bright were uneasy. Cass's principal utterance was a triumph of equivocal statement. "The general," wrote one auditor, "made a very creditable speech against the bill by way of assigning reasons for voting for it. Directly after the performance was over, I met a wag, and asked him if he had heard the speech; and he replied he had, and it was the best freesoil speech, to hang an anti-freesoil vote upon, that he had ever heard." [59] The *National Intelligencer* declared of the bill that

56 Washington correspondence dated February 16 in *Missouri Republican*, February 24, 1854.
57 Schurz, *Reminiscences*, II, 30.
58 N. Y. *Tribune*, March 7, 1854; *Cong. Globe*, 33d Cong., 1st sess., App., 336
59 J. B. Bowlin, April 21, 1854; Buchanan Papers.

"many of its supporters had publicly and privately expressed their aversion to the proposition, and their deep regret that it had ever been brought forward." [60] Friends of Buchanan congratulated him that he was safe in England and need take no position. The whole effort, wrote one, is "evidently a bid for the Presidency on the part of Douglas, and I hope he may be foiled." [61]

The closing debate in the Senate filled a dramatic all-night session on March 3–4. John Bell opened it with a long attack on the bill. Various others were heard. A number of members were intoxicated, paying frequent visits to an anteroom where eatables and drinkables were provided. William Pitt Fessenden's speech excited Southern resentment, and twice Butler of South Carolina (who was particularly "exhilarated" and profane) advanced toward the Senator from Maine with flushed face and clenched fists. Weller's bombastic discourse showed the effect of liquor. At eleven o'clock, the majority having refused an adjournment, Douglas took the floor. His tremendous speech—tremendous in length, vigor, and ill-temper—was an impressive exhibition of physical endurance, for it lasted until nearly three in the morning. But it was less impressive in intellectual quality. The published reports, wrote the New York *Tribune* correspondent, "convey but a faint idea of its violence and vulgarity." To a courteous exclamation of Seward's he replied, "Ah, you can't crawl behind that free nigger dodge." His harangue, full of colloquies with various Senators, struck the fastidious Everett as unforgivably coarse and ungentlemanlike. [62]

Once more Douglas reviewed and tried to answer all the objections to the bill. He declared that the organization of Territorial governments was overdue, for a hundred thousand people crossed Kansas every year by the emigrant routes and needed protection. He reiterated that the old principle of Congressional intervention which produced incessant agitation had been supplanted in 1850 by the new, fair, and truly democratic principle of popular self-government. He pointed out that he had long stood for this principle, that he had repeatedly asserted it in the debate of 1850, and that in a speech late that year before a turbulent Chicago crowd he had stated it even more emphatically. He termed the repeal of the Missouri Compromise "a mere incident" of his bill, and accused his opponents of the grossest misrepresentation when they assailed his means instead of openly resisting the object itself.

But the essential weakness of Douglas's position was confessed in his repeated resort to irrelevant personalities. He knew that he could never prove his point about the supersedence of the Missouri Compromise. He knew that in all his talk of the popular sovereignty principle in 1850 he had never dared say

60  *National Intelligencer*, May 24, 1854.
61  George Sanderson, Lancaster, February 24, 1854; Buchanan Papers.
62  N. Y. *Tribune, Herald*, March 7, 1854; Everett's MS Diary, March 3.

that it would be applied to the Louisiana Purchase country. He knew that he could never prove his assertion that Kansas was in no danger of reduction to slavery—for already exultant Missouri slaveholders were boasting they would gain control of it. He knew that he could not explain his change of front between the Nebraska bill of 1853 and that of 1854. To give his final speech a specious show of force, he filled a great part of it with wrangling attacks upon Seward, Sumner, and Chase. He quarreled with Seward about New York's attitude toward the Missouri Compromise, charging that the Empire State had been the first to violate that so-called compact. He assailed Chase for slander, falsification, and forgery. He stigmatized Sumner's catchword about Northern men with Southern principles as a disreputable insinuation. Finally, he more than intimated that Chase and Sumner had found their way into the Senate by base means. He must be permitted, he rapped out, to tell Chase that "I did not obtain my seat in this body either by a corrupt bargain or a dishonorable coalition"; to tell Sumner that "I did not enter into any combinations or arrangements by which my character, my principles, and my honor, were set up at public auction or private sale in order to procure a seat in the Senate of the United States!" [63]

As dawn peered into the chamber, Houston was uttering his words of warning and protest. A hurricane was raging throughout the North, and would continue to rage; if, as some said, this controversial measure would give no new slave State to the South, why not jettison it for the sake of national harmony? The South had never asked for a repeal of the Missouri Compromise. "I, as the most extreme Southern Senator upon this floor, do not desire it. If it is a boon that is offered to propitiate the South, I, as a Southern man, repudiate it. I reject it. I will have none of it." His final plea for the sake of the Union, *"Maintain the Missouri Compromise!* Stir not up agitation! Give us peace!" was still echoing when, at a few minutes before five o'clock, the Senate proceeded to vote. "Aye!" called Adams, Atchison, Badger, and Bayard; "No!" said Bell—and the bill passed by thirty-seven ayes to fourteen nays.

63  For a different view see Milton, *Eve of Conflict,* 141. "In a single speech he had torn away the Abolitionists' foundations; he had shown and forced them to admit that their contention that the Missouri Compromise was a compact was a sectional lie; he had proved that the North had repudiated it within a year of its making, that the faithless had no right to expect further compliance from the faithful." The reference is to the fact that a Vermont member on February 12, 1821, had sought to debar Missouri unless she came in without slavery, and that 61 Northern men had voted for this amendment while 33 voted against it. But of course the amendment was defeated; of course Missouri came in with slavery; and under the arrangement of 1821, which need not be called a compact, the South gained its advantage while that of the North was incompletely fulfilled. The vital question was not whether the legislation of 1820–21 was a "compact." That word had no constitutional or legal meaning whatever. The vital question was whether an arrangement sanctioned by thirty years of national approval, and throughout that time regarded as a working compromise, had been superseded by the Compromise of 1850.

Had all Senators been present, wrote Edward Everett, who had gone home exhausted at half-past three, the vote would have stood forty to twenty. Other polls differed; but in any event, the victory was overwhelming.[64] As the Senators, some exultant, some despondent, but all exhausted after their continuous session of seventeen hours, filed down the Capitol steps, they heard the boom of cannon fired by Southern enthusiasts roll over the sleeping city. The sombre Chase turned to Sumner with his memorable prophecy: "They celebrate a present victory, but the echoes they awake shall never rest until slavery itself shall die." [65]

## [ IV ]

For a time many questioned whether the bill would pass the House. Feeling in that chamber was intense. Each side was making immense exertions. "The result is doubtful, but Mr. Douglas and the President are hand in hand, Wellington and Blucher," reported a Washington observer to Buchanan, adding: "There is no doubt of the feeling at the North, decided hostility in every form of expression." It was even said that Pierce, frightened by the horrid genie that Douglas had released from the urn, could and would make a new issue. Some bold coup, perhaps with regard to Cuba, would be staged to divert the public mind from Kansas.[66]

With the fall elections at hand, with the North in complete revolt, with the South half-apathetic, Representatives were much more responsive to home influences than Senators. The Northern Whigs in the House stood solidly opposed to the bill. The Northern Democrats divided almost equally. An overwhelming majority of members from the slave States espoused the measure, and the Lower South in particular was practically a unit. Altogether, sectional lines were drawn with much more distinctness in the House than the Senate. In the end, only nine slave-State votes were cast against the bill, three Democratic and six Whig, and of these, all but one came from North Carolina, Virginia, and the border.

The opposition of all Northern Whigs and a good half of Northern Democrats was a direct reflection of the popular mood. These men saw the hostile petitions which rained upon the Speaker's desk. They heard the incessant

64 Toombs, Bright, and Pearce of Maryland would have voted aye; *National Intelligencer*, March 7, 1854. The Washington *Sentinel* thought the final vote would have been 42 to 18; May 27, 1854. No Southern Democrat voted nay—Houston being absent; only two slave State Whigs, Bell and Clayton.

65 J. W. Schuckers, *Chase*, 156. John Jay had written Chase nearly a month earlier: "We swear . . . to fight on and fight ever, until Congress has gone to the *farthest limit of its power* for the extinction of slavery . . ." Hart, *Chase*, 146, 147.

66 J. D. Andrews, March 21, 1854; Buchanan Papers.

drum-fire of editorials and speeches. By March, too, time had been given for legislature after legislature to speak out on the subject—and some had spoken in no uncertain terms.

Ten free-State legislatures were in session early in 1854, and nine slave-State legislatures. In Maine, resolutions assailing the Kansas-Nebraska Bill passed the Senate 24 to 1, and the House 96 to 6. In Rhode Island, the legislature unanimously passed condemnatory resolutions. In Massachusetts, hostile resolutions passed the Senate unanimously, and the House 246 to 13. New York passed resolutions instructing the delegation in Congress to oppose the bill by a vote of 23 to 6 in the Senate, and 80 to 27 in the House. The Wisconsin legislature, by large majorities, passed resolutions opposing the bill. Thus five of the ten free States were emphatic in their censure. But almost equally significant was the result in the other five, controlled by Democratic majorities. In Pennsylvania the legislature, after considering the subject, prudently declined to take a vote. The Democratic majorities in New Jersey practised the same avoidance. In Ohio the majority persistently kept the subject tabled, obviously fearing either to break with the Administration or to defy public sentiment. The California legislature, strongly Democratic, refused to take any action. Only one Northern State passed resolutions of approval. This was Illinois, where Douglas's supporters plied whip and spur. Douglas made much in his Senate speeches of this supposed endorsement. But his opponents pointed out that the affirmative vote (14 to 8 in the Senate, 36 to 22 in the House) was only half of the full strength of the legislature; 50 in a total membership of 100.[67]

Meanwhile, in the slave area the legislatures generally reflected the prevailing indifference by avoiding the subject. Georgia and Mississippi alone adopted resolutions of approval, while the Tennessee Senate endorsed the principles of the bill. But the legislatures of Maryland, Alabama, Louisiana, Texas, and Kentucky adjourned without taking action.[68]

Nor were other tokens of public opinion wanting. In Connecticut both the Democratic and the Whig State conventions voted resolutions against the bill. This was the more striking in that Connecticut, a land of traditional conservatism where certain manufacturing groups did a large Southern business, had given Pierce its electoral votes, and had elected Toucey in place of Roger S. Baldwin on a platform of Union-saving acceptance of the Compromise of 1850. The two conventions were condemning the course followed by Toucey and Representative Ingersoll.[69] Many Connecticut editors had received government

67 "Many an assemblyman, with the rising storm of opposition and agitation, came shortly to regret his vote in favor of the resolutions; John Reynolds, 'the old ranger,' publicly recanted his vote." Cole, Era of the Civil War (Centennial History of Illinois), 121, 122.

68 Summary in N. Y. Courier, quoted in National Intelligencer, April 18, 1854.

69 National Intelligencer, March 2, 1854; the Whigs were unanimous and even the Democratic vote was overwhelming. See N. Y. Tribune, March 20, 1854.

largesses for printing or other favors, and had followed a servile course. When the editor of the Hartford *Times* printed anti-Nebraska letters from a Democratic writer, Pierce himself told Connecticut visitors that he would discipline the author.[70] And in Pierce's own State, the first to hold an election after the bill was introduced, the Administration received a severe check. In the March election for governor the Democratic majority was cut by fully two-thirds, from about 5,500 to about 1,500, while the Democratic majority of 89 in the House was wiped out. Pierce men had insisted that the Nebraska question was in no sense an issue in the election, but the popular antagonism to it was unmistakable.[71] Douglas showed how hard this election had hit him—so thought some correspondents.

In Pennsylvania, the Democratic convention met early in March to renominate Governor Bigler. Administration forces, abetted by Simon Cameron, endeavored to get the convention to endorse the principles of the Nebraska bill. Pierce, indeed, looked to Pennsylvania for his main support. His workers were actively on the scene. They utterly failed. "At least three fourths of the Convention were determined to let Judge Douglas and the National Administration fight their own battles," wrote one of Buchanan's lieutenants. They meant to keep the issue out of the approaching State campaign. "There is evidently a very strong feeling among the people in favor of the sacredness of the Missouri Compromise. . . ." Bigler and his principal adviser, Jeremiah Black, were—according to another observer—not pulling anybody's chestnuts out of the fire. They heard Douglas's and Pierce's emissaries, grunted, and went ahead with resolutions that endorsed nothing beyond the Baltimore platform. They knew that Wilmot's old district and other freesoil areas were all aflame.[72]

As for Michigan, the election in Detroit, Cass's own city, gave a Whig anti-Nebraska candidate for mayor a majority of more than a thousand, though the Democrats usually carried the city by nearly that margin. The Detroit *Times,* special organ of the old-line Democracy, declared itself firmly convinced that the party in the State was hostile to the bill, that the people of Michigan generally opposed it, and that if it passed the agitation would reach a height never before known.[73] In Ohio, William Allen, an old Jacksonian Democrat who had been in the Senate for a dozen years ending in 1849, came out against the bill; aided, as George W. Manypenny wrote Douglas, by fusionists, Free Soilers, and Whigs.[74] When the legislature balloted for a Senator in succession to Chase, the Democrats finally united upon George E.

70  F. L. Burr, March 30, 1854; Welles Papers.
71  N. Y. *Tribune,* March 17, 20, 1854.
72  George Sanderson, March 20, J. C. Van Dyke, March 23, 1854; Buchanan Papers.
73  *National Intelligencer,* March 18, April 15, 1854.
74  February 22, 1854; Douglas Papers.

Pugh. But this selection, as numerous leaders asserted, was taken without reference to the Nebraska issue, and Pugh denied a statement by the Washington *Union* that he had authorized it to say he was for the bill.[75] From Illinois came word that a formidable coalition against Douglas was emerging. A friend of the Little Giant wrote from Jacksonville as early as January 28 that "we are going to have trouble," and that the Whigs, Free Soilers, and some of the Democrats would be united against the principles of the Nebraska Bill.[76]

Most portentous of all for the Democratic Party was the revolt under way in New York. Only eight of the eighty-eight German papers of the State supported the measure. Marcy's friends, who had some trouble in persuading him not to resign his Secretaryship of State in protest, were in arms. So conservative a Democrat as James T. Brady, spokesman for the best element among the Irish, returned from Europe to condemn the "wanton and wicked" bill, which he described as "the joint production of a profligate Administration and an ambitious intriguer." Brady, a distinguished lawyer who had been the Hard candidate in 1853 for the attorney-generalship of the State, delivered himself of one scorching sentence. He hoped, he declared, that he would yet see the presidential chair filled by some man really fit for it, "and that the descending gradation of the incumbents which has for some years injured our national reputation may not be continued by adding to the succession of the incompetent and unworthy one whose only reliance for success will be founded on his unscrupulous use of the artifices by which a selfish demagohue elevates himself at the expense of detriment, if not disgrace, to his country!" [77] Of the twenty-one Democratic Congressmen, twelve opposed the measure.

The Democratic State Committee, meeting in Albany early in April, adopted resolutions censuring Pierce for rewarding the enemies of the Compromise of 1850, and applauding Francis B. Cutting and other New York Representatives who had voted for a full and free discussion of the Nebraska bill. Nobody doubted that the fall elections for governor would find the Democratic party split, and see voters rebuke the Administration with savage emphasis.[78]

The central figure of the Missouri coalition was of course Benton, never more Roman than now. He knew that his speeches in the House would cost him his seat, smash all his prospects for a return to the Senate, and estrange many old associates. But he made the chamber ring with his attacks, and rallied all his Missouri friends. His contempt for Douglas was intense.

75  Washington *Union*, March 8, *National Intelligencer*, March 14, 1854.
76  M. McConnell, n.d., Douglas Papers.
77  Letter to Rufus W. Peckham, June 29, in *National Intelligencer*, July 4, 1854.
78  *National Intelligencer*, April 15, 1854; Alexander, *Political History of New York*, II, 190ff.

"He won't do, sir!" he exploded when somebody mentioned Little Giant's aspirations for the presidency. "His legs are too short, sir. That part of his body, sir, which men wish to kick, is too near the ground!" [79]

Benton gave it out that he was preparing a tremendous set speech. He would require about four hours, he said, and if the House would not grant him that time, he would adjourn to the rotunda; nay, if the crowd were too great, he would speak in the grounds. His wit sparkled dangerously. The whole country repeated his remark about the bill having a stump speech in its belly, for that precisely hit off Douglas's clause explaining its true intent and meaning. Three dogmas afflicted the land, he declared: squatter sovereignty, non-intervention, and the impotence of Congress to legislate upon slavery. This bill asserted all three, and then knocked each one in the head with the two others. "It is an amphibiological bill, stuffed with monstrosities, hobbled with contradictions, and Badgered with a proviso." There could be no question that the German element of Missouri, with many other freesoilers, were enthusiastically behind Benton.[80]

Even in California the Democratic party was split, partly by the Nebraska bill, partly by the rivalry of Wm. M. Gwin and David Broderick, and partly by other local factors. It was a picturesque and stirring contest for power that these two men waged. Gwin, a tall, courtly Southerner by origin, a close friend of Robert J. Walker, and a favorite of slavery leaders in Washington, had brilliant abilities. He had gone to the Senate in 1849, in the same year with Frémont, and represented the Southern element which for a time dominated California politics. A leader of refinement and courtesy, used to the best society, he was a cool, adroit, and masterful manager of men. Broderick was a complete contrast. Trained in politics by Tammany Hall, a friend of the notorious Bill Poole, and onetime foreman of a New York fire-engine company, various Eastern reverses had sent him to California to seek his fortune. His burning ambition was to return east a Senator. He was domineering, coarse-mannered, and subject to fierce outbursts of wrath. But by his strong animal magnetism, his imperious temper, and his ruthless use of Tammany methods in politics, he had built up a powerful organization.

While Senators Gwin and Weller supported the Nebraska bill with all their strength, Broderick, who resented the way in which Gwin had diverted most of the California patronage to Southerners at the expense of the New York and

79 J. T. Mason, July 29, 1854; Buchanan Papers.
80 J. C. Bowlin, April 21, 1854, Buchanan Papers; *Cong. Globe*, 33d Cong., 1st sess., 560. On the Whig side in Missouri Edward Bates was conspicuous in the movements of protest. To him Douglas's bill was barren of all good, and the fruitful source of all the evils that followed. Floyd E. McNeil, *Lincoln's Attorney-General, Edward Bates*; MS doctoral dissertation, University of Iowa.

Middle Western element, took sides against him. He gave violent utterance to anti-Nebraska and anti-Douglas sentiments. With him stood his friend Governor John Bigler, who also had ambitions for the Senate.[81]


[ V ]


While the struggle in Congress went into its last phase, and while Northern massmeetings and burnings in effigy continued, the dramatic case of the fugitive Anthony Burns lit up the passions of the hour like a beam from a suddenly opened searchlight. Nothing better showed the change in the Northern temper. Henceforth freesoilers would take a more unyielding position on the fugitive slave issue. "The South is violating the Compromise of 1850," they said. "Very well, *we* shall certainly take no pains to observe it." [82]

Burns, the property of Charles T. Suttle of Alexandria, Va., had early in 1854 smuggled himself aboard a vessel and escaped to Boston. His master. tracing him by a letter he sent his brother, followed in pursuit. On May 24 Burns was arrested by the Federal marshal, and confined in the courthouse, which was surrounded by chains to exclude the indignant populace. Next day, fettered and closely guarded, he was brought before Commissioner Edward G. Loring for examination. Richard H. Dana, Jr., who had volunteered to act as his counsel, begged for a delay, and the case was postponed until the 27th. "He is a piteous object," Dana noted in his diary, "rather weak in mind and body, with a large scar on his cheek, which looks much like a brand, a broken hand from which a large piece of bone projects, and another scar on his other hand."

On the night of the 26th an abortive attempt was made to rescue the slave. Faneuil Hall that evening was filled with an immense crowd, the greatest that young Thomas Wentworth Higginson ever saw in the building; Theodore Parker and Wendell Phillips delivered inflammatory speeches; and they and Higginson planned to lead the audience forth in an overwhelming attack on the courthouse. While the speechmaking continued some man in the audience suddenly proposed an adjournment—for the reason, he said, that a mob of Negroes was trying to rescue Burns. A general rush was made to the court-

81  James O'Meara, *Broderick and Gwin: A Brief History of Early Politics in California.*
82  "The free States," declared the venerable Josiah Quincy at the Whig convention in Boston on August 16, "agreed in 1789 to be field-drivers and pound-keepers for the black cattle of the slaveholding States. . . . They have multiplied their black cattle by millions; and are every day increasing their numbers and extending their cattlefields into the wilderness. Under these circumstances, are we bound to be their field-drivers and pound-keepers any longer? . . . Are you the sons of the men of 1776? or do you 'lack gall to make oppression bitter?'" N. Y. *Tribune,* August 21, 1854.

house square, where the attackers finally broke into the building. In the mêlée a teamster who had been sworn in as special deputy was shot dead; but the marshal's officers finally expelled the assailants, and nine of them were jailed.

While Boston hummed with excitement, and two artillery companies of militia, a company of United States troops, and a company of marines were all brought into the city, the examination before Loring commenced. It lasted all that Saturday, and three days of the following week. Each day the courtroom was filled with the marshal's guard, whom Dana describes as a gang of about one hundred and twenty bullies, blacklegs, convicts, prize-fighters, and other scum of the community. Meanwhile, marines, regular troops, and police guarded the building, so that men had to pass four or five cordons in order to reach the courtroom. Dense crowds filled up the surrounding streets. On Monday six or eight hundred Worcester men, carrying a banner inscribed "Worcester Freedom Club," joined the concourse. Much resentment was felt because the claimant had chosen to plead his case before Loring, the respected probate judge of the county and lecturer in law at Harvard, who was a Whig and a known opponent of the Nebraska bill. This was done, they grumbled, with the design of insulting Bostonians as offensively as possible. Dana was assisted in defending the slave by Charles M. Ellis, an able, earnest attorney. On the other side were B. F. Hallett, as Federal attorney, and a lawyer to represent the owner. On May 31 Loring bowed to the plain letter of the law by deciding that Burns must be surrendered, and on June 2 he was formally delivered to his master.

But how? Wide-scattered circulars had summoned the yeomanry of New England to gather in Boston. Crowds poured in from all the neighboring towns. Crepe was strung across many buildings. The church bells tolled. A mighty concourse lined the ways to express their shame and indignation. Among those present was James Freeman Clarke. "I saw," he writes, "from the window of John A. Andrew's chambers, the lawyers' offices hung in black. I saw the cavalry, artillery, marines, and police, a thousand strong, escorting with shotted guns one trembling colored man to the vessel which was to carry him to slavery. I heard the curses, both loud and deep, poured on these soldiers; I saw the red flush in their cheeks as the crowd yelled at them, 'Kidnappers! Kidnappers!'" Another onlooker was the conservative attorney George S. Hillard. The city had been turned into an armed camp, he wrote his friend Francis Lieber, to do the dirty work of tying hand and foot a poor wretch who had recovered his natural birthright of freedom. "How odious and hateful the whole thing looked! Think of the same apparatus in the case of a Christian slave escaped from Algiers! When it was all over, and I was left alone in my office, I put my face in my hands and wept. I could do nothing less." [83]

The significance of the Burns affair did not lie in the fact that it required an imposing display of military force and an expenditure variously estimated at from $40,000 to $100,000 to return one slave to Virginia. It lay in the revelation of a wholly altered Northern attitude. The Kansas-Nebraska bill had convinced multitudes that the South was faithless to its pledges and determined to extend the slave area. From that moment the Fugitive Slave Act was worthless throughout most of the North.

Coincident with Burns's hearing three slaves but newly escaped from Maryland were seized in New York and returned. The press gave the episode indignant columns, the *Tribune* published an editorial, and a meeting of protest was held.[84] In Syracuse that week tremendous excitement reigned when two citizens received telegrams saying that a marshal would pass through on the late afternoon train with a recaptured slave. Bells were rung, a crowd gathered, and the arriving train was stormed by two thousand angry people— who found the telegram without foundation. In Manchester, Vt., lived a Negro barber who admitted that he had escaped from his master twelve years earlier. Word reached the Vigilance Committee in Boston that this master was coming north to reclaim the man. A watch was set up at the Boston hotels, and when the owner registered at one, men were set to shadow him. Meanwhile the committee started two couriers to Manchester, which they reached at two in the morning. The citizens at once made up a handsome purse, and by noon the barber was on his way to Canada.[85]

A dramatic episode had advertised Wisconsin's feeling. News reached Milwaukee one March morning that a fugitive slave, captured near Racine by his owner and a Federal marshal, had been brought handcuffed to the Milwaukee county jail. The streets filled with indignant men. A crowd gathered at the jail. Lawyers by the dozen, busily searching the precedents, soon filed both a demand for a writ of habeas corpus and a civil warrant for damages sustained by the Negro in his capture. That afternoon ringing bells summoned the citizens to the courthouse square, where speeches were made, resolutions were passed, and a vigilance committee of twenty-five was appointed to watch lest

83  June 2, 1854; Lieber Papers, Huntington Library. In the immense literature on the Burns case the most important sources are John Weiss, *Theodore Parker*, II, Ch. 20; C. F. Adams, *Richard Henry Dana*, I, Ch. 14; James Freeman Clarke, *Anti-Slavery Days;* and C. E. Stevens, *Anthony Burns, A History* (1856). On the Sunday following the rendition, the clergy of Massachusetts spoke out with almost united voice. Ezra Stiles Gannett preached with fervent indignation, while the sermon of Theodore Parker, printed in the *Commonwealth* and sold in extra sheets, had an enormous circulation. N. Y. *Tribune*, June 19, 1854.
84  N. Y. *Tribune*, May 27-29, 1854.
85  N. Y. *Tribune*, June 15, 1854.

the prisoner be spirited away by stealth. On any alarm, they were to call out the entire population. A few days later Madison dispatches announced that the citizens had liberated the man, and that the owner was glad to decamp after being charged in court with assault and battery.[86]

Similar episodes followed in other parts of the Northwest. When late in 1854 more than a dozen fugitive slaves were protected from capture by the populace of Chicago, who refused to let the marshal make an arrest and overawed the militia, a down-State paper commented that this was quite natural. "Before the repeal of the Missouri Compromise, in all contests between the slaveholders and abolitionists our sympathies were decidedly in favor of the former; but since that act of treachery we have not one word to say. . . . One year ago there were thousands of men who would have aided you slaveholders in the capture of your slaves, who now say hands off—non-intervention is the policy—let the slaveowners and the abolitionists fight it out." [87]

All over the North the news was the same. A fugitive slave reached Medina, N. Y.; the people hid him, supplied him with money, and hurried him into Canada. Another was found hiding in the outskirts of Poughkeepsie. He was soon on the train, with funds in his pocket, for British soil. "Though all the Douglasites in Christendom should appear in this city armed to the teeth," wrote one Poughkeepsie man, "no fugitive could be dragged or hammered back into servitude." [88] Early in June B. B. French, Pierce's close friend and commissioner of public buildings in Washington, visited the White House. Sitting at the President's table, he watched Pierce open his letters, and heard him read an anonymous epistle beginning: "To the chief slave-catcher of the United States. You damned, infernal scoundrel, if I only had you here in Boston, I would murder you!" This was outrageous, as was French's counter-assertion that he would really glory in putting ropes around the necks of Wendell Phillips, Theodore Parker, and other traitors.[89] But Edward Everett understated the change when he noted that whereas numerous conservative men had once been willing to support even this repugnant law, now none but officers would help execute it. Many were actively obstructing it, like the Worcester hotel proprietors who refused to quarter some Southern slave-seekers, and the Worcester citizens who threatened them with tar and feathers if they did not leave town.[90]

What had been radical opinion in the North now became general opinion; Douglas had converted more men to intransigent freesoil doctrine in two

86  Milwaukee *Sentinel*, March 13, 17, 1854.
87  Warsaw, Ill., *Express*, December 21, 1854.
88  N. Y. *Tribune*, June 29, 1854.
89  June 4, 1854; French Papers.
90  Everett, MS Diary, May 27, 1854; New York *Tribune*, June 12, 1854.

months than Garrison and Phillips had converted to abolitionism in twenty years. One illustration of the sudden change in the intellectual climate was supplied by the meeting of the American Anti-Slavery Society in New York early in May. The abolitionist leaders were as hysterical as ever. Wendell Phillips splashed vitriol in every direction—at John Mitchel ("British tyranny . . . has crushed the manhood out of him"); at Edward Everett ("he represents money and the fashionable pulpits"); at the cotton manufacturers ("busy at Lowell and Lawrence in making a tariff that shall fill the United States Treasury full enough with surplus funds to buy up all the real virtue there is in Washington"); and at State Street ("does not care if you plant slavery in Nebraska and annex all China, provided you will let it make one per cent a month in peace"). Garrison and Samuel J. May called for the dissolution of the Union. Once such a meeting would have met with derision and possible violence. Only three years earlier a mob headed by the Democratic politician Isaiah Rynders had broken up the abolitionists' Tabernacle meeting and virtually driven them from the city. Only two years earlier every hall had closed its doors to them, and they had to assemble in Syracuse. But now they were made welcome in one of the city's handsomest churches. Crowded and sympathetic audiences of respectable citizens listened to their discourses. Their boldest utterances, recently so shocking, were heard without visible dissent.[91]

## [ VI ]

The battle in the House did not really begin until May 8. Cutting of New York, a prominent member of the "Hard" faction, had succeeded on March 21 in getting the bill sent to the committee of the whole, where it was placed at the bottom of the calendar, with half a hundred bills ahead of it. The vote by which this was accomplished, 110 to 95, showed the danger in which the measure lay. Many doubted whether it could be resurrected during this session of Congress. But Douglas exerted every effort; the Administration seconded him, announcing through the *Union* that the Federal patronage would be used in the fight; and word went round that defeat of the bill would be defeat of the party. The Cabinet, except for Marcy and McClelland, put their shoulders to the wheel, and Jefferson Davis and Caleb Cushing exerted their great powers to the utmost. While the bill remained locked up in the committee of the whole, loyal Democrats were being forced into line behind it.

From May 8th to 22d, the House was in a blaze of excitement as the majority leaders tried to force a vote. Everybody then knew that the Douglas forces could carry it; everybody knew that speechmaking availed nothing;

but the minority fought every inch of ground. Douglas's deputy in the House was Richardson. The Little Giant himself was frequently a visitor to the floor. But the ablest advocate, both as debater and parliamentary manager, was Alexander H. Stephens. Often compared with John Randolph of Roanoke—to whom his gaunt body, small, sickly-looking form, beardless, wrinkled-parchment skin, and shrill voice gave him a certain physical resemblance—he was quite as formidable as a speaker. What he lacked in vituperative wit and literary finish he made up in the directness, simplicity, and logical force of his utterances. He was terse, pointed, and frequently dry, loading his speeches with facts which he had mastered at the cost of prolonged research. He loved to impale an opponent not on a felicitous comparison or a quotation from the classics, as Randolph did, but on some forgotten fact of history or statistical detail. Nobody in the House was more expert in analyzing an issue, or in giving a quick, brief statement of a complicated subject; and no member could be more bitterly partisan than Stephens when he was aroused. Auditors found something fascinating in the aspect of this bloodless, mummified figure, rising spectrally to his nearly six feet in height; something delightful in his piercing yet musical voice, which at times took on a swelling intensity, at times broke into a rapid recitative, and at times died away like the wind in a grove of pines. He was as much the dashing Marmion of the House contest as Douglas had been the Boabdil of the Senate.

Stephens insisted that the South had never accepted the Missouri Compromise restriction except as a vanquished party. He argued that when the North refused in 1850 to let the Missouri line be extended to the Pacific, "the South was thrown back upon her original rights under the Constitution." The section then determined that the territorial restriction should be abandoned both above and below the line of 36° 30'. Thereafter the issue was to be taken out of Congress, into which it had been improperly thrust, and referred to the people directly concerned. This was the root principle of all our republican institutions —"that the citizens of every distinct community or State should have the right to govern themselves in their domestic matters as they please. . . ." And was it not true, Stephens asked, that the free States, with double the population of their rivals and the heavy European immigration to boot, would have an enormous advantage over the slave States? Did the North not trust the colonizing energy of its own people on this issue?

For the opposition, the ablest speeches had been delivered before the final struggle began. Hunt of Louisiana employed both economic and political arguments. The South could never gain any new slave territory from the bill; why, then, force it on a riotously angry North? Benton went over all the historical ground, and once more pointed out that the bill was full of contradictions. He was against this shilly-shally, willy-won'ty, don'ty-can'ty style of legislation. But he rose to his best heights in denouncing the utter needlessness of the bill: [92]

"What is the excuse for all this turmoil and mischief? We are told it is to keep the question of slavery out of Congress! Great God! It was out of Congress, completely, entirely, and forever out of Congress, unless Congress dragged it in by breaking down the sacred laws which settled it! The question was settled and done with. There was not an inch square in the Union on which it could be raised without a breach of compromise. The Ordnance of '87 settled it for all the remaining part of the Northwest Territory beyond Wisconsin; the compromise line of 36° 30' settled it in all the country north and west of the Missouri to the British line, and up to the Rocky Mountains; the organic act of Oregon . . . settled it in all that region; the acts for the governments of Utah and New Mexico settled it in those two Territories; the compact with Texas . . . settled it there; and California settled it for herself. Now, where was there an inch of territory in the United States on which the question could be raised? Nowhere! Not an inch! The question was settled everywhere, not merely by law but by fact. . . . No way for Congress to get the question in, for the purpose of keeping it out, but to break down compromises which kept it out!"

Time and again the contest between the two nearly equal sides threatened to break forth in physical violence. Lewis D. Campbell of Ohio headed a group which maintained a bitter filibuster. He and various Southerners taunted each other ferociously. Once all discipline broke down; an angry, gesticulating crowd surrounded him; weapons were drawn; and a Virginia member was with difficulty restrained from personal assault. Only the vigorous action of the Speaker, who ordered the sergeant-at-arms to use the mace of the House, had the irate Virginian arrested, cut off debate, and declared the sitting adjourned, prevented a general and perhaps bloody fight. But at last the opposition was worn down. In the final scene, on May 22, Stephens assumed charge, and by an adroit parliamentary stratagem which even the Charleston *Mercury* denounced as destructive of the rights of minorities, carried the bill to victory.

"Nebraska is through the House," he exultantly wrote. "I took the reins in my hand, applied whip and spur, and brought the 'wagon' out at eleven o'clock P.M. Glory enough for one day." [93]

The final vote was 113 ayes to 100 nays. Of the Northern Democrats, forty-four were for the bill, and forty-two against. Of the Southern Democrats, fifty-

---

92 *Cong. Globe,* 33d Cong., 1st sess., App. 557ff. Together with Hunt and Benton, Etheridge of Tennessee deserves credit for his courage in opposing the bill. An attractive portrait of Hunt, who was a great friend of Clay, and who next to John A. Campbell was for many years perhaps the brightest adornment of the New Orleans bar, is drawn in Thomas Hunt's privately-printed *Life of William H. Hunt* (1922).
93 The *Mercury,* quoted in *National Intelligencer,* June 1, 1854.

seven voted aye, and only two no. All the Northern Whigs, forty-five in number, were against the bill. Of the Southern Whigs, twelve voted for it and seven against. "The great agony is over!" ejaculated the Georgia *Union*. "We trust the South is satisfied. As for the North, we honestly believe she has achieved *a perfect triumph*, if her people only had the good sense to see it."

## [ VII ]

And what was it that Congress had enacted? Over and beyond its repeal of the Missouri Compromise restriction, it had passed one of the most equivocal measures, as the Georgia *Union* suggested, in its long history. It had enacted a popular sovereignty principle which was susceptible of two diametrically opposed interpretations. Most Southerners maintained that the bill permitted the people of a Territory to decide the issue of freedom or slavery only when they had attained a condition which entitled them to seek admission to the Union under a State Constitution. The Cass-Douglas interpretation was that they might decide it much earlier, long before applying for Statehood. Franklin of Maryland told the House that the bill contained an "intentional equivocation," "the phraseology being framed with a full knowledge that the gentlemen of the North would place one interpretation on it and the South another." Similar language was used by the Charleston *Evening News*, which remarked: "The essential value of the Nebraska Bill to politicians is, that it is a skilful specimen of that species of political non-commitalism which has of late become so valuable in perpetrating substantial and systematic departures from the first principles of our republican organization." This journal, believing that the popular-sovereignty principle deceived and injured the South, remarked that the only real question was whether the slaveholding area should be kicked and humiliated openly, as Northerners wished, or kicked only *sub rosa*, as the Southerners implored.[94]

Thus even while the North was fierily denouncing the new law, many Southern Democrats were also muttering angrily against it. If the Cass-Douglas principle were to prevail, if a Territorial legislature were to be allowed to pass laws hostile to slavery, then they had bought repeal of the Missouri Compromise restriction (always, they held, unconstitutional) at too high a cost. We accepted that restriction, said Millson of Virginia, the one Southern Democrat who stood beside Benton in opposition, because it was fastened on us by others, and was accompanied with some equivalent advantages. But this new restriction "is to be rivetted by ourselves, and we are to submit to sacrifices of opinion and interest for the privilege of doing it!"[95] Most Southerners, however, meant to

94 May 18, 1854.
95 *Cong. Globe.*, 33d Cong., 1st sess., 726.

see that the Cass-Douglas principle should not prevail. Senator Jones of Tennessee put the matter in a nutshell two years later:[96]

"He (Cass) voted for the Kansas-Nebraska Bill; so did I. . . . We voted for the identical clause proving the existence of squatter sovereignty according to his view, and proving directly the reverse according to mine. What was it? That the people of the Territories should be left free to form and regulate their domestic institutions in their own way, subject to the provisions of the Constitution. That Senator believes the Constitution gives them the power, and therefore he voted for it; I do not believe it, and therefore I voted for it. What followed? We agreed to refer that debated question to . . . the Supreme Court of the United States."

Northern anger, widespread Southern dissatisfaction, a fierce contest on the Kansas plains, a nascent schism between two schools of the Democratic party, an embitterment of sectional relations—these were among the direct consequences of the Kansas-Nebraska Act. Henceforth Douglas would have to fight on two fronts, one already blazing fiercely, the other reserving its fire. Against the freesoil attack he had measurably steeled himself, though the revolt of those Northern Democrats who, as they left the party, flung back stinging epithets, found him less well prepared. But the radical Southerners led by Jefferson Davis were determined never to give way to the Douglas interpretation of the new measures, and never to abate their contention that neither Congress nor the local legislature had any power to interfere adversely with slavery in a Territory. Some journals, like the Chicago *Times*, were saying that it required positive law to establish slavery in such an area; very well—the radical Southerners would demand such law. They, too, were ready to offer battle when the time came.

For the time being it was simply the more desperate phase of sectional enmity which counted. Everywhere freesoilers shared the spirit of Greeley, crying, "We of the North have not sought this struggle, but if it is forced upon us, why, we are ready!"; the spirit of John Jay, who declared: "We accept the gauntlet thus thrown down to the free States. I am ready for the fight between slavery and freedom." [97]

Both sides were prepared to wage a desperate struggle for Kansas. And in the background larger forces were at work, destined to determine the outcome of this particular issue and of others allied with it; forces generated by the great developments in the fields of agriculture, transportation, industry, and labor. We have said that some slavery leaders hoped to bulwark the old combination of South and Northwest, and to use a jutting salient of Missouri-Kansas slave territory to so orient most of the trans-Mississippi and trans-Missouri region

96  Cong. Globe, 34th Cong., 3d sess., 151.
97  N Y. Tribune, March 2, 1854; Hart, Chase, 146, 147.

that its commercial, social, and cultural outlook would be southward to St. Louis and New Orleans, not eastward to Chicago and New York. That was a legitimate dream. But the issue would be decided by the deeper economic and social forces of the time. The outcome of the sectional competition which now came to a head in Kansas cannot be understood without some study of the impact of these forces; and to this subject we must now turn.

# 5

## Two Blades of Grass

THE FIRST rancors of the Kansas issue burned fiercest in Congress, and the inflammation soon spread to the Missouri border; but the future of the new Territory was not to be settled in either place. It was on a broader stage that the drama played itself out to its tragic denouement. Its determinants were the forces which shaped the future of the whole American heartland. Here fate was already "choosing sweet clay from the breast of the unexhausted West" to make new heroes; and it was the activities and outlooks of the humble millions who overran the genial, level-lined prairies all the way from the Miami to the Niobrara which fixed the nation's destiny.

The wealth most easily within reach of the busy American population was landed wealth, and the most expansive interest of the nation was its agriculture. A full generation before 1850 settlers had broken across the Appalachians to debouch in an insatiable horde from the land of forests into the land of prairies. Now the movement was rising to its climax. This was the period of what (if we permit ourselves to invent convenient phrases) we may call the Northwestern Surge, filling the upper Mississippi Valley with tillers who wrought a revolution in grain and meat production, and created a hungry new market for the industry-pocketed coast. It was equally the period of the Eastern Readjustment in agriculture, creating a more intensive farm economy in the North Atlantic area to interlock with the rising urban industrialism. The Lower South meanwhile was making the most of its old system, with a generally fixed acceptance of an economy based on a few great staples: the Southern Stasis.

Of these forces the Northwestern Surge proved the most decisive for the American future, altering the whole national balance socially, economically, and in the end politically. First came the rush of settlers, scattering their homesteads over the landscape, separated in rigid rectangular areas of a quarter-section to a section or more; a uniform pattern which placed its mark on the minds of the dwellers. They wrestled with frost and blizzard, flood and fire, tough soil and insect pest, until they developed stubbornness, angularity, and reflective self-reliance. They kept and deepened their native piety. Hard after them came the glistening lines of the railways, and the establishment of a complementary relation between seaboard manufactures and prairie food production. There arose a great new East-West nexus north of the Ohio River; and this marriage of the North Atlantic with the Upper Mississippi Valley was an even more potent event than it seemed.

[ I ]

Agriculture remained the dominant occupation of America, increasing in vigor as farm production diminished in Great Britain and other parts of western Europe. The rural population in 1850 was 17,394,000 or almost three-fourths of the whole; and the westward movement helped keep farming paramount. Since the development of new lands engrossed so much of the capital, labor-supply, and constructive energy of the country, our industrial revolution was slowed in reaching completion. The surpluses of hands, money, and inventive skill were all cut down by tasks of pioneering. According to the census of 1850, some five thousand millions in capital was employed in agriculture (counting the land and slaves), while more than two-thirds the laboring forces was devoted to rural pursuits. The farmer was the nation's most representative figure.

A generation earlier that typical figure might have been found in some New England squire like the shrewd, sturdy Maine countryman in whose home C. A. Stephens grew up, within sight of the White Hills. Well-educated, prosperous, and benevolent, the squire and his thrifty wife presided over a large household of girls and boys. Near by was the trim, quiet village, with clustering houses, three or four churches, some stores, a tannery, a grist-mill, and a flourishing academy. The farm was a place of simple plenty; its house, food, clothing, and mental fare all plain, substantial, and good. Squire Stephens, who took a Congregational view of the Bible and a Whig view of the Constitution, believed in a stock of plain, substantial truths. Though innovations came slowly, he was not the last to adopt a new cornplanter, or to substitute a kerosene lantern for the old whale-oil device. The farmhouse boasted of thirty or forty books: the Bible, *Pilgrim's Progress*, Walker's *Dictionary*, a *Surveyor's Guide*, a few histories, and some novels of Scott, Cooper, and Jane Porter. When the village schoolmaster suggested an encyclopaedia, the squire encouraged the children to help earn the $125 required for a sixteen-volume *Britannica*. Such outdoor amusements as fishing, hunting, and nutting, and such indoor pursuits as church entertainments, a debating society, and "sociables," gave ample occupation. The squire took an interest in politics, and Hannibal Hamlin was a fast friend. Whatever the deficiencies of this New England farm as a business institution, it was a school of character. Hard-work, thrift, and self-denial were part of the daily routine; ethical views were taken of all questions, and morals taught by precept and example; while the youngsters had to show self-reliance, courage, and a capacity for accepting hard knocks. Such homes left their mark on a whole generation.[1]

But by 1850 the representative figure of American agriculture would have to be sought farther west. He could no longer be described in terms of the pioneer generation made familiar by the Lincoln story—that was too crude; nor could he be described quite as Lew Wallace and William Dean Howells drew the rural society of their Ohio and Indiana boyhoods—that was too civilized. Mary Austin's description of the farm people of Macoupin County in Illinois of the fifties comes nearer the mark. Still better is the record given us by James Baldwin's *In the Days of My Youth*.[2]

Here is a sober, hardworking Quaker farmer of Indiana, living in a log cabin with stick-and-clay chimney—but with the skeleton of a new frame house near by. About it stretch the "big woods," especially dense along the watercourses; but he has two large cornfields dotted with charred stumps, a "new deadenin' " of girdled trees shows where more fields are being cleared, and still other areas are marked for tillage. Already an orchard is well grown. The farmer's speech is Hoosier dialect. Yet like the Yankee squire, he is proud of his shelf of books: the *Journals* of George Fox and John Woolman, Walker's *Dictionary*, standard texts like Noah Webster's blue-backed spelling-book, Pike's *Arithmetic*, and Lindley Murray's *English Reader*; some volumes of McGuffey; old classics like *Robinson Crusoe*; and in due time, Dickens. Though his daily dress is blue jeans, he has a "go to meetin' " suit of drab homespun and a gray beaver hat in which he takes on a mien of dignity. This family too enjoys plain but ample food, western in flavors: hot corn dodgers, fried pork, roasted-wheat coffee, plenty of vegetables and pies, foaming new milk. Along with grain and meat, the farmer sends to market some vestiges of the dying pioneer age—such as bundles of coonskins and muskrat hides. In most respects life on the farm is pinched and arid enough. Wabash society is ignorant; prejudices against fiction, plays, and new ideas are immovable; bigotry is general. But the idealism of Fox and Penn still runs strong, while the current of a great movement rapidly catches up the

1  C. S. Stephens, *Stories of My Home Folks*. Agriculture was never regarded in strictly economic terms; it was a way of life, a school of character. Writers of the period, whether in the Jeffersonian or Crèvecoeur tradition, credited it with inculcation of manly independence, integrity, resourcefulness, patience, and stability. See Greeley's *Recollections of a Busy Life*, 295ff.; Herbert A. Kellar, ed., *Solon Robinson, Pioneer and Agriculturist*, II, 102.

2  Agriculture was dominant in every sense. According to the census of 1850, the capital invested in manufactures, mining, the mechanic arts, and fisheries was less than one-seventh that invested in agriculture; $527,300,000 against $3,967,000,000. The number of free males over fifteen employed in agriculture was given by the same census as 2,400,000 or nearly as many as in all other occupations combined. The rural population was estimated at 17,394,000 or three-quarters of the whole.

whole household: copies of the *National Era* are treasured, and when the Fugitive Slave Act is passed, the farm becomes a station on the underground railway. Here, too, rural pursuits were a school for character.

Nothing better illustrated the preponderant place held by agriculture among American activities than the eagerness of the most eminent political and literary figures to identify themselves with it. Here, they seemed to say, was the broad, healthy base of American life. Presidents, Senators, and governors all appeared at agricultural conventions and fairs. Emerson was glad to discourse to the Middlesex Agricultural Society on "The Man With the Hoe," a lecture published far and wide, while Lincoln travelled to Madison to address the Wisconsin Agricultural Society—championing the small farm, and giving shrewd, homely reasons for his distrust of big holdings.[3]

Daniel Webster was ever prominent in agricultural activities; when he visited Great Britain in 1839, his only speech was at an agricultural dinner in the beautiful hall of Queen's College, Oxford,[4] and he was frequently in evidence at similar American gatherings. Whenever the United States Agricultural Society held an important meeting in Washington, the President, be it Fillmore, Pierce, or Buchanan, was likely to be there. At the New York State Fair in Rochester in 1851 the sixty thousand visitors had an opportunity, after inspecting threshers, mowers, and flax-breakers, to hear Stephen A. Douglas. His long discourse abounded in confident if sometimes erroneous apothegms. "Planting and farming are the mutual allies of each other"; the repeal of the British corn laws "was a triumph achieved by the American cotton grower over the feudal aristocracy of the Old World"; as a cheap food, "Indian corn has no longer any real competitor in British markets than the now uncertain crop of potatoes." He foresaw a great future for oil and candles made from the fat of the "prairie whale" or hog. Naturally, he paid repeated tributes to "the illustrious race of cultivators" exemplified by Washington, and to the "scientific and practical" farmers of his own day. Southern statesmen were equally assiduous in addressing planters' conventions, and one of Jefferson Davis's best-read speeches was made at the Augusta county fair in Maine. Even the press of the great cities gave an astonishing amount of space to farming. Not merely because of their wide rural circulation, but because city folk had country backgrounds and connections, the *National Intelligencer*, New York *Tribune*, Springfield *Republican*, Boston *Atlas*, and Chicago *Tribune* devoted no small part of their contents to farm topics.

That agriculture was the main foundation of the American economy, and

3 Emerson's address was widely published (in the N. Y. *Weekly Tribune* of October 9, 1858, for example) and commented upon. Lincoln's might be regarded as a protest against such swollen holdings as those of Jacob Strawn and Michael Sullivant in Illinois.

4 Caroline LeRoy Webster, *Mr. W. and I.*, 52.

that it gave American life much of its wholesome tone of industry, frugality, and integrity, no observer could doubt. And yet the nation's farming fell far short of complete health, for if one distinguishing feature was its immense productiveness, another was its immense wastefulness.

No other land under the sun threw into the world's markets such huge aggregate crops, and no other so recklessly laid waste its soil. The average size of rural holdings was fairly large; according to the 1850 census, 203 acres. Most farms were not so much tilled as exploited. This was partly a result of the fact that American farmers were compelled to economize labor just as British farmers were compelled to economize land. Englishmen visiting the United States were struck with the waste of land while Americans visiting England were struck with the waste of labor.[5] But the ignorant or wilful devastation of great fertile tracts, most conspicuous in the South but visible almost everywhere, was carried to an indefensible extreme. Every year of the fifties average crops of seven hundred million tons of seed cotton, and two hundred and fifty thousand tons of tobacco and sugar, were mined from the soil.[6] It required no great skill to take virgin land, and extract bread, meat, and textiles. Bad plowing, bad drainage, waste of manures, and the cropping of the same field to corn, or cotton, or tobacco, for ten, twenty, or thirty years, till the soil broke down, might almost be called the rule.

One writer, after a rough survey, computed that the deterioration of the soil since white settlement began had detracted at least half a billion dollars, in prices of 1851, from its value. "There are whole counties, and almost whole States," commented the New York *Tribune*, "which would once have yielded an average of twenty bushels of wheat or forty of Indian corn to the acre, yet would now (unmanured) average not more than twenty of corn and five of wheat. 'The virtue has gone out of them.' They have been gradually robbed of their fertility by false, miserable, wasteful culture."[7] Another student, writing in the *National Intelligencer* of 1852, estimated that of the one hundred and twenty-five million acres of tilled land in the country, four-fifths were rapidly being depleted, and only one-fifth were being sustained or improved. The destruction of land, he remarked, passed through several stages. In the first phase few if any worried about the depletion; in the second, random and uncertain efforts were made to supply fertilizers, such as lime, potash, guano, gypsum, and manure; while in the third the owners became genuinely alarmed. Already, he thought, all the older States, both North and South, had advanced into the

5 Cf. William Saunders, *Through the Light Continent*, 227, 228; Arthur Cunynghame, *A Glimpse at the Great Western Republic*, *passim*. Britons also noted that since labor was scarce, it was driven hard, and farmers worked from four A.M. till after dark.
6 These are rough median figures from the censuses of 1850 and 1860.
7 April 3, 1851.

second stage.[8] But careful observers believed that while farsighted farmers in these States annually restored certain values to the soil, they did not as yet compensate for the elements that were being consumed by deep plowing and heavy cropping. The cream of the land, wrote Isaac P. Roberts later in his *Autobiography of a Farm Boy*, was sold for a pittance.

## [ II ]

The Northwestern Surge was much more than a matter of population advance alone, though that was its main component. The increase in the number of people dwelling in the North Central area between 1850 and 1860, reaching 3,693,000, was very nearly as great as the whole population of the country at the first census. This increment was greater than the population of New England when the Civil War began. It raised the population of the North Central States and Territories to 9,097,000. Another year or two, and there would be ten millions in the region bounded by Ohio and Michigan on the east, Kansas and Minnesota on the west. This was roughly equivalent to the numbers in New England and the North Atlantic States combined. It was greater than the white population of all the slave States. The American map was tilting; the center of gravity was moving toward the great upper valley.

Illinois had fewer people in 1850 than Massachusetts, but ten years later, with 1,712,000, it had very nearly half a million more. Its population had more than doubled in the decade. So had the population of Wisconsin, which by 1860 exceeded 775,000, and was greater than New Jersey's. As for Iowa, its population more than trebled, rising from less than 200,000 to 675,000. Ohio, with 2,340,000 people, became the third State of the Union.

What gave this population growth its tremendous significance, as wood trails turned into roads, as canals linked up the rivers and lakes, and as railways carried their clattering cars westward, was the fertility of the soil, and the rapid improvement of farm machinery. Most of the prairie land, turned up in wide, flat, shallow furrows by the powerful "breakers" that required ten or twelve oxen to drag, was marvelously rich. The glacial drift which underlay the surface in Ohio, Indiana, and the greater part of Illinois, thicker than anywhere else in the country, provided a soil of even quality, notable richness, and remarkable endurance.[9] Both the drift country and loess sheets of Wisconsin, Minnesota, and Iowa were almost equally valuable. Here was a broad section that, properly tilled, would without fertilizers yield the pioneer farmer thirty bushels of wheat and seventy of corn. Of course it was seldom properly

8 "L," September 25, 1852. For a British view of this soil-destruction, see Robert Russell, *North America: Its Agriculture and Climate* (1857), 93ff.
9 Nathaniel S. Shaler, *The United States*, I, 105.

tilled. But even so, the average corn crop in Ohio, Indiana, Illinois, and Iowa ran about thirty bushels to the acre during the fifties, while in the South the return was only sixteen bushels an acre. Just before the Civil War, the per capita value of food crops for the Upper Mississippi Valley averaged $75 as against $45 for the nation as a whole. While the Great Valley had wide stretches of poor land, such as the hills of southern Illinois and the broken, forested country of northern Wisconsin, as a whole it was the garden of the republic.[10]

The invention or adaptation of special farm implements for the prairie country had been in full blast by the thirties. The age of home-made devices— cornshuck mattresses, hand-hewn plow-beams, blacksmithed cart-wheels, whittled ox-yokes like that from Lincoln's knife which hangs in the library of the University of Illinois—was giving way to the factory age. An ingenious young Vermonter, John Deere, went to Illinois with his smith's tool-kit in 1837, settled at Grand Detour, and began repairing the farmers' machinery. He quickly noted that the Eastern plows did not scour properly in the heavy Western soil, and undertook some improvements. Before long he was making plows with a share and mold-board of sheet steel, and with wrought-iron standard and white-oak beam and handles. An eager market developed. Mexican War days found Deere selling a thousand plows a year. Then he moved his manufactory to Moline on the Mississippi, induced Pittsburgh firms to begin manufacturing cast-steel plates for him, and increased his output. By 1857 he was marketing ten thousand plows annually.[11] The year that Deere reached Moline, Cyrus H. McCormick arrived in Chicago to arrange for the largest plant yet erected beyond the Alleghenies. In the next dozen years, he manufactured 31,252 reapers—and Deere and McCormick together made the Middle West the nation's greatest wheat-producing area.

The production of improved farm machinery was of course a national and even an international process. The East was as busy as the West. The exhibits at the New York State Fair at Rochester in 1851 included literally hundreds of plows of various models, numerous wheat-drills, a variety of mowers, good horse-rakes at ten dollars which Greeley thought equal to the cumbrous British horse-rakes selling for fifty, and Wheeler's horse-powered threshing-machine, which would separate 150 bushels of grain in a day.[12] British inventors were indefatigable, while in far-off Australia the settler John Ridley devised in 1842

10   C. M. Thompson, "Southern Food Supply, 1859-60," quoted by Avery Craven, "Agricultural Reformers of the Anti-Bellum South," *Am. Hist. Rev.*, XXXIII, 302-314; Sir James Caird, *Prairie Farming in America; National Intelligencer*, March 17, 1855.
11   R. L. Ardrey, *American Agricultural Implements*.
12   The farm machinery exhibit at the Crystal Palace Exhibition in New York in 1853 included not only Hussey's, McCormick's, and Denton's reapers, but a model of the California combine, "an immense double machine, represented to be capable of cutting, raking, and binding the wheat all at the same operation." N. Y. *Tribune*, July 18, 1853.

the grain-stripper, as important for that continent as McCormick's invention for America.

But by the fifties the westward march of farm-implement manufacturing was a notable fact. McCormick's Chicago plant left Obed Hussey's reaper factory in Baltimore so far behind that long before the Civil War the embittered Eastern inventor was practically out of business. Ketchum's successful mowing-

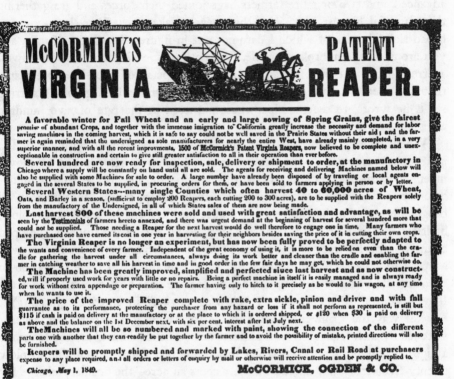

McCormick, Ogden & Company, Poster of 1849.

machine, so improved by 1851 as to cut an acre an hour, was made in Buffalo, and Manny's mower at Freeport, Ill. Residing at Waddam's Grove in Illinois, John H. Manny became an important manufacturer of reapers as well, turning out his machines at various places in the North and West; and he fought with McCormick one of the greatest patent battles of the decade, in which Lincoln and Edwin M. Stanton played a part as counsel.[13] Denton's self-raking reaper was made in Peoria. The Western market had become the most lucrative in the country.

As plows, reapers, mowers, rakes, and threshing-machines poured from the

13  W. T. Hutchinson, *Cyrus Hall McCormick*, I, 431-452; Beveridge, *Lincoln*, I, 575-583.

workshops, the prairies became covered with them. Reports came east in 1857 that single Illinois counties were yielding more than a million bushels of wheat. One writer pictured a midsummer scene.[14] "The clatter of the reaper on every side strikes the ear. Look around and count; twelve, fifteen reapers, each with four horses attached, requiring at least eight hands to gather what each lays in numberless sheaves. Ride to the next knoll; the work is here a little further advanced, and two or more farmers have joined their forces and are gathering the bountiful harvest into ricks; they never make stacks here, but long and broad ricks the size of which I dare not put in figures. Another half-mile, and you are upon the unbroken prairie." An enthusiastic visitor to the Northwest averred that at one time he had counted 164 reapers, followed by more than a thousand men, women, and children, harvesting the golden grain. A stirring sight, he wrote, to see the ripe wheat garnered at the rate of two hundred acres an hour! [15]

When James Caird, M.P., visited the agricultural fair at Springfield, Ill., in 1858, he was struck by the array of serviceable farm machinery. Sulky plows, ingenious corn-planters and wheat-drills, a self-scouring disc, a hand washing-machine, and a chain-bucket pump, extremely cheap, simple, and efficient, all caught his eye. On the endless level prairie near Urbana he saw a steam-plow, built to turn six furrows at once, that was ready for testing. Indeed, the open country, with no trees or hedges to break its sweeping fields, seemed so well adapted to power cultivation that the State Fair offered a prize of $3,000 in 1859 for the best steam-plow, and $2,000 for the next best, to which sums the Illinois Central added $1,500. A "plowing engine" invented by Joseph W. Fewkes was the main entry, and its performance at Freeport was eagerly watched by men from all over the Northwest. The machinists' committee made a highly favorable report, declaring that the implement appeared able to plow twenty-five acres a day at a cost of 62.5 cents an acre—the ordinary charge for breaking virgin prairie being $2.50 an acre. But the officials declined to make the award without further proof of efficiency. Good one and two row corn-planters came in so rapidly that by the Civil War they put in most of the Western crop.

Everybody could see that the next great step in Western farming would be the invention of a grain-binder. To tie the cut grain by hand was too laborious. At the Freeport fair two entries attracted buzzing knots of farmers— a reaper from Auburn, N. Y., which bound the wheat by wire, and another, invented by the tireless John H. Manny, which tied it with a hempen string, fastened at the end by a small cast-iron hook.[16]

14  *National Intelligencer*, September 26, 1857.
15  *Idem*, January 14, 1858.
16  N. Y. *Weekly Tribune*, September 17, 1859.

New Orleans at the Apogee of Its Cotton Traffic

St. Anthony's Falls, Minneapolis. 1856

## [ III ]

With population, fertile soil, and machinery, the Mississippi Valley bade fair to become the chief granary and meat-larder of the world. One of the most interesting pages in the official life of Cyrus McCormick is devoted to a map correlating reaper-sales, railroad extension, and wheat-production in Illinois, 1849–59. The three kept close pace; and while population rose 101 per cent in the decade, wheat-yields rose 159 per cent.[17] Caird's verdict on the boundless possibilities of the Northwest was particularly gratifying to that section. The astute Scot was in some respects the foremost agricultural expert of the world. He had made an agricultural survey of the United Kingdom, publishing his findings first in the London *Times* and then in a book which was accepted as the most valuable work on British agriculture since Arthur Young. He had directed the attention of British capitalists to the agricultural resources of Ireland, thus helping raise that island from depression to prosperity. Whatever he wrote received respectful attention. His tour of Canada and part of the United States in 1858 resulted in the graphic volume, *Prairie Farming in America*, which emphatically argued the superiority of the upper Mississippi Valley over Canada for land-hungry emigrants from Britain. His honest and perfectly sound opinions were of course bitterly attacked by Canadian promoters and journalists, who falsely accused him of holding an interest in the Illinois Central.[18]

The westward expansion registered itself first in a great increase of corn production, and then in a pronounced rise in wheat-growing and cattle-raising. The forties saw corn the ruling monarch of the upper valley; the fifties, with the reaper becoming common, found wheat seizing almost an equal suzerainty. The census of 1840 had reported a crop of 377,532,000 bushels of corn the previous year, and this grew by the next census (the crop of 1849) to 592,071,- 000 bushels—an increase of 58 per cent. In the same decade the production of wheat increased less than 20 per cent, from 84,823,000 bushels to 100,486,000. Naturally, these figures convinced some observers that corn would soon become the most profitable staple of the country. Indeed, one writer contended that the obliteration of two-thirds the maize crop would do the nation greater harm than the destruction of all the cotton. Census returns also demonstrated that corn was more profitable in the Middle West than in any other section—much of the crop reaching the market in the form of pork, and some as whiskey. But in the fifties wheat had its innings. This decade saw the nation's wheat-produc-

17 Hutchinson, *McCormick*, I, 468.
18 See defense in Chicago *Press and Tribune*, quoted in *National Intelligencer*, July 28, 1860. Of other British travellers, Arthur Cunyngham, Robert Russell, and William Ferguson (*America by River and Rail*) made good agricultural observations.

tion rise by seventy-five per cent to more than 173,000,000 bushels, while corn-production gained only about forty per cent. Wheat culture had not merely increased in older parts of the Northwest, but had flowed out across Iowa into Kansas and southern Minnesota.

Corn was likely to be the first food crop of the prairie settler. So long as communications were poor, it would remain favored, for it could be driven to market on the hoof. But as agriculture gained a strong footing and communications improved, wheatfields multiplied. In Kansas, after some experimenting, it was found that winter wheat flourished. By 1857 one of the earliest settlers was writing that he had never known a wheat crop there that was not fair, and that he believed wheat a surer crop than maize. Steadily the rich Middle West drew ahead. In 1860 Illinois was by far the leading corn State, with Indiana, Ohio, and Missouri running neck and neck behind. Illinois, Indiana, and Wisconsin then led the nation in wheat production, with New York and Pennsylvania (suffering from the midge, winter-killing, and soil depletion) hopelessly behind.[19]

Meanwhile, the Northwestern Surge also carried the center of livestock marketing to Chicago, St. Louis, and Milwaukee. Climatically, the zone which follows the fortieth parallel from the Eastern seaboard to the Rockies is one of the world's best areas for beef-production. Here stock can be fattened more rapidly, and mixes its lean and fat, marbling the flesh, more evenly, than in belts to the north or south. In colder regions cattle use large quantities of feed simply to maintain animal heat, and their dark-colored meat shows no proper mixture of fat. In the hot Southern belt beef tends to become stringy, and the fat to form solid layers of tallow.[20] What one historian has called the American Beef Belt stretches, at its widest extent, from the 36th to the 43d parallel. By the middle fifties a good many shrewd men were grasping the value of the rolling Western plains as a cattle area. An observer who published his conclusions in the Louisville *Courier* asserted that beyond the Missouri the open tall-grass country would be valuable primarily for cereal production, and the short-grass or buffalo-grass country as a grazing area.[21] The corn-belt stretching from Ohio through Iowa was of course ideal for hog-growing.

Every elderly New Yorker could remember when the cattle slaughtered in the metropolis had come from neighboring areas, and when drovers from Westchester, Connecticut, New Jersey, and Long Island had brought their

19 J. C. Malin, "Beginnings of Winter Wheat Production," *Kansas Hist. Quart.*, X, No. 3. The *Democratic Review*, January, 1849, pp. 76–82, discussed the changing agricultural situation and remarked: "The power of cotton over the financial affairs of the Union has in the last few years rapidly diminished, and bread stuffs will now become the governing power."

20 J. W. Thompson, *Hist. of Livestock Raising in the U. S.*

21 July 22, 1856; quoted by Malin, *ut supra*.

lowing herds to the cattle-market at Bull's Head Village, just off the Boston Post Road in what is now lower Manhattan. But by the middle fifties more than half the cattle killed in New York, Philadelphia, and Baltimore came from the Middle West. In 1855, according to an expert in the trade, these three cities slaughtered about 285,000 head, while Boston took 10,000 more. Fully half the total, or 150,000 head, were shipped by rail from the huge area bounded inclusively by Ohio and Illinois, Kentucky and Michigan. The Erie alone carried 56,789 cattle, and the Hudson River Railroad 48,503. The same area sent the Eastern markets by rail at least 600,000 live hogs.[22]

Great herds of cattle were regularly driven overland as well. The cost of rail transport was so high—$195 or $200 for a car (holding fifteen large steers) from Chicago or Indianapolis to New York—that many Westerners preferred the highway. To drive steers all the way from Illinois to New York, feeding them on corn, cost in 1853 about thirteen dollars apiece. But if they were pastured on roadside grass and in hired meadows, taking sixty days for the journey to Philadelphia and seventy to New York, the cost could be kept much lower, or only $5 to $9 a head.[23] Just how many came overland we do not know. Great numbers of beeves were partially fattened on the corn and grass of Iowa and Illinois, and then finished off in Ohio, Pennsylvania, or New York. The large Eastern cities by 1860 looked to the Middle West for most of their meat; and by that time the reduced rates of the through railroads were ending the long, hard trans-Allegheny drives.

Naturally, meat slaughtering (and especially pork packing) tended also to move westward. Illinois, as the keystone State of the Middle West, possessing the greatest railroad center, was the logical seat of the industry. It was a heavy producer of beef. One stockman, B. F. Harris of Urbana, claimed for a time the title of cattle-king of the country. On his four-thousand-acre farm he raised annually about five hundred cattle and six hundred hogs; and in 1853 a hundred of his beeves, weighing just short of a ton each, took the premium at the world's fair in New York.[24] Another grower, Isaac Funk of Bloomington, sold fourteen hundred head of cattle in one lot in 1854; still another, Jacob Strawn, for years dominated the St. Louis beef market. But it was for pork that Illinois was becoming most famous. The number of hogs raised in 1850 fell a little short of two million and by 1860 exceeded two and a half million. European observers remarked that while Western cattle were inferior to theirs, Western swine were much inferior. While towns like Alton and Peoria became great slaughtering centers, Chicago was achieving worldwide fame for her meats. Curing had been

22 S. G. Rennick, *Report on Cattle Transportation*, 1856; *N. Y. Tribune*, April 12, 1856; Bouck White, *The Book of Daniel Drew*.
23 Patent Office *Report*, 1853.
24 Chicago *Tribune*, quoted in *National Intelligencer*, May 8, 1856.

done in such slovenly fashion before 1850 that European buyers had rebelled, but it was rapidly improved.[25]

Throwing a canal southwestward in 1848 to link Lake Michigan with the Illinois and the Mississippi, throwing railroad after railroad, like spokes of a half-wheel, across to the Mississippi, throwing the Illinois Central southward, Chicago was soon in a position to bring the cattle, sheep and hogs of the West to her yards. When in 1852 the city cheered the first flag-bedecked trains of the Michigan Central, spanning the 270 miles to Detroit, and heard the first whistle of the Michigan Southern (soon to be part of the Lake Shore-New York Central system), it enjoyed two competitive lines to the Eastern seaboard. Chicago was thus able by the year of the Kansas-Nebraska Act to fix the prices for cattle and hogs for the entire region west of Cincinnati and north of St. Louis. Its packing-houses grew steadily in number and size. City regulations drove the noisy pens and reeking abattoirs out to the south branch of the Chicago River. Along the sluggish stream the stockyards widened, the packing-plants sprawled in ever-larger units, and the railroad tracks multiplied. The smoke of the lard-rendering furnaces rolled black across the town, and when the wind blew from the south the reek of offal, blood, and manure came with it. By 1861, Chicago was the greatest general meat-packing center of the world.[26]

The growth of Eastern manufacturing and merchandising, and of Western grain and meat production, were reciprocal processes. Hundreds of little towns that had been self-sufficient as to food in 1820, drawing all they needed from horse-haul radius, were by 1850 thriving, hungry cities, buying food from afar. Gone were the days when Alexander Hamilton could grow his vegetables in the huge kitchen-garden of his suburban "Grange," and when Nicholas Biddle could bring a winter's supplies from his neighboring farm. The London *Economist* pointed out that the consumer population of America was rising fast in proportion to the producers. "It is now some time," it declared in 1855, "since the States of New York, Pennsylvania, and others in the East ceased to produce as much grain as they consume, and every year adds considerably

25  Cole, *Era of the Civil War*, 83; British Consular Reports, FO. 5/519, William Mure, April 5, 1850; P. W. Bidwell and J. I. Falconer, *Ag. in Northern U. S. 1620–1860*, pp. 388ff.
26  Bessie L. Pierce, *Chicago*, II. Attention was being paid in the West to blooded stock. Caird, visiting the fair at Springfield, Ill., found shorthorn cattle of good quality, and thought one cow would have taken a prize in any English show. The exhibitor had a shorthorn (Durham) bull imported from Lord Ducie's stock the previous year. "The large stock farmers of the west, who are the really moneyed men," wrote Caird, "are taking great pains to improve the quality of their cattle by the importation of the best English blood." Yet large areas in eastern Illinois, as rich as any in the world, were still without settlers. N. Y. *Weekly Tribune*, March 26, 1859. In 1859 national attention was attracted by a sale of blooded cattle in the Kentucky bluegrass region, fifteen miles from Lexington. Among those present were Vice-President Breckinridge, John J. Crittenden, and Ezra Cornell, with buyers from all over the East. Durham cattle, Cotswold and Southdown sheep, and several race-horses, one of which brought $15,000, were sold. N. Y. *Weekly Tribune*, June 11, 1859.

to the quantity they require from the West. Again, California, where the crops in the present year are deficient, has become a large additional channel for the surplus of the Western States." All this was correct. The East was changing its emphasis from grain to other staples. The government had lately reported that the keen California demand had levied a heavy toll on the number of Missouri cattle and raised their price two hundred per cent. New York city, with only 313,000 mouths to feed in 1840, had 814,000 people in 1860.[27]

In older parts of the Northwest, too, population was shifting from food-production to food-consumption. Cities and towns were beginning to cluster thickly in Ohio. When Easterners complained in 1854 that beef was atrociously high, an observer in central Ohio pithily wrote that it was true; that his district would furnish it cheaper if it could; but that they had their home markets to supply. He could take any visitor to hills which had once commanded a view of eight or ten herds, but now showed as many smart villages, filled with buyers instead of graziers. "Not only have great numbers of cities and towns grown up among us like mushrooms, but we have hundreds of railroads . . . which keep in employ thousands of hands, receiving high wages, which enable them to pay high prices for meat, and they want nothing better than fresh beef. . . . Our consumers have increased faster than our growers." [28]

## [ IV ]

The Northwestern Surge, raising the competitive level of agriculture and giving it a profit-basis in place of the once widely established subsistence-basis, forced a thorough-going readjustment of tillage in the Middle Atlantic and New England areas. Farmers in these regions found themselves unable, with old crops and old methods, to meet the pace set by the prairies and plains. Many of the strongest, most energetic, and most enterprising moved west. In its report for 1852 the Massachusetts Board of Agriculture pointed to the increasing importation of foodstuffs from the West, and the decrease in farm production at home. Although tilled lands had slightly expanded during the previous decade, cereal crops had fallen by more than 600,000 bushels a year; and although the pasturelands had risen by more than a hundred thousand acres, the number of neat cattle had remained practically stationary, that of swine had dropped by 17,000, and that of sheep by more than 160,000. The board contrasted the thrift, industry, and skill conspicuous in the State's manufactures with the low condition and slow progress of its farming.

One broad aspect of the Eastern Readjustment was the movement toward

27 *Economist,* quoted in *National Intelligencer,* October 6, 1855; Patent Office *Report,* 1853.
28 *National Intelligencer,* May 9, 1854.

an intensified agriculture, recognizing the Western primacy in meat and grain, the rise in land values, and the special demands of the new industrial towns. Half-deliberately, half-instinctively, farmers turned to milk and cheese; to winter-keeping apples for the cities and for export—Baldwins, Jonathans, and Rhode Island Greenings; to Green Mountain and Early Ohio potatoes; to strawberries, gooseberries, and blackberries; to cauliflower, beets, cabbages, and carrots.[29] In Connecticut and Massachusetts by 1855 about 1,870,000 pounds of tobacco were grown. Buckwheat and broomcorn brought Yankee farmers many a dollar. With such crops they could make the most of their land. The average size of York State farms dropped sharply in the fifties, while the value of buildings and equipment rose. By the end of the decade the New England farm averaged but little over 100 acres.

The "milk sheds" of Boston, New York, and Philadelphia also began to emerge—districts that were now shipping milk in metal containers by way of rail and steamboat. Orange and Putnam County milk in New York and Bucks County milk in Pennsylvania were obviously preferable to the stuff sold by the nauseous city dairies. The Harlem Railroad carried about 15,000,000 quarts of milk into New York in 1847; about 25,000,000 quarts in 1861. Much of the Hudson, Mohawk, and Delaware valleys, too, was slowly turning into an immense orchard. Farmers in many areas took to specialties, some old and some new; maple sugar had long been familiar, while cranberries, which did not appear on the official crop returns of Massachusetts in 1845, sold for more than $135,000 ten years later. Turnips, Swedes, and mangolds for cattle-feeding became profitable crops.[30]

By a natural evolution, the dairy industry developed swiftly from a purely household basis into a highly organized business with many well-capitalized units. John Burroughs, like many another lad of the time, recalled seeing his mother lift the great masses of golden butter from the churn with her ladle, piling them in a big butter-bowl with the drops of buttermilk standing upon the glistening surface. Then the butter was worked, washed, and packed; the spring product going into fifty-pound tubs to be shipped as fast as churned,

29 Ephraim Bull, a goldbeater by profession, made a hobby of grapes in his little garden on Fayette Street, Boston, later removing to Concord for room. Anxious to produce a stable variety that would be large, sweet, long-keeping, and early enough to face New England's autumn frosts, he fanatically pushed forward his experiments with an early-ripening specimen of the wild northern fox grape (*Vitis labrusca*). For eleven years in Concord this monomaniac planted, selected, and tested his stock. Raising 22,000 seedlings, he found twenty-one worthy of preservation. In 1853, in the Massachusetts Horticultural Hall, he triumphantly exhibited the Concord grape. But commercial nurseries soon stepped in and wrested his trade in seedlings from him, leaving him an embittered old man. On his grave in Concord cemetery is a stone with the accusatory epitaph, "He sowed, others reaped."
30 Robert West Howard, *Two Billion Acre Farm*, 86–105; Patent Office *Report*, 1861, 216ff.; *National Intelligencer*, June 10, 1856; Bidwell and Falconer, 368–386.

the summer product placed in hundred-pound firkins to be held over till November. To sell six or seven thousand pounds of butter a year, at prices which rose slowly from twelve cents to eighteen or twenty cents a pound, was considered very satisfactory. This was small business, and countless housewives, taking a weekly supply from cool spring-houses to their village customers, did a smaller trade still. But in the Hudson Valley, in Connecticut, and in parts of Rhode Island and Massachusetts large dairy farmers arose, increasing in numbers and scope. As cities grew and demand multiplied, a business basis became easier to reach. Better cattle were bought—Ayrshires, Devons, Guernseys, Holstein-Frisians—and within a generation after 1850 the average yield of milk climbed from 166.5 to more than 300 gallons a year.[31]

The cheddar cheese of Connecticut and up-State New York was so good that long before the fifties a large export trade had developed. It, too, was at first produced on a household basis. But in 1853 the first cheese factory was built in Oneida County in western New York, and 1860 saw over thirty in operation. The sixties were to spread them in hundreds all over the map.[32] Meanwhile, vegetable-canning was becoming an important Eastern industry. The bottling of food had commenced in Europe early in the century. An Englishman, Peter Durand, had presently improved upon the process by packing fruits and vegetables in "tin canisters"—iron or steel containers plated with tin to protect them from rust. His method reached America before 1820, and "tin canisters" soon became "tin cans." At first the principal foods thus preserved and marketed were lobsters and oysters, with some fruit jellies and preserves. But a Maine whaler who wanted fresh vegetables for his crews at sea suggested the canning of sweet corn, and about 1846 or 1847 the first successful consignments were ready. Doubtless this skipper, whose name was Isaac Winslow, never guessed how important a path he was blazing. In 1848 the S. S. Pierce Company of Boston began to handle the product at a wholesale price of thirty-three cents a can, and a brisk demand arose. Before many years, canneries throughout the Atlantic States were busy turning out corn for a rising world market—and beside them sprang up first pea-canneries and then tomato-canneries.

Livestock breeding was an attractive field for hundreds of Eastern agriculturists. "It is said, with undoubted correctness, that more horses are now sold for two thousand dollars and upward than were sold for two hundred dollars

31 Burroughs, *My Boyhood*, 16–18; Joseph Schafer, *Social History Amer. Ag.*, 135, 136; Howard, *Two Billion Acre Farm*, 97.
32 Gail Borden, working in the old Shaker community at Lebanon, N. Y., had his first tins of condensed milk ready in 1853, and obtained his patent in 1856. But it was not until 1860 that he began manufacturing in quantity, and selling his unsweetened condensed milk from white carts in New York at twenty-five cents a quart. Borden Papers, Univ. of Texas Archives; Clarence R. Wharton, *Gail Borden, Pioneer*.

and over twenty years ago," a writer upon New England agriculture declared in 1861. Throughout this decade New England and New York were areas from which blooded stock was taken to the South and West. George Wilkins Kendall, intent in 1852 upon a great wool-growing enterprise on the cheap Texas lands, went to Vermont for his pure-blooded Merino sheep, and to Scotland for his collies and shepherds. At the great horse show at Springfield, Mass., in 1853, sales of blooded horses at from $500 to $1,500 were commonplace. The two great strains of New England horses, the Morgan and the Black Hawk, which combined the qualities of good driving and saddle horses with those of steady work animals, were in keen demand. This was the decade in which Frank Forrester's classic work on *The Horse and Horsemanship in the United States and the British Provinces* (1857) found an admiring public. As for cattle, a keen competition among the Durham, Devon, Guernsey and other breeds, which were now being grown in large numbers in the Northeastern States, helped to elevate the standards of breeding.[33]

Poultry farming was by no means neglected in the East, and particularly near the cities. The early fifties witnessed a veritable poultry mania, which ran riot over Europe and America alike. Originating in a genuine desire to improve breeding standards, it culminated in an extravagant speculation in blooded fowls. British fanciers frequently paid eight or ten guineas for a single pair of chickens, and sometimes forced the price to fifty guineas or higher. At the Boston Fowl Show in 1852, three Cochin Chinas were sold for $100, a pair of gray Chittagongs fetched $80, and three gray Shanghai chicks brought $75. Oriental fowls, obviously, reached the highest levels. One Boston fancier in the single year 1853 sold $25,000 worth of poultry. His orders from the Lower South often came in sums varying from $500 to $1,500, and one of his single shipments to Louisiana amounted to $2,230. The "hen fever" found its historian in one Beekman. "It is very certain that people were mad on the subject of hens," he wrote, "and that they acted extravagantly, crazily, and too often with the rankest dishonesty of intention." But the mania gave a genuine stimulation to the poultry industry.[34]

### [ V ]

Another aspect of the Eastern Readjustment was the growing crusade for scientific tillage and scientific soil-restoration. This, indeed, was a national movement; it was vigorously pushed in the border States and the older cotton

---

33 Patent Office *Report*, 1861, p. 256; Kendall, June 22, 1852, to Franklin Pierce, Pierce Papers.
34 See the article on the poultry mania in *Hunt's Merchants' Magazine*, May, 1855.

States; but it was unquestionably strongest and most effective in the North Atlantic and New England areas.

For two full generations the scientific impulse had been gaining strength. Ever since a few gentlemen in and near Philadelphia, meeting in 1785, had set up the Philadelphia Society for Promoting Agriculture, since John Taylor of Carolina had written his *Arator* articles in 1803, and since the Baltimore postmaster, John Stuart Skinner, had established the pioneer agricultural journal, the *American Farmer*, in 1819, centers of illumination had grown in number. They diffused a flickering, misty light, but they at least made the circumambient darkness visible. Some reformers, like Job Roberts, author of *The Pennsylvania Farmer* (1804), were simply practical men who loved progress and hated waste. Roberts showed that by careful cultivation and the use of lime, phosphates, and manures, sixty bushels of wheat could be grown to the acre. His gospel was summed up in a sentence: "Fifty acres of land, properly managed, will produce more than five hundred, badly conducted." He believed with Goldsmith that every rood of ground should support its man, and assured farmers that niggardliness with labor and fertilizer meant poverty. "Praise large farms," he quoted Virgil, "but cultivate a small one." Such practical men were useful. But already true scientists, who knew something of soil chemistry as founded by Sir Humphrey Davy and developed by Justus von Liebig, and who eagerly followed the experiments which John Bennett Lawes of Rothamstead, England, systematically began in 1843, had arisen.

In New England no worker was more earnest or intelligent than Marshall P. Wilder, chairman of the Massachusetts Board of Agriculture, who during the fifties was also head of the only great national farmers' organization. In Pennsylvania J. R. Tyson; in Maryland, Charles B. Calvert; in Virginia, Edmund Ruffin; in Georgia Dr. William Terrell; in New York (after 1851), the prolific Solon P. Robinson—these were among the agricultural leaders of the seaboard States. Greeley said that he had left the farm because in his boyhood it offered merely work for an ox. This alert group, of whom Wilder, Ruffin, and Robinson were the salient leaders, meant to lift farming high above that level.

It was as promoter and organizer that Wilder, a versatile, multifariously active man, left his mark. Born the son of a village merchant in New Hampshire, he had an indefeasible taste for rural pursuits; and though he entered business, went to Boston at twenty-seven, and was partner in a number of successive commission firms, as soon as he earned a competence he followed his natural bent. Setting up a nursery at Dorchester, he began to develop new varieties of pears, roses, and other fruits and flowers. As head of the State horticultural society, he issued the call which brought about the formation (1848) of the American Pomological Society, which long did more than any other agency to stimulate the country's fruit-growing interests. He then took steps which resulted in the establishment of a State board of agriculture (1852), of which he was appointed senior member. Thanks chiefly to his initiative, this body issued a series of valuable reports.

But there seemed a crying need for some national organization in the field. From time to time prominent men, including Stephen A. Douglas, had proposed the formation of one. In pursuance of resolutions passed by the Massachusetts board and other farm bodies, Wilder issued invitations for a convention at Washington, and the United States Agricultural Society (1852) was the result. He was at once chosen president; Daniel Lee, an official of the Patent Office, became secretary; relations were established with the three hundred agricultural societies of the country; and before many months passed the first number of a handsome 144-page quarterly journal was before the public. The organization seemed an assured success.

Indeed, the United States Agricultural Society made such steady growth that in 1858, when Wilder was succeeded by Tench Tilghman of Maryland, its executive committee announced arrangements for opening a permanent office in Washington, collecting a library, and issuing a monthly bulletin. The annual meetings, accompanied by exhibitions or fairs, attracted throngs of visitors. When the third was held in Boston in 1855, the speakers invited included Everett, Choate, Winthrop, and Sumner. The fourth exhibition the following autumn in Philadelphia brought to that city a quarter of a million visitors, representing every State from Texas to Maine. On the gala day, under a brilliant October sun, a hundred thousand people presented what seemed to some newspaper writers the grandest spectacle they had ever seen.[35] Louisville was host to the fifth annual exhibition. As head of the Massachusetts board, Wilder had contrasted the backwardness of agriculture with the enterprise which stamped most other departments of labor. But, believing that the country would soon see the necessity of promoting experimentation and education, he hailed the opening of a new era. "The old worn-out systems of cultivation which have been followed by father and son, and from generation to generation, are now to be swept away, and science is to take its place in aid of honest industry." [36]

If Wilder was an organizer, honest Solon Robinson was primarily a writer. Of Connecticut birth, a descendant of the Pilgrim pastor, he had become a shopkeeper and land-dealer in northern Indiana, where his formation of a settlers' union for protection against land-speculators won him the title of "king of the squatters." Beginning in 1837, this jack-of-all-trades—country

35　*National Intelligencer,* October 21, 1856.
36　*Report,* Mass. Bd. of Ag., 1852; presidential address, June 25, 1852.

editor, justice of the peace, postmaster, town planner, farmer—contributed voluminously to agricultural journals. His restlessness, ill-health, and numerous business interests led to a remarkable series of travels, and his genial, homely essays of rural observation in almost every State, published in the *Cultivator, Prairie Farmer*, and *American Agriculturist*, made him almost an American Arthur Young. He, too, believed that agriculture needed systematic organization and government help, and played no small part in the United States Agricultural Society. But he attained his widest influence when in 1853 he became agricultural editor of the New York *Tribune*, which through its weekly edition reached scores of thousands of the most intelligent farm homes in the country. Far more than Greeley, Robinson was a practical farmer, with a Westchester farm which furnished the basis for many of his articles. More fertilizer, deeper plowing, better draining and fencing, use of the best tools— such were his constant exhortations.[37]

Edmund Ruffin of Tidewater Virginia was organizer, writer, and scientist all in one. His career dated from the days when, discontented with the poor yields of the farm to which he brought his bride after the War of 1812, he adopted Sir Humphrey Davy's suggestion that acidity of soil might be corrected by applications of marl. Successful experiments led him to prepare a volume on *Calcareous Manures* (1832), which ran through five editions; to establish a good farm journal, the *Farmer's Register;* to organize a county agricultural society; and to undertake the secretaryship of the State board of agriculture. Writing innumerable papers, delivering countless speeches, serving as head of the State agricultural society, he filled the decades 1840–60 with useful endeavor.

Like others, Ruffin drew a strong contrast between the exhausting and the conserving systems of agriculture. He turned the worn-out lands of his "Marlbourne" into a magnificent estate, where he made large profits from wheat, corn, and livestock grown with well-supervised slave labor. He found most Virginians conservative and unappreciative; but when the passionately progressive James H. Hammond invited him to make an agricultural survey of South

37 H. A. Kellar's two well-edited volumes of Robinson's selected writings cover the years 1825–1851; a compilation of his N. Y. *Tribune* writings would be useful. By 1860 New England had at least eight good agricultural journals, of which the *New England Farmer*, issued weekly in Boston with Simon Brown as editor, was the oldest and perhaps the best. In New York City, Orange Judd was owner and editor of the *American Agriculturist*, a large and finely-printed monthly which was in its nineteenth year, and probably had a larger circulation than any other farm journal in the land. Almost as celebrated was the *Horticulturist*, once edited by A. J. Downing, and now conducted by Peter B. Mead. Other farm journals of the Empire State were the *Country Gentleman*, published weekly at Albany; the *Cultivator*, a monthly, and Moore's *Rural New Yorker*, a weekly issued from Rochester. First place in the Middle West was taken by John S. Wright's *Prairie Farmer*, a weekly more than twenty years old; and first place in the South was probably held by the *Southern Planter*, published in Richmond by Augustus Williams. Demaree, *Agricultural Press*; N. Y. *Weekly Tribune*, December 1, 1860.

Carolina in 1843, he prepared a report which contributed powerfully to Hammond's movement for Carolina crop-diversification. Year after year Ruffin overtaxed his frail body in an effort to make the Southern farmer and planter more careful, more energetic, and at least modestly scientific. But it was not these activities which brought him to his tragic end. His semi-fanatical loyalty to the South demanded political outlets, and by 1850 he was a fiery protagonist of slavery and State Rights. A leader of Cato's sternness, a man who would break but not bend, a Puritan who had shown grim satisfaction in watching John Brown die, he took his own life when the spirit of John Brown triumphed.[38]

Other rural leaders of future renown were appearing. A young Scot, William Saunders, who reached America in 1848, was rapidly making a reputation as a landscape architect when in 1855 he contributed an article to the *American Farmer* picturing an organization such as the National Grange later became. That dream he was to pursue until it became a reality. Another young Scot, Peter Henderson, established a market-garden and greenhouse near Jersey City, opening in 1853 a New York office where he took orders for plants and seeds. He was shortly fixing a new standard through the vitality and purity of his seed, and the merit of the new plants which he introduced. By his researches, and the essays which he frequently contributed to magazines, he powerfully aided in discrediting the ignorant, selfish, and slipshod methods of the old horticulture. A young German, Eugene Woldemar Hilgard, a graduate of Heidelberg, reached America in 1855 equipped with an expert knowledge of chemistry, geology, and botany. First employed as chemist in the Smithsonian Institution, he soon became assistant State geologist of Mississippi; and studying soils, vegetation, water-supply, and mineral fertilizers, he printed in 1860 a report which, though not distributed until 1866, gave Mississippi agriculturists their first true knowledge of these subjects. An Ohio farmer, Jacob S. Leaming, began in 1856 some experiments in selecting seed-corn for productivity and early maturity which notably increased the yields on the fast-widening areas which his grain reached. In every State, indeed, a select body of men accepted Edward Bates' dictum: "The perfect success of agriculture depends on land, labor, and learning." [39]

While the rich soils of the Northwest seemed as yet to require little replenishment, the older lands of the seaboard States needed fertilizer, and a prominent feature of the Eastern Readjustment, registered in a Pacific guano-rush that might almost be compared with the gold-rush and copper-rush, was

38 Avery Craven, *Edmund Ruffin, Southerner*, does full justice to this remarkable figure.
39 Speech to Missouri Agric. Soc., *National Intelligencer*, October 13, 1855. It was often pointed out that British farmers had more learning and got better yields. Our agriculturists "work too much and think too little," said one Yankee expert. Harry J. Carman, "English Views of Middle Western Agriculture, 1850–1870," *Agricultural History*, January, 1934.

a systematic application of nitrogen—along with phosphates and potash—to worn-out farms. Liebig had shown in a series of London lectures in 1840 that plant life contained nitrogen as well as hydrogen, carbon, and oxygen. He erroneously believed that it drew this element from the atmosphere by means of ammonia carried by rainwater. At Rothamstead, Lawes and his associate Henry Gilbert proved that the addition of nitrate of soda to the soil spectacularly improved the crops of wheat. Before the forties ended, artificial fertilizers were on the market in both England and America. Von Humboldt had long tried to introduce guano into Europe for fertilizer, but it had first been imported there for chemical use. When farm journals and agricultural societies began to popularize the new scientific discoveries of Lawes, Liebig, and certain French chemists, a keen demand for the cheap natural nitrogen sprang up. Shipload after shipload began to come in from the Chincha Islands, lying off the Peruvian coast, where veritable guano cliffs existed. By 1857 a hundred thousand tons a year were being brought to the United States.[40]

Within twenty years after 1850, in fact, British and American ships had taken some eight million tons of guano from the Chinchas alone. Other vessels searched the Pacific, the American Guano Company fetching fertilizer from Baker's and Jarvis Islands. Enthusiasm for the product rose to extravagant heights. "Whole counties of the South, previously exhausted by bad farming, have been speedily renovated by the use of this Peruvian dust," declared the New York *Tribune*, "until it is doubtful whether the annual depreciation of Maryland, Virginia, and the Carolinas through slavery is not compensated by the extensive and steadily increasing use of guano." [41] As much might be said for some New England and North Atlantic districts.

Guano, costing about $50 a ton on the seaboard in the early fifties, was always reckoned expensive. When the Peruvian government placed a high export price on the crop, with various restrictions, an instant outcry arose. Farmers of the border States, protesting that they could no longer afford the precious fertilizer, met in an indignant convention at Wilmington in March, 1856; and a larger gathering, representing farmers from New York to the Carolinas, was held in Washington the following June. A committee which called on President Pierce was told that the government had taken every possible step for their relief, but without avail.

Indeed, the State Department had long shown great interest in guano supplies. When Daniel Webster was its head, he had conducted a little controversy with Peru over the Lobos Islands, and his successor Marcy had not neglected the subject. Now Congress, in the summer of 1856, passed an act

40 Howard, *Two Billion Acre Farm*, 101, 102; Address by J. R. Tyson, *National Intelligencer*, January 7, 1857.
41 May 24, 1854.

providing that any American citizen might take peaceable possession in the name of the United States of any uninhabited island containing guano deposits and not in the possession of another government. This, the first step for the acquisition of overseas holdings in our history, resulted in the occupation of Howland's, Baker's, Jarvis, and Christmas islands, with thirty-odd others of lesser value—many later abandoned. The Peruvian envoy, De Osma, was stung by the farmers' threats of forcibly overthrowing his government's "monopoly" into publishing a defiant letter.[42]

Ideas of soil-maintenance, as the guano mania proved, were still crude and elementary. As time passed, considerable feeling grew up against guano, veteran farmers declaring that it was a stimulant rather than a true fertilizer, imparting temporary power but likely to leave the soil weaker in the end than ever.[43] Certainly it was not to be applied indiscriminately. Gradually a knowledge of the nitrogen-storing value of clover and other plants spread. Gradually, too, a specific adaptation of mixed fertilizers to different soil types was learned by farmers who had once simply spread marl and guano without previous tests. By the middle sixties more than a hundred fertilizer factories in the Baltimore-New York area were selling patent compounds of phosphate, nitrogen, and potash. But even simple ideas of fertilizing were usually better than none; and the constant preaching of men like Solon Robinson, who urged the use of manure, ashes, bonedust, lime, guano, nightsoil, dead leaves, plaster, and swamp-muck, helped the East to readjust its agriculture. "Nothing but manure," asserted Robinson, in arguing for more stock-growing, "is wanted to renovate the worn-out lands of Connecticut."[44] He might have added that the tile-drainage crusade instituted by John Johnson, a Scot who had settled near Geneva, N. Y., was also of the highest value in this section.

[ VI ]

"Our present system," the Hon. J. Foster Marshall told the State agricultural society of South Carolina at its second annual fair at Columbia in 1857, "is to cut down our forest and run it into cotton as long as it will pay for the labor expended. Then cut down more forest, plant in cotton, plough it uphill and downhill, and when it fails to give a support leave it. . . . Then sell the carcass for what you can realize, and migrate to the Southwest in quest of another victim. This ruinous system has entailed upon us an exhausted soil, and a dependence upon Kentucky and Tennessee for our mules, horses, and hogs, and

42  S. F. Bemis, *Diplomatic Hist. U. S.*, 402; see the *National Intelligencer*, June 12, 1856, for the De Osma controversy.
43  *National Intelligencer*, January 16, 1858.
44  Kellar, *Solon Robinson*, II, 420; Howard, *Two Billion Acre Farm*, 104.

upon the Northern States for all our necessaries from the clothing and shoeing of our negroes down to our *wheelbarrows, corn-brooms and axe-handles.*" [45] He was but repeating what other South Carolina leaders, notably George McDuffie in 1840 and James H. Hammond in 1843, had told the agriculturists of the Lower South. Their advice, too, he echoed in urgent terms: plant less acreage in cotton, diversify your produce, and fertilize your land. Specifically, he said, they should put a quarter of their cotton land in wheat and corn, manure it heavily, and raise all their own pork, beef, and horses.

There had been a Southwestern Surge, but it had taken place long before the Northwestern movement. In the five years 1815–20, almost half a million Americans moved southwestward. They brought statehood to Mississippi in 1817 and to Alabama in 1819; they filled up Louisiana (which had become a State in 1812), spilled into Arkansas (which by 1820 had 14,000 people), and began to settle Texas. This huge migration had one ruling passion—cotton. The earliest settlers in the Gulf area and lower Mississippi Valley had grown grain, livestock, fruits, tobacco, and sugar, but now the lands were covered with fleecy white. Thus was built up the great domain of King Cotton. The irresistible tide of settlement rang the knell of the Jeffersonian dream for the South. For Jefferson had believed that America should become great through a vigorous population of yeomen farmers, each growing substantially what he needed to make himself independent; his own breadstuffs and meat for food, textiles for clothing, and timber for housing. He believed, too, that ultimately slavery might be abolished as a dire wrong to the weaker race, and a clog upon the finer development of the nation. Instead, the tremendous expansive thrust which cotton gave to Southern agriculture entrenched a one-staple money crop in great areas, leaving the grower dependent on other regions for tools, garb, and grain; the yeoman farmer made room for the aristocratic-minded lords of many acres; and slavery became a 'permanent' institution. [46]

By comparison with the dynamic Northwest and refronting East, much of Southern agriculture by 1850 seemed locked in a static frame. Everywhere progressive men were trying to shake and reshape it, but with indifferent and uneven success. That the slavery system tended to keep the South an almost exclusively rural area; that it confined agriculture largely to a few great staples like sugar, tobacco, and cotton; and that it forced many of the less efficient freemen into the demoralizing status of poor whites—these are familiar truths. [47] But slavery was far from being the only factor. Poorer communications than in the North; a less productive soil, by and large, than in the prairie regions; a climate less conducive to hard, sustained labor; a slower rate of population

45  Address, November 11, 1857, issued as pamphlet.
46  Gray, *Agriculture in the Southern United States*, II, 691ff., 861ff.
47  Cf. Robert R. Russel. *Economic Aspects of Southern Sectionalism, 1840–61.*

increase, all had their effect in reducing the pace and scope of change. The South carried the burden of a tariff which at its highest rate was painful, and at its lowest irritating. Operating largely on a debtor economy, accumulating but small financial reserves, and leaving too much of the crop proceeds in the hands of Northern brokers, bankers, and merchants, Southerners felt it necessary to mine quick profits out of the soil. Then, too, the large planters of the Lower South maintained a special standard of living, almost a reproduction of the English landed-gentry order, which impelled them to exploit to the utmost the soil resources of the region.[48]

Of the fifteen slave States, only nine produced any considerable amount of cotton; and it was in these nine that agricultural methods became most nearly stagnant. The planters of the Lower South, because of their dependence on cotton, sugar, rice, and tobacco, their frequent changes of overseers, the high Negro death rate, and the steady deterioration of their land, were in a somewhat more precarious position than those of the Upper South. Yet despite frequent reverses, they tended constantly to enlarge the scale of their operations; and this expansion was from the economic standpoint the worst feature of the system. They were deluded victims of the before-mentioned policy of buying more slaves to grow more cotton to buy more slaves for making more cotton. In prosperous times they were irresistibly tempted to enlarge their labor force and landholdings, and in hard times they had no spare money for diversification. There grew up a stolid and even defiant acceptance of this order of affairs as immutable; some men labored for change, but the majority were inert.

The South had fallen into a rut—a concentration of attention upon cotton and a few other staples, a centralization of slaveownership in a decreasing proportion of the population, an expansion of units of production, and a bad financial system. John Randolph's maxim, "Pay as you go," was ignored. "One great cause of the incessant struggle to make large cotton crops, to the neglect of every other interest, is the reckless habit of contracting debts," said George McDuffie in 1840. "Negroes are purchased upon credit, and the planter is thus furnished both the means and the motives for unduly and disproportionately enlarging his cotton crop. As cotton is the only crop that will command money, and as money is the most pressing want of a man in debt, everything is directed to that object." [49] One sagacious Southerner remarked that he outstripped his neighbors because they began at the wrong end of the year: they purchased necessities at the beginning on credit and paid at the end with heavy interest, while he bought at the end for cash. Debt was in fact a reason commonly

48 Avery Craven, "The Agric. Reformers of the Ante-Bellum South," *Am. Hist. Rev.*, XXXIII, 302-314. Cf. James C. Bonner, "Genesis of Agricultural Reform in the Cotton Belt," *Journal Southern History*, IX, 474-500, which deals with the need and the reformers.
49 Anniversary Oration, State Agric. Soc., 1840, issued as pamphlet.

assigned by Southerners for sticking to one ready-cash crop, and not infrequently their creditors insisted on this course.

From the days of John Taylor of Caroline in Virginia and the indefatigable George Jefferys of North Carolina, the South had no lack of agricultural reformers. While their work was most fruitful in the border region and the upper South, it was far from unimportant elsewhere. The roll has been called by a careful student of Southern history. Theoderick McRoberts of the *Virginia Farmer;* A. G. and William Summer of the *Southern Agriculturist,* in Laurensville, S. C.; Daniel Lee and other editors of the *Southern Cultivator* of Augusta, Ga.; N. B. Cloud and Charles A. Peabody of the *American Cotton Planter,* its office in Montgomery; J. M. Daniels, R. B. Gooch, and F. G. Ruffin of the *Southern Planter,* in Richmond; J. D. B. De Bow of the New Orleans *Commercial Review;* and above all, Ruffin. To this list should be added Thomas Affleck, a Scot, who from his large commercial nursery and plantation in Mississippi exercised a wide influence; transferring his residence in 1857 to Texas, but continuing his experiments and writings. We have noted that Affleck not only preached careful accounting methods, but published two well-planned plantation account-books (one for cotton and one for sugar growers) to facilitate the keeping of records. He inveighed against the folly of Southern reliance on the North for supplies. Especially after his removal to Texas, he urged greater attention to breeds of livestock; and holding that the prime need was for an animal that would put on flesh rapidly, and then not fret it off on the way to market, he recommended the Durhams, Devons, and Herefords.[50]

In Maryland, Virginia, and North Carolina the progress toward better agricultural methods was fairly comparable with that in the North Atlantic States.[51] Ruffin's influence in the Old Dominion grew until the Richmond *Whig* asserted that "thousands" were indebted to him for their prosperity, the Petersburg *News* declared that he had done more for Virginia than any other man living, and the United States Agricultural Society gave him honorary membership for driving the "garb of barrenness and desolation" from his State.[52]

50 Fred C. Cole, "Texas Career of Thos. Affleck," MS Dissertation La. State Univ. Library. Mention should also be made of William Terrell, of Sparta, Ga., who sat in Congress 1817–21, and took a lifelong interest in better farming. "To him more than any other man," said the Savannah *Republican* when he died in 1853, "are we indebted for the organization of agricultural societies and State fairs, and for the improved stock of horses and cattle now observable in all parts of the State."

51 One Virginian, the venerable G. W. P. Custis, addressing the United States Agricultural Society in 1854, pointed to the immense advance in his lifetime. When in his youth the old Arlington sheepshearing was established to improve sheep culture, it was thought wonderful if a yearling sheep produced twelve pounds of wool. In those days one of his plantations with a hundred hands on it had yielded seven to nine thousand bushels of wheat a year; now he expected to take fifteen or twenty thousand. *National Intelligencer,* February 25, 1854. For Custis's own defects as a farmer, see Douglas Freeman, *R. E. Lee,* I, 129, 130.

52 Craven, *Ruffin,* 89, 90.

The papers of quite another Ruffin—Judge Thomas Ruffin of North Carolina—are full of notes on agricultural improvements. An applicant for a farm managership assures the judge in 1855 of his belief that many changes for the better might be introduced into North Carolina. He has read various scientific works; and "to be brief, I will say that my whole theory of proper farming consists in clover, the free use of concentrated manures, and a proper *rotation of crops.*" A friend about the same time informs Ruffin that he is ordering the much-advertised Rescue grass seed, and Dr. Battey's boasted potato from Rome, Ga., while he has bought six tons of Mapes's improved superphosphate at $70 a ton. Various notes refer to the use of guano, marl, and other fertilizers, and to the introduction of the osage orange for hedges. From the University of North Carolina in 1854 comes word that an agricultural course, emphasizing soil chemistry, had been introduced. These papers reveal the vigor of the State agricultural society, and the wide influence of William D. Cooke's *Carolina Cultivator.*[53]

But in most parts of the South the way of the innovator was hard. No such revolution could be effected by machinery as harvesters, cornplanters, and new plows brought to the Northwest. Farm equipment was meagre. The middle fifties witnessed an effort at a mechanical cotton-picker,[54] but it was far in advance of its time. Experiments with a machine to convert cotton into merchantable yarn on the plantation also failed. Cotton meant endless toil, necessarily by hand. The Northwestern farmer might sow his wheat in October, and have little more care until his gaily-painted reaper clattered into the field the next July. But the cotton-planter started his plows in January, and from then until August waged an incessant war with men and mules, hoes and plows, against the luxuriant grass of the Southern climate. In autumn the prairie farmer might sit down at leisure to roast turkey and apple-pie, but the cotton-grower's Negroes were in the field from dawn till dusk picking their crop boll by boll. Nor was it easy to find new products. Perhaps the most significant experiment was announced in 1854 from Galveston, where a Mr. Shepherd had succeeded in pressing oil from the cottonseed previously considered a mere nuisance. He found that a hundredweight of seed yielded from twelve to fifteen pounds of oil which, properly clarified, was as good as sweet oil for machinery, and better than ordinary lamp-oil for illuminant, while it could be sold at one-third or one-half the price. What was more, the cake from the pressed seed was valuable for feeding livestock.[55]

Certain progressive tendencies were visible in parts of the South—a stirring of life, enthusiasm, and new ideas. Northern Virginia and wide tracts of

53  J. G. deR. Hamilton, *Papers of Thomas Ruffin*, II, *passim.*
54  MS Diary of W. P. Gould, December 30, 1856, Ala. State Dept. of Archives and Hist.
55  Galveston *Journal*, July 6, 1854.

Maryland, abandoning tobacco as a one-crop system, saw large estates broken up into small farms and plantations, attracting some Northern immigration, and conducing to greater efficiency. General grain and stock farming was introduced, with some dairying, and these areas began to take on the thrifty, progressive look of southern Pennsylvania. Small farms multiplied also in Tennessee and Kentucky. North Carolina brought a good deal of rich alluvial land into cultivation by drainage. While Northwestern Virginia and the Shenandoah Valley continued to be one of the rich wheat-growing regions of the country, the district about Norfolk was already gaining fame for its truck-gardening, selling its products in Baltimore and Washington. The Piedmont country of both Virginia and North Carolina found profit in general farming and in cattle, hogs, and sheep. During the fifties the two newly developed States of Arkansas and Florida showed a specially notable increase in cattle and hogs, while Texas was clearly on the way to becoming one of the great livestock areas of the country. The fifties found the number of horses and mules in Texas more than quadrupled; the number of cattle similarly multiplied by four; and the number of sheep increased more than sevenfold. The piney-woods frontier in Mississippi was also a notable cattle-raising country, where immense herds subsisted on the coarse grass and reeds growing among the long-leaf pines and along the creeks; and the lasso or catching-rope, the periodical round-up, and the horse-outfit of the cowboy had a development here paralleling that on the Texan plains.[56]

Already the Southwestern cattle-drive was beginning. Texas was crowded with cattle; the East and Northwest offered an eager market, and the overland trails were being blazed. By the later fifties Texas cattle were crossing the Mississippi in large numbers at various points between Hannibal and Keokuk. An early driver has left in the University of Texas archives his graphic record of how he bought cattle on credit in Coryell County for ten or twelve dollars a head. "It was all an experimented venture with us, we had no certainty as to where we could find a market, or what we could get for the beeves, it was all guesswork we had no news from the outside world, about matters of this kind, like we have now, but one thing we did know, and that was that the country was full of fine fat beeves, and the citizens wanted a market opened so they could get the money for them. . . ." On his second drive he encountered "what we then called a blewtailed norther, they were very common in Texas forty to sixty years ago," and lost all the money he had made on the first; but even this second venture "was a success, as far as the citizens was concerned as it put over two thousand dollars in money in circulation in the county, in ex-

56 Gray, *Southern United States*, II, 924–942; W. H. Sparks, *Memories of Fifty Years;* Gordon Linthicum, *Autobiography, Miss. Hist. Soc. Pubs..* IX.

change for their beeves, which no one else had attempted to do." [57] While this buyer did not go as far north as Illinois, others did. The first through drive from Texas to Chicago was probably made in 1856—and soon the bellow of long-horns was familiar along the lake front.

But despite the stirrings of progressive ideas, despite the merited popularity of such monthly periodicals as the *Southern Planter* issued from Richmond and the *Southern Cultivator* published at Augusta, despite the work of the State fairs,[58] the South as a whole continued in its unhappy rut. It is easy to overestimate the improvement effected by Edmund Ruffin and other leaders in the seaboard States. Some lime was used in the upland country, and marl where available in the tidewater, but otherwise, except among a few wealthy agri-culturists, the essential features of Southern tillage were altered much more by the breakup of estates than by new principles.[59] And in the Lower South they were hardly altered at all. A note of desperation had crept into the appeals of some early reformers. "We cannot contend with the planters of Alabama and Mississippi," declared George McDuffie, "in a wild and destructive system, by which even they have sunk under embarrassment and ruin, with all their advantage of soil and climate. . . . While they are exhausting their soil and preventing the natural increase of their slaves by a reckless system of pushing and driving, let us improve the fertility of the one by resting and manuring it, and increase the number of the other by moderate working, and by providing everything necessary for their health and comfort." [60] But although South Carolina was sorely in need of crop diversification, it did not come; and still less did it come elsewhere in the Deep South. The extent of Southern de-pendence on the Northwest for corn meal and pork has sometimes been over-stated, but the dependence had existed and it continued to exist.

The general Southern prosperity of the fifties made it easy for the section to accept its old pattern as fixed. Some men proposed increasing the land area by annexations; others proposed increasing the slave supply; but few demanded a new system.[61] Certain results of the old system were deplorably plain. By the census of 1850, Georgia, North Carolina, and Virginia had 22,192,000 acres

---

57  John H. Chrisman, MS Reminiscences, 1864–65.

58  The Montgomery correspondent of the *National Intelligencer*, writing in the fall of 1858 of the State fairs of Alabama, Tennessee, Georgia, South Carolina, and Mississippi, spoke of the prizes awarded a new cornplanter, cottonpress, and other implements. "These annual festive occasions are producing their legitimate effects upon the Southern people. Already one who has been in attendance upon them since their inception a few years since can see, in the improved foreign and domestic breeds of cattle, the blooded horses, the ingenious plantation implements, the better systems of cultivation, the neater farm arrange-ments, that the beneficial effects of these gatherings are being impressed upon the hearts and the hands of the masses." November 11, 1858. This was partly a rhetorical flourish.

59  R. H. Taylor, *N. Ca. Hist. Rev.*, 1932.

60  Anniversary Oration State Ag. Soc., 1840.

61  Gray, *Southern United States*, II, 936.

of improved land, and Illinois, Indiana, and Ohio 19,938,000. But the cash value of the farms in the three old States, with their improvements (and depletions) of two centuries, was only $380,100,000, while that of the three new States was $591,300,000. The middle fifties found James L. Orr plucking the same string that McDuffie had struck a quarter century earlier. The planter, he said, tried only to increase the number of his cotton bales, forgetting every-thing else—and how little of his roll of money was left when he had paid the merchant, corn-grower, and stock-drover! A variegated agriculture would bring with it personal supervision, system, order, and economy in small matters, all neglected in producing one great staple. As matters stood, wrote Orr, the planter grew poor even while he seemed to be handling large sums, the farmer of the border amassed wealth more rapidly, and within a generation, the popula-tion of Tennessee and Kentucky would be far richer than the orgulous baronial society of the Lower South.[62]

## [ VII ]

Progressive farmers who recalled that Washington had recommended, in his last annual message, vigorous Federal action for the promotion of agriculture, found it deplorable that hardly even the first step had been taken in that direc-tion. Representative Eben Newton, a farmer-lawyer of Ohio, proposed early in the fifties that an agricultural office should be established to collect statistics, procure and distribute seeds and plants, maintain a chemical laboratory, and make itself generally useful. But since his bill, providing for five employees in all, would have involved an annual outlay of slightly more than ten thousand dollars, Congress recoiled from the idea. When Stephen A. Douglas addressed the national agricultural convention held in Washington in June, 1852, he objected to any bureau or department as certain to become a nest of meddle-some, incompetent politicians. Instead, he suggested, the Smithsonian Institution should devote itself to agriculture. As it stood, that scientific agency yielded no practical results; "abstruse and theoretical subjects were all the professors busied themselves about"; and it seemed likely to become odious to the public. Douglas wished Henry and the eminent Smithsonian scientists to turn im-mediately to farming, geology, and mechanics, with an eye not to theory but to grassroots utility! Fortunately, nothing was done in this direction; and in fact, nothing was done at all.

We have noted that the agricultural activities of the Patent Office, the sole national agency in the field, were meagerly supported. In the dozen years before 1850 the annual appropriations had climbed slowly from $1,000 to $4,500.

62 Address, S. Ca. Institute, *National Intelligencer*, June 5, 1855.

This driblet was the government's scientific patronage of the central activity of the nation, of an industry which in 1850 yielded products worth one and a third billions of dollars. But with this pitiful stipend the Office accomplished wonders.

Its greatest achievement, beyond doubt, was the introduction of the sorghum cane or "Chinese sugar cane" into the country in 1854. Seeds had been sent from China to France, where an agent of the Office, collecting information and products, saw it thriving. A distribution among members of Congress followed so that experiments might be made in all parts of the Union. They proved highly satisfactory. The following year the Office obtained a larger shipment of seed by way of South Africa and London, and quantities of sorghum molasses were soon being barrelled in the United States. As the government predicted, the plant took an important place in farming both North and South.[63] The Office also distributed seeds of the kohlrabi (described as a vegetable reminiscent of both the cabbage and cauliflower), of the "Cassabar" melon, and of improved varieties of beets and turnips. From France and Hungary it brought new types of wheat, and from Italy barley. Whenever better varieties of corn were produced (for example, the Brown corn, an improvement upon the King Philip corn of New England), it described their merits and faults. In 1856 it sent an agent to investigate the grasses of every State in the Union. Following in Jefferson's footsteps, it introduced choice varieties of French figs in the hope that the South and Southwest would take them up.[64]

Financially starved as it was, the Patent Office carried on a wide correspondence with farmers. It gained some useful information from our consuls abroad —one of Douglas's pet ideas was that these officers should be required to collect all the information possible regarding crops and modes of production. It published occasional statistics of yields, which never had more than general accuracy, and were sometimes called grossly misleading, but which represented a gallant effort. Midway in the fifties it deputed a naturalist, Townsend Glover, to study insects beneficial or pernicious to a wide range of farm products, and he shortly presented a useful report on the joint-worm, then ravaging border wheatfields. Altogether, the Office deserved better support than the tiny appropriation to which it had attained by the middle fifties. But the rule of Americans in that era was to add cautiously and slowly to governmental activities. Lieutenant Matthew Fontaine Maury, one of many who perceived that a good weather bureau was needed in Washington, presented through the *American Farmer* in 1855 a plan for a general system of meteorological observations. As much might be done for agricultural and sanitary meteorology, he believed, as for that of the sea, and he besought farmers and planters all over

63  *National Intelligencer*, December 25, 1856.
64  Annual Reports.

the Union to exert pressure upon Congress to furnish a basis—that is, a central office with a staff—for the work.[65] His idea bore no immediate fruit.

Yet little by little something was done to lay foundations for a future Department of Agriculture, a future Weather Bureau, and future colleges of agriculture. If literary, theological, and technical colleges, why not colleges for farmers? This question was asked by editors of farm journals, publicists like Greeley, Solon Robinson, and Marshall P. Wilder, alert educators, and a good many plain husbandmen. Slowly the movement gathered strength. The Maryland legislature in 1856 passed a bill authorizing the establishment of an agricultural department or college at the University of Maryland, with at least three professorships. The next year it was announced that Michigan had created a college of agriculture at Lansing, with a small endowment from the sale of some salt-spring lands held by the State, and with an appropriation of $20,000 annually for the first two years. Greeley complained that while Prussia boasted of half a dozen agricultural colleges, New York lacked even one, and that the legislature had again and again voted down proposals for an institution. When a correspondent remarked that it was the farmers (distrustful of taxes and theory) who had defeated the bill in the legislature of 1851, while city members had voted for it, Greeley sadly admitted that this was true.[66]

The most imposing and fruitful movement, however, was that for national aid to a general chain of State institutions. The legislature of Illinois, spurred on by Jonathan B. Turner, one of the "Yale band" who many years before, standing under the New Haven elms with only the stars as witnesses, had pledged themselves to go to the prairies as missionaries, in 1853 urged Congress to endow an industrial university in each State by a grant of public lands amounting to at least $500,000 apiece. Other men were fired by the same grand conception. In 1855 Justin S. Morrill, whose father had been a farmer and blacksmith, entered Congress, and two years later he introduced a land-grant bill. President Buchanan promptly vetoed it—but in due time it was to be revived.[67]

## [ VIII ]

When the shadow of impending civil conflict fell across the land, the United States, then much the richest agricultural nation in the world, could look back upon a decade of general prosperity for planter and farmer. For the cotton-grower the skies were clouded chiefly by factors connected with the single-

65 Maury's letter, dated August 25, 1855, is in the *National Intelligencer*, September 18, 1855.
66 See *U. S. Agric. Misc. Pub.* 251 (1937), *History of Ag. Experimentation and Research in the U. S. 1607–1925; National Intelligencer*, March 4, Nov. 1, 1856, for the Maryland action.
67 M. T. Carriel, *Turner*, 74ff.; Parker, *Morrill*, 278ff.

crop system and institution of slavery. For cereal and meat producers of the Northwest the principal adverse factors were the high costs of transportation and marketing. There were times when prices dropped to cruelly low levels. Thus early in 1858, when America and Europe were suffering from an economic depression, Western farmers complained that it was difficult to get even forty cents a bushel for wheat or twenty for corn; and an Eastern editor exclaimed, "Wheat forty cents a bushel in Illinois, and flour nine dollars a barrel in Washington!" [68] Yet the general rise of prices, stimulated by gold mining, the worldwide elevation of standards of living, the growth of cities as immigrants poured in from Europe, and the keen Old World demand resulting from the abrogation of the British corn laws, several short crops, and the Crimean War, kept most farmers well satisfied. When the Allies moved against the Czar, not merely did millions of men go under arms, but the usual flow of grain from the Danubian and Baltic areas was suspended.

Indeed, in the middle fifties prices of breadstuffs rose so steeply as to give serious concern to workingmen and the urban middle class. The fall of 1855 found large grain operators in Chicago buying wheat at the rate of 100,000 bushels a day and paying $1.50 a bushel; while newspapers in Lincoln's Springfield recorded sales of wheat at $1.69 a bushel, and new corn at twenty-five cents.[69] Though the total wheat crop that year was estimated at 175,000,000 bushels, and the corn yield was exceptionally good, purchases for German, British, and French account were so large that market quotations continued to rule high. "The prices of flour have been enormous for more than a year," grumbled a New York correspondent. "They are still far too high for the general good." They remained high for two years. In the early autumn of 1857 wheat was fetching $1.80 to $2.12 a bushel in New York, corn 80 cents, and oats 52 to 57 cents.[70]

By the close of the decade fully two-thirds of the good tillable land of the country had been effectively occupied. Beyond the Mississippi, the State of Missouri had 1,182,000 people; Iowa had 675,000; Texas had 604,000; and Arkansas counted 435,000. Minnesota, Kansas, and Nebraska contained 300,000 more. As population moved westward, so did transportation. "We have long iron arms extending far into the productive West," wrote Greeley. Great areas were still to be opened up: the wheat lands of the Dakotas, the range country

68 *National Intelligencer*, January 14, 1858.
69 *Idem*, November 8, 29, 1855. The apex of the Crimean War demand found Grinnell, Minturn & Co. of New York, with other merchants, buying largely for foreign account. In the fiscal year 1855–56, exports of breadstuffs came to very nearly sixty million dollars, equivalent to about half the value of cotton exports, and amounting to almost one-fifth of the entire foreign exports of the country. This gave an impetus to Northwestern growth. "With due notice of the foreign demand," said the *Bankers' Magazine* (February, 1857), "the wheat regions of the United States can enlarge their product from fifty to one hundred per cent in two or three years."
70 *National Intelligencer*, October 11, 1855; N. Y. *Tribune*, September 21, 1857.

extending from Texas to the northern Montana boundary, the central valley of California, the wide reaches of Oregon and Washington. That was a task for the next generation. Meanwhile, the Eastern Readjustment would have to be pushed forward, and the work of Ruffin, James H. Hammond, and Thomas Affleck given deeper root in the South.

But the dominant fact of the decade had been the Northwestern Surge— the huge folk-movement that had lifted the number of dwellers in the dozen States now called the North Central group from four and a half millions to

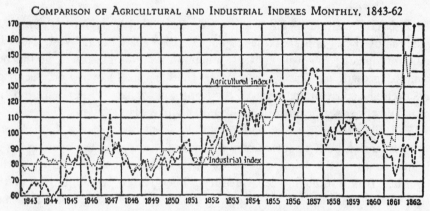

COMPARISON OF AGRICULTURAL AND INDUSTRIAL INDEXES MONTHLY, 1843-62

Note the marked price-rise at the time of the Crimean War.

From A. H. Cole, "Wholesale Commodity Prices in the United States, 1843–62," Review of Economic Statistics, February, 1929.

more than nine millions. Cotton was king, said the South. But was it?—or would it long remain so? It was roughly computed at the close of the fifties that the Northwestern section was producing about two hundred million dollars in exchangeable values a year, and the South was producing about four hundred millions.[71] But the Western rate of growth was so much more rapid than that of the South that this difference was being steadily cut down. If the old river-system link between the Gulf and the Northwest could have been maintained as a dominating factor, the surge of the decade would not have seemed adverse, but beneficial, to Southern interests. But it was not maintained. Instead, the trend of communications and the interchange of raw materials for manufactured goods created, as we have said, an east-west nexus of ever-growing strength.

In the wake of the folk-movement into the Northwest, and indeed to a great extent accompanying it, came the rails; and their superiority as a means of communication over old modes of water-transport made them not merely a great economic and social force, but a political factor of the first consequence.

71 *Annual Cyclopaedia,* 1861, p. 107.

# Web of Transport

"THE RAILROAD FEVER," remarked the Philadelphia *North American* in the fall of 1855, "appears rather to increase than abate in the West. The vast results of opening the iron lines of communication, as illustrated in the un-exampled growth of Chicago and other cities in the Lake region, seems to have excited a spirit among some of the rising towns that will not rest until the Great West is fairly gridironed with railroads like Massachusetts." [1]

Well might men speak of vast results. Railroad building was fundamental to the expansion both of agriculture and manufacturing, to the opening up of the new lands of the West, and to the creation of a national market as distinguished from a thousand local markets. The greatest economic fact of the fifties was the throwing of a network of rails from the Eastern seaboard into the upper Mississippi Valley, giving the course of trade a new direction, and establishing a broad basis for exchange of the products of the prairie plow with those of the North Atlantic workshop. The shouting and hammering of track-layers resounded along the seaboard, through Appalachian defiles, and deep amid the cottonfields of Alabama and Mississippi—but above all, across the prairies of the Old Northwest. In the brief space between the elections of Zachary Taylor and Franklin Pierce, 1848–52, the length of the lines open for travel practically doubled. The head of the census bureau, writing to the French Government early in 1852, reported that the United States then had some 10,800 miles of railway built, with almost 10,900 building; and by the end of the fifties, he predicted, it would possess at least 30,000 miles of finished track. He was right, for it then had 30,626. [2]

The pride or ambition of every community was a shining track and the lively whistle of a well-laden train, with the accompanying statistics of crops hauled, mills built, and values enhanced. What does the railway do for farmers? asked the Athens (Tenn.) *Post* in 1855. Before the railroad reached eastern

---

1 Quoted in *National Intelligencer*, October 13, 1855.
2 J. C. G. Kennedy, March 1, 1852, to Jules Cartin, French Minister of Public Works, printed in *National Intelligencer*, March 13; *U. S. Statistical Abstract*.

Tennessee, it answered, the three counties of Bradley, McMinn, and Monroe grew less than twenty-five thousand bushels of wheat, and sold it for less than fifty cents a bushel. But the fall of 1855 found them growing four hundred thousand bushels, and selling it for a dollar.

And what could a railroad do for a large city? To this query the *National Intelligencer*, a few months later, gave its answer. "If ever there was a blessing sent in good time to any spot upon earth," it exclaimed, "the Baltimore & Ohio Railroad has proved such to Baltimore. The building of this pioneer road has saved it and the property-holders from impending ruin and desolation. Instead of being on the decline, as it was from the years 1817 to 1830, we now behold it in the full tide of prosperity, and all its greatness is yet to be developed." This was done, it added, "by the wisdom, energy, and untiring perseverance of the good and true men who conceived and those that forced through almost to completion this road, the greatest of the great enterprises of its day; for at that time the idea of building a railroad to the Ohio was a thing chimerical and beyond belief; that the iron horses should ever meander the Cheat River, and with unheard of speed, harnessed to a ponderous iron load, dash safely across the Allegheny Mountains, was too preposterous for the wildest imagination. But what was then a dream is now chronicled history, and Baltimore has a population of two hundred thousand souls and is seventy-five millions richer." [3] This picture was not overdrawn. Baltimore, which was not a great manufacturing center, enjoyed a rich Southern and Western trade in all sorts of consumers' goods, a trade which the railway had created. The Erie Canal in 1825 had given New York a paramount place among seaboard cities, but the B. & O. kept Baltimore prosperous. [4]

Railroad building in America had been slow until after the effects of the panic of 1837 fully wore off. From 1830 to 1848 only about six thousand miles of rails were laid. Then, with foreign investment, the westward movement, rising industrial production, California gold, and immigration, came a great leap forward. In the years 1849–57, nearly seventeen thousand miles were built. [5] The North Central States were far and away in the lead, the Northeastern States came second, the South Atlantic States were third, and the Old Southwest stood fourth. To anyone who looked at a railroad map it was plain that this railroad building tended to link the Northeast and Northwest together; to make the citizens of Indiana and Illinois, Iowa and Wisconsin, look

3 September 6, 1856.
4 S. F. Van Oss, *American Railroads as Investments*, 268ff.; Edward Hungerford, *The Story of the Baltimore & Ohio*, I, 268–316.
5 The first great impulse, said the Washington *Union* of May 31, 1850, came with the year of European famine, 1847, when prices of farm products soared and exports were heavy.

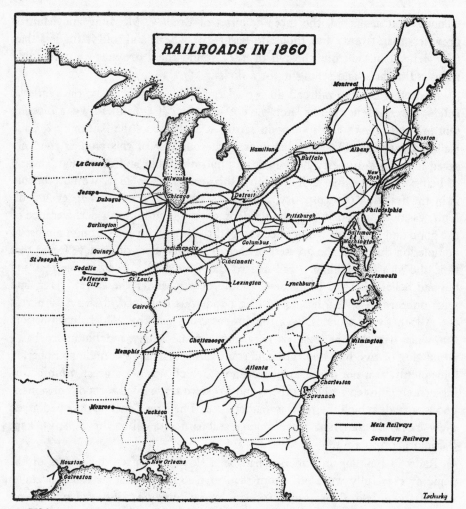

*This map, neglecting some short lines, pertains to the beginning of 1860.*

toward New York and Philadelphia, rather than down toward the Gulf. By the end of 1857 the lines stretching westward had reached the Mississippi at ten points. Four roads, the New York Central, Erie, Pennsylvania, and Baltimore & Ohio, were already young giants, and lusty rivals for the traffic of the central valley.[6]

[ I ]

Native and foreign capitalists joined hands with States, counties, and cities in providing funds to maintain this "railroad fever." Such an alliance was

6 Caroline E. MacGill and collaborators, *Transportation in the United States Before 1860*, 487–550.

indispensable, for building at the rate of two thousand miles a year required larger sums than the country had thrown into any previous endeavor. In level parts of the South and Northwest construction costs averaged little if anything over $20,000 a mile; but in the Middle Atlantic area they rose to $40,000, and in New England to $45,000. The United States was still poor in working capital, and the general growth of the nation created innumerable demands for money.[7]

The loyalty of States and cities to their special railway projects was often impressive. Instances could be found in Virginia and Illinois, in Buffalo and Savannah. But we may best cite the way in which Baltimore staunchly supported the great road over which a succession of her ablest citizens, Philip E. Thomas, Louis McLane, and Thomas Swann, presided, and of which the universally esteemed Benjamin H. Latrobe was principal engineer. When in the fall of 1851, with five thousand men and twelve hundred and fifty horses pushing the road on its last lap to the Ohio, and with payroll charges alone reaching $200,000 a month, its solvency trembled in the balance, the new generation of merchant princes and bankers which had arisen in Baltimore doggedly shouldered the burden. Such men as Johns Hopkins and Robert Garrett were determined that it should never fail. Maryland had done her share in furnishing credit and cash; Virginia, on condition that the road run west from Harper's Ferry on the south bank of the Potomac, had subscribed heavily—though it later withdrew its support; and so had Wheeling. Baltimore had grown so rapidly in the forties that citizens boasted that the $3,500,000 originally subscribed by the city had been more than returned in the enhanced value of realty. Wheeling had been placed on the map by the line. Now everybody agreed that the mighty final effort must be made. The whole of Maryland thrilled as on Christmas eve in 1852, at Rosby's Rock, the last spike was driven, and two glittering lines of iron connected the Ohio at Wheeling with tidewater at Baltimore, 379 miles distant. After a quarter-century of effort, victory had been won.[8]

More than a year earlier the Erie, the longest continuous railroad line in the world, had been opened from end to end with a ceremonial journey by Fillmore's Cabinet. Its 537 miles of track had cost $23,580,000—for that time a colossal sum. Uniting the Atlantic and the Lakes by a well-built roadbed hewn

7 A salient figure in collecting capital for railroads was Jacob Little, a native of Newburyport, Mass., who made a fortune in New York as an exchange and specie broker, and then turned to the new railroad movement. For a time, "every successful project for a new railway had him for a director, manager, or friend; if he said nay, the scheme fell to the ground." He became known as the Railway King before the name was bestowed on Hudson in England. See sketch in *Harper's Weekly*, September 18, 1858. Forbes, the Boston capitalist, entered the railroad field in 1846; Sarah Forbes Hughes, *John Murray Forbes*, I, 118. The figures on construction costs here given are from Kennedy's letter cited above.

8 Hungerford, *Baltimore & Ohio*, I, 198ff. A four-column description of the opening of the Baltimore & Ohio from Cumberland to Fairmont, Va., with special train, cannon salutes, and banquet, is in the *National Intelligencer* of July 13, 1852.

through hilly country and flung across the Delaware and Susquehanna, with bridges and viaducts of solid masonry, it had been under construction for nearly twenty years. The State advanced six millions, which it later made a gift, and the energetic S. B. Ruggles and other projectors raised the remainder by selling securities. They had contended with sore difficulties. The charter had been won only after a bitter struggle with the Canal Ring at Albany; the jealous northern counties, fearful that the Erie Canal would lose some of its traffic, had stipulated that the line should operate only in New York State, and should not connect with any Jersey or Pennsylvania railroad; and the panic of 1837 had dealt the builders a heavy blow. The road touched no populous city, and its six-foot gage proved a terrible handicap. Its projectors, however, were indomitable men.

It was a curious road, the Erie. It followed no established trade route or important river valley; its terminals were two mere hamlets, Piermont on the Hudson and Dunkirk on Lake Erie; and its management was not of a kind which commanded high public confidence.[9] Nevertheless, New York was proud of it. That same year of 1851 found a much more modest line, the Hudson River Railroad, open all the way from New York to East Albany; while in 1853 nine small roads linking Albany and Buffalo were consolidated into the New York Central. Complete union of the Hudson River and the Central was to wait for many years, until the strong hand of Cornelius Vanderbilt took control at the close of the Civil War; but meanwhile fairly speedy through transit was provided for both passengers and freight. It was cheap transit, too, for charges were slashed heavily to meet river and canal rates. For some years passengers were carried between New York and Albany at an average of a cent a mile.[10]

Philadelphia and Pennsylvania, lagging behind their rivals in New York and Maryland until they faced total eclipse, finally threw themselves with desperate frenzy into the provision of a really efficient trunk line. The opening of the Mexican War found freight still being hauled across the State by a crude combination of short railroads, canals, and inclined planes. An eighty-two mile railroad ran from Philadelphia west to Columbia on the Susquehanna; there the passenger took a boat on the Central Pennsylvania Canal to Hollidaysburg at the foot of the Alleghenies; thence he was lifted over a thirty-six and a half mile stretch, rising to nearly 2300 feet, by a series of inclined planes; and at Johnstown he took another canal-boat for Pittsburgh. Dickens had described the somewhat alarming mode of hoisting the cars over the mountains.

But however picturesque, this State-built system was so costly that Pitts-

9 E. H. Mott, *Between the Ocean and the Lakes, The Story of Erie*, 86–114. The bad track caused thirty serious accidents in 1852. See Edward Hungerford's spirited *Men of Erie*.
10 Vanderbilt became a director in the New York & Harlem in 1857; W. J. Lane, *Commodore Vanderbilt*, 185.

Flat-car, Canal Boat and Inclined Plane in Pennsylvania.

burgh manufacturers who wanted to send goods to New York sometimes routed them down the Ohio for transshipment at New Orleans. Of course in midwinter, when the canals were frozen, the system was entirely paralyzed. Meanwhile, the State lost heavily on its investment.[11] Indignant citizens held massmeetings to demand a continuous railroad from Philadelphia to Pittsburgh. The Baltimore & Ohio offered to build a branch line from Cumberland into Pittsburgh, and in 1846 obtained a charter for it from the Pennsylvania legislature; but this provided that if the promoters of an all-Pennsylvania railroad obtained subscriptions for $3,000,000 and began construction of thirty miles before midsummer of 1847, the Baltimore & Ohio would lose its rights.

The challenge was met. A Pennsylvania Railroad Company was formed. By hectic effort, selling sixty thousand shares at fifty dollars apiece, it satisfied the legislative conditions. The directors made a shrewd choice when they appointed J. Edgar Thomson, a thoroughly trained civil engineer of old Pennsylvania Quaker stock, to superintend the project. Some authorities had de-

11  John W. Starr, Jr., *One Hundred Years of American Railroading*, 113.

clared a railroad over the Alleghenies impossible. By finding practicable grades, building tunnels, and laying out the Horseshoe Curve, Thomson confuted such experts. Work was pushed with great rapidity, and early in February, 1854, the first through trains passed between Pittsburgh and Philadelphia. Both cities believed their fortunes made—and a great new east-west link had been forged.[12]

If speculative mismanagement was the hallmark of the Erie, sagacity and thrift stamped the Pennsylvania. The new railroad had cost only about $16,000,000, and even in an unfinished state it paid six per cent.[13] Its managers soon executed a spectacular coup. In 1857 the State offered all its "main line" properties—the Philadelphia-Columbia railroad, the portage railroad, the canals—at auction; an upset price of $7,500,000 was fixed; and just one bid was made, J, Edgar Thomson tendering precisely $7,500,000. This repaid the State for about half its cash investment.[14] Alongside Thomson a brilliant young man, of tremendous physical vitality and mental alertness, Thomas A. Scott, was rising to prominence. Beginning as station agent for the new railroad, he had worked his way up to become by 1853 superintendent of the Altoona-Pittsburgh division; and after the purchase of the State properties he became general superintendent. In 1860 Thomson told him that he was promoted to be first vice-president. Scott protested that he was not eligible, for a vice-president must have held ten thousand dollars' worth of stock for a half year. "You must be mistaken, Mr. Scott," replied Thomson with a twinkle. "The books show that two hundred shares of stock have been registered in your name for a longer period than six months."[15]

In some lights the most important historical fact of the time was that by 1855 four railroad systems connected three different Atlantic ports by east-west lines with the area beyond the Alleghenies; the Erie and the still loose Hudson River-New York Central system serving New York, the Pennsylvania serving Philadelphia, and the Baltimore & Ohio serving Baltimore. All these lines ran north of the Ohio. All of them naturally reached out for extensions into the heart of the Middle West. They were helping fix the broad outlines of a Middle Atlantic-Northwest relationship which seemed to leave the South isolated and lonely. The story of the means by which they gained their Middle Western extensions, and of the counter-measures undertaken by the South, is of great significance. Equally significant, and much less known, is the story of the hidden factors which helped make the east-west traffic far more important than north-south traffic.

12  W. B. Wilson, *History of the Pennsylvania Railroad Company*, I, 150ff.; MacGill, *Transportation in the U. S.*, 388, 389.
13  N. Y. *Tribune*, February 9, 1854.
14  Slason Thompson, *Hist. Am. Railroads*, 115; *National Intelligencer*, June 20, 1857.
15  Philadelphia *Press*, May 21, 1881.

The First Roundhouse at Martinsburg on the B. & O.

## [ II ]

The opening of the four main links between the Atlantic and the Western waterways would alone have kindled men's imaginations and inspired scores of cities with dreams of grandeur. But it coincided with another mighty stimulant, the inauguration of the era of Federal land grants.

The sponsors of the Illinois Central first unlocked the gates. In 1850 the Illinois delegation in Congress, including Douglas and Shields in the Senate and McClernand, Bissell, and Wentworth in the House, with various allies, eagerly pushed through a measure by which large tracts of public land were made available to Illinois, Mississippi, and Alabama for transfer to railroad corporations. Douglas had adroitly disarmed Southern opposition by linking the interests of the Mobile & Ohio Railroad project to his own venture. The Illinois Central was thus endowed with some 2,595,000 acres along its right of way; and with Robert Rantoul of Massachusets, agent for a group of Eastern capitalists, as its chief promoter, it was rapidly brought under construction. Ten thousand laborers, among them a host of Irish paddies, were set to work. By the end of 1854 the main line from Chicago to Cairo, with most of the Chicago-Galena branch, had been put into operation. While this main line was the first great north-south railroad of the country, it was not destined to unite South and Northwest; for until the very eve of the Civil War no railroad was completed through Kentucky, and even then no bridge spanned the Ohio at Cairo. Indeed, its immediate effect was to tie Southern Illinois, which might easily have gravitated into the orbit of St. Louis, to Chicago. The railroad laid open for development a wide expanse of the most fertile land of the continent. Before it was constructed, land had gone begging at the government's minimum price. But within a half dozen years after its completion, the road had disposed of 1,300,000 acres and was rapidly selling more at from $6 to $25 an acre—so much had it raised values.[16]

The way having thus been blazed, a swarm of applicants settled upon Washington. All the new States had their frantic suppliants. A vast amount of jealousy, backbiting, logrolling, pressure-group hammering, and political maneuvering appeared. Missouri and Arkansas, with their proposed links in future transcontinental systems, were the first to profit; then, beginning in 1856, nearly all the public-land States. The movement threatened to over-stimulate railroad-building, with unhappy financial consequences. It threatened to build up corporations of menacing size in the youthful West, which (as

16 P. W. Gates, *The Ill. Cent. R.R. and Its Colonization Work*; Robert Rantoul, *Letter to Robert Schuyler on the Value of the Public Lands of Illinois*, 1851; J. B. Rae, "Development of Railway Land Subsidy Policy in the U. S.," MS Dissertation, Brown Univ., 1936.

the New York *Tribune* remarked with a shrewd prescience of the days of railroad legislatures and Senators), might hold the prosperity, and even the political character and destinies, of some States in their hands. Certain Democratic leaders who had been foremost in denouncing monopolies were now encouraging companies which would infallibly monopolize large tracts of land.[17]

Grant after grant, however, was made under avid public and corporate pressure. In the seven years following 1850 the Federal government donated almost twenty-one million acres for railroad construction in the Mississippi Valley. In the last two of these years, no fewer than forty-five Western railroads had their outstretched hands filled. It was clear that the land-grant roads promoted settlement; but they did so at a price—land that had been a dollar and a quarter an acre going up to ten, twenty, or even thirty dollars. No grant should be sealed, insisted Greeley, except on condition that the land was promptly sold at not more than government prices.[18] Efforts were made to hold a sectional balance, and of the eight States benefited in 1856 four were Southern and four Northern. But naturally the Northwest, as the seat of the most energetic construction, fared better than the slave States.[19]

Meanwhile, some of the States and cities furnished financial aid of their own with a liberality which they later rued. Tennessee, Georgia, and Florida among others all spent not wisely but too well. North Carolina by the fall of 1854 had incurred a debt of $4,130,000 by appropriations and bond-endorsements for railroads, roads, canals, and river improvements, the chief item being $2,000,000 for the North Carolina Railroad. Virginia, with her cities and people, offered largess with unstinted hand. Governor Henry A. Wise, urging in 1857 that the State apply twenty-five millions in the next ten years to public works, gave a good summary of what it had already done. After detailing the expenditures on various canals, he went on: [20]

And her railroads are numerous and extensive. Norfolk has penetrated North Carolina by 80 miles, costing one and a half million, and has another road to Petersburg of 80 miles, at a probable cost of one and a half million; Petersburg has connected herself with North Carolina's great southern route, by 63 miles, at a cost of one million; and with Richmond, by 22 miles, at a

17  Various Western journals campaigned for a law to curb the monopolization of great tracts of land by speculators. The Dubuque *Herald and Express* called for a tax-discrimination program, exempting from taxes $500 to $1,000 worth of improvements made by any actual settler. Such a law in Michigan, it said, had resulted in throwing very large tracts on the market. Quoted in Warsaw, Ill., *Bulletin*, January 24, 1858.

18  N. Y. *Weekly Tribune*, March 6, 1852.

19  Roy M. Robbins, *Our Landed Heritage*, 147ff.; see the speech of Representative John Letcher of Virginia, *Cong. Globe*, May 21, 1856, for criticism of the legislation.

20  April 12, 1857, to R. Lacouture; *National Intelligencer*, May 21, 1857.

cost of $1,150,000; and with Lynchburg, by the South Side road, of 123 miles, at a cost of $1,975,000. Richmond has penetrated the Roanoke Valley to Danville, 143 miles, at a cost of four millions; has reached the Tennessee line by the Southwestern road 204 miles, at a cost of five and a half millions; has touched the Potomac by her Fredericksburg road, 76 miles, at a cost of one and three quarters millions; has nearly completed her Central road, by 180 miles, at a cost of four and a quarter millions; has her York River road in progress, 38 miles, at a probable cost of one million; and has 34 miles of road in operation of her coal mines, at a cost of something less than a million. Alexandria has her Orange road complete to Gordonsville, 88 miles, at a cost of two and three quarters millions; and, crossing the Central, is reaching south to Lynchburg, 30 miles, at a probable cost of $1,200,000 and has her Manassas road penetrating the valley to Harrisonburg, 139 miles, at a cost of three and a half millions. . . .

These . . . are in addition to the great works now in progress on State account, the Blue Ridge and the Covington & Ohio road, 247 miles, at a probable cost of sixteen millions.

But the best example of what public and private effort could accomplish was furnished by New England. Massachusetts held a great railroad jubilee in the autumn of 1851, attended by President Fillmore, Secretary Webster, Lord Elgin, then Canadian Governor-General, and other notables, who were entertained by a great procession, a civic feast, and an aquatic parade. This celebrated the completion, within twenty years, of seven main lines of railroad with more than a thousand miles of track and a capital of fifty-two millions. Massachusetts boasted that outside of England, no other area of equal size in the world was so criss-crossed by rails. Not a single town of five thousand was without railway communications, and hardly a neighborhood was beyond sound of the locomotive whistle.[21] The Yankees had special reason to celebrate, for their capital was an indispensable element in most Northern construction. Benton remarked in 1856 that he had lately travelled from west of the Mississippi to the Penobscot, seventeen hundred miles. "Every inch of the distance was a tribute to the enterprise of New England; for the whole distance I rolled over roads which New England enterprise had made." [22]

The railroad craze, lasting until the panic of 1857, gave sanguine men an impression that almost anything could be achieved. It reached its greatest extravagance in some of the plans for transcontinental lines. New Orleans, Little Rock, Memphis, St. Louis, Chicago, and St. Paul were all eager to see a Pacific Railroad built to their portals, and all ready to believe that it would be easy to fling it over plain and mountain. At a railroad convention in St. Louis in 1849, with Douglas presiding, Thomas Hart Benton had aroused the assemblage to a

21 N. Y. *Weekly Tribune*, September 27, 1857. Alvin F. Harlow in *Steelways of New England*, 143ff., 236ff., describes in detail the building of various lines.
22 Speech at New England Society dinner December 22, 1856; *National Intelligencer*, December 25. For British aid, see C. H. Jenks, *Migration of British Capital*.

high pitch of enthusiasm by a speech urging that the nation rise above local and sectional jealousies in laying the iron road from sea to sea. He coined the phrase that was later to be inscribed on his orient-facing statue: "There is the East— there lies the road to India." [23] A little later, as a champion of Missouri interests, he boldly advocated the investment of a hundred millions in a central route, with the national government, the State, St. Louis, and private investors all sharing the cost. Other men, in the South, the Northwest, and on the Pacific coast, talked of even larger plans, and of three or four roads at a hundred millions apiece.

The fundamental question in dealing with the Pacific Railroad, however, was neither its precise route through the unsettled Far West nor the mode of defraying its cost. It was the question of Eastern connections. The road must necessarily be like a projecting girder supported by a truss. Until that truss was stable, well-knitted, and powerful, it was premature to talk of the westward extension. The main task of the fifties was to fill up the railroad network between the Appalachians and the Missouri-Mississippi waterway.

[ III ]

The four main trunk lines from the Atlantic coast had broken through to Dunkirk, to Buffalo, to Pittsburgh, and to Wheeling, where each tapped a main water route into the Middle West. But when would interlocked rail connections to the Chicago-Indianapolis-St. Louis area be established? And would the traffic that rolled over the connecting lines be profitable?

It was not long before an answer to these questions was forthcoming. The Michigan Central Railroad, with a main line running westward from Detroit, had been chartered in 1846. Thrust forward by enterprising men, in 1850 it reached almost within hailing distance of its Chicago goal. But there it met an equally enterprising and dogged rival in the Lake Shore & Michigan Southern Railroad, building westward from Erie, Cleveland, and Toledo. This line also came almost within hailing distance of Chicago. The two corporations battled savagely in the legislatures of Indiana, Illinois, and Wisconsin, and in the city council of Chicago, while their workmen fought along the tracks. They created a deadlock that prevented either from obtaining an Illinois charter or Chicago franchise, and during 1851 remained halted at the Illinois boundary. Finally the Michigan Central formed an alliance with the Illinois Central by which it was allowed to pass its trains over the I. C. tracks from Calumet into Chicago. It thus emerged the victor, and beginning in May, 1852, established the first through line from Chicago to Detroit and the East.

23  W. M. Meigs, *Thomas Hart Benton*, 421, 422.

But of course the Lake Shore also quickly gained access to the city. Indeed, it did better, for in 1854 it completed a northward extension into Milwaukee. Both the New York Central and the Erie, connecting with the two lines, could now send passengers and freight direct from the seaboard to the Illinois prairies.[24]

Meanwhile, the Pennsylvania Railroad was intent upon a connection with lines west of Pittsburgh—and it was not long kept waiting. In the fall of 1854 the Ohio & Indiana Railroad was completed from Pittsburgh to Fort Wayne, Indiana. An excursion train filled with Pennsylvanians and Ohioans reached Fort Wayne to find its ten thousand inhabitants wildly celebrating the occasion. An extension to the Western metropolis soon gave the Pittsburgh, Fort Wayne & Chicago, as it was renamed, a length of 470 miles, and a valuable traffic.[25] At the same time a number of small railroads were being linked up (very loosely and haphazardly, to be sure) to furnish a zigzag line between St. Louis and the East.

The year 1855 thus found citizens of both Chicago and St. Louis congratulating themselves that they could now journey to the Atlantic coast without setting foot in a boat or a horse-vehicle. One hardy citizen explained that year just how easy it was. He had breakfasted with his daughters in St. Louis, transacted business there for two hours, and caught a morning train to Terre Haute and Indianapolis. Thence he travelled to Dayton, Columbus, Zanesville, and Wheeling. From the last-named point, stepping aboard a Baltimore & Ohio train, it was a delightful journey to Baltimore. He had made the whole trip, about 886 miles, in one day and twenty-two hours, at a cost of only $25.30. The roads he found in good order, and the conductors all "perfect gentlemen."

Indeed, the Baltimore & Ohio that summer sold through tickets from Baltimore to Chicago for $20.50, to St. Louis for $28.50, and to Memphis (reached by a mail steamboat from Cincinnati) for $26. A year earlier the Michigan Southern had advertised in New York newspapers that passengers could leave at seven in the morning by either the Erie or Hudson River railroad, and, connecting at Dunkirk or Buffalo with "lightning express trains" on the Lake Shore Railroad, could be in Chicago at nine-thirty the evening of the next day. Patrons, declared the agent with an obvious grimace at the Michigan Central, "will not be subjected to the numerous and vexatious delays occasioned by low water as on other routes." The Michigan Central, however, was pounding its own drum with a notice that it was selling tickets over the

24 MacGill and others, *Transportation in the United States*, 539–548; Van Oss, *American Railroads*, 384–400.
25 Pittsburgh *Gazette*, quoted in *National Intelligencer*, November 23, 1854.

only direct and continuous line of railroad from New York to Chicago and the Mississippi River. And, it added with a sneer at its rival, they could "thus avoid the long and vexatious journey around the south shore of Lake Erie." [26]

Before long, moreover, the Baltimore & Ohio was destined to gain as direct a connection with the Mississippi Valley as the Hudson River-New York Central system, the Erie, or the Pennsylvania. One of the greatest railroad achievements of the decade was the construction of the Ohio & Mississippi Railroad from St. Louis to Cincinnati. Two groups of capitalists had broken down in the effort. Then a new and more powerful body, including the New York merchant William H. Aspinwall, the rising Ohio attorney George Hoadly, and E. S. Gould, assumed control of the line and completed it. The full road was 340 miles long, of which these "associates" built the last 105 miles in less than six months. Together with the Cincinnati & Marietta and the Northwestern Virginia, it afforded continuous communication from St. Louis to Washington.

When the first trains left the Mississippi for Cincinnati in May, 1857, newspapers all over the border region published enthusiastic editorials. A special excursion train from Washington brought out Lewis Cass, then Secretary of State, the French Minister (Count Sartiges), and Mayor Thomas Swann of Washington, who were welcomed with due ceremony at Marietta by Governor Salmon P. Chase. Nobody, said Cass, could appreciate the changes of the time better than he, for, as a green schoolboy just out of Exeter Academy in New Hampshire, he had migrated to Marietta in the closing days of 1799. He could recall when a horseback trip from Marietta to Baltimore had taken twenty days. "Within a few feet of where we stand," he said, "I landed more than half a century ago, a poor young adventurer. . . . Fifty-seven years ago all the Northwest Territory contained only thirty thousand people; now its limits include six millions. The man is now living whose axe felled the first tree of these forests, and there are men now alive who will not pass away until the United States has attained a population of one hundred millions." The train continued to St. Louis for another rousing celebration.[27]

By these iron bands the Atlantic Coast and the upper Mississippi Valley were being stapled together. The linking of the numerous roads, some small, some large, plainly foreshadowed the day when the four powerful trunk lines —New York Central, Erie, Pennsylvania, Baltimore & Ohio—would unite East and West. The rivalry of the principal roads with one another and with the waterways offered some guarantee that rates would be kept low, and that every effort would be made to improve facilities. Already it was plain to astute

26 Advertisements in the N. Y. *Times,* January–February, 1854.
27 *National Intelligencer,* May 16, June 8, 9, 1857.

railroad managers that the huge volume of bulky freight produced in the upper Mississippi Valley, the fast-swelling mountains of meat, corn, and wheat, constituted the richest prize of American commerce. At an early date the scope of the traffic astonished beholders. "Few persons who are not in a position to see it," declared the Toledo *Blade* early in 1854, "can form an adequate idea of the amount of travel through this city by railroad. Night before last *thirteen* carloads of first-class passengers went west in one train. The number could scarcely be less than 700. Three trains pass through each way daily, and we are told that a fourth train is in contemplation. There is probably no road in the country doing a better business than the Cleveland & Toledo. The freight business is becoming large and will be immense when proper arrangements for its transportation between Cleveland and the New York lines shall have been perfected." [28]

[ IV ]

And what of the South? It was all too plainly being shouldered aside— and yet it made heroic efforts. The two important east-west lines which Southerners completed in the fifties were those which linked Memphis with Savannah and Charleston in one direction, and with Richmond and Norfolk in another. The original dream of Charleston had been a splendidly equipped railroad running from that port northwest to Louisville and Cincinnati; a road which would annex the Northwest to the Southeast. Had this project been pushed to completion with the energy thrown into it in the thirties, the whole psychology of Charleston and the Lower South might have been altered, for a close union of the upper Mississippi Valley with the South Atlantic would have engendered a nationalist feeling. But the terrible cotton crisis at the end of the thirties and the death of the two chief initial promoters brought disaster.[29] The fifties ended with nothing but indirect and very inconvenient communications between Charleston and the Ohio.

In the spring of 1857, however, Memphis and Charleston celebrated the completion of railroad connections by way of Atlanta and Chattanooga, which now became important junction centers. Excursionists from the coast hastened

28 Quoted in N. Y. *Tribune*, March 30, 1854; the Cleveland & Toledo was part of the Lake Shore system. As late as 1853 the State Engineer of New York, W. I. McAlpine, had predicted in his annual report that the impending completion of railroads would wrest from New Orleans most of its pork trade. This prophecy, wrote the British consul in Chicago on April 30, 1859, has been "amply fulfilled." FO 115/216.

29 These promoters were the eminent Robert Y. Hayne, and Abraham Blanding. The panic of 1837 also played a part. Hayne's death tragically came when he was prostrated by fever at the end of the first day's session of a stormy stockholders' meeting at Asheville. U. B. Phillips, *History of Transportation in the Eastern Cotton Belt 1860*, 168–220; T. D. Jervey, *Robert Y. Hayne and His Times*; MacGill, *op. cit.*, 433.

to Memphis; glowing speeches were made, describing the road as the greatest of all Southern achievements; and wonderment was expressed when the return train accomplished the seven hundred and fifty miles to Charleston and Savannah in fifty-two hours.[30] The most important section of the line to Charlestonians was that tapping the cotton districts of Georgia. A year later the linking up of various minor roads opened a through communication from Memphis through Chattanooga and Lynchburg to Richmond and Norfolk. A convention of railroad officials had been held to arrange a timetable free from long detentions. The schedule adopted enabled Memphis passengers to travel to or from Richmond in fifty-eight hours, and to or from New York in a little less than four days. This was a great blessing to men bound for the Southwest, who previously had journeyed by steamboat or stagecoach. The last gap to be closed was a little strip of about seventy miles on the Lynchburg-Knoxville line, and great were the rejoicings when the final spike was driven.

Yet the South lagged behind the North, and some of the gaps in its system remained deplorable. The connections of the Lower South with the North were slow, crooked, and inconvenient. When the Civil War began, Texas and Arkansas had no line joining them with Missouri, and men bound for St. Louis had to travel by horse, or to go across country to the Mississippi and catch a boat. No line ran from eastern Tennessee or eastern Kentucky into Ohio. And farther down the map, what extraordinary lacunae appeared! It was impossible to travel by rail from New Orleans to Mobile, or from Baton Rouge to Vicksburg. The connections between Memphis and Richmond, or Memphis and Charleston, were outrageously roundabout and difficult, especially when compared with the direct connections between St. Louis and Baltimore, or Chicago and New York. When Senator Slidell left New Orleans for Washington, he had to journey north into Tennessee or Missouri and then turn eastward. As late as the summer of 1859 the meandering New Orleans-Washington railway route, by way of the Jackson, the Tennessee, and the Virginia railroads, was interrupted by a gap in the Mississippi Central line which stagecoaches had to fill in. Not until just before Lincoln's election, indeed, was continuous rail travel from New Orleans to New York, by way of Jackson, Chattanooga, and Lynchburg, possible; and with the best of luck it took three and a half days. Or the traveller might go by way of Jackson, Cairo, and Cincinnati, taking slightly longer.[31]

Southern railway building suffered from obvious disadvantages. The population of the section was widely scattered, and the social economy nearly static,

30  *National Intelligencer*, May 12, 1857.
31  New Orleans *Picayune*, January 27, July 28, 1860. The Mississippi Central gap was closed January 31, 1860; till then the Washington-New Orleans mails, nominally carried by government contract in four and a half days, were often vexatiously late.

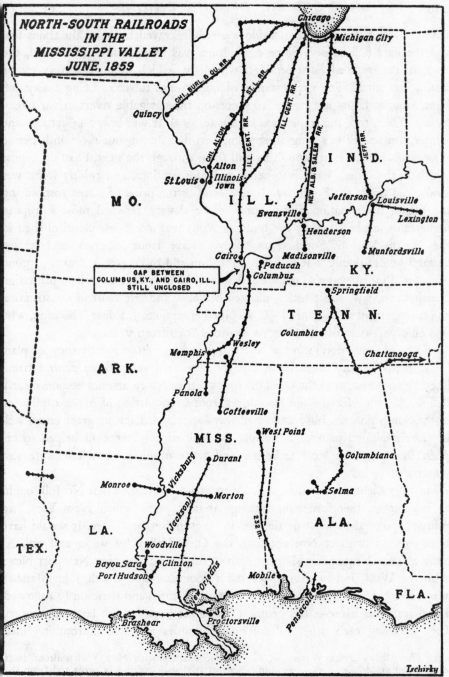

NORTH-SOUTH RAILROADS
IN THE
MISSISSIPPI VALLEY
JUNE, 1859

GAP BETWEEN
COLUMBUS, KY., AND CAIRO, ILL.,
STILL UNCLOSED

*The gaps in Mississippi and Kentucky are noteworthy; New Orleans, Vicks-burg and Memphis still had only a river connection with the northwest.*

This map and other railroad maps which follow **are** drawn from data in Appleton's *Railway Guide.*

with the result that passenger traffic was small. Travellers found the trains few and the cars half-empty. Since agriculture was insufficiently diversified, the regional exchange of farm products was slight, which meant that way-station traffic was small. The great staples of cotton and tobacco, being bulky but light, were in large part hauled to points on the navigable rivers, never closed by ice. Then, too, the traffic was highly seasonal. It was heavy in autumn and winter, but scanty in spring and summer, so that during one six-month period most roads had to earn enough to pull them through the next. Floating capital which in the North went into better railroads, stations, and rolling stock was swallowed up in the South by slavery—and as the price of slaves rose during the fifties, the situation grew worse. Since slavery repelled most European immigrants, unskilled labor for building roads was much less plentiful than in the North. Various Southerners believed slave labor superior, and it was certainly more docile; but it was hard to find and to keep.[32] A dearth of good managerial talent was also manifest. Most of the able men went into plantation management, law, and politics, disliked business, and left railroad construction and management to eccentrics—or to Northerners like J. Edgar Thomson, who was chief engineer of the Georgia Railroad for fifteen years.

Railroad construction in the South suffered also from a deficiency of plan. Short roads aplenty were built, but the section developed no *central* trunk lines. Whereas north of the Ohio the four great east-west arteries became clearly defined, drawing freight and passengers from a reticulation of minor capillaries, in the South no such busy main highways appeared. Lack of great cities, lack of clearly-defined natural pathways, and lack of commerce all helped to explain this fact; but local jealousies and want of directing talent were also important.

In 1857 Lieutenant Matthew F. Maury, who maintained that Norfolk ought to have taken that leadership among Atlantic ports which New York had usurped, pointed to what he deemed the reason for the failure. It would have been easy to connect Norfolk with the Ohio Valley by water and rail. As early as 1810 Virginia legislators began to think of connecting Newport News with the West, and in 1811 appointed a commission of which John Marshall was a member. But no broad plan was ever laid down and tenaciously followed. Local jealousies arose—"the people of Virginia have for the last half century been accusing each other of sectional jealousies and uncompromising local

32 The Albany attorney John V. L. Pruyn, connected with New York railroad interests, talked at Mobile in 1855 with an officer of the road which was projected from that city to Cairo. "The whole distance is 496 miles—109 miles completed, and 40 more will be within 90 days. The residue to within 20 miles of the Ohio River is nearly all funded. Mr. Childe spoke highly of slave labor—it is slow, he says, but steady, and there are no quarrels or strikes." Pruyn Diary, March 19, 1855; N. Y. State Library.

prejudices." What was the result? Most of the railroads south of the James were of the five-foot gauge, and those north of it were four feet eight and a half inches. When and if a road was built from Covington to connect with the Lynchburg line, then Ohio Valley freights might reach Norfolk; but only by passing over five railroads, each a separate and independent concern. Maury's outburst against the local prejudices of the Virginia railroads is worth quoting alongside Governor Wise's gratulations over the work Virginia had done: [33]

There are no two of them that touch each other that can without quarreling pass passengers and baggage; much less can five consecutive roads pass from one to the other their cars, locomotives, freights, and engines. The Central Railroad was at first built as a local tributary to the Richmond & Fredericksburg road; yet these two roads could not get along together. They quarreled about this very thing of freights and cars passing from one road to the other; and the result was that the Central disconnected itself from the other, and laid its rails right alongside those of the Richmond & Fredericksburg, and thus from a tributary it became a most active competitor and opponent.

The same thing occurred in the case of the Alexandria & Orange and the Manassa Gap Road. The latter was a tributary. It has now gone or is going off into opposition. And the agent at the railroad office here tells me if I want to pay to Weldon I cannot pay or check through. I pay from here to Richmond, and then am left with my baggage to scramble as best I may to the Petersburg depot. Arrived in that city, I am again left to "paddle my own canoe" to the next depot, some mile or two off. . . . There is not a spirit of accommodation and coöperation on the roads of the State to pass the citizens of the State from one road to the other; and if not with passengers between two roads, how can it be with whole trains of cars and freight, engines and conductors, over a chain of five roads?

In vain did a body of ambitious Virginians throw themselves into the project of developing Norfolk as a great port, with railroads reaching on the one hand into the Ohio Valley and Lower South, and a direct steamship line on the other to Europe. The men laboring for this "disenthralment" of the South included Maury, President J. R. McDaniel of the Virginia & Tennessee Railroad Company, F. B. Deane, William B. Preston, and Ambrose Dudley Mann, being the before-mentioned lawyer of West Point training who had occupied various diplomatic posts and who was Assistant Secretary of State under Pierce. They held conventions at Old Point Comfort and Bristol, Tenn.; they opened subscriptions for their "steam ferry line" from Norfolk to Europe; they published newspaper articles; they exchanged innumerable letters.

"As to the natural advantages of position, depth of water, and accessibility by land and sea," declared Maury, "Norfolk has no competitor among the

33 *National Intelligencer*, November 11, 1854.

seaport towns of the Atlantic." [34] Preston went abroad in 1858 to enlist foreign interests. But the old local jealousies persisted, direct-line communication with the West was never really obtained, and capital could not be found for the steamship enterprise. Not one Virginian or Tennessean in a hundred, lamented a friend of Mann's in 1857, understood the movement.[35] An agent that summer sold shares in the steamship enterprise to President Buchanan, Secretary Howell Cobb, and other members of the Cabinet [36]—but the outbreak of the Civil War found the undertaking still half inchoate, and still without substantial footing.

Nor was the South really successful in developing serviceable north-south trunk lines in the lower Mississippi Valley. The great Gulf ports, Mobile and New Orleans, were eager to save themselves from two distinct economic threats. One was offered by the ambitions of Charleston and Norfolk; for if these Atlantic ports really built up strong lines reaching through the Lower South, farewell to half the cotton trade of the Gulf ports! The other threat was presented by the steady Eastern conquest of Northwestern trade.

Beginning in the forties, both the Gulf cities bestirred themselves to encourage railroads which would meet this double challenge. The Mobile & Ohio, chartered in 1848, was slowly built northward through Mississippi, just west of the Alabama line; how slowly is indicated by the fact that only thirty miles of the projected 440 were completed in 1852.[37] Help came from State and local subscriptions, and from a Congressional land-grant the value of which was estimated as high as $6,500,000. Finally the road reached Cairo in 1859, connecting with the Illinois Central—but much of it was not yet in condition to operate.[38] New Orleans businessmen, obtaining a charter for their road in 1850, met with a series of difficulties and discouragements. Planters were indifferent, merchants skeptical; natural obstacles were many; capital was timid. Direct communication was finally achieved with Columbus, Ky., in 1858— but this line, too, was in poor operating condition. Neither road offered a link with the Northwest comparable to the roadways built from the Eastern ports. They saved for Mobile and New Orleans a certain amount of cotton traffic that might otherwise have flowed to Charleston, Wilmington, or Norfolk, but

34 Letter to R. L. Maury, September 20, 1854; Maury Papers.
35 See letters of F. B. Deane, Overton Bernard, and others to Mann; Mann Papers, N. Y. Hist. Soc.
36 This agent, M. J. Kelley, wrote that Buchanan signed with alacrity, as did Howell Cobb; Floyd and Toucey were more reluctant; so was McClelland at the Interior Department, who thought the Cabinet could more freely grant favors if not shareholders; while Cass refused. August 19, 1857; Mann Papers.
37 R. S. Cotterill, "Southern Railroads and Western Trade," *Miss. Vall. Hist. Rev.*, III, 434; MacGill, *op. cit.*, 474.
38 Actually the road was not really open until early in 1861; *Appleton's Railway Guide*, 1860, 1861. No bridge existed at Cairo for many years to come.

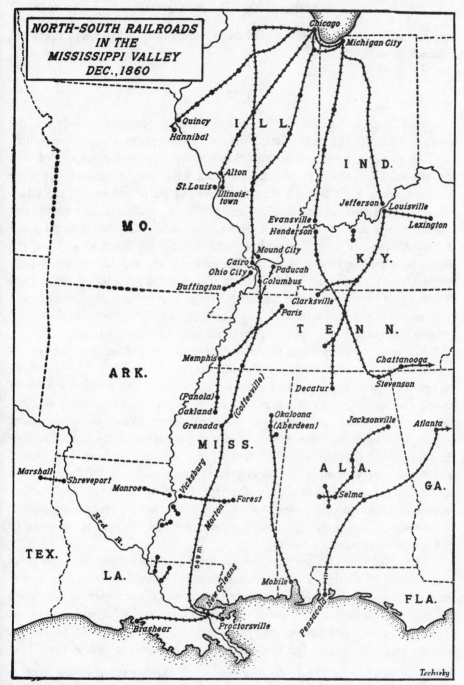

NORTH-SOUTH RAILROADS
IN THE
MISSISSIPPI VALLEY
DEC., 1860

*East-west connections (as from St. Louis) not included. No bridge crossed
the Ohio at Cairo.*

they furnished no nexus between Southern merchants and Northern grain and livestock growers.[39]

## [ V ]

In the silent but grim, intense, and unsleeping competition between the South and East for the trade of the Northwest, a competition which had widely ramified political implications, the Southerners held one trump card, the Mississippi. They failed to develop railroads which could compete with the Northern trunk lines. But the mightiest river system of the world, the Ohio-Mississippi-Missouri waterways, rolling southwest, southeast, and south, and draining every part of the nation's great central valley, emptied into the ocean at New Orleans. It poured its yellow flood through the heart of seven of the fifteen slaveholding States. It made Minnesota, Iowa, and Illinois the natural neighbors of Arkansas and Louisiana. It traced three glimmering paths from Pittsburgh at the forks of the Ohio, St. Paul at the falls of St. Anthony, and Fort Benton in the far Northwest, down to the great delta country. Why could not this trump card be played to give the South the winning hand?

River steamboating reached its magnificent apogee in the fifties. No pageantry of the time surpassed that of the Western rivers. The mile-long expanse of boats smoking and throbbing at the St. Louis and New Orleans levees; the motley crowds of passengers—fur-traders, immigrants, soldiers, cotton-planters, land-speculators, gamblers, politicians, British tourists, Indians, and plain farmers; the avalanche of pork, grain, tobacco, cotton, and hides that the Illinois, the Cumberland, the Washita, the Arkansas, and the Red poured into the central Mississippi stream, cramming every deck; the lordly pilots, the hardbitten captains, the profane mates, the chanting roustabouts; the fierce races as the firemen tied down safety valves, the hands crammed fat-pine into the roaring furnaces, and the passengers cheered—all this was romance in its day, and will be romance forever.

Visitors to New Orleans never forgot the five o'clock hour when the great boats, one after another, swung into midstream; the levee boiling with excitement as the line of twin chimneys poured murk into the red evening sky, while calliopes roared, flags waved, hands chorussed "De Las' Sack," and the tardiest passengers, with bodyservants carrying flowered carpetbags, hurried aboard. Many a girl never forgot her first sight of such a saloon as that of the *Grand*

39 Cf. T. D. Clark, *A Pioneer Southern Railroad*. Southerners lacked staying power in railway enterprises, complained the New Orleans *Picayune*. "The most important undertakings have flagged and fallen. . . . How little interest is taken here in the affairs of the Southern Pacific Road—an enterprise that is destined to elevate New Orleans into a metropolitan city!" August 12, 1859.

*Republic,* its Belgian carpet specially woven in one piece three hundred feet long, and its white pillars, endless mirrors, and softly wavering candelabra, a vista of radiance, presenting a scene of fire and snow. When scores of black servants spread the tables for dinner, and the passengers seated themselves before shining napery and silver and multicolored fruits and flowers, the long cabin seemed palatial. The night views from the deck enchanted such travellers as Lady Wortley. "Hundreds of lights are glancing in different directions from villages and plantations on shore, and from the magnificent floating palaces of steamers that frequently look like mountains of light and flame, so brilliantly are these enormous leviathans illuminated inside and outside."

The Western steamboat of the fifties was essentially a combination of some features of the deep-water steamer of the coast and some humble traits of the oldtime river keelboat. As invented by Henry Shreve, who built the archetype of the fleet at Wheeling in 1815, it was composed of the engines, boiler, and saloons of a steamship placed on a flat keelboat hull. This unconventional craft united speed with space, while its draft was so shallow that it could 'run on a heavy dew.' Twelve feet or 'mark-twain' was more than ample water. By the fifties most of the steamboats were built at Pittsburgh and Cincinnati, though St. Louis, New Orleans, and other cities had their hallmarks. Curiously enough, the most famous single yard was long found at Jeffersonville, Indiana; a yard established by an English immigrant named Howard, who turned out his first Ohio River boat about 1829, led his competitors in one improvement after another, and with his son and grandson was finally credited with more than half of the oldtime river boats.[40]

Decade by decade the vessels became larger and sturdier; their engines, at first cobbled together by ignorant mechanics, grew more dependable. In the days of Mrs. Trollope they had been ugly, unpleasant, and dangerous, but by the fifties they were gaudily handsome, comfortable, and fairly safe.

Unlike the railroads and the ocean shipping, river steamboats demanded no large capital. When numerous boats were crushed at St. Louis early in 1854 by masses of floating ice, the loss proved but trivial. Newspapers spoke of the *Garden City* as "altogether the finest boat at the landing," yet she had cost only some $40,000. The *F. X. Aubrey,* plying the Missouri, "a splendid specimen of river architecture" which had been built only the previous spring, had cost but $32,000. Other crushed vessels were valued at from ten to twenty thousand each.[41] Two years later New Orleans witnessed one of her worst levee conflagrations. Some torches on a steamer which was trying to force her way into a line of closely-packed boats set fire to a pile of pinewood on another

40  Garnett L. Eskew, *The Pageant of the Packets,* 87.
41  St. Louis *Democrat,* February 3, 1854.

vessel. The two most expensive vessels lost, the *Natchez*, famed in river legend, and the *Charles Belcher*, one of the largest afloat, were valued at $85,000 and $83,000 respectively; but the others were appraised at only ten to twenty thousand each. Such figures explain why a steamboat could often pay for herself in two or three years.[42] Hudson River vessels were also inexpensive, and even the fine steamers on the Sound, where George Law and Commodore Vanderbilt were rivals, cost but $150,000 or $160,000.[43]

The Western rivers, unlighted, ill-charted, full of snags, rocks, stumps, and wrecks, their channels constantly shifting, were dangerous paths of commerce. In the middle fifties it was estimated that the destruction of property by the various impediments to navigation totalled three million dollars a year, and that on the lower Mississippi alone, from St. Louis to New Orleans, it reached two millions. Westerners constantly urged the improvement of the principal streams. For decades the government acted only spasmodically, policing the channels for a season or two, and then selling the snagboats and abandoning the stream to nature. In 1856 Congress witnessed a tremendous combat over the issue of internal improvements. A phalanx of Northerners and border men—Crittenden, Seward, Douglas, Cass, Stuart, Pugh—who favored tidying up the rivers met in fierce onset an array of Southerners: Mason, Toombs, Clay, Hunter, Adams, Biggs. One item was an appropriation of $100,000 for the Mississippi; another $50,000 for the Tennessee. Butler declared that no confederacy on earth could stand when the majority began levying tribute on a minority. Toombs argued that the Western people were rich and should improve their own streams; they took the profits from the Mississippi's trade, and should meet the expenses. But the appropriations, aided by logrolling, went through.[44]

The Mississippi's thousand-mile tributary to the eastward, the Ohio, had developed an impressive traffic, the number of boats fit for service in 1857 (including barges and flatboats) being about 900, and their annual commerce being valued at $140,000,000. Coal, lumber, and farm products made up most of the freight. But passenger revenues were important; even in 1851 about 960,000 fares were paid to or from the four principal ports, Pittsburgh, Wheeling, Cincinnati, and Louisville.[45]

42  New Orleans *True Delta*, February 4, 1854.
43  Lane, *Commodore Vanderbilt*, 74.
44  *Cong. Globe*, July 29, August 4, etc., 1856. Pierce's veto of the rivers and harbors bill of 1854 aroused the sternest resentment in the Northwest. Many voters of the section concluded that his motive was the same as that of Southerners in opposing homestead legislation, and in forcing through the Kansas-Nebraska bill—to injure the Northwest. See Madison J. Kuhn's MS dissertation, *Economic Issues and the Rise of the Republican Party in the Northwest*, Univ. of Chicago Library.
45  *Special Report* of Secretary of War to House, January 22, 1857.

The Pittsburgh & Cincinnati Packet Line, which provided daily service between the two largest Ohio River cities with seven packets averaging 230 feet in length, was the most important single agency. Its big fast boats carried from 300 to 350 people apiece with clocklike regularity. They were credited during 1852 with transporting some 12,000 passengers and 30,000 tons of freight apiece. The line, well-managed by an executive committee of seven, was really a loose coöperative organization of individual boat-owners, who agreed on schedules of rates and sailings. These owners acted together, for example, to help press the famous Wheeling Bridge case, still remembered for the eminence of its counsel (Edwin M. Stanton against Reverdy Johnson), and the interest of its legal points.[46] Pennsylvania charged that the bridge, construction of which had been authorized by Virginia law, was an obstruction to interstate commerce. The Supreme Court early in 1852 upheld this view, decreeing that the bridge must be raised to a greater height; but this verdict was nullified by a law which Congress passed within six months.[47]

Traffic on the upper Mississippi was very different from that on the lower reaches. It, too, reached a striking development. In 1857 and again in 1858 more than a thousand arrivals of steamboats were reported at St. Paul, where ten years earlier there had been fewer than fifty! [48] The very earliest up-river steamboats had depended upon fur-traders with their skins, soldiers with their stores, and a trickle of explorers. Treaty-goods for the Indians also had importance. Then as the fur-trade slackened, minerals provided a good substitute. Galena, which in the thirties was a typical wild-and-wooly mining town and remained an important center, sent her lead pigs down the Mississippi literally by millions. The lead output of the country rose from seventeen thousand tons in 1840 to twenty-two thousand in 1850, then sinking to about sixteen thousand in 1860.[49]

Lumber, too, soon began to furnish a valuable freight. The mills of the St. Croix Valley were becoming famous by 1855, one established at Stillwater in that year turning out millions of feet of white pine annually for the St. Louis market. Throughout the fifties the wheat of Iowa and Illinois, Wisconsin and Minnesota, was transported downstream in large quantities. In that decade, moreover, the influx of settlers grew to such a torrent that passenger revenues became as important as freight returns; frequently more important. One steamboat, the *Milwaukee*, in 1857 collected five-sevenths of its receipts from passengers. Among the colonists crowding her decks may have been a few

46 E. M. Sellers, "The Pittsburgh and Cincinnati Packet Line Minute Book, 1851–53," *Western Pa. Hist. Mag.*, December, 1936.
47 Charles Warren, *The Supreme Court in U. S. History*, 1936 ed., II, 234–236.
48 *National Intelligencer*, December 3, 1857.
49 *Statistical Abstract U. S.*, 1940, p. 778.

tourists, for as early as 1845 George Catlin had designated the boat trip to the Falls of St. Anthony as the "Fashionable Tour." Up the river went plows, harrows, reapers, window glass, groceries, and drygoods to stock the infant settlements. Down the river came the products of the fast-expanding farms. This northern traffic was far more variegated than the transportation of the lower river, which was confined mainly to cotton, grain, and meat.[50]

Why was it that the South, holding the outlet of the nation's central river system as its trump card, failed to win the glittering prize of Northwestern trade? The explanation involves a number of factors that have received little attention.

[ VI ]

In one sense the conflict transcended a mere clash of sectional interests; it was a conflict of two eras and two economies. The old age of river transport and small shipments was giving battle to the new age of rail transport and mass shipments. It was a conflict between St. Louis and New Orleans, allied with the old commercial economy, on one hand, and Chicago, Philadelphia, and New York, allied with the new commercial economy, on the other.

So long as the old era lasted, St. Louis and New Orleans flourished. Some of the reasons why these two cities became great ports are manifest from a glance at the map; others are not. New Orleans dated its real greatness from the year 1817, when the steamboat *Enterprise* demonstrated the possibility of carrying cargo upstream to Louisville in three weeks or less, as contrasted with the three months formerly required; from the rapid settlement of the Southwest in the years after 1815; and from the liberation of Latin-American trade by the revolutionary movement of the same period. St. Louis obviously occupied a crossroads position, standing on a median site where the trade of the Rivers Ohio, Missouri, Mississippi, and Illinois (which reached almost to Lake Michigan) could pour into its lap. Placed near the point where the Missouri and Illinois emptied into the Mississippi, it had deep water below, comparatively shallow water above. Large steamboats of heavy draft could not ordinarily ascend above St. Louis, while small steamboats of light draft found it economical to discharge cargo there into roomier craft. St. Louis therefore became a natural point for breaking freight. Its merchants handled consignments to and from the lower Mississippi on one side, and the upper Mississippi, the Missouri, and the Illinois on the other. Most river pilots were specially trained for either the section above St. Louis, or the section below, and made the city a terminal point.

50  William J. Petersen, *Steamboating on the Upper Mississippi; Commerce and Navigation of the Valley of the Mississippi for the Use of the Chicago Convention* (1847).

It enjoyed another natural advantage in the sloping limestone bluff on which it was placed, a natural quay far superior to the shore facilities at Dubuque, Quincy, Memphis, Natchez, or other river points.

These facts help explain why St. Louis, which in 1804 was a village of one hundred and eighty houses, and which laid its first pavement, a stone sidewalk, in 1818, rose swiftly to be the chief commercial emporium of the West. The year 1831 had found sixty different steamboats plying from its levees, and the year 1835 one hundred and twenty-one. By 1850 it was one of the world's greatest ports of exchange. Its merchants carried on a huge wholesale and jobbing trade throughout the whole region of Western waters. Its packets made regular sailings to Cincinnati and Pittsburgh, to Beardstown and Peoria, to Dubuque and St. Paul, to St. Joseph and Kaw Landing, and to Nashville on the Cumberland—on six major water routes. Traders from the South congregated here to buy pork, corn, and machinery. Pioneers on the overland route outfitted for their long journey. The Far Western trade in pelts and furs was still valuable. In 1855 nearly seven thousand arrivals and departures of steamers were recorded. When the river threatened to silt up the port, the Federal government intervened and the masterly engineering work of Robert E. Lee preserved it unharmed.[51]

The hamlet of Pierre Laclede had become by the fifties one of the imposing cities of the country, its brick buildings stretching along six and a half miles of the river front, and extending back for three or four.[52] River travellers thirty miles away could see the cloud of wood and soft-coal smoke that the steamboats and manufactories threw like a dense pall over the city; they could hear from afar the rumble of its wharves. It was the city not only of important political leaders, Benton, Frank P. Blair, and Edward Bates, but of respected and enterprising merchants. Those who looked for a hustling business spirit there and in New Orleans could easily find it. Both cities had busy stock exchanges. Both had large commodity markets; St. Louis specializing in grain, meat, tobacco, furs, and hemp, and New Orleans in cotton. Both had their crowded commercial streets, like Canal in St. Louis and Carondelet in New Orleans, where cotton and grain factors, buyers, brokers, weighers, classers, and samplers swept by in a steady stream, the air was thick with prophecies and quotations, and fortunes were made by traders standing on the curb. Both had their scenes of thundering hurly-burly, and the picture that George W. Cable drew of antebellum New Orleans might have served equally for its Missouri sister: [53]

51 Douglas S. Freeman, *R. E. Lee*, I, 172–180.
52 Galusha Anderson, *A Border City During the Civil War*, 2.
53 In *Dr. Sevier*.

Drays, drays, drays! Not the light New York things; but big, heavy, solid affairs, many of them drawn by two tall mules harnessed tandem. Drays by threes and by dozens, drays in opposing phalanxes, drays in long processions, drays with all imaginable kinds of burden; cotton in bales, piled as high as the omnibuses; leaf tobacco in huge hogsheads; cases of linens and silks; stacks of rawhides; crates of cabbages; bales of prints and of hay; interlocked heaps of blue and red ploughs, bags of coffee, spices, and corn; bales of bagging; barrels, casks, and tierces; whiskey, pork, onions, oats, bacon, garlic, molasses, and other delicacies; rice, sugar—what was there not? Wines of France and Spain in pipes, in baskets, in hampers, in octaves; queensware from England; cheeses, like cartwheels, from Switzerland; almonds, lemons, raisins, olives, boxes of citron, casks of chains; specie from Vera Cruz; cries of drivers, cracking of whips, rumble of wheels, tremble of earth, frequent gorges and stoppage. . . . We are a great city, said the patient foot-passengers.

But the coin, alas! had its obverse. Against advantages had to be set off disadvantages. As long as shipments were of comparatively small bulk, and financed by comparatively small investments, the two great Mississippi ports lorded it over their competitors. When shipments swelled to enormous proportions, requiring the most modern warehouse and transfer facilities, and when their handling demanded tens of millions, other cities drew to the front.

As a port, St. Louis was hampered by frequent low-water stages in summer and by ice in winter. From August to the close of November the channel of both the Missouri and upper Mississippi often furnished but four or five feet of water, which meant that it was useless. From the beginning of December until the middle of March, navigation of the upper Mississippi and Missouri was suspended by cold. Even if ice did not form early, no guarantee of safety existed and steamboats seldom ran. The same risks were encountered as far south as Cairo. Thus the season of dependable navigation above St. Louis (or even Cairo) lasted a bare six months. Most of the corn crop on the Missouri, Illinois, and upper Mississippi was not husked until ice was closing the rivers, and the pork fattened upon this corn was not ready until later still; while the major part of the beef was also for winter shipment. The Missouri was so unsafe for downstream navigation at night that underwriters' rules compelled southbound steamers to tie up at dusk. At certain river-stages pilots on the Illinois and upper Mississippi also had to order the boats anchored overnight. In low water no steamboat could safely pass the Des Moines or the Rock Island rapids, where the river fell over sharp limestone ledges. Altogether, for all-year handling of cereals, pork, beef, and other products, the railroads offered the upper Mississippi Valley immeasurable advantages over the steamboats.[54]

54 See the interesting *Report* of the Select Senate Committee on Transportation Routes to the Seaboard, 43d Cong., 1st sess., Report 307, Pt. 2, 1874. The statement on behalf of the Kansas City Board of Trade, pp. 639–643, shows how risky, uncertain, laborious, and unsatisfactory river navigation was.

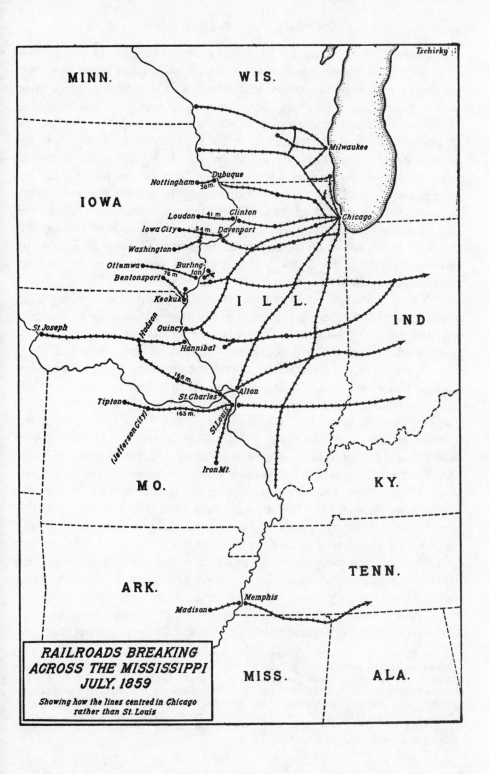

Tschirky

MINN.    WIS.

Milwaukee

Dubuque
Nottingham    38 m.

IOWA

Loudon    41 m.    Clinton
Iowa City    54 m.    Davenport

Washington

Ottumwa    Burling-
Bentonsport    76 m.    ton

Keokuk    I L L.    IND

Hudson    Quincy
St. Joseph

Hannibal

168 m.

Tipton    St. Charles    Alton

163 m.    St. Louis

(Jefferson City)

Iron Mt.    KY.

MO.

ARK.    TENN.

Madison    Memphis

RAILROADS BREAKING
ACROSS THE MISSISSIPPI
JULY, 1859

Showing how the lines centred in Chicago
rather than St. Louis

MISS.    ALA.

Similarly, New Orleans found grave natural handicaps in the tortuous ninety-eight mile channel connecting her with the ocean, and in the bars which the muddy river deposited at the delta entrances. The natural depth of water on the outside bar was about sixteen feet in summer, eighteen in winter. Government engineers made assiduous efforts to deepen the channel, but the tremendous force of the current and the immense mass of silt made any material improvement impossible in this period. During low water five or six ships often stuck on the bar; whereupon one large fleet collected inside and another outside until the river rose high enough to end the blockade. It was estimated that if a draft of twenty-five to twenty-seven feet had existed, three times as much grain could have been shipped from New Orleans. But the fetters were not to be stricken from the port until James B. Eads in the seventies, overriding the doubts of army engineers, performed his brilliant feat of constructing the jetty system in the South Pass.[55]

All river ports suffered, moreover, from the difficulty of handling bulky products on shores where the water rose and fell unpredictably—a gamut of 41.4 feet being registered at St. Louis between floodmark and extreme low-water mark.[56] With the engineering and financial resources then available, it was impossible to build satisfactory shorefront elevators. Warehouses had to be placed safely above high water, which meant that they were far above ebb-mark steamboats, and that handling costs were high. The inferior transfer facilities involved heavy loss from breakage of boxes and leakage of barrels. Climate was also an adverse factor. While Memphis and New Orleans interests denied that their hot, humid summers were more injurious to wheat and corn than those of Chicago or New York, it was unquestionably true that butter, lard, tallow, cheese, and meats quickly deteriorated or spoiled. The loss on flour passing through New Orleans was estimated at from twenty-five to fifty cents a barrel. That city, with its high transfer charges and insurance rates, made a weak commercial partner for St. Louis.[57]

Altogether, the river age of transportation was a crude, primitive, and wasteful age. That bustling confusion which so impressed Cable was partly sheer inefficiency; the phalanxes of drays, the stacks of bags, crates, and barrels, represented a costly mode of transferring and storing freights. A visitor to the St. Louis levee in 1856 was similarly impressed. "Along a winding shore, for

55  *Idem*, 812–849. The New Orleans Chamber of Commerce complained bitterly of the constant and heavy losses sustained from the bar. But the same Chamber did little to provide proper port facilities. "Crescent" complained in *De Bow's Review* of 1850 that the city had not built one great work. It was time for New Orleans citizens, he wrote, to realize that the goods of the West were fast moving to the Northeast and the Southeast. Vol. VIII, 589.
56  I. Lippincott, "History of River Improvement," *Jour. Pol. Economy*, XXII, 644ff.
57  *Idem; Report* Senate Committee on Transportation, 849; Wyatt Belcher, *Economic Rivalry of Chicago and St. Louis*, 1850–1880.

an extent of two miles, nothing is to be seen but hogsheads of tobacco, boxes of hardware, and bags of corn; every description of merchandise, in fine, raw or manufactured, either pouring into the capacious holds of steam vessels or being disgorged therefrom. The levee seems like an anthill of human and equine industry." [58] It never struck the observer that much of this industry meant a type of rehandling that the better-organized system of railroads, grain-elevators, and trackside warehouses in the Northern cities avoided.

And back of the railroads, elevators, and warehouses of the Great Lakes area stood a panoply of Northern money and credit that the South could not match. New Orleans in particular suffered heavily from lack of capital. Money that might have accumulated in its banks and been invested in its ports facilities went instead into slave property and the opening up of new lands as old areas decayed. The city had so limited a body of grain-traders, and such weak credit-resources, that a few boatloads of grain or meats depressed the market. Northwestern shippers learned this, and preferred Chicago. [59] Midway in the fifties *De Bow's Review* pointed out that the East was not only investing large sums in railroads, canals, lake shipping, elevators, warehouses, and other improvements, but in addition supplied generous funds for moving the Western produce to market. Eastern bank-drafts and other credit instruments were as important in the development of Western trade as locomotives and cars. The South had no surplus capital to throw into such channels. All its money was drawn into agrarian investments. The *Review* further noted that New York, Boston, and Philadelphia were all great centers for importing European goods; and the Northwestern grain-shipper found there brokerage firms which, acting in conjunction with the great banks, efficiently shipped his consignments abroad and meanwhile granted him liberal credits. [60]

[ VII ]

Chicago swiftly rose to be *par excellence* the railroad city of the United States. The great north-south wall of Lake Michigan, jutting three hundred miles into the heart of the prairies, forced all east-west traffic to pass around its southern tip; and this tip was the natural point for breaking all lake-and-land traffic. In 1850 Chicago had not a mile of railroad. By 1855 it boasted of being the terminus of 2,200 miles, radiating in every direction, and draining traffic from some 150,000 square miles. The city, said the *American Railroad Journal*, saw at least a hundred heavy trains arrive and depart daily. [61] Already it was

58 N. Y. *Weekly Tribune*, April 12, 1856.
59 Lippincott, *loc. cit.*
60 *De Bow's Review*, XIX (1855), 689.
61 Quoted in Warsaw, Ill., *Express*, February 1, 1855.

probably the largest grain-exporting market in the world. Railroad construction continued until by 1860 Chicago was the center of eleven main lines and a score of branch or extension lines, aggregating nearly 5,000 miles in length.

The Father of Waters had for ages been tributary to the Gulf; but by a spasmodic effort in the fifties Chicago made all its upper stretches subservient to the lakes and the Atlantic. On an August day in 1852 throbbing bells and booming cannon in Rockford announced that a railroad had been flung halfway from Chicago to the Mississippi. Next year a line was open to Galena on the river; part of it the property of the Galena & Chicago, part that of the Illinois Central. A year later still a gay celebration at Rock Island marked the opening of the first continuous connection between that river town and the Great Lakes. A third road to the Mississippi, the Chicago & Northwestern, was completed to a point opposite Clinton, Ia., in 1855.

River traffic above the Keokuk rapids had now been seized. It remained for Chicago to drive two more railroads southwestward to the Mississippi in the area that St. Louis regarded safely her own. One line, the Chicago, Burlington, & Quincy, ran aslant the State to connect the lakes and river at the point where Illinois projects farthest west. It reached Burlington in 1855 and Quincy at the beginning of 1856. The other, the Chicago & Alton, spanned a still greater distance to tap the Mississippi at the port where Elijah Lovejoy had been murdered—a port which for a time had hoped to eclipse neighboring St. Louis.[62]

In short, before the end of 1856 five different roads, in the language of railroad-celebration orators, enabled the iron horse to take his morning draft from the crystal waters of Lake Michigan and slake his afternoon thirst on the banks of the Mississippi. They diverted eastward from Galena, Dubuque, Rock Island, Quincy, and Alton a vast amount of freight that would otherwise have moved down the river. And still longer lines were stretching out beyond the Mississippi. One, the Chicago & Northwestern, began running its trains into Cedar Rapids, Ia., before the end of the decade, meanwhile building on west toward Council Bluffs. Another, the Hannibal & St. Joe, was completed across northern Missouri in the early weeks of 1859. Sometimes treated as a Missouri achievement, it actually conduced to the prosperity of Illinois and particularly Chicago. Being practically an extension of the Chicago, Burlington, & Quincy, it annexed—so the Chicago press boasted—all of northern Missouri to the domain of the windy city, thus weakening St. Louis. The Missouri Pacific, St. Louis's own pet scheme, made slower progress, and failed to reach the Missouri River before the war.

"While we in St. Louis have been fighting about the slavery question,"

62  R. E. Riegel, *Western Railroads*, 96, 97; Cole, *Era of the Civil War*, 42, 43; R. C. Overton, *Burlington West*, 31–44.

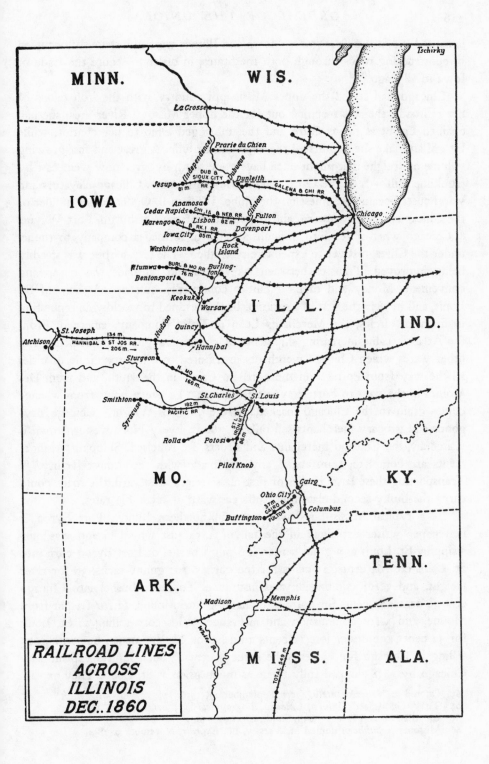

RAILROAD LINES
ACROSS
ILLINOIS
DEC. 1860

lamented the St. Louis *Inquirer*, "Iowa and Illinois were industriously occupied in constructing roads through both the States, in order to secure the trade of Iowa to Chicago." [63]

Chicago had seized the upper Mississippi country with the iron talons of her railroads; she was reaching out for the upper Missouri River area; she had chained Egypt as far as Cairo and the unbridged Ohio to her chariot; while by rail and lake she dominated the Wisconsin traffic. A great and fast-growing volume of freight that might once have gone south by river now went east by trunkline railroads or the Great Lakes-Erie Canal route. Chicago elevators and warehouses became the finest on the globe. William B. Ogden, chief builder of the Chicago & Northwestern, and regenerator of the Pittsburgh, Fort Wayne, & Chicago when it fell into difficulties in 1859, formed a company to tunnel under the Chicago River to expedite city traffic.[64] The city harbor was steadily being improved. Transfer between lake boats and railroads was cheap and convenient. Money and credit facilities continually outstripped those of St. Louis, and in 1857 the first of a series of banks destined to worldwide reputation in financial circles, the Merchants Loan & Trust Company, emerged. From the Atlantic came increasing shipments of consumers' goods, implements, and other wares which Chicago merchants distributed to a hungry circle of cities all the way from Portage on the north to Cairo on the south, and from Des Moines in the west to Fort Wayne on the east. "To every point from whence comes grain to the Chicago market," wrote John S. Wright, "Chicago dry-goods and grocery merchants sell bills of goods. Every Northwestern town is visited by the Chicago merchants and orders are solicited. Shipping arrangements are complete; transfers, if any, are made with the utmost facility." [65] Transporting these large bodies of first-class freight westward, the roads could carry the bulky second-class foodstuffs eastward at favorable rates.

At a typical Mississippi River town in northern Illinois, Port Byron, a newspaper writer explained in the fall of 1854 just why Chicago was outstripping St. Louis as a grain center. To put a bushel of Port Byron corn into St. Louis cost 64 cents; 25 cents for the corn, 6 for gunny-sacks, 30 for river freight, and 3 for commission and insurance. To put a bushel into Chicago cost 46 cents; 25 cents for corn, 6 for hauling into Moline, 12 for freight from Moline, and 3 for commission and insurance. With corn selling in St. Louis for 52 cents, the dealer lost 12 cents a bushel on his shipments; but with corn selling in Chicago for 55 cents, he made 9 cents.[66] Such figures explain why Chicago by 1858 shipped fully twice as much grain as St. Louis. They explain

63  Quoted in *National Intelligencer*, September 27, 1856.
64  T. W. Goodspeed, *Univ. of Chicago. Biographical Sketches*, I, 48, 49.
65  Lloyd Lewis and Henry Justin Smith, *Chicago*, 110, 111.
66  *Missouri Republican* quoted in Warsaw, Ill., *Express*, November 9, 1854.

why, though New Orleans remained the chief port for cotton and enjoyed nearly all the export trade in tobacco from Kentucky, Tennessee, Illinois, Indiana, and Missouri, the grain and pork of the Northwest flowed to Europe by way of Chicago and New York.

Even by the middle fifties the primacy of Chicago was clear to all. An eloquent report was made to the British government under date of January 9, 1857, by its consul in the city, Edward Wilkins. For the year just past he chronicled a torrent of wheat and corn, the entry of 6,128 vessels, and the receipt of four hundred and fifty million feet of board lumber, or twice as much as two years previous. "Chicago," he wrote, "may now be considered established as the chief depot for the receipt of domestic and foreign merchandise imported for consumption in the States and Territories west and northwest, and as the granary and primary market for the agricultural products of these regions." And alongside this may be placed an earlier utterance by a writer in *De Bow's Review*, explaining why New Orleans was steadily being outstripped. The city was cursed by unhealthful climate and high living-costs, while it could provide only for slow heavy freight, and could not give year-round service for that. Meanwhile, with New Orleans ten days from New York, and at times almost cut off from St. Louis and Louisville, "a great network of railroad is growing up, binding all the middle, northern, and western States." [67]

The parallels had conquered the meridian lines of commerce. Had the South developed its manufactures, had New Orleans pushed its railroads to the northward energetically, had St. Louis flung a line into Iowa, the story might have been different. As it was, by 1860 the Northwest and Northeast marched arm in arm.

## [ VIII ]

Great Lakes commerce was an important precursor, auxiliary, and competitor of the railroad in developing the Northwest. By 1855 these deep, cold waters carried almost 350,000 tons of shipping. The value of the lake vessels, according to the House committee on commerce, was then almost fifteen million dollars, while in 1854 the fleet had carried freights worth more than six hundred millions. Until the Civil War more than nine-tenths of the lake tonnage was powered by sail, and the schooners on Erie, Huron, Michigan, and Superior, the product of numerous local yards, often possessed a grace and speed that Yankee shipbuilders might have envied.

67 *Report* Senate Committee on Transportation, 846; for Wilkins, FO 5/678; for the eclipse of New Orleans, *De Bow's*, VIII, 444ff.

The lake passenger trade reached the height of its glory in the fifties, for a great part of the human flood overspreading the Northwest still preferred to travel westward from Buffalo or Erie by boat. Henry Schoolcraft, journeying from Mackinac to Detroit in 1838 in the new vessel *Illinois*, had described her as something like a floating parlor, where every attention and convenience was promptly provided,[68] and since then the steamers had been improved. The handsomest of the lake vessels by the middle fifties, the *Western World*, was 348 feet long, with powerful engines and beautiful interior fittings. She and her peers, the *Plymouth Rock*, the *Western Metropolis*, and others, with several hundred staterooms each, competed in luxury and entertainment for those who could pay.[69] Down the green lakes they slipped with dancing, gambling, flirtation, and feasting, the musicians in the ballrooms thrumming their guitars to the song:

> Old Huron's long, old Huron's wide,
> De engines keep de time.

But the staple of the passenger trade was made up of businessmen, prospectors, mechanics, California-bound emigrants, and above all, horny-handed, hardheaded men from Europe, Lower Canada, New England, and the Middle Atlantic States bound westward for cheap farms. Among those from overseas in 1849 had been little wide-eyed John Muir, whose Scottish father chose Wisconsin as his destination when in Buffalo he saw dozens of lake boats filled with plump-kernelled wheat from that new State. At Cleveland these migrants espied a lusty little industrial city of New England aspect; at Mackinac blanketed Indians standing beside bark wigwams; at Milwaukee and Chicago raw boom cities impinging on the raw prairie. Sometimes the colonists found the lakes as dangerous as the river steamboats. When in the summer of 1852 the passenger ship *Atlantic* collided in Lake Erie with the new cargo boat *Ogdensburg*, and sank in thirty fathoms, two hundred and fifty passengers, many of them Norwegian settlers, perished.

Ore was already becoming a specialty of the lakes. The barriers to its free passage were thrown down when on April 19, 1855, the sluice gates first opened to let Superior waters flow through the Sault-Ste. Marie Canal into Huron. Credit for the remarkable feat of building this canal goes mainly to Charles T. Harvey, who as a twenty-three-year-old Vermonter had come west to Michigan in 1852 to sell scales for the Fairbanks Company of St. Johnsbury. At the Soo, while recovering from the curse of primitive areas, typhoid fever, he looked about him. Great stacks of copper and iron ore were piling up along

---

68  Quoted in Landon, *Lake Huron*, 350, 351.
69  Walter Havighurst, *Long Ships Passing, passim.*

the Superior shores because the new mining companies could not get them down to the smelting centers in Ohio and Pennsylvania. The impediment was a mile of shallow, boiling water, falling over its rapids nineteen feet. For nearly a century men had talked of a bypass canal, and a ditch had been dug by the Northwest Fur Company in 1798 to let its canoes around. But the difficulties had daunted everybody.

Harvey saw the absurdity of letting a single mile of shallow rapids block a thousand-mile waterway—one narrow neck obstruct all water passage from Minnesota to the Atlantic. Returning to Vermont, he talked with the Fairbanks managers. His driving enthusiasm enlisted their support, and they were hard-driving men themselves. A company was organized with prominent New Englanders and New Yorkers guiding it. The president was Erastus Corning, one of the master spirits in the consolidation that resulted in the New York Central system; another leader was John M. Forbes, chief architect of the Chicago, Burlington & Quincy. Young Harvey became general agent and chief engineer. Even with the aid of the land grant which Congress voted, the task was titanic. The nearest large base of supplies, Detroit, was 450 miles away; the nearest machine shop was half as far distant at Saginaw; the winters were of Arctic severity. But Harvey mustered a force of brawny workers which he tried to keep at 1,500 men; and fighting against snow, ice, howling gales, temperatures 35° below zero, epidemic disease, accidents, and stoppages of supplies, he pushed the work forward; sometimes sighting his level by the dancing glare of the Aurora Borealis. After two years of exhausting toil, the task was finished.

Destiny hung like a golden star above the brig *Columbia* on the sunny August day when, clearing Marquette harbor, she set her course across Superior to the Soo, her hold filled with mounds of red iron ore. It was the first bulk shipment through the new canal. Behind her the Marquette iron range was humming with activity, brawny Cornishmen and Irishmen swinging their picks; before her waited the iron mills of Cleveland and Pittsburgh, their smoke blackening the valleys of the Cuyahoga and Monongahela. Marquette grew into a city, its streets curling up over the green hills. Sailing vessels like the *Columbia* made room for larger steam freighters, first conventional in shape, then long and lean as a Pittsburgh stogie. New and richer deposits of iron ore were found around the southern and western rim of the lakes. That busy pioneer Peter White, the chief figure in developing the Cleveland Mine and making the Cleveland Cliffs Company famous, had signed the bill of lading for the first six-barrel ore shipment from Marquette to Cleveland in 1852; he was to live to see Lake Superior float forty-two million tons of iron ore eastward in a single season.

When the panic of 1857 smote the country, the lakes carried 106 side-wheel steamers, 137 propeller-driven steamers, and more than a thousand sailing ships. Some were filled with copper from the Keweenaw peninsula, that wild tip thrust into Superior, where Houghton (named for the Michigan State geologist whose scientific reports had brought swarms of prospectors into the country), Hancock, and Calumet had sprung into thriving towns. Some carried iron ore. Some transported lumber and bales of furs. But above all, they did a brisk summer trade in the grain, flour, meats, and other farm products that rilled out of ten thousand farm communities in the Northwest, and that were gathered by railroad into the lake ports—Chicago, Milwaukee, St. Joseph, Toledo, Cleveland. This summer trade helped keep railway rates within bounds. It made Buffalo the greatest milling center of the time.

Carrying so immense a commerce, the lake shippers could well demand government improvement of their channels. See how much we haul, they argued; the wealth of our freights is greater than that of all the imports and exports by ocean. They estimated the value of the lake vessels shipwrecked in the eight years ending June 30, 1855, at $8,852,000.[70] The wretched St. Clair flats were a veritable graveyard for ships. There was not a harbor on Lake Michigan in 1855 to which a vessel might run in a storm with any assurance of safe entry. Even in a slight gale, no craft drawing more than eight feet could pass the Chicago harbor entrance.[71] Yet the government was collecting more in revenues on the lakes than Congress was appropriating for their harbors and lighthouses.

When the Democratic platform in 1848 denied the constitutionality of a general system of internal improvements, fresh-water interests of the West angrily resented this "salt-water interpretation" of the Constitution. Cass, who was bitterly attacked in his own region for failing to attend a Chicago convention on internal improvements, had to vindicate himself by a speech of 1851 demanding appropriations for the lakes. Douglas laid down the thesis that adequate internal improvements should be paid for by tonnage duties. But the Southern wing of the party remained adamant, Butler and Mason opposing dredgers on Lake St. Clair just as they fought snagboats on the Mississippi. Keen resentment was felt throughout the Northwest when the rivers and harbors bill of 1854 failed under Southern enmity. Gales of unprecedented severity that winter, with staggering losses, led the Pittsburgh *Gazette* to declare scornfully that while our lakes have been whitening with the sails of our bold merchants, "our legislators have been hairsplitting about the power to build lighthouses and beacons." [72]

70 *Report*, House Commerce Committee, 1855.
71 *National Intelligencer*, September 6, 1855.
72 Quoted in *National Intelligencer*, December 23, 1856.

Calhoun, in his reverberating Memphis address, had indicated his willingness to regard the Mississippi as an arm of the ocean, but the great lakes possessed a far better title to that constitutional and physical position. Their deep-water trade had its beginnings when in 1844 the brigantine *Pacific* sailed from Cleveland with a cargo of wheat for Liverpool. At least two other lake vessels made long ocean voyages in the next decade. But the real opening of the transatlantic grain traffic may be dated from the summer voyage of the steamer *Dean Richmond* in 1856 with 14,000 bushels of wheat from Chicago and Milwaukee for Liverpool. It was a profitable trip. The British gave the vessel an enthusiastic reception; the London *Times* published much of its log; [73] captain and crew were lionized; and the grain sold well above ordinary levels. Liverpool next year returned the visit by sending to the lakes a schooner laden with iron, hardware, pottery, and other manufactures. Chicago rose to the occasion. A grand salute was fired, British flags were unfurled, and the captain was greeted by all the city leaders. When the ship hoisted sail with a full cargo of hides, a delegation of a hundred merchants and aldermen crowded her decks, while a throng cheered her three times three.[74] Chicago took intense pride in this evidence that she might send ships to any part of the world.

But it was the cheap, efficient, and convenient connection of Chicago and the Northwest with the East which was most important. Both sections felt that the water transportation was an important auxiliary of the railroads. This fact was attested in 1854 by the decisive vote of New Yorkers on the proposal to enlarge the Erie Canal, which as replanned by S. B. Ruggles and others on the foundation laid by DeWitt Clinton, was then estimated to be only two-thirds completed. The *Herald, Evening Post,* and other newspapers united in attacking the canal as obsolete, stagnant, and extravagant. It was compared to an old stagecoach running alongside a modern train. The *Tribune* contrariwise argued that traffic had almost steadily risen, that Rome-haul was busy with boats and barges, and that every day of navigation saw approximately ten thousand tons of freight carried at cheap rates.

The vote for enlargement was absolutely overwhelming; some 65,000 to 5,000, or thirteen to one! [75] As traffic between Northwest and East rose, all agencies of transport were needed. By 1860 the huge Upper Mississippi Valley, the fastest-growing region of the country, definitely faced east, not south; it definitely belonged to the railroad and deep-draft steamship age, not the river age.

73  September 26, 1856.
74  Chicago *Free Press,* August 6, 1857.
75  N. Y. *Tribune,* February 9, 18, 1854.

## [ IX ]

The discomfort of American railroads was a theme of universal complaint. Britons, appalled by the flimsy stations, rough roadbeds, and overheated, dirty cars, seldom failed to compare the lines unfavorably with their own; though a few preferred the sociable cheerfulness of the American coaches. Not a few American travellers were equally murmurous. Edward Everett, journeying in the spring of 1857 from Albany to Buffalo, found the greatest neglect of comfort along the whole way. Only once were the passengers told how long the train would stop; only once or twice did it stop long enough to alight. When they reached Syracuse, the fact that they were to dine there was not announced. "I had but one opportunity to relieve myself between seven a.m. and 8 p.m.," Everett grumbled. "How absurd to sacrifice not merely all comfort but common humanity to speed!" [76] That fall he went from Cleveland to Boston. His train was nearly an hour late in starting, and did not reach Buffalo in season to connect with the Albany train. Determining to endure a night journey, he waited six hours for a midnight train that was again nearly an hour late in starting, and reached Albany too late for another connection. After waiting another six and a half hours, he boarded his third train, and half-dead with fatigue, was deposited in Boston at two-thirty in the morning, to find that his trunk had been left at Palmer.

Another inveterate lecturer, Horace Greeley, sprinkled the pages of the *Tribune* with his outbursts of wrath. He once summed up the most urgent and crying outrages. The first was the constant missing of connections: timetables were arranged with too little margin for junction points, in an effort to persuade passengers that they would get through quickly, and then they failed to get through at all! If, he grumbled, the scheduled time between New York and Chicago were increased by three hours, actual running time would be reduced. His second grievance was the bad ventilation. Every train was a moving pest-house, an antechamber of death, where customers were poisoned wholesale. The third outrage was lack of time for meals, the ten-minute interval allowed for lunch or dinner being ruinous alike to good manners and good digestion. Finally, no notice was given of the length of stoppages. Conductors, halting the trains for half a minute at one place and ten minutes at another, never took the passengers into their confidence.[77] Travelling west in 1859 by the Erie, Greeley for the third time in his busy life took a sleeping car. He found it intolerable: the stove was red-hot, the ventilators were closed, and the air was stifling. Two

76 MS Diary, April 14, 1857.
77 N. Y. *Tribune*, March 16, 1854.

or three grand-jury presentments of car manufacturers for manslaughter, he thought, might work a reform—nothing else could.[78]

Though railway accidents were not so costly of life as steamboat accidents, they aroused much denunciation. In 1856 they cost 115 lives, while shipping disasters on rivers, lakes, and sea took 439. One wreck of that year, on the North Pennsylvania Railroad, killing 62 people and injuring about 100, was the worst thus far known on American lines.[79] The better railroads made somewhat spasmodic efforts to improve both the comfort and safety of travel. While at the opening of the decade most lines depended upon wood for engine-fuel, the "experiment" of using coal made rapid headway. The boldest pioneer was William J. Palmer of the Pennsylvania, whose success with anthracite persuaded other corporations to follow his example. The Providence & Worcester Railroad, typical of other Eastern companies, announced in 1857 that by converting both its freight and passenger engines to coal it had cut the cost in half and made great gains in convenience and time.[80] That summer representatives of various railroads met in New York to form the American Association for the Improvement of Railroad Machinery, its object being to find better equipment by experiment, competitive trial, and comparison of verified reports.[81] Year by year the best roads installed more double track, lengthened their sidings, and purchased sturdier locomotives. The Baltimore & Ohio, among other lines, boasted that it had its own telegraph system. This enabled it, by the use of a master clock in the Camden Station in Baltimore, to keep time on the whole railroad absolutely uniform, and brought the trains under more perfect control. Nevertheless, an English expert in 1857 found that the signal arrangements at American stations were generally poor, and was astonished that the telegraph was so little used in railroad work.[82]

The most imperative need for safety and efficiency, as various inventors saw, was a good braking system. A train of heavy cars running thirty miles an hour might come in sight of an open drawbridge half a mile ahead; the engineer had just sixty seconds to stop it. Sounding "down brakes" on his whistle, he could only wait for his crew to do the impossible with their crude hand-brakes, madly running from car to car and desperately twisting a wheel to tighten a chain. The fast express between Washington and Baltimore, which often

78 Idem, May 28, 1859.
79 National Intelligencer, January 3, 1857.
80 Idem, July 25, 1857. Palmer was destined to an important railroad career. His conversion of the Pennsylvania and other lines to hard coal gave these Northern systems a great advantage over Southern wood-burning lines when the Civil War came on. See I. H. Clothier, ed., Letters of Wm. J. Palmer 1863–1868; Jeannette Turpin, ed., General William J. Palmer.
81 National Intelligencer, September 8, 1857.
82 Idem, November 8, 1856. Report of Captain Galton to British Privy Council on American railroads, summarized in De Bow's, XXII, 608ff.

exceeded thirty miles an hour, carried only two brakemen. This was enough for the ordinary station stops, but insufficient for an emergency. In 1857 a Virginian, Angus U. McDonald, invented a steam-brake, to be operated by the engineer from his cab, but it failed to give satisfaction.[83]

Not a little pride was taken by various corporations in their engineering achievements. Americans paid tribute to the Victoria Bridge across the St. Lawrence at Montreal, completed late in the fifties at a cost of seven million dollars; a structure almost two miles in length, resting upon twenty-six stone piers, with a central span of 330 feet. Planned for the Grand Trunk Railroad and carried out by British engineers, it was called one of the wonders of the world—"the crowning work of modern civil engineering," said the Boston *Atlas*.[84] Some American feats, however, were of nearly equal note. When in 1857 the Virginia Central pierced the Blue Ridge with a tunnel almost a mile in length, the result of seven years of continuous labor, the South rang with applause.[85] At that time work on the Bergen Hill tunnel of the Erie was progressing rapidly. It was more than four-fifths of a mile long, and twelve hundred workmen, using five hundred kegs of blasting powder a month, were driving it through hard rock. A still greater enterprise, the four-mile tunnel under Hoosac Mountain in western Massachusetts, was projected as early as 1852, and actually begun in 1855.

The sad fact remained that down to the Civil War neither the lower Ohio nor the Mississippi below Rock Island had a railroad bridge—a grievous deficiency. It was not until the middle seventies that St. Louis gained by the Eads bridge uninterrupted transit with the East. Moreover, the American railroads obviously possessed less substantiality and finish than those of Europe. The lightly-ballasted roadbeds, the ill-buttressed bridges, the numerous curves and grades, told of construction carried out with an eye for haste and cheapness. While a British road might well cost two hundred thousand dollars a mile, and the London & Northwestern came to more than three hundred thousand dollars, the ordinary American railroad cost only from twenty to forty-five thousand.[86]

## [ X ]

The question of railroad profits or losses defies easy generalizations. Many roads which seemed highly prosperous in the early fifties were thrown into difficulties, if not bankruptcy, by the panic of 1857. At the height of this storm the

83  *National Intelligencer*, August 8, 1857.
84  *Idem*, March 3, 1857; Charles Mackay, *Life and Liberty in America*, II, 207–209.
85  *National Intelligencer*, March 3, 1857.
86  *House of Commons Return*, 1855.

civil engineer Charles Ellet, Jr., said that most railroads were really unprofitable, and that a thoroughgoing reform in their rate structures was needed.[87] Little expert study had at this time been given to costs and revenues. Rate wars between rival lines had already proved disastrous. It was becoming clear that while capital charges on American roads were lower than on British, operating costs were higher. It was also clear that the management of many American lines was incompetent.

The New York Central and the Erie, for example, conducted a competition which at times reached cutthroat intensity. The Central (which then ran only from Albany to Buffalo) announced early in 1855 that, in conjunction with the Hudson River boats and Hudson River Railroad, it would carry passengers from New York to the lakes at from $4 to $7.50 each. The Erie promptly slashed its fares to meet these rates. Impartial observers were aghast at such ruinous competition. "It is singular," commented the New York correspondent of the *National Intelligencer*, "that these two roads cannot be conducted upon an enduring peace basis instead of the periodical warfare which has hitherto prevailed." Two years later President Charles Moran issued a circular calling attention to abuses in railroad management, the chief of which arose from the frantic effort of various lines to divert traffic from its rivals. Unless prompt and thorough reforms were effected, he thought it probable that nearly the entire amount invested in railroads, estimated at about seven hundred million dollars, would ultimately prove valueless.[88] Two of the four principal roads carrying anthracite from the mines to the seaboard were thrown into heavy difficulties by the panic of 1857. The Reading could not meet its current debts; the Lackawanna, similarly embarrassed, had to carry through a hasty readjustment. Yet they enjoyed a heavy traffic. The great trouble, said experts, was that they charged but an average of $1.50 a ton. Year after year they stayed in the old rut, "each overburdened with trade, each possessing more business than it knows how to manage, each jealous of the other's prosperity and seeking to destroy it, and so adjusting their charges as to render . . . prosperity reciprocally impossible." [89]

There was but one means of escaping rate-wars—by agreement; and the fifties witnessed the earliest of those railroad compacts which were ultimately to make pooling almost universal.

The battle of the Erie and Central in 1855, for example, helped to bring about a midsummer convention of representatives of twenty-three railroads at Buffalo. At this gathering the two great rival systems of the State failed to reach an agreement; but to reduce competitive costs, the roads pledged themselves to

---

87 Letter dated October 15, 1857, in *National Intelligencer* October 17.
88 *National Intelligencer*, August 6, 1857.
89 Ellet, *ut supra*; see also his pamphlet, "Report on the Tariff of Toll for the Virginia Central Railroad," 1858.

dispense with "runners" and outside freight-agents, while in the interest of fairness they outlawed all exaggerated handbills and posters. An important Southern convention was held the following year. Officers representing the principal rail and steamboat lines met at Ashland, Va., primarily to arrange for greater speed, cheapness, and certainty in travel. Improved timetables were adopted between Richmond and Wilmington, and Washington and Montgomery, arrangements being made by a committee for express service on the latter line at about twenty miles an hour. The fare from Washington to New Orleans was cut from $53 to $48. After urging that twenty miles (exclusive of stoppages) be made the standard speed everywhere, the convention adjourned to meet again at Augusta, Ga., in the spring of 1857. From these agreements to coördinate schedules, standardize speed, and make saner arrangements for freight-solicitation, it would be but a short step to rate-making agreements. Indeed, a conference of four magnates, Erastus Corning of the New York Central, J. Edgar Thomson of the Pennsylvania, Charles Moran of the Erie, and the imperious young John W. Garrett of the Baltimore & Ohio, was held in Washington for rate-making purposes early in 1859.

But as yet rate-making was a chaotic rule-of-thumb affair. The rapid growth of railroads during the fifties left their business upon an improvised, hastily arranged, and largely experimental basis.[90] Though most lines had a general freight agent who made charges his special care, and a set of toll-sheets which seemed to give shippers rough uniformity of treatment, in practise the widest variations and grossest irregularities existed. Local freight-agents, especially at competitive points, grabbed for traffic by concessions that varied with the season and the shipper. Large manufacturers got special rates, secret and arbitrary, which were denied to small manufacturers. Discriminations between man and man, noncompetitive and competitive cities, long-haul freight and short-haul freight, were already common. Investigations held at a later date (notably the inquiries in Ohio and Pennsylvania in 1867) showed that rebating had been common in the later fifties. One Pennsylvania ironmaster who testified that he had begun shipping in 1855–57 declared that rates had always been "entirely arbitrary," and that ironmakers had consistently made "a special or private bargain" with freight-agents.

In short, all the rate-making abuses that subsequently produced so fierce a

90 Trunk lines which tapped the Middle West by 1860 showed a disposition to discriminate against median points like Pittsburgh and Buffalo in favor of shippers who sent through freight from St. Louis, Chicago, and Indianapolis. We find the large milling interests of Buffalo and Rochester grumbling that the high rates on flour to the seaboard were ruining them. A thousand barrels of flour from Chicago could be put into New York cheaper than the combined cost of carrying wheat from Chicago to Buffalo, and flour from Buffalo to New York. N. Y. *Weekly Tribune*, February 18, 1860. See *National Intelligencer*, February 1, 1859, for the rate conference in Washington, forced by B. & O. rate-slashing.

public outcry, and that did so much to promote the concentration of manufacturing in certain cities, and to stimulate the growth of ever-larger industrial units, had a nascent existence by 1860. They were a natural product of the still-unchecked competition of a great proliferation of rapidly built lines.[91]

The high operating costs of American roads as compared with British were of course quite natural. Maintenance-of-way costs on lines hastily built through half-settled country were higher than—indeed, a good deal above double—British costs. Fuel charges were again more than double the British average. The wage bill, for lines of equal mileage, was perhaps half again as high. Finally, the average speed of the English railroad was probably one-fourth greater than that of American lines, a fact which reduced handling costs. The New York *Evening Post*, using the best available figures, estimated in 1858 that the total annual operating expense of American railroads was $171,000,000, while the expense of an equal length of British lines would be but $100,000,000.[92]

Yet some American railroads enjoyed dazzling prosperity. Conspicuous in the list stood the Baltimore & Ohio. The middle fifties found it handling a tremendous volume of livestock, flour, dressed meats, grain, and other produce from interior Ohio and western Virginia. It had become a huge artery pouring the bounty of the West into the lap of the East. The managers found it necessary to sign urgent orders for new rolling-stock, and to construct or lease larger facilities for shipping freight by sea to New York and Boston.[93] The gross revenues in 1855 reached $3,711,453, and deduction of $2,110,000 for operating expenses left net revenues of slightly over $1,600,000. The directors were able to lay down an eighteen-month program for paying off all the floating debt, completing amortization arrangements for the funded debt of $5,328,000 and creating an adequate sinking-fund for Baltimore's loan of $5,000,000; meanwhile maintaining a dividend rate of six per cent.[94]

Next year the road did a larger business than ever, both freight and passenger earnings increasing so heavily that the gross revenues rose about $700,000. The exuberant directors in December declared a dividend of thirty per cent in scrip, convertible into six per cent bonds the following summer; and though the Maryland and Baltimore authorities took legal measures to thwart this step, and prolonged litigation followed, the dividend was finally upheld. Even in 1857 and 1858 the annual reports were satisfactory. To be sure, the panic struck the road hard. Freight rates sank to unprecedentedly low levels. But the expenses were retrenched, and an adequate net revenue remained. Moreover, in these years one of the ablest railroad captains of the century, John W. Garrett,

91 Nevins, *John D. Rockefeller*, I, 259–267.
92 Quoted in *National Intelligencer*, September 25, 1858.
93 Baltimore *Sun*, quoted in *National Intelligencer*, December 25, 1855.
94 *Annual Report*, 1855.

emerged to leadership, first as the most active member of the board and in the fall of 1858 as president. The son of a Baltimore merchant, he showed an Aladdin-like skill in meeting difficulties and maintaining the vigor of what for a whole quarter-century men called "Garrett's road." [95]

Another flourishing railroad was the richly endowed Illinois Central. At the close of 1856 it had more than seven hundred miles in operation, and the steady settlement of Illinois was lifting its revenues to princely levels. Though it had received more than $10,700,000 from the sale of land, it still held some 1,700,000 acres, which Eastern newspapers enviously reported were already worth twenty-three or twenty-four million dollars.[96] The Federal grant, declared the *National Intelligencer*, "will pay the whole cost of the road and and leave a surplus of $8,000,000, besides the entire stock of the road free to the stockholders, which will pay a dividend, as the directors estimate, of eight per cent. The stock is now selling for $137." [97] High dividends were paid without interruption. Another Western line, the Dubuque & Pacific Railroad, projected to run from the Mississippi westward 330 miles to Sioux City on the Missouri, was pronounced in 1857 the richest railroad in the world. It had a grant of 1,250,000 acres, and its lands were believed superior to those of the Illinois Central. The managers counted on selling them, once the road was completed, at $15 to $25 an acre. For years a third Western venture, the Galena & Chicago, paid the highest consistent railway dividends in the country—eight to twelve per cent every six months.[98]

Such profits do much to explain the eagerness with which men fed the "railroad fever" by large investments. In the summer of 1860 John P. Kennedy wished to buy some securities. A business friend recommended certain of the best seven per cent railroad bonds; the New York Central was selling slightly above par, and several other good roads below it. Under these circumstances, some smaller lines obtained funds for construction only on extortionate terms. The backers of the road from Alexandria to Charlottesville, Va., for example, in 1856 got a much-needed loan of $70,000 only by parting with $100,000 in face value of seven per cent bonds; paying half of one per cent in commissions, and getting the money in seven equal monthly instalments, though the interest commenced at once! [99]

The cost of the rapid railroad expansion, as we have noted, was one reason why capital moved so slowly into manufacturing. The provision of communications for a national market necessarily had to precede the rise of great national

95  Hungerford, *Baltimore & Ohio*, I, 327–330.
96  *Annual Report*, 1856.
97  March 31, 1857.
98  Cole, *Era of the Civil War*, 41.
99  J. S. Barbour, July 10, 1856; Wm. C. Rives Papers.

industries. But the two processes might have kept in closer step but for the glittering gains promised by the "railroad fever." Why pour savings into iron mills, precariously competing with the British industry, when the Baltimore & Ohio furnished six per cent dividends, and the Illinois Central eight per cent? Why invest in textile factories when the Galena & Chicago paid sixteen to twenty-four per cent a year, and the Lackawanna in 1860 offered eighteen per cent in stock-scrip to atone for its recent suspension of dividends? [100] New Englanders estimated that in the twenty years 1837–57 the railroads of their section had swallowed up approximately $150,000,000 in capital; that Massachusetts alone had invested $100,000,000 in roads centering in Boston. The railroad investment in that section was one-third greater than the banking investment. "It is this enormous demand for capital," stated the Boston *Journal*, "which has kept up the rates for interest so long, and although the demand for the New England States is nearly at an end, it is still very heavy elsewhere . . ." The estimate that by 1859 fully a billion dollars (much of it, of course, drawn from abroad) had gone into railways indicated why sprawling America seemed slow in rearing mills and factories. Some thought the panic of 1857 produced primarily by over-investment in railroads.[101]

[ XI ]

Already many transportation problems of the future were lifting their heads. Scores of communities, especially in the closing years of the decade, complained of excessive freight charges. Railroad men, pointing to a pamphlet on the subject by Captain William H. Swift, argued that they were really too low. But who could say what constituted a fair rate? As rebating and other discriminations spread, grumbling became common. In 1856 the mayor and board of trade of Dubuque, Ia., assailed the Illinois Central for numerous practises ("every species of petty warfare") unfair to Dubuque, and favorable to its rival Dunleith. This was because the Illinois Central, allied with the Dubuque Packet Company, was interested in the warehouses, hotel, and ferry at Dunleith.

And to an increasing extent, men arraigned the lusty young corporations for their efforts to influence the State legislatures. Throughout the decade the Pennsylvania Railroad seemed to be knee-deep in politics. Its acquisition of the State's transportation facilities at a low price was the fruit of an adroit campaign of pressure and propaganda, begun as early as 1852.[102] Simon Cameron soon

100 Bogen. *The Anthracite Roads*, 89.
101 Boston *Journal*, quoted in *National Intelligencer*, April 16, 1857, estimated $700,000,000; the railroad convention at Buffalo in March, 1859, more than a billion. The estimate of T. C. Cochran and William Miller, *The Age of Enterprise*, 83, is over $1,500,000,000 by 1860.
102 William Prindle, January 10, 1853; Cushing Papers.

formed a political partnership with the line. The Erie was potent at Albany, and the Illinois Central at Springfield. But the company whose political activities invited the strongest denunciation was the Camden & Amboy. When in 1854 it sought from the New Jersey legislature not merely a twenty-year renewal of its charter, but an enlargement of its monopolistic position, the New York and Philadelphia press raised a loud outcry. The upper house passed a bill intended to prevent the building of any competitive road whatever. Editors attacked the "monopoly swindle"; public meetings were held; and the head of the line, Commodore Robert F. Stockton, was assailed as a public enemy. Representative Bissell of Illinois demanded in Congress: "Why, is the State of New Jersey itself anything except a railroad company? Or a sort of fixture or attachment to such a company? I believe her entire sovereignty is kept by the railroad company, or the directors thereof." [103] Greeley called these directors the rulers of the State. The bill was beaten, but sage observers believed the defeat only temporary. "The company will have to elect another legislature to extend their monopoly," observed the *Tribune*.[104]

Early in 1860 the New York legislature took up an important bill for the regulation of railway rates. It prescribed that each freight-carrying road should make up "a complete classification, as it shall rate the relative value of transportation of the property carried," designating the classes as first, second, third, and so on. The highest rate charged should not be more than three times the lowest —though certain commodities, including ore, coal, meats, milk, and garden vegetables, were exempted from the act. Surcharges were limited. All rates were to be publicly posted, copies were to be filed with the State government, and they might not be changed at all within five days of filing, or thereafter by more than thirty per cent. Rebates and drawbacks were forbidden. So were combinations with another company to transport freight at a lower rate than that company would otherwise charge. All railroads were required to carry the products of the State at the same mileage rates as freights originating outside— a requirement which brought impassioned protests from the Erie and Central, which were trying to get Western freight away from the Baltimore & Ohio and the Pennsylvania by offering special low rates. The penalties for violation were severe; fines running from $250 to $1,000 imprisonment, or both. When the bill failed, agents of the Erie and Central, which had lobbied strenuously, were accused of defeating it by corrupt methods.[105]

103  N. Y. *Tribune*, March 1, 1854; *Cong. Globe*, 33d Cong., 1st sess., p. 498 gives slightly different language.
104  N. Y. *Tribune*, February 25, March 3, 20, 1854.
105  The Chamber of Commerce of the State of New York, with many merchants anxious to sell in Chicago, Milwaukee, and St. Louis at low through rates, joined the railroads in protesting against the bill. But it rallied much support both up-State and in the metropolis. N. Y. *Weekly Tribune*, February 18, 1860.

## [ XII ]

In any broad picture of American transportation in this period, three salient facts catch the eye. One is simply the rapidity and energy with which the whole region between the Missouri River and the Atlantic was being provided with a network of communications. Such a provision, creating the greatest and richest national market in the world (for during this decade the population of the United States passed that of Great Britain), had to precede the establishment of a powerful manufacturing industry. The task was being accomplished; a smaller part of the national capital would presently be needed for new transportation lines; and the country could turn a new page in its development. The second fact is the emergence of a set of "railroad problems," connected with rates and competition, which anybody could see would soon become intermixed with politics. But the fact of most immediate importance was the completeness, closeness, and modernity of the great transportation web which was binding the agricultural Northwest with the industrial, mercantile, and financial East.

Binding the agricultural West and industrial East; but just what was the industrial picture?

# 7

## The Rising Industrialism

COULD THE UNION endure?—that was the anxious, all-pervading question that faced the politicians. Could a truly national utilization of the country's resources be achieved?—that was the major question confronting business leaders. The wisest statesmen wished to strengthen the Union by sectional adjustment, fair laws, and the creation of a fraternal spirit; the ablest business leaders wished to operate without thinking of State and regional lines. Both impulses were nationalistic. The expansion of the forties, with the acquisition of Oregon, California, and the Southwest, enhanced the magnitude of both tasks. Just as it presented the politicians with a wide range of territorial problems, it presented businessmen with challenging new difficulties of scale. Huge vacant areas were to be settled, far reaches were to be covered by rails and telegraphs, and the scope of business organizations touching the West was to be doubled. But whereas observers often feared that the political problem might prove insoluble, nobody doubted that business would successfully exploit the wealth of the continent. The imperial domain of farmland, cattle ranges, timber, and minerals roused the appetites of a people already materialistic, and quickened the hopes of a society already sanguine.

Year by year, moreover, the advance of technology and invention strengthened the country for its work of economic conquest. Even as the troops of Taylor, Kearny, and Frémont added to American distances, improvements in the railroad and telegraph shortened them. Even as the rapid settlement of new Western lands drained old communities of half their manpower, new machines for factory and farm halved the general manpower problem. The result was that nothing checked the business exuberance of the time except the occasional panics that were half the result of its own excesses. To be sure, the industrial advance created as many problems as it solved. In time it would be seen that many a valuable invention resulted in a temporary evil of technological unemployment; that the interests of agriculture, railroading, and manufacturing would be hard to adjust; and that the task of controlling destructive competition without setting up dangerous monopolies would tax men's resourcefulness.

But as yet the country was in the honeymoon of fresh and boundless resources combined with a fast-expanding technology.

"A great though silent revolution in our National Industry," said the New York *Tribune* in the spring of 1860, "has for forty years been in progress."[1] The industrial revolution might be in its early stages, but it was well under way. A worldwide phenomenon, it was certain under any conditions whatever to transform the republic. No crisis was needed to bring it to fruition. Borrowed from England, it metamorphosed one land after another: Germany, Japan, France, Belgium, Italy, and eventually Russia. If the United States had one entrenched landed group, the Southern planters, who opposed a rapid industrialization, Germany had an equally powerful element of opposition in her junkers, and Japan another in her daimios. Decade by decade, ideas and inventions were more rapidly transferred from one country to another. The Bessemer process no sooner aroused the curiosity of British ironmasters than Abram S. Hewitt's New Jersey iron mill was experimenting with it: Goodyear's vulcanizing method was hardly made known in America before it was seized upon in England. The irresistible sweep of industrialization could nowhere be stopped, and nowhere long delayed. Had the United States remained at peace in the sixties, that decade would have witnessed a tremendous acceleration in the growth of manufacturing and trade, just as the fifties displayed an immense advance over the forties.

It is doubtful whether the Civil War had anything like the accelerating effect upon the industrial revolution that is commonly supposed. The great elemental forces, revolutionary in nature and worldwide in operation, are far more important than cataclysmic impulses confined to a single land. While wars stimulate certain phases of national evolution they retard others. The Civil War accelerated the mass production of clothing and shoes, but it did nothing to spur the growth of the new petroleum industry, which would have taken a prodigious forward leap in any event, and it actually retarded the iron and steel industry. The conflict demanded relatively small quantities of iron, slowed down the construction of railroads, which had been using most of the iron produced, and created conditions inimical to adoption of the Bessemer-Mushet process of steelmaking. In a review of the thirty years, 1850–80, of our industrial efflorescence, still other facts might be assigned for reducing the role of the Civil War. The wartime boom furnished a partial stimulus to industrial

1 N. Y. *Weekly Tribune*, April 21, 1860. The great leap forward began about 1850. Of that year the *Preliminary Report of the Eight Census* (1860; pp. 76, 77) says: "The spirit of enterprise abroad was very strong, and the impression that prices were to rise by reason of the depreciation of gold was prevalent; hence the general desire to operate, in order to avail of the anticipated profits. Industry of all descriptions was very active and productive, and there was never a period when national capital accumulated so fast."

expansion and change; but its extremes bred a panic and depression, 1873–78, which chilled experiment and growth. Had no war occurred, a more equable, more steadily maintained progress could well have brought the industries of the nation to the point they actually reached in 1880.

In America the underlying forces of the industrial revolution were simply irresistible. The wealth of natural resources; the energy of the people; the flow of invention; the provision of cheap labor by heavy immigration; the supply of capital by savings, gold-and-silver discoveries, and European investment—all this combined like a chain of bellows to make the forge roar. To a considerable extent a sixth factor, government encouragement, was discoverable. Federal and State aid subsidized railroad building, which in turn directly stimulated the iron and lumbering industries, and indirectly vitalized a hundred other forms of manufacturing. Certain tariff aids furnished by the government were important to nascent industries. The government, finally, kept taxes low, and maintained a hands-off attitude which protected businessmen from interference.

## [ I ]

As industry expanded, its interlacing roots and branches made a powerful contribution to the unification of the country. With every step in growth, it more emphatically demanded the whole nation for its demesne. The fact that the Northeast was becoming mainly industrial while the South remained overwhelmingly agricultural rendered these areas complementary rather than antagonistic. In some respects they needed each other more distinctly than if they had been alike. Northern and Southern merchants, manufacturers, and railroadmen struggled almost to the last against sectional disseverance. Iron-makers of the North wanted higher tariffs, but they were unwilling to estrange the Southern railroad builders, bridge-contractors, public-works officers, and others with whom they constantly did business. Northern textile manufacturers also wanted tariffs, but not at the cost of angering the section on which they depended for raw materials. The war was caused primarily by social, moral, and political, not economic forces. Industrialism did not weaken the Union, but strengthened its fabric. It was not dissatisfied with its opportunities for growth during the fifties; it had reason to be content, and fairly remained so.[2]

The steady rise of the corporation was one great fact of the period. Jacksonian democracy had attacked monopoly, especially in the fields of banking and transportation, by substituting for special charters the general State law of incorporation. New York's general incorporation act of 1811 had been liberal for its time; but the famous law of 1848, based on a new State constitution,

2  Cf. Nevins, *Abram S. Hewitt*, 185, 186.

roughly marked the beginning of an epoch. Within the next dozen years all the Northern and Northwestern States took similar action, and the corporations set up under these new laws were numbered by tens of thousands. Of all the business corporations of the country in the first half of the nineteenth century, nearly half were established during the fifties.[3] As they multiplied, they made all forms of business life more impersonal.

Once the master of a factory had labored among the machines with his hands, the head of a store had helped the clerks make sales, the ironmaster had known all his workmen by their first names. The owner of a business had been personally responsible to the public for its operations. But now corporation heads sat aloof in offices, and absentee owners were common; while for the misconduct of many a business nobody seemed responsible. "The corporation has neither a body to be kicked nor a soul to be damned," men said disgustedly. With the growth of impersonality came a decline in morals. These "artificial creatures," a Massachusetts legislative committee noted in 1850, would treat laborers and the public in a way that flesh-and-blood men would not.[4] Already, too, men were beginning to feel and fear the power of interlocking corporate groups. The fifteen Boston families united in the "Boston Associates" controlled by 1850 one-fifth of the nation's cotton spindles, almost a third of the Massachusetts railway mileage, approximately two-fifths of Boston's banking capital, and two-fifths of the State's insurance capital.[5]

In a sprawling, inchoate nation, industrialism was by far the most powerful force making for a greater degree of organization. The fast-growing corporations were the strongest coherent groups in the land. The farmers were unorganized. Labor was unorganized. Professional groups, apart from the clergy and physicians, were unorganized. Retail business was unorganized. To observant men, the country seemed invertebrate. National authority was still poorly centralized in any of its numerous offices. It might be set at naught in almost any area by the imperfections of its machinery, the clashing authority of the States, and the high-tempered individualism of the citizens. State authority was positively exercised in only a few channels, such as education and road-building, and even there but partially and spasmodically. The Protestant churches, however loosely powerful, were ill-organized, for their tradition was generally hostile to centralized authority, and their steady westward march had tended to strengthen the local autonomy of congregations. Business alone was developing organization on a general scale and of a powerful type. The first trunk-line

3 Thomas C. Cochran and William Miller, *The Age of Enterprise*, 70; C. M. Haar, "Legislative Regulation of New York Industrial Corporations, 1800–1850," *New York History*, April, 1941.
4 Massachusetts House Docs., No. 153.
5 Vera Schlakman, *Economic History of a Factory Town*, 35ff.

railroads, the strongest banks, the shipping-lines of Cornelius Vanderbilt, the Michigan mining-companies, the Trenton and Pittsburgh iron corporations, were islands of organization in a restless sea of multitudinous unorganized activities. They alone pointed to the highly organized republic of the future.

Already industrialism was creating a special array of leaders. A business type was becoming as prominent in the United States as in Europe; keen-witted, incisive of speech, with ready energy and an air of being up-to-date or ahead of it. The type had long been familiar in London, Manchester and Liverpool, and had grown important in Boston and New York, in Lyons and Hamburg. Within a generation Lafcadio Hearn was to discover it in the industrial metropolis of Japan, where, as he wrote, "the man of Osaka is said to be recognizable almost at sight." [6] Eastern seaboard cities had first produced the American congener, but he was now abundantly identifiable in Pittsburgh, Cleveland, St. Louis, and New Orleans. In gait, thought, and speech the keen trader or organizer met the competitive pace of the time. He could furnish expert information about products, transportation, and prices all over the map; adaptable to any company, he could be refined with clergymen, jocose with sportsmen, or common-sense with farmers and merchants.

In energy and talent such men were superior to the average professional man or politician; already the best brains of America were going into business. In populous communities they were becoming the dominant American type. A generation earlier the typical American had been rural—leisurely, ruminative, conservative, and thoroughly honest; now he was urban and commercial— hustling, quick-witted, progressive, and sometimes of an elastic moral code.

Since the merchant, who had long exercised leadership in business, was yielding pride of place to the entrepreneur, a transition between the two was afforded by the merchant turned entrepreneur. Such a man as Elihu Townsend, who died at his Union Square home in 1853, represented the supersedence admirably. For long years he was simply a partner in a plain, substantial mercantile house.[7] Then he assumed leadership in one great undertaking after another. He was one of the little group who chartered the New Haven Railroad and took its first stock. When the panic of 1837 halted the Erie, he stepped forward to aid it and brought in other moneyed New Yorkers. He was one of three men who built the Atlantic Dock in Brooklyn, costing nearly a million. He owned a large cotton mill in Brooklyn, and was interested in other factories. He had given substantial support to the development of Cairo, Ill.; while in his last days he evinced a keen interest in promoting the Mexican Ocean Mail and Inland Railway to shorten the journey to California by six to ten days.[8] A still more

6 *Gleanings in Buddha Fields*, 136.
7 Nevins, Townsend & Co.
8 N. Y. *Tribune*, June 28, 1852.

striking illustration of the cycle of economic change is offered by the Lawrence family. The mother of Amos and Abbott Lawrence passed many hours each day at her spinning wheel or hand loom. In 1807 Amos came to Boston with twenty dollars in his pocket, and the next year Abbott joined him. Their firm, at first a mercantile and importing house, presently turned to manufactures; and the name of Lawrence soon became synonymous with textiles the world over.

Even yet, to be sure, the dignity of the merchant was tremendous. Every bright boy in the East knew that Edwin D. Morgan, who was elected governor of New York in 1858, had become wealthy in the wholesale-grocery trade; that H. B. Claflin, another merchant of Yankee birth, whose huge drygoods business removed to larger quarter in the shadow of Trinity steeple in 1853, had built his fortune on the rule of the lowest possible margin of profit; and that Charles L. Tiffany had turned the sale of jewels, silverware, and bric-a-brac into a fine art, winning the plaudits of all lovers of beauty. A large proportion of the men engaged in all branches of business had begun life by "clerking" in some mercantile house. Marshall Field, for example, after some training in a small store in Pittsfield, Mass., became in 1856 a salesman in a wholesale drygoods house in Chicago, and before the Civil War was a partner.

The drygoods trade in particular enjoyed an eminent position, such names as William E. Dodge and A. T. Stewart diffusing an almost magical aura. Its special distinction was largely traceable to the high purchasing power and varied tastes of American women. In Europe few were able to buy silks and satins, moirés, taffeta, and furs, of varied design. In America a very large number of women made such purchases constantly. British travellers marveled at the great stores in New York and Philadelphia, with frontages of five hundred to seven hundred feet, plate-glass windows, and marble pillars; they exclaimed over the seven-million-dollar business that Stewart did annually in the early fifties in his Chambers Street store. The tastes of Louisbourg Square and Fifth Avenue were spread through towns and villages by *Godey's Lady's Book* and its like, by advertising, and by travel. The plainest woman aspired to a few annual touches of fashion, and even on the Kansas frontier the wives of log-cabin settlers knew what was being worn on Independence Square. Hence it was that the merchant princes of Eastern cities remained among the most admired of Americans.

Yet the trend was toward transportation and manufacturing as the largest single sources of wealth. The firm of Phelps, Dodge & Company had a not untypical history. Both Anson G. Phelps and his son-in-law Dodge were originally merchants; but they expanded their interests into manufacturing, mining, and railroading, and the fifties found their mill town of Ansonia flourishing. More and more of the ablest young men were drawn into manufacturing with very brief preliminary training.[9] The later years of the decade found John D. Rockefeller a clerk in a mercantile establishment, and Carnegie (whose mother had once kept a "sweetie shop" in Scotland) with the Pennsylvania Railroad; but industry called to both with irresistible voice.

[ II ]

The capital invested in manufacturing, according to reports, almost doubled between 1850 and 1860, rising from $533,200,000 to $1,009,000,000, or by 89.4 per cent. This increase represented the largest ten-year investment thus far made in American history. Not even in the Civil War decade was so high a *percentage* of growth attained. The expansion was the more striking in view of the fact that throughout the decade, except for the single year 1858, the balance of trade was against the United States. Where did the capital come from? Home savings counted for much. So did foreign investment and reinvestment; as early as 1853 the Secretary of the Treasury estimated that foreign holdings, including state and national bonds, amounted to more than $222,-000,000. But that dazzling piece of national good fortune, the discovery of gold in California, was one of the most important factors. For the ten years the nation's production of gold had a value aggregating no less than $533,118,000. This aureate stream helped meet all adverse balances in foreign trade, lifted prices as with some giant hydrostatic lever, and stimulated all branches of the national economy. During the whole history of the country from 1792 down to the finding of the first yellow flakes in Sutter's mill-stream, only about twelve hundred ounces of gold had been mined. Now in ten years very nearly twenty-seven million ounces were produced.

But it is the question of the investment of this capital which interests us. What national resources were used, and how were the arts of fabrication applied to them? The basic materials for machine industry were coal and iron. Though most Americans knew that the republic was marvelously endowed with both, they were not used by 1860 on a scale which Britons would have called extensive. Why was this, and what were the prospects for the future?

Americans liked to boast that they had three-fourths of all the coal reserves of the world, and that their fields were thirty-six times as great as those of the British Isles. Such statements were wild guesses, but the optimism which they expressed was legitimate. Nevertheless, on the eve of the Civil War only eight States mined more than a hundred thousand tons of coal annually, and the entire nation did not lift fifteen million tons. Great Britain's production was roughly

9  D. S. Dodge, *Memorials of William E. Dodge*, 21 ff.; Carlos Martyn, *William E. Dodge*, 68–81.

five times as large, and that of little Belgium was more than three-fifths as great. Though Pittsburgh lay upon a huge bituminous bed stretching far about the city and covering many millions of acres, its upper seams alone offering an almost illimitable wealth of fuel, it lagged far behind several British cities in coal-utilization. Alabama and Missouri possessed an immense store of coal, but in 1860 the Alabamans mined barely ten thousand tons, and the Missourians less than four thousand.

Among the reasons for this tardiness were the vast stores of cheap firewood, the ease with which foreign coal was imported, the wide diffusion of population and industry, the considerable use of local waterpower in the North, and the mildness of the Southern climate. Railroads were largely wood-burning, and steamboats almost exclusively so. The gas-works of New York and other Eastern cities (for this was the age of gaslight) used shiploads of coal from Great Britain for years after the Civil War.[10] Innumerable towns of New England, Pennsylvania, and New York employed waterpower for factories, flourmills, and sawmills—supplemented at need by cordwood. But as the timber of the coastal plain was depleted, as population thickened, and as industry grew less primitive, the demand for coal naturally increased. While Van Buren was President, the Welshman David Thomas built the first successful anthracite iron furnace in the country. The growth of canals and railroads was soon making coal cheaper in many communities than firewood. The Reading Railroad supplied hard coal at low rates to industries and households of Philadelphia, while the Delaware, Lackawanna & Western, tapping the northern deposits, brought anthracite at low cost to New York city. Other coal roads assumed growing importance, and it did not escape notice that the shrewd Moses Taylor, head of the City Bank, unhesitatingly seized an opportunity to buy control of the Lackawanna.[11]

In iron, we meet the same story of enormous deposits and relatively slow exploitation. Veins of ore were scattered over the Middle Atlantic States, the wild country encircling Lake Superior and upper Lake Michigan, and the Southern Appalachians. But the fifties found only the mines of Pennsylvania and New Jersey as yet industriously worked. Until the Civil War, the Schuyl-kill Valley was to remain the heart of the business. Despite the immense national resources in this field, the iron-mining industry in 1860 was not so far advanced as that of Great Britain had been twenty years earlier; for the United

10 Sir S. Morton Peto, *The Resources and Prospects of America*, 184. The later fifties found a trade monthly, the *American Gas Light Journal*, published in New York. It declared in 1859 that an aggregate capital of fifty millions or more was employed in the gas industry, and that the dividends of numerous companies had long been ten per cent a year, with occasional extra dividends of ten or even twenty per cent.

11 Jules I. Bogen, *The Anthracite Railroads*, 85–89.

States dug only nine hundred thousand tons, and even allowing for quantities taken by foundries from their own lands and not reported, the total fell below that of the British in 1840. The production of pig-iron was likewise smaller than that of Great Britain twenty years before. Once more the main reasons for the nation's tardiness were simple. Since the railroads wished cheap iron, tariffs were kept low. Great quantities of British iron were imported at minimum rates, keeping native output at a slender volume. The lack of a *regular* demand was a telling element; for being dependent on the railroads, many ironmasters prospered or suffered according to the fortunes of a notably speculative field of industry. The high cost of labor and of money were also deterrents. Moneyed men would not invest capital in iron manufacture, or workmen their labor, while more profitable and agreeable openings were available.

For both the coal and iron industries, the growth of transportation, the sweep of settlement across the treeless prairies, and the rise of machine industry were prerequisites for any large-scale progress. By 1860 these factors were all being supplied.

A network of railroads made it possible to speed coal to remote points, while the roads themselves required ever larger supplies of iron. A railroad used from eighty to a hundred tons of iron per mile in rails alone, costing, at an average of $50 a ton, from $4,000 to $5,000, while spikes, switches, bridges, and trestles added to the demand. As rails wore out every few years, replacements were heavy. The rapid expansion of the railway system added to the permanent demand. It is easy to see why both British and American ironmakers competed so eagerly for this market. The rising cities of the Middle West required coal for fuel, and iron for innumerable uses. By the middle fifties it had been found that iron made on the headwaters of the Ohio could be sold in the interior for less than British prices; and immediately after the Civil War, an English visitor found that there was an insatiable demand for "almost any amount of it." Americans, this observer noted, then made their own rails, bar-iron, boiler-plate, nail-plate, wire-rods, and sheet-iron; they forged their own anchors, manufactured their own car-wheels, and turned out their own stoves and furnaces. Locomotive factories like that of the Baldwins in Philadelphia, and tool-factories like that of Ames Brothers in Massachusetts, were equal to any of Europe. The American factories for sewing machines, firearms, and farm implements were the best in the world. Year by year, naturally, the country needed more of its own iron and anthracite.[12]

Throughout the fifties the Cooper-Hewitt works at Trenton showed how

---

12  Peto, *Resources and Prospects of America*, 175ff. As coke was developed into a substitute for anthracite, and high-quality Lake Superior ores were made accessible, Pittsburgh became the chief iron center. Marvin W. Schlegel, *Franklin B. Gowen*, chs. 1, 2.

much a versatile and enterprising ironmaster could accomplish despite high labor costs and keen foreign competition. Superior iron for long-lasting rails; iron for John A. Roebling's new wire-mill; iron for structural beams in large public and private buildings; iron for bridges; iron for fencing; iron for Federal ordnance—these were some of Hewitt's specialties. News of the Bessemer process reached the United States in the late summer of 1856. The *Athenaeum*, which circulated widely in America, published Bessemer's paper on the manufacture of steel without fuel on August 23; while a brief account of the discovery appeared in the New York *Tribune* of September 16 and the *National Intelligencer* of the 18th. In December, and again in the following January, the new process was unsuccessfully tested by Hewitt at Phillipsburg, N. J. Most American and British ores were not immediately adapted to it, and mechanical and chemical adjustments had to be made before it proved generally acceptable.[13] Another enterprising establishment was the Cambria Iron Works of Johnstown, Pa., which gained renown as a practically self-sufficing unit; for the property embraced about twenty-five thousand acres, with iron ore, coal, limestone, and firebrick clay all abundant. By 1859 the Cambria's blast furnaces were capable of making eight hundred tons of pig-iron weekly, while its rolling mill, the largest in the country, could turn out seven hundred tons of finished railroad iron every week.[14]

[ III ]

Invention seemed an American pastime. By 1850 American sewing machines, telegraphs, reapers, Colt revolvers, vulcanized rubber, pressed glass, and circular saws were famous. On each a whole industry had been founded. The shoe-pegger, the steam fire-engine, soda-water, ether as an anaesthetic, and the Hoe press all had an important effect upon society—and all were famous by 1850. The greatest sight in Washington, to multitudes of visitors, was not the Capitol but the Patent Office. In 1854 the number of patents was one-fifth greater than in 1853, and in 1856 it was one-third greater than in 1855. The government in 1854 issued fifty-six patents for harvesting implements of various kinds, thirty-nine for seed-planters, and sixteen for plows. The next year it issued forty for sewing machines, thirty-nine for seed-planters, and sixteen for plows. A year later still it issued forty for sewing machines, thirty-one for looms, and nineteen for locks. America being still primarily an agricultural country, inventors were most active in making farm appliances. But they concerned themselves ceaselessly with steam engines, heating apparatus, illuminating devices, and a thousand

13  Nevins, *Hewitt*, 125-132.
14  N. Y. *Weekly Tribune*, June 18, 1859.

other matters. Invention was not a pastime at all, but a business. The hope of fortune, the ambition of growing rich, lured the inventor on.

It was natural that America, with her great distances to conquer, should lead the world in inventions concerned with transportation. Locomotives and cars made in the United States had virtues all their own. The inequalities of the tracks, the steepness of the grades, and the sharpness of many curves required engines very different from those used on the straight, level, and solidly-built railroads of Europe. These special demands gave birth to the "equalizing lever," which divided the shock of a bumpy roadbed between the two opposite wheels to which it was attached; the swivel truck at the front of the locomotive, which easily followed the curves of an abruptly swerving road; the eight-wheel design, distributing the weight of the engine over a larger area; and the "basket" mode of construction, loose yet strong, which gave the engine flexibility in meeting torsions and stresses.[15]

American rails, again, were quite unlike Britain's. When Robert L. Stevens went to England in 1830 to buy rails for the Camden & Amboy, he whittled out a model of the world's first T-rail, which soon became standard in the United States. Fastened to the ties by a spike instead of a costly "chair," it saved tremendous sums in construction.[16] American cars till about 1840 were in the main the small-bodied, partitioned carriages which fitted European conditions. Then builders lengthened the car, removed the partitions, enlarged the body, and began installing conveniences. Within a dozen years the standard car was nearly fifty feet long, the body occupying forty-two feet and the platform and buffers the remainder. The best cars had woodwork of black walnut, white oak, or birch, seats unholstered in flowered plush, and windows of imported plate glass. These roomy, open coaches were more comfortable for long journeys, seated more passengers, and suited the democratic spirit of the people.

When the Virginia Central was built over the Blue Ridge, its chief engineer, Charles Ellet, Jr., congratulated M. W. Baldwin & Co. of Philadelphia upon the stalwart performance of their locomotives. In winding around the spurs and over the summit, the road climbed as much as 295 feet in a mile, and described curves which were only three hundred feet in radius. Yet the twenty-eight-ton engines drew heavy trains without difficulty. "They have climbed the extraordinary grades and turned the abrupt curves of this road in all kinds of weather," wrote Ellet, "including storms and sleet, when the rails have been covered with frost and ice and the cuts have been filled in places several feet deep with snowdrifts." [17] Since American locomotives had heavier trains to haul than those of Europe, traversed rougher roadbeds, and used inferior fuel, they needed more

15  Roger Burlingame, *March of the Iron Men*, 252-255.
16  A. D. Turnbull, *John Stevens, An American Record*, 501.
17  *National Intelligencer*, November 27, 1855.

frequent repairs. But foreign observers agreed that several American companies made engines as good as any abroad.[18]

Some of the manufacturers, indeed, won an international repute. Besides Matthew Baldwin, who had made one of the very first locomotives in the country, and whose works turned out more than fifteen hundred before his death in 1865, William Mason and Holmes Hinkley, both inventive New Englanders, deserve to be remembered. Mason, apprenticed at thirteen to a cotton manufacturer, had an artistic streak, which evinced itself in portrait painting and violin playing. Turning from the making of improved textile machinery, in which he scored his first great success, to larger fields, he began early in the fifties to build locomotives at Taunton, Mass. They came to be recognized the world over for their symmetry of design and mechanical excellence. His locomotive No. 25, placed in service in 1856, was exhibited under its own power at the Baltimore & Ohio centenary sixty-one years later. Hinkley, another pioneer, who had built his first locomotive in 1841 for the Portland, Saco & Portsmouth Railroad, turned out more than six hundred by the beginning of 1856. The Norris, the Rogers, and the Amoskeag Works also deserve mention. Of fifty-eight locomotives listed by the C. B. & Q. Railroad in 1858, seventeen were already coal-burning.[19]

Equally did the United States lead the world in the invention of farm machinery. The large potential market, the keen interest of the farm press in new devices, and the well-attended exhibitions of State and county agricultural societies, all stimulated an incessant activity. A small improvement in a straw-cutter enabled one inventor to realize $40,000 in profits from a single western tour; a new model for a threshing machine was sold by another inventor for $60,000.[20] Compared with foreign designs, American farm machinery was distinguished by lightness and simplicity. Bulky, heavy machines would not work well on rough land, while complicated mechanisms were useless in areas distant from repair shops and spare parts. Costly implements, moreover, were unsuited to a nation where land was cheap, most farmers had little capital, and holdings were of moderate size.

American plows, cornplanters, wheat-drills, revolving rakes, cultivators, and other horse implements were excelled in no part of the world. For a time American threshing-machines had been imitated from British models, but before 1850 such makers as the Pitts Brothers were producing the best models (still none too good) known anywhere.[21] By the end of the decade sulky or riding plows were

18 Peto, *Resources and Prospects of America*, 282.
19 *Dictionary of American Biography*; E. S. Hungerford, *The Baltimore & Ohio Railroad*, II, 91; pubs. of the Ry. and Locomotive Hist. Soc.
20 Peto, *Resources and Prospects of America*, 103.
21 Burlingame, *March of the Iron Men*, 234.

being introduced, enabling boys of fourteen to do the heaviest ordinary plowing. At the Crystal Palace exhibition in London (1851) it was noted that for many articles of rural use, the ingenuity, utility, and cheapness of the Yankee entries easily bore off the palm. Besides wooden pails and the like, wrote one visitor, "our handled axes, hay-rakes, grain cradles, scythes and snathes, three-tined hay-forks, solid steel hoes, road-scrapers, posthole augers, fan-mills, smut-mills, sausage cutters, sausage stuffers, tinman's tools, permutation locks, wheel cultivators, carpenters' tools, currycombs, corn-brooms, portmanteaus and trunks, ice-cream freezers, axletrees, paint-mills, and many other things of universal use here, but in the shape and conveniences which we have given them utterly unknown in Europe, established for our industry a character independent of and unlike that of any other nation." [22] The picks and shovels of Ames Brothers, for which the California and Australian goldfields furnished an extensive new market, were unsurpassed. Many a Briton turned from admiring inspection of a Yankee clock to find his wife equally pleased with a Yankee churn.

The sewing machine, too, had its hour of triumph in London, which it deserved not merely as an invention but as a product of American manufacture. A number of experimenters in different lands had worked on the problem of a practical machine; and the first to succeed on this side of the Atlantic was Elias Howe, Jr., whose patent was dated September 10, 1846. Seldom has a device been so rapidly developed. Though numerous subsequent patents were granted various men, all machines using two threads to make a lock-stitch were subject to Howe's basic claim; and he wisely granted licenses to sub-manufacturers, exacting from each a fee for every machine. The press in 1859 stated this to be five dollars. At that time the principal manufacturers, all paying the royalty, were Wheeler & Wilson, I. M. Singer & Co., and Grover & Baker. They, with smaller manufacturers, turned out in twelve months of 1858–59, according to Howe's own statement, a total of 37,442 machines. Englishmen asserted that two of their inventors, Fisher and Gibbons, had devised a lock-stitch sewing machine before it was invented in America. But they had to admit that in making the machines the United States was unquestionably first. Whereas in England the lowest price for a lock-stitch machine was £22, American machines could be imported into Scotland, not covered by the English patent, for about half that sum. And whereas 1859 found only about ten thousand sewing machines in England, the United States was making nearly four times that number every twelvemonth. In fact, Wheeler & Wilson alone sold in one year nearly sixteen thousand machines. Their cost, ranging from $50 to $150 apiece, placed them beyond the reach of the poor, but all middle-class families regarded them as a necessity.

22 *National Intelligencer*, February 3, 1852.

It was the reaper, however, which won the most signal triumph at the Crystal Palace. Before the public trials were held the London *Times* had derided McCormick's queer-looking contrivance, remarking that it looked like "a cross between a flying-machine, a wheelbarrow, and an Astley chariot"; but its competitive performance quickly converted all skeptics. On a gloomy, chilly, drenching day at Tiptree Heath, July 24, 1851, it moved efficiently through the heavy wheat while its two rivals failed.[23]

"Before it," wrote the elated Horace Greeley, "stood John Bull, burly,

Demonstration of the safety device of the Otis Elevator at the Crystal Palace Exhibition.

dogged, and determined not to be humbugged; his judgment made up and his sentence ready to be recorded. Nothing disconcerted, the rough, brown, homespun Yankee in charge jumped on the box, starting the team at a smart walk, setting the blades of the machine in lively operation, and commenced raking off the grain in sheaf-piles ready for binding, cutting a breadth of nine or ten feet cleanly and carefully, as fast as a span of horses could comfortably step. There was a moment, and but a moment, of suspense; human prejudice could hold out no longer; and burst after burst of involuntary cheers from the whole crowd proclaimed the success of the Yankee 'treadmill.'"[24] Obed Hussey's reaper, which had choked in the wet grain of Tiptree Heath, made a favorable

23  William T. Hutchinson, *Cyrus Hall McCormick*, I, 389.
24  N. Y. *Weekly Tribune*, August 21, 1851.

showing on a subsequent harvest tour of Britain, and Prince Albert ordered two Hussey machines for his estates.

McCormick, who had patented his machine in 1834, was more than an inventor; he was one of the builders of the Middle West. His reaper, a product of the grain-growing Valley of Virginia, had obviously required a larger world. At first he had made little effort to push his production. In 1842, after much labor to remedy faults, he sold only seven machines, and in 1843, only twenty-nine. But he began to engage New York, Ohio, and Illinois firms as sub-manufacturers to turn out reapers for those States, and his own invasion of the prairies soon followed. With a sure vision of the future, he planted his manufactory in 1847-48 in Chicago, then a city of about seventeen thousand people, where he soon concentrated all construction under his own direction—for he found that distant licensees had sold inferior machines. His younger brothers joined him there, capital was obtained from the railroad-builder William B. Ogden and others, and before 1860 the establishment, with several hundred mechanics in three large buildings turning out more than five thousand reapers a year, was one of the most famous manufactories in the country. The price of a combined reaper and mower in 1854 was $155. McCormick, a man of boundless energy, with that combination of force, determination, and combative prejudices associated with the Ulster Scots, sought for improvements, expanded his production, travelled far and wide to advertise his wares and spur on his agents, conducted lusty court battles over patents, and thrust his fist into Democratic politics. The number of his competitors, exceeding thirty in 1850 and a hundred ten years later, testified to the richness of the market. But he maintained an easy primacy, and to him more than anyone else belonged the credit for the ever-widening acreage of wheat and oats that rolled under the prairie winds, the ever-swelling shipments of grain and flour that left the lake ports.[25]

Of all branches of manufacture, that of farm implements showed the most striking increase in the fifties, rising from a little less than seven millions in value to a little less than eighteen, or 160 per cent. And this manufacture followed the westward march of farm population. Already the first and second generation of farmers in the area between the Alleghenies and the Missouri were spending generously to augment their production and lessen their toil.

Whereas in 1850 not quite two million dollars' worth of agricultural implements were produced in the Western States, in 1860 the figure exceeded $8,700,000. By the latter year the value of implements and machinery used on American farms (cotton gins, vehicles, and hand tools not included) was nearly $250,000,000, and the demand was steadily increasing. Production for rural

25  Hutchinson, *McCormick*, I, 453ff.

buyers ramified in many directions. One of the largest of the early Chicago fortunes, that of Silas B. Cobb, was founded upon a harness manufactory.[26] The industrial history of Quincy, Ill., a typical Midwestern manufacturing center, presents some interesting illustrations of the way in which the growing farm population was served by Western enterprises. A four-year-old stove factory in 1854 made seven thousand cooking-stoves and three thousand parlor-stoves, with a retail value of ten dollars apiece. That same year the manufacturer of a portable corn-mill sold thirteen hundred machines for twenty-five dollars each; while other firms were making threshers, corn-shellers, and burr mills for grinding feed. The little Mississippi River city, so newly risen from the wilderness, also listed in 1854 fifteen wagon and plow shops, which manufactured nearly 1,400 wagons, carts, and buggies, 3,500 plows, and a large quantity of harrows and scrapers.[27]

Other branches of heavy industry made but slow progress. The astute S. Morton Peto observed that the manufacture of stationary steam engines, for example, was strangely backward, being even after the Civil War "still in its infancy." [28] Outside the fields of agriculture and transportation, machinery was tardily developed. This was largely because European and particularly British makers supplied such an abundance of good machinery at low prices that only heavy tariff walls could guarantee an adequate market to Americans. But the iron-manufacturers, striving to enlarge their sphere, did show considerable ingenuity in making construction materials.

Their most noteworthy innovation was the large-scale production of iron beams and girders for buildings. James Bogardus of New York, after taking out a number of patents for new devices in cotton spinning, sugar grinding, bank-note-engraving, and the like, and after winning a $2,000 prize for the best machine for engraving postage stamps, had turned to the use of cast iron for the frames, floors, and supports of buildings. In 1850 he erected a five-story factory which was said to be the first complete cast-iron building in the world.[29] Patenting his method, he put up many other iron structures in the larger cities. But since cast-iron beams had to be thick and heavy to meet the strain, and even then tended to buckle, other men experimented with wrought iron, which Robert Stephenson had used for his great Menai bridge in Wales in 1849. When the erection of Cooper Union began in 1854, wrought-iron beams rolled at Trenton by specially designed machinery were employed; this being

26 T. W. Goodspeed, *Univ. of Chicago Biog. Sketches*, I, 147–170.
27 H. L. Wilkey, "Infant Industries in Illinois," *Journal Ill. State Hist. Soc.*, XXXII, No. 4. Chicago by 1855 had nearly 1,500 people employed in its iron, machinery, and stove industries alone. The total capital invested in its manufactories was then placed at $6,363,400, and the total employees at 6,288. *Hunt's Merchants' Magazine*, XXXV, 177.
28 Peto, *Resources and Prospects of America*, 141.
29 *Dictionary of American Biography*.

the first building in which a grid of rolled wrought-iron supported the heavy flooring of extensive rooms. Trenton wrought-iron beams were used in Harper Brothers' new building after their disastrous fire of 1853, and the Federal government was soon employing them all over the country. Much credit was due to Secretary James Guthrie of the Treasury and the head of the Bureau of Construction for instituting tests, and insisting thereafter on the many structural advantages of iron.[30] By 1856 the Cooper-Hewitt beams had been ordered for more than a hundred Federal and many State buildings, and were increasingly sought by those who wished strong, fire-resistant, and comparatively light materials.[31] According to the Harrisburg *Pennsylvanian*, government orders had given a marked stimulus to private demand for iron, and had "already brought up the American production from 500,000 to nearly 1,000,000 tons per annum."[32]

## [ IV ]

It was to be expected that in a land of forests the American sawmills and planing-mills, seen at their best in Maine and Michigan, should excel all others. The British Commissioners at New York's imitative Crystal Palace exhibition gave them special praise. Wood-pulp paper was being used by at least two newspapers, the Philadelphia *Public Ledger* and Providence *Journal*, in 1854. Meat-packing and grain-milling of course developed with great vigor in the North and West. Both were still in a rather rudimentary stage; efficient wheat-grinding machinery had yet to be patented, while chilled meats were unknown. Nevertheless, by 1860 the hog-slaughtering establishments of Cincinnati and Chicago had evolved the conveyor-belt system and the differentiation of labor which were to become so prominent a characteristic of American manufacturing.

Now and then a particularly striking product of American ingenuity in the use of abundant primary materials appeared, as in Gail Borden's meat biscuit. A rugged, versatile Southwestern pioneer, by turns soldier, farmer, surveyor, stock raiser, map maker, land agent, customs collector, and what not, Borden was struck by the difficulties which migrating settlers encountered in carrying adequate provisions, and by the plethora of meat on the Texas ranges. At the London exhibition of 1851 he showed two very ordinary barrels of unsavory looking hardtack which he called meat biscuits. While most visitors passed them by unnoticed, British government officials inspected them with keen interest. Borden told army men that he had discovered a process of preserving

30 Report, Senate Manufactures Committee, February 20, 1857.
31 Nevins, *Hewitt*, 113–116.
32 Quoted in *National Intelligencer*, July 8, 1856.

animal food by extracting in concentrated form all its nutritious elements, mixing them with flour, and baking the result in an oven in the form of crackers. A pound of this preparation contained the nutriment of five pounds of meat; so that all the valuable essence (fats excepted) of more than five hundred pounds of good fresh beef, with seventy pounds of flour, could be packed in a twenty-two-gallon cask. The biscuit was easily preserved in all climates and over long periods of time, without attracting insects or growing mouldy. "I am from Galveston," said Borden proudly, and he described the

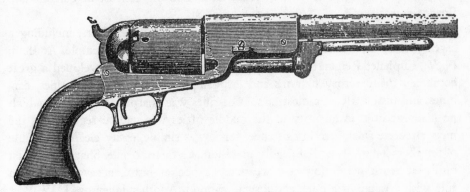

The Colt Walker model .44 revolver, first made in 1847.

vast Texas plains, covered with cattle waiting to be converted into this convenient meat-biscuit. The Crystal Palace authorities gave him what many an exhibitor would have paid a thousand pounds to obtain, a great or council medal. And though his meat biscuit was not destined to prove a commercial success, on his way home Borden, seeing how much some of the immigrant children aboard his ship longed for milk, was started on the train of thought that led to condensed milk.[33]

It was inevitable, too, that in a country with a wide frontier to advance, firearms should have some points of special perfection. The hunting rifle of the Pennsylvania and Maryland frontier had helped to win the Revolution. Samuel Colt's revolvers, their merits blazoned to the world by the Mexican War, were soon used all over the globe. When in 1853 Colt established a factory at Milbank, England, the *United Services Gazette* predicted a keen demand. "What is so useful as a protection against the Indians, Mexicans, wild animals, and the robbers of California," it declared, "must prove equally efficacious against the dacoits of Burmah, the ruffians in Australia, the people of the hills north of the Punjab."[34] British tests showed that while Birmingham arms had

33  See *National Intelligencer*, January 15, 1852; Borden Papers, U. of Texas Archives.
34  Quoted in *National Intelligencer*, December 24, 1853.

a high percentage of defective pieces, Colt's revolvers failed but once in two thousand five hundred trials. His Hartford factory, where he was one of the pioneers in the mass production of standardized parts, and where his precision tools reduced variations to a minimum, flourished under the orders rained upon it during the Crimean War and afterward. By efficient salesmanship, selling his wares to Indian-fighters, to Mormons, Irish Fenians, Kansas emigrants, fiery Southerners, and apprehensive European nations, Colt built up in the fifties one of the largest arms factories in the world, and became a millionaire. Like Rockefeller and Ford in a later day, he manifested a strong distrust of bankers and finance-capitalism.[35]

The Whitney works in Connecticut also made fine revolvers, including a seven-shooter with rifled barrels which was strong, light, and simple. At Ilion, N. Y., Eliphalet Remington, son of a farmer and mechanic, developed a great combined manufactory of arms and farm implements, turning out rifles, carbines, and pistols. But the most famous of rifles was Sharpe's. One model which he manufactured in quantity in the middle fifties was widely regarded as the most effective small arm in existence, for it was simple, easily cleaned, capable of ten shots a minute, and of deadly precision at a quarter-mile. Sharpe was then busily at work perfecting new weapons—a pocket pistol, a cavalry pistol, a rifle with a range of a mile, and a small cannon. Another inventor, J. W. Post of New York, patented a repeating rifle which in 1856 was said to be capable of thirty discharges a minute.[36]

In a land of common schools and fairly high literacy levels, where publishing was an extensive business, the making of printing-presses offered tempting business opportunities. Those designed and built by Richard M. Hoe attained an international fame. Brought up in the press-room of his father, an English immigrant, young Hoe followed his sire in making improvements on English machines, and in 1845–46 turned out type-revolving presses based on new patents of great originality. When in 1847 he installed for the Philadelphia *Public Ledger* a cylinder press capable of printing 8,000 papers an hour, something like a newspaper revolution resulted.[37] One journal after another adopted his machinery. In 1856 he shipped a six-cylinder press to London for *Lloyd's Weekly Newspaper*, which instantly ordered a duplicate. Nearly every newspaper proprietor in London, with crowds of other people, visited the shop to see it work. The London *Times* was then printed on a press which, with a staff of twenty-seven men, made 11,000 impressions an hour. But Hoe's press produced 15,000 impressions with a staff of only seven or eight, and the *Times* forthwith ordered a ten-cylinder model from America.[38]

35  Jack Rohan, *Yankee Arms-Maker*, Chs. 17–24.
36  *National Intelligencer*, June 23, 1855.
37  James H. Harper, *The House of Harper*.
38  Robert Hoe, *Short History of the Printing Press*.

## [ V ]

In the arts of design youthful America naturally followed behind her European sisters. Yet designers of real talent could be found, and some of them made happy use of native ideas, forms, and materials. The handsome capital which Tennessee erected during the fifties at Nashville was adorned by a gilt-and-bronze chandelier, said to be the largest ever made, from the workshops of Cornelius & Baker in Philadelphia. It effectively employed buffaloes, a soaring eagle, and Indian figures, gracefully modelled, surrounded by stalks of maize, cotton, and tobacco.[39] Though European glass was in general far better than American, the tradition of Stiegel and his Bristol hands was not forgotten; a Brooklyn manufacturer of flint glass received a first prize at the London Exhibition for wares of greater purity and brilliance than any others of the same type. Pittsburgh glass (the city by 1857 had thirty-three workshops with nearly two thousand employees) was known around the globe.[40].

The Europeans who had a low opinion of New World craftsmanship were astonished when the Crystal Palace awards for the best square pianos were carried away by Nunns & Clark in New York, Chickering in Boston, and Myers in Philadelphia. The making of pianofortes, then about fifty years old in the United States, had languished until 1822, when Nunns & Clark set up their business. A year later Jonas Chickering, trained under an older manufacturer, had commenced business in Boston. By 1852 New York city alone had more than a hundred piano manufacturers, and few of the larger centers of the North were without one. Nunns & Clark occupied an entire New York block on Third Avenue between Twenty-fifth and Twenty-sixth Streets, where they had two five-story workshops, seasoning-yards, and some houses for workmen. They prided themselves upon keeping their sounding-boards of native spruce from seven to ten years before use. Chickering not only built up a huge factory —his Tremont Street building was said to be the largest edifice in the country after the Capitol—but hit upon many improvements. To make it easier to keep grand pianos in tune, he had a full cast-iron frame made to sustain the tension, thus opening a new era in piano manufacture.[41] So important was the piano market that at the annual fair of the American Institute in 1852 a large section was given up to an impressive display by some twenty instrument-makers. Mechanical skill was united to artistic taste in a way that even German piano-makers could admire.[42]

39 *National Intelligencer*, August 21, 1855; the chandelier still hangs, a work of arresting beauty.
40 See Brooklyn advertisement in N. Y. *Weekly Tribune*, August 28, 1858; Arthur Bining, "The Glass Industry of Western Pennsylvania," *Pa. Mag. Hist. and Biog.*, December, 1936.
41 *Dictionary of American Biography*.
42 N. Y. correspondence in *National Intelligencer*, October 23, 1852.

But nobody ever questioned the ingenuity of the American inventor or industrialist. Goodyear's india-rubber fabrics were ingenious. He even made some beautifully colored and printed school globes from inflated rubber, refusing a lavish offer from the Sultan of Turkey for them because they were not quite perfect. Connecticut clocks were ingenious. Schooley's patent refrigerator, widely sold by the middle fifties, was ingenious; it utilized the principle later so effective in refrigerator cars, forming a current of cold air which expelled the warm air from upper vents.[43] The artificial ice-making machines (Cincinnati by 1856 had an artificial ice factory, worked by steam) were ingeniously adapted to the hot American summers. An ingenious electric locomotive, long in advance of its time, was invented in 1851. The Otis elevator, product of an ingenious Vermont mechanic employed in a Yonkers factory, dates from 1852— it being more slightly in advance of its time.

And the products of American locksmiths were marvels of ingenuity. At the London Exhibition a quiet, unobtrusive agent for the bank lock made by Day & Newell in New York suddenly became a figure of renown. This man, named Hobbs, found that the public paid little attention to his lock. He decided to call attention to it by demonstrating that he could pick any rival lock with ease. A sober committee assembled one morning to see him attack a lock which one of the best English makers had specially devised to secure important state papers. Within a few minutes, using a simple instrument taken from his vest pocket, he triumphantly threw it open. He then transferred his attention to a shop window in Piccadilly, where a lock had long been exhibited with an offer of £200 to anybody who could invent an instrument to pick it. Hobbs presented himself, made suitable arrangements, and had arbiters appointed. He then set to work, swiftly opened the lock, and by unanimous decision received the reward. Thenceforward, he was one of the lions of the exhibition, and had no difficulty in collecting a crowd about his glass case. From the Queen down to the plain workingman, everybody was eager to see his lock! [44]

All this American ingenuity was not difficult to explain. For one reason, while most workers in old countries merely perfected the patterns used by their fathers, the novel conditions of the American scene encouraged workmen to strike out unconventional patterns. The variety of circumstances met in the raw continent tested men's resourcefulness, and the free atmosphere of social and economic life placed a premium on boldness. But an equally important characteristic of American industry, its trend toward mass-production, was asserting

43 *National Intelligencer*, June 19, 1856.
44 See letter of S. N. Dodge, secretary of the United States commission, in *National Intelligencer*, January 10, 1852.

itself. As population grew and as railroads brought more and more people within easy reach, incentives to large-scale production increased.

A salient example was offered by the shoe trade. In 1843 all the manufacturers of Milford, Mass., one of the principal shoe centers of the nation, turned out only 150,000 pairs of footgear; but in 1852 a single firm there made 135,000 pairs. Even yet, however, a boot passed through not fewer than twenty hands before being finished. In New York, Underwood & Godfrey, inventors of the so-called Hungarian boot, owned in the early fifties a large factory on Pearl Street. But it depended largely on the initial labor of widely-scattered household workers. Half-made boots came in by the car load and cart load from piece-workers throughout the State; and the finishing was then done largely by hand. In one room fourteen sturdy treers, with sleeves rolled up, were proud of their ability to tree nearly three hundred cases of boots in a week! [45] The inefficiency of this system was evident. Lyman R. Blake, who had been one of the pioneers in setting up sewing machines in clothing factories, and who had organized a stitching room in a Massachusetts shoe-plant, invented in 1858 a machine to sew the soles of shoes to the uppers. Once this proved a success, the development of mass-production shoe factories was easy; and in 1859 Gordon McKay, a machinist of true business genius, who saw the possibilities of the device, undertook to promote it.[46] Boston during the fifties became the largest boot and shoe market in the world, far outselling any other city. By 1857 the Hub had more than two hundred wholesalers and jobbers in the business, and their annual sales approached thirty-five million dollars.

The arms factories, which had been the first American plants to attain mass-production based on a high standardization of rapidly-fitted parts, still held their special distinction. The Springfield arsenal was one of the chief industrial spectacles of the nation. To produce a complete musket, nearly three hundred machines and five hundred distinct mechanical processes were required; but so rapid was the operation that, beginning with raw material, a finished firearm could be turned out every eighty minutes.[47] The watch industry of the country, however, was copying and improving upon Eli Whitney's methods. At the beginning of 1850 there were probably not a thousand American-made watches in the country. A small number had been made at different times and places, and during the War of 1812 the industry had seemed about to take firm root, but capital had never been attracted to the business, and English and Swiss importations had met the demand. Then in 1850 the first watches were made by the use of automatic machinery producing standardized parts, precision-made,

45 National Intelligencer, March 5, 1853.
46 Dictionary of American Biography.
47 National Intelligencer, October 29, 1856.

and in 1853 superior watches appeared on the market at $40. The manufactory of Appleton, Tracy & Co. at Waltham soon led the world. It carried the division of labor to a new pitch of perfection. Every part was a facsimile of the like part in every other Waltham watch of the same size, so that the man who broke a spring, wheel, pivot, or balance-staff need only send the type-number of his watch to the factory to obtain a replacement. Since the fast-growing body of employees put the parts together with great speed, prices were low and quality was high.[48]

On William Chambers's visit to Cincinnati in 1853, he was impressed by the gigantic scale of a furniture factory in that city. Chairs were turned out at the rate of about 125,000 a year, the two hundred and fifty hands working in departments, some sawing, some planing, some mortising, some painting and varnishing, and making much use of machinery. He found another establishment producing about a thousand bedsteads a week. At Lynn, Mass., he was told that division of labor and employment of machines made it possible for that town to manufacture four and a half million boots and shoes yearly. The managers of Ames's shovel factory at North Easton, Mass., were proud of the skill with which they had organized the hands in their dozen or more connected workshops. Before a shovel was completed, according to *Hunt's Merchants' Magazine* for 1856, fifty different sets of employees had dealt with it. "Each one has a separate and distinct process to perform, and is taught that and no other." The sugar refineries in New York, according to the same journal, had developed remarkable expertness in the application of machinery to the mass-production of sugar. Engines hoisted the raw material to the tops of the buildings, where it was liquefied and passed through a series of processes on its downward journey.

The sewing machine of course lent itself to a slow transformation of the clothing industry to a partial mass-production basis. The census report of 1860 pointed out that "the vast demand for ready-made apparel of moderate cost has developed an enormous and growing trade." In Chicago alone the wholesale and retail trade in ready-made garments amounted to $2,500,000 annually. Rough work-clothing for men probably constituted the staple of this trade; one Western observer spoke of the demand by boatmen and emigrants. However, the dressmaker was to a perceptible extent being replaced by factories operating on a quantity level. The spring of 1857 found an enterprising manager in New York keeping 175 sewing machines at work on hoopskirts, and steadily increasing his force. The *Tribune* estimated that three-quarters of the sewing in the city would soon be done by machine, and much of it by organized workshops.

48  N. Y. *Weekly Tribune*, March 6, 1858; H. C. Brearly, *Time-Telling Through the Ages*, Ch. 13.

The city then had scores of such shops making cloaks, mantillas, and the like, and seventy-eight making hoopskirts; and while this number did not compare with the four thousand manufacturers of men's clothing, it was not negligible.

Dozens of inventions, indeed, large and small, were quickly exploited for mass-production. The gold pen, for example, had been perfected by an American, John L. Hawkins. He had long sought a nib which might be soldered to gold, would be hard yet flexible, would carry ink well, and could easily be cleaned; and while resident abroad he profited by British experiments to make a gold pen pointed with iridium (1834). But this so-called invention was less important than the industrial use made of it. By 1850 two factories were humming in New York and Boston; and with ingenious machinery fabricating more than a hundred thousand pens a year, the retail price was only $2.50.[49]

## [ VI ]

Thus the industrial revolution was being pushed forward along a wide front; Yankee ingenuity marrying itself with facilities for large-scale production, and utilizing the nation's wealth of raw materials to supply a market that the railroad and steamboat were fast making truly national. Barrel-making had been a local business, slow and costly. But by 1857 anybody could buy for $700 a machine which in a few minutes transformed a piece of timber into a set of barrel staves and heads at the low cost of two and a half cents a barrel.[50] Perhaps the machine was still inadequate; but it at any rate pointed the way toward an indispensable auxiliary of the petroleum, flour, whisky, turpentine, and many other industries. As the fifties ended, shoemaking machinery was still definitely inadequate. But it was being improved so rapidly by Gordon McKay and others that the men would soon say, with little exaggeration, that the leather was put in at the end of one row of machines and came out finished footgear at the other; so rapidly that a single Yankee factory would soon be producing more shoes than the thirty thousand bootmakers of Paris.

Once industrialism was firmly planted, it advanced with ever-accelerating rapidity. In Massachusetts, for example, the value of manufactures was first estimated in 1837, and was then $86,282,000. By 1845 it fell just short of $125,-000,000. Ten years later it was $296,000,000—and expert observers thought that

49 N. Y. *Tribune*, February 25, 1850. Evert Duyckinck in his MS diary for October 9, 1857, mentions the prospectus for a typewriter invented by Samuel W. Francis, the keys of which could be moved at the rate of seven letters a second. "An ingenious contrivance of convenient size . . . ," he writes. "The adjustments are very neat. How Milton having readily learnt to manage the keys would have rejoiced in this mode of composition, so consonant with this favorite organ."
50 *National Intelligencer*. March 28, 1857.

really accurate returns would have shown a product of $350,000,000. In other words, within less than twenty years the manufactured products of the rocky little State had probably quadrupled in value. It was significant that while the capital employed in the decade 1845–55 had just doubled, rising from about sixty millions to about one hundred and twenty millions, the number of employees had grown only from 153,000 to 246,000; machines, that is, were doing more and more of the work. An official commentator declared that the industrial growth of Massachusetts during the decade "is believed to be without a parallel in the history of the world." [51] An interesting illustration of the speed with which New England was being industrialized was revealed by a fire which swept part of Brattleboro, Vt., in 1857. Not long before, Brattleboro had been a sleepy country town. But the fire destroyed a paper mill, a cabinet factory, a rule factory, a large melodeon factory, and a machine shop—and this was only about half the mechanized business of the little city. Brattleboro had become a manufacturing center.[52]

Obviously, more capital and energy would have been thrown into industry but for the steady westward drive. Money was urgently needed to open the Middle West and Far West; to construct railroads, break and stock the prairie farms, move the fast-swelling crops, and build the villages and towns that thrived upon agriculture. Money so invested paid quicker, surer returns, in general, than did capital in the ordinary mill or factory competing with European industries. As the West became settled and its railroad network grew fairly complete, a larger share of the nation's savings and borrowings could be diverted to manufacturing. Throughout these years, the trans-Allegheny region was a great vacuum which sucked down its throat labor, brains, enterprise, steam power, and surplus funds. The nation was kinetic—a nation on the march; its frontier was geographical, whereas the frontiers of Great Britain, Germany, and later Japan were industrial. It was not until society became more static, until cheap land, with all its prospects of unearned increment from a fast-rising population, became less of a lodestone for capital, until seven per cent factory stocks became as attractive as seven per cent railroad bonds, that industrialization could make its most rapid progress.

The general advent of that new period coincided with the end of the Civil War, for 1870 was to find the line of well-settled farms pushed far beyond the Missouri River. Because it did roughly coincide with Appomattox, many observers have exaggerated the share of the Civil War in producing or accelerating the industrial revolution. It must be said again that this revolution would probably have completed itself at much the same time, though not in just the same way,

51  *Idem,* May 24, 1856.
52  *Idem,* September 8, 1857.

had there been no war. It must be repeated that if we examine the accelerating pace, measured in percentages, of industrial growth, if we consider the fact that the war retarded some elements in the great transformation while it stimulated others, and if we weigh the additional fact that the war boom contributed to a terrible post-war depression, we may well conclude that a peaceful America would have grown as fast industrially as the America of history did.

## [ VII ]

Industry found one great stimulant in the more than half-billion-dollar gold production of the decade, which stimulated confidence, raised prices, and helped provide capital for new enterprises; but after 1846 it lacked the additional assistance of a high protective tariff. This was not for want of assiduous campaining by Northern makers of railroad iron, textiles, and miscellaneous wares. Could the Whig Party have gained full control of Congress and the presidency, protectionist legislation would probably have been forced through. But the Democrats never ceased to hold at least one chamber, while after 1853 they were in continuous possession of the White House. The agricultural interests of the South and West in this particular effected a tacit alliance; and many Southern leaders regarded even such low tariffs as existed as an unequal and unfair tax on the rural sections. Faced with this obstructive front, the complaints of manufacturers were twofold. In the first place, they argued, duties were at all times too low; in the second place, they were on an ad valorem basis, which meant that they fell lowest of all in times of glut and depression. But American tariff policy was geared to the demands of the dominant primary industries, not of secondary and tertiary production.

The foreign commerce of the United States, like its industrial production, roughly doubled during the fifties. In view of the panic of 1857 and its sequels, it is rather impressive to find that in 1860 imports and exports reached $687,-000,000, as against $317,000,000 in 1850. The great export staple was cotton; but grain came next, and in such increasing quantities that it promised to become cotton's rival. The chief imports were manufactured goods, with textiles first, iron (in rails, bars, rods, pigs, and castings) second, and the finer miscellaneous manufactures following. Britain was far and away the best customer of the United States, and the largest seller to it. The generally unfavorable balance of trade gave needless worry to many people who did not see that the country was stocking itself with both consumers' goods and durable goods in a perfectly healthful fashion, and that the nation paid for its excess of imports over exports in simple and logical ways; by the earnings of the large merchant marine, the commissions of merchants in the re-export trade, and the specie and bullion brought from Latin-America and the Orient. The investment of European capital in American enterprises was also a compensating factor.

Since American prosperity depended largely on foreign trade, it was sharply affected by the wars, the economic vicissitudes, and the commercial policy of other lands. No small rôle in the good times of 1850–56 was played by the repeal of the British corn laws. When the State Department submitted to Congress an exhaustive four-volume report on commercial relations compiled by its statistician, Edmund Flagg, much attention was directed to the pages upon comparative tariffs. They brought out clearly the dependence of both the cotton and breadstuffs trade on the open British market, which admitted these staples without a penny of duty—though the British did place a heavy tariff on American tobacco. Flagg's report praised the "enlightened" policy of Great Britain, asserting that it had demonstrated within a brief period of five years that England could best compete with the merchant marine of other nations by placing the trade of every port, at home and in the overseas colonies, upon the freest possible footing. The success of British manufacturers, backed by British commercial diplomacy, in expanding the world market for cotton goods year by year, meant much to American cotton producers; Alabama planters lived better because Manchester sold more and more "shirts for black men." [53] And as British population grew, so grew the American grain trade. In the year after the corn-law repeal, 125,000 quarters of American wheat passed through the London market alone.[54]

Since the cotton trade possessed great political importance, it merits a special word. In the five years 1851–55, the United States exported an average of more than a billion pounds of cotton annually, of which roughly seven-tenths went to Britain, and two-tenths to France. The British did not use at home quite all they bought, reëxporting about a sixth of it to the continent—principally to Central Europe and Russia. But the amount they did use made cotton manufacturing by far the most important industry in the British economy. A great part of the whole British income was derived from the fabrication of this raw material.

Taking the decade of the fifties as a whole, British experts estimated that the shipments of cotton goods comprised from two-fifths to five-ninths of their total exports, while cotton textiles also constituted an important element in their domestic trade. About one-seventh of the whole population of the United Kingdom, or four million people out of twenty-nine million, were regarded as dependent upon the cotton industry. In 1860 England, according to the best figures available, had thirty-three million spindles as against twenty million in

53 Cf. Clapham, *Economic History of England*, I, 480–482.
54 *Idem*, I, 500.

the entire world outside. It is easy to see that the South, anxious to have her British market maintained, and eager also to keep the price of manufactured goods low, had a double reason for hostility to protective tariffs. It was abundantly clear to cotton and grain shippers that Britain could not long buy huge quantities of their commodities if Americans did not purchase large amounts of woolens, the finer cotton textiles, railroad iron, and miscellaneous manufactures from the United Kingdom.

Hence the tariff remained static, and primary commodities continued to be the principal American exports. The outcries of Northern ironmasters,[55] textile manufacturers, and other industrial leaders were incessant. Such journals as the New York *Tribune* never desisted from their high-tariff crusade. Abbott Lawrence, writing in 1850, sounded a note which was destined to echo throughout the ensuing decade. Since the repeal of the tariff of 1842, he said, imports had steadily exceeded exports. California gold and American securities were being used to meet the excess. "The spindles of Manchester and ironmasters' machinery are digging gold every hour, without the risk and trouble of going to California. The effect of our revenue laws, with the introduction of gold from the Pacific, has been so far and will in my opinion continue to [be to] stimulate the labor and productive power of every country but our own. . . . Congress should without delay adopt a moderate tariff of specific duties. The industry of our own country should be protected." Such pleas were all in vain.[56]

Yet special products of American ingenuity, from wooden pails to sewing machines, did find their way abroad in growing quantities. Nor did manufacturers fail to try to exploit markets in far-off fields. The principal object

---

55 During the thirties practically no railroad iron was made in the United States, and almost none in the early forties; it came from England, and the cost averaged in 1842 about $100 a ton. In that year Congress laid a protective duty to encourage iron-making. A number of furnaces and mills were constructed under what their owners called an implied promise of future protection. Many of them went into operation during 1845 and 1846, and the owners credited this home competition with effecting a reduction in the price of rails to about sixty dollars a ton. Then the Walker Tariff of 1846 reduced the duty to 30 per cent ad valorem. The iron manufacturers charged that this duty was further diminished by falling on artificially low prices stated in foreign invoices—indeed, fictitious prices. They also charged that English manufacturers took advantage of the situation to prostrate the American manufacturer, underbidding the Americans on all contracts and selling inferior rails as low as $40 a ton until they utterly destroyed the rolling of rails in America. This accomplished, they advanced the price of rails to $80 a ton, and for several years held command of the American market at this high rate. It was charged by the ruined American manufacturers that $60 a ton would have been a fair price. About 1853, the high market brought a few American rolling-mills back into operation; and by the beginning of 1856 this domestic competition had again reduced the price of rails to $58–60. See the well-informed letter on the recent history of the industry by an ironmaster in the *National Intelligencer*, February 21, 1856. Material on the abortive efforts of the iron mills to gain better tariff rates may be found in Nevins, *Hewitt*. A good picture of the conditions ruling in the mills in this period is presented in the *Autobiography* of John Fritz.
56 September 27, 1850; Everett Papers.

of the Perry expedition of 1853 was to find whaling havens and possible trade outlets. Just after the frigate *Susquehanna* arrived at Hong Kong from Yedo with reports of Perry's treaty, a Chinese correspondent of the New York *Tribune* wrote that he had seen a long list of American goods likely to be wanted in the island kingdom—textiles, hardware, stoves, glassware, carpeting, firearms, clocks, and leather goods.[57] South America also was viewed with sanguine eye. Here the best customer was Brazil, which sold the United States increasing quantities of coffee, and took in return considerable amounts of breadstuffs, with some fabricated goods. The total annual trade with Brazil by the middle fifties fell little short of twenty million dollars. In Chile and Peru adventurous Yankee engineers vied with Britons in laying out railroads, building bridges, and opening mines; while a visitor in 1855 found smelters, gristmills, public buildings, warehouses, and similar works credited to Americans. The railroad then under way between Santiago and Valparaiso had been planned by William Wheelwright of Massachusetts and surveyed by American engineers, though a Briton was superintending the construction. Two important mining railroads, one connecting Tacna with Arica in the nitrate region, and the other the Copiapo & Caldera, which was surveyed by Allan Campbell of New York, had been placed in the hands of Walter W. Evans of New Jersey as engineer and principal builder. It was hoped that as this transportation development proceeded, American trade would follow in its wake.[58]

Industrialism, beginning to remake America, had among its advantages the nation's rich natural resources, an inventive if not expertly trained body of machinists and experimenters, a growing fund of capital, a reservoir of cheap immigrant labor, and a market that was steadily becoming less local and more national. It met with difficulties and handicaps aplenty; but the idea that it was not making sufficiently rapid progress would never have occurred to most of its leaders and would never have gained the assent of the mass of the population. Slowly and unsystematically, but steadily, surely, and fruitfully, it was transforming the republic. Year by year it rendered the North more powerful in

57 N. Y. *Tribune*, June 13, 1854.
58 *National Intelligencer*, July 31, 1855. The New England trade in ice was an interesting example of Yankee ingenuity in primary industry and commerce. Frederic Tudor made the first shipment in 1806, taking ice from his father's pond near Lynn, loading 130 tons of it in the brig *Favorite*, and sending it to Martinique. Despite some heavy losses in the early years, the trade grew. Other men, especially in the later thirties, engaged in it; the Oriental market was opened; and it became one of the mainstays in maintaining the Calcutta trade of New England. In 1846 New England sent out 75 cargoes, of 65,000 tons; in 1856 the trade had increased to 363 cargoes of 146,000 tons. This ice went to Southern ports, to Latin-America, to Australia, and to the Far East. Merchants in Batavia sipped their stingarees with Boston ice; officers of Bombay stirred it into their punch; grandees of Buenos Aires used it to ice their fruit. The Boston Board of Trade applauded a report by a committee upon the trade, glowing with pride. The pride was justifiable, for the Yankees had taken water and climate, and created a commercial staple of great value. *Report*, Boston Board of Trade, 1857.

relation to the South, and supplied the States from Pennsylvania to Maine with the means of knitting the Northwest to themselves. But to understand the method by which this alliance was achieved, we shall have to turn to other aspects of the economic picture; in particular, to the flood of immigration which in 1846–61 helped place one great forcing-draft under American industry with an ample body of labor.

# 8

## Immigrants and Toilers

HERMAN MELVILLE, keenly scanning the docks at Liverpool, was impressed by nothing (as he wrote in 1849) so much as the confluent tides of emigration which he saw streaming westward. Aboard the British and Yankee ships bound for Montreal, Boston, and New York, tramped a variegated army: Irishmen with knee-breeches, high-crowned hats, and blackthorns; Germans with caps, short jackets, and meerschaums; Scandinavians with gay waistcoats, and sober Britons. Girls from Cork and Munich fingered their rosaries, while countrymen of Knox and Calvin sang Protestant hymns. Plows that had scored the hills of Transylvania were being carried to Wabash prairies, and wheat that had waved yellow in Warwickshire was taken to seed the Iowa valleys. The manner in which America was being settled, wrote Melville, should forever extinguish national prejudices. "We are not a narrow tribe of men . . . whose blood has been debased in the attempt to ennoble it, by maintaining an exclusive succession among ourselves. No: our blood is as the flood of the Amazon, made up of a thousand noble currents all pouring into one. We are not a nation, so much as a world." [1]

The immigration of the thirties had fallen just short of 600,000. That of the forties leaped up to a figure nearly three times as great, 1,713,251; and that of the fifties rose again to 2,598,214.[2] The first four years of the decade poured population across the Atlantic in a thick stream. During 1851, the number of foreigners entering the country was 351,550; during 1852 it was 372,725; during 1853 it was 368,643; and in 1854 it reached 427,833. Such a tide disturbed many American observers. They saw how many of the aliens were ill-educated or illiterate; how low were their living standards; how readily they responded to demagogues; how naturally the Irish and some others congregated in city slums and mill towns, and how clannish were many German and Scandinavian settlements in the Northwest.[3] But it was also plain that the newcomers brought

1 *Redburn,* ch. 33.
2 *Statistical Abstract of the U. S.,* 1940, p. 99.
3 The report of the House Committee on Foreign Affairs in 1856 on "Foreign Criminals and Paupers" (34th Cong., 1st sess. House Report No. 359), draws a distressing picture.

an energy, ambition, and industry that powerfully accelerated the nation's development.

The question whether in the long run immigration really meant an increased population is debatable, but for the time being it greatly augumented the nation's working force. Most of the immigrants came from the British Isles (1,338,093 for the decade) and Germany (951,667), with Scandinavia, Switzerland, and Holland furnishing nearly all the rest. Indeed, as yet more than ninety-five in a hundred of America's alien-born were drawn from the north and west of Europe. At the end of the decade, four distinct areas existed in which immigrants constituted more than thirty per cent of the population. These were the Eastern seaboard cities from Boston to Baltimore, full of Germans, Irish, and other newcomers; the upper Middle West, particularly Wisconsin, Minnesota, and Chicago; the Mormon settlements in Utah; and much of central and northern California, where Australians, Britons, and other adventurous wanderers mingled with Chinese and Kanakas. "What a glorious New Scandinavia might not Minnesota become!" exclaimed the Swedish novelist Fredrika Bremer, and a New Ireland and a New Germany seemed equal possibilities.[4]

Marked variations of flow were of course visible in this huge folk migration. Like a series of rumbling seismic disturbances, the European food-shortages and political revolts of 1845–48 sent tidal waves of hungry, discontented people across the Atlantic. The high point reached in 1854 remained a record mark for nearly two decades. But that was a year of depression in the United States, and news of the distress brought a decline. Recovery followed, to be still more sharply checked by the panic of 1857, and immigration then remained low until the outbreak of the Civil War. One factor in the flow was constant, the attracting force of American freedom and social equality. Three other factors varied unpredictably in strength: the propulsion of political unrest in Europe, the still more important thrust of economic hardship, and the pull of economic opportunity in the United States, strong in days of prosperity and weak in depression. A study of available documents suggests that an important rôle was played by the amount of money that the alien-born were able to send to bring over relatives and friends.[5]

When in the years 1847–54 the migration reached its height, it was the wonder of Europe and America alike. Emigration from the British Isles em-

4 *Homes of the New World*, 56, 69. Milwaukee by 1857 was more than half Teutonic; the Germans had three newspapers, one theatre, several militia companies, and countless taverns. *Irish News*, August 1, 1857.

5 See Edwin C. Guillet, *The Great Migration*, exceptionally good for "the British background" and the hardships of transit; Marcus Lee Hansen, *The Atlantic Migration, 1607–1860*, in which ch. 13 specially deals with this period; Harry Pratt Fairchild, *Immigration*, ch. 4; and Edith Abbott, *Historical Aspects of the Immigration Problem: Select Documents*.

ployed a fleet of a thousand vessels, aggregating 800,000 tons. Old World observers found the outgoing flood of 1854 particularly impressive. All the railroad stations of Ireland that summer seemed crowded with people flocking to Canada, the United States, or Australia. "Every boat that leaves the quays," remarked the Dundalk *Sentinel*, "carries off numbers of persons from this and the adjoining counties on their way to the United States, the passage money in most cases being paid on the American side of the Atlantic." Waterford and Tuam newspapers chronicled the departure of thousands. "Before the end of the year," lamented the Galway *Packet*. "Ireland will be literally deserted, and the silence and desolation which now brood over Connemara will be visible in the more populous districts of the country." Some perplexed editors believed the restlessness of the population an unreasoning mania. It seems wholly illogical, remarked the Sligo *Chronicle*, "when we consider the present prosperous state of the country and the accounts continually received of the sad disappointments experienced by thousands who were happy and comfortable at home." [6] Many wondering descriptions of the migration might be culled from English and German journals. In the single month of June fifty-one emigrant ships left Liverpool with 21,767 passengers, the movement from the Mersey in the quarter which ended that month breaking all records.

The Crimean War reduced emigration in various ways: by a shipping shortage and soaring transatlantic fares, by higher farm prices in Great Britain and prosperity in neutral European lands, and by the embargo which some countries declared on the departure of men of military age. But peace returned, the year 1856 and the first part of 1857 were a boom period in America, and the resumption of the departures—with ships again plying their old routes, and shipping agents and land promoters hard at work—again impressed Europeans. Altogether, more than a quarter of a million people were landed in America during 1857. "The extent to which emigration still goes on," wrote a Dublin correspondent on October 15, "is perfectly astounding." [7] Laborers were scarce in Ireland and wages high; more land than ever was being tilled, crops were good, and prices excellent; Ballinasloe Fair had never been so crowded or bidders so eager. Yet still emigrants gathered for debarkation.

Similar news came from Germany. The New Yorker *Abend-Zeitung* believed that before 1857 ended, Germany would send over the population of two or three petty states. Despite general prosperity at home, news was coming from all parts of the country, even from Prussian and Pomeranian areas theretofore strangers to the emigration fever, of parties gaily moving to the ports. Most of the migrants were well-to-do farmers and mechanics. "Their reason

6 All these journals quoted in *National Intelligencer*, June 22, 1854.
7 To the New York *Courier;* quoted in *National Intelligencer*, November 23, 1857.

for emigrating is not want or oppression, but rather the reverse, an excess of prosperity; an unaccountable rage for speculation, or a desire to acquire wealth more rapidly, has induced thousands of people considered well off among their neighbors, to turn their backs upon their homes and set out for the west." [8]

Though somewhat tardily felt, the panic of 1857 cut off immigration like sluice-gates closing a flume. Even in good times employment had frequently been difficult to find. "If two hundred thousand come over to us annually," the New York *Tribune* had warned in 1851, "there will be at least fifty thousand of them who will need good counsel and aid in their quest of Something to Do." [9] What jobs could a shipload of men freshly landed from Hamburg or Liverpool procure when New York had "forty thousand waiting and begging for work" already? Greeley suggested that the city should take the initiative in finding work, and send newcomers even hundreds of miles to accept it. It was better to advance railroad fares than to take these aliens into almshouses, or see thousands of them become vagrants and beggars. [10] As the last months of 1857 brought gloomy news of American wage-cuts, unemployment, and hunger, and as remittances declined, Europeans determined to stay at home. The next year saw immigration drop by half; and in the two years just before the war it remained nearly static at that low level. [11]

Two million people could not flow from Europe into America in a single decade without profound effects on the economy of both continents. When in the first half of the fifties Ireland's population was reduced by roughly half a million, the country benefited by steadier employment, better wages, and ampler food supplies. Similar gains were reported from Germany. Of course other factors contributed to the heightened prosperity of Europe. The repeal of the English corn laws helped Irish farmers, the flood of Californian and Australian gold stimulated investment and industrial expansion, the growth of railroads created new markets; but migration unquestionably raised Old World living-standards. [12] Irish workhouses which had sheltered 186,000 people in 1852 held only 84,500 three years later. [13] Meanwhile, the number on outdoor relief fell to less than one-third the old total. The chief cause for this was the rising labor-demand in the wake of the great exodus; wages, farm prices, and agricultural enterprise had all improved. [14]

8 Quoted in *National Intelligencer*, May 30, 1857.
9 Weekly *Tribune*, September 20, 1851.
10 Francis Bowen in an article in the *North American Review*, 1852, LXXIV, 221–232, argued that immigration tended to reduce wages to the European level of "a bare sufficiency for subsistence from day to day."
11 Hansen, *Great Migration*, 305.
12 Hyde Clarke in the (London) *Bankers Magazine*, 1853, XIII, 731ff., enumerates all these contributory causes.
13 *Report* of the Irish Poor-Law Commissioners, 1855–56.
14 See article in *National Intelligencer*, September 20, 1856.

Moreover, no sooner did the emigrants establish themselves than they began sending large sums home. It was authoritatively estimated that New South Wales in 1854 remitted £1,600,000 to the United Kingdom to promote emigration. According to a report on British emigration published in 1856, the sums sent to Ireland from American immigrants in the previous seven years amounted to £8,393,000, and in the last three years to about £3,500,000. In 1853 no less than £1,439,000, or nearly seven million dollars, was transferred from America to Ireland through the banks, quite apart from sums sent by private hands.[15] Indeed, much emigration operated on a revolving-fund basis, those who went abroad sending back money for connections who in turn remitted funds for a fresh crop of settlers. But much of the money was kept in the homeland. Many a Connemara cabin and Rhineland cottage was made more comfortable by American dollars.

The United States needed labor no less than Europe needed room, and as the newcomers built their energy and ambition into the republic, it was clearly the gainer. It would be easy to compile long lists of names later famous. Among Irish immigrants of the forties were three brothers named Ford; John Ford sought a home in Michigan, and a grandson was presently born there to be named Henry Ford.[16] Thomas Veblen emigrated from Norway in 1847, settling on the Wisconsin frontier under conditions of terrible hardship. His son Thorstein was born ten years afterward. The rich gifts which the German forty-eighters offered the United States were quickly illustrated by such men as Carl Schurz, Dr. Joseph Goldmark, Henry Villard, and Friedrich Kapp. Schurz's and Villard's careers are too well known to require characterization. Goldmark rapidly gained distinction by his work as physician, research chemist, and manufacturer of explosives. Dr. Kapp, who like the others had been identified with the republican movement in Germany, immediately became editor of a German newspaper in New York, and in 1858 issued his valuable life of von Steuben, an admirable example of German scholarship.[17] The Anglo-

15 Francis Bowen, *Principles of Political Economy*, 2d ed., 1859, p. 207. William Newmarch, the English economist and statistician, read a paper on the subject at the British Association meeting in Glasgow, 1855. Immigrants also *carried* money back. The packet ship *Daniel Webster*, sailing from Boston to Liverpool in the summer of 1855, carried about four hundred passengers, nearly all returning migrants who had accumulated property in the United States, going back to spend or invest in the old home land. Some carried drafts for several thousand dollars. Boston *Journal*, quoted in *National Intelligencer*, August 30, 1855. In this year, according to official British reports, 11,402 persons returned to the United Kingdom from America, and 4,419 from Australia; *National Intelligencer*, June 24, 1856. In the panic year 1857 the remittances to Ireland fell to £593,165. See the annual reports of the British Emigration Commissioners, which show the largest annual amount in the decade as £1,730,000 in 1854, and the smallest as £472,000 in 1858.

16 The Ford family was however of English origin.

17 The names of the Willkie family and Adolph Brandeis belong among the immigrants of this period; cf. Alpheus T. Mason, *Louis D. Brandeis*, ch. 1. The Brandeis family, though city people, "thought first of American land; like Jefferson, they associated freedom with agriculture."

Scottish and Canadian immigration, in no real sense alien, constantly brought in its Partons, Carnegies, and James J. Hills.

But it was as a great reservoir of labor that immigration was most immediately important. The spiritual gifts, the cultural enrichment, were mainly to emerge later. Most of the arrivals were ablebodied men and women in the prime of life. Of the 224,500 admitted in 1856, only 31,000 were ascertainably below ten years of age, and only 20,000 above forty.[18] That is, the overwhelming majority were and would long remain useful. It was again and again pointed out by European officials that most of the people leaving for America were young and vigorous.[19]

The fact that the newcomers were in their most productive years was evident to anybody who watched the Irish navvies on the railroads, the Welsh and Cornish miners in the Pennsylvania coal fields, or the British, Scandinavians, and Germans on the lines of travel to Western farms. The same fact was demonstrated by the figures of births. Foreign-born parents were highly prolific. Of the 32,000 children born in Massachusetts in 1854, only 16,470 were of American parentage, the remainder having parents one or both of alien origin. During the previous five years the number of births to purely American parents had not increased by one thousand, while the annual births of alien or half-alien parentage had risen by more than five thousand. "At the same rate," said the Newburyport *Herald*, "shortly we shall have more children born in Massachusetts from foreigners than from natives." The editor went on to say that in Suffolk County the births in foreign-born families were already more than twice as numerous as in American-born; that in Boston the Irish stock was increasing with far greater rapidity than the native stock; and that in Lawrence, Lowell, Fall River, Taunton, and even Worcester the same preponderance of children born to immigrants was well established.[20] Old Massachusetts, her main labor-supply Irish, was becoming Celtic!

It was observed that the Irish influx was solving the servant problem in most of the Northern cities. Less and less would native Americans serve as domestics, coachmen, or gardeners. But the Irish would, and a Bridget was to be found in thousands of kitchens. The Celtic tide had so completely driven Negro servants out of most Northern hotels that their persistence in some Saratoga establishments excited comment.[21] It was British, German, and Scandinavian

18 *Report* Statistical Bureau of State Dept., 1857, on immigration during 1856; 20,000 were "age not stated."
19 Parliamentary Tables on Irish Emigration to 1857.
20 Quoted in *National Intelligencer*, January 3, 1856. Young Henry Cabot Lodge, participating in the Boston battles of North End and South End boys, the old stock and the new, found that the Irish lads were growing the more numerous.
21 William Chambers, *Things as They Are in America.* Chambers, delighted by the fine interiors of some New York houses, with beautifully carved marble mantels and walnut panelling, credited much of the work to French and German artists who had migrated to America.

labor, along with that of the older American stock, which broke the prairie sod and created innumerable tidy farms. The English and Scottish immigration naturally supplied many skilled workmen. An English factory foreman was as familiar in parts of America as on the European continent, and Scottish engineers were a worldwide tribe. It was an able Welsh mechanic, John Griffith, who was John Fritz's chief lieutenant in building the Safe Harbor rail-mill and blast-furnace on the Susquehanna (1849); it was an Englishman,. William Barrow, who as foreman in the Cooper-Hewitt mills designed the new machinery for rolling large structural beams.[22] James Caird, M. P., travelling in the Northwest late in the fifties, was gratified to find how high stood the reputation of the Scottish immigrant for skill as well as industry and integrity. Unlike most of the Irish and many of the Germans, he reported, they never occupied menial positions or toiled as day laborers, but acted as machinists, artisans, or small entrepreneurs.[23] Many Britons, like the incisive journalist E. L. Godkin and the eloquent preacher Robert Collyer, stepped at once into professional eminence.

As for the Germans, the fact that a multitude brought special skills with them was attested by the rise in the fifties of tailors, capenters, and mechanics, unions—the Chicago Arbeiter Verein, for example, being organized in 1857. Leadership in the musical field was quickly assumed by Germans. Their managerial enterprise was illustrated all over the American map, even to the Pacific coast; it was a German immigrant who in 1852 founded Seattle by building a sawmill on its site, and such Germans as Adolph Sutro, Claus Spreckels, and Henry Miller (who with Charles Lux in 1857 founded a slaughter-house in San Francisco, and eventually became one of the cattle-kings of the West) were leaders in the development of California. Young Frederick Weyerhaeuser, destined to write his name across the greatest timber empire in the United States, migrated from near Mains in 1852, and found work in a Pennsylvania brewery. Like the Anglo-Scottish element, the Germans conspicuously nourished liberal principles, which in the Middle West particularly had a leavening influence. At Alton, Ill., the *Freie Blätter,* a radical weekly, carried on the anti-slavery crusade of the martyred Lovejoy; at Davenport, Ia., the *Demokrat,* "the low German Bible," was equally outspoken, swinging in 1856 to the Republican side. German skill and thrift enforced respect for these ideas.[24]

22  Fritz, *Autobiography,* 65; *Nevins,* Hewitt, 114.
23  *Prairie Farming in America* (1859).
24  Albert B. Faust, *The German Element in the United States,* I, 505-511; "Bunyan in Broadcloth, The House of Weyerhaeuser," *Fortune,* April, 1934; H. B. Johnson, "German Forty-eighters in Davenport," *Iowa Journal of History and Politics,* XLIV, 3-53. The Turner societies encouraged mental as well as physical training.

As yet practically none of the immigration was of the contract labor variety, and little was assisted by steamship companies or land-selling railroads. Yet by the middle fifties a labor surplus was visible, and bitter complaints arose that employers were encouraging the influx simply to keep wages at low levels. Manufacturers, mining-companies, and railroad contractors, it was charged, favored an indiscriminate admission so they might continue to exploit the workers. "Indeed," wrote one observer, "it is no secret that immigrants, or rather foreign workers, have become an article of importation, professedly for the purpose of providing for the deficiency of supply in the labor market, but in reality with the intention of obtaining efficient workers at lower wages." Senator Robert H. Adams of Mississippi, once an apprenticed cooper, adverted in 1856 to "the injurious and depressing effects upon the labor of our country-men." Yet in general, there was singularly little objection to immigration on the ground that it took bread from American mouths. The dominant view was that the country offered room and verge for all.[25]

The most important body of directed immigration was that which under the Mormon aegis helped to build up the nation's one great planned community, Utah. "Bound for the Great Salt Lake" was the title which Dickens gave in *The Uncommercial Traveller* to a vivacious description of a shipload of British folk about to leave a London dock for the Far West. Their Mormon shepherds had made shrewd provision for them, and Dickens grew warm in praising the management of the vessel, the comfort of the quarters, and the hopeful dignity of the wayfarers. Their conversion, he noted, seemed but skin-deep; what they obviously wanted was not the Mormon faith but a bright new chance. In the emerald isle the Irish Pioneer Emigration Fund, to which Palmerston, Shaftes-bury, the Earl of Carlisle, Horace Greeley, Judge Roosevelt, and many Irish leaders contributed, systematically sent over hundreds of persons in the fifties; "specially selected on account of good character and industrious habits, in the expectation that the persons so assisted will, according to the usual generous practise of Irish immigrants, also send for or otherwise greatly help the rest of the family in Ireland." The Fund kept an eye upon its protégés in the New World, and proudly chronicled their success in remitting money home and paying for the passage of relatives. But this was a very limited type of planning.[26]

25 Adams's statement is in *Cong. Globe*, June 16, 1856. In addition to Bowen's previously-cited essay in the *North American Review*, see *Emigration, Emigrants, and Know-Nothings*, by a Foreigner (1854); a volume by an intelligent English immigrant who gave facts from his own observation showing that the unrestricted influx hurt labor.

26 *Irish News*, June 20, 1857. The women sent over by the Fund, averaging twenty years of age, expected to earn $100 a year plus board in America as against $18 at most in Ireland. The men did still better. The majority went in groups to New York, Chicago, Detroit, and other cities, where Catholic priests and Protestant ministers often took them in charge.

The immigrants of course brought something more than brains and ambition, muscle and ideals; they imported a certain amount of capital. How much it was nobody knew, but unquestionably it more than counterbalanced the remittances sent "home." A few clues to its amount we do possess. "It is said," wrote a careful New York journalist in the spring of 1856, "that the passengers brought to this port today by the ship *Matilda* from Antwerp, 264 in number, brought with them in the aggregate about three quarters of a million dollars, equal to over $2,840 a head." If this was true, it was very unusual. It had been reported the previous fall that 6,555 immigrants who reached New York in a single week brought in about $245,000, which meant an average of only $38 for each passenger.[27] A shipload of eight hundred Mormon 'converts' arriving in Boston in 1857 carried, according to the captain's estimate, some $20,000 in British gold, which would average $25 apiece.[28] The Dublin correspondent of the New York *Courier* that same year computed the funds taken out of Ireland at only £4 a head. No doubt the Germans were better supplied, and no doubt the British brought most of all, for their living standard was the highest in Europe. Even at an average of forty dollars apiece, the immigration of the fifties meant a transfer of well over a hundred millions in cash capital.

Then, too, some brought goods. A number of emigrant guidebooks suggested carrying tools, household appliances, firearms, and for gentlefolk even a pianoforte; while many a jewel, painting, and piece of plate was lovingly transported overseas. Chippendale and Biedermeier furniture crossed the main. Late in the forties a British adviser urged his countrymen to take over some good Cleveland horses, or Durham cattle. MM. Erckmann-Chatrian in their charming tale of *L'Ami Fritz* draw a vignette of a party of Bavarian peasants en route to embark for America, their two large country wagons bulging with household goods; and Carl Schurz recalled seeing almost precisely this same scene in the Rhineland of his boyhood. But what the immigrant chiefly gave to America was his strength, his skill, and his aspirations.[29]

[ I ]

It need not be said that this vast indiscriminate immigration had its darker aspects, arousing antagonism and apprehension. If its better elements contributed to the building of the nation, its worst parts swelled the volume of pauperism and crime. Beyond question, many European communities at different times took more or less systematic steps to ship undesirables to the New World.

27  New York corr. in *National Intelligencer*, May 17, 1856; October 25, 1855.
28  *Idem*, May 9, 1857. Castle Garden figures 1855-56 indicated an average capital of $68; Prussian figures 1844-59 an average of $180. Eight Census, *Population*, p. xxii.
29  See Francis A. Evans, *The Emigrant's Director and Guide*; Guillet, *Great Migration*; Schurz, *Speeches, Correspondence, and Political Papers*, I, 49.

Earlier in the century the practise of "shovelling out the paupers" from various parts of the United Kingdom had met the reprobation of William Cobbett. The English pauper emigration probably reached a peak in the early thirties, when numerous parishes in ten counties were raising money to send away the "redundant population." [30] Switzerland in the middle fifties shipped over so many impoverished, criminal, and otherwise inutile persons that our Minister, Theodore S. Fay, protested sharply; with the result that the government sent a formal circular to the cantons asking them to desist. At about the same time a stream of Belgian undesirables aroused the anger of the consul at Antwerp, and of Mayor Fernando Wood of New York. Informing the Belgian authorities that the convicts and unemployables whom they were sending across would be immediately returned to the port of debarkation, Wood asked the Commissioners of Emigration for stringent precautions to halt this "most infamous practice." The commissioners thereupon informed Belgium that inasmuch as more ships with a criminal and worthless element had been arriving from Antwerp than from any other port, and as agents in Antwerp were known to be forwarding dangerous persons, Belgian vessels would thereafter receive special investigation. Some German states were also serious offenders. The Württemberg authorities took umbrage in 1855 on learning that transported paupers would be sent back, for this meant that all their expense was in vain! [31]

To be sure, some reports of European dumping were exaggerated. When our consul at Antwerp warned New York authorities to investigate the ship *Leopold I*, they found his monitions overdrawn. Although most of the ship's passengers were poor, the commissioners were assured that they had an aggregate of at least $50,000.[32] And of course some of those who arrived in the most abject need ultimately made the best citizens. The early story of several thousand eager German settlers in Texas, sent out by an "Adelsverein" which grossly mismanaged their slender resources, was one of painful destitution, and for a time former barons were eager to push wheelbarrows in Galveston for a subsistence. Yet they shortly mastered all obstacles, their settlements became models of thrift, and soon many accumulated small fortunes.[33]

30 Guillet, *Great Migration*, 31.
31 *National Intelligencer*, April 24, May 12, 1854, May 10, December 4, 1855. Mayor Wood was about to deport a dozen Belgian undesirables early in 1855 when the courts interfered. He wrote in high indignation to Representative John Wheeler, expressing fear that the city could thereafter do nothing to stop the entry of criminals and paupers. The country, he declared, was in danger of being flooded with unfit persons sent over by the German, Belgian, and Swiss authorities. *National Intelligencer*, February 22, 1855. A National Society of German Emigration which had its headquarters in Leipzig admitted that various Continental governments had actively exported unemployables and criminals, but averred that Saxony had taken no part whatever in this disgraceful proceeding.
32 *National Intelligencer*, June 7, 1855.
33 *Idem*, March 18. 1854; Faust, *German Element*, I, 493–498.

Nevertheless, the evil was real and great. Much evidence might be cited to show that Europe encouraged and even assisted the emigration of malefactors. Some caustic comments were evoked by a meeting in 1849 of the great philanthropist Lord Shaftesbury (then Lord Ashley) with some two hundred professional thieves of London—one of his objects being to induce them to emigrate.[34] Nor was this all. When New York began to exclude the physically unfit, foreign governments undertook to get them in anyhow. William Hunter of the Department of State in 1855 warned various cities: "The circulars issued by the emigration agents in the interior of Germany caution immigrants who are deformed, crippled, or maimed, against taking passage to New York, and advise them to go by way of Baltimore, New Orleans, and Quebec, where the laws prohibiting the landing of immigrants of the above classes do not apply." [35]

Near the close of 1854 the New York Association for Improving the Condition of the Poor referred in scathing terms to the burden of foreign-born indigents. In the year ending December 1st, it had been compelled to aid more than 15,500 families. Of all the immigrants landed in New York since the spring of 1847, it declared, no fewer than 617,000 had received help from the public purse, at a total cost of about $2,250,000. "Most of the beggars who swarm our streets, besiege our dwellings, and persistently demand our alms are immigrants of the kind described." [36] Mayor Wood's message to the Common Council in January, 1855, declared that an examination of criminal and pauper records showed conclusively that but a small proportion were native-born. One of the city's heaviest burdens, considering direct cost alone, was the support of these unfortunates. "Certainly, we have the power to protect this city against the landing of so vile an addition to our population."

Similar complaints could be extracted from the reports of municipalities, charitable bodies, and amateur sociologists along the whole North Atlantic coast, and as far west as Chicago and St. Louis. In Boston, for example, President Ephraim Peabody of the Society for the Prevention of Pauperism declared in 1849 that more than two-thirds of the Massachusetts paupers were foreigners. While people in Ireland felt that the flower of their population went to America, leaving the unfit behind,[37] Americans fancied that the lees of Europe were flowing to their shores. Stricter laws and sterner inspection certainly were needed. But obviously the pauperism and criminality raised an insoluble question: how much of it was attributable to depravity and weakness

34  Washington *Daily Republic*, June 16, 1849.
35  Quoted by Senator Adams, *Cong. Globe*, June 16, 1856.
36  Annual Report, 1854.
37  Francis Hackett, *Ireland*.

engendered by European social evils, and how much to neglect, abuse, and social maladjustments in the new American environment?

New York police reports in the fifties showed that Irish-born girls furnished much the largest single element among the prostitutes of the city;[38] but for prostitution New York was at least as much responsible as the Irish. The same reports exhibited the Irish as far in the lead among criminals. In a typical quarter, May–July, 1858, of the 17,328 persons arrested 10,477 were natives of Ireland, 2,690 natives of the United States, 1,621 natives of Germany, and 666 natives of England. But intoxication caused the main group of arrests, and for saloons, grogshops, and general incitement to drunkenness New York was again as much responsible as the Irish patrons. Many a British and German mother trembled at the thought of her child entering the slums of Boston or New York, or encountering the rough, dissolute boom cities of the West. Responsible immigrant leaders were troubled by problems of environment.

Irish, Germans, and English in particular deplored the tendency toward congregation in Eastern centers. The *Irish News* in New York frequently urged unskilled labor to hire out to farmers to gain proficiency, and then move West. An Irish Emigrant Aid Convention which met in Buffalo in 1856 to consider means of alleviating Irish destitution, declared that a propertyless class was growing up in America like that which imperilled the social fabric of Europe. It proposed the adoption of some systematic plan for colonizing large bodies of Irish Catholics in homogeneous communities on the land. This would benefit society "by removing large masses of men from the demoralizing influence of swollen cities, and bringing and retaining them within the salutary influences of the church and school." When a committee on Canadian settlement suggested the possible choice of sites in the Ottawa Valley, the Toronto Orangemen held a meeting at which three thousand people adopted an emphatic protest! But it was unfortunate that alien-born and native Americans alike paid so little attention to the systematic guidance of newcomers.[39]

Those who did attend to them were the sharpers, profiteers, and political manipulators. Exploitation of the immigrant, as the inflow rose in volume, became a major business. It began with the shipping lines, where overcrowding, bad diet, and lack of elementary sanitary precautions were all too common. Whether the emigrant ships were American, British, or Continental, little was done until the middle fifties to enforce decent conditions. From time to time epidemic disease took a horrifying toll. This was the fact in 1847, called by the London *Times* "the black year of emigration," when dysentery, smallpox, measles, and "ship fever" disastrously smote the great concourse bound from

38 *Quarterly Reports,* Deputy Supt. of Police.
39 *National Intelligencer,* February 14, 26, 1856; *Irish News,* June 20, 1857, and ff.

the United Kingdom to America. Out of every hundred persons, sixteen or seventeen died in transit. The total loss of life in the year's battle for a new home, 17,445, was greater than that at Gettysburg or the Wilderness, or on any field of the Crimean War. Huddled like cattle in narrow quarters, eating poor food badly cooked, sometimes wallowing in filth, with fetid air and little water, the emigrants yielded readily to any infection. Subsequent years showed a certain improvement, but not much. From Hamburg, from Antwerp, from Liverpool, too many suffered the fate described by one Irish voyager: "dyin' like rotten sheep thrown into a pit, and the minit the breath is out of our bodies, flung into the sea to be eaten up by them horrid sharks." [40]

Shipwreck and fire, moreover, were all too common. When the American ship *Floridian* went ashore on the east coast of England in 1849, in an icy gale and a heavy sea, only four out of about two hundred German laborers and mechanics survived. That same year the American vessel *Caleb Grimshaw* caught fire near the Azores with more than four hundred passengers, chiefly immigrants, of whom many were lost and the remainder endured terrible suffering. Especially shocking was the disaster to the German-owned ship *Austria*, which burned to the water's edge in mid-Atlantic in the late summer of 1858. Some five hundred immigrants lost their lives. The gross mismanagement of the panicky officers found a counterpart in the inefficiency of the home authorities. The proprietors had thought the immigrants of so little consequence no list was made of most of the steerage passengers, and no care was taken to instruct, quarter, feed, or protect them; they had been herded aboard like so many dumb animals, and left to take care of themselves when calamity fell. The American press called for a law requiring owners of ships to publish a complete roster of passengers on the day of departure. [41]

A transfer of the immigrant traffic from sailing vessels to steamships or to "steam-and-sail," which grew pronounced by the later fifties, helped improve conditions, for the steamships were generally larger and better-found. While sailing ships still carried most of the passengers in 1860, their predominance was being cut down. Only large corporations could operate expensive vessels with powerful engines, and these companies squeezed out the oldtime rapacious skippers. After the release of British steamers from Crimean War duty, Americans lost more and more of the business. In the first six months of 1856 a little more than a thousand steam-carried passengers arrived at New York,

40 Guillet, *Great Migration*, 89–98; Marcus Lee Hansen, *The Immigrant in American History*, ch. 2; R. G. Albion, *The Rise of New York Port*, ch. 16.

41 Philadelphia *Public Ledger*, quoted in *National Intelligencer*, October 2, 1858; Guillet, *Great Migration*, 134, 135. Doubtless the hardships of the voyage as well as the new country contributed to the early death of many immigrants. J. S. Buckingham estimated that one-third died within three years; *America, Historical, Statistic, and Descriptive*, II, 93.

against some 54,000 who were sail-carried. In the first half of the following year nearly 10,500 were steam-carried against some 75,000 sail-carried. Some much-needed protective legislation was also tardily passed. A series of vivid articles in the New York *Tribune* on the sufferings of immigrants led Hamilton Fish to press the Senate for an investigating committee. This body, which he headed, submitted a report in the summer of 1854, with a bill to cure the more flagrant evils. The committee recommended that ships be compelled to forfeit the passage-money of every immigrant who died at sea; that the provision and cooking of food be made the duty of the ship, not the passengers; and that no ship be allowed to bring in more than two passengers for every five tons' weight in summer, or two for every six tons' weight in winter. The New York legislature also acted. In the spring of 1855 it authorized the Commissioners of Emigration to set aside a special landing-place, Castle Garden being forthwith designated.[42]

This restriction of immigrants at the port of New York to one landing, from which the clamorous tribe of runners, ticket-agents, and boarding-house sharps was rigidly excluded, was of the utmost importance. Once ashore, immigrants had previously been pounced upon by a pack of harpies. The frauds and outrages had shocked a legislative committee, which found that hotels, railroads, land-promoters, and others had hired foreigners to act for them; "the German preying upon the German—the Irish upon the Irish—the English upon the English." [43] For an exorbitant price an unsuspecting immigrant would be given a neatly-printed ticket, with a picture of a steamboat, railway train, and canal packet on it, and assured that he was getting rapid first-class passage to a western destination. Actually he was being given the cheapest and slowest passage.[44] He would be taken to a lodging-house which rooked him; he would be overcharged for every article he bought; he would be deluded with false offers of employment. The Commissioners of Emigration estimated that in 1854 these swindlers plundered immigrants in New York of two and a half millions in money and property; with the result that thousands of the newcomers fell upon charity.

Under the new order, about half the immigrants landed bought transportation from supervised agents within Castle Garden walls. [45] The authorities also ameliorated the lot of immigrants who had been herded aboard the night boats to Albany with no sleeping quarters but the hard deck, no proper sanitary

---

42 New York *Tribune*, August 4, 1854, summarizes the recommendations; for movement toward steam carriage see Guillet, *Great Migration*, 233–248; *National Intelligencer*, October 2, 1858.
43 Friedrich A. Kapp, *Immigration and the Commissioners of Emigration of the State of N. Y.*, 62–64; cf. B. Moran, MS Diary, March 19, 1857.
44 Mann, *The Emigrant's Complete Guide to the U. S.*, 57.
45 *National Intelligencer*, April 3, 1858; 149,257 out of the first 370,000 entering.

arrangements, and no shelter from rain and cold. The *Tribune* had estimated that their exposure cost three thousand lives annually. "It is our deliberate judgment," it stated, "that no negro-trader in the South would permit a cargo of his human chattels to be carried for a single night with as little regard for their health and comfort—to say nothing of decency—as is regularly evinced in the transportation of free white emigrants from this city to Albany." [46]

That the position of the ordinary newcomer was far from unhappy is amply demonstrated by a multitude of personal narratives. A little money, a little hard sense, a little friendliness of mien, carried the vast majority into safe havens. An alien might fall upon actual beggary for a time, as Hans Mattson did, selling the very clothes from his back, and yet push forward, like this indomitable young Swede, to become a wealthy and respected leader among his own people. [47] But the general carelessness and frequent brutality in the treatment of the immigrant, going beyond even the ordinary American recklessness of health, property, and life, was a blot upon the national record. Sometimes it was so felt. The *Tribune*, in the course of its creditable campaign, made much of such cases as that of the Scottish immigrant Alexander Torrens, who was proved by a coroner's inquest to have died of actual starvation in a sailing-ship passage of more than seven weeks; his brother testifying that they did not get above one-half the provisions for which they had bargained with the officers of the *Constellation*. [48] But more frequently nobody cared. A friend of William C. Rives wrote of a young man who fell overboard from an Ohio River steamboat:

I saw him as he fell over, I saw the expression of unutterable misery and despair with which, on rising, he beheld the boat sweep rapidly by him, I saw his frantic struggles. . . . Instead of *cutting* the rope by which the little boat was fastened a half-minute was consumed in untying it. Without the delay he would have been saved. The boat arrived but ten seconds too late. I afterwards related the incident to one of the officers of the boat who was asleep at the time of its occurrence. With much apparent nonchalance, he remarked: "A Dutchman, I suppose." I answered in the affirmative. "Well, nothing lost," was his reply. [49]

[ IV ]

The influx of immigrants naturally tended to keep the wages of unskilled labor low and to retard labor organization. While a cardinal fact of American life was the general shortage of skilled labor, gluts of unskilled workers were

46  September 9, 1854.
47  Hans Mattson, *The Story of an Emigrant*, 21ff.
48  August 23, 1853; thirty-six passengers, mostly children, died on the voyage.
49  John C. Rutherfurd, Frankfort, Ky., November 3, 1848; Rives Papers.

all too frequent. Not merely did immigration contribute to such recurrent labor surpluses as those which Greeley lamented, and which he used as arguments for throwing open the Western lands to settlers without charge. The general temper of the immigrants was conservative on labor matters. They wanted work and a living; they did not want agitation and organization. Many had fled from Europe to escape the restrictions of gilds and trade-unions, and to be free to make their own bargains. As believers in individual effort, during this particular period (for with later immigrant stocks came changed outlooks) the great majority took little interest in Owenite or Fourierist communities, or in labor aggregations.[50]

But even without the immigrant tide, the conditions of the time would have been unfavorable to labor organization: the loose texture of society, the old American tradition of individualism, the dislike of corporate responsibilities, and the paucity of highly skilled workers, all operated to retard it. The remarkable growth of unions in Jacksonian days had been brought to an abrupt halt by the panic of 1837, and the movement was slow to revive. Some of the energies that might have been drawn into it were flung into the anti-slavery crusade and other reforms instead. Few national labor organizations existed in the fifties; no attempt was made to federate them, after the precedent set by the National Trades Union of the middle thirties; and they regarded with indifferent eye the mass of laborers outside their own crafts. Only one eminent labor leader emerged, William H. Sylvis, and he not until after the panic of 1857.[51] The overwhelming majority of workers, including practically all the unskilled, had no protection save that given them by the abundance of cheap land, the keen demand until 1857 for hands in expanding the transportation system, the public disapproval of employers who paid less than a living wage, and the general fluidity of American life, friendly to a "new start." At various times and places these protections were substantially worthless.

Only in crafts where a high proficiency obtained, where some sense of comradeship existed, and where the rewards of "joining" were plain, did unions easily spring into life. At the beginning of the fifties the printers, a

---

50 Hansen, *Immigrant in American History*, 86–88. Yet already evidences of the radicalism later associated with foreign-born workers were visible. Some refugee forty-eighters from France, Italy, and Germany believed in Communism. When early in 1858 Orsini made his famous attempt to kill Napoleon III, meetings of radicals were held in various American cities to honor the would-be assassin. One Sunday gathering in New York, attended by about three hundred foreign-born, was roundly denounced by the press; *National Intelligencer*, April 20, 1858. The New York Allgemeine Arbeiter-bund, a union of German workingmen, declared that it was under the necessity of waging obstinate war against German elements demanding revolutionary action; its officers maintaining that senseless radicalism would ruin honest workmen, and that reforms should be won through the ballot-box. This was a premonition of the struggle between Marxists and Lassalleans. *Ibid.*
51 Jonathan Grossman, *William Sylvis, Pioneer of American Labor*, 22–44.

hard-bitten, well-read, alert body of men, made plans for a national organization based on the numerous local unions. Good book and job printers, with the newspaper "swifts" who could set eighteen hundred ems of brevier an hour, were well paid. Orion Clemens, Mark Train's brother, received ten dollars a week in St. Louis at a time when board and room cost a third of that sum. They wished to maintain the enviable status of their craft, and in 1852 their International Typographical Union, a body that Ben Franklin would have applauded, began its long and august life. The stone-cutters, another skilled and tough-minded group, formed a similar organization in 1854. An iron-molders' union arose in Philadelphia in 1855, with a young journeyman, son of a poor wagon-maker, rising at once to be its leading spirit. This before-mentioned "Bill" Sylvis, unselfish, indefatigable, had dreams of a great national organization of ironworkers, and perhaps of all labor. Times grew hard after the panic, and labor was depressed. But he and his friends signed a call for a national convention, and in the summer of 1859 the Iron-Molders International Union was born. In that same year a national union of machinists was born, with the only Congressional charter ever given such a body.[52]

Four small, uncertainly-managed, and decidedly weak national unions, touching the four industries of printing, masonry, ironmaking, and machine-work—this was the sum of interstate labor organization. Yet it was a beginning. The four bodies can hardly be blamed for particularism, and certainly had no choice but to leave the unskilled and unorganized to shift as they best could. The one service they could do the labor movement was to develop and use their own strength, knowing that if they succeeded they would find imitators.

It was inevitable that most of the strikes called during the fifties should fail because of inadequate organization and the surplusage of urban labor. A stoppage on the Baltimore & Ohio in 1853 wrested better terms from the company, and sent a wave of strikes across the East, some thirty breaking out in May in New York city alone. But four years later the same railroad crushed a walkout by hiring large numbers of new workers, while militia suppressed some rioting in Baltimore. A strike on the Erie proved equally unsuccessful. Indeed, the many labor disturbances which followed the panic of 1857 won few gains for hard-pressed labor. In 1859-60, when times were growing better, the workers in a number of Massachusetts shoe-factories spontaneously joined in an impressive movement. First some local successes were won; then the impulse spread across the State, until one-fourth of the forty thousand operatives had quit work. Great excitement reigned; tumultuous processions filled the streets; militia had to be used to quell several riotous outbreaks; and the

52  John R. Commons and associates, *History of Labor in the United States*, I, chs. 6, 7.

press exhibited a strong partisanship. A Unitarian minister in South Natick lost his pulpit because he exhibited sympathy with the workers. But though a few sporadic readjustments were effected, the strike was in general a failure.[53]

Unions hastily organized, unprovided with reserve funds, and badly led, could accomplish little against wealthy corporations. A seasonal labor glut appeared every winter in the largest cities. Though 1851 was reckoned a prosperous year, the *Tribune* found New York filled that fall with hungry thousands looking for jobs. "Europe pours her surplus millions in armies upon our shore and their first cry is for Work! Work! Our own country meets this host by another as needy and as willing." The metropolis had fifty thousand persons, some highly skilled and not a few with professional training, "but all destitute, unemployed, desperate, and threatened with starvation, eagerly pressing the inquiry, 'Can't you find something for me to do?' " [54] Flinty employers took the most unscrupulous advantage of an overflowing labor supply. The Cohoes mills, in the dark summer of 1857, advertised for five hundred men to clean and repair the mill canals. Soon after dawn about six hundred gathered at the gates. The owners then announced that the men would be expected to work sixteen hours a day! Half assented, but the other half angrily declared they would starve first; and a desperate battle between the two bands ensued, with many injured.[55]

Already the employers' blacklist was a familiar device. Seventeen female employees of the Middlesex mill at Lowell in 1850 sent the Massachusetts legislature a petition declaring that they had taken work under an agreement to remain one year, but had felt that this contract was voided when the company summarily cut their wages by one-quarter. They had left the mill. What was the result?—a ruthless persecution. "Some of us went to work for other companies, but these companies soon received our names and we were immediately turned off. Some of us applied for work where hands were wanted, but were informed that they could employ 'none of the turnouts from the Middlesex,' and many who labored with us have been obliged to leave Lowell and seek their bread, we know not where, on account of the persecution carried on against them by the Middlesex Company." [56]

[ II ]

At the bottom of the industrial system was a body of sweated, underpaid women, of overworked children, and of hard-driven day-laborers, whose lot

53  Cole, *Irrepressible Conflict*, 152.
54  N. Y. *Weekly Tribune*, November 22, 1851.
55  Troy *Times*, quoted in *National Intelligencer*, July 9, 1857.
56  Quoted in Mobile *Herald and Tribune*, April 6, 1850.

often seemed worse than that of dumb beasts. It must be judged by the standards of the time, but even then it excited commiseration and indignation.

The position of the New York needle-worker was probably worse than that of her London sister. The Philadelphia *Bulletin* in 1855 preached a sermon from an advertisement: "To Let, to a single female, with Sunday board, an unfurnished front attic." Some friendless creature must find a home in that bare attic, with but one day a week in which she could eat a meal under her own roof. There were contractors in the city, wrote the editor, who recruited needlewomen and paid the wretched toilers in their employ but six or eight cents for the labor upon each garment. "Tom Hood's Song of the Shirt would be as appropriate in our midst as it is in London." [57] That same year the trial of a New Yorker prosecuted for sweating poor workingwomen brought out evidence that some of them had labored three days to earn thirty-six cents. [58] A spasmodic effort had been made by New York shirt-sewers several years earlier to set up a coöperative shop, for they complained that the scale set by the 'monopolists' made it nearly impossible to gain daily bread; but the effort broke down. [59]

It was true then, as later, that women lived in two worlds; one of guarded domesticity, the other a harsh world with the motto, "Work or starve," which might often better read, "work *and* starve." They were generally uninstructed; they found few departments of labor open, and these nearly all blind alleys; and they competed in an overstocked market. Constitutionally timid, they were bullied and cheated. The lower orders of men cheated them in coarse, violent ways, the upper orders with more finesse—but the result was the same. Just after the Civil War it was authoritatively stated that New York alone had thirty thousand women who labored twelve to fifteen hours a day, and whose income rarely exceeded thirty-three cents. [60] Clerks, laundrywomen, and factory girls were as badly off as seamstresses. In the middle forties a writer had pictured the scene at a jobber's door as a poor needlewoman knocked with her bundle. "It is now Saturday night. Since last Monday morning this poor female has labored with her needle fourteen hours in each day, and never closed her eyes in sleep till after midnight. 'Let us see,' says the employer, 'six pairs of pants at thirty-seven and a half cents a pair, is $2.25'; and that amount he doles out to the poor, unfortunate, lonely widow. . . ." [61] Servant girls were often driven mercilessly. Rising at five, they were expected to labor

57　Quoted in *National Intelligencer*, October 25, 1855.
58　N. Y. correspondence of *National Intelligencer*, February 27, 1855.
59　N. Y. *Weekly Tribune*, April 26, 1851.
60　*Nation*, February 21, 1867.
61　*Elements of Social Disorder: A Plea for the Laboring Classes in the U. S.*, by a Mechanic (1844).

till ten or eleven at night, and were lucky to get a half-day off on Sundays.[62]

As for child labor, it was still practically universal. After great effort, a few legislatures were induced during the fifties to pass laws interdicting the employment of children under ten in manufacturing, mechanical, or mercantile establishments. But such statutes were ill-enforced. Indeed, for decades after this time the open violation of such laws by New England factories was notorious. Truant officers who went to the great mills found that every one of them kept children at work under the legal age, and without regard for the provision requiring a certain annual term of school-attendance. As late as 1880 one child in eleven in Massachusetts between five and fifteen had never stepped inside a school.[63] The newsboy was already a social problem in city slum areas; the vagrant youngster a greater one. To be sure, a specially tough "victim" of child labor frequently did well. Thomas J. Burrill, born on a farm near Pittsfield, Mass., while still a small child was put to work in a cotton mill, and when his family removed to Illinois, he combined farm work with toil at the loom. Then, struggling for an education, he rose to be one of the most notable scientists of his generation. Only the tough, however, escaped being broken.

Pamphleteers and journalists constantly inveighed against the labor evils of the time. One described the hardships of laborers paid seventy-five cents for a day's toil—a frequent figure in and just after 1857; of girls who, earning $1.50 a week, struggled on the brink of prostitution; and of other women making twenty-five or thirty cents a day. Since no workman earning only two or three hundred dollars annually could support four or five children, youngsters in poor homes simply had to be put to hard toil at twelve or earlier. Yet the number of laboring men who made less than $200 a year probably exceeded, in both the forties and fifties, those who made more than $300.[64] For this reason, few children over twelve were found in schools in any industrial community.

In New York at the beginning of the decade at least eleven thousand men and women, and perhaps twice that number, worked at boot and shoe manu-

---

62  N. Y. *Weekly Tribune*, April 26, 1851.

63  E. E. Brown, "Children's Labor: A Problem," *Atlantic Monthly*, December, 1880. Early in 1854 a cartridge factory in Ravenswood, Long Island, blew up, killing sixteen persons. The striking fact was that thirteen of the slain were children; two boys of ten, four of twelve, and several more of thirteen. New York *Tribune*, January 20, 1854. In New York, as in London, children served as crossing-sweepers.

64  *Elements of Social Disorder*. One unregarded figure of the time was the farm laborer. Long hours, backbreaking toil, and a pittance in wages were his lot. A writer praising Michael Sullivant's ten-thousand-acre estate near Homer, Ill., wrote that his hired labor breakfasted at five-thirty, went to the fields at once, had dinner sent them in the field, and worked until sunset, receiving $12–13 a month and found most of the year, and $15–18 in harvest. N. Y. *Weekly Tribune*, April 14, 1860.

facture. Nearly all had to troop from shoe-seller to shoe-seller asking for work, and were obliged to take it on the harshest terms. They were unemployed for weeks together, and their wages at best were shabby. Yet the shoe-dealers made high profits, one firm pocketing a profit of $100,000 a year on a million dollars' worth of business. It is significant that the New York *Tribune* suggested that the remedy lay in coöperative cobbler-shops and coöperative shoe-stores; not in strikes.[65] Workers in the car manufactories of the country, about six thousand in number, toiled from seven A.M. to six P.M. daily, or eleven hours. The skilled hands—carpenters, upholsterers, painters, metal-workers—got $1.50 to $2 a day, according to capacity, while others were paid a dollar.[66] Yet this was a preferred industry!

Sailors and other maritime workers, as always, felt a jagged harrow tooth. These were years when shipping was enjoying one of its greatest booms, with American clippers showing their heels to foreign rivals, designers proud of their superiority, and many yards full of cheery clank and bustle. Yet wages were so low that young fellows who had cruised for two years would return to find only two hundred dollars due them, while even this pittance was hard to keep. Lower Manhattan was filled with sailors' boarding-houses of the worst type. These establishments, in Cherry and Water Streets near the East River, in Washington Street near the Hudson, and elsewhere, offered every temptation to drink, gambling, and prostitution. After carousing for a week or fortnight, most sailors were penniless again.[67] Life aboard many American vessels was a veritable hell, and though maltreated sailors, flogged, starved, overworked, and underpaid, could appeal to the law for redress, those who did so—like the abused crew Charles Nordhoff described in *The Merchant Vessel*[68]—met such tardy and costly justice that they usually rued their act.

Most readers are familiar with R. H. Dana's account in *Two Years Before the Mast* of the brutal skipper Frank Thompson, 'a regular down-easter johnny-cake' who flogged capable hands out of sheer meanness of temper, knowing that resistance on the high seas could be treated as a crime. But the brutish, squalid life of many seamen is seldom mentioned in the glowing record of American maritime exploits. A system of harsh exploitation had grown up under the manipulations of so-called "shipping masters." Whenever a sailor fell into debt ashore, the only way he could get free was to go to one of these gentry, who found a berth, drew advance wages, paid the debt with a handsome commission,

65   March 1, 1850.
66   N. Y. *Tribune*, July 29, 1853.
67   "If you once get moored, stem and stern, in old Barnes's grog-shop, with a coal fire ahead and the bar under your lee, you won't see daylight for three weeks!" R. H. Dana, *Two Years Before the Mast.*
68   P. 284ff.

and put the man abroad ship to work out his time. The system caused great distress, for sailors had to take what jobs they could get and submit to usurious exactions. In 1857 some prominent shipowners, to the accompaniment of a press crusade, tried to break it down. But it proved impossible to eradicate the evil. The "shipping masters" told the owners that men would not go aboard with an advance, and remained in control of the situation.[69]

## [ III ]

What could be done to improve the condition of labor? Effective unions, which since the crusade of William Leggett in New York and the pleas of Robert Rantoul in Massachusetts had a legal foundation in the most important States, were the prime desideratum. But for the reasons noted they were yet impossible. As for immigration-restriction, no important American leader yet proposed it. Where could men turn?

Albert Brisbane, in two-hour discourses heard by large crowds, urged labor to turn to coöperative manufacturing and selling.[70] Numerous experiments were attempted, particularly in the Ohio valley. Pittsburgh at the beginning of the fifties had several coöperative glassmakers' establishments, all prosperous; in Wheeling a nail-cutters' association owned its own mill; in Cincinnati an iron-molders' association ran its own stove-factory and store, keeping members steadily at work while other molders were unemployed for a quarter of the year. Shoemakers and even printers fell into the movement. But coöperation, though retaining devoted adherents, failed really to flourish. While the badly-managed establishments failed, the efficient shops tended to pass into the ownership of their superintendents.

Political agitation could accomplish little for labor. The movement for a ten-hour day had its political aspects; enlightened men generally agreed that the fourteen- or fifteen-hour day exacted by some New England mills was barbarous, and legislators were elected on a program of reduction. Early in the decade Massachusetts and other States passed laws for an eleven-hour day which employers were willing to accept, if only to avoid sharper reductions. In a few States the ten-hour schedule found legal sanction, but it was hard to enforce.[71] Such self-advertised labor champions as the noisy mayor of New York, Fernando Wood, were essentially futile figures. Moved by the complaints of a seamstress who made only a dollar and a half for a week's hard work, while her employer took a profit of three or four dollars on her

69 *National Intelligencer*, July 23, 1857.
70 See his *Association; or a Concise Exposition of the Practical Part of Fourier's Social Science* (1843).
71 Commons and associates, *Labor in the United States*, I, 536–547.

handiwork, Wood vowed that he would break up this swindling sweatshop system if it took all his time and salary. But of course he was helpless.[72] "Imposing demonstrations" were equally useless. One was held at Metropolitan Hall in 1853 to support the claim of New York workingmen for a fair wage; their woes having been advertised by a strike of housepainters who, after being promised two dollars a day for the active season, had just been cut to $1.75. Stating that they could not earn more than $390 a year, the painters asked how they could support a family on that sum.[73]

"Land and Labor Reform" was a popular cry of the day; newspapers inveighed against land-monopoly and labor-bondage; and conventions were held to promote the double crusade. A gathering at Albany in the late summer of 1851, attended by delegates from the whole Hudson Valley, declared for free homesteads, the ten-hour day, and a five-hour day for all children under sixteen. Chairman R. Manning of the State committee was especially emphatic on the third point. He lived in the factory town of Cohoes. Here, he said, he saw so much of the sufferings of small children toiling endless hours in the mills that if the oppressions were not soon abated, he would oppose the erection of another plant.[74] But the professional men, editors, and politicians who attended these gatherings could do little; what was needed was action by the workers themselves.

Throughout the fifties Eastern journals were full of exhortations to laborers and mechanics to go west. Many of these allocutions were inspired by land-speculators, but many were altruistic. Greeley was conspicuous in the agitation, arguing that mass-settlement on free homesteads would draw off from the cities their superabundant labor supply. It was of course true that the West was full of opportunity not only for would-be farmers, who had to possess some capital, but for wage-earners.

In the year of numerous Eastern strikes, 1853, one observer wrote that railroad labor in the Mississippi Valley was getting from $1 to $1.25 a day, though board was only $1.50 to $2 a week, and that contractors and foremen complained of the scarcity of able-bodied men for railroad labor.[75] The rapid growth of the Northwest frequently drove wages in various areas to levels which were reckoned high by Eastern standards. From the Wabash to the Des Moines, from Cairo to Duluth, craftsmen of all types were in keen demand; painters, plasterers, druggists, bakers, tailors, shoemakers, and blacksmiths. The smaller cities offered a more favorable field than Chicago, Milwaukee, and St. Louis, which had their own labor gluts and seasonal unemployment. Whenever a

72 National Intelligencer, July 19, 1855.
73 N. Y. Tribune, August 24, September 1, 1853.
74 N. Y. Weekly Tribune, September 6, 1851.
75 N. Y. Tribune, July 6, 1853.

new city like Superior, Wis., experienced a boom, carpenters and masons could command from $2.50 to $3.50 a day, and even hotel waitresses $4 a week. A mechanic in such a thriving little municipality could soon become independent. If he liked, he could purchase a farm near by on credit. "The West," wrote a wandering Philadelphian, "is full of examples of what has been done and is now being done by poor men, mechanics, and particularly young men." [76]

But all the available evidence indicates that Western farmlands did not to any important extent operate directly as a "safety-valve" for discontented Eastern labor. The safety-valve idea had possessed a wide currency from the days of Franklin, Jefferson, and Hamilton, all of whom gave it interesting expression. That Western agriculture drained off a great deal of labor which, but for the cheap lands, would have gone into unskilled or semi-skilled pursuits in industry, is unquestionable. Countless boys like the hero of *Vandermark's Folly*, who foresook the Erie Canal for an Iowa farm, turned their backs on the uncertain labor-markets of the East to establish flourishing prairie homes. That the Western towns and cities, with their multitude of little factories, shops, and stores, attracted a great many Eastern wage-earners and craftsmen, year by year, is also unquestionable. But it is highly questionable whether any considerable body of Eastern wage-earners and artisans, finding their lot oppressive, went straight to Western farms. Some, of course, did, but the evidence indicates that they were not numerous. A thin steady seepage took place, but not any great sudden gush of migration. [77]

76 *National Intelligencer*, January 29, 1857.
77 Already the controversial material on the "escape-valve" theory, first fully enunciated by Frederick Jackson Turner in his famous essay on "The Significance of the Frontier in American History," is very large. Sol Davidson and Carter Goodrich, in their studies in the *Political Science Quarterly* for June, 1935, March, 1936, have stated some interesting conclusions. They assert that "the movement of eastern wage-earners to western lands was surprisingly small"; that "too few wage-earners left the industrial centers to exert any marked influence on the labor situation"; that "even when the obstacles to working-class settlement were partially removed by assisted and organized migration, the numbers did not swell into a really substantial stream"; and that "when eastern workers did attempt to take up land they appear very frequently to have failed, and returned home discouraged." It is their opinion that "once American industrialism was well established . . . the overwhelming proportion of workers lived out their lives within its confines," and that if American workers did have better opportunities than their European fellows, "it would appear that more of the explanation lies in the rapid growth of manufacturing employment than in the presence of a distinct frontier." Fred A. Shannon has supported this attack. He concludes ("The Homestead Act and Labor Surplus," *Am. Hist. Review*, July, 1936) that the frontier movement was not from city to farm, but from farm to farm, and that when people did leave their home States, they usually settled in not more than one State removed. Murray Kane ("Some Considerations of the Safety Valve Doctrine," *Miss. Vall. Hist. Rev.*, XXIII, 1936) believes that most of the emigrants to the West were farmers, because industrial conditions did not permit workers to accumulate enough capital to migrate; and that the relatively few workers who did migrate did so during times of prosperity, not depression. However, the Turner theory has been upheld by Joseph Schafer ("Some Facts Bearing on the Safety Valve Theory," *Wis. Mag. of Hist.*, December, 1936), and others.

In short, many Eastern farm boys became Western farm owners; many Eastern town craftsmen became Western town craftsmen; but few Eastern wage-earners, comparatively speaking, became Western farmers. In general, tillable land was taken not by discontented urban mechanics and laborers, but by men hailing from rural environments. The Irish Emigrant Aid Convention might discuss settling thousands of laborers in Ontario or Wisconsin; but actually they remained in the cities. The ragged workmen of New York might gather in the bitter March blasts of 1856 to discuss free homesteads; but few really wanted to take the plow-handle in hand. They left that to sons of the soil or to hardy immigrants. For that matter, the testimony of nearly all observers shows that the immigrants of this period (and particularly the German immigrants) chose areas already well opened in preference to the newest frontiers. The pioneering was done mainly by old-stock Americans of rural antecedents.

If the labor movement of the forties had been defensive, that of the fifties was more aggressive in temper. The craft organizations of various cities, formerly nothing but mutual-benefit associations, grew into bargaining unions. Though still ready to flirt with political action and producers' cooperation, they increasingly centered their attention on fighting the employers. Leaders began to talk of the perpetual antagonism between labor and capital. Slowly, by strikes, boycotts, and the threatening demands of city trades' unions, they developed a technique for improving wages and hours. This new realism estranged reformers like Greeley, who asserted a natural law of supply and demand in labor. The panic of 1857 fell with such weight on these unions that various authorities have written that the labor movement ended the decade practically in nothingness. Happily, this is not entirely true. The workers had learned something about the emptiness of most talk of a community of interest between labor and capital, about the importance of fixing attention on wage and hour demands, and about means of forming compact fighting organizations. It was high time.


[ IV ]


If the period was dark for labor, and especially for the unskilled worker, it was bright for industry. Abundant labor was one of the foundation-stones for the rapid expansion of manufacturing and transportation. Factory owners, railroad builders, and other employers of the time had a full supply of cheap and willing help which they could drive for long hours. The mill-hands, the paddies laying tracks, the child workers in the Cohoes barracks, the needlewomen shivering in attics, the iron-puddlers, the anthracite-miners, all meant production at high levels, profits at stimulating rates. The cheap labor supply, continually fed from Europe, was a great forcing draft for industrialism.

It must be remembered that two important facts constantly mitigated the harshness of the system: one the plenitude of opportunity for ambitious, thrifty men, and the other the personal kindliness of many employers. In countless corners the Horatio Alger story was being enacted. In a multitude of small shops, mills, and mercantile establishments the owner still worked as a comrade with his men. Even when a manufactory grew large, the paternal tradition was likely to be strong. Samuel Colt, for example, allowed nobody in his Hartford arms factory to work more than ten hours a day, while he insisted that his hands should take a full hour for their noonday meal. He provided washrooms with soap and towel. He built perhaps the first social center furnished by any American employer, his "Charter Oak Hall," its recreation room well stocked with games and its reading room with books, newspapers, and magazines. He organized a bank, and encouraged his employees to set up a debating forum. When, opening a willow-furniture factory, he imported German workers to operate it, he built for them a model village which was almost a reproduction of the hamlet near Potsdam whence most of them had come. Here they had homes of the sort in which they had always lived, recreations which they loved, and above all, the orchestra which had always given them their principal avocation.[78]

On the other hand, the outlook of many employers was brutally illiberal, while as corporations grew larger their management became more impersonal and exacting. The fourteen- or sixteen-hour day of the textile mills was not only inhumane but wasteful. Workers were numb with exhaustion before they left the machines. A little experiment would have shown that the ten-hour day was in the long run more productive. Yet as the movement for shorter hours overswept New England it was savagely fought. Franklin Pierce, attorney for New Hampshire textile interests, received piteous pleas in 1848–49 from the great Merrimac Valley corporations for aid in withstanding reform. "We cannot operate our mills upon the ten hour system (*sic*) only at a *loss—great loss—* and to the utter destruction of our property," wailed one owner. "Genl Pierce you can at once perceive how impossible it would be for us to run but ten hours where our neighbors in Massachusetts are working as they now are— it cannot be done and our property would be worthless." He hoped that "everyone should be left to exercise his rights uncontrolled," and added: "Our Corporations want friendly feelings with the rulers of the State—we do not

78 Rohan, *Colt*, ch. 18.

want to be antagonistical with them." [79] Up to midsummer of 1853 Rhode Island textile workers toiled from thirteen to sixteen hours a day for $4 to $4.50 a week. A new law then fixed ten hours as a day's work, but it was generally disregarded. The workers were willing to toil for eleven hours; the manufacturers met, consulted, and offered them eleven and a half. When some operatives still insisted on an eleven-hour limit, French-Canadians were brought in to take their places. The majority had no choice except acquiescence. [80]

Whether the New England country girls who filled the textile mills were badly overworked and underpaid was a question upon which debate raged hotly, its answer depending upon the standard set as fair. The "Waltham system" of strict moral and physical care of the mill-girls had been instituted to destroy the popular belief, based on European experience, that factories exercised a debasing influence on women. For a time the Lowell mills really possessed that idyllic side which Lucy Larcom describes in *A New England Girlhood*. Girls of strong pioneer stock, used to hard work, flocked to the factories to broaden the economic opportunities of their sex; they were vigorous, active-minded young women (Emerson said that New England children were born "with knots in their brains"), and their flower-boxes, their poetry tacked to the looms, their French and German classes, their debating society, and their creditable magazine the *Lowell Offering* impressed the country. Most of them, like Lucy Larcom, had no intention of staying in the spinning rooms for life. At night they studied botany or read Carlyle's *Hero-Worship* with a firm intention of becoming schoolteachers, writers, or wives.

Then as the years passed the Lowell and Lawrence mills lost their early bloom. Discipline hardened; a permanent class of mill operatives, less ambitious and hopeful, grew up; the towns became crowded, ugly factory centers. As late as 1850 many of the country girls still protested that they were happily used. We average at least two dollars a week beyond our board, wrote one; we never labor more than twelve and a half hours a day; we have pie for breakfast and meat for noonday dinner; we can school ourselves in our spare time; some of us save money for marriage, some for opening a shop, some for a trip to Washington to see the Patent Office and shake hands with the President. [81] This was the utterance of a young woman glad to escape from the

---

79 Robert Read, Manchester, December 9, 1848; Pierce Papers. The N. Y. *Tribune*, May 18, 1854, in an editorial on "Hours and Strikes" said that ten hours was a fair day's work. "We may add that it is now the all but universal rule among mechanics in this city, and we presume it is in most others."

80 Centreville, R. I., correspondence in N. Y. *Tribune*, January 7, 1854.

81 Clementine Averill in N. Y. *Tribune*, March 19, 1850. The *Lowell Offering*, which in 1840–49 filled seven volumes, was not only the first periodical conducted by factory girls, but the first magazine written exclusively by women in the whole world. Harriet H. Robinson, *Early Factory Labor in New England*, 20. The 2,500 girls in white dresses with

unending, unpaid toil of the farm. But a darker side of the picture was becoming prominent.

The situation which had then emerged in most mills was described by experienced observers in very different terms. Women at Lowell got $2 a week and men $4.20 a week above their meagre board; the corporation paying the boarding-house keepers 17½ cents a day for each woman's food and lodging, and 25 cents for each man. Working hours extended from early light to seven-thirty in the evening, with two half-hour intervals for breakfast and dinner; supper being eaten after work. All boarding-houses were closed at ten; keepers had to report on the conduct, conversation, and church-attendance of inmates; and any marked infraction of decorum brought dismissal. Some companies met part of the wage-roll on orders on company stores which sold goods at exorbitant costs. Employees were urged to put their small savings into savings banks whence the corporations might draw it for capital. No system could have been better devised to get a high return from labor.[82]

The working force had fewer and fewer of the high-minded, independent-spirited Yankee girls, for they, able to find better openings elsewhere, had left when wages fell and the atmosphere became cheerless. It contained more and more of Irish and "low-class" operatives. The responsible pioneer managers of Francis Cabot Lowell's day had given way to absentee owners and capitalists, interested primarily in profits. Practically all the companies could well have paid better wages and granted shorter hours. The thirteen principal textile mills of New Hampshire had in 1848 a combined capital of $11,660,000, and employed nearly ten thousand hands. The average annual dividend on this large capital from the beginnings of the industry (one mill was twenty-two years old, one twenty-one) was 7.85 per cent. Yet the average monthly pay of each operative inside the mills was only $22.61, while hands doing piecework outside received even less. Throughout the expanding factory world a pronounced tendency toward the degradation of the worker was visible.[83]

Early in the century William Sprague of Rhode Island had converted his gristmill into a cotton factory, growing wealthy before he died in 1836. His sons, owning huge mills at Natick Falls, Aquidneck, and Arctic, grew richer still, and a handsome grandson, lifted to prominence by his great fortune, was elected governor late in the fifties. Yet this wealthy family still insisted on the thirteen and a half hour day, and paid but $4 a week.[84] Nathan Appleton, who

parasols who lined up to greet President Jackson were of pure Yankee stock; the coming of immigrants did much to change the conditions of labor. George F. Kenngott, *The Record of a City: A Social Survey of Lowell*, 18–27.

82 *Washington Union*, May 2, 1850.

83 Statistics compiled by Judge Parker of Nashua; Franklin Pierce Papers, Vol. II Norman Ware, *The Industrial Worker, 1840–1860*, ch. 7.

84 Benjamin Knight, *Hist. of the Sprague Family in R. I.*; N. Y. *Tribune*, January 7, 1854

did as much as any man to build up Lowell and Lawrence in Massachusetts and Manchester in New Hampshire, was a singularly enlightened man; scrupulously honest, interested in science and the Massachusetts Historical Society, a liberal giver to good causes, and an affectionate father-in-law of Longfellow. But though not particularly anxious to amass great wealth, he showed no such zeal in raising wages as in trying to raise tariffs.[85] Clearly, employers could not be trusted to safeguard the interests of workers; that could be done only by strong unions, still in the womb of the future.

And in a land careless of human life, industrial accidents were frequent. Few employers took proper precautions for safety. One of the long-remembered disasters of the time, the collapse of the Pemberton Mills at Lawrence, was, alas! all too typical of lesser occurrences. At dusk one January evening, when all hands were still on duty, a defective pillar gave way, precipitating roof, walls, and machinery upon seven hundred and fifty workers. In the first frenzied efforts at rescue, a searcher overturned a lantern on some oil-soaked cotton, and the ruins sprang into flames. Girls caught in the debris began singing hymns, and "Shall we gather at the river?" rose in a wild chant as the flames engulfed them. "The startled Merrimac rolled by, red as blood beneath the glare of the burning mills, and it was left to the fire and to the river to finish the chorus." [86]

85  R. C. Winthrop, Memoir in *Mass. Hist. Soc. Proc.*, V, 249–306.
86  Elizabeth Stuart Phelps, *Chapters from a Life*, 91.

# 9

# Kansas and the Break-up of Parties

HAD THE UNITED STATES possessed a government of the parliamentary type, the tidal wave of antagonism lifted by the Nebraska Act would quickly have forced the ministry to appeal to the country. The vote, as the fall elections of 1854 proved, would have gone against it with smashing force, and repeal of the offensive legislation would doubtless have followed. But under the American system of government the surge of popular condemnation accomplished nothing toward undoing the action just taken. It was possible to effect a radical change in the next House, but the Senate and President would still block the path. As matters stood, the repeal of the Missouri Compromise was a *fait accompli*. Very little chance existed that adverse action could be taken within a decade; none whatever that it could be taken before 1857–58; and before then the fate of Kansas would have been decided.

It was necessary for men to accept the situation, and inevitable that they should deal with it in the spirit of the defiances exchanged by Seward and Douglas as the Nebraska debate closed. "Come on, then, gentlemen of the slave States," Seward declaimed; "since there is no escaping your challenge, I accept it in behalf of the cause of freedom. We will engage in competition for the virgin soil of Kansas, and God give the victory to the side that is stronger in numbers as it is in right." Chase, equally aroused, proclaimed that a great new party would be formed to combat the workings of the Act. "I accept your challenge," responded Douglas. "Raise your black flag; call up your forces; preach your war on the Constitution, as you have threatened it here. We will be ready to meet all your allied forces." [1]

## [ I ]

Kansas proper, an undulating plain of some eighty thousand square miles, gently sloping from west to east, was the quarry for which the two sections

[1] *Cong. Globe,* 33d Cong., 1st sess., Appendix, 788. Kansas Territory, stretching over much of what is now Colorado, of course covered a considerably larger area than Kansas today. Fort Leavenworth, Scott, and Riley guarded its 126,000 square miles.

were now to strike and struggle. The land of "smoky waters," so-called from the pensive blue haze which in autumn veils the forest recesses and hangs above the placid streams, dropped from an elevation of four thousand feet on the west to nine hundred in the Missouri Valley.[2] The eastern third, a rich prairie region diversified by valleys, limestone ledges, and woods of elm, cottonwood, sycamore, and walnut, was the immediate prize. Beyond this, by imperceptible transition, the country merged into the great plains, a semi-arid plateau country of scanty vegetation, its level monotony broken only by detached knobs and buttes. A great central valley was seamed by the Kansas River, running the entire four hundred miles of the Territory, and opening into the Missouri. South of this lay the fertile Neosho Valley, and the less important watersheds of the Osage and Verdigris. North of the Kansas ran the Republican and Big Blue rivers, reaching up into Nebraska. The entire Territory lay west of Missouri, and for the most part this slave State was separated only by an imaginary line. The northern third of the boundary was supplied by the Missouri River, flowing sinuously down to the southeast, but elsewhere no natural frontier existed.

When the Congressional debates of 1854 ended, few Americans did not know that the Kansas climate, though often fiercely hot in summer and cold in winter, was healthful and even bracing; that the dark clay loam of the upland prairies and sandy clay of the river bottoms were generally fertile; that the vast pasturages of buffalo grass could be transformed into richer areas of millet, timothy, and clover; that abundant soft coal supplemented the timber; and that the region was attractive to both stockgrowers and general farmers. Time was to prove that corn, winter wheat, oats, grasses, and vegetables were the best prairie crops, while the plains were ideal for cattle. But Missouri slaveholders hoped to make hemp and tobacco profitable—and hemp was indeed grown with some temporary success. The "crook-backed oxen" that Coronado had found in that region still roamed in millions, their meat and hides no unimportant resource.

Could slavery gain a strong footing in Kansas? It was powerful in precisely that part of Missouri from which its influence could most effectively be exercised. The six contiguous counties of Platte, Clay, Ray, Jackson, Lafayette, and Saline, three north of the Missouri River and three south, had in 1850 a free population of 56,726, and a slave population of 17,357; the slaves constituting 23.5 per cent of the whole, as against not quite 13 per cent for all Missouri. It was popularly believed in this district that by some sort of unwritten compact among national leaders, Kansas was to be made slave and

---

2  See J. J. Ingalls, "Kansas, 1541–1891," in W. E. Connolley, *A Collection of the Writings of John James Ingalls.*

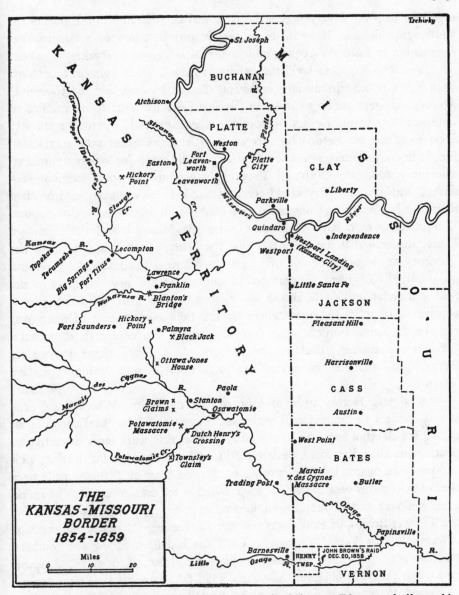

THE
KANSAS-MISSOURI
BORDER
1854-1859

Miles
0    10    20

*Ray, Lafayette, and Saline counties, all on the Missouri River, and all notable
for slave population, lie immediately east of those named on the map.*

Based on a map drawn by James C. Malin for the *Atlas of American History.*

Nebraska kept free.[8] Many early pro-slavery settlers later testified to this fact.
In Atchison's own county, Platte, and to some extent elsewhere, a militant

3 "Howard Report"; 34th Cong., 1st sess., House Report No. 200 pp. 926, 1124.

eagerness to plant slavery across the river had been fanned to life during the Washington debates. It found expression in proclamations of a fanatical determination to hold the region, and in denunciations of everything Yankee.[4]

Those who hoped to weld the country to the Southern system took heart from half a dozen circumstances. Several thousand (some said ten thousand) Missourians were ready to stake out claims. The Missouri River dominated transport to and from Kansas. Missourians expected to hold a natural monopoly upon most services needed by inflowing settlers; the steamboats, stages, and freight lines, the hotels, sawmills and gristmills, the stores for supplying lumber, machinery, food, and clothing.[5] They might use this monopoly to favor proslavery immigration. They could certainly use it to make money and to plant their own border towns along the Kansas bank—each town a basis of operations.

Products would have to be sent down the Missouri, and the Baltimore *Patriot* declared that the mere fact that the hemp, tobacco, and grain of the Territory must go out through St. Louis tied Kansas to the South. "God and geography have given the commercial control of the new country to the Southern States, and all the British abolitionists in New York or Canada cannot deprive us of it."[6] The area where slavery flourished best in Missouri was right on the Kansas borders, while Iowa settlements were comparatively remote. "Present appearances," declared the Glasgow, Mo., *Times*, three weeks after Pierce signed the Nebraska Act, "are in favor of Kansas becoming a slave Territory."[7]

But adverse factors were at least equally numerous. Where were proslavery settlers to come from? Arkansas, Texas, and New Mexico were all calling for slaveholding immigrants, and the two first were more attractive to Southerners than Kansas. A veritable "Texas fever" had set in, drawing rich and poor westward. When a brother of Senator Clay of Alabama rode over the Southwest this year to spy out its possibilities for cotton-planting, he found a tremendous influx of people who, hearing of good cheap land, had set out for the Trinity, Brazos, or Red rivers without further ado. "I passed hundreds of movers going to Texas," he wrote.[8] Utah also had been calling for Southern settlers—yet with fifteen thousand people she had but thirty slaves. Suppose, wrote one St. Louis observer, Missourians did take five thousand slaves across to Kansas. What would be the result? "It weakens slavery in Missouri, where it is now *insecure*. Every slave removed from Missouri reduces the proportion of

4 Fort Leavenworth correspondence dated September 18, 1854, in N. Y. *Tribune*, October 4, 1854.
5 J. C. Malin, *John Brown and the Legend of '56*, ch. 24, discusses the economic basis of the Kansas controversy.
6 Quoted in N. Y. *Tribune*, July 19, 1854.
7 Quoted in N. Y. *Tribune*, June 30, 1854.
8 Hugh Lawson Clay to C. C. Clay, December 15, 1854; Clay Papers, Duke Library.

slaves to the free; for there is no slave immigration into Missouri to replace them, while the places of the free who leave will in a few months be entirely filled from the east." [9] Many Missourians of Southern birth, like Edward Bates, were hostile to any spread of slavery, and hoped to see it extirpated in Missouri herself within a generation.

Slaves, moreover, were difficult to remove. There need be no fear Kansas will go for slavery, wrote an Arkansas correspondent of the Cleveland *Herald*, "for while one Southerner gets ready to 'tote his traps, plunder, and niggers' into Nebraska, a dozen Northerners will be there ploughing before him." [10] They were expensive to keep. "A healthy negro man costs now in Missouri some $1,200," later explained a citizen of that State. "Capital is worth here at least ten per cent, so that his cost to the owner, without reckoning expenses of food, clothing, medicine, and shelter, is $120 per annum." But a freesoil settler could hire an intelligent, efficient, industrious German for $100 a year, and get twice as much out of him.[11] And would Kansas crops really foster slave labor? Southerners could not foresee that despite every effort to introduce hemp and tobacco, these products would disappear before 1870 from the official list of Kansas crops; [12] but they could well fear such a result.

Two other considerations were to prove of the highest importance. One was the dependence of slavery upon psychological factors. It was not an ordinary economic commodity, flowing freely into areas of demand. Far from it; as sensitive as a hothouse plant, it shuddered at every drop in the moral temperature. Men hesitated to risk it in any area where the prevailing sentiment might soon change to enmity. A pro-slavery speaker at Independence, Mo., pointing out that any migratory Southern slaveholder would certainly prefer Texas, where his human chattels were safe, to an undecided and at least part-hostile Territory, asserted this summer that the South had been gulled by the cunning Yankees; that the dream of a new slave State was an utter delusion.[13] The other cardinal consideration involved was capital. To settle in a raw, harsh country like Kansas took money. The newcomer needed to buy land—and the best land, with timber and water, soon cost five to ten dollars an acre; he must build a cabin; he needed to hire four yoke of oxen to break up his prairie; he had to have horses, a cow, some heifers, and pigs; and he must purchase wheat for seed, and orchard trees. The farmer who had only $500 or $1,000 was hard put to establish himself, while the man with $4,000 or $5,000 could

9 "Letters for the People in the Present Crisis," by a St. Louisian (1855); pvt., Huntington Library.
10 Quoted in N. Y. *Tribune*, July 17, 1854.
11 "C.I.B.," Marthasville, Warren County, Mo., May 19, 1858, in N. Y. *Tribune*, June 5. 1858.
12 Malin, *John Brown and the Legend of '56.*
13 One Colonel Hall, quoted N. Y. *Tribune*, July 15, 1854.

have a prosperous homestead within two years. And the East and Northwest possessed far more settlers with cash capital than Missouri and the South.[14]


[ II ]

Conflict on Kansas soil was inevitable. It is almost futile to inquire which side first used threats or force, for both contemplated coercive measures from the beginning.

Popular sovereignty was stricken down, said Douglas later, by unholy combinations in New England to ship rowdies and vagabonds to Kansas with Bibles in one hand and rifles in the other, to shoot down the friends of self-government. It was destroyed by Northern machinations to carry elections by the use of emigrant aid societies. "In retaliation, Missouri formed aid societies too; and she, following your example, sent men into Kansas, and then occurred the conflict. I condemn both, but I condemn a thousandfold more those that set the first example and struck the first blow." [15] This became the general Southern view. The freesoil view was that long before the Kansas bill passed, border Missourians had been organizing "Blue Lodges," "Social Bands," "Sons of the South," and like bodies to take possession of the Kansas country. Some said that border measures to seize Kansas had been planned as early as 1850. In that year W. G. Kephart, an Ohioan representing the American Missionary Society who crossed Kansas, published allegations that slavery was already trickling into the area, and he repeated his warnings in the *National Era* in 1853.[16]

It seems clear that threatening speech was first used by Missourians. Atchison, in that Westport address in 1853 in which he had said he would rather see Nebraska in hell than have it admitted as a free State, spoke of using violence. If Northern vermin came in to "take up those fertile prairies, run off your negroes, and depreciate the value of your slaves here," he trumpeted, "you know how to protect your own interests; your rifles will free you from such neighbors.... You will go there, if necessary with the *bayonet* and with *blood*." B. F. Stringfellow's law-partner, one Able, said in a Fourth of July oration the following year: "I am ready to go, the first hour that it shall be announced that the emigrants have come, and with my own hands, will help to hang every one of them on the first tree."[17] An association formed at Weston, Mo., resolved

14  Cf. Greeley's observations, N. Y. *Weekly Tribune*, June 18, 1859.
15  *Cong. Globe*, 36th Cong., 1st sess., 915; February 29, 1860.
16  See the letters of Governor John W. Geary to President Pierce, *American Historical Review*, X, 124, 350-354; Greeley, *The American Conflict*, I, 235; and the long letter by Kephart, N. Y. *Tribune*, June 17, 1854.
17  Lawrence *Herald of Freedom*, February 21, 1857, gives both Atchison's and Able's speeches.

on July 20, 1854, that it would hold itself ready, whenever called upon by any settler, to enter Kansas and help remove any and all persons brought there by Northern emigrant aid societies. But such vaporings were of little moment; it was acts that counted.

The nation in the spring of 1854 saw launched two irrepressible movements which were certain to produce a serious collision on the Kansas plains. In the Northeastern States a movement to help freesoil emigrants settle in Kansas

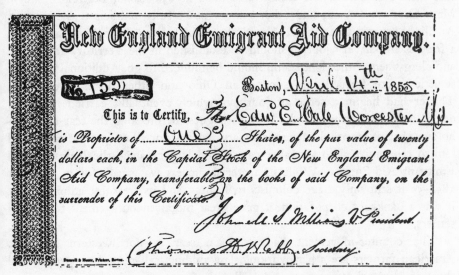

A share of stock in the New England Emigrant Aid Company, issued to Edward Everett Hale.

Courtesy of the Kansas State Historical Society, Topeka.

gained rapid headway. Its principal promoter, Eli Thayer, an educator, business-man, and politician of Worcester, Mass., on April 26, 1854, incorporated the Massachusetts Emigrant Aid Society; the Massachusetts legislature (of which he was a member), though one-third Democratic, granting its charter by unanimous vote.[18] The program of the Society was to raise capital, advertise the advantages of Kansas, recruit well-organized bodies of settlers, and send

18 Thayer's *A History of the Kansas Crusade, Its Friends and Its Foes* (1889), combines a record of the society's work with a biting attack upon Garrison and the other abolitionists who (he says) first attacked the effort, and then claimed credit for its successes. The Lawrence *Herald of Freedom* in 1857 published "A Complete History of Kansas" by in-stalments. It states that an early emigrant aid society was formed in Washington in June, 1854, with J. Z. Goodrich of Massachusetts as president. The American Settlement Company in New York, which attempted to settle a county and founded Council City, was very active for a time. See issue of February 28, 1857.

them west to townships where the society would help build mills, hotels, schools, and churches. From the investment in land and structures Thayer, who combined great gifts as salesman and promoter with marked incapacity as executive or organizer, hoped the organization might reap a profit.

Arriving in New York on May 27 to solicit stock-subscriptions, within a few days Thayer obtained pledges of more than $100,000.[19] Many leading Bostonians, headed by Charles Francis Adams with a subscription of $25,000, lent their aid. The whole capital was fixed at $5,000,000. Beginning late in May, Greeley, Bryant, and other editors powerfully publicized the scheme. Auxiliary organizations, they declared, should be formed throughout the North; a fearless anti-slavery journal should be established in the Territory forthwith; and clergymen of the right stamp should be induced to go. Additional emigrant societies were formed that summer in Ohio and other States. Meanwhile, Thayer had begun a series of journeys which eventually carried him over 60,000 miles, delivering hundreds of harangues. Before long the fear of stockholders that they would have a pecuniary liability for all obligations compelled him to reorganize with a smaller capital and larger name—the New England Emigrant Aid Society. While its material success was small, for in the year 1854–55 it sent only 1,240 colonists to Kansas, and its treasurer admitted that it was a bankrupt corporation, it gave great moral encouragement to freesoil settlers.[20]

The counter-movement had its main seat in northwestern Missouri. American farmers are a hardworking, law-abiding, self-respecting people, and those of Missouri were no exception. But all river-bottom country accumulates a certain drifting, vagabondish, irresponsible population. The Missouri River counties dominated by Atchison had but recently emerged from the pioneer stage; Jefferson City, halfway across Missouri, had not been made the capital until 1826, and various county names—Cass, Bates, Atchison, Buchanan—indicated the newness of the land. Much of the population had the unfettered individualism and reckless turbulence characteristic of the frontier. Moreover, an excitable, speculative, greedy element had been brought into northwestern Missouri by the business of outfitting emigrant trains, supplying western troops, and plotting boom towns. Indian-traders, cattle-dealers, buffalo-hunters, and vendors of arms and provisions crowded into Independence, Westport, Platte City, St. Joseph, and Rockport. They had made the most of the Oregon migration, the Frémont and other expeditions, the stream of goldhunters, and the army posts. W. T. Sherman, visiting Fort Leavenworth in 1852 partly to

19  Philip S. Foner, *Business and Slavery*, 97.
20  Thayer, *The Kansas Crusade*, chs. 2 and 3; Wilson, *Rise and Fall of the Slave Power*, II, 466; Avery Craven, *Coming of the Civil War*, 357.

inspect cattle for the troops, found Weston "the chief town," and noted that land-speculation had burned the fingers of some army officers.[21]

This motley population wanted Kansas settled in such fashion as to produce the richest returns in the shortest time. Many had never paid much attention to law, and if called across the river into Kansas they would pay still less.

Even before the Nebraska bill became law, border men had slipped in hundreds across the Kansas line and took claims to much of the best acreage. This was not, as many Easterners supposed, the token of a conspiracy to annex Kansas to slavedom. Ordinary "sooners" had but limited interest in slavery-extension and still less in national politics; their eyes were upon the land.[22] Like most frontiersmen, they thought they had a natural right to any neighboring district opened to settlement. Some wanted to remove their families to the new sites as soon as convenient; some hoped to establish preëmption rights and later sell them; many wished to own one farm in Missouri and another in Kansas. They did not at first worry about Yankee competition. But in June news of the huge five-million-dollar Emigrant Aid Company reached northwest Missouri with natural exaggerations and distortions. Many supposed the five millions was all in hand, though actually when the year closed not twenty thousand dollars had been collected. This rich corporation, they believed (and all corporations were disliked by Westerners), would employ its vast resources to hold Kansas by force and rob the poor Missourians of their birthright. Rumors sprang up that lawless Irishmen and other rowdies would be sent out to carry off slaves. Many honest farmers who never thought of carrying Negroes with them into Kansas deeply resented the abolitionist abuse of slaveholders and the operations of the underground railroad.[23]

Border Missouri sprang into activity. Politicians, editors, and aggressive slaveholders roused their neighbors to meet the freesoil peril. On June 3 a belligerent meeting at Westport sounded a defiant warning, and two days later another at Independence took more threatening measures. The Westport gathering organized a society of Missourians for mutual protection; declared that its members meant to carry slaves into Kansas, and protect them there; invited other citizens of Missouri and Arkansas to do likewise; and called upon

21 *Memoirs*, I, 89.
22 E. L. Craik, "Southern Interest in Territorial Kansas," *Kansas Historical Colls.*, XV, 348ff. A correspondent of the Troy (N. Y.) *Whig* wrote from St. Joseph, Mo., on June 13, 1854, that the border rush into Kansas would eclipse the California rush. "Camps are formed, and tents are dotting all the hills and valleys. Thousands are waiting the permit to cross. Large numbers have organized for mutual protection and defense, and have crossed the river, and are locating claims and staking out farms." These Missourians, who would kill anyone who squatted on their claims, "calculated certain" to have slavery in Kansas.
23 Mary J. Klem, "Missouri in the Kansas Struggle," *Miss. Valley Hist. Assn. Proceedings*, IX, 393–413; Lucien Carr, *Missouri*, 244–248.

all men interested in the future of Kansas to rally "that we may avail ourselves of the great advantages which the contiguity of the new Territory at once gives to us, and *entitles us,* in moulding the government and institutions of the future State." [24] The Independence meeting organized a vigilance committee to repel any infringement of the rights of Southern settlers, directed it to act with stern severity if any occasion demanded its intervention, appointed a committee of correspondence to advertise the advantages of Kansas throughout the South, and earnestly called on the citizens of all border and western counties not merely to organize, but take "action, that we may meet and repel the wave of fanaticism which threatens to break up our border." [25] As word of these steps spread throughout the country, some Missourians were shocked, but others applauded. On June 10 a band of pro-slavery squatters near Fort Leavenworth, Kansas, met to declare that no protection could be given to "abolitionists" as settlers.[26]

Such threats were quite inexcusable. Citizens of the North had a perfect right to band together for the peaceable colonization of Kansas; the systematic organization of colonies in America had a tradition running back to 1607 and 1620. But the rough, hotheaded Atchison soon went further still. He knew that his chances for reëlection to his Senate seat were poor, and saw that an appeal to pro-slavery feeling in Missouri might strengthen them. His was the chief name in a call for a meeting at Weston, in his own Platte County, on July 29. This gathering not merely completed the formation of the Platte County Self-Defensive Association, but proclaimed its readiness to enter Kansas whenever called upon "to assist in removing any and all emigrants who go there under the auspices of the Northern Emigrant Aid Societies." [27] Similar meetings, convoked by Atchison and certain pro-slavery confederates like B. F. Stringfellow, were held at other border points during the summer. An ingenious plan for securing the Kansas country was meanwhile being matured. Missourians were well aware that Kansas was deficient in wood and water. By taking possession of the timber claims along the streams, they believed they could dominate the economic and political destinies of the country; for who could farm a Kansas holding without wood for building, fences, and fuel, and water for stock? [28]

24  Text in *National Intelligencer,* June 22, 1854; italics mine.
25  *National Intelligencer,* June 27, 1854, quoting Independence *Agrarian,* a Democratic paper, in criticism.
26  W. M. Paxton, *Annals of Platte County, Mo.,* 178.
27  S. A. Johnson, "The Emigrant Aid Companies in the Kansas Conflict," *Kansas Hist. Quarterly,* VI, No. 1, 21ff.; Lawrence *Herald of Freedom,* February 21, 1857.
28  Malin, *John Brown and the Legend of '56,* pp. 506, 507. The Lawrence *Herald of Freedom,* October 31, 1857, contains a long article on Atchison and Stringfellow as the principal fomenters of strife in Kansas, and on S. S. Jones, Westport livery-stable keeper who became sheriff of Douglas County, Kansas, as their chief tool.

Evidently, lamented the Warsaw (Ill.) *Weekly Express*, a typical North-western journal, Missouri, Arkansas, and other Southern States will make a systematic attempt to force slavery upon Kansas; and it added that "we have but little doubt that these efforts will be successful."[29] Labor being scarce, slaves would be in demand as hands, and in many Kansas communities a few rich slaveholders would soon control the opinions of their poorer neighbors.

[ III ]

These first repercussions of the Nebraska Act were ominous enough. The press North and South began to take sides. News that before the end of July, 1854, Thayer's first company of about thirty Eastern emigrants had reached the beautiful site of Lawrence, Kan., pitched their tents, and begun building houses, elicited indignant comments from many slave-State editors. This pioneer group, cheered by an immense crowd when they left Boston, had received ovations in Worcester, Albany, Rochester, and other points along its journey. Thayer was recruiting a second and larger company. During 1854 he was to send out five parties totalling about 750 people.[30] Quite equal indignation was meanwhile expressed by Northern editors over the lawless course of the Missourians who had crossed the boundary, selected farms, placed marks on them, and then, without effecting any real residence, banded together to make their preëmption permanently good. The Lawrence settlers defiantly received a threatening visit from armed Missourians who invited them to leave immediately.

By September Kansas had its own militant journals. From Leavenworth was issued the *Kansas Herald*, a Democratic sheet professing but not practising neutrality on the slavery issue; from Wakarusa circulated a freesoil organ, the *Herald of Freedom*, destined to a large influence and fame.[31] Its editor, G. W. Brown, late of the Conneautville, Pa., *Courier*, had begun soon after the introduction of the Nebraska bill to enlist colonists for Kansas. He mustered about three hundred and with the help of Thayer took all but twenty of them west. Bringing his press and twelve hundred full subscriptions, Brown was ready to appeal to Northern sentiment. He scattered his paper throughout the North; and "wherever read," he boasted later, "it did its work, and a heavy emigration

29 June 22, 1854.
30 Thayer, *Kansas Crusade*, 69–73; Godfrey T. Anderson, "The Slavery Issue as a Factor in Massachusetts Politics From the Compromise of 1850," MS Dissertation, Univ. of Chicago. In the years 1854–62 the Emigrant Aid Company, with Amos A. Lawrence as treasurer, raised and spent $136,000. E. E. Hale, *Memories*, II, 156.
31 N. Y. *Tribune*, October 4, 1854.

followed as a matter of course, to gain the cheap lands of Kansas and aid in rolling back the tide of slavery." [32]

Late summer found the tide of emigration rapidly augumenting. Every steamer from St. Louis was crowded, while the ferries at Weston, Fort Leavenworth, and other points did a rousing business with migrants arriving on foot and by horse. Already strong indications of freesoil ascendency were visible. A correspondent of the Chicago *Democratic Press* reported in June that the desperate efforts of Missourians to stimulate large-scale settlement were meeting no success, and that many intelligent slavery men admitted they had no chance. [33] "I know it to be a fact," wrote a settler the next month, "that very few slaveholders have carried their slaves into Kansas"—for they were afraid to; and he added that a number of Missouri fireaters in an Independence hotel had been overheard expressing a dismal conviction of defeat. [34] Still another correspondent, writing the Milwaukee *Sentinel* early in September, declared that it seemed the universal opinion in Missouri, and almost the universal wish, that Kansas should become free. He did not believe the slavery propagandists who were slyly averring that if they were citizens of the Territory when the referendum was taken, they would vote to exclude slavery. "At the same time, we are assured by those who have been over the Territory and have lived in it since it was opened . . . that nine-tenths of the whole number of claimants, from both North and South, will vote for freedom. *Kansas is sure to be a free State.*" [35]

A full Territorial régime was duly established in the fall of 1854. President Pierce selected as first governor Andrew H. Reeder, a corpulent Democratic lawyer of Easton, Pa., who had never held office. [36] He did not reach Fort Leavenworth, where he established temporary executive quarters, until October 7. Samuel D. Lecompte of Maryland was appointed chief justice; Rush Elmore of Alabama and S. W. Johnston of Ohio associate justices; and Daniel Woodson of Arkansas secretary. The governor was vested with broad powers to set the machinery going. Pending election of a legislature, he could take a census, fix the temporary capital, define election districts, and appoint election dates. It was a sad blunder to name an unknown provincial attorney, selected only because Postmaster-General Campbell thought he might strengthen the party in

32 George W. Brown, *False Claims of Kansas Historians*, 7–10. Edward Everett Hale wrote a guide, *Kansas and Nebraska*, which emigrants found full of valuable information.
33 Quoted in N. Y. *Tribune*, June 29, 1854.
34 Letter dated July 25 in N. Y. *Tribune*, August 2, 1854.
35 N. Y. *Tribune*, September 25, 1854.
36 The Easton Congressional district had given Pierce more than five thousand majority, and had sent by a still larger majority Asa Packer, later founder of Lehigh University, to Congress, where he valiantly supported the Kansas-Nebraska bill. Reeder had also warmly espoused that bill. Easton *Argus*, quoted in Charles Robinson, *The Kansas Conflict*, 139.

northeastern Pennsylvania, to so responsible a post. It was a worse error to put another unknown, the bibulous, hot-tempered, partisan Lecompte, into the chief judicial post. Kansas needed men of national prestige.[37]

Reeder was so anxious to demonstrate his impartiality that when in the capitol at the time of his appointment, according to the Washington *Union*, he assured Southern leaders that he would have no more scruples in buying a slave than a horse, and regretted only that he lacked money to purchase some and carry them to Kansas.[38] But however coarse in some respects, he was a man of energy and ability, who labored courageously to see that popular sovereignty was given a fair trial. He found from 1,500 to 2,000 adult males in the Territory, with more rapidly arriving. The slavery men, who knew their temporary advantage might prove brief, exerted heavy pressure upon him to call an immediate election for a territorial legislature. But he refused, wishing first to investigate the situation, and after a tour, contented himself with arranging merely for the election of a delegate to Congress. A shower of denunciation fell upon him. When a meeting in Platte County, Mo., denounced his course, he published a letter declaring himself responsible to the people of the Territory alone, and ready to resist all outside interference. Then ensued the first clear indication of the way in which popular sovereignty could be abused.

On election day, near the end of November, 1854, more than 1,700 Missourians illegally crossed the boundary to vote. On horseback, on foot, and in buckboards, carts, and wagons, the well-armed slavery men crowded the river ferries in the upper counties and the muddy roads in the lower. Some went to the nearest polls while others pushed well into the interior. The more conscientious drove a stake, marked a tree, or signed a claim-register in a feeble effort to validate their votes, while others took a mere mental resolve to be settlers—or simply damned the Yankees, and let it go at that. Proper judges of election were set aside in one polling place after another. Of the 2,871 votes cast, it was later estimated that only 1,114 had been legal. Out of 604 ballots marked in one notorious centre, 20 were legal and 584 illegal. By these means John W. Whitfield gained an overwhelming majority as delegate; a tall, sinewy, good-looking Tennesseean, till now an Indian agent.[39]

The Missourians had taken all too literally Atchison's injunction only a few weeks before the election: "When you reside within one day's journey of the

---

37  Nicolay and Hay, *Lincoln*, I, 403; James Campbell, June 29, 1854, in Bigler Papers.
38  Washington *Union*, quoted in Greeley, *American Conflict*, I, 236, 237.
39  The evidence on this election is contained in the "Howard Report"; 34th Congress, 1st sess., House Report No. 200. pp. 3–100. As the majority report in this document states, the settlers took little interest in this election, not more than half of them voting. This was because the settlements were scattered over a wide exent of country, the delegate was to serve only a short term, and the question of freedom or slavery was not distinctly in issue. For impartial comment on the election, see Leverett W. Spring, *Kansas*, 40–42.

Territory, and when your *peace*, your *quiet*, and your *property*, depend upon your action, you can without an exertion send five hundred of your young men who will vote in favor of your institutions. Should each county in the State of Missouri only do its duty, the question will be decided quietly and peaceably at the ballot-box." [40] Whitfield was a respectable aide of Atchison's, and since all the settlements thus far made outside Lawrence and its environs were of Missouri sympathies, could easily have been chosen by a fair vote; but the episode augured ill for the future. Plainly, Missourians were ready to assume that tomahawk claims carried an implied right of citizenship. This was canonical frontier practise, as Iowans demonstrated when they, too, poured across the Missouri River to elect a delegate and a legislature for Nebraska Territory. For that matter, what *was* a legal vote? The Kansas-Nebraska Act gave the ballot in the first election to every free white male above twenty-one who was an actual resident of the Territory, but prescribed no term of residence whatever. In subsequent elections the legislative assembly was to define the qualifications of voters. More precision in the enabling act would have helped to avert trouble.

Yet as all autumn human rivulets continued pouring into the new land, conflict actually counted for less than excitable onlookers in the South and East supposed. Most true settlers were primarily interested in the all-engrossing task of making a living—or making money. Interesting stories of business enterprise could soon be told. The town of Fort Leavenworth was founded by thirty-odd settlers who chose a site on the river just below the military reserve, bought out all claimants, and spent $2,400 in clearing 320 acres for the municipality. Almost overnight they had a sawmill, printing office, stores, hotel, and boarding houses, while the 175 shares of stock were selling at $300 to $500 apiece.[41] Among Eli Thayer's first party were Dr. Charles Robinson and S. C. Pomeroy, destined later to be governor and senator respectively; and while Robinson helped found Lawrence, Pomeroy purchased the Union Hotel in Kansas City.[42] A body of Missourians organized July 27th to found the town of Atchison. Freesoil men were obviously strongest in southern Kansas, and slavery men in the north, just opposite Platte, Clay, and Buchanan Counties. But as new groups kept arriving from many States, odd juxtapositions became frequent. After all, these men were all Americans. The Independence *Agrarian* ridiculed the idea of general strife: [43]

"Those who will take the trouble of making a short excursion into the Territory will find here and there the oddest kind of association. For instance, he may find a Yankee, a Tennesseean, and a Missourian all cozily sheltered in

40   William Phillips, *The Conquest of Kansas,* 43; Robinson, *Kansas Conflict,* 93, 94.
41   *National Intelligencer,* October 5, 1854.
42   W. H. Miller, *History of Jackson County, Mo.,* 423, 424.
43   Quoted in *National Intelligencer,* October 5, 1854.

the same cabin, and living together as harmoniously as a prairie dog, a rattlesnake, and an owl. They all seek to better their condition in life, and to secure, if so be they can, the little lordship of one hundred and sixty acres of mother earth, whereon to propagate no matter what, but opinion least of all things. The Yankee (shame on his education!) has never heard of the famous Boston Propaganda; the Tennesseean has barely 'hearn tell' of Mr. Calhoun and the rights of the South; and the Missourian thinks the rights of the West will be amply vindicated if he can get his favorite quarter-section."

Before the end of 1854 Thayer's Emigrant Aid forces had sent six regular companies into Kansas, besides encouraging the Pennsylvania cohort and scattered detachments from Ohio and other States.[44] Some companies were small when they left Boston, but picked up recruits at half the important stops between Worcester and Chicago. One body arrived in St. Joseph with a brass band, looking "comfortable and happy." [45] Early autumn found the *Kansas Herald* declaring that while Missourians still constituted a majority of the population, arrivals from other areas were fast wiping out their preponderance.[46] Many Easterners, traversing Missouri fearful that they would meet desperadoes with knives and revolvers, were delighted to find instead a welcome from leading citizens. Active slaveholders were willing to sell them livestock and vehicles, protesting that they favored emigration from South and North alike. Indeed, most of the newcomers were of such moderate temper that the *Liberator* lamented in the summer of 1855 that hardly a single abolitionist could be found among them.

"I have yet to see the man," testified one citizen of Wakarusa Settlement, "who has not expressed himself in favor of all the emigration from the East that could be induced to come, and *four fifths* of the *actual settlers* are in favor of Kansas being a free State." [47] Thayer, speaking at the Tabernacle in New York, asserted that for all their claim-staking, the Missourians by midsummer had not moved one slave into Kansas. Nor would they give slavery root, he added, for Northern emigration would be kept up in a steady exodus.[48]

"Up to this time," declared the *Kansas Herald* as November opened, "the people of Kansas have dwelt together in the utmost harmony and good neighborhood." [49] Yet it could not be denied that the tone of various western Missouri newspapers and leaders was threatening. Ferocious articles and speeches against the "nigger stealers" were common in Platte and other counties. At

44 *Herald of Freedom*, March 10, 1855, quoted in Robinson, *Kansas Conflict*, 91, 92.
45 St. Joseph, Mo., *Gazette*, September 13, 1854.
46 September 29, 1854.
47 N. Y. *Tribune*, August 29, 1854.
48 N. Y. *Tribune*, August 3, 1854.
49 Quoted in *National Intelligencer*, November 7, 1854.

various meetings noisy radicals overawed the moderates who deprecated agitation of the slavery question. A great deal of tinder was lying about loose, and a few furious agitators on each side could soon put it in a blaze. In New England and the South, jealous sectionalists watched eagerly for the first spurt of flame.

[ IV ]

Like a great catalytic agent, the Nebraska bill, to the chagrin and anger of its father, had meanwhile been crystallizing the nation's parties into new forms. Chase's bold prediction that the independent Democrats and Northern Whigs would unite in a powerful new party was being verified. This, Douglas sternly asserted, meant "civil war, servile war, and disunion."

Bryant, for nearly thirty years a Democratic editor, declared that the party of Jefferson and Jackson which this year he abandoned forever had met a staggering blow. "The result is inevitable; Seward is in the ascendency in this State and the North generally; the Democratic Party has lost its moral strength in the free States; it is stripped of the respect of the people by the misconduct of those who claim to be its leaders." [50] The poet-editor hesitated for a short time to espouse a new party, fearing it might be shortlived. Then, on August 8, 1854, in a leader headed "Freedom's Battle: The Only Way to Win It," the *Evening Post* challenged all freesoil Democrats to help erect an organization which would oppose an impassable barrier to the admission of any more slave states. To the freesoil Whigs, Greeley offered the same challenge. "When the mask fell off the faces of the Nebraska conspirators," he wrote,[51] "and revealed Badger, Geyer, James C. Jones, and the entire Whig delegation from Kentucky —not to mention Toombs, Stephens, and Clingman, who had deserted long ago—plotting and caucussing with Hunter and Mason, Butler and Orr, Bayly and Atchison, Douglas and Bright, for the overthrow of the Missouri Restriction, it was clear enough to all discerning vision that old party distinctions were superseded and meaningless." Hundreds of other freesoil editors, and thousands of freesoil politicians and agitators, joined in a great drive for a Fusion or Anti-Nebraska Party.

For evident reasons, it was impossible to use the Northern branch of the Whig Party as a nucleus for the new organization. A staunch remnant of leaders stuck by the familiar banner and tenets. "The Whig party still lives," declared the New York *Commercial Advertiser*, "and will live so long as there are intelligence and patriotism in the country." Many conservative men, best repre-

50 Nevins, *Evening Post*, 249.
51 N. Y. *Tribune*, October 16, 1854.

sented by the sage, staid *National Intelligencer*, deeply valued the national character of the party, and hoped that when the storm passed a fraternal union of Northern and Southern Whigs could be restored. They fervently disliked all freesoil firebrands. In addition, many professional politicians wished to maintain the existing party machinery intact. A fusion with freesoil Democrats and

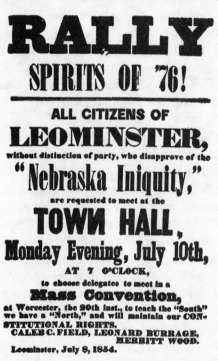

# RALLY
## SPIRITS OF '76!

ALL CITIZENS OF
# LEOMINSTER,
without distinction of party, who disapprove of the
## "Nebraska Iniquity,"
are requested to meet at the
# TOWN HALL,
## Monday Evening, July 10th,
AT 7 O'CLOCK,
to choose delegates to meet in a
### Mass Convention,
at Worcester, the 20th inst., to teach the "South"
we have a "North," and will maintain our CON-
STITUTIONAL RIGHTS.
CALEB C. FIELD, LEONARD BURRAGE,
MERRITT WOOD.
Leominster, July 8, 1854.

Call for a meeting on the "Nebraska Iniquity."
Courtesy of the American Antiquarian Society, Worcester, Massachusetts.

others would mean new machinery; some members of the Whig National and State Committees would be displaced; and others would find themselves outranked by parvenues. Men who had toiled for long years to gain a Whig standing which would entitle them to office rejected the idea of losing their prestige, precedence, and political capital by entering a new party. To such politicians the "fusion" movement meant professional suicide. Thus both patriotic and selfish reasons, idealistic and materialistic motives, counselled a last effort to maintain the grand old entity of Adams, Webster, and Clay.

The fusion movement in some States therefore embraced merely outright seceders from the Whig and Democratic ranks, who left the old party structures intact. In other areas members of the Whig party rose en masse to convert it into a fusion organization, their element easily dominating the freesoil Democrats who joined them. Natural forces dictated the course of events. In such States as Ohio, Indiana, and Iowa in the Middle West, Vermont and Maine in New England, the Whig party was so weak that few men felt a stake in its maintenance, while freesoil sentiment was fervent and general. A headlong rush from Whig to fusion organizations was natural in such districts. But in Massachusetts and New York, where the Whigs were in power; in Pennsylvania, where they recently had been, and hoped to be again; and in the border States where freesoil feeling was weak, the Whig Party remained strong. These States, it was to be noted, contained five great commercial centres—Boston, New York, Philadelphia, Baltimore, and St. Louis. Such cities had business reasons for treating the South considerately, while their merchants and capitalists were naturally conservative.

Certain Southern Senators had declared during the Nebraska debate that they supported the bill because it would leave the freesoilers no further ground for troublemaking; because, as Douglas put it, it would "deprive these agitators of their vocation." [52] Such statements cannot be taken seriously, for the act gave agitation a permanent basis and made it thrice-potent. On May 25, the Democrats of Indiana held their State convention with Senator Bright, Pierce's docile lieutenant, as the dominating figure. It passed resolutions endorsing the Nebraska bill. Next day a large and spirited convention of freesoil Democrats, meeting in Indianapolis with George W. Julian among its conspicuous members, denounced the bill as a wanton violation of pledged faith and a coldblooded conspiracy against humanity and republican principles. Meanwhile, throughout the Northwest and New England, preparations were under way for placing vigorous fusion parties in the field. Conscience Whigs, Proviso Democrats, Free Soilers, were all to be united in a great new party.

By the middle of July, union or fusionist conventions had been called in Vermont, Ohio, Indiana, Michigan, Iowa, and Wisconsin. In several of these States, notably Indiana and Ohio, the Whig Party for all practical purposes now ceased to exist. No Whig State conventions were held, and no Whig tickets were put in the field. [53] The fusionist convention in Indiana (July 13) chose Judge Thomas Smith, an oldline Democrat, as its presiding officer; adopted resolutions condemning the Nebraska bill, pledging united action against the extension of slavery, and calling for prohibition of liquor; and nominated candidates for State offices. In the Ohio convention on the same day, held at Columbus with nearly every county represented, former Democrats under Chase locked arms with former Whigs under Joshua Giddings; resolutions

---

52  *Cong. Globe*, 33d Cong., 1st sess., Appendix 325–338.
53  See review, N. Y. *Tribune*, October 16, 1854.

denouncing the Nebraska Act and slavery extension were adopted; and candidates for State office were named. Some observers thought the movement largely inspired by selfish politicians. Ohio's veteran Whig leader Tom Corwin later bluntly remarked of the Nebraska bill: "And do you not see how gladly it was seized upon by those who have been trying to form a Northern party for years?" To others the movement seemed a singularly pure expression of public feeling.[54]

In Massachusetts the fusionists held the first of two conventions at Worcester in July. The delegates present, estimated by the hostile Boston *Courier* at not more than eight hundred, and by the friendly *Traveller* at twelve to fifteen hundred, represented chiefly the middle and western parts of the State, fewer than two hundred having come in the special convention train from Boston. Four-fifths of the gathering were veteran Free Soilers of the old '48 stamp, Democrats and Whigs being rare.[55] A stiff set of resolutions was adopted. The party militantly declared that it would labor "to bring the administration of the general government back to the national principle of liberty; to repeal the fugitive slave bill; to restore the prohibitions of slavery in the Territories of Kansas and Nebraska; to prohibit slavery in all the Territories; to resist the acquisition of Cuba, or any other territory, unless slavery therein shall be prohibited; to refuse the admission into the Union of any more slave States; to abolish slavery in the District of Columbia; to protect the constitutional measures of opposition to slavery." It stood, that is, for some tenets whose application Mississippi and other States had declared would be cause for secession.

Old-line party organs correctly declared that these far-reaching doctrines were not at all representative of Massachusetts feeling. The leaders were seizing upon the strong feeling against the Nebraska Act to advance extreme demands. But when the convention met again at Worcester on September 6, Sumner, the lion of the occasion, spoke for an hour and a half, and practically the same set of resolutions was readopted. Henry Wilson was nominated for governor, with Increase Sumner for lieutenant-governor.[56]

A fusionist convention at Wolfborough in New Hampshire early in September drew an assemblage of two or three thousand men. Ichabod Goodwin presided, and speeches were made by S. P. Chase, John P. Hale, Amos Tuck, and others, denouncing the Nebraska Act and calling for a union of parties. Everyone recalled that the New Hampshire legislature had passed a vote of

54 *National Intelligencer*, July 18, 1854; Julian, *Giddings*, 321; Chase, *Diary and Corr.*, 260–263.
55 See Springfield *Republican*, July 21–25, for critical comment on the gathering as respectable but "wanting altogether in leading representative men."
56 Boston *Traveller*, Springfield *Republican*, September 8; *Liberator*, September 15, 1854.

censure on a Senator and Representative in Congress who supported the Nebraska bill, and had warmly commended two Representatives who opposed it. That State, quick to learn scorn of President Pierce, was plainly turning its back on the Democracy.[57]

In New York the political pot meanwhile boiled furiously, and as always the situation was singularly mixed. Greeley had favored dissolving the Whig party and organizing an anti-Nebraska or fusion party, with a joint ticket of former Whigs and former Democrats. Seward, Weed, and a majority of other Whig leaders, with their heavy investment in the existing party, wished to retain its name and organization.[58] A split took place. Henry J. Raymond, Preston King, Greeley, Moses H. Grinnell, Hiram Barney, and others of both old parties were prominent in a rousing anti-Nebraska Convention which met at Saratoga on August 16th. An impressive roster of delegates was present. Observers expected to see a new party organized and a platform adopted. Instead, after an exciting debate, the convention decided to await action by the Whigs, and to meet again at Auburn on September 26.

When the Whigs gathered at Syracuse on the 20th, Greeley and many other freesoilers were present. Indeed, the editor, who never fully realized that his *Tribune* desk was far more important than most elective posts, hoped to receive the nomination for governor. It went instead to Myron H. Clark, reformer, friend of the workingman (he had once been a cabinetmaker), and staunch advocate of the Maine law. Henry J. Raymond was named for lieutenant-governor. The platform, with Seward's cordial agreement, was trenchantly anti-Nebraska. It denounced Douglas's bill, endorsed the course of Seward, Fish, and the New York Representatives who had resisted it, attacked popular sovereignty as a quack device "too flimsy to mislead any but those anxious to be deluded," and declared that repeal of the Missouri restriction had freed the party from any obligation to support the old compromises with slavery. Presented with such a candidate and such resolutions, the fusionists had no choice but to fall into line. Greeley, indeed, called the platform "as noble as any friend of freedom could have expected." [59]

At their adjourned convention at Auburn, therefore, the fusionists accepted the Whig nominees. They drew up a platform of their own, decidedly radical in character, which Clark and Raymond at once accepted. Seceding freesoil Democrats accepted Clark and his platform, and so did a temperance convention. Practically speaking, a broad fusion ticket had been put in the field. The unhappiest group behind it were those conservative or "silver gray" Whigs

57  *National Intelligencer*, September 5, 1854.
58  Horace Greeley, *Recollections of a Busy Life*, 314; Bancroft, *Seward*, I, 366ff.
59  Alexander, *Political History New York*, II, 201.

who felt that their party convention, under Seward's inspiration, had become altogether too "ultra" on the slavery issue, and that their nominees should never have accepted the Auburn resolutions.

"We are in the position of a party having no candidates,' said their metropolitan voice, the New York *Commercial Advertiser*. It did not wonder at the tempest of agitation evoked by Douglas. "But who supposes that the storm is never to spend itself and be succeeded by a calm? . . . The reaction is as certain as the return of the seasons. . . . We would counsel our Whig conservative friends, therefore, to wait and see what next year will bring forth." [60] That view was shared by Fillmore's organ, the Buffalo *Commercial Advertiser*, by James Watson Webb's *Courier and Enquirer*, and by the Albany *Register*. But the great majority of Whigs were with Seward and Greeley, Clark and Raymond. They endorsed the declaration now vehemently made by many fusion gatherings, that no new slave State could ever enter the Union; a declaration that filled many Southerners with fury.

The clearest instances of conflict in New York between the freesoil fusionists and the Whigs were observable in certain Congressional districts. In Buffalo the old-line Whig nominee, S. G. Haven, was opposed by a fusionist; so in the Canandaigua district and elsewhere. "In most places the arrangements are made without any pretence of a concealment," said the Buffalo *Commercial Advertiser*. "In fact, the Freesoilers, in most places where they are in a minority, as they are in this Congressional district, have no hesitation in avowing their determination to disregard all party obligations, and to bargain with the Democrats, hard or soft, to achieve the defeat of all candidates who are not of their stripe." [61]

In Pennsylvania, those staunch freesoil Democrats, David Wilmot and his law-partner and successor in Congress, Galusha A. Grow, were prompt to attempt a fusion party. But their laborious negotiations achieved only a partial success. Both the freesoil Democrats and Whigs nominated tickets; and though the former group finally withdrew and urged support of the Whig nominee for governor, James Pollock, this, as Greeley put it, "was very different from having one ticket at the start, and that nominated on the distinct anti-Nebraska platform." [62] The Democratic convention refused to endorse the Nebraska bill, and the Democratic candidate William Bigler, very much on the defensive, labored amain to persuade the voters that national issues ought not to enter into State elections. In California the situation was highly confused. The Whigs there, always weak, clung to a conservative platform, refusing to take ground

---

60  Quoted in *National Intelligencer*, October 26, November 4, 1854.
61  Quoted in *National Intelligencer*, October 26, 1854.
62  N. Y. *Tribune*, October 16, 1854.

against the Nebraska bill at all, while the Democrats split into two parties, one freesoil, the other supporting the Administration.

Obviously, if a new national party were to be formed, it required a better name than "fusionist" or "anti-Nebraska." Spontaneously and almost simultaneously, numerous men and organizations proposed the appellation "Republican." In Washington on the morning of May 9, just after the House took up the Kansas-Nebraska bill, about thirty Representatives who had been called together by Israel Washburn of Maine met in the rooms of two Massachusetts members, Thomas D. Eliot and Edward Dickinson, at Mrs. Cratchett's boarding-house, Sixth and D Streets. They agreed that nothing but a new party could offer any genuine hope of arresting the expansion of slavery, that it should be formed at once, and that "Republican" would make an appropriate name. One influential outsider, Dr. Gamaliel Bailey of the *National Era*, who had been insistently urging a fresh organization, was present.[63] On July 6, at the call of ten thousand citizens, a great mass-meeting of fusionists was held in Jackson, Mich., in a grove of oaks. This historic gathering, in which Zachariah Chandler was a conspicuous figure, adopted a platform, nominated candidates, and named the new political organization the Republican Party. The Worcester convention of fusionists in Massachusetts on July 20 declared that "we hereby form ourselves into the *Republican Party* of Massachusetts," and urged a national convention.[64]

Thereafter the name rapidly became popular. The Ohio and Wisconsin conventions had adopted it even before the Massachusetts gathering. In Illinois and other States a series of local meetings of fusionist groups in August and September accepted it.[65] Recalling the principles and traditions of Jefferson (Greeley had suggested Democratic-Republican as the proper appellation), it appealed even more strongly to former Democrats than former Whigs. As time passed various legends concerning the origin and authorship of the name sprang up. The honor of first proposing it has been claimed for a New Yorker, Alvin E. Bovay; the "birthplace" has been variously designated as Pittsburgh, Pa., Strong, Me., and Exeter, N. H., where Lincoln's old Congressional associate Amos Tuck is said to have suggested it.[66] But the name was so obvious and

63  Francis Curtis, *The Republican Party*, I, 178–181. Dr. Gamaliel Bailey, editor of the Washington *National Era*, brought about this caucus of Northern Congressmen. He was anxious to see a new agency created. "Party names and party prejudices are the cords that bind the Samson of the North," he wrote. The gathering, agreeing to give the Northern fusion the name "Republican," recalled that Jefferson was after all the author of the Northwest Ordinance. James S. Pike, *First Blows of the Civil War*, 233, 234; Wilson, *Rise and Fall of the Slave Power*, II, 410, 411.
64  Springfield *Republican*, July 21, 1854.
65  Beveridge, *Lincoln*, II, 264.
66  See *Proceedings* of New York State Historical Assn., IX, 99–105, for Bovay; C. W. Dahlinger, *Western Pa. Hist. Mag.*, IV, 1–10, for Pittsburgh; A. J. Turner, *Genesis of the Republican Party*.

logical, both as the counterpart of "Democratic" and the repository of Jeffersonian associations, that it was almost inevitable; while the party really had a
thousand birthplaces that fateful summer, for fusionists, anti-Nebraska men,
and freesoilers met in a thousand places.

## [ V ]

Meanwhile, the general disintegration of parties expressed itself in a portentous new phenomenon, with grave social and religious as well as political
implications—the rise of the Know-Nothings or Native Americans. This mush-
room party, formidably rapid in growth but born with seeds of decay which
made it shortlived, sprang from a complex of causes.

The mixture of honest convictions and ignorant prejudice which had given
birth to earlier ebullitions of nativism—for example, the Native American movement which elected a mayor of New York in 1844—was easy to revive. It had
remained quietly active in various Atlantic cities through the forties and early
fifties; in 1844 it chose Lewis C. Levin, a lawyer and editor of Philadelphia,
to Congress. When immigration rose to unprecedented volume after the Mexican
War, the apprehensions, jealousies, and bigotries that make up nativism rose
with it. The greater part of the Irish immigration and a large part of the
German was Catholic. These foreign-born citizens were prompt to take a share
in politics, the Irish in the great Eastern cities, the Germans wherever they
spread in city or country. Their dress, manners, strange habits in eating and
drinking, and resistance to assimilation aroused irritation. German athletic
organizations wore a military mien that many found disquieting. It was obvious
that many Irish in particular were prone to disorderliness, and responded readily
to the blandishments extended them by the baser politicians, nearly always
Democratic. It was obvious also that immigrants, not subjected to adequate inspection at ports of entry, contributed far more than their due share to the
almshouses, asylums, hospitals, and prisons of the seaboard States, imposing a
considerable burden upon taxpayers.

Various secret societies with picturesque names—Sons of '76, Sons of Sires,
the Druids, the Foresters, and so on—had sprung up to combat the supposed
machinations of Catholic immigrants. Some of them drifted into politics, chiefly
under Whig auspices. Then in 1852–53 these nativist organizations gradually
coalesced into a single party, at first officially termed "The Order of the
Star-Spangled Banner," but which Greeley named the Know-Nothings—for
members of the order, when questioned, were instructed to profess utter
ignorance.

This emergence of a broad national organization coincided with the ill-advised visit of the papal nuncio Mgr. Gaetano Bedini to settle a controversy which had arisen between certain Catholic congregations and the higher ecclesiastical authorities as to the ownership of church property. Angry critics declared that the Pope was impudently arrogating control over the property of American citizens on American soil. An Italian ex-priest, Gavazzi, launched a crusade against the nuncio. "Forty-eighters" from Germany, Austria, and France seized the opportunity to help foment anti-papal demonstrations. Bedini was almost mobbed in Boston, Baltimore, Pittsburgh, and Cincinnati, and had to perform much of the later part of his tour clandestinely. The new organization also gained strength from Pierce's appointment of Judge Campbell, a Pennsylvania Catholic, as postmaster-general. It was stimulated by various Irish riots in New York; for example, an outrageous outbreak on July 4, 1853, when a parade of the Hibernian Society in the ninth ward degenerated into a street-mêlée. The Irish, out of mere exuberance, irritated by a runaway horse which disordered their procession, assaulted peaceable citizens, and "a fearful scene ensued" until platoons of police came on the run, arresting thirty-six men. More serious rioting took place in the last weeks of 1853.[67]

By the summer of 1853 the Native Americans had begun to throw off their secrecy. In August, for example, Baltimore witnessed a demonstration by several thousand men in Monument Square. The crowd bore aloft transparencies reading: "We Ought to be More Americanized"; "Americans, Organize—Your Country Calls"; "The Bible in our Public Schools"; "The Public Schools as They Are"; "We Want no Foreign Military Organizations"; "Eternal Separation of Church and State." The speakers included both Marylanders and Pennsylvanians. And when early in 1854 the Kansas-Nebraska bill was brought forward, the shock it gave lent new strength to the Know-Nothings. Both North and South, Whigs who felt their old party craft sinking under their feet looked about for a refuge. They did not wish to enter the Democratic ranks, and if conservative in temper, they objected to the new fusion party.[68]

The nativist movement bore a direct relationship to the spectacular rise in the alien-born population, which increased by 84 per cent during the fifties, and the Irish portion of which settled mainly in or near the three important debarkation-points of Boston, New York, and Philadelphia. Millions resented Celtic clannishness, the solid Celtic vote, and the violence of Celtic hoodlums. Orestes A. Brownson, who had joined the Catholic Church a decade earlier,

67 Henry Slicer, chaplain of the Senate, sent Buchanan on June 10, 1854, a description of the reasons for the Know-Nothing movement. He thought Bishop Hughes more responsible than any other man—he had irritated Protestants; the demand by Catholics in various localities for a share of the public school funds, though invariably defeated, had aroused much indignation; the visit of the papal nuncio had contributed; and the controversy between Hughes and Senator Cass was not to be ignored. There were still other factors.
68 National Intelligencer, August 25, 1853; Billington, Protestant Crusade, chs. 12, 13.

thought a defensive reaction against alien radicalism equally natural. "When we consider," he stated in his *Quarterly Review* of July, 1854, "that a foreign population at a rate of a quarter of a million or more is annually poured in upon us, with foreign manners, foreign tastes, usages, and habits, and by far the larger part of them imbued with erroneous notions of our institutions, and prepared to push democracy to extreme radicalism, few of us can deny that there is at least some cause for apprehension, especially since our natural-born citizens are already to a fearful extent animated by an ultra-democratic spirit." This outcry against alien-radicalism was to be heard through the coming generations; after the rise of Marxism in the seventies, following the Haymarket riot, in response to the Sacco-Vanzetti affair; but Brownson, whose Catholicism was highly conservative, had a special definition of radicalism.

As a matter of fact, anti-Catholic feeling was rather stimulated by a feeling (which refugees of '48 did much to propagate) that the Church was on the side of reaction and tyranny in Austria-Hungary, Italy, France, Spain, and other lands. John Mitchel in his *Citizen* maintained that Brownson's ultramontane and anti-republican opinions had done more than anything else to kindle hostility to the Church as a reactionary force.[69] "Since '48 you have regularly enlisted yourself on the side of all the tyrants of Europe," ran his accusatory statement. It had some force. Brownson had written in January, 1851: "European democracy is mere wild anarchy." At an earlier date (July, 1849) he had declared: "When infidelity, heresy, and schism are clearly and directly crimes against society, they are justly punishable by the civil authorities." It was alleged by his opponents that he had done much to give other Catholic periodicals, such as the *Freemen's Journal* and the *Shepherd of the Valley* (St. Louis) an anti-democratic tone. S. F. B. Morse's vitriolic brochure on the *Foreign Conspiracy against the Liberties of the United States* was running through its seventh edition by 1855.

Suspicion of Catholicism was also stimulated during 1854 by an interesting clash between Senator Cass and Archbishop Hughes of New York. On May 5, Cass delivered an earnest speech in the Senate on the religious rights of Americans residing or travelling abroad, based largely on an excellent report made the previous session by Joseph R. Underwood. He emphasized the withholding of certain human decencies from Protestants in various Catholic countries. When an American woman died in Matanzas, Cuba, the only place available for the interment of Protestant bodies was a vile hole where corpses were tossed indiscriminately together, and where a mound of corruption had arisen. To bury elsewhere, even in private ground, was punishable with a fine of $2,000, and to take the body away from the island without permission (rarely

69 Quoted in N. Y. *Tribune*, July 14, 1854.

if ever granted) involved another fine of $1,500. Cass spoke also of the denial of religious liberty represented by the Madiai case, which had aroused much feeling in America and Britain, and had led to a public meeting in New York called by Luther Bradish, Hugh Maxwell, Hiram Ketchum, and other prominent citizens. The Madiai couple, man and wife, had been imprisoned in Florence merely for owning and reading a Protestant Bible. Bishop Hughes explained that Tuscan laws prohibited the establishment of "domestic conventicles" for the purpose of converting Tuscan subjects from the established religion. He did not defend the arrest, but thought it no such offense as the burning of the Charlestown convent in enlightened Massachusetts.[70]

Unlike some later nativist organizations, such as the A.P.A. and second Klan, the Know-Nothings mobilized their principal strength in the great cities, and for a time sought chiefly to win local and municipal victories. They failed to plant their roots deeply enough in the South to gain a strong political position. Many Southern Whigs for a time became Know-Nothings, and the movement showed great force until checked by a spectacular election in Virginia. But the number of immigrants in the South was comparatively small, Catholics were few outside Maryland and Louisiana, and except in these States, the party lacked materials for sustenance. Even in Tennessee, where it made great play for a time, Andrew Johnson—who said, "Show me a Know-Nothing, and I will show you a reptile on whose neck every foot ought to be placed"— soon checked it. In the North, however, the organization showed in 1854–56 an astonishing vitality and strength. For a time nothing seemed able to oppose it. It swept a great part of New England, almost conquered New York, and grew powerful even in the Ohio Valley.

Its first spectacular victories were won in Pennsylvania, the seat in the forties of the American or United American party. "Have you heard of the new political combination called the Know-Nothings?" demanded a Lancaster friend of Buchanan in the spring of 1854.[71] "Their operations, in the few instances in which they have acted, were secret and hidden, and very successful." He went on to describe their interference in a Lancaster election of school directors. A rumor had sprung up that they were about to strike one of their sudden fierce blows in order to defeat two Catholics and a foreign-born Swedenborgian. It soon became evident that they were working with immense energy. The three men were overwhelmingly defeated. "These 'Know-Nothings' act in perfect concert, it would seem; but where they meet and how they are organized, no one can tell. It is said they were summoned, on this late occa-

70 See the pamphlet comprising the "Speech of Cass on Religious Freedom Abroad"; "Letter of the Most Rev. Archbishop Hughes on the Madiai"; "Letter of Hughes in Reply to Lewis Cass," etc. A copy is in the Huntington Library.
71 A. L. Hayes, May 8, 1854, to Buchanan; Buchanan Papers.

sion by triangular bits of black paper dropped about, or posted on alley fences."

Then in June came the Philadelphia election. A coalition of Know-Nothings, Whigs, freesoil Democrats, and temperance men swept all before them, electing their candidate for mayor by eight thousand majority. For a minor office one of Postmaster-General Campbell's special friends was defeated by eleven thousand votes. The coalition carried a large majority of both the select and common councils. "The Know-Nothings are rampant in this city," a Lancaster friend wrote Buchanan late in June. "But the country, thank God, is right. . . ." The Philadelphia election, however, encouraged activity in every quarter. In July Daniel T. Jenks of Philadelphia sent Buchanan the ominous news: "The 'Know-Nothings' are organizing in every county of the State, I am told wherever there is a town of any size." [72] Governor Bigler, hearing from all parts of the commonwealth, concluded that nativist feeling was much stronger and deeper-seated than in 1844. "I have always opposed the Irish combination," he wrote.

The sudden impact of Know-Nothingism on political affairs filled many observers with foreboding. No one could tell how powerful the new party might become. "The Whigs are desperate—ready to ally themselves with any faction—many democrats are soreheaded, having failed to secure Government patronage, etc.—this new order, so far, is secret and intangible—they talk of their *principles,* but they avow none—and the clandestine manner in which they proceed, fills timid people with alarm—and even *old politicians* are led away, *by fear,* or *desire of favour*—they are a kind of 'Gunpowder plot' undiscovered, until, without even hearing the explosion, candidates proscribed by them, find themselves like 'Mohammed's Coffin' suspended in mid-Heaven, or like Haman, dangling from a Know Nothing gallows." So Henry Slicer analyzed the situation this spring.[73] Postmaster-General Campbell wrote privately, with deep feeling: "This order is one of the most dangerous that has ever arisen in the politics of our country. A secret society, bound together by the most horrible oaths—they swear never to vote for a foreigner or a Catholic to any office." [74] His only comfort was in thinking that its existence might be brief. Shrieks of fear and anger from New York, Massachusetts, and Pennsylvania announced the discovery by old-line politicians that both States might be won by the Know-Nothings. In New York by autumn no fewer than seventy

72 George Sanderson, June 22, Jenks July 7, 1854; Buchanan Papers. Light on the grounds for old-stock irritation against the Irish is thrown by Thomas D'Arcy McGee's *History of the Irish Settlers in North America* (1855); a book which urged the Irish to preserve their native characteristics, to strengthen Catholicism, and to resist "every effort to exalt the Anglo-Saxon over the other races here."
73 June 10, 1854, to Buchanan; Buchanan Papers.
74 June 12, 1854, to Buchanan.

thousand voters were said to be enrolled on the Know-Nothing books, though not all were dependable. In Massachusetts the summer enrolment was estimated at fifty thousand, and the fall enrolment at seventy thousand or more, outnumbering all rivals. Meanwhile, by a determined effort, battling against Administration pressure, the Know-Nothings elected John T. Towers mayor of Washington.

### [ VI ]

It was a season of political effervescence and change; new impulses, prejudices, and principles were making the currents of American thought boil and spout; and under all the giddy, foaming surface eddies lay a profound disturbance—the upheaval caused by the collision between the old force of nationalism and the new force of sectionalism. Douglas's bill was like a jetty suddenly thrown into the central bed of a river; spray shot up, rapids roared, whirlpools formed. Many lovers of the Union were drawn to the Know-Nothings by their strong nationalistic principles. The amiable Clayton of Delaware, deeply distressed by the conflict of North and South, helped disband the Whig Party completely in his State and led it into the Native American fold as a new *national* party. Orestes A. Brownson emphasized this important aspect of the new organization. In his *Quarterly Review*, he declared that Americans resented the attacks of foreigners on the dominant Anglo-American stock. They resented the assumption that naturalization was a right, not a privilege. They resented the violent and radical tendencies of many foreigners. "We beg our naturalized citizens and foreign residents to bear in mind that the Native American sentiment is but the sentiment of American nationality, and that it is their duty as well as their interest to respect it, and not to ridicule and vituperate it." [75]

Greeley's *Tribune* and other sober newspapers constantly drew a distinction between the healthy element of national feeling in the Know-Nothing Party, and the unhealthy element of anti-alien, anti-Catholic prejudice. In so far as the movement was directed against the abuses and evasions of the immigration laws, alien voting, Irish violence at elections and the like; in so far as it was aimed at maintaining the free public schools, in distinction from parochial schools, as a solvent of various national stocks, and a great unifying and democratizing force; in so far as it was directed against the possibility of papal interference in American affairs (for, wrote Greeley, most Catholic writers "maintain not merely the Pope's supremacy in spirituals, but his authority to draw the line between spirituals and temporals; and when that is conceded, there is very little

75  July, 1854.

left")—many editors thought it sound.[76] Cass's learned speech on Protestant troubles in obscurantist Catholic countries had expressed a widespread and justifiable resentment. In so far as the new party was bigoted and hate-ridden in religious and "racial" matters sensible observers held it most pernicious.[77] Other observers thought the Know-Nothing impulse beneficial as tending to loose old party trammels. The people, later wrote Gideon Welles, "were justly tired of the old party combinations and discipline"; many entered the new movement "with a view of relieving themselves of fetters that they could not otherwise easily cast off"; and the result might well be good.

For potent if rather obscure reasons a natural sympathy existed among temperance men, anti-slavery men, Whigs, and Northern Know-Nothings. Temperance advocates could not forget that the Democratic Party generally, and the Irish-Americans almost universally, were opposed to their cause. The Irish-born were perhaps the most intemperate group in America, yet their leaders did little to defend them from the saloon. The New York *Tribune* spoke out plainly on this subject. "The fact that the Catholics of this country keep a great many more grogshops and sell more liquor in proportion to their number than any other denomination, creates and keeps alive a strong prejudice against them." The Church, it added, does not use its moral power wisely in this field. "It is liquor which fills so many Catholic (as well as other) homes with discord and violence, darkens newspaper columns with so many accounts of Irish rows, brawls, and faction-fights, fills our prisons with Irish culprits, and makes the gallows hideous with so many Catholic murderers. For while the foreign-born population of our country is scarcely a sixth of the whole number, it appears that a large majority of the crimes against life, at least in the free States, are committed by this faction, and most of the culprits evince by their choice of spiritual advisers that they are Catholics."

As for the anti-slavery movement, the Irish were again open to the charge

76 And so did many politicians. A. G. Brown wrote December 17, 1854, to C. C. Clay, Jr.: "Our fellow citizens of American birth will have to Americanize themselves a little more. The business of giving Irish votes and German votes and French votes will have to cease. We ought to have none but American votes—American votes from foreign and native born citizens, I care not which. Another thing—German societies and Irish societies and all such as indicate a greater devotion to the fatherland than the land [of] adoption will have to be abandoned. It is not wonderful that our people (natives I mean) should be jealous of a power that shows in its outward conduct that it loves Ireland more than America." Clay Papers, Duke Library.

77 Note the remarks of J. M. Davidson, editor of the Havana (Ill.) *Squatter Sovereign*, October 14, 1859: "In all efforts of the Know-Nothings, or any other body of men, to repel the interference of Romish priests, or their abettors in political affairs, we can and will most heartily join; but at the same time we must insist on the application of the like rule to a certain class of Protestant priests and their underlings (*qui capet ille facit*), who are today more dangerous to the peace and perpetuity of the Union than all the priestly minions of Rome in the land, because the more numerous, and the more powerful for harm, and not a whit less scrupulous in their treasonable designs."

of consistent hostility to it. Nine-tenths of the 45,000 subscribers for the *Citizen* launched this year by the Protestant Irish-Nationalist John Mitchel, were Irish Catholics. It was one of the most violent defenders of slavery in this country. A pro-slavery tone pervaded the *Irish American*, which boasted of 20,000 subscribers, and certain other periodicals. Irish dislike of the free Negroes was notorious. "How the Irish rushed en masse to the polls of our State only seven years ago," wrote Greeley, "to vote down the right of colored men to the elective franchise! No other class of our citizens was so zealous, so unanimous in its hostility to Equal Suffrage without regard to color. 'Would you have your daughter marry a naygur?' was their standing flout at the champions of democracy irrespective of race and color." [78] The German-Americans, on the other hand, were overwhelmingly anti-slavery in feeling. So were the Scandinavian-Americans. But it was the Irish who counted for most in the East. And much of the Democratic press attacked Know-Nothingism as a product of the same psychology that produced abolitionism. [79]

Finally, some Whigs drew from their aristocratic and conservative tendencies a marked affinity for Know-Nothingism. In the large Eastern cities the Whigs had been the party of property, decorum, and class-feeling. The circles in Boston, New York, and Philadelphia which adored Clay and hung with eager attention on Webster's after-dinner speeches, the groups depicted in the diary of Philip Hone and the letters of John P. Kennedy, had a natural dislike for the aliens sweeping in at the ports. They looked on the excitable Irishman as a menace to social order. The firemen's fights in New York and other cities alarmed them. Still greater was their dislike of the "radical" ideas propagated, as they thought, by those whom Brownson denounced as "German infidels and Italian patriots" [80]—ideas they believed of demagogic tendency. Freethought, socialism, and the general temper of 1848 in Europe, jarred upon them. They disliked the liberalism of Kossuth and Mazzini, the tendency to push democracy to extremes. The wealthy John Bell of Tennessee, who believed that the foreign influx threatened to undermine national institutions, turned to support an aristocratic Know-Nothing candidate for governor.

Altogether, it is not difficult to understand why for a season Know-Nothingism flourished and the lines separating Native American, Whigs,

78 N. Y. *Tribune*, August 26, 1854.
79 Cf. Washington *Union*, August 18, 1853.
80 Brownson's *Quarterly Review*, July, 1854. Michael Doheny published a long article in the *Irish American* attacking Brownson as "a pious baboon," and John Mitchel repeatedly assailed him in the *Citizen* as the friend of tyrants, the author of an "outrageous caricature" of Catholicism. Brownson, who had been aptly termed the Boston Boanerges, retorted in kind, calling the *Irish American* "a ribald sheet." Inasmuch as Brownson now held distinctly ultramontane views, the controversy was closely analagous to the quarrels of liberal and conservative Catholics in Europe. Mitchel, though a Protestant, had many Catholic backers. See N. Y. *Tribune*, July 14, 1854, for long controversial quotations on both sides of the issue.

freesoilers and Maine law men became hazy. This party maelstrom abounded in contradictions. The nationalism of the Know-Nothings and the sectionalism of the freesoilers, the conservatism of the old-line Whigs and tne radicalism of many fusionists, were in sharp conflict. But a general demand for "reform," for change, and a widespread belief that America suffered from intruding aliens and from expanding slaveholders gave the seething elements a temporary cohesion. This was certain to disappear as each group insisted sharply on its own creed. More and more the Republicans, whose creed was the sanest and most constructive, were to emerge as dominant. And as time developed the essential weakness of the Know-Nothings—for national and religious tolerance are absolutely basic elements in American life, while attacks upon alien groups and upon religious sects defeat themselves by making these groups and sects more militant, more clannish, and more suspicious—the voters were sure to fall away from it and its organization to lose strength.[81]

The Know-Nothing organization was open to serious criticism, also, for its highly undemocratic character. Its apparatus of lodges and councils enabled a few men in strategic positions to control policies and name candidates. In New York this year the State convention, for example, was managed by elements from the metropolis and its suburbs, the northern and western counties counting for nothing. Had all the councils been fully represented, nearly 1600 delegates would have been present. But only 953 attended; of these only 482 took part in selecting a candidate for governor; and the nominee received the votes of but 243. The grand council of each State exercised autocratic powers, and the grand council of the nation threatened to become more dictatorial still.

The Know-Nothing movement, moreover, had three degrees, which gradually suffered some erosion, but temporarily gave it a caste structure. Members of the Know-Nothing Society, who must be Americans born and without Catholic taint, constituted the powerful general corps of the party. They were pledged to vote as the society determined—and always for native-born Protestants alone. Organized in secret lodges, with passwords, degrees, signs, and handshakes, they were supposedly an adamantine brotherhood to

---

81 Two views were taken of the relation of the Know-Nothing movement to the anti-slavery cause. One was that it did great harm; people, according to this view, had become sick and tired of the old party dogmas and leaders, Douglas's bill had aroused the free spirit of the North, and a general uprising was at hand—when this new issue was interposed to divert and distract the friends of freedom. The other view was that the Know-Nothing movement offered a good halfway house between the old parties and the new one. Henry Wilson, who joined it for a time, states this emphatically: "Hundreds of thousands, who cared less for its avowed principles than for the higher claims of justice and humanity, and had little faith in its permanency, were willing to use its machinery to disrupt the Whig and Democratic parties, in the confident hope that out of the disorganized masses would come a great political party, antagonistic to the dominating influences of the slave power." *Rise and Fall of the Slave Power*, II, 419, 420. This second view was the sounder of the two.

check "the stride of the foreigner and alien," and to thwart "the deadly plans of the Jesuit and the Papist." Whenever asked as to their principles or objects, they were to respond, "I know nothing." A second-degree circle, of more select nature, comprised members eligible for office within the order; and a third-degree group, more eclectic still, offered material for offices outside the organization. But as we shall see, two irresistible forces, popular antagonism to excessive secrecy and to hierarchal lines, and the political necessities of a fast-growing party, compelled the abandonment of much of the mumbo-jumbo, the restrictive formality, and the group-demarcation of early days. As the party grew larger, it grew looser in structure, and adapted itself more to special local and State conditions.[82]

During this brief summer of political agitation hatreds and antagonisms flamed high. The conflict between Nebraska men and anti-Nebraska men was sore enough. Old friendships were ruptured, old associations broken, for men previously temperate denounced each other as cheats and knaves. And the constant, jarring conflict between Know-Nothings and the alien-born produced nastier episodes. Wicked and designing politicians, wrote G. S. Hillard to Francis Lieber, were fomenting these clashes. "You have noticed that two Catholic churches in New England have been destroyed, and I am afraid that there may be bloody encounters between the natives and the Irish, if this sort of thing goes on." [83] A religious riot occurred in Brooklyn on a Sunday afternoon early in June, some Irishmen attacking a procession of Native Americans, and provoking a general encounter which reportedly left two men dead. A little later a worse disturbance took place in Newark. Here an imposing procession of the American Protestant Association Lodges of the State, some two thousand people with bands, flags, and mottoes, came into collision with hostile Celts, and before the fighting ended one man had been slain, many were badly wounded, and a Catholic church was gutted.[84]

## [ VII ]

How fiercely the freesoil sentiment of the North had been aroused was demonstrated by a hundred episodes this summer and fall. Three Southerners who visited Detroit to recover a fugitive slave met the now universal hostility. When they applied to prominent attorneys for legal aid, with an offer of fees running up to $2,000, a peremptory refusal was given. "As the South is de-

---

82 See Darrell Overdyke, *The American Party in the South* (Duke University doctoral dissertation, MS, in Duke Library); the long and frank article on the order signed "United Forever" copied from N. Y. *Times* in the N. Y. *Tribune*, October 11, 1854.
83 July 11, 1854; Lieber Papers, Huntington Library.
84 N. Y. *Tribune*, June 28, 1854.

termined to have the slave laws her own way," wrote a Detroit citizen, "men are determined to allow her to get them executed as she best can." [85] Pennsylvania and Ohio sent thickening news items about the operation of the underground railroad and the successful escape of slaves. In Boston men applauded a butcher who refused to sell meat to E. G. Loring, the commissioner who had assisted in the return of Burns. Massmeetings, political parades, and rallies showed that the free States were ablaze.

When Douglas, on the adjournment of Congress in August, set out for the West, he found manifestations of indignation at every turn. Already, in June, he had visited New York to encounter a chilly reception; the applause at his meeting in City Hall Park coming, if we may believe the *Tribune*, only from some knots of "Fourth Warders, bhoys, Rynders' followers, and government lackeys." Now at Trenton, N. J., he was booed by a crowd of hostile workingmen, for a local labor leader named Skelton was a vigorous anti-Nebraska man.[86] Similar episodes occurred elsewhere. As Douglas had said, he could have travelled from Boston to Chicago by the light of fires kindled to burn his effigy. In Cleveland his image was hanged on a tree in the Public Square, with a placard denouncing "Douglas and Doughfaces, the *Plain Dealer* and Nebraska." The freesoil newspapers were filled with attacks on "traitor Arnold," "Judas," and the like.

He reached Chicago to find the entire press save for the recently-founded Chicago *Times* under his friend James W. Sheahan, the entire Protestant clergy, and fully three-fourths of the citizens, deeply antagonistic. Some friends, frightened by the ugly public temper, had advised him to stay away from the city. The general hostility did not diminish when it was announced that he would speak in his defence at North Market Hall on the evening of September 1st.[87]

There was reason for this public distrust. It had been rumored for several

85 N. Y. *Tribune*, June 28, 1854.
86 Rodman M. Price, June 9, 1854, to Douglas; Douglas Papers, U. of Chicago.
87 Douglas had compact bodies of friends in most of the principal cities of the State working busily for him. In Springfield, for example, the postmaster, Isaac R. Diller, was a staunch adherent. When the Nebraska bill passed he congratulated Douglas on "the crowning glory of your life." The strength and depth of the local feeling in Douglas's favor, he wrote, were immense. "Old men who have grown gray in the ranks of Whiggery, threw up their hats [and] huzzaed for you, when I announced to them from the postoffice window that the Nebraska bill had passed." All this time the *Illinois State Journal* was attacking the bill with as much vigor as Eastern freesoil papers. Simeon Francis was its editor. "*Sim* was away during the greater part of the time of the Nebraska discussion," explained Diller, "and his sanctum was occupied by a one-horse lawyer and Yankee schoolmaster named Moore, who has so completely committed his paper that *Sim* finds he is in for it, and hammers away at your 'diabolical iniquity' in a style only equalled by his great prototype [Greeley]. He is in a tight place, and so is 'our member,' as he will discover when he makes his appearance on the stump in the next Congressional canvass." Diller, May 31, 1854; Douglas Papers, U. of Chicago. The member for the Sixth District was Richard Yates.

weeks that Douglas was planning an assemblage which would enable him to boast of widespread Chicago support. The city had a good central park suitable for public massmeetings, and an excellent central auditorium, South Market Hall, ordinarily used for smaller gatherings. Considerable astonishment was therefore expressed when it was announced that the meeting would take place north of the river, in the centre of the Irish district, at a little-used hall that could not accommodate more than twelve hundred people.[88] Chicago then had a population of about seventy thousand, of whom at least ten thousand would wish to hear the speech. Various Douglas men let it be known that his well-organized Irish adherents would deal roughly with any hecklers. These statements naturally aroused the anger of numerous Know-Nothings in the city. In Philadelphia on July 4 Douglas had denounced the Know-Nothings as a sectional party whose nucleus was "a secret society bound together by the most solemn and terrifying oaths," and had declared that all Democrats would stand firm against the "allied forces of Abolitionism, Whiggism, Nativism, and religious intolerance, under whatever name and on whatever field they may present themselves." [89] Filled with resentment, Know-Nothings now declared that Douglas's intention was to hold a packed meeting under the protection of bullies, have it vote resolutions glorifying himself and his measures, and blazon them to the world as the sentiment of Chicago.

Feeling in Chicago and indeed the whole Northwest had been irritated, moreover, by the defeat of homestead legislation at the hands of Southerners. This area was eager to see the prairies and plains thrown open to free settlement. A bill granting 160 acres to actual settlers who had occupied and cultivated the land for five years had passed the House in March. The vote had been sectional rather than partisan. Only one adverse vote came from the Northwest; only three favorable votes from the South Atlantic region. Citizens of Illinois had hoped for a great impetus to settlement, railroad building, and trade. But Southern members of Congress, seeing nothing to gain and much to lose, were adamant. The bill, wrote J. L. M. Curry of Alabama to Senator C. C. Clay, was outrageous. "It is a fine theme for mouthing demagogues. Kill it off." He saw in it a departure from old Jeffersonian strict-construction tenets, a rich inducement to corruption, and a flagrant injustice to Southern copartners in the national domain. Clay was equally opposed, and summed up Southern arguments with slashing vigor. Apart from his constitutional objections, he felt that the measure would greatly injure the slaveholding region.

"Our lands are generally poor," he wrote confidentially to fellow-Southerner, "those in the North and West generally rich. Settlers in Southern States would

88 See the two Chicago letters in N. Y. *Tribune*, September 8, 1854.
89 James W. Sheahan, *Douglas*, 264-271.

thus receive a barren gift compared with settlers in Northern States. But sagacious self-interest would prompt poor men, dependent on their manual labor for support, to go north to the best lands. We would thus lose in population and the North would gain what we lost. Again, the South pays at least three-fourths of the duties of the government, and has to supply the deficiency of a dollar in the treasury caused by giving away a dollar's worth of land; the South must pay seventy-five per cent in taxes while the North paid but twenty-five per cent and yet gained more land, better land and more population. Thus the South would lose by the free farm policy in land, money, and population. Besides, it would prove a most efficient ally for Abolition by encouraging and stimulating the settlement of free farms with Yankees and foreigners pre-committed to resist the participancy of slaveholders in the public domain. The 'Emigrant Aid Societies' now organizing in the North will flourish and multiply under the fostering aid of such federal legislation." [90]

Closing ranks against the bill, Southern Senators defeated it. They passed a substitute measure sponsored by Hunter of Virginia, providing for a form of preëmption under which twenty-five cents an acre would be payable at the end of five years. The House refused to consider the substitute—and the homestead bill failed. Resentment over this fact, and over Southern opposition to efficient rivers and harbors legislation, naturally accentuated the North-western hostility to the Kansas-Nebraska Act. Douglas would have to explain not only himself but his Southern allies.

As the date for his meeting approached, Douglas and his friends made strenuous efforts to produce an imposing display in his favor. Emissaries were sent to neighboring counties to urge all his devotees to attend. Talk in saloons and hotels indicated that trouble was brewing. A noted out-of-town politician declared that unless the Senator was assured a fair hearing, adequate forces would be massed to see that he got it. A Chicago supporter threateningly growled: "Douglas will be heard—a thousand six-shooters will be on the ground for that purpose." [91] Other threats of force, enunciated by Douglas men, were met by Know-Nothing counter-threats. The more influential and conservative citizens of Chicago had from the first discountenanced any violence, but they were not opposed to such demonstrations as would show the real feeling of the city.

The morning of the first opened with feeling at high pitch. Reports were current of an overwhelming force of armed Irishmen, and of sales of revolvers and pistols that had emptied every arms store. Wentworth's *Democratic Press*, formerly a warm supporter of Douglas but since the introduction of the

90  C. C. Clay Papers, Duke University.
91  Warsaw, Ill., *Press*, September 7, 14, 1854; letters from Chicago.

Nebraska bill his implacable opponent, was rebuking his followers for their threats. The *Tribune* called upon the people, if a packed audience occupied North Market Hall, to hold a greater meeting just outside it. It must be realized that Chicago still had a good many frontier characteristics: a city built chiefly of wood, distinctly frowsy in appearance, its streets unpaved or ill-paved, its wooden sidewalks sheltering swarms of rats, its railroads and boats constantly bringing in crowds of immigrants, its labor force occasionally turbulent, its whole atmosphere rough and ready.[92] It also had a large body of high-minded, Puritan-tempered citizens, who could set their jaws hard, and whose detestation of the Nebraska bill knew no bounds.

Early that afternoon ships in the river and harbor lowered their flags to half-mast. Soon after six all the churchbells began tolling; "and above the sound of every other, and as if consciously and by authority proclaiming the great voice of the city, came the solemn booming of the big city bell." [93] As citizens poured along the roadways to the meeting, their grave, earnest demeanor impressed every spectator. The night was clear, still, and hot. A platform had been erected before the hall, and eight or ten thousand people were soon packed in front. Mayor Milliken was to preside. Political and personal friends of Douglas, including District Attorney Thomas Hoyne, Postmaster Isaac Cook, and John L. Peyton of Virginia, an adviser of the Senator, took their places on the stand. Special trains had brought some hundreds of Douglas men from downstate, chiefly Springfield, who clustered near the platform. For the rest the crowd, according to the Chicago *Tribune*, was "composed, in a very large degree, of the very best classes of our community; our mariners, shippers, merchants, mechanics, and professional men." The *Tribune's* reporter emphasized their good humor.[94]

Douglas began by saying that he wished to elucidate the Nebraska Bill. He was satisfied that nobody in his audience understood it. (Three hearty groans.) The bill had never been published in any of the city's journals (laughter and groans) until that morning it had been printed in the Chicago *Times* (groans and hisses). Amid constant interruptions, he proceeded to argue that the Kansas-Nebraska Act was right, because based on the great American principle of popular sovereignty; and with a defiant air he read the "stump speech" clause embodied in the bill. He further argued that the repeal of the Missouri restriction was in accordance with the declared views of Illinoisans.

92 Warsaw, Ill., *Press*, September 14, 1854; D. B. Sanger, "The Chicago *Times* and the Civil War," *Miss. Valley Hist. Rev.*, XVII, 557–580. The Douglas forces had to have an organ quickly when the *Press* went anti-Nebraska. They took over a struggling sheet and converted it into the *Times* under Sheahan, Isaac Cook, and Daniel Cameron.
93 Chicago letter in N. Y. *Tribune*, September 8, 1854.
94 Chicago *Tribune*, September 2, 1854.

Why? The Missouri Compromise not only prohibited slavery north of 36° 30', but by implication was a contract to permit it south of that line. Freesoilers and Northern Whigs had expressly pledged themselves in 1848 against any more slave States, and therefore against the Missouri Compromise. Cass's followers were at the same time pledged to popular sovereignty in the Territories. Who of all his audience was in favor of admitting slave States south of that line? They were all opposed to the Missouri Compromise, and consequently to geographical limitation. They had all declared in favor of the *principle* of the bill, and he had therefore carried out their views. He had once been in favor of the Missouri line, and had sought to extend it, but after the great adverse decision of 1848 had yielded his own convictions. Was it fair to censure him for carrying out their own declared principles? [95]

This argument, which occupied the first three-quarters of an hour, was too obviously inaccurate and sophistical to convince the hostile majority of the audience. Every statement by Douglas that seemed to have a pro-slavery tinge was received with groans, hisses, and cries of "No." As orator and crowd grew warmer, both began to lose their tempers. Douglas commenced to pepper his discourse, according to the Chicago *Tribune* reporter, "with the most insulting epithets which the resources of billingsgate could furnish," and with "ungrounded accusations against the character of our city and citizens." [96] Auditors commenced to interrupt him more frequently. Laying aside his manuscript, he began to bandy retorts with the crowd. He dared any man who held certain views to give him his name; he spoke of threats against his personal safety; he denounced the *Tribune* as a mendacious sheet (three cheers for the *Tribune*, and three groans for the *Times*); and giving way to passion, shouted that he would silence the "mob" or stay there until morning. His tormentors burst into song:

> We won't go home until morning,
> We won't go home until morning!

At the end, Douglas was transported with rage. He assailed the Know-Nothings, evoking a new chorus of groans. He refused to answer questions about his vote on the Rivers and Harbors bill. Finally, he declared that it was useless to proceed and he would go home (cries of Good, Good). He would be heard again, but for the present he would leave the stand to the mob. Jamming his hat on his head, his features dark with anger, he shouted: "It is now Sunday morning; I'll go to church and you may go to hell!"—and shaking

95 Idem; N. Y. *Tribune*, September 8, 1854, regular Chicago correspondence; N. Y. *Herald, Express*, and other papers, September 3–9, 1854.
96 September 2, 1854.

his fist at the audience, he strode off the stage.[97] The comment of the Chicago *Journal*, more judicious than the *Tribune's* taunting editorial on his "humiliation," was not unfair: [98]

We regret very much that Mr. Douglas was not suffered to proceed without interruption and conclude what he had to say upon the subject, but at the same time do not hold him blameless in the premises. He came among an excited constituency, who felt that he had deeply wronged them, to speak in self-vindication, but at the very outset of his remarks assailed their intelligence, and charged them indiscriminately with not having read the Nebraska Bill, and being ignorant of its provisions. Instead of asking them to "hear him for his cause, and be silent that they might hear" he constantly appealed to the immense throng for answers to the interrogatories propounded, boasted of being an older resident of the State than a majority of the meeting, and wound up with charging those who had come in obedience to his summons to hear him with being an ungovernable mob. We submit to the friends of Senator Douglas whether such a course was calculated or *intended* to secure for him a respectful hearing. We ask any candid reader whether Senator Douglas is not himself accountable for fanning excitement which he knew existed to a fury which drove him from the stand?

While the nation's press rang with the story of the Chicago meeting, orthodox Democratic newspapers condemning the "outrage" and freesoil journals applauding the "manly demonstration," Douglas carried his campaign down State. He spoke at Rock Island, Geneva, Quincy, and other towns. Careful local preparations were made for most of these appearances: handbills posted in English and German, a band sent about to neighboring towns, a preliminary procession held.[99]

Everywhere he met tokens of the widespread disapprobation; sometimes burning effigies and denunciatory placards, almost universally a chilly, critical crowd. Never again did he lose his temper or challenge his audience, though he heaped venomous epithets upon the "Abolitionists," "Black Republicans," "Know-Nothings," and "Nigger-lovers." Gradually he perfected a speech which he repeated over and over—essentially his closing Senate speech, with changes adapting it to the prairies. He spoke of the two rival principles, one geographical and sectional, the other based on self-government and hence national; of his long fealty to the former, and his attempts to extend the geographical line to the Pacific; of his final acceptance of the national principle instead; of its application to new Territories in the Compromise of 1850; of its logical appli-

---

97   Chicago *Tribune*, September 2, 1854; cf. the accounts in Milton, *Eve of Conflict*, 175ff, and Johnson, *Douglas*, 258, 259.
98   Quoted in N. Y. *Tribune*, September 8, 1854.
99   Douglas Papers, U. of Chicago; Quincy, Ill., correspondence of N. Y. *Tribune*, October 19, 1854.

cability to Kansas and Nebraska; of the importance of the development of the West; and of the certainty that for physiographic reasons slavery could never long exist there. A number of down-State newspapers, led by the *Illinois State Register* (Springfield), Peoria *Press*, and Quincy *Herald*, closed around his banner. He was rather dubiously aided, too, by one notable figure from outside. Cass came to Chicago for a speech, which, like his recent Senate effort, ostensibly pleaded for the Kansas-Nebraska Act, but actually told heavily against it.

For a time, unopposed by any freesoil orator of consequence, and supported by all the batteries the Democratic regulars could muster, Douglas made progress. His audiences grew larger and more friendly.[100] Then a dramatic confrontation advertised to the State the fact that an arresting new figure had stepped upon the political stage. On October 3, when the opening of the State Fair brought thousands pouring into Springfield, Douglas delivered his oft-rehearsed arguments in the hall of the House at the State Capitol. The next day, in the same place, and to very nearly the same audience, Abraham Lincoln, whose appearance had been advertised by a shower of circulars, rose for a three-hour argument of masterly vigor, breadth, and philosophic outlook. Lincoln was of course still a staunch Whig; practical rather than speculative in intellect, and always moderate, he kept cautiously aloof from a Republican convention which Owen P. Lovejoy and others assembled in Springfield at this very time. But both his ambition for the Senate and his detestation of Douglas's doctrines impelled him to a carefully studied reply.

This reply, which when repeated twelve days later in another city became known as the "Peoria speech," dealt with the "naked merits" of the repeal of the Missouri Compromise. In part Lincoln's discourse was an historical exposition; in part an argument posited upon moral, social, and economic foundations. It was this argument which possessed the intellectual originality and moral force which we associate with Lincoln. His historical pages were a lucid demonstration that the Missouri Compromise had remained valid after the legislation of 1850; that the organization of Nebraska did not require its repeal, any more than the prior organization of Iowa and Minnesota had required it; that the Utah-New Mexico Acts had applied to those Territories and no other; and that so far was Congress from accepting a "universal principle" in legislation that it had never applied that principle to the spot nearest at hand, the District of Columbia. But much more novel and telling was the second half of his speech.

Lincoln remarked that he could not but hate that declared indifference to the spread of slavery which masked a covert zeal for it. "I hate it because of the monstrous injustice of slavery itself. I hate it because it deprives our

100  Beveridge, *Lincoln*, II, 238.

republican example of its just influence in the world, enables the enemies of free institutions with plausibility to taunt us as hypocrites, causes the real friends of freedom to doubt our sincerity, and especially because it forces so many good men among ourselves into an open war with the very fundamental principles of civil liberty, criticizing the Declaration of Independence, and insisting that there is no right principle of action but self-interest." He did not know what to do about slavery where it existed, and if all earthly power were given to him, he would be puzzled as to his course. Systems of gradual emancipation might well be adopted, but he would not criticize the South for its tardiness in accepting them. But he did know this: that slaves were not property in the sense that a hog was property. The South itself had recognized that fact when it helped to forbid the bringing of slaves from Africa under penalty of death; when it placed the domestic slave-trader under a harsh social ban; when it admitted that the 430,000 free blacks of the country needed no owners, but had a natural right to themselves. Equal justice to the South might require that every Southerner should be allowed to take his horse or pig to a new Territory; it could not require that he be allowed to take black men, who were property in Mississippi, but not property in Illinois.

But what of the sacred right of self-government? That doctrine, said Lincoln, is absolutely and eternally right, but it had no just application of the sort which Douglas attempted. Douglas had asserted that the freesoil argument amounted to this—that the white men of Nebraska are good enough to govern themselves, but not good enough to govern a few miserable Negroes!

"Well," replied Lincoln, "I doubt not that the people of Nebraska are and will continue to be as good as the average of people elsewhere. I do not say the contrary. What I do say is that no man is good enough to govern another man without that other's consent. I say this is the leading principle—the sheet-anchor of American republicanism." This principle should be extended with the growth of the republic, while slavery, its antithesis, should be kept within its original bounds. And after stating categorically that the Missouri Compromise ought to be restored, for until that happened no man would ever trust in a national compromise, Lincoln declared that the worst feature of the Kansas-Nebraska Act was not its betrayal of a thirty-year-old compact; it was its betrayal of the spirit of free institutions:

I particularly object to the new position which the avowed principle of this Nebraska law gives to slavery in the body politic. I object to it because it assumes that there can be moral right in the enslaving of one man by another. I object to it as a dangerous dalliance for free people—a sad evidence that, feeling over-prosperity, we forget right; that liberty, as a principle, we have ceased to revere. I object to it because the fathers of the republic eschewed and rejected it. The argument of "necessity" was the only argument they ever admitted in favor of slavery; and so far, and so far only as it carried them, did they ever go. . . .

"Little by little, but steadily as man's march to the grave, we have been giving up the old for the new faith. Near eighty years ago we began by declaring that all men are created equal; but now from that beginning we have run down to the other declaration, that for some men to enslave others is a "sacred right of self-government." These principles cannot stand together.

Here was a voice, fresh as the prairie world itself, such as no man had raised in the East. It lifted the argument at once to a new plane; to the level of high moral considerations. It tested the Kansas-Nebraska Act not by old laws, compacts, and precedents, or by new expediencies, but by those fundamental principles of freedom, right, and humanity on which the republic had been founded. Not all could appreciate that voice; among those who never understood its argument was Douglas, whose mind was closed to the highest moral considerations as some ears are deaf to the finest harmonies of music. But among the plain people of Illinois were multitudes who instinctively comprehended its force.

## [ IX ]

East and West the State campaigns rolled swiftly to their end. Long before election day came the Democrats knew that they were confronting disaster. It proved to be cataclysmic. In New York the party had split asunder, and Greene C. Bronson, whom the Administration had dismissed as head of the customhouse, took the field as an anti-Pierce Democrat against the regular nominee Horatio Seymour.[101] This made the defeat of both almost certain. The fusionists won all along the line, electing Myron H. Clark the next governor. Of the thirty-one Congressmen chosen, twenty-nine were Anti-Nebraska men! An effulgent morning sun thus threw its rays upon the forward path of the Republican Party. Greeley, exultant over the victory and irate over his failure to gain office, spurned the Whig leaders by announcing the dissolution of the political firm of Seward, Weed & Greeley. No man was quicker to feel the drift than the political wizard Thurlow Weed himself, as shrewd in calculating chances as he was supple in intrigue and stratagem. From this moment he turned to enter the Republican camp, and began to shape history—

101 Ex-Senator Dickinson tartly characterized the faction which had nominated Seymour: "Its Convention in Syracuse, though containing worthy men, was under the control of the Government appointees—tenants of the New York custom house, who were there crammed like Christmas turkeys with government bread and butter to sing hosannas to the wisdom of the Administration who fed them." They blindly supported this Administration, "which had no more future than a katydid." Speech at Delhi, N. Y., September 29, 1854.

to make possible the triumph of the party in 1860—by skillfully maneuvering the New York Whigs toward the new organization.[102]

In Pennsylvania, too, the Whig-Know-Nothing coalition, gaining confidence as the canvass advanced, showed a spirit and energy that the Democrats totally lacked. Three years earlier the State had placed Bigler in the governorship by a majority of some 8,000; now it turned him out by 37,000. The alliance carried the legislature, and elected twenty-one Anti-Nebraska men to Congress against four Nebraska men. Men had to look far back in history to find any parallel to this political revolution. The Congressional district of Wilmot and Grow, which had given Pierce a majority of 2,500 in 1852, now gave the Whig candidate Pollock a majority of more than 4,000.

The Administration stood rebuked in one of its chief strongholds, and machine Democrats turned toward Buchanan as their only hope. It was a significant fact that the leading political opportunist of the State, sly Simon Cameron, grown wealthy as railroad contractor, banker, ironmaster, and general businessman, and eager to regain his seat in the Senate, now suddenly forsook the Democratic fold and carried his talents and prestige into the Know-Nothing camp.[103]

Equally striking was the Know-Nothing victory in Massachusetts. The Bay State Whigs, condemning the Nebraska Act, had renominated Washburn for governor, while the Know-Nothings (who were joined by many moderate freesoilers) named a young and talented former Whig, Henry J. Gardner.

102   The result in New York left Marcy discredited, as Gideon Welles was quick to point out: "His grasping selfishness and over-management have been rebuked, and must have been attended with some humiliation. If not a subordinate in the Cabinet, or destitute of magnanimity, he would not have permitted Dix to be so improperly treated. Certainly he has gained no laurels in his present position, and the attitude of New York is itself fatal to any aspirations he may have entertained for the Presidency. Whatever reputation he may have acquired under Polk, he has forfeited under Pierce. Had he withdrawn from the Administration when it adopted the Nebraska schism as a part of its policy, he would have been himself formidable." Welles believed Seward had also erred in clinging so long to the Whig Party, and in insisting on a strict Whig ticket. He should have pursued a bolder policy. "Had he been truly great he would not have lost such an opportunity to exhibit high qualities; but he is evidently only a partisan and demagogue." November 25, 1854, to Preston King; Welles Papers, L. C.

In New York city this year Fernando Wood, an accomplished corruptionist, was elected mayor on a good government platform; and he was soon in arms against the Pierce Administration. Samuel Pleasants, MS Life of Wood.

103   The prohibition issue played a large rôle in this Pennsylvania campaign. The legislature in the spring of 1854 passed a law to submit the question of State prohibition to the people in the fall election. Bigler was noncommittal on the subject. His opponent James Pollock gave warm approval to the proposed prohibitory law. He promised to favor "every measure of moral and political reform" sanctioned by the legislature; and most temperance leaders therefore urged support of Pollock. On the eve of election, both prohibition and anti-prohibition forces were confident. It turned out that although Pollock was elected, prohibition had lost in the plebiscite, by a vote of 163,457 noes against 158,318 ayes. Asa E. Martin, Pa. Mag. of Hist. and Biog., July, 1925, Vol. 49, pp. 195-230.

The new organization amazed all beholders by its strength.[104] "The Know-Nothings are far more numerous than is generally supposed," wrote the Worcester correspondent of the New York *Tribune* as the canvass approached its end. "They will form an overwhelming majority in all our cities and large towns—in Boston, Salem, Worcester, Springfield, New Bedford, etc.—and will be found numerous even in the smaller towns. They expect to cast 50,000 votes this fall. . . ." [105] Actually the Know-Nothing-Free Soil alliance cast more than 80,000 votes, or sixty-three per cent of all ballots, bearing Gardner into power by a tidal sweep, with a Know-Nothing legislature behind him. The Whigs were reduced to 27,000 votes; the Democrats to less than 14,000; while the Republicans did not reach 7,000.[106]

Robert C. Winthrop was filled with dejection. "Our K. N. lodges," he dolefully informed the novelist Kennedy, "have been controlled by the most desperate sort of Free Soil adventurers. Henry Wilson and Anson Burlingame have ruled the hour. Our Governor-elect had to *qualify* for the candidacy by advocating a *fusion* between the Whigs and the Abolitionists. Our members of Congress are one and all of the ultra-agitation Anti-Slavery Stamp." The personnel of the Know-Nothings he pronounced "repulsive." Even Governor Gardner was "not of the family of Gardners to which I belong, either by pedigree or principle." [107] Such conservatives as Winthrop shortly lamented the election of Henry Wilson, self-educated farm hand and cobbler, to the national Senate. The meaning of the result was plain to impartial judges. "The tremendous smashup in Massachusetts," wrote Gideon Welles, "must annihilate the idea of continuing the Whig Party in existence."

All Yankee-land was moving toward a radical freesoil position. For years the Democrats had enjoyed a large majority in Maine. This fall it melted into nothingness, the Anti-Nebraska Fusion Party carrying every Congressional district, and making Anson P. Morrell governor by an overwhelming majority. Vermont responded to the same irresistible swing. The Republican candidate for governor ran far ahead of the Nebraska nominee, and the legislature showed

104 The Know-Nothings really dominated this Massachusetts coalition. "Many of the Free Soilers," wrote the Boston correspondent of the N. Y. *Tribune* September 25, "joined the 'Know-Nothings' at an early day in the expectation of being able to control that organization, and thereby make it contribute to the defeat of the Whigs. But I am inclined to believe that those who went out to shear will come back shorn."
105 N. Y. *Tribune*, August 10, 1854.
106 The Democratic State Convention in Massachusetts had left the nation thunderstruck by the asininity of its resolutions. It had the effrontery to say that the Administration "has confirmed the fraternal feeling among the States" by its recent legislation. It had the folly to assert that the Constitution recognized the power of the people, "whether in State, county, town, district, or Territory," to control their own institutions. For text see *National Intelligencer*, October 10, 1854. The idea that counties and towns might regulate slavery was a novelty indeed.
107 Winthrop, October 27, 1854, January 3, 1855; Kennedy Papers.

a three-quarters majority for the Anti-Nebraska elements. Douglas's birthplace of Brandon sent a freesoil representative to Montpelier. In New Hampshire the legislature was revolutionized, and the way was thus opened for placing the redoubtable John P. Hale, Pierce's most unrelenting opponent, in his old place in the national Senate. Upper New England, in fact, was completely conquered. Only in Connecticut and Rhode Island could Democrats still hope for aid—and there not for long.

Nor was the story different in the Northwest. The Democratic candidates were mowed down in the October contest in Ohio and Indiana. Every Congressional district in the former State, and all but two in the latter, thirty in all, elected anti-Nebraska men. The sweep constituted a dramatic political revolution. In 1852 both States had gone Democratic by wide margins; now the anti-Nebraska State ticket was carried in Ohio by 70,000 and in Indiana by 10,000. As for Illinois, Douglas's friend W. A. Richardson wrote him just before election day that all was lost. He reported the Know-Nothings more numerous than anybody had anticipated. In the Quincy district he knew of twenty lodges, and the smallest number of former Democrats in any of them was twenty. "The disasters in Penn., Ohio and Indiana have driven from us every doubtful vote. The state is lost at least for a time and I see plainly before me all the pleasures of private life." [108] Though reëlected, he was mainly right. November saw the Know-Nothings and Republicans secure a majority of the legislature on joint ballot, while five of the nine Congressional seats went to Anti-Nebraska men. It was clear that the next legislature would replace Douglas's friend Shields in the Senate by an opponent of the Administration.

In Iowa, too, a Democratic senator was doomed. The Anti-Nebraska party polled a large majority for its gubernatorial candidate, the courageous James W. Grimes, who had proclaimed "*war and war continually*" against the abandonment to slavery of a single foot of soil now consecrated to freedom"; and it chose a legislature certain to crush Douglas's follower A. C. Dodge, whose senatorial term expired the following March. And in California the September voting gave San Francisco to the Know-Nothings, who were destined shortly to sweep the State.[109]

108  November 5, 1854; Douglas Papers.
109  In Michigan, Cass, following the precedent he had set in the Senate, made a speech in favor of the Kansas-Nebraska Act which impressed every hearer as a powerful argument against it. This was at the Detroit City Hall, November 4th. One paragraph, for example, read: "It was . . . contended that the South could not enjoy their equal rights of settlement upon the public lands unless a comparatively small portion of its population, say 350,000 out of more than six millions, could take their slaves with them; or, in other words, that every man, from every State of the Union, had a right to take all his property to the public domain, and there hold it—whiskey, banks, or anything else—although prohibited by the local law. A true answer to this pretension is, that if any man, North or South, holds property not recognized as such or prohibited by the local law, his remedy is to be found,

The election, like an exploding flare, lighted up the effects of Douglas's impetuous stroke—a stroke which had benefited nobody; spread destruction far and wide; and for national peace and harmony substituted angry hatreds and bitter jealousies. Some other issues had counted for a little: the defeat of the Homestead bill, the maladroit conduct of foreign relations, general discontent with the incompetent Pierce. But the Nebraska Act had easily been paramount. The Democratic party was left battered and disfigured, with large elements in all the Northern States deserting its ranks. The Whig Party had been broken into Northern and Southern fragments. Of these the Northern portion had so far disintegrated that in a number of States the party had completely disappeared, and the Southern fraction was being assiduously wooed by the Democratic press and politicians.

Men everywhere talked of the early extinction of the Whig faith. While Democratic newspapers were full of semi-exultant editorials on the death of the great rival organization, Republican journals teemed with sadder obituary notices. In a series of articles, Horace Greeley traced its rapid decline from 1850 to 1852. It "was destroyed," he believed, "by the successful attempt of the anti-progressive majority in the last national convention to place it, at least nominally, on a pro-slavery platform." When the Fillmore-Webster groups in the North joined with the Southern Whigs to insist upon endorsement of the Fugitive Slave Act, he thought, its demise became certain. Its stunning defeat that fall, and the shock of the Nebraska bill, had merely hastened its fatal illness. "We consider the Whig Party a thing of the past," declared the *Tribune*, "and hope soon to see at least all of the nominally free States moving on to triumph under a banner bearing on its folds the Republican name. . . ."[110]

Many Southern Whigs were disconsolate. Their party had suffered heavy blows in their own section; in North Carolina, for example, the Democrats won a victory which made certain the exit of the veteran Senator Badger from public life—an able man, a loyal lover of the Union. Yet some conservative spirits felt sure they could keep Whiggism alive, if only it could count upon Northern allies. "I have come to the conclusion," wrote George S. Bryan from Charleston to John P. Kennedy, "that the Nebraska excitement will soon die out—that it will not harm the country, that it will very properly turn out the majority of the Northern Democrats, who hoped to profit by it, and it will then have served its office and lost its vitality. But where will the Whig Party be?

not in the violation of it, but in the conversion of such property into money, the universal representative of value, and to take that to his new home, and there commence his work of enterprise in a young and growing community." *National Intelligencer*, November 16, 1854.
110 N. Y. *Tribune*, October 3, 1854.

The country will not suffer. But can we of the South maintain brotherly relations with men whose power is based upon sectional agitation, *against our section?*"

Such men felt bitterly toward Douglas, believing that his Nebraska bill had been "a transparent speculation upon the passions of the South"; they thought scornfully of the weak, timid, time-serving course of most Southern Whigs on that measure; but their principal chagrin arose from the snapping of another great link of national feeling. They longed passionately for a party which, in Rufus Choate's words, carried the flag and kept step to the music of the Union—and where now was that party?

111  Kennedy Papers.

# 10

## Cuba, Ostend, and the Filibusters

AN ADMINISTRATION which blunders in home affairs is likely to blunder also in foreign relations. The temptation to seek a diversion from domestic embarrassments in overseas adventures is ever-present and highly dangerous. A tendency to rash pyrotechnics was the special weakness of Pierce and the Cabinet officers whom he so imperfectly controlled. As the Gadsden mission and the appointment of Soulé to Spain indicated, they took up the thread of foreign policy where Polk had dropped it; and from the beginning a determined group of Southern leaders looked forward to sectional profit in Cuba, Mexico, or Central America. The change from the dignity and caution of the Whig Administration, from the circumspection of Fillmore, the reserve of Webster and Everett, to the erratic energy and headlong expansionism of Pierce, Cushing, and Jefferson Davis, was abrupt and in some ways alarming. The sober Marcy would do his utmost to keep State Department policy moderate, but he could always be overruled in the White House or in Congress. The braggadocio of "Young America," the rampant nationalism of Douglas, the Anglophobia of Cass, and the Captain Bobadil temper of the filibusters, together with the slaveholding appetite for new lands, made the diplomatic barometer point to "Stormy."

The most troublesome, dangerous, and tempting spot in our foreign affairs was Cuba; the island which John Quincy Adams had said in 1832 would probably prove indispensable to the continuance and integrity of the Union itself, and which Webster had declared in 1843 we could never permit a really strong Power to occupy. To many Southerners the acquisition of Cuba had been an implicit issue in the election of 1852, and they regarded the Democratic victory of that year as a triumph for the imperialist policies which would bring the long-coveted prize into our grasp. Pierce's promise in his inaugural address that his Administration would not be restrained "by any timid forebodings of evil from expansion" still rang in many ears.

Yet in obedience to the rule that a precipitate temper always defeats itself, by its Kansas foray the Administration had gone far toward cancelling any

Cuban adventure. To millions of Northerners slavery expansion on the breezy Western plains was bad enough without joining to it slavery expansion into the opulent Caribbean. When Pierce, Davis, and Cushing committed themselves to Douglas's bill, they all but cut off every chance of tropical acquisitions. Had the Missouri Compromise been left intact, peremptory measures against Spain might have been within the limits permitted by public sentiment. But after the fateful January of 1854, an aggressive movement southward would utterly have wrecked the Democratic Party in the North, and divided the country into two mutually hostile halves. The expansionists soon had reason to rue their lost opportunities.

### [ I ]

If Cuba attracted the Southern expansionists while Whig leaders sat in the White House, it was certain to excite a keener cupidity as soon as the Democrats took office. The rejection of the three-power guarantee and the election of Pierce naturally aroused Spanish apprehensions. Madrid took hasty steps to propitiate British anti-slavery sentiment and to render the island less tempting to Americans. Near the close of 1853 Don Juan de Pezuela was sent to Havana as the new captain-general. On December 20–25, he issued decrees which more rigidly interdicted the slave trade; which authorized the importation of African and other labor as "apprentices" to lessen the shortage of hands; and which decreed the immediate liberation, with permanent residential rights, of *emancipados* (illegally imported Negroes) taken as prizes before 1835. News of these decrees aroused a spasm of anger in the South. Many concluded that Spain, with British backing, was about to create a great free-Negro dependency at their doors.

Then the simmering Cuban pot came suddenly to a boil when on February 28, 1854, the American steamer *Black Warrior*, stopping at Havana on her regular New York-Mobile run, was seized by the Spanish authorities. The ground assigned for this drastic action was the ship's failure to report to the custom-house that it had cargo in transit; a technicality the more unreasonable because the vessel had entered Havana thirty-odd times in the same way. The real reason for the seizure lay elsewhere. The filibustering ventures of Quitman and Lopez, the constant American talk of annexation, and the machinations of a busy Cuban Junta in New York, had deeply irritated the Havana authorities. Suspicious lest contraband arms be smuggled in, they were now showing they could give blow for blow. American revenue laws were also full of technicalities, and in recent years two Cunard steamers had been seized at Boston for irregularities of which owners and officers were quite ignorant, and not released until a heavy bond had been posted. But while American authorities could be trusted to deal justly with shipowners, Spanish officials and courts were capriciously unfair. The order for confiscating the vessel, issued in haste and in defiance of the long-established usage of the port officials, was an outrage.[1]

Within fifteen days President Pierce sent Congress a special message of minatory tone. Recent years, he wrote, had furnished many other instances of Spanish aggression, violations of American rights, and insults to the flag; this "wanton injury" was simply the climax; the offending party "is at our doors, with large powers for aggression," while "the source of redress is in another hemisphere," and if his demand for immediate indemnity failed, he would not hesitate to use any authority and means which Congress might grant in order to obtain satisfaction and vindicate the national honor. The Washington *Union* broke into a rash of epithets. Stock of the Cuban Junta in New York shot upward. Never before, gleefully announced the New York *Courier and Enquirer*, had the plans of that body been so well advanced. Enough ammunition was stored in New York "to supply an invading force which could sweep the island of Cuba from east to west in thirty days," while officers and men were eager and well drilled. "Now," ejaculated the New York *Herald*, "is the time to get Cuba." Washington rumor had it that the Administration meant to pick a quarrel with Spain, and to recommend either reprisals or the repeal of the neutrality laws as regarded Cuban insurgents. There is no question that Attorney-General Caleb Cushing, upon whom Pierce leaned heavily for counsel, was ready to seize any pretext for a rupture with Spain.[2]

Happily, moderate sentiment everywhere, and especially freesoil sentiment throughout the North, was in no mood to permit an artificial and needless conflict with the proud Spaniards. The Washington *National Intelligencer*, New York *Evening Post*, and other powerful journals scoffed at the belligerent frothings of the Washington *Union* and New York *Herald*. If we have any just complaint against Spain, wrote Bryant, our government will know how to deal with that nation in a manner worthy of its dignity and of modern civilization. When Representative Gilbert Dean proposed repealing the neutrality law of 1818, Joshua Giddings asked just why Administration politicians supported non-intervention in Kansas and intervention in Cuba. Men pointed out that war might be hazardous with only one first-class steam frigate in the navy, and that in Japanese waters.

In his cool way, Marcy took charge of the situation. While determined to

1 "Justice" in *National Intelligencer*, March 18, 1854; Bemis, *American Secretaries of State*, VI, 188.

2 Pierce's Message, March 15, 1854; Washington *Union*, quoted in *National Intelligencer*, March 23, 1854; N. Y. *Courier and Enquirer*, quoted in *National Intelligencer*, March 16, 1854; N. Y. *Herald*, March 9, 1854; Everett, MS Diary, March 13, 1854.

have justice, he was no war-hawk. On March 17th he sent a special messenger to Madrid with moderate instructions for Soulé, who was authorized to demand satisfaction for an act that had interfered with American rights, menaced national security, and involved the possible loss of $300,000 worth of property. Warning Soulé of the inevitable Spanish procrastination, he bade him obtain as prompt an answer as possible. Meanwhile, Marcy wrote Buchanan in London that it was desirable to let the Foreign Office know that, in his opinion, Spanish insolence was encouraged by a belief that Britain and France would furnish Madrid support in any difficulty.[3]

The episode was meat and drink to the explosive, intriguing Soulé. Though still under explicit instructions that the time was not ripe to ask Spain to sell Cuba, he had been eager to move for its acquisition, and convinced that if he had a large fund of secret service money to use in the Cortes, he could effect a purchase. Moreover, a crisis had just occurred in Spanish home affairs, for a military revolt at Zaragoza, though quickly crushed, resulted in the proclamation of martial law throughout the country. Describing this crisis in a letter written just before the *Black Warrior* seizure, he suggested that it offered a significant opportunity, and asked for new instructions and larger powers. At this moment, in March, 1854, the outbreak of the Crimean War gave Britain and France enough worries without any thought of backing Spain in Cuba. Altogether, the theatrical envoy must have rubbed his hands when he heard of the seizure. He could now attempt to obtain the island under threat of war, presenting Madrid with a choice of surrender or a breach of relations.[4]

Studying the *Black Warrior* documents sent him by Marcy, Soulé requested an interview with the Spanish foreign minister, the dull, honest, cool-headed Calderon de la Barca, long envoy in Washington. The two met on Saturday, April 8. Presenting Marcy's demands in writing, Soulé asked an early reply. Holy Week began next day. Time was needed to translate the American papers. Yet Tuesday found the impatient minister despatching Calderon a second note which laid down new and peremptory conditions. An indemnity of $300,000 must be paid; all persons responsibly concerned in the wrong, even to the Captain-General, must be dismissed; and unless the demands of the American government were met within forty-eight hours, he would regard

3 *National Intelligencer*, N. Y. *Evening Post, passim;* Joshua Giddings in *Cong. Globe,* 33d Cong., 1st sess., 647; Marcy to Soulé, March 17, 1854; State Department Instructions, Spain, Vol. 15, No. 10; Marcy to Buchanan, March 12, 1854, in Buchanan Papers. The Washington *Sentinel,* March 29, 1854, quoted an article of the London *Times,* dated January 23, on the sad condition of the American fleet. "It seems to have been recently discovered, or 'realized,' that the navy of this great naval power has no substantial existence. . . . Our correspondent remarks in plain language, that the whole United States navy, if it could even be got to sea at all, could be demolished in twenty minutes by a French or English squadron. . . ."
4 M. B. Fields, *Memories of Many Men,* 82; Bemis, *op. cit.,* VI, 192.

them as rejected. Secretary Horatio J. Perry, who bore the note to Calderon, is reported to have drawn out his watch, remarking: "It is now twelve o'clock. At this hour two days hence, I am instructed to say, I shall call again. If the reply is not ready—." [5]

This second note went far beyond Soulé's instructions, for Marcy had said nothing about a fixed time-limit or about the dismissal of Cuban officials. It was outrageously discourteous, was quite unjustified by the slight Spanish delay, and plainly looked toward provoking a rupture. But Calderon had taken Soulé's measure, and knew Washington well enough to guess what the attitude of the State Department and American people might be. First he consulted the Spanish Cabinet, and those oldtime associates of the Tripartite pact proposals, Britain and France. Then, shrewdly surmising that Soulé had acted without authority, he sent a calm reply. Since time was needed to learn the Cuban version of the episode, he wrote, he could not yet act on the American demands. Frankly and caustically, he expressed a suspicion that Soulé's precipitancy sprang not from any wish to redress pretended injuries, but from a desire to seize a "pretext for exciting estrangement, if not a quarrel, between two friendly powers." It is evident, Calderon remarked to the sympathetic British minister, "that Soulé has but one object, and that is a quarrel." The French envoy urged Spain to reinforce Cuba at once.

In a series of exchanges, Calderon made the most of delay; and finally, on May 7, the Spanish government announced its final decision on the *Black Warrior* affair. By this time the vessel had been restored to its owners, and a mere fine of $6,000 (not excessive when compared with the American penalties twice imposed on the Cunard company for technical infractions) exacted. Calderon pointed this out, announced a royal remission of the fine, denied that the American flag had been insulted, and refused to pay any indemnity. His argument had its weak passages, but the fuming Soulé could only forward it to Marcy, who received it on June 2.[6]

Even before that time the State Department had begun to take certain larger considerations into view. Marcy was discouraged from pursuing a stringent policy by the unfortunate results of Soulé's rashness in overplaying his hand, and by pressure from the British government for an arbitration of differences. At the same time, he was deeply impressed by the possibility that the Crimean War, and above all the mounting internal crisis in Spain, offered a real opportunity for acquiring Cuba by purchase. Reliable reports arrived of intense distress among the Spanish masses, republican manifestations against the un-

5 State Department Dispatches, Spanish, Vol. 39; Bailey, *Dip. Hist. Amer. People*, 319; *Harper's Magazine*, XL, 900, May, 1870; Vilá, *Historia*, II, 75ff.

6 Bemis, *op. cit.*, VI, 196, 197; *Harper's Magazine, ut supra;* Amos A. Ettinger, *Mission to Spain of Pierre Soulé*, 260ff.

popular Queen Isabella, communist outbursts in Catalonia and other provinces, and in short a general ferment. "Spain," one revolutionary orator had declared, "means to teach Europe how to be free!" Penury, misery, and discontent reigned throughout the peninsula. The treasury was on the verge of bankruptcy, and indeed kept itself solvent this spring only by borrowing at the atrocious rate of twelve per cent; the army, maintained at an annual cost of about fifteen million dollars, could not be reduced without courting general rebellion; internal improvements had long been grossly neglected for want of funds. If the Spanish government sold Cuba it could restore its credit, cut down its military expenses, and invest money in much-needed highway and railroad construction.[7]

At the same time pressure in the Deep South for drastic action against Spain increased. The now-familiar clatter of accusations against the British and Spanish governments for their supposed plot to introduce a flood of Negro "apprentices" into Cuba, extinguish slavery there, and "Africanize" the island by making it another Haiti, an uproar that was largely part of the filibustering system and a studied effort to provide excuses for new buccaneering enterprises, was being renewed. The Cuban Junta in New York, planning a fresh invasion with Quitman and others, had whipped up a feverish excitement in certain Southern circles. Many slaveholders believed that the best way to acquire Cuba would be to bring about a successful revolution there, the sooner the better; and Mississippi and Louisiana had bold groups of filibusters straining at the leash.

The *Black Warrior* affair had no sooner broken than adroit leaders persuaded the Louisiana legislature to pass resolves urging the national government to take vigorous measures to prevent the establishment of prejudicial influences near the South and to extend the limits of American sovereignty. Slidell responded by the delivery of a ringing speech in the Senate on May 1. He and his colleague Judah P. Benjamin warned the country that this greater, nearer Haiti would be a deadly peril to Southern white supremacy. Should America remain a passive spectator until the fatal blow had been struck? Never, declaimed Slidell; authorize the President to suspend the neutrality legislation of 1818 and 1838; allow patriots like Quitman free scope; and individual enterprise would quickly furnish men and materials to help the native population of Cuba to overthrow their transatlantic tyrants. In less than six months, he predicted, the flag of freedom, the lone star, would wave over the entire island.[8]

Numerous Southern leaders and journals took up the cry, for the belief

7 See Paris correspondence, dated September 26, in *National Intelligencer*, October 14, 1854; *Blackwood's Magazine*, "Spanish Politics and Cuban Perils," vol. 76, 477ff, October, 1854.

8 *Cong. Globe*, 33d Cong., 1st sess., 1021ff, 1298ff.

that Britain and France would do anything to prevent Cuba from falling into American hands had been widely inculcated. But Senator Clayton, who as former Secretary of State had familiarized himself with the subject, declared the charge of projected "Africanization" totally empty. While it was true, he said, that if an insurrection in the island, aided by American invasion, should threaten its loss, the Spanish authorities might proceed to the extremity of freeing and arming the slaves, he was certain that at the moment they contemplated no emancipatory step whatever. Not merely a large number of Northern newspapers, but such self-respecting Southern journals as the New Orleans *Bee* and *Bulletin*, Mobile *Tribune*, and the Charleston *Mercury*, derided or assailed Slidell's proposal. To fight a manly war for due cause was one thing; to encourage filibusters in greedy marauding and plundering adventures was quite another.

It was of course true that Lord Palmerson and other British statesmen had urged upon Spain, among other measures for securing the good-will of the Cuban population, the emancipation of the slaves. It was true that British and French liberals supported emancipation everywhere; true that the London *Times* and *Journal des Débats* of Paris pointed out that since Southerners coveted Cuba for new slave States, emancipation would instantly deprive the island of its attractions. But this was very different from proposing the "Africanization" of Cuba. Moreover, both the Spaniards in Cuba and the governing groups in Spain had recoiled in horror from the idea of emancipation. The Madrid Cabinet this very spring asserted the maintenance of slavery to be indispensable to Cuban prosperity. Pierce's consul in Havana has left a long memorandum relating how during 1853–54 he was constantly urged by Southern expansionists and their Cuban allies to make trouble; how they implored him to discover a secret treaty proving that Britain and France had guaranteed the island on condition that the slaves should be liberated; and how they assured him that if he found such a treaty, they could use it in Washington to produce immediate war. He confidentially offered $100,000 for an authentic copy of such a compact—in vain, for it did not exist.[9] The Spanish officials in Havana were up to some queer tricks, and the new Captain-General seemed bent for a time on measures that would have freed many veteran slaves; but Pezuela was soon recalled to Spain. No marked change of policy actually took place.

Nevertheless, Slidell, with his tall figure and rather impressive head—dome-like brow, whitening hair, square chin, and crafty eyes—was much in evidence at the doors of the White House and State Department, for he never rested in

9 *Idem*, 1299, for Clayton's speech; cf. *National Intelligencer*, May 20 quoting Southern newspapers, May 16 quoting Madrid *Gazette* dated April 13 and Paris correspondence dated April 27, 1854; Consul A. M. Clayton, undated MS, Claiborne Papers, U. of N. C.

his quest of Cuban annexation. He urged Secretary Marcy to obtain frequent and expert reports from the London and Paris legations. He suggested that more use be made of Belmont at the Hague for ascertaining the Franco-British plans. Attending a White House conference early in June, with Mason, Douglas, Jefferson Davis, and two others present, he besought the President to reassure the South, by a special message to Congress, that he meant to pursue an energetic policy. Pierce suggested that Slidell himself might telegraph the district attorney in New Orleans that immediate and decisive measures would be taken respecting Cuba, but the senator rejected so futile a step. At the very least, he declared, Marcy ought to make a public statement. Instructions to this effect were given the Secretary, but delays ensued. Before long Slidell became convinced that the President, weakly good-natured in making promises but quite undependable in executing them, would never act with energy. While the Senator continued to bring pressure upon both President and State Department, and to bombard Buchanan in London with letters, it was with declining hopes.[10]

[ II ]

Yet already, at the beginning of April, Marcy had taken a moderate forward step. Until this time he had clung to the view that Soulé must await a favorable moment to press Spain for a cession; but now in response to the minister's request for fresh instructions, he wrote that the hour might be ripe, that a large cash offer should be made, and that if it failed, the minister should move to bring about Cuban *independence*.

The date of this definition of a new policy, April 3, goes far toward explaining its curious terms. Written just after Marcy had received Soulé's report on the boiling internal situation in Spain, and just as he knew that the Crimean War was beginning, it naturally showed a desire to exploit these favorable factors. But having just received word that the Cuban authorities had restored the *Black Warrior* and its cargo, Marcy also knew that threats could obtain nothing. Slidell, as his reference to the lone star flag showed, was talking in terms of at least temporary Cuban independence. Marcy therefore instructed Soulé, whenever he thought circumstances favorable, to propose a treaty for the purchase of Cuba. If, however, he failed to buy the island for a reasonable sum, offering not more than $130,000,000, he should not drop the matter. "You will then direct your efforts to the next most desirable object which is to detach that island from the Spanish dominion and from all dependence on any European power." He added that "if Cuba were relieved from all transatlantic connection and at liberty to dispose of herself as her present interest and

10  L. M. Sears, *John Slidell*, 107ff.

prospective welfare would dictate, she would undoubtedly relieve this government from all anxiety in regard to her future condition."

While some writers have construed the word "detach" as suggesting the use of force, surely Marcy's meaning was pacific enough. If Spanish pride recoiled from the idea of selling the island jewel to the United States, the government might by some means (whether by Soulé's intrigues with various factions, by Daniel Sickles' suggestion of a five million dollar grant to the avaricious and powerful Queen Mother, Maria Cristina, or by a large American payment to the Spanish treasury), be induced to declare Cuba free and independent.[11]

Unhappily for Marcy, he had in Soulé an agent who was certain to behave with reckless irrationality. The Secretary also had behind him a pliable President, constantly influenced by the Cabinet expansionists Davis, Dobbin, and Cushing, and by Postmaster-General Campbell, who hated England and believed that Spain was under her thumb. At the other end of Pennsylvania Avenue, Marcy had to confront Slidell, Benjamin, A. G. Brown, and others panting for war. It is not strange that the nation's foreign policy was fluctuating and impulsive, finally reaching by a tortuous path that disreputable climax still famous as the Ostend Manifesto.[12]

In this policy of pure opportunism, what could be done to encourage Spain to sell or "detach" Cuba? The June conference of Davis, Slidell, Douglas and others at the White House apparently helped Pierce to decide on a dramatic step: he would send an extraordinary commission to Madrid to make a solemn and impressive appeal to the Ministry. Gossip reported that the commissioners would be Howell Cobb and George Mifflin Dallas, men of strong personality, political experience, and acquisitive ideas. Their task would be to join Soulé in telling the Spanish leaders that American acquisition of Cuba, or at least its liberation, had become a commercial and political necessity; that this alone could put an end to filibustering and other irritations; and that America would pay a handsome compensation. The special mission would prove that Washington was ready to exhaust all peaceable modes of action before resorting to the "extreme measures" which Marcy mentioned to Soulé as possible.

From one standpoint something could be said for such a mission. Soulé's duel, backstairs intrigues, and theatrical posturings, capped by his popgun

11  Bemis, *op. cit.*, VI, 193; Marcy to Soulé, State Department Instructions, Spain, Vol. 15.
12  State Department Secret Book No. 2; Special Missions Book Vol. 3; Dispatches, Spain, Vol. 39; Washington corr. N. Y. *Herald, Journal of Commerce, Express*, June, July, 1854. Senator A. G. Brown wrote a friend on June 29 that now was the time for a bold stroke; that Secretary Dobbin predicted annexation within a year; and that he would be sure of it if only Pierce had a backbone. Claiborne Papers, Miss. State Archives. Postmaster-General Campbell was thoroughly jingoist. Earlier (March 14) he had written that if Britain did not cease her meddling in Cuba, "our people will be in arms from Maine to Texas." Buchanan Papers.

ultimatum, had ruined his usefulness for any tactful negotiation. While Madrid would no longer listen to him, it might turn an attentive ear to Cobb and Dallas. On the other hand, a special mission would be worse than useless unless preliminary work gave it some probability of success, for it would simply subject our diplomacy to humiliation. Moreover, could even the genial Cobb and urbane Dallas get along with touchy Soulé, who prepared to resign as soon as he heard of their errand?

For a variety of reasons the extraordinary commission soon had to be given up. Everything went wrong for the expansionists. Slidell's attempt to suspend the neutrality laws failed; when Pierce asked Congress on August 1 for additional powers in reference to Spain, he was rebuffed; Mason wrote home that Madrid would regard the commission as a public repudiation of Soulé; and the Nebraska storm was becoming a cyclone which made it impossible to trifle with Northern opinion. By mid-August the harassed Pierce dropped the scheme. What new step could then be taken? The *Black Warrior* affair was becoming such ancient history that Marcy, while replying to Calderon in a long and extremely able summation of the American case, had found it expedient to instruct Soulé to do nothing more in the matter. The proper course, obviously, was to recall the sputtering Minister, send over some such strong and tactful a diplomat as William C. Rives, and entrust him with a free hand. August Belmont kept insisting that active, prompt, and courteous steps might still prove effective. As the secretary of legation, Horatio J. Perry, was soon confidentially writing Marcy, Soulé's policy had been an abysmal failure. Not one individual of influence in any party would accept a proposition from him; he stood utterly isolated. "He is in many respects a superior man," reported Perry, "but as a diplomatist he has missed his career." [13]

As July closed the time would have been auspicious for dispatching a new Minister, for that month the Spanish Cabinet fell, and a strong progressive government under one of Spain's few genuine statesmen, Baldomero Espartero, took power; Calderon shortly giving way to a new Foreign Minister named Francisco Pancheco. A new Spanish representative arrived in Washington. Unfortunately, political reasons made the recall of Soulé difficult; it would look weak to the Southern expansionists—and he was not wanted at home!

In sheer desperation, Pierce and his advisers, while keeping Soulé in office, determined on another dramatic step: a conference of the Ministers to London, Paris, and Madrid. They had failed with bluster over the *Black Warrior;* they had found a high commission impracticable; and now they fell back on this hasty confab. What did they think it could accomplish? Since Anglo-French

13  Ettinger, *op. cit.,* 277ff.; Belmont, April–August, 1854, Buchanan Papers; Mason, July 23, 1854, Marcy Papers.

authority in Madrid seemed to be tremendous, perhaps the three could devise ways of moulding French and British opinion (particularly the latter) to bring pressure on Spain. Perhaps three second-rate brains could strike out one first-rate idea! At any rate, Marcy in two notes dated August 16 gave Soulé fresh instructions. In Spain, he was to watch the party shifts intently for any opportunity to propose radical changes in the political situation of Cuba. In his forthcoming conference with Buchanan and Mason, he was to exchange counsel, and to "secure a concurrence with reference to the general object." That same day Slidell wrote Buchanan that the three Ministers were to meet for consultation, and that in view of the Rothschild influence in Paris and Madrid, he had suggested to Pierce that Belmont be brought into their counsels either personally or by correspondence. Presumably, these men could exchange ideas on the attitudes of Britain, France, and the international financiers. They could canvass the various chances of a lucky grab at Cuba, as by revolution in Spain, revolution in Havana, bribery of the Queen Mother, use of money in the Cortes, pressure from Spain's numerous creditors, and what not; chiefly what not.[14]

## [ III ]

The prime responsibility for this ill-advised arrangement, which had hardly one chance in ten of achieving any useful result and fully nine chances of doing great harm, falls upon Pierce. Caleb Cushing may have advised him, but all the official and unofficial correspondence speaks of the plan as the President's. Marcy tells us that a combination of factors, including Buchanan's reiteration of his old views regarding the probable success of measures of economic pressure upon Spain, and Daniel Sickles' arrival from Europe in mid-August with news of a Spanish revolt, the authors of which might accept American gold, led the President to believe that the conference "might possibly result in something favorable." Inasmuch as Marcy disliked Soulé and his ways, thought Mason a pompous windbag, and regarded Buchanan rather contemptuously, it is very unlikely that he expected anything from the meeting. He had taken so little pains to keep Buchanan and Mason posted on Spanish affairs that the latter had protested, and he had half apologized to them. Slidell was unquestionably prompting the Administration to general action. Still cherishing his original plan of enlisting European financiers to exert pressure upon Madrid, and fired with the fears of the Lower South regarding the

14 State Department Instructions, Spain, Vol. 15, Marcy, August 16 (Nos. 18, 19) to Soulé; Perry to Marcy, September 6, 26, 1854, Marcy Papers; Bemis, *op. cit.*, VI, 200.

"Africanization" of Cuba, he was steadily urging some forward step. But he shared Buchanan's views regarding the impolicy of the conference.[15]

For on this point Buchanan was unwontedly emphatic, making repeated protests. Only financial pressure could succeed, he wrote Pierce on September 1st. "Our great means of accomplishing this object is to bring the creditors of Spain into our views by an appeal to their self-interest." He held that Belmont would be the best agent in the movement, that other diplomats could contribute little if anything, and that it would be particularly unfortunate for Soulé to absent himself from Madrid at a time of continuing crisis.[16]

The chief objection to the conference was that such a meeting of the nation's chief European envoys, held when Washington had just been openly bullying Spain, and when the South notoriously had its eyes fixed on the Cuban quarry, would excite general suspicion and apprehension. Europeans did not trust our rough-and-ready diplomacy. They believed that Brother Jonathan was growing altogether too aggressive. Buchanan, realizing this, was horrified at the original plan for meeting in Paris. This city was the whispering gallery of Europe; French espionage was perfect; and the envoys' discussions would become nearly as much public knowledge as if they conferred in the Champs-Elysées. Do leave the matter to quiet correspondence, he urged Pierce. With adroit help from Belmont and a little Treasury money, he could obtain the names of the principal holders of Spanish bonds, and probably induce them to unite in an effort to prevail on the Spanish Government to sell Cuba to the United States. But they should move softly, for capital was timid, American intentions had aroused much question, and even the exploratory journeys of Dan Sickles of the London legation, who had gone first to Washington and then to Paris and Madrid, had excited unpleasant comment. As the President persisted in his plan, however, Buchanan reluctantly assented; and arrangements were made by Soulé for a meeting to take place at Ostend on October 9.[17]

Though it was important that the meeting be kept as quiet as possible, circumstances threw a perfect blaze of publicity upon it. The fiery-tempered Soulé during August involved himself in fresh quarrels and scandals, more spectacular than ever. The new and more democratic government under Espartero was presumably much to his taste, and was even said to have promised him a favorable ear. When the press gave Espartero a banquet on August 13, Soulé sent a letter in which he insolently took sides in Spanish political affairs. He referred to the former government as a "shameless despotism" which had

---

15 See particularly Marcy's letter to Soulé, August 16, 1854, on Pierce's responsibility, State Department Instructions, Spain, Vol. 15; House Exec. Docs., 33d Cong., 2d sess., No. 93; Nichols, *Franklin Pierce*, 366–371.
16 Buchanan to Pierce, September 1, 1854; draft in Buchanan Papers.
17 *Idem*; Ettinger, *op. cit.*, 355, 356.

"crushed the freedom of thought"; hailed the recent overturn with "holy enthusiasm"; assailed "the perfidies and the treasons" of Espartero's enemies; and gave Spanish liberals the felicitations of "Young America." The bad taste of this performance was duly noted by European leaders, and elicited anguished groans from various American papers. But already Soulé was intriguing against the very government which he was heaping with panegyrics! The last days of August brought a brief, abortive republican insurrection in Madrid, in which the American minister had a hand. Though he wildly denied any participation, there is evidence that he had helped plan the uprising, in the hope of getting a due reward for his aid; that he had spent large sums of money, which the British minister reported came not from the American government, but from private associations and individuals; and that one of his closest freinds, his second in the famous duel, had been active on the barricades. All Madrid believed that, using money from European liberals and American filibusters, Soulé had been a ringleader in the revolt; and a graphic essay in *Blackwood's Magazine* shortly pictured him as the semi-piratical accomplice of the rebels.[18]

The result was that Soulé hastily departed from Madrid amid a violent press controversy which attracted international attention. The *Diario Espanol* on August 30 carried an article accusing him of having fomented and aided the recent disturbances in Madrid not merely with advice, but with material support; he retorted with a letter stuffed with epithets—"perfidious insinuations," "tools of tyrants," "infamy"; the *Diario* replied in kind; and a general shindy ensued. Other journals flew to arms, so that the *Diario* was able to boast of the "unanimous manifestations" of the Madrid press against the sinister influence universally attributed to Soulé in the late disturbances. It correctly blamed him for a situation which might delay indefinitely the settlement of outstanding Spanish-American difficulties.

Arriving in France, Soulé, as a Frenchman by birth, a violent republican, and a hater of Louis Napoleon, was closely shadowed by the secret police. The foreign office had daily reports on his visitors. By a perverse fate, the irrepressible George Sanders, apostle of Young America, who had been touring Europe, chose this moment to deliver from London a long and withering "Address to the People of France" against Napoleon III, urging all Gallic

18 *La Presse*, September 3, 1854; London *Times*, September 6, 1854; *Blackwood's Magazine*, Vol. 76, 477ff, October, 1854. But many observers thought that the *Black Warrior* affair was practically settled. The new Espartero-O'Donnell government considered Cuba in a perfect state of defense, and O'Donnell had commanded there long enough to know. "The troops at present there are upwards of 20,000 infantry, 1,000 cavalry, and five or six batteries of artillery. The infantry are among the best in the Spanish army, and the whole force are inured to the climate." So the N. Y. *Citizen*, October 7, 1854.

patriots to rise against the despot. You have now tasted tyranny to the lowest dregs, he wrote. "Strike!" The month of September found a whole group of American diplomats in Paris. A. Dudley Mann, Assistant Secretary of State, was there; Soulé; Sickles; Lewis Cass, Jr., from Rome; Daniel from Turin; O'Sullivan from Lisbon; and Belmont from the Hague—with Buchanan expected soon to arrive. Of these men, Assistant Secretary Mann was remembered as a secret agent to Hungary during its recent revolt, and a confirmed agitator for European republicanism, while O'Sullivan was a notorious intriguer. No wonder European governments were anxious and disturbed! In sober fact, most of the men had come without prearrangement, young Cass being in town on private business, and Daniel to escape cholera. But Mann inspired gossip by a silly trip to Bayonne to talk of Cuban affairs with Soulé; O'Sullivan made foolish statements; while many people recalled that Sanders was an intimate friend of Kossuth and Garibaldi (who had first met at his house in London), of Mazzini, Saffi, Louis Blanc, and other radical leaders. He was an active participant in all kinds of revolutionary intrigues. The British press of course gibed at this "conclave of cuteness." Were the Yankees about to annex Monaco? [19]

Naturally, as the diplomatic trio gathered in Ostend, the Brussels *Echo* and other Belgian journals blazoned their arrival to the world, while the French and British press began printing rumors of plots and strokes. Buchanan, Soulé, and Mason, evidently annoyed by the publicity, left after three days for Aix-la-Chapelle, where they continued their conversations until ·October 18. D. K. McRea, American consul in Paris, acted as secretary.

As a result of the conference, Soulé, Buchanan, and Mason (who hardly counted) agreed upon a semi-secret letter or memorandum which McRae as special messenger promptly bore to Washington. This was the famous Ostend Manifesto, which ought to be called simply the Aix-la-Chapelle dispatch. Soulé had arrived equipped with an elaborate document, which he astutely handed to Buchanan with a request that the latter revise and perfect it. Persuaded by Soulé's arguments, beguiled by the Louisianian's personal charm, and influenced by his own political ambitions, Buchanan copied it with various changes and additions. It was then recorrected by Soulé, while Mason made a few verbal alterations. "Judge Mason," later wrote an officer of the Paris legation, "can scarcely be held accountable. It depended very much whether it was before or after dinner that he signed the paper." Apparently Buchanan contributed

19 See the review of the entire controversy in *Diario Español*, September 19, 1854; *National Intelligencer*, October 31, 1854; for Soulé in France, Paris correspondence dated October 6 in N. Y. *Times*, October 24, 1854; Sanders' letter dated October 4 published in full in N. Y. *Times*, October 27, 1854. On the meeting in Paris, see Paris correspondence dated October 2, in *National Intelligencer*, October 19, 1854; Sickles, Paris, September 23, 1854, to Buchanan; Buchanan Papers.

to the final draft most of the economic passages, while Soulé was the author of the sections which called for the spoliation of the Spanish nation.[20]

It would have been well had this famous dispatch never been written. Marcy had wished the Ministers to confer upon the best means of acquiring Cuba by purchase, or of procuring its independence; instead, they dealt with the whole question of Cuban policy, and proposed, in the most reprehensible manner, the possible use of force to seize possession of the island. Two distinct recommendations contained the gist of the so-called manifesto. One was a declaration that the government should make an earnest and immediate effort to buy Cuba at a large but unnamed price. The second was a statement that if the offer was rejected, the United States must consider the question whether continued Spanish possession of Cuba would endanger American peace and security. "Should this question be answered in the affirmative, then by every law human and divine, we shall be justified in wresting it from Spain, if we possess the power. . . . Under such circumstances, we ought neither to count the cost, nor regard the odds which Spain might enlist against us. . . ." This went far beyond Marcy's recent suggestions. Whereas he had intimated that Cuba might be detached and made independent, the trio proposed that under certain circumstances it should be wrested from Spain to *keep*.[21]

To speak of well-considered reasons in connection with Soulé would be absurd, but the impulses which moved him are easily defined. He had long enunciated the economic arguments which, as now rephrased by Buchanan, constituted the first half of the dispatch; the arguments that Spain should sell Cuba, with its chronic recent deficits, for a good price, should use most of the money to build a modern railroad system connecting her with the rest of Europe, and should employ the residue to pay her debts. Repeatedly, as his friend M. B. Field tells us, he had used these arguments with Maria Cristina. His addition of a threat of naked force sprang from his defeats and chagrins of the past six months. He had tried to use the *Black Warrior* affairs to provoke a conflict, and had been deeply humiliated when his little private ultimatum was rejected and the American demands were rebuffed. He had plotted with the republican leaders in the August revolt on their pledge that, if they came into power, they would sell Cuba; they had been defeated, and his plots and duplicities had been exposed. He knew that his diplomatic career was ended. In his mortification and anger, he wanted Spain consigned to perdition. Violence was second nature to him. Violence would be sweet revenge. All else having failed, violence might succeed. If our demands mean war, he wrote Marcy, let it be war while the powers of Europe are engaged in their stupendous struggle.

20 Bailey, *op. cit.*, 316; *Harper's Magazine*, XL, 901, May, 1870; draft, Buchanan Papers.
21 House Exec. Docs., 33d Cong., 2d sess., 93.

As for Buchanan, his motives were more complex. Essentially a weak, timid man, he found Soulé's personal force, and his ability to combine intense vehemence with honeyed words, overwhelming; while always there gleamed before his eyes the portals of the White House. He knew that a spirited attitude with respect to Cuba would gain him Southern support—as it did. Time proved that both Young America and the Cotton States credited him with the main authorship of the manifesto, and were proportionately grateful. His own interpretation of the document was less aggressive than Soulé's.[22]

European contempt and irritation, as the three ministers returned home from Aix, were candidly expressed. "The diplomacy of the United States," observed the London Times, thinking of Soulé's antics, George Sanders's pronunciamento, and a recent attempt by Dan Sickles to draw the banker-philanthropist George Peabody into a duel because he had given a Fourth of July dinner where the Queen's portrait was displayed and Washington's was not, "is certainly a very singular profession." By mid-November the American press was full of conjectures as to the contents of the manifesto. The New York Herald had one version, the Times another; while various other garbled summaries found their way into print. Finally, on March 3, 1854, Marcy found it necessary to send the full document to Congress, arousing a perfect furor.

Spanish indignation was naturally intense; British and French scorn was expressed in no uncertain terms; but the hottest attacks came from American pens. "Manifesto of the Brigands" was the New York Tribune's title for an article boiling with anger over this "buccaneering document," with its proposals "to grasp, to rob, to murder, to grow rich on the spoils of provinces and toils of slaves." Here once more, exclaimed the freesoil press, we see the brutalizing march of slavery. Spain will not be bullied into parting with her property, and so it must be stolen from her! Most men agreed that Soulé was never quite sane when his vanity was pricked, and that Buchanan was stalking the presidency. "Atrocious" was the adjective used by Bryant's Post. Nor were highminded Democrats silent. Senator Cass among others voiced a fervent hope that such an act of rapacity as the seizure of Cuba would never stain our annals.[23]

There is no reason to doubt the sincerity of the sense of shock which Secretary Marcy himself expressed. Little over a year earlier, in his instructions to Buchanan with regard to the intervention of Britain and France in Cuban affairs, he had spiritedly denounced the suspicious attitude of these countries. "In our territorial expansion," he wrote, "international law has been observed,

22  M. B. Fields, Memories, 83; cf. Ettinger, op. cit.; Nichols, Franklin Pierce, 585ff.
23  London Times, December 6, 1854; N. Y. Times, November 13, 1854; "Manifesto of the Brigands," in N. Y. Weekly Tribune, March 8, 1855; N. Y. Evening Post, March 6, 1855; McLaughlin, Lewis Cass, 315.

the rights of others rigorously respected; nothing, in short, has been done to justify the slightest suspicion of rapacity." He had spoken of honor, of honest intention, and of readiness to submit national policy to the most scrupulous examination. Now, in a long letter of rebuke to Soulé, dated November 13, 1854, he repelled the suggestion that Spain be offered a choice of cession or seizure. Mere failure to obtain a cession, he declared, would "not involve imminent peril to the existence of our government" and would hence demand no action. At the time he wrote this, the Administration had just received a staggering blow in the fall elections, while the sudden sweeping rise of the Know-Nothing Party made the acquisition of a Spanish-speaking and Catholic island more unpopular politically in large areas than ever. Moreover, Marcy, with fixed presidential ambitions of his own, had no reluctance to overturn the Cuban *carreta* in which Buchanan was gliding toward the White House. But the Secretary was really a man of character, who expressed privately as well as publicly the reprobation which he unquestionably felt.

Such a robbery, he wrote a friend, "would degrade us in our own estimation and disgrace us in the eyes of the world." [24]

The tempestuous diplomatic career of Soulé was now approaching its squalid end. For a time Napoleon III refused to let the intriguing diplomat traverse France to return to Spain, but finally relented. The European press had published in full the *Diario* charges upon his connection with the republican revolt, and press correspondents, the diplomatic corps, and the Ministry had all been investigating them. The Cortes debated the subject, and one pamphleteer promised explicit facts, dates, and names. The Madrid correspondent of the London *Times* declared that full evidence was available of the truth of the charges. When Soulé reached Madrid, he naturally found the atmosphere glacial. His secretary, Horatio Perry, had quarreled with him, and a new controversy was about to break; a controversy in which Perry would spread before the American public full data upon the minister's unfitness for diplomatic life. Soulé must have found the rebuke contained in Marcy's letter of November 13 devastating, for in addition to its rejection of the manifesto's proposals, it declared that in his *Black Warrior* demands he had gone altogether too far when he called for the dismissal of Cuban officials. His disobedience of certain instructions from Washington was about to be revealed. In resentful frustration, the peppery Minister resigned just before Christmas in 1854. He had furnished a memorable illustration of the folly of hasty political appointments.[25]

24 Marcy to Buchanan, July 2, 1853, Washington *Union*, March 8, 1855; Marcy to Soulé in N. Y. *Weekly Tribune*, March 8, 1855; Bemis, *op. cit.*, VI, 215.
25 *L'Independence Belge*, quoted in *National Intelligencer*, January 24, 1856; London *Times* quoted in N. Y. *Tribune*, September 22, 1854; Ettinger, *op. cit.*, 458ff.

## [ IV ]

If London kept a watchful eye upon American movements in Cuba, Washington was similarly vigilant with respect to British movements in Central America. The two greatest commercial nations of the globe took an equal interest in a region already important for transit and obviously destined to be the seat of a great interoceanic canal. An uneasy diplomatic area, it was the chief seat of friction between Britain and America; friction the more important because many politicians affected to see Britain (and her temporary ally France) interfering with American interests in numerous parts of the hemisphere.[26]

The Mexican War, the nation's exuberant growth, and the general prosperity stimulated a xenophobia and especially Anglophobia which now and then gave Congress a veritable field-day of ramping oratory. Early in 1855, for example, Cass, Mason, and others loosed a series of broadsides against the "interference" of European powers with the western continent. These powers, they declared, had tried to block American expansion in Texas; they were blocking it in Cuba; when the United States attempted to make a commercial convention with Ecuador, representatives of France, Britain, and Spain had protested; the French and British consuls in Santo Domingo had taken measures to end the war between that republic and Haiti with a condition that the Dominicans should promise never to lease Samana Bay; consuls of the same powers had brought pressure in Hawaii to prevent King Kamehameha from entertaining any idea of annexation to the United States; and so on. According to Mason, the British had behaved with special perfidy on the Nicaraguan coast by provoking the United States to an attack on an undefended town. They had claimed some vague protectorate over the Mosquito Indians; had rechristened the port of San Juan del Norte as Greytown; and had put its people in such an equivocal position that they did not know whether they constituted a responsible political community or not.

"In order to protect our people and the honor of our country," said Mason, "the town was battered about their ears on a very recent occasion by a gallant officer of the American navy. It was well done."[27]

While no legitimate complaint could be made against Anglo-French efforts to preserve the existing status of Cuba, Santo Domingo, and Hawaii, there was some ground for accusing Britain of Central American encroachments. We have seen that the United States, while admitting the British right to a re-

26 "I am confident that the Administration intends to insist that G. B. shall cease from all intermeddling with Central America," Secretary Marcy wrote on a slip of paper, on the afternoon of December 30, 1853; and gave it to Senator Clayton, authorizing him to use it in debate. Clayton Papers.

27 *Cong. Globe*, 33d Cong., 2d sess., 832ff.

stricted area in Belize or British Honduras, objected to any more extensive claims. By the Clayton-Bulwer Treaty both nations had agreed not to occupy, colonize, fortify, or exert dominion over Nicaragua, Costa Rica, Guatemala, or other parts of Central America, exclusive of the Belize settlement. But as Clayton himself vehemently asserted, the British nevertheless began enlarging their foothold. They expanded their protectorate over the Mosquito Indians to the eastward of Honduras and Nicaragua, and asserted title to half a dozen small islands in the Bay of Honduras, making the group in 1852 a crown colony. Marcy opposed these aggressive steps. He, like Clayton before him, insisted that Great Britain should withdraw, and desist from her meddling in the area. But all efforts under Pierce to compose the difficulties broke down. It was not until 1859–60 that the British Government finally ceded the Bay islands and Mosquito protectorate to Honduras.

Meanwhile trouble broke out at Greytown, or San Juan del Norte, the little port at the mouth of the San Juan River on the Caribbean coast of Nicaragua. It was a port with a good deal of history; ships had once sailed from Spain to it and straight up the San Juan to Granada on Lake Nicaragua—almost to the Pacific; Nelson had attacked it in the *Hinchinbrook;* it had figured in various civil conflicts. From the Atlantic its white dwellings and warehouses showed up amid ragged palm trees and deep green vegetation, while in the distance, faint against the sky, gleamed the volcanoes of the Nicaraguan uplands. As we have noted, the British had temporarily seized the place by an armed expedition from Jamaica in 1848, at the moment when it seemed possible that the United States was about to acquire most of Mexico; and they had soon relaxed their grip. Now practically self-governing, it was a town of only four or five hundred people, including a number of former Californians, traders from Britain, France, and other countries, and two or three score Jamaica Negroes. It was important, however, as commanding the Nicaraguan route across the Isthmus, which used the San Juan River, and hence the seat of a good deal of commercial activity.

When California was opened up, Cornelius Vanderbilt began promoting commerce by way of Nicaragua in opposition to George Law's line by way of the Panama route. Setting a line of fast ships in motion, he organized a Nicaraguan corporation, the Accessory Transit Company, which shortly fell into the hands of two scheming promoters, Charles Morgan and C. K. Garrison. These get-rich-quick gentlemen (a too-frank flatterer of Garrison told him that he was "so smart it took twenty men to watch him") ousted Vanderbilt during his absence in Europe. On his return, the Commodore swelled with wrath. Between volleys of profanity, he dictated an incisive letter. "Gentlemen," it read: "You have undertaken to cheat me. I won't sue you, for the law is too slow. I'll ruin you." He forthwith began to "bear" the stock, while he threw his support behind a new Panama line with fast, cheap steamers.

The Accessory Transit Company, under its two unscrupulous heads, meanwhile fell into a dispute with Greytown, which had set up as a "free city." The company appropriated some harbor land; the city demanded that it be converted into a quarantine station; the company refused; and according to some dubious accusations, a boatload of company stores was then carried off by a marauding party.[28]

At this point a petty but arrogant and scheming diplomatic officer of the United States, Joseph W. Fabens, seized the opportunity to play a directing rôle. As commercial agent at Greytown, in close touch with the Transit Company, he sent Marcy some inflammatory dispatches. A ship-captain of the Transit Company, with deliberate brutality, killed a Negro pilot; and when the Greytown authorities sent an officer to arrest the culprit, the American minister to Central America, Solon Borland, who happened to be in town, protected him. Disorders broke out (the citizens alleged that Borland had made offensive speeches), and the minister was cut by a flying bottle. Secretary Marcy at once hurried the warship *Cyane* to the port, ordering the captain to consult the fiery Fabens, and to teach the people that the United States would not tolerate such outrages. Commander George N. Hollins arrived, conferred with Fabens, and obviously acting at his instigation, demanded payment of $24,000. When it was not forthcoming, he gave notice of a bombardment.

In vain did a British naval officer there protest that the inhabitants and houses were quite defenseless, that much British and other foreign property would be destroyed, and that the act would be without civilized precedent. In vain did the inhabitants first offer entreaties and then flee. Hollins opened an intermittent two hours' bombardment of the wretched little place, and landing a party, completely destroyed it. Nobody was slain, but the property damage ran as high by some estimates as three millions.[29]

Marcy was taken aback when he learned what had occurred. He had wanted reparations and an apology, not a resort to violence. "The place merited chastisement, but the severity of the one inflicted exceeded all expectations," he wrote Buchanan. The half-hearted excuses of the Administration were not convincing. Northern feeling was deeply stirred, and countless editors, clergymen, and plain citizens expressed deep indignation. "We cannot recall any public question," snorted the New York *Tribune*, "with regard to which there has been such unity of opinion. Journals habitually opposed on every other subject, representing every shade of party feeling, every divergence of interest,

28 W. J. Lane, *Vanderbilt*, 94, 108–138.
29 The full correspondence was laid before Congress by Pierce on July 31, 1854.

and every antagonism of nationality, concur to declare the destruction of San Juan a needless, unjustifiable, inhuman exercise of warlike force. Conservative and radicals, Whigs and Democrats, Americans and foreigners, all agree on this one thing—all express the same horror and disgust." Lord Clarendon, the British Foreign Minister, a calm man of great friendliness toward America, seized Buchanan by his coat-lapels and declared the outrage one without modern parallel. The indignation over this wanton and barbarous act had something to do with the refusal of Congress to arm Pierce with extraordinary powers in dealing with Spain.[30]

Despite Senator Mason's charges of British provocation, it seems clear that the Greytown bombardment possessed no earthly connection with the dispute over Britain's Mosquito protectorate. That protectorate, being intended primarily to shield the Mosquito tribe from Nicaraguan oppression, involved no real exercise of British jurisdiction; and certainly no British authority existed in Greytown, which had its own *de facto* government. It also seems clear that the murderous American steamboat captain was a disreputable fellow; that Minister Borland was quarrelsome and overbearing; and that Fabens behaved precisely as if he had been a paid officer of the Transit Company—which he very likely was. It was shortly demonstrated that J. L. White, president of the company, had written Fabens from New York on June 16 that Hollins was about to leave for Greytown; that "you will see from his instructions that much discretion is given to you"; that "it is to be hoped that it will not be so exercised as to show any mercy to the town or people"; that "if the scoundrels are soundly punished, we can take possession, and build it up as a business place, put in our own officers, transfer the jurisdiction, and you know the rest." It seems to be true that the town had been orderly and well-governed, that it had been controlled mainly by American residents, and that the alleged theft of company goods was generally disbelieved.

The company, in short, had deliberately picked a quarrel; and Fabens had then gulled the State Department and Navy into destroying the place for the benefit of the notorious sharpers who wished to build their own well-controlled port on its ruins. A French merchant, P. A. Barriel-Beauvert, appealing to the American press for redress, listed many commercial houses—French, British, Spanish, German, Italian—which had been ruined, and described the suffering of the inoffensive inhabitants, left without food or shelter, as heartrending.[31]

In another instance, American bullying failed of its goal. Early in 1855

30 Marcy to Buchanan, August 8, August 25, 1854, Buchanan Papers; N. Y. *Tribune*, July 29, 1854.
31 *National Intelligencer*, September 2, 1854; and September 8 for E. L. White, New York and California Steamship Line, to Fabens, dated June 16, 1854; N. Y. *Tribune*, July 26, 29, August 2, 3, 1854.

reports began circulating in the press that the government had sent a special commissioner, William L. Cazneau, to Santo Domingo to negotiate for the sale or cession of part of the republic, Samana Bay being specially desired. A treaty which Cazneau induced President Santana to favor was concluded. But the National Representation rejected it, and at this Cazneau became incensed. The sloop-of-war *Falmouth* had been lying in Samana Bay; Cazneau sent the government a note declaring he would give them just twenty-four hours to reconsider acceptance of the treaty; and he plainly expected the captain to support him. But the prudent skipper refused to lend himself to this coercive measure, and slipped away, whereupon the legislature defiantly stood its ground. It did well, for the British consul reported that Cazneau had laid plans to throw a large body of immigrants into the island to Americanize it.[32]

## [ V ]

Filibustering and rumors of filibustering filled the whole of the Pierce Administration. This unhappy activity began with the inglorious foray of William Walker, "the gray-eyed man of destiny," into Lower California in 1853; embraced much sporadic plotting against Cuba, in which the irrepressible Quitman was again concerned; included certain Nicaraguan adventures of the intriguing Fabens and Colonel H. L. Kinney; and reached its climax in Walker's temporarily successful descent upon Central America in 1853. Most of these lawless enterprises elicited on one hand the applause of thoughtless or selfish onlookers, especially in the South and West; on the other the condemnation of discerning men, particularly in the North and East. To many, the idea that war and bloodshed should be carried into the territory of unoffending neighbors seemed desperately criminal and immoral. To others, Quitman appeared a truehearted American toiling for legitimate national aggrandizement, while Walker was a gallant leader striving to establish in Central America a nation to which his energy and genius might impart the love of liberty, industry, and order, and if possible the prosperity, which marked the United States. Many Cubans thought of Quitman as a liberator; many Nicaraguans, sick of the long civil strife between Leon and Granada, deemed Walker a constructive builder.[33]

But in any impartial view, the filibustering was indefensible. And unquestionably the Pierce Administration showed a censurable want of vigilance. "These expeditions," scathingly remarked the London *Times*, "do not receive the sanction of the American government, are not equipped by its funds, will not

32 Letter of Cazneau from Santo Domingo, February 16, 1855, in N. Y. *Tribune*, March 17, 1855; Br. consular report, FO 23/19, No. 38.
33 See Representative Percy Walker on Quitman, *Cong. Globe*, 34th Cong., 3d sess., Appendix, 99ff.

be conducted by its officers, but their preparation is nevertheless well known to the President and his Administration, and receives no check in that quarter." [34]

Walker's reckless incursion into Lower California proved to be only his rehearsal for larger efforts. Personal magnetism, iron determination, a keen mind, and a good education made the man an effective leader of desperate causes. A Tennessean by birth, with a Scottish father and Southern mother, he had received careful training first in medicine and then the law, to which he added the polish of European study and travel. He might have had a successful professional career; but restlessness took him to California, and the vacuity, disorder, and tropical splendor of the nearest Latin areas fired his imagination. He dreamed of colonizing Lower California and Sonora with American settlers. With a little band of forty-five he left San Francisco in the autumn of 1853 to begin his conquests. The party landed at La Paz in Lower California, shot five or six Mexicans, seized the governor, proclaimed a republic, and sailed for Magdalena Bay and further aggressions. Two mutineers were ruthlessly executed. But scanty rations, guerrilla warfare, hardships, and disease took a heavy toll of lives. With a mere handful of exhausted followers, Walker was finally glad to struggle back into American territory, and surrender to our border forces. His final exploits included the theft of some mission plate, the murder of a rancher who refused to give up his sheep, and the slaying of seven or eight Cocopa Indians.

"All the preparatory steps for this piratical undertaking," observed the Philadelphia *Public Ledger*, "were made in the territory of the United States, directly under the notice of the officers of our government." On his return northward, San Francisco greeted Walker with honor. Brought to trial for violating the neutrality laws, before a judge who openly proclaimed his admiration for these men who had gone forth to rebuild the broken altars and rekindle the fires of liberty in Mexico, and a jury which sympathized with any American who tried to "civilize the Greasers," he was promptly acquitted; while the fines imposed on two of his associates were never paid. It is not strange that he was soon planning a far greater stroke, an expedition which, if his Napoleonic star gleamed brightly, would make him dictator of all Central America and Cuba to boot.[35]

The same summer of 1853 which found Walker collecting recruits for Lower California saw Quitman, now out of office and looking for employment, visiting the East to consult with the New York Junta for the liberation of Cuba. His native Rhinebeck, N. Y., hailed him joyously. But his principal

34 London *Times*, October 25, 1855.
35 Philadelphia *Public Ledger*, quoted in *National Intelligencer*, December 17, 1853; L. Greene, *The Filibusterer: The Career of William Walker*, 46-48; W. O. Scroggs, *Filibusterers and Financiers*, 52ff. Los Angeles *Star*, April 15, 23, 1854.

business was with Sr. Domingo de Goicuria, treasurer of the Junta, who commanded large sums and expected to collect more. Quitman engaged to gather forces for a descent on Cuba in consideration of reward of a million dollars, to be paid when the enterprise succeeded; while he interested various retired army officers and others, some of whom received sums in hand running up to ten thousand dollars. All this later gave rise to pointed newspaper sneers at pocket-patriotism and sordid libertarianism. Quitman took care to consult important Administration officers, among them no doubt his old comrade-in-arms Jefferson Davis; and they gave him to understand that the government would not merely take a hands-off position, but would regard his undertaking with distinct sympathy. The Junta at once began to collect stores of arms and ammunition. A motley body of recruits was soon being enlisted. While most of them came from the Gulf States, a large force—some said a thousand—was raised in Kentucky.

Unquestionably the movement had some connection with the demand of the Louisiana legislature, so quickly taken up by Senators Slidell and Benjamin, for repeal of the neutrality barriers against filibustering; it may even have had some connection with the disposition of Davis and Cushing in the capital, and of Soulé in Madrid, to exploit the *Black Warrior* affair to the point of war. Patriots under Cuban palms heard of it with elation. They anxiously awaited the arrival of the first armed parties, led by Americans who had marched to Mexico City, to raise a banner emblazoned, "Death to the Tyrant and Liberty to Cuba." Marcy was kept well informed of all this, for he had his secret agents, including one Charles W. Davis whom he sent to Cuba.[36]

But Quitman and his associates acted with the indiscretion characteristic of all filibusters. The spring of 1854 found the lower Mississippi Valley buzzing with gossip about their intended expedition. The Memphis *Whig* learned from confidential sources that nearly a million dollars was available; that between 80,000 and 90,000 stand of arms had been collected; that the filibustering committee had about ninety field-pieces; and that eight steamers and four sailing vessels had been engaged to sail on twenty-four hours' notice. Quitman would command; his second would be a Northern man with Southern principles who had been brigadier-general in the Mexican War, a governor since, and was now a high civil officer; and one General Gonzales would be third in rank. Veteran officers of the Lopez expedition were helping make preparations. All in all, nearly fifty thousand men had been enrolled. The expedition, predicted the *Whig*, would probably sail about mid-July, 1854, land in Vuelto Abajo, and march on Havana. With perhaps ten thousand men thrown into the first effort, and thirty or forty thousand more to follow, success was deemed certain.

36 N. Y. *Sun*, June 6, 1855; Claiborne, *Quitman*, II, 195; *National Intelligencer*, July 3, 1855. For Davis's report on "Africanization" see *Consular Dispatches, Havana*, XXIX.

At this time Spain was feverishly reinforcing her Cuban garrison. A collision would upset all Marcy's hopes for peaceably "detaching" Cuba. As news of Quitman's plans was sent by the Spanish authorities to Washington, the Administration was galvanized into action; it notified Quitman to halt, and on June 1 Pierce issued a proclamation warning that the neutrality laws would be strictly enforced and violators would be prosecuted.[37]

Stern judicial action was also taken. At the spring term of the Federal Circuit Court in New Orleans Judge John A. Campbell charged the grand jury to pay special heed to the laws against filibustering expeditions. Northern communities, he pointed out, were being required to enforce the Fugitive Slave Act; but how could they be expected to do so if the South declined to halt expeditions that Northerners abhorred as piratical, lawless attempts to secure an unfair sectional advantage? The jury, after examining witnesses, reported that filibustering meetings had been held, that Cuban bonds had been sold, and that the money was being used to finance a revolutionary design. Judge Campbell then took action to place Quitman and two other leaders under bond for nine months to obey the neutrality statutes. Once later, in the spring of 1855, Campbell instructed the grand jury that the American people could not allow their peace to be disturbed by the cabals, intrigues, and plots of adventurers and juntas.[38]

Even yet, however, the filibusters hoped to fish in the troubled waters of American-Spanish relations. A new war-scare, slightly shopworn but grisly enough to serve, raised its head in April of 1855. A Spanish warship, the *Feronola*, had halted some American vessels in Cuban waters to make sure of their good character; Commodore McCauley was sent into the Gulf with a squadron led by the *San Jacinto;* and report had it that he was to sink or capture any Spanish vessel that might interfere with American shipping. Broadsides roared from all the bellicose Southern journals. We trust our new Minister in Madrid will speak emphatically, growled the Richmond *Enquirer.* He should tell the dons "that the first Spanish man-of-war which has the temerity to discharge a gun at a vessel belonging to citizens of the United States, not within a marine league of the territory of Spain, will be treated, if found, as piratical vessels ever have been." The Washington *Union,* more warlike than ever, teemed with the language of menace, insult and denunciation toward Spain. No time should be lost in preparing for a final and successful struggle for Cuba, declared a South Carolina editor. "The slightest provocation should be seized as the cue for bold, energetic, and successful action."

---

37 Memphis *Whig,* quoted in *National Intelligencer,* June 22, 1854.
38 H. G. Connor, *John Archibald Campbell,* 92–93, 96–97; *National Intelligencer,* May 24, 1855, "A Judge Worthy of the Ermine."

Gossip had it that the Davis-Cushing war-party in the Administration had again gained control of Pierce, and that the Secretary of the Treasury was making a desperate fight against them. If Guthrie is opposed to the war policy of the Cabinet, said the New York *Sun*, it would be more honorable for him to resign than continue a futile obstruction and betray Cabinet secrets to his friends. The conservative press, led by the *National Intelligencer*, New York *Evening Post*, Philadelphia *News*, and nearly all commercial organs, broke into protest against these evidences of a secret war policy. To still the clamor, the *Union* finally had to publish what was obviously an officially-inspired article declaring that its bluster and bellicosity did not represent any Administration views, and that President Pierce contemplated no steps which did not have the approval of all his Cabinet.[39] Senator Slidell, fuming over the failure of his schemes, and blaming Jefferson Davis for lack of energy, began urging his Mississippi friends to elect Quitman to the upper chamber as a defender of Southern rights.

While this final scare faded away, quarrels broke forth among the frustrated filibustering elements. The Cuban Junta, disappointed, humiliated, believing itself the victim of swindling and treachery, persuaded the New York *Sun* to publish an article which was half defense, half accusation. It declared that $150,000 of Junta money had been thrown away upon the charters of three steamboats whose treacherous owners had apparently first pocketed the money, and then informed the government of the filibustering scheme; that other large sums had been wasted upon unusable arms; that still others had gone without visible result to Quitman's associates. Goicuria, trying to exculpate himself from the charge of mismanagement, assailed Quitman for failure to comply with his brilliant promises, and for lack of decision, energy, and boldness. His story, pathetic enough in one light, showed that the deluded Cuban patriots and their friends had spent more than $330,000 without anything to show for it but bafflement and scandal. The press had talked of an enthusiastic leadership, of coffers with a million or more, of an army of fifty thousand; but the truth was that the great enterprise had never enlisted more than 2,500 men, that it could not arrange to transport even that many to Cuba, and that it was constantly crippled by internal quarreling. And to complete the discomfiture of Junta and filibusters, word shortly came that Commodore McCauley was genially dining in Havana with the Captain-General! [40]

A misty, flickering light hangs over the next figure to appear in the chronicles of the adventurers of Gulf and Caribbees; so mysterious a figure that one almost

39 Richmond *Enquirer*, April 16, 1855; *National Intelligencer*, April 19, quoting S. Carolina press and Philadelphia *News*; April 15, quoting N. Y. *Sun*; April 21, "The Kitchen Cabinet Cut Adrift"; N. Y. *Evening Post*, April 17; Washington *Union*, April 20, 1855.
40 N. Y. *Sun*, June 18; *National Intelligencer*, August 9, October 9, October 30; files of N. Y. *Journal of Commerce*, June-October, 1855.

doubts he was honest flesh and blood. Henry L. Kinney, a Texan promoter apt in turning his hand to anything (Walker termed him "the mule trader") was a seeker for both wealth and empire. Somehow he got hold of certain dubious land titles in Nicaragua, and with the aid of a hastily-formed corporation, proposed to colonize and develop these tracts. When it appeared that the titles were dubious or worse, he took J. W. Fabens, of Greytown fame, into partnership, and changed his plan. Fabens had obtained title to large Nicaraguan tracts; additional land was to be purchased; and another New York corporation, the Nicaraguan Land and Mining Company, was chartered to open mines, cultivate the richest acreage, cut mahogany, and otherwise exploit the district. They hoped, said Kinney, who was a man of the Mulberry Sellers type, to establish freight and passenger boats, build villages, erect hotels, "and in fine, to settle and clear up the country and bring its productions into market." The district lay in the elevated, healthy tablelands; coal had been discovered; while above all, it was in the vicinity of productive gold-mines.[41]

Alas for Kinney's dreams! The Nicaraguan minister protested to Marcy in violent terms. "New filibustering persons of high standing are mixed up in the iniquitous scheme," he wrote ex-Secretary Clayton on January 6, 1855. He denounced the selfish commercial interests which, he said, meant to take possession of all of Nicaragua. "I never could believe that the American people and the American government would act toward us in such a shameful manner, and avail themselves of the weakness of our people who have proffered to be, honestly and sincerely, a good and true friend of your country." He knew positively, he added, that several persons connected with Kinney's scheme were in close touch with President Pierce. When Marcy did nothing, poor Marcoleta resorted to newspaper publications. He had documents, stated the New York *Herald*, to prove that under the guise of peaceful colonization, the well-armed promoters would attempt the overthrow of the Nicaraguan government.[42]

Though Kinney protested that this was not true, and that the vessel he was equipping carried no arms, the evidence was against him. He had written to Marcy of establishing municipal regulations for his colony, which indicated a repudiation of Nicaraguan sovereignty. Moreover, sending a friend in Texas a letter which appeared in the Brownsville *American Flag*, he declared that only a few hundred Americans would be needed to take control of all that country: "I intend to make a suitable government, and the rest will follow." The people of Greytown had requested him to take control of the place, he

41 Kinney to A. B. Corwine, late U. S. consul at Panama, April 17, 1855, in *National Intelligencer*, April 24, 1855, quoting N. Y. *Evening Post*.
42 Marcoleta to Clayton, January 6, 1855, Clayton Papers; Marcoleta to the press, April 21, in *National Intelligencer*, April 24, 1855; N. Y. *Herald*, April 21, 1855.

explained, and he would establish himself there first. "They are anxiously looking for me. This will be the point from which I shall start." [43]

This was a bit too barefaced, and the steamer *United States,* which was to
carry the emigrants out, was detained in New York, while President Pierce
summarily dismissed Fabens from his official post. Kinney was brought before
Judge Kane in Philadelphia, and gave bail for $4,500 to appear for trial two
months later, with the understanding that the expedition need not be delayed.
Both Kinney and Fabens were also cited to appear before the district court
in New York, and Fabens did so, but his companion was absent. It transpired
that he and various associates had slipped away from New York on June 6,
1855, in the schooner *Emma.* After many vicissitudes, they reached Greytown
to find that the Nicaraguan president had declared them outlaws; but Kinney
protested in a conciliatory letter, pleading that he had only peaceful aims.

He had arrived full of hope, for Fabens and thirty other colonists were soon
to come, and despite the fierce enmity of the Accessory Transit Company, he
expected to make rapid progress. His first step was to obtain a larger tract of
land. "I have just completed the purchase of thirty million acres of the most
magnificent country in the world," he wrote a friend on August 16, "a country
which, I venture to predict, will before many months teem with the enterprising
and industrious masses of the United States and Europe. . . . There are three
hundred miles of seaboard belonging to it, and further back an elevated table
land, healthy in climate, and capable of producing every staple of the tropic or
temperate zones. Sugar, coffee, tobacco, cochineal, and cocoa are produced in
abundance, in addition to the substantial supplies of cattle and grain required
by the exigencies of a large population."

Truly an imperial domain; but just how good was his title? It rested upon
the grant which years earlier the drunken, profligate "king" of the Mosquito
Indians had given to two Jamaicans named Samuel and Peter Shepherd; and
the British government had set aside all the king's gifts on the ground of his
notorious inebriety. Kinney held but a cloudland estate. Nevertheless, he took
up quarters in Greytown; when Fabens's party arrived, they drafted a plan of
administration; he had himself elected "civil and military governor"; and his
American followers were put in a long list of subordinate positions. Having
had a printing-press sent down, he began publication of a journal, the *Central
American.* The autumn of 1855 found him trying to get his titles validated by
the Nicaraguan government. But his hour was nearly over, for the bolder and
abler William Walker—of whose activities we shall speak later—had appeared
on Nicaragua's western strand.[44]

43  Kinney's protest in *National Intelligencer,* May 3, 1855; Kinney to Marcy, February 4,
in *National Intelligencer,* February 10, 1855.
44  Kinney to unnamed friend, August 16, quoted in *National Intelligencer,* September 11,
1855; Greene, *op. cit.,* 140.

## [ VI ]

The one great diplomatic achievement of the Pierce Administration, the Canadian reciprocity treaty of 1854, was to be credited more largely to the energy of a special mission under Lord Elgin than to the State Department. We have seen that in the late forties and early fifties new troubles had arisen over that perennial source of discord, the Canadian fisheries. When provincial officers began to exclude American vessels from the inshore fisheries of Laborador and Newfoundland, hardbitten Yankee skippers set to arming their craft. Immediately after taking office, Pierce sent a naval force to the troubled quarter to protect the American boats. Not a little war talk, though poohpoohed by sober men, broke on the American air that summer. The British took a conciliatory attitude. "Perish all the cod and mackerel in the ocean— fine eating though they are," exclaimed *Punch*, "before we go to war with Brother Jonathan for a cause as scaly as any fish can be that have no scales." The fact was that with the Crimean War in the offing, the British Government had every reason to seek a peaceable solution for the difficulty; while it was given further stimulus in this endeavor by the circumstance that Canada, suffering heavily from the repeal of the British corn laws, the American tariff, and other adverse factors, was in such economic distress that not a little sentiment for annexation to the United States had arisen.[45]

A special British effort seemed necessary to achieve a general agreement before the fisheries difficulties provoked real anger, and to soften the economic policies of the United States before Canadian discontent became dangerously acute. London therefore instructed the Canadian governor-general in May, 1854, to proceed to Washington to make what bargain he could. He was given a free hand on condition that any concession from Great Britain and Canada must be matched by a corresponding concession from the United States. This governor-general was James Bruce, eighth Earl of Elgin. He was the son of the rescuer of the Elgin Marbles, the son-in-law of that Lord Durham whose name is connected with the report which marked so signal an advance toward the institution of dominion self-government, and the brother-in-law of Dean Stanley; a short, stout, jolly Scot of great wisdom, tact, and humor, full of hard sense and racy anecdote. A hearty supporter of provincial autonomy, he had rapidly become the most popular man in Canada.

When he arrived in Washington, he was warned by Pierce and Marcy that a treaty for a permanent settlement of the fisheries issue and for Canadian-American reciprocity would be difficult if not impossible to carry. But the situation was not completely hopeless. The Canadians could offer fishing

45 *Punch*, quoted in Bailey, *op. cit.*, 295, 296; L. B. Shippee, *Canadian-American Relations, 1849–1874, passim.*

privileges, the Americans tariff reductions—and so a bargain might be struck. The President and Secretary of State made it clear that if the Senate would assent to a compact, they would interpose no obstacle; and Elgin set resolutely to work on the most remarkable piece of lobbying ever executed by a British envoy.[46]

"I find," remarked his brilliant young aide Laurence Oliphant after a few days, "that all my most intimate friends are Democratic Senators." "So do I," dryly replied Elgin. He made himself immensely popular by his democracy of bearing, brilliant repartee, and graphic stories; not to mention his entertainments at the British legation, with an ample store of liquors and cigars. Before long Democratic senators were loud in assurances that if all British lords were like him and would become naturalized Americans, they would soon run the country, and that it was a pity he was not born an American so that he might become President. "Certainly," commented Oliphant, "it would not have been difficult to be more eligible for that high office than the respectable gentleman who then filled it." The mission was in Washington just as the Kansas-Nebraska Bill was passing. This fact gave Oliphant an opportunity to record some illuminating anecdotes. For example, he was at Hamilton Fish's house for dinner when Toombs in his most pompous manner informed Lord Elgin:

"Yes, my lord, we are about to relume the torch of liberty upon the altar of slavery."

Whereat Mrs. Fish, with her most winning smile and her sweetest tones, broke in archly:

"Oh, I am so glad to hear you say that again, Senator; for I told my husband you had made use of exactly the same expression to me yesterday, and he said you would not have talked such nonsense to anybody but a woman."

Before a fortnight had expired, Lord Elgin was able to assure Marcy that if the Administration would redeem its promise to conclude a treaty of reciprocity, it would find two-thirds of the Senate, including numerous leading Democrats, ready to assent. The process of "chaffing Yankees and slapping them on the back," as Oliphant put it, had succeeded. On June 5 the reciprocity treaty, the first that the United States had ever made with any nation, was signed in Washington. Marcy himself had not only used his influence with Senators, but had written to various businessmen asking them to support the compact. The Boston Board of Trade pronounced the treaty one of the most valuable to commercial and industrial interests ever made. It received general approval, and after a perfunctory debate, was duly ratified by the Senate early in August.[47]

---

46  L. Oliphant, *Episodes in a Life of Adventure.*
47  Margaret O. Oliphant, *Memoirs of Laurence Oliphant,* I, 42, 118–120.

"We are tremendously triumphant; we have signed a stunning treaty," wrote Oliphant, and the same statement might have been made by Marcy. It was one of those ideal treaties in which both nations win much, and neither surrenders anything of consequence. Americans gained the right to fish the inshore waters of all the Atlantic colonies except Newfoundland; they acquired also the use of the St. Lawrence and the Canadian canals between the Great Lakes and ocean. The Canadians achieved the rather empty right to fish along American shores as far south as the thirty-sixth parallel, below Chesapeake Bay. Of far greater value, they won the free entry of a long list of their products into the American market. These were in the main natural products of sea, land, or mine; and Elgin might well feel pleased that Americans consented to take without duty the furs, lumber, and coal, as well as the farm staples, of Canada. As an offset, the British provinces were to admit free the tar, pitch, turpentine and rice of the South, with unmanufactured tobacco. The treaty was to endure at least ten years, after which it might be abrogated by either party upon twelve months' notice. While the New York *Tribune* was critical, most other prominent American newspapers applauded it; and so did the London *Times*, remarking that international trade, like mercy, blesseth him who gives and him who takes.[48]

While it was primarily as a fair all-round bargain that the treaty slipped smoothly through the Senate, certain extraneous factors lent assistance. Unquestionably some Northern Senators supported it in the hope that it would lead to the ultimate annexation of Canada. Some Southern Senators, hostile to any such union, may have voted for the treaty in the converse belief that by alleviating the economic distress of Canada, it would postpone or avert annexation. Having just gained so much from the Kansas-Nebraska Act, various Southern leaders unquestionably felt that New England's ruffled feelings might be calmed by an arrangement which gave such indisputable benefits to the fisheries of the Northeast. And to make sure that all the needed votes would be impounded, the State Department called in an experienced diplomatic agent and lobbyist, Israel D. Andrews, and furnished him with means to pursue his task; he in good time showing that he had spent $118,000 in various ill-defined but useful ways. The same experienced agent had already employed much effort and money in making certain that the provincial legislatures in Canada would accept the treaty; his influence upon opinion in the Maritime Provinces being especially valuable.

But however curious some of the methods used in making this treaty—champagne, chaffing, and hard cash—it was an unquestioned boon both to Canada and the United States, and a noted landmark in the history of the progress of the three great English-speaking countries of the North Atlantic toward that partnership which in the next century provided one of the central fortresses of civilization.[49]

### [ VII ]

At first glance it may seem curious that a Secretary so able, experienced, and hardworking, so elevated in character and patriotic in aim as William L. Marcy, should have left his name on so infelicitous a chapter of foreign relations. Not merely was the record full of blunder and failure; the tone of our diplomacy was aggressive, opportunistic, and provokingly selfish. Had our policy shown more honesty, more simple decency, it would have been both more reputable and more effective.

The immediate fault lay in the division of counsels and responsibility which has too often characterized the conduct of our foreign relations. The weak President, dominated by Jefferson Davis and Caleb Cushing, continually interfered with State Department affairs. Even a stronger personality than the fast-aging, decrepit Marcy would have found it impossible to withstand such pressure. When Gadsden was appointed minister to Mexico it was at Davis's instance, and Davis informed Gadsden of the appointment before he heard of it from Marcy. When Soulé was appointed minister to Spain it was over Marcy's protest, and at the instance of Caleb Cushing, "Young America," and the slave-holding expansionists. These two appointments determined the character of vitally important transactions, and Soulé's in particular gave Marcy an impossible tool with which to work. Nor could Marcy ever know just when Slidell and other Congressional leaders, buttonholing the President, would dictate policies to which he had no choice but to subscribe.[50]

Behind this immediate division of counsels lay other factors: the appetite for conquest created by the Mexican War; the interest in expansion bred by slavery; the chauvinism which a Jefferson Brick press, a Young America school of politicians, and a backwoods pugnacity had engendered; the rampant belief in New World democracy and contempt for Old World tyranny which dated back to the Revolution and to its historical and political glorification; the restlessness of a migratory population; the want of experience, tradition, and balance in the diplomatic service. Foreign relations were a field in which the desire for sectional advantage operated strongly and a sense that the rewards of victory in Mexico had proved disappointing impelled many Southerners to further adventures. The level of American morality in international dealings

49  On Israel D. Andrews, see Bailey, *op. cit.,* 297; Shippee, *op. cit.,* 76, 77.
50  P. N. Garber, *The Gadsden Treaty,* 74–81; Fuess, *Cushing,* II, 159–161; Ettinger, *Soulé,* 151, 152.

was neither perceptibly below nor above that of British, French, Russian, and Spanish morality. Power-politics of an unblushing type dominated all international relations, and no nation dared cast stones at the glass walls of its neighbor.

The unhappiest results of our American arrogance and blundering in foreign affairs were not seen abroad; they were visible in the domestic sphere. The obvious desire of the Pierce Administration to seize Cuba, the failure to halt Central American filibustering, and the greedy eyes bent in some government circles on Sonora and other Mexican states, excited constant suspicion and distrust in the North. All this persuaded large freesoil elements that the "slaveocracy" was essentially aggressive and expansive, and that determined steps were necessary to halt it. The constant frustration of all expansionist schemes, meanwhile, and the steady scolding by freesoil editors and politicians, irritated countless Southerners, and gave them a conviction that their interests would never be protected until they were free from Northern meddling and nagging. Each misstep, each defeat, in foreign policy, deepened the sectional chasm at home. A strong President, a harmonious Cabinet, and such deference to principle as some earlier Administrations had shown in dealing with foreign problems, would have strengthened the fabric of the Union; but while Pierce and his advisers were in power, no statesmanlike act lifted men's eyes to loftier aims either at home or abroad.

# 11

# The Year of Violence: 1855

THE QUESTION whether the first fruits of Douglas's squatter-sovereignty principle would be sweet or bitter was soon answered. It bore apples of Sodom in the shape of violence, intimidation, cheating, wholesale stuffing of ballot-boxes, and the erection of two rival governments in Kansas, one based on fraud and the other frankly extra-legal; with an inevitable deepening of sectional animosities both North and South. The materials were being laid in Kansas during 1855 for a smoulder of civil war which, as armed bodies of men began entering the Territory from various parts of the Union, would flare in 1856 into a crackling blaze. Nor can there be any doubt as to the primary responsibility for the inflammatory lawlessness which marred the first efforts to erect agencies of self-government in Kansas; it clearly lay with the border leaders of Missouri. Douglas declared in 1857 that he still thought the Kansas-Nebraska Act statesmanlike: "Subsequent reflection has strengthened and confirmed my convictions in the soundness of the principles on which I acted, and the correctness of my course. . . ." Upon this statement events had already furnished an adequate commentary.[1]

[ I ]

The success of the pro-slavery settlers and their Missouri allies in electing a delegate to Congress in the fall of 1854 attracted national attention. The next steps in territorial affairs were to take a census, choose a legislature, and adopt a code of laws. All this could and should have been done without conflict. But it is not difficult to explain why the Missouri groups acting under the inspiration of Atchison felt it necessary to embark upon illegal courses, and loose a brood of dragons to feed on the plains alongside the buffalo.

The rough border elements believed that it was essential to the maintenance of slavery in Missouri (where about half the State's fifty thousand slaves lived in the range of counties bordering on Kansas) that the new Territory become

[1] Speech at Springfield, Ill., June 12, 1857; *National Intelligencer*, June 30, 1857.

slave.[2] They believed, as a manifesto of western Missourians at Lexington shortly stated, that one object of Douglas's bill had been to bulwark the institution in Missouri, and that this object would in the normal course of affairs have been achieved. They held (as the convention also stated) that when the freesoilers lost their fight for Congressional intervention, they had substituted active intervention by the Northern States. This emigrant aid movement, they declared, did not send out true settlers; it sent out mercenary hirelings, a body of military colonists who were to subjugate Kansas and take exclusive possession thereof. It was a duty to repel these Hessian bands of anti-slavery fanatics. All this was the negative side of the border movement; the positive side was summed up by John W. Geary, Pierce's ablest governor, when he said that the Missouri border manifested "a virulent spirit of dogged determination to *force* slavery into this Territory." [3]

The morbid belief of Atchison, B. F. Stringfellow, and other Missouri border leaders that Kansas would be flooded with Yankee "abolitionists," "negro thieves," and "philanthropic knaves," bore no relation to the facts.[4] They conjured up a vision of emigrant aid societies transporting a horde of fanatics into Kansas to deprive the Missouri farmer of his "natural rights" to an adjacent area. Such persons were criminals, insisted the Leavenworth *Herald*. With Dogberry gravity, it argued that when any group banded together for an object detrimental to the welfare of others, this was conspiracy, and conspirators were lawbreakers. Freemen of the South, Pioneers of the West! exhorted the Westport *Frontier News* early in 1855: Will you stand impotently by and see "abolition tyrants," marched by Greeley and Eli Thayer into the Missouri Valley, ruin this hesperidean garden, and destroy the whole institution of slavery? [5] Yet all this Yankee-phobia was, as time proved, as absurd as the demand for violent actions was brutal.

The fact was that New England could and did contribute little to the population of Kansas; that other States of the northernmost tier sent relatively few people; and that a heavy majority of settlers during the fifties came from the Ohio Valley and the middle country east of the Appalachians. By the census of 1855 in Kansas, it appears that the Upper North, from Maine to and including Iowa, furnished only 15.7 per cent of voters living in the Territory, the Lower South only 1.6 per cent, and the intermediate States (with Missouri) 75 per

2 34th Cong., 1st Sess., House Report No. 200 (hereafter called Howard Report), 838ff. One witness here testifies that the fears of Missourians were partly excited by a letter of the editor of the *Herald of Freedom* stating that one of his objects in coming to Kansas was to make it a free State.
3 December 22, 1856; Pierce Papers.
4 Atchison's speech at Weston, 1854, quoted by Charles Robinson, *The Kansas Conflict*, 93, 94.
5 February 17; quoted by Robinson, *Kansas Conflict*, 102.

cent. This was in the very infancy of the Territory, and the figures are open to considerable question. But the more accurate census of 1860 tells a similar story. It shows that the Upper North from New England to Iowa had contributed but 16 per cent; the Lower South only 13.5 per cent; while the intermediate States (with Missouri) had furnished 59.5 per cent. Discerning officers of the New England Aid Society were quick to realize that while they might bestow much leadership and moral vigor upon Kansas settlement, with some financial strength, the Northeast was too distant to send any large body of men.

"We are too far off," wrote A. A. Lawrence dejectedly in 1856; "we can pay some money and we can hurrah; but we cannot send you men—men of the right stamp. The Western States will furnish them, if you have them at all." [6] All the roaring of Atchison's fire-eaters against Yankee abolitionists was beside the point. The New England Emigrant Aid Society had sent not more than 750 people to Kansas in 1854; it sent not more than 900 in 1855, and fewer of them actually settled.

Indeed, it may be said that the battle for Kansas was fought and won years before any settler put foot on her soil or Atchison and Thayer began to rally their respective camps. It was won when the population of the Ohio Valley and the middle country generally, with its strong tendency to move westward along parallels of latitude, accepted the principle that slavery injures a pioneering race of small farmers growing mixed crops. It was won when Ohio, Illinois, and Indiana became freesoil, when Kentucky, Tennessee, North Carolina, and Western Virginia nurtured powerful non-slaveholding elements, and when Pennsylvania and New Jersey became confirmed in their rejection of slavery. This was the area destined to populate Kansas. As part of the Northwestern Surge, it sent beyond the Missouri River wave after wave of men determined to own no slaves and permit no slave-marts. They, and not Yankee abolitionists, composed the irresistible invasion that Atchison had to fear. On Washington's birthday, 1854, jubilant crowds at Rock Island, Ill., celebrated the opening of through railroad traffic from the Atlantic to the Mississippi. "From 50,000 to 100,000 people crossed the Mississippi ferries last season," wrote the Rock Island correspondent of the New York *Tribune*, "but they are only a small portion compared with those who are to come this season." Trains were soon running to Iowa City, a track was being planned to Council Bluffs, and the flood of freesoil settlers was steadily swelling.

The one hope that the slavery forces possessed of gaining Kansas was to send in an equal or greater force of Missouri and Arkansas slaveholders. But Arkansans, with their own State yet half-unsettled, tarried at home, and the two

6  February 12, 1856; quoted in Malin, *John Brown and the Legend of '56*, p. 514. See the excellent summary in ch. 25 of this volume.

censuses tell an eloquent story of the swamping of Missouri elements. In the 1855 registry of voters, Missouri furnished 47.6 per cent of the total of 2,905. In the 1860 census of population, Missouri furnished but 10.6 per cent of the total of 107,209. The foreign-born population of Kansas by 1860 exceeded Missouri's contingent.

Far from being imbued with Garrison-Greeley ideas, the dominant population which settled Kansas had a strong distaste for all persons of color. It took no sentimental views whatever of the Negro. The majority, wrote a New York settler named John Everett, "would dislike and resent being called abolitionists." [7] They would have recoiled from the idea of making Kansas a haven for runaway Missouri slaves. But they were immovably opposed to slavery. They wanted no colored people among them, bond or free—a disposition which they shared with the great majority of Illinoisans, Indianians, and Ohioans. Most settlers were not hostile to slavery as a Southern institution; they felt no antagonism to their brethren in the Cotton Belt; they disliked Yankee fanatics; but they wanted Kansas a free State. Left in peace, they would probably have made it a free State of Democratic faith and mild Southern sympathies —like California.

The conditions of Kansas settlement were neither Eastern nor Southern, but distinctively Western; conditions that made no appeal to cotton-belt planters or New England townsfolk, but which hardy farmers of the wide median region from Wheeling and Pittsburgh to St. Louis and Quincy accepted as natural. To live in a straw tent, to shake with chills and fever, to burn buffalo-chips, to forage for rabbits and berries, to endure, build, and prosper—such pioneering had the essential breath of freedom. A Boston woman, lucky in possessing a cabin of "shakes" near Lawrence, its inner walls pasted over with newspapers, was appalled by the fierce western winds, which shook the frail edifice till it seemed about to fall; by the prevalent typhoid, malaria, and digestive ills; by the rough fare of bread, milk, and small game. The want of good wells, the crowding of invalids in rooms half-freezing, half-roasting, the abundance of vermin, were dismaying. At night she listened to noises which slowly lost their power to terrify. "Far off across the river, in my wakefulness, I hear the whoop of the Indian, or the echo of a rifle; or quite as often, the sound of hungry and quarreling wolves." [8] Already immigrants were finding that cattle, corn, wheat, potatoes, pumpkins, and beans, on small holdings well tilled, were their best reliance. It was not a land for the slaveholder or his antagonist the anti-slavery agitator.

What a tragedy it was that a great adventure in settlement which might

7 January 25, 1856; quoted by Malin, op. cit., 515, 516.
8 Six Months in Kansas, by A Lady (H.A.R.; 1856), 99.

have been full of comradely enterprise, and which might have knit Northerners and Southerners together as in Illinois and Indiana, was given so Balkan a hue by the issue of slavery!

For the moment slaveholding Missourians were full of confidence. Atchison's chief lieutenant of the Missouri border, B. F. Stringfellow, penned a long letter to Clingman and four other Southern members of Congress which the press of all sections published far and wide at the beginning of 1855. Kansas would certainly be a slaveholding State, he wrote. The soil favored slavery; the chief staples of the region were most profitable when produced by slave labor; slaves in adjoining Missouri paid so well that they were let at higher rates than anywhere else in the Union; Missourians had already settled in Kansas in large numbers; slaves were safer there than in the old South, for they were farther from the underground railroad. While the letter was a bid for a strong Southern emigration, it expressed an honest conviction. It was significant that Douglas and his associates had ceased to assert that slavery would never go into Kansas or flourish there. A violent pro-slavery weekly founded at Atchison on February 3, 1855, the *Squatter Sovereign*, sought a wide Southern circulation as a propagandist organ.

The census of Territorial inhabitants and voters taken by Governor Reeder's officers early in 1855 indicated a population of about 8,500, of whom 242 were slaves. This was scattered sparsely over about 20,000 square miles.[9] Such a population justified the election for a legislature which the governor ordered for March 30th. His proclamation stated the boundaries of districts, the voting-places, and the names of election judges. Determined that the contest should be fair, he appointed justices of the peace and constables from each faction, while in most election districts, especially along the Missouri frontier, he selected as judges two freesoilers and one slavery man. Rigid rules were laid down. Judges were placed on oath, constables were ordered to attend and maintain lawful procedure, and it was emphasized that all voters must be actual residents, possessing no other homes.[10]

But with the incitement of Atchison, who had remained absent from the Senate this winter to make sure of victory in Kansas, Missourians again broke through all restraint. Rumors were broadcast that the Emigrant Aid Society meant to send twenty thousand Easterners into Kansas to control the vote, and the border rose to forestall them. By this time a widespread secret society, called variously the "South Band," "Sons of the South," or "Blue Lodge," gave organization to the Missourians. No fewer than five thousand men, many

9 *National Intelligencer*, May 31, 1855; Howard Report, 9.
10 The testimony of Reeder before the Howard Committee, pp. 933–947 of the Howard Report, is very full on this and other elections.

identified by a badge of hemp, poured across the line. One company of about a thousand, collected from eight Missouri counties, well armed, with flags, music, and two field-pieces, encamped near Lawrence on the eve of the election. Atchison himself led a body of about eighty, armed to the teeth, who "demolished considerable whiskey" en route. By a variety of illegal expedients—threats, force, repeating, the ousting of fair judges, and counting of illegal ballots—the intruders gave all but one of their candidates a nominal majority. The whole pro-slavery vote was 5,427, and the freesoil vote 791, with 92 scattering.[11]

Of the votes cast, subsequent investigation showed that only 1,410 were legal, while 4,908 were illegal. Atchison had exhorted his company in rough Cromwellian vein: "There are eleven hundred coming over from Platte County to vote, and if that ain't enough we can send five thousand—enough to kill every God-damned abolitionist in the Territory."[12] The investigation also presented evidence which indicated that if the election had been restricted to actual settlers, it would have seated a freesoil legislature. Though the Missourians excused themselves on the ground that they came to "rebut" illegal Yankee votes, a more outrageous violation of the principles of popular sovereignty would have been impossible to find. But the bold attempt to seize control of the Territory seemed for a time successful. Reeder, who had apprehended fraud, would no doubt have acted vigorously and promptly had early information of the election-day violence reached him, and had he comprehended the extent of the illegality. But his proclamation had furnished only five days for sending in notices of contest. Moreover, the governor was placed under heavy pressure by the threatening pro-slavery forces; indeed, he said later that his life had been continuously threatened since the preceding November.[13]

A majority of the men who claimed election promptly sought him out at the executive office he had established at Shawnee Mission, near the junction of the Missouri and Kansas, and almost opposite the thriving town of Westport, Mo., now part of Kansas City, to demand certificates. A freesoil committee drew up a formal written protest. The pro-slavery claimants threatened the

11 Howard Report, 30–33.
12 See testimony of Dr. G. A. Cutler, a Tennessean by origin, Howard Report, 357. Cutler protested against the illegal voting, and was told by one of a wagon-load of men from Platte County, Mo., that "Atchison had helped to make the bill, and had told them they had a right to vote, and he knew a God-damned sight better than I did." Report, 358.
13 Spring, Kansas, 52, 53; Robinson, Kansas Conflict, 121, 122; Howard Report, 936. The St. Louis Republican gave a telegraph dispatch from Independence, dated at nine A.M. on March 31, to show how the election had been carried: "Several hundred returning emigrants from Kansas have just entered our city. They were preceded by the Westport and Independence brass bands. . . . They gave repeated cheers for Kansas and Missouri. They report that not an anti-slavery man will be in the legislature of Kansas. We have made a clean sweep." Published also in Atchison Squatter Sovereign. April 10. 1855.

governor's life so fiercely that he formed a bodyguard of personal adherents, and when he gave judgment on April 6, it was in the presence of two armed groups; his guard fingering their revolvers on one side of the room while slavery men rattled their knives and pistols on the other. The claimants maintained that the governor had exceeded his legal authority when, in his proclamation, he established a residential qualification for voters; that they had as valid a right to vote as newcomers from the North; that he had no power to exact oaths from judges or voters; and that the new legislature was the only body competent to decide contested election cases.

Much distressed, Reeder gave certificates to about two-thirds of the claimants. Not knowing the scope of the frauds, he set aside the result in the only six districts in which adequate proofs were forwarded to him; and new elections being ordered in these places, all but one were carried by the freesoil forces. In mid-April, convinced by mounting evidence that the coming legislature was a child of violence and chicane, Reeder set out for the East to arouse public sentiment, and to warn the Administration.[14]

Had a resolute and impartial man sat in the White House, his errand might have accomplished something, but as it was it proved futile. Remaining in the East about two months, the distraught governor made numerous public statements, and in his home city of Easton delivered a singularly frank address.[15] Speaking as an early and consistent believer in the Kansas-Nebraska Act, he declared the recent election scenes shameful. "Kansas has been invaded, conquered, subjugated by an armed force from beyond her borders, led on by a fanatical spirit." Thus overborne by numbers, the settlers of the Territory must appeal to the American sense of justice. He could not indict the whole people of Missouri, for the authors of the outrages "were the fanatic leaders and corrupt and reckless presses of some half-dozen border counties who had inflamed, excited, and deceived their own people." But if Missouri did not deal sternly with these interlopers, he said, then the nation should maintain its plighted faith by dealing sternly with them.

Alighting from the cars in Washington, Reeder called at the White House almost daily for two weeks. He talked at length with Pierce, describing the illegal interference of Missourians in the two elections, denouncing their use of intimidation and force, declaring that they were determined to deprive Kansans

14  Reeder's testimony, Howard Report, 936–946, is explicit on his Eastern trip. The proslavery organ in Kansas, the *Squatter Sovereign*, rejoiced over his departure. "There is such a feeling rising in the Territory against the Governor that only his absence will prevent a general outbreak," it said. "Revolution is in every mouth; and if the President still persists in forcing Reeder upon us, God only knows what the consequences will be." April 3.

15  Easton, Pa., *Argus*, May 3, 1855, gives a corrected report of this speech obtained from Reeder himself. The governor referred to the indignation caused by the Kansas news. "He had found along his whole route the same familiarity with the facts, and the same state of indignant excitement."

of self-government, and pleading for decisive action. His reception was characteristic. Pierce seemed to share his indignation. He expressed himself highly pleased with the governor's course, endorsing in unequivocal language all that he had done. Kansas, he lamented, had given him greater anguish than anything since the death of his son; it haunted him day and night, and was the great overshadowing trouble of his administration. He seemed ready to act conscientiously. Yet his warm words and cordial gestures meant nothing, for no conviction lay behind them. He was ready to yield to the nearest and sternest pressure. A hint of his real attitude crept forth when he remonstrated with Reeder for the "unnecessary" warmth of his Easton denunciation of the Missouri invasion, and for not attacking the "illegalities" of the emigrant aid people as well—though Reeder knew of none.[16]

Returning to Kansas late in June, Reeder found the pro-slavery legislature ready to make startling use of its power. He had called the body to meet on July 2 at Pawnee City, a hundred miles inland from the Missouri boundary. A good stone assembly hall, with ample accommodations for board and lodging was available. But the legislature at once adjourned, in defiance of the governor, to Shawnee Mission, a few miles from the Missouri line. Here, with the editor of a pro-slavery journal as speaker, they addressed themselves to the task of putting slavery in full possession of the Territory. The revised statutes of Missouri were adopted as the general law; officeholding was limited to pro-slavery men; any person who asserted that slavery did not legally exist in Kansas was made subject to imprisonment at hard labor for not less than two years; while anyone who helped a slave to run away, or who aided in circulating any book, magazine, or paper that incited slaves to conspiracy or rebellion, was punishable by death. Even to harbor or conceal a fugitive slave was ground for ten years' imprisonment. A detestably partisan and unfair election law was passed. Governor Reeder vetoed one bill after another, but was systematically overridden.[17] Fair-minded Southern newspapers like the New Orleans *Bulletin* denounced the laws as outrageous, while so good a Democrat as Senator Weller of California later pronounced the worst of them violations not only of the organic act but the Federal Constitution, and of such infamous character that

16 Howard Report, 937, 938. Reeder also talked with the Secretary of the Interior, McClelland, and General Wilson, Commissioner of the Land Office. Of the latter Reeder writes: "He was profuse in his expressions of approval of my course, but expressed himself deeply solicitous as to the probable consequences of my return to the Territory."
17 The proceedings of the legislature were followed with special closeness by the St. Louis *Democrat* and *Republican*, while New York papers had correspondents in the Territory. The Leavenworth correspondent of the N. Y. *Journal of Commerce* was specially impartial. I have consulted files. Of the law by which the legislature appointed all local officers—sheriffs, constables, attorney, tax assessors, and so on—for six years, the St. Louis *Democrat* said: "A more infamous invasion of the rights of any people, a more unwarranted assumption of power not delegated, was never perpetrated by any assembly that ever sat in even revolutionary France." August 29, 1855.

Congress ought to wipe them out.[18] They in fact largely defeated themselves, for during the stormy ensuing year no prosecutions took place under them.

It was not law, but lawlessness, that was most to be feared. The country had been shocked to hear in April that the Parksville *Luminary*, a moderate newspaper in a border town of Platte County, Mo., had been "abated" by a mob which wrecked its office, threw the press into the Missouri River, and would have tarred and feathered one of the two owners had his wife not interposed. The journal was offensive because it had not attacked Northern immigrants as abolitionists and "white slaves," but had impartially welcomed all honest settlers; while one of the proprietors owned a hotel where freesoil migrants sometimes sheltered. More specifically, it had published an editorial denouncing the extremists on both sides. Kansas had fallen into disorder, it said; polling-places had been violated by pistols and bowie-knives; and legislative claimants were threatening to cut Reeder's throat from ear to ear if he did not give certificates. George S. Park, the editor, a Vermonter by birth who had gone south and fought under Houston in Texas, at once announced that he would hold his ground.[19] Before the month ended a public meeting in Leavenworth, attended by excited men of both parties, broke up in disorder as a freesoil lawyer resented a blow by shooting a pro-slavery politician dead. Slavery enthusiasts in that town held a gathering early in May which adopted violent resolutions, and appointed a vigilance committee to deal summarily with any settlers who meddled with slaves or criticized slavery.

## [ II ]

By midsummer the open rupture between Reeder and the pro-slavery leaders had riveted the attention of the country. The legislature not only memorialized President Pierce for the governor's removal, but held a joint session for the public attachment of signatures. Some citizens even called for a special election to choose a popular-sovereignty governor in his stead. Reeder stood firm; a freesoil address to Congress declared that he had fearlessly pursued the path of duty amid a storm of menace and destruction under which many men would have quailed.[20] But he was being fiercely assailed in Washington, where urgent demands were made upon Pierce for his elimination. Atchison had seen Pierce, pressed for dismissal in the most excited manner, and declined to take a refusal.[21]

18  *Cong. Globe*, August 26, 1856.
19  St. Louis *Intelligencer*, April 21, contains a full account of the destruction of the press; St. Louis *Democrat*, May 5, has Park's long statement to the public.
20  This memorial is in *National Intelligencer*, May 19, 1855.
21  Howard Report, 938.

Most unfortunately for his spirited fight, Reeder had gravely compromised himself by land speculations. Together with two Federal judges in the Territory, Elmore and Johnston, and a Colonel Isaacs, he had made contracts for the purchase of four large tracts reserved to half-breed Kansas Indians; submitting them on January 10, 1855, to G. W. Manypenny, the Indian Commissioner, for confirmation. Manypenny's relations with Southerners were close; he had aroused much suspicion when in 1853, purchasing titles to Indian lands in Kansas, he had neglected to extinguish some in Nebraska—thus leaving the northern line for a Pacific railroad blocked; and he could not have been ignorant that Atchison and others wanted Reeder ousted. Within a week, on January 15, he recommended to Pierce that the contracts be disapproved. He described them as a disreputable and demoralizing attempt to forestall competition in the purchases of these valuable reserves, an effort to monopolize the land, and a scheme to cheat the half-breeds.

In vain did Reeder protest that the sellers were educated French-Indian traders and keen businessmen, that they made as shrewd bargains as any full-blooded whites, that they had themselves set the price of the lands, and that this price was four- or fivefold the amount which the government was paying the Shawnee tribe for better tracts. Certainly one would-be seller, Aubrey, was a very astute trader indeed. The Indian agent in the Territory insisted that Reeder had cheated the very people he was sworn to protect, had carried out his land operations under pretext of examining the country to district it, and had taken adroit steps to prevent fair competition. When Reeder went East, he explained the matter to Pierce, who professed himself satisfied; but later the President demanded a written statement, and peremptorily dismissed Reeder. The truth seems to be that the governor had acted with indelicacy and impropriety, but not dishonesty, and that his enemies briskly seized the opportunity to overthrow him.[22]

Executive opposition to the Shawnee Mission legislature swiftly vanished. All hope of dislodging it was gone. And to make the prospect for a fair administration of the territory still worse, the character of the judiciary also changed. Judges Elmore and Johnston were removed, and in their places Pierce appointed Sterling G. Cato of Alabama and J. M. Burrill of Pennsylvania; but Burrill died before taking office, and no effective successor arrived until 1857. The two active judges in 1855–56, Cato and Lecompte, were therefore extreme pro-slavery men.

A new executive, Wilson Shannon, a Cincinnati attorney who had been Democratic governor of Ohio and a signally blustering, tactless minister to

22 Full text of the correspondence among Reeder, Manypenny, and Indian Agent Clarke is in the *National Intelligencer*, June 21, 1855.

Mexico, was at once sent west. He accepted, he said later, with great reluctance, and only on the urging of political friends.[23] Arriving at Westport and Shawnee at the beginning of September, he made speeches to slavery crowds which showed that his course would be precisely the opposite of Reeder's, for he announced that he regarded the Shawnee Mission legislature as a perfectly valid body, and all its laws as binding. Turning to the slavery issue, he declared his belief that since Missouri and Kansas were adjoining States, and since the immense trade up the Missouri must lead to perpetual intercourse between them, it would conduce to the avoidance of quarrels and border feuds if their institutions should harmonize. "He was for slavery in Kansas." [24] Shannon at once fraternized with the slavery party, and imbibed all their dark suspicions of the free-state men.

These events filled one important observer, the clearheaded Thomas Hart Benton, with disgust. Indignant over the armed invasion of Kansas by border interlopers, he took comfort in thinking that only a small part of Missouri, and that part Atchison's, had anything to do with it. But he believed that Congress should take notice of the disgraceful proceedings, and repudiate the Kansas legislature and all its doings. When Reeder was dismissed, he indulged in a still angrier outburst. The Pierce Administration, he commented, was taking the side of the "disreputable legislature," endorsing the mode of its election, and sanctioning all its conduct. The land speculations were a mere pretext. They had been known to the government the previous January, Benton correctly remarked, and if the governor was to be ousted it should have been then; but he was kept on while he seemed likely to be useful, and removed only when he had boldly obstructed the slavery extremists. Reeder was at least on the side of law and order; and in overthrowing him, Pierce assented to the destruction of every principle in the Nebraska Act, and of every argument on which it was founded.[25]

[ III ]

But if left without any other defense, the freesoil settlers had their own strong right arms, and they now prepared to use their unquestioned majority

23 See Shannon's letter on his record, *National Intelligencer*, November 29, 1856. His appointment was August 10, 1855. "Governor Reeder's removal," wrote the New York correspondent of the *National Intelligencer* in the issue of August 2, 1855, "is the universal theme of the press in this part of the country, and the sentiment expressed upon it is almost unanimously one of condemnation." Even the pro-Administration *Journal of Commerce* deplored the removal as an implied acquiescence in the acts of a legislature which had outraged conservative sentiment by its violence and disregard of propriety and duty.
24 St. Louis *Democrat*, quoted in *National Intelligencer*, September 18, 1855; the statement was long remembered—Greeley's *American Conflict*, I, ch. 17.
25 Benton to John M. Clayton, July 29, August 2, 1855; Clayton Papers.

strength. On September 5, a "Free State Convention" assembled in Big Springs, a hamlet of shake-cabins and log huts not far from Lawrence, and organized under G. W. Smith as president. Among its hundred delegates two men stood forth in special prominence: ex-Governor Reeder, who made a lively speech, and was nominated for delegate in Congress, and James H. Lane, a tall, swarthy, powerful-looking demagogue who had been a member of Congress from Indiana, voting therein for the Kansas-Nebraska Act, but who had now come

# FREE STATE
# CONVENTION!

**All persons who are favorable to a union of effort, and a permanent organization of** all the Free State elements of Kansas Territory, and who wish to secure upon the broadest platform the co-operation of all who agree upon this point, are requested to meet at their several places of holding elections, in their respective districts on the 25th of August, instant, at one o'clock, P. M., and appoint five delegates to each representative to which they were entitled in the Legislative Assembly, who shall meet in general Convention at

## Big Springs, Wednesday, Sept. 5th '55,

at 10 o'clock A. M., for the purpose of adopting a Platform upon which all may act harmoniously who prefer Freedom to Slavery.
The nomination of a Delegate to Congress, will also come up before the General Convention.
Let no sectional or party issues distract or prevent the perfect co-operation of Free State men. Union and harmony are absolutely necessary to success. The pro-slavery party are fully and effectually organized. No jars nor minor issues divide them. And to contend against them successfully, we also must be united.—
Without prudence and harmony of action we are certain to fail. Let every man then do his duty and we are certain of victory.
All Free State men, without distinction, are earnestly requested to take immediate and effective steps to insure a full and correct representation for every District in the Territory. "United we stand; divided we fall."
By order of the Executive Committee of the Free State Party of the Territory of Kansas, as per resolution of the Mass Convention in session at Lawrence, Aug 15th and 16th, 1855.

**J. K. GOODIN, Sec'y.**      **C. ROBINSON, Chairman.**
*Herald of Freedom, Print.*

Call for A Free State Convention, 1855.
Courtesy of the Kansas State Historical Society, Topeka.

to the Territory for a larger career. One of the ablest, and by far the most picturesque, of early Kansas leaders, Lane had a personality so compelling, a tongue so persuasive, an energy so tireless, that to many uncritical men he seemed a genius. Though unprincipled and often unscrupulous, a selfish opportunist and a political turncoat, he did some valiant service for freedom. While ill-schooled and ignorant, he spoke so admirably that (as John J. Ingalls later testified) "the electric shock of his extraordinary eloquence thrilled like the blast of a trumpet; the magnetism of his manner, the fire of his glance, the studied earnestness of his utterances found a sudden response in the will of his audience and he swayed them like a field of reeds shaken by the wind." His adventurous temperament, love of strife, and consuming ambition instinctively led him to see in Kansas a theatre for reckless action. The chief objects of this histrionic manipulator, full of stock tricks, but of unresting industry in building up his political following, were simply prestige, power, and money. It was later said that Douglas had persuaded him to go to Kansas to take the Democratic side, but that on arriving he found the free-state position more promising. He liked to attend revivals and get himself reconverted for the effect on the church vote; he told Southerners he was a Kentuckian and Westerners he was of Hoosier birth; he dabbled in land deals and resorted to desperate money-raising dodges. From the moment he appeared in Kansas he took his place with S. C. Pomeroy and Charles Robinson as one of the three freestate leaders. More militant than they, he was ready to drill troops and lead them to battle.[26]

The convention, bent on organizing the anti-Missouri elements into a Free-State party, began by repudiating the charge of abolitionism, asserting its opposition to the admission of free Negroes or mulattoes, and denouncing any interference with slavery inside any State. Dictated by Jim Lane, these resolutions were intended to reassure freesoilers of conservative views or Southern sympathies. But in additional resolutions written by Reeder, the delegates went on to assail the armed bands which had robbed Kansas of the right of suffrage and self-government, and to declare that "this miscalled legislature . . . have trampled under foot the Kansas bill, have defiled the power of Congress, have libelled the Declaration of Independence, violated the constitutional bill of rights, and brought contempt and disgrace upon our republican institutions at home and abroad." They further resolved that they owed no obedience to the enactments of the spurious legislature, and would defy it; and that if peaceful remedies should fail, matters might be pushed to "a bloody issue." Reeder delivered a fiery speech, closing with a stanza of Halleck's "Marco Bozzaris." Finally, the convention took steps not only to hold their own election for delegate in Congress, but to bring together a new convention at Topeka September 19th, which was to discuss the question of a constitution. Already the establishment of a State government and admission to the Union were ideas uppermost in the popular mind.[27]

26 Much has been written about the picturesque Lane. See W. G. Clugston, *Rascals in Democracy*, ch. 5, for a sharp recent estimate; W. E. Connelley's brief *James Henry Lane;* the enthusiastic biography by John Speer; and two scholarly estimates, L. W. Spring's "The Career of a Kansas Politician" in *Am. Hist. Rev.*, October, 1898, and W. H. Stephenson's "Political Career of General James H. Lane" in *Kan. State Hist. Pubs.*, III, 1930. Clugston also gives an estimate of Robinson and Pomeroy.

27 But the important achievement was the establishment of a political party, for which the resolutions provided a platform; Malin, *John Brown and the Legend of '56*, p. 517. "While the freestate movement is an apparent necessity," wrote the New York *Times* correspondent from Kansas City under date of December 4, 1855, "and seems to be our only salvation, I can never enough regret that it has fallen, to the extent it has, into the hands of demagogues like Col. Lane and his immediate followers, who have been far more anxious for the instant

Thus when Shannon, taking up his residence in Kansas, used the cool autumn days to examine the situation, two rival parties glowered at each other and two hostile systems of government were coming into existence. Freesoil men detested Shawnee, and slavery men derided Big Springs. Left to themselves, the Kansans might have conquered their difficulties peaceably. But every transaction on those windy plains now caught public attention from Fundy to Florida. While the Northern press rang with denunciations of the fraudulent and despotic Shawnee legislature, the before-mentioned convention of western Missourians drew up an address to the nation, signed by Governor Sterling Price, Judge W. B. Napton, and Congressman Mordecai Oliver, rehearsing all the reasons why Kansas *must* be a slave State, and declaring that any refusal to admit her because of slavery would mean the breakup of the Union.

## [ IV ]

Politically, the first half of 1855 showed no brightening of the skies for the Pierce Administration. East and west, sentiment was hostile; and the year opened with a spectacular defeat to Douglas's party in the Illinois Senatorial contest.

The returns from the fall election of 1854 had made it plain that the Illinois legislature would probably choose an anti-Nebraska man in place of James Shields, the Irish-born politician, jurist, and Mexican War veteran who had gone to the Senate in 1849. The mixed character of the opposition to Shields, chiefly Whigs, but partly anti-Nebraska Democrats and "abolitionists," made prediction as to his successor difficult. Douglas being from Chicago, down-State areas felt entitled to the other seat. Lincoln was an aspirant, and to render himself eligible resigned his place in the legislature. When the balloting began in joint session on February 8, 1855, with 51 votes necessary to a choice, he took the lead with 45 against Shields's 41. Lyman Trumbull—a scion of the illustrious Connecticut family who had gone west, associated himself with Governor John Reynolds, taken up practice at Alton, and been elected to Congress as an anti-Nebraska Democrat—received five votes, and Governor Joel A. Matteson, a Nebraska Democrat, had one.

It is likely that Lincoln would have won had not five anti-Nebraska Democrats stubbornly refused to vote for any Whig. For some time the balloting proceeded with little change. On the sixth poll Shields still had 41 votes; Lincoln had dropped to 36; and Trumbull had risen to eight. Intense excitement reigned, for the entire State regarded the contest as momentous. Seeing that it

---

creation of offices, whose honors and enrolments it is their especial care to monopolize, than for the real quietude and prosperity of the fair land they have transformed into a political hunting-ground." This was but too true.

was impossible to make headway with Shields, the Nebraska Democrats then dropped him and threw all their strength to Matteson, who on the seventh ballot received 44 votes, and on the eighth 46—more than any other aspirant had thus far obtained, and only five votes short of a majority.[28]

This was alarming, for Matteson's friends were ultra-Nebraska men who attacked Shields as an old fogy of the Cass type. They declared that he had advised against the introduction of the Nebraska bill, had voted for it reluctantly, had opposed the Gadsden treaty, and was out of touch with Young America generally. Matteson they lauded as the staunchest possible advocate of popular sovereignty.[29] At the same time, Matteson himself had been so noncommittal on the Nebraska issue that he appealed to some anti-Douglas Democrats. Moreover, as a self-made man with a wide range of interests, he was deservedly popular. He had been active in promoting railroad construction, had shown keen interest in the Illinois and Michigan canal, and was concerned in various banks. Few men had done more than this native of upper New York to "build up" the State. Yet if he went to Washington he would give increased strength to Douglas and Pierce.

At this critical moment Lincoln saw that a sacrifice of his ambition was imperative and that his vote must instantly be thrown to Lyman Trumbull. "Evening had come," state Nicolay and Hay;[30] "the gas was lighted in the hall, the galleries were filled with eager women, the lobbies were packed with restless and anxious men. All had forgotten the lapse of hours, their fatigue and their hunger, in the absorption of the fluctuating contest." The roll-call of the ninth ballot showed only 15 votes for Lincoln, 35 for Trumbull, 47 for Matteson. Amid painful excitement and in a silence such that spectators scarcely breathed, Judge Stephen T. Logan, Lincoln's nearest and warmest friend, arose and announced the purpose of the remaining Whigs to decide the contest, whereupon the entire fifteen changed their votes to Trumbull, who was thus elected. The Democrats were astounded and dismayed, for they regarded Trumbull as an arch-traitor, and knew that he would relentlessly attack the Nebraska Act.

To Douglas personally the result was a heavy blow. His correspondence shows that he had helped concert the Matteson coup more than a fortnight before the balloting began. "Your dispatch of the 21st is read," wrote a Springfield friend.[31] "I shall do all in my power to have our friends abide by the position they have taken. But I assure you that stronger efforts were never made for

28 Horace White, *Life of Lyman Trumbull*, 42–44; Cole, *Era of the Civil War* (Centennial History of Illinois), 134. A long letter in the *National Intelligencer*, February 15, 1855, describes the contest. "Gen. Shields would have been reëlected," it said, "had he voted against the Nebraska bill." For the ballots see Beveridge, *Abraham Lincoln*, II, 285–287.

29 *National Intelligencer*, February 15, 1855.

30 *Abraham Lincoln, A History*, I, 389, 390.

31 Thomas L. Harris, Springfield, January 25, 1855; Douglas Papers.

any man than are now being made for Matteson. He is a strong worker for anyone when he starts—a stronger for himself than I supposed he could be—he is working up strength all the time. Shields can count but 43 votes certain, and his best probabilities count but 46. If he can get another one I don't know where it is to come from. We can get nine votes, neither one of which I suppose Shields can receive. . . . M. tells all of them, that he will act with you and for you from beginning to end. . . ." It was bad enough to have the coup fail; it was worse to have such a hard-hitting Yankee as Trumbull, an old party associate driven into revolt by Douglas's pet measure, and a man who openly denounced Douglas as a demagogue, triumphantly enter the Senate. Loyal Sheahan, the Washington friend who had been sent west to found and edit Douglas's organ, the Chicago *Times*, wrote him that Trumbull would be a continuous thorn in the flesh.

"The deed is done," he exclaimed.[32] "The severest blow we have received has been given us. . . . The most dreaded result has been accomplished. Wentworth, Snowhood, Long, Williams, Fuller and all the other traitors to the party and to you, have got what they wanted. They will be bold and defiant in their treason. They have got that which I wrote one month ago they sought, a democrat who will be administration man enough to stand between them and you for their protection. Trumbull is your personal enemy. His ambition will lead to such position as they wish him to take—your enemy and their protector."

Douglas, always a fighter, impulsively telegraphed Sheahan to announce forthwith the candidacy of Shields for the governorship, and to accompany the announcement with a suitable editorial. But Sheahan, who wished Shields to run for the seat Trumbull was vacating in the Alton Congressional district, wisely expostulated.[33] The gubernatorial election did not take place until the fall of 1856. Shields could not properly sustain a candidacy through eighteen months, a year and a half. Moreover, he would not wish to remain out of office for that period. In the end, Shields ran neither for the governorship nor for Congress. He was engaged at the time in a speculative land-buying scheme with Douglas, and we find him urging the Senator to pay up a debt of nearly a thousand dollars, "for I mean to continue getting warrants as soon as a few of them are issued and they become cheap, which will be most likely last of June or middle of July. Now dear Douglas you must not disappoint me in this. You know how much depends upon it. I will do a great season's work if I live and you do this."[34] Presently he became a resident of Minnesota.

It was a gloomy spring and summer for Douglas. Sentiment in the North and Northwest remained generally hostile to him. The outrages committed by the "border ruffians" in Kansas were bringing his much-touted principle into

32  February 8, 1855; Douglas Papers.
33  February 17, 1855; Douglas Papers.
34  March 13, 1855; Douglas Papers.

discredit. In Kansas his friend Atchison, after a bitterly fought contest, had failed of reëlection to the Senate, the place going after some delay to James S. Green. This was a body-blow indeed! [35] In Illinois the able lieutenant-governor, Gustave Koerner, had made strenuous efforts to get the legislature to instruct the Senators to restore the Missouri Compromise. "Such is the mettle of the little Dutchman," wrote a disgusted legislator, "who we are compelled to address Governor." Chicago and all northern Illinois seemed almost solidly hostile. Sheahan wrote of the metropolis as "this god-forsaken city," and reported that the *Times* was struggling desperately for life. "There is a deep-set determination to break us down by withholding advertisements, etc. I meet it by bold defiance." [36]

Evidences that the tide of opinion continued to run strongly against the Nebraska Act cropped up on every hand. In Pennsylvania, for example, the wily Simon Cameron on February 9 addressed a long public letter to a member of the legislature. Until the previous year Cameron had been a loyal Democrat, and as a good hater of Buchanan had shown himself most cordial toward the Pierce Administration; but now he revealed himself as a radical freesoiler. He declared that he was utterly opposed to the Nebraska Act, and that if elected to the Senate he would vote for restoration of the Missouri Compromise and labor to repeal the fugitive slave law. "The passage of the Compromise measures," he wrote, "was acquiesced in by the North, and I had hoped the questions growing out of it had been settled; but as the South has been the first to violate it, I hold the bill subject to revision, and will act with the North upon this and all questions connected with the subject of slavery." [37]

The general repute of the Pierce Administration was illustrated by a witticism which John P. Kennedy picked up from an old Negro and retailed to his wife. "He said, 'Pierce came in wid *little* opposition, and is going out wid *none*.'" [38]

In the South, to be sure, the Democratic Party in general remained firm. One spring election aroused sharp national interest, and from it Pierce could

35 The Blair family labored with might and main against Atchison. "The struggle here to elect a Senator is desperate," Frank Blair wrote from Missouri on May 28, 1855, adding of Atchison: "I am not certain that money is not being used to accomplish his election. The administration would not hesitate to buy up any member who could be purchased." But by autumn sentiment had changed. "I found that there has been a sharp reaction in this State against Atchison and his banditti," Frank Blair wrote his father on October 23, 1855. Atchison was then under accusation of having joined the Know-Nothings; Blair Papers, Princeton Univ.

36 F. D. Preston, H. of Reps., Springfield, January 21, 1855; Douglas Papers. One reason why Matteson was not elected Senator was that this would have promoted Koerner at once to be governor. Sheahan, February 8, 1855; Douglas Papers.

37 This is in *Facts for the People of the South, or Know-Nothingism Exposed*, pvt, 1856. Cameron's freesoil pledges showed that he expected Pennsylvania to become Republican.

38 March 1, 1855; Kennedy Papers.

draw a delusive gleam of hope—the Virginia contest for governor. Henry A. Wise as the Democratic nominee, a true gentleman, a man of the world, and something of a scholar—for he had graduated from Washington College in Pennsylvania, and had read widely—faced a Know-Nothing candidate, Flournoy, who was also supported by the Whigs. The battle seemed for a time extremely close, and most observers believed till near the end of the canvass that Flournoy would win. But Wise displayed a matchless energy and ability in stump speaking. Short, spare, and physically frail-looking, he spoke with an assiduity and vehemence that were extraordinary, and he knew how to appeal to the popular judgment and feeling. He denounced Know-Nothingism as the spawn of Boston abolitionism, the unconstitutional and un-American product of Theodore Parker and Wendell Phillips. Had not Lafayette, a foreign Catholic, sacrificed everything for America, he asked, while the native Protestant Arnold was bartering his country's liberties? He also struck a wise constructive note. Advocating internal improvements, and calling for a universal system of common school education, he bade his auditors to drop their local bickerings and lift the Old Dominion, the home of Washington, Jefferson, and Madison, from the dust in which it grovelled. His appeal, wrote an Ohio traveller who heard him at Parkersburg, "set the blood dashing through my veins like a mountain torrent," while its effect on the cheering Virginians could be seen "in their glistening eyes and heaving chests."

As the canvass reached its climax, political circles in Washington became almost as excited as in the hottest presidential campaigns. Anxiety as to the result was stimulated by the huge amounts wagered on the contest.[39] Religious issues played little part in the battle, though Wise assailed the intolerance as well as the secrecy of the Know-Nothings. It was noteworthy that sectional animosities and extreme State Rights doctrines were also allowed to sleep, though again Wise accused the Know-Nothings of an abolitionist taint.[40] He gave his appeal an attractive reform coloring by dwelling on the importance of agricultural progress and industrial development. But the primary question was whether a powerful nativist party rising on the ruins of Whiggism was to dominate the most influential of the slave States and so gain an all-important vantage point for sweeping half the section. When Wise triumphed by a majority of 10,180, thus effectively stemming the Know-Nothing advance in the South, the rejoicing of all Democrats was exuberant.[41]

Pierce shared this exultation. "The result of the election in Virginia," he

39 *National Intelligencer*, May 29, 31, 1855; N. Y. *Herald* latter half of May. For the Ohio report of Floyd's oratory, see *Ohio Arch. and Hist. Quarterly*, XXXIX, 673–682.
40 Robert M. T. Hunter's papers disclose a frank jealousy of Wise, tending to split the State Rights men.
41 Barton Wise, *Life of Henry A. Wise*.

wrote Douglas, "has put a new face upon the prospects of the Democratic Party—the only party which carries no dark lantern and gives its time-honored banner to the breeze. . . ." [42] Wise, coming to Washington, was serenaded by a tumultuous crowd who cheered his denunciation of the Know-Nothing "Sam." While Sam might achieve victories in the North, he said, that sinister figure could win no real victory in the land of Jefferson. "I knew he could not stand before the pibroch and trump of liberty. He might live in the land of the secret ballot, but he could not survive the *viva voce* of the people of Virginia." [43] Democrats everywhere, still half-stunned by the reaction against the Nebraska Act, began to pluck up hope. The Whig Party was dying; the Republican Party was but an infant; and this portentous Know-Nothing apparition began to look like a Wardour Street knight with lath sword. Despite the record of the coarsest, most erratic, and most barren administration in the nation's history, the Democracy might yet win in '56.

## [ V ]

Indeed, the year 1855 witnessed an unmistakable decline in the power of that Know-Nothing organization which still boasted how during the previous fall it had elected nine governors, and 104 of the 234 members of the national House.[44] Its capacity for mischief alone remained strong. All its efforts to create a vigorous national organization proved half abortive; but the dragon's teeth it had sown began growing a thick crop of hatred, riot, and outrage.

Looking to the next presidential contest, nativists already began to talk of a possible Whig and Know-Nothing fusion on Millard Fillmore. The patent fact was that Know-Nothingism itself was bankrupt of statesmen; it had less political talent of high order than any other third party in American history; but it controlled so many votes that it could offer a tempting bait to able men in other camps. Sam Houston was also frequently mentioned. Honest Gideon Welles, detesting all secret political orders and all proscription of men because of birth or faith, early this year met the Texan, and talked frankly with him about the growing gossip that he was a Know-Nothing and a favorite for the nomination. "He gave me to understand that he 'knew nothing' about them, other than that some had talked of him as a 'Sam.' I said to him that they had an undoubted right to support whom they pleased for any office, and that it could not be expected, or desired, nor wished, that any good candidate should repel them, if they were disposed to vote for him." [45] Fillmore was out of reach of

42   May 28, 1855; Douglas Papers.
43   *National Intelligencer*, May 29, 1855.
44   *Know-Nothing Almanac, or True Americans' Manual*, 1856, pp. 62, 63.
45   Welles to Preston King, April 23, 1855; Welles Papers.

interviewers, for he sailed for Europe in May, 1855, to be absent more than a year; but that he was as receptive as Houston could hardly be doubted.

June brought the first stormy national convention of the Know-Nothings or American Party in Philadelphia, held behind closed doors. Among the crowd of mediocrities a few delegates of modest distinction, notably Henry Wilson, Governor Gardner of Massachusetts, and Schuyler Colfax of Indiana, stood out. One E. B. Bartlett of Kentucky was chosen president. It was known that a sharp battle would take place over the platform, for various State pronouncements had revealed an acrid disagreement upon slavery. While conventions in Massachusetts and New Hampshire had adopted strong anti-slavery resolutions, the New Jersey convention had evinced warm friendliness to the South, and in Illinois a tumultuous session had terminated in complete disruption.[46] The burning question in Philadelphia was whether anti-Nebraska resolutions should be adopted. Gardner and Wilson declared that unless this were done, the party could carry not a single village in Massachusetts; the New York *Express*, metropolitan organ of the party, argued that the moment the slavery issue in any form affected the organization, it ceased to be American and became sectional.[47]

The party readily agreed on planks demanding exclusion from office of persons of alien birth and education, a twenty-one-year term for naturalization, and resistance to the "aggressive policy and corrupting tendencies" of Catholicism. But on slavery it divided. A majority of the platform committee brought in a report deploring Whig and Democratic agitation of the slavery question; declaring it the imperative duty of the American Party to give peace and perpetuity to the Union; and asserting that the best guaranty of this was to "maintain the existing laws upon the subject of slavery, as a final and conclusive settlement of that subject in spirit and in substance." This acceptance of the Nebraska Act was underlined by an express declaration that Congress ought not to legislate upon slavery in any Territory. The minority report demanded a restoration of the Missouri Compromise, or, if that were impracticable, the exclusion by Congress of any would-be slave State formed out of any part of the area formerly subject to the Missouri restriction. Delegates representing fifteen slave States, with California and New York, signed the majority report, and delegates from twelve free States the minority document.

The efforts of peacemakers like Kenneth Rayner of North Carolina to hold the two factions together completely broke down. When the majority platform was adopted, the delegations of twelve Northern States, Henry Wilson at their head, indignantly withdrew. If the party persisted in proving recreant to freedom, declared Wilson, he would "shiver it to atoms."[48] The seceders, repre-

46  *National Intelligencer*, May 8, 1855.
47  Quoted in *National Intelligencer*, June 14, 1855.
48  Elias Nason and Thomas Russell, *Henry Wilson*, 121.

senting all New England and all of the old Northwest Territory, at once published a declaration of principles, the first two of which demanded the uncon-
ditional restoration of the Missouri Compromise prohibition, and national protection of all Territorial settlers in the free and undisturbed use of the ballot.
Some observers expressed astonishment that the free State delegates should not
peaceably accept the status quo, including the Nebraska arrangement. Yet in
view of home sentiment neither compromise nor evasion was possible. The
Indiana delegation in withdrawing expressed regret that the majority had
promulgated a platform which could have no other effect than to increase the
fury of the conflagration which the Nebraska Act had kindled.

Following the convention, in State after State the Know-Nothings lost
ground. "As a nation," wrote Abraham Lincoln this summer, "we began by
declaring that 'all men are created equal.' We now practically read it, 'all men
are created equal except Negroes.' [49] When the Know-Nothings obtain control,
it will read: 'All men are created equal except Negroes, foreigners and Catholics. . . .' " This succinctly stated the primary reason why good citizens turned
away from the party. As Henry A. Wise had asked, why was it necessary to
excite violent animosity against Catholics when they numbered fewer than
700,000 among the 14,235,000 church members or persons using church facilities;
to arouse a harsh prejudice against the foreign-born when they were but 2,210,-
000 against 17,740,000 native-born? [50] The want of political principle in the new
party was provoking. Why wage war on the religion of Charles Carroll of Car-
rollton and Chief Justice Taney, asked that distinguished Virginia lawyer and
banker, Thomas S. Gholson, and say nothing whatever about such real issues as
the tariff, the banking system, and internal improvements? "It is much to be
feared that the originators of this new Order are moved more by *hope of place*
than *fear of the Pope*." [51] The party was showing a certain capacity to appear
all things to all men. In Louisiana it was cordial to native-born Catholics and in
the Middle West to foreign-born Protestants; and such local inconsistencies did
not improve its national reputation.

Few facts of the time, indeed, were more heartening than the expressions of
fervent liberalism which Know-Nothing dogma evoked from representative
Americans in all sections. "In my humble opinion," wrote J. L. M. Curry of
Alabama, "Nullification, secession, U. S. Bank, Mexican War, and such like
existing questions were harmless to the government in comparison with this
stupendous and far-reaching leprosy. This manner of carrying political questions

49  Letter to Joshua F. Speed, August 24, 1855; Nicolay and Hay, *Works*, I, 216–219.
50  James P. Hambleton, *Biog. Sketch of Henry A. Wise, With a History of the Political
Campaign in Virginia*, 9, 10.
51  Letter of Thomas S. Gholson in Richmond *Enquirer*, April 25, 1855; pvt., Huntington
Library.

—this terrible system of espionage—this imitation of the most odious practises of European despotism, will, as certainly if it continue unchecked, bring about the ruin of our government and the failure of our republic, as night follows day." His Baptist principles revolted against any interference with freedom of private judgment. "To go back ten centuries and proscribe religious faith, to institute an inquisitorial star chamber commission in a republic, to render free speech dangerous, to choke up the spontaneous convictions of an immortal soul, is what I fear." [52] The Know-Nothing convention of Louisiana, meeting in July, summarily rejected the Philadelphia platform as it applied to Catholics. "We shall forever continue to protest against any abridgment of religious liberty," it proclaimed, adding that "we condemn any attempt to make religious belief a test for political office." [53] Pelting attacks on the organization came from Walt Whitman, James Russell Lowell, Bryant, Greeley, and other publicists, while Samuel Bowles called it "in the last degree reprehensible." [54]

Nor did the party's tendency toward machine and boss rule fail to breed enmity. Many who originally sympathized with its objects respecting naturalization and the exclusion of the alien-born from high elective office were estranged by its political methods. The grand president of the order in New York, for example, under the constitution adopted in June, 1854, exercised almost despotic power. He was empowered to appoint one deputy for each county; this deputy was authorized to create any number of lodges and administer oaths to the members; and the lodges in turn selected delegates who met in the grand council to make rules and choose officers. A small oligarchy thus controlled a great membership.[55] One New York assemblyman, a repentant adherent, declared that the party was managed by schemers and demagogues; even by men, he was sorry to say, "whose names are enrolled upon the calendars of crime." [56]

The refluent tide in the fall elections of 1855 left the Nativist craft lying half-stranded in sandy shallows. Though thousands in New England and elsewhere voted the Know-Nothing ticket without sympathy for the party's peculiar ideas, simply because the majority of anti-Nebraska voters were ranged under its banner, the "Americans" failed to obtain a majority of the entire vote in a single Northern State. Municipal and county elections illustrated the same trend toward decay. One after another, Chicago, St. Louis, Trenton, Hartford, New Haven, and other cities which the Know-Nothings had ruled swung against them. While it was unquestionable that the "Americans" would play a

52  June 30, 1854, to C. C. Clay; Clay Papers, Duke Library.
53  National Intelligencer, July 14, 1855.
54  Merriam, Bowles, I, 124.
55  Speeches in the Assembly of the State of New York in Exposition of the Know-Nothings, pvt, 1855; Huntington Library.
56  Speech of D. C. Littlejohn in N. Y. Assembly, February 5, 1855.

powerful rôle in the campaign of 1856, it was also certain that they were a transitory body.

Each party found something to encourage it in these autumn elections. The Republicans won by far the most important victory by their triumph in Ohio, where Chase was rewarded for his effective Senate battle against Douglas by being elected governor; his vote being 146,106 against 130,887 for his Democratic competitor, and 24,237 for the Whig nominee.[57] The Know-Nothings could point to New York, where in a light vote their candidate for secretary of state had a small lead over the "fusion" candidate, with the Democracy badly defeated because of the split between Hards and Softs. Had the Democrats been united, they would have won.[58] In Maryland, too, the Know-Nothings elected a heavy majority of the house of delegates, while in California they swept a highly confused board. As for the Democrats, they picked up crumbs of comfort in minor Pennsylvania elections, and a bit of hard crust in Maine, where the Republican Party entered the lists with the burden of the prohibition law on its shoulders, and hence went down in defeat. Pierce was foolishly delighted by this tiny victory.

"I saw the President soon after my return," wrote his friend B. B. French, "and he was glorifying the Maine election as a great Administration triumph, *on the Kansas issue!* I told him he was mistaken, I thought, and he told me I was politically crazy. He said that N. H. Conn. N. J. Ill. Ind. Iowa and several other free States would follow Maine, and in one year the Democratic Party would be stronger than ever it was before, and the Union stand firmer and more permanent than ever. I told him I hoped he was right as to the Union, but must beg leave to doubt. He was very much excited, and very sanguine. . . ."[59]

Democrats of more realistic mood than Pierce found no roseate glow in the prospect. As an omen of the future, Chase's triumph in Ohio, where the new legislature would be Republican by more than two to one, was worth a hundred Maines. Everything pointed to the fact that in a clear battle with the anti-Nebraska forces, the Democrats would lose all New England and New York, and would find even Pennsylvania debatable ground. The one Democratic hope was that the battle would not be clear-cut; that it would be three-cornered. The Know-Nothings offered a temporary middle ground to bewildered Whigs, old-fashioned conservatives, and men of Union-saving views who wished to suppress all sectional issues. The incongruous fusion of these groups with rabid

---

57 *National Intelligencer*, October 22, November 1, 1855. Chase had advised his friends to soft-pedal their opposition to the Know-Nothings. "My idea is fight nobody who does not fight us. We have enemies enough in the Slaveholders and their aiders." *Diary and Corr.*, 270.
58 The Know-Nothing candidate had 146,001 votes; the Fusion, 135,962; the Softs, 90,519, and the Hards, 58,394. *National Intelligencer*, November 22, 1855.
59 To H. F. French, September 23, 1855; French Papers.

nativists could not long endure, but it might serve to dish the Republicans. They would need dishing. If anyone asked at the end of 1855 what political figures the year had tossed into prominence, the answer was obvious: they were Lyman Trumbull, Salmon P. Chase, Henry Wilson, and Henry A. Wise. Three of the four were Republicans.

[ VI ]

The Know-Nothing Party had sown the whirlwind by exciting fell racial and religious prejudices, and the crop was beginning to ripen. Its anti-foreign orators denounced all alien peoples—China's "abject slaves"; France's "giddy and fickle population"; Russia's "serfs"; the dukes, lords, and earls of old England, "our ancient enemy and natural rival"; the "degraded" peoples of Southern Europe, crushed by "the incubus of Popery." They lamented that immigration was making the United States "the common sewer of the world." Jesuit intrigue, they warned, was trying to "subject our country to the dominion of the Roman hierarchy." [60] The fearful burden of pauperism, crime, insanity, and vice was all attributed to aliens. Many declared that political Romanism had already proved its power, for the Catholics had defeated Clay in 1844, and had forced Campbell into Pierce's cabinet.[61] Books of the type of Maria Monk's *Awful Disclosures* found a ready market. A publisher of 114 Fulton Street, New York, one Edward Walker, advertised the twentieth thousand of an enlarged edition of *Dr. Dowling's History of Romanism*, with 800 pages on Catholic errors and menaces. He issued a 400-page volume, *A Voice to America, or The Model Republic, Its Glory and Fall*, descanting on the danger from aliens, easy naturalization, and Rome.[62] A Nassau Street publisher was peddling a spiteful diatribe against Catholicism called *Startling Facts for Native Americans*. Venomous tracts and pamphlets were innumerable.

Fuel was added to the flame this year by a savage controversy between Erastus Brooks of the New York *Express* and Archbishop John Hughes over the church property question; while other men falsely charged Hughes with using his influence on behalf of the "Soft" faction of the Democratic Party.[63] Four State legislatures, in New York, Ohio, Massachusetts, and Connecticut, with much acrimonious discussion, enacted laws restricting the property-holding rights of the hierarchy.

60 All this in the July 4th Oration of Vespasian Ellis, 1855, to American Party adherents; *National Intelligencer*, July 7, 1855.
61 *The American Textbook for the Campaign of 1856*; pvt, Baltimore, 1856.
62 *Walker's Book-Catalogue*, 1855.
63 Henry A. Brann, *John Hughes*, 124–126. For the atrocious behavior of the "Nunnery Committee" of the Massachusetts legislature in 1855, see Ray A. Billington, *The Protestant Crusade, 1800–1860*, pp. 414, 415.

It is not strange that violence ensued. At the beginning of April a bloody election riot took place in Cincinnati between the Know-Nothings and foreign-born elements, chiefly Irish and Germans. A fierce scrimmage for possession of a cannon, and the destruction of ballot boxes in two wards, marked the combat.[64] Chicago had a riot over the liquor laws, with an anti-alien tinge. The August elections in Louisville presented disgraceful scenes of bloodshed and incendiarism. A number of houses and shops were destroyed, a German brewery was burned, and fifteen or twenty people lost their lives. According to the Louisville *Journal*, the riots were occasioned by indiscriminate and murderous assaults committed by foreigners, chiefly Irish, upon inoffensive citizens, peaceably at work;[65] but the *Journal* was a Know-Nothing sheet, and other accounts laid partial blame on the native-born. A reporter for the Louisville *Courier* recorded dreadful scenes of mob frenzy. He described poor women fleeing with their children and their little treasures brought from the old country; terror-stricken men hiding themselves in corners; furniture smashed, houses swept by flames, and the people fearful all next day that every shout might be the signal of a new attack. But worst of all were the wanton murders:[66]

Seeking to escape death from the flames, the wretched inhabitants reached the streets only to meet death in another form. As soon as one appeared at a door he was fired at and generally killed. A number were taken off badly wounded, and others, shot to pieces, returned to the burning houses, preferring rather to be burnt than to meet the infuriated mob. One man escaping in woman's clothes was detected and shot. Another who came out covered with a blanket and leaning on the arm of his wife was torn away and deliberately shot. To escape from within to the street without being killed was almost a matter of impossibility. How many of these miserable people, thus caged in their own houses, were burnt alive, there can be no computation. The blackened and charred remains of some have been discovered.

This was merely the beginning. Election riots, with much loss of life and property, the direct result of the Know-Nothing agitation, occurred during the next three years in Baltimore, New Orleans, Washington, and other cities. In Baltimore particularly the spectacle of strong bodies of Democrats and "Americans," each armed with muskets, pistols, knives, and clubs, swaying in battles which terrorized large parts of the city, attracted national attention. The Know-Nothings introduced a new element of violence into American political contests, and one which it required a generation to eradicate.

64 *National Intelligencer*, April 5, 1855.
65 Quoted in *National Intelligencer*, August 11, 1855.
66 *Idem.* For facts on the violence aroused by the Know-Nothings in New Orleans, St. Louis, Lawrence, Mass., and other places, see Billington, *Protestant Crusade*, 421.

## [ VII ]

Violence was also the note of the year in foreign relations. The adventures of Quitman had happily proved abortive, and the operations of Kinney inconclusive; but these men were thrown into eclipse by the brilliant successes of William Walker, who in the latter half of 1855 made himself master of all Nicaragua. Kinney was left without support or prospects, for the new ruler regarded him with hostility.

Walker outfitted his expedition quite openly in San Francisco. He equipped the leaky old brig *Vesta* with a deckhouse and other conveniences, recruited about sixty heavily-armed "emigrants," and sailed on May 4th, actually using the crew of the revenue cutter *Marcy* to help him bend his sails. He made no secret of his intention of invading Nicaragua—the term is justified, though he was invited by one faction—and taking a hand in the civil conflict then raging in the exhausted republic. Early in June he reached Realejo on the west coast, joined forces with a somewhat larger body of insurgents, and began hostilities with the government army. Many of his men were Mexican War veterans, each was armed with a Mississippi rifle, two Colt's revolvers, and a bowie-knife, and they thirsted for combat. Within a month Walker had given the Legitimists a taste of his prowess. Attacking a force of five hundred, his party of fifty-five all but routed them, inflicting two hundred casualties with but slight loss to itself. A series of marches followed, in which the insurgents lost a small number of men, and the Legitimists many.[67]

The superior weapons, energy, and leadership of the Americans quickly gave them full control of the country. Four and a half months after landing, Walker had captured the capital, Granada, dispersed the enemy, and become virtual dictator. Under terms of peace which he formally signed with General Ponciano Corral, a native figurehead was set up as provisional President, while Walker was recognized as general-in-chief of the armies.[68] This marauding expedition, deplorable in itself, was still more unfortunate as a precedent which might encourage other restless American spirits to undertake similar enterprises. Walker, who was little better than a freebooter, had sacrificed American lives, impressed American steamers to aid him in his undertaking, and injured American property. He had done a grievous wrong to the Nicaraguan people. Worst of all, his lawless course, unchecked by his own government, had brought the

67  Laurence Greene, *The Filibuster: The Career of William Walker*, 62ff.
68  The best account of all this is in Walker's book of 1860, *The War in Nicaragua*, supplemented by W. O. Scroggs, *Filibusters and Financiers*. The *National Intelligencer*, November 8, 1855, has a long account of the battle of Rivas, describing how "the Americans lost but ten of their men in six hours' fighting; of the enemy upwards of one hundred were killed on the spot."

probity, good faith, and peaceful intentions of the American nation into discredit throughout Europe and Latin America.[69]

Large reinforcements promptly came out from California. Scenes of excitement were witnessed in San Francisco when the Transit Company steamer *Uncle Sam* sailed with a new troop of adventurers and about three hundred stand of arms—part of them stolen from the Manhattan Fire Company in San Francisco and the militia armory of Sacramento, which had been entirely divested of weapons and ammunition. The wharf was densely packed, and numerous men who wanted to get aboard and join Walker failed to find a place. Our chargé in Nicaragua, Wheeler, at once publicly acknowledged the independence and sovereignty of the new republic, and assured the Walker-Rivas government of the "kind regards and good wishes entertained towards it by the Chief Magistrate of the United States." This cordiality was not diminished even when General Corral was shot in the plaza at Granada on November 7th on a charge of treasonable correspondence. His arrest, trial, and execution had all taken place within eighty hours.[70]

That important economic and political interests stood behind Walker was clear. Some Eastern groups disliked his advent to power. "He has complete control," wrote a New Yorker, "of that great Nicaragua route of travel between the Atlantic and Pacific, which will have to be abandoned, if he is not forcibly obliged to change his conduct; for at present the route is not safe either for persons or property. He has already seized some of the treasure that came by a previous steamer, and the last arrival from San Juan did not bring a dollar of gold, as shippers at San Francisco would not trust any of their treasure through the territory occupied by this filibuster; and, until some favorable change takes place, the route will of course be avoided by both passengers and shippers of bullion." [71] The banking house of Lucas, Turner & Co. in San Francisco wrote the Metropolitan Bank in New York that they had not sent an expected consignment of specie by the *Sonora* because Walker had established himself at San Juan del Sur, and his pseudo-government "might levy a tax probably of a hundred per cent on the transit of treasure through his dominions—a consequence not unlikely to arise from his necessities, if not from the positive piratical

69  But many Americans hoped for constructive work from Walker. He may fail, said the New York *Evening Post;* "but there is reason to believe that in Nicaragua at least the sceptre has departed from the degenerate descendants of the Spanish conquerors, and that the destiny of Central America is now more manifestly than ever placed in Anglo-American hands. An efficient republican system may yet be adopted there under Yankee auspices, and the perplexed 'Central American question' . . . may be settled by the irresistible law of modern colonization." Quoted in *National Intelligencer*, December 1, 1855.

70  Walker explains in *The War in Nicaragua* that he decided in Corral's case that mercy to one would be injustice to many.

71  San Francisco *Herald*, quoted in *National Intelligencer*, October 18, 1855.

character he and his associates established in their former government of Sonora." [72]

But the Accessory Transit Company, with the unscrupulous Charles Morgan and C. K. Garrison still in control, rejoiced when Walker triumphed. The president of the company promptly penned a letter of congratulation to the stockholders. Eighteen months of civil war, he wrote, had ended in the restoration of peace in Nicaragua. Business would again prosper. "The revolution is now over. The new government, friendly to the company and respecting its vested rights, will at all times be ready to protect it should protection be required, and we shall no longer have to invoke the aid of our own government. The isthmus is free from disease, and the future of the company promises a business as successful as can be desired." The Philadelphia *News* pointed out the alliance between Walker and the Transit Company. Any veil which covered the company's assistance was too transparent to afford a disguise. "The forced loan paid by its agent at Virgin Bay to Walker; the stoppage of one of its steamships on Lake Nicaragua by an unarmed schooner belonging to Walker and his allies, the Nicaraguan rebels, together with many other acts no better disguised, are all matters understood by everybody who has given any attention to the subject." [73]

And what was the Transit Company's motive? It was bound by charter to pay ten thousand dollars a year to the Nicaraguan government, and was in arrears on these sums since 1849, while it owed still other payments. It expected to be relieved from these dues by the friendly Walker, while it anticipated advantages in land-grants and other favors.

As for Southern expansionists, they were jubilant over Walker's success. New recruits steadily dribbled into his army, for his position on the Isthmus made it possible for adventurous young men to embark as "passengers," and from every boatload travelling through Nicaragua he obtained a few. A public meeting was shortly held in New Orleans to raise money for his war-chest. Pierre Soulé expatiated on the sufferings of the Nicaraguan people, the duty of Americans to fly to their aid, and the greatness of Walker in meeting the occasion. In Gallic rhetoric he pictured the glories of manifest destiny, the future greatness of Central America, and the happiness of the Gulf States when the "Young South" should realize its dream of expansion. Pointing to British cannon levelled at New Orleans from the Bay Islands, he asserted that "the Monroe Doctrine must and shall be enforced." Walker would of course be opposed by "the evil spirit in the North," for the North hated expansion southward. But if properly aided he would in a few weeks "sweep the Costa Ricans

72 *Idem.*
73 November 7, 1855.

like dust from the face of the earth"; would gain the joyful coöperation of Honduras and San Salvador; and would bring into existence a grand Central American federation linked with the United States. He declared Walker's $250,000 bond issue an admirable investment, and the crowd at the St. Louis Hotel forthwith bought several thousand dollars' worth.[74]

Throughout summer and fall, reinforcements openly left for Walker's standard. The leader kept in San Francisco a regular recruiting and financial agent, Charles Gilman, who had lost a leg in the Lower California expedition. One ship, the *Cortez*, left San Francisco with fifty-five men aboard, and a large stock of firearms and ammunition. The depression that had settled down upon placer mining in California stimulated enlistment. "Indeed, if accounts may be trusted," commented the New York *Evening Post*, "every steamer of the Transit Company not only drops the regular detachment of Walker men, but also a score or two of 'through' passengers from the gold regions, who yield to the fascination of settling in a new country and founding a new republic." It was not until the closing days of 1855 that Pierce by special proclamation warned citizens not to enlist for military operations in Nicaragua.[75]

[ VIII ]

Most disturbing of all was the stormcloud which lowered dark on Kansas hills and prairies, and which now began to mutter thunder and send forth fitful spears of lightning. All summer an armed collision between freesoil settlers and pro-slavery forces had become increasingly probable. When the so-called Wakarusa War of December, 1855, opened, battle and carnage seemed likely to begin at any moment. They were avoided only by the frantic efforts of a few leading men, but all the materials for guerrilla fighting remained.

The Wakarusa War might better be called the Wakarusa Demonstrations; a demonstration by Missouri border men against the freesoil center of Lawrence, and a counter-demonstration by the Lawrence garrison against the "border ruffians." These threatening movements were not provoked by the constitutional convention which the freesoil men held at Topeka between October 23rd and November 11th, with James H. Lane as president and thirty-four delegates in attendance. This body drew up a serviceable constitution, which prohibited slavery after July 4, 1857, placed the temporary capital at Topeka, and provided

---

74 *National Intelligencer*, May 6, 1856.
75 December 8, 1855; just in time to prevent the sailing of a steamer from New York with between three and four hundred Nicaraguan adventurers. *National Intelligencer*, December 25, 27, 1855. But Pierce was still willing to favor the Walker regime. It was recognized the following May in order to discourage the British from supporting Costa Rica and other Central American nations in attacking Walker. Marcy opposed the recognition, but was overridden. Bemis, *American Secretaries of State*, VI, 230.

for a list of State officers. Submitted to popular vote on December 15, the document was adopted by an overwhelming majority, 1,731 to 46. The election of officers was set for January 5, 1856, when Charles Robinson was chosen as "governor." Whether justified or unjustified by circumstances, whether a discreet or rash move, the effort of the freesoil men to perfect a government which they could place in effective rivalry to the "bogus" Shawnee Mission legislature did not at first create violent resentment. Slavery men in the Territory and Missouri simply sneered at it as a fatuously illegal performance, carrying no weight whatever. The Topeka Constitution was at once forwarded to Washington, where it was certain to find favor with the House, but to meet with contemptuous rejection at the hands of Senate and President.

Nor was ill-temper provoked by any act of Charles Robinson, who though an abolitionist was fairly moderate on most issues. Jim Lane, with his vein of malignant cunning, had failed in a bit of maneuvering that he hoped would give him the nomination for governor. The sagacious Robinson behaved circumspectly, urging upon the Topeka leaders the avoidance of any collision. Still more cautious was Amos Lawrence, writing from Massachusetts that rough policies would be indefensible and that forbearance was imperative.

What provoked the grim threat of irregular warfare was the rapid solidification of parties in the Territory. The successive meetings of the freesoil men at Big Springs and Topeka gave the Free-State Party a firm organization under effective leadership. Slavery men had expected to continue carrying everything with a high hand. They awoke from a dream of general enemy submission to find the freesoil settlers firmly organized, with leaders in Lane, Robinson, and Pomeroy whose iron determination and quick resourcefulness made them more than a match for Atchison and Stringfellow, with a growing number of energetic freesoil newspapers, and with potent allies in Northern editors and politicians. The stream of immigration constantly augmented their numbers. So long as the anti-slavery settlers had lacked unity, they were weak; but the new Free-State Party swiftly made them powerful and self-confident. To resist this organization, the slavery men met at Leavenworth on November 14, with Governor Shannon present, to organize a Law and Order Party. The crisis on the Wakarusa, a little stream flowing into the Kansas not far from Lawrence, followed a fortnight later.[76]

The details of the Wakarusa Demonstrations, long celebrated by Kansas historians and sung by Kansas bards, need not detain us. A general impression existed among slavery men, and was shared by Shannon, that the Free-State forces had a secret military organization to resist the laws and attack Southern

---

76 Leverett W. Spring, *Kansas*, 79–81; Robinson, *The Kansas Conflict*, 181–211, give accurate succinct accounts of the Wakarusa disturbances. For the crystallization of parties, see Malin, *John Brown and the Legend of '56*, 517, 518; Lawrence *Free State*, March 3, 1856.

settlers; and that a firm show of authority was needed to overawe the malcontents. A swift, hard stroke by the militia that Shannon was forming would accomplish the desired end. It would stop the machinations of what the Leavenworth gathering called "the abolition, nullification, and revolutionary party." The murder on November 21st of a young Free-State settler named Charles M. Dow set in motion a startling train of incidents. As the murderer fled to Shawnee Mission, men mustered on both sides. One of the Free-State leaders was arrested by the sheriff of Douglas County; he was rescued by his friends; and the sheriff asked the governor to call out three thousand men and enforce the laws. Only a small body of Kansas militia were ready to respond, but fully 1,200 armed Missourians, eager to teach the Free-State men a memorable lesson, marched to Shannon's assistance. Some estimates placed the Missouri army at much higher figures. They flooded into the country south of Lawrence, stopped citizens, fired hayricks, drove off horses and cattle, and prepared to level the Free-State town to the ground.[77]

But they were brought to a pause by militant preparations to give them a hot reception. Six hundred armed settlers quickly gathered in Lawrence, with more slipping in every hour. They began brisk drilling. Entrenchments were dug and five small forts constructed. Robinson was named commander-in-chief, and Lane made second in command. "Our fighting spirit is fully up," wrote a correspondent to the New York *Evening Post*. "The great difficulty is to restrain our men from making a sally upon the camp on Wakarusa."

On the other side blood ran just as hotly. Missourians chafed for battle, and one of their leaders expressed fear that when they fought their way inside Lawrence, they could not be restrained. "My deliberate opinion," wrote another, "is Lawrence will soon cease to be a habitable place." Both sides were inflamed by reports of murder and pillage. The Missourians heard that the "abolitionists" were burning the houses of pro-slavery people right and left, and driving women and children half-naked into the wintry night. Free-State men accused the "ruffians" of bloodshed and rapine. Had an attack on Lawrence begun, the loss of life might have stunned the country. Col. E. V. Sumner, commander of the national troops at Fort Leavenworth, refused to do anything without specific orders from the inert President.

But an attack was not begun. Shannon, hastening to Lawrence on December 7, interposed, and with the support of the alarmed Atchison, sought to bring about a peaceful settlement. What he observed of the Missourians on one side— he called them "a pack of hyenas," and declared them quite uncontrollable—

77 The murder of Dow and ensuing events are fully treated in Howard Report, 1042–1065. The sheriff involved, S. J. Jones, appears in this testimony as a blustering, threatening fellow. "These men that came along with me we expected would have a little fun," he said; and at another point, "By God, I will have revenge before I see Missouri."

and of the cool, shrewd Free-State leaders on the other, contributed greatly to his education. For the first time he began to throw off pro-slavery influences, and to discern that the freesoil settlers had their own case, and a good one. In the end Shannon signed a treaty with Robinson and Lane; a document in which the two Free-State chiefs declared that they had no intention of supporting any organization to resist the laws, while Shannon asserted that he had not called upon the Missourians for aid, but they had come of their own choice.[78] The armed forces on both sides disbanded.[79]

In this almost bloodless collision, the Lawrence men carried off the moral advantage. They had stood their ground, and forced the Missourians to retire. But the words in which Atchison exhorted his followers to accept the result did not augur well for continued peace. "If you attack Lawrence now," he said, "you attack as a mob, and what would be the result? You would cause the election of an abolition President, and the ruin of the Democratic party. Wait a little. You cannot now destroy these people without losing more than you would gain." Plainly, the battle was but postponed.[80]

78  This notable document is printed in full in Robinson's The Kansas Conflict, 202, 203.
79  "We are of the opinion that the Kansas bubble has burst, and that the people on both sides of the Western border are now enjoying the quiet of their homes, talking and jesting over the incidents of the late campaign," said the St. Louis Intelligencer of December 13, 1855. It believed that "what with cold weather, rain, hunger, and second sober thought," the peace would stick. But the Lexington, Mo., Citizen of December 7 printed some rather ominous correspondence. S. H. Woodson, a slavery leader, had written from Independence on December 3 urging all friends to start for the seat of war. "There is no doubt now in regard to having a fight. We all know that a great many have complained because they were disappointed when here before in regard to a fight. Say to them now is the time to show game; and if we are defeated this time, the Territory is lost to the South." On the other side, the N. Y. Evening Post printed a letter written from Lawrence while five hundred freestate men were drilling there and breathing fire and gunpowder. "The fighting spirit is fully up," it declared. "The great difficulty is to restrain our men from making a sally upon the camp on Wakarusa." When the dispersal came, a good many were disappointed at missing the fun of battle, and hoped for better luck later.
80  Spring, Kansas, 97, 98; Cf. Senator Butler in Cong. Globe, March 5, 1856.

# 12

# Crisis in Kansas and Washington

FROM THE wintry slopes of the Wakarusa valley all eyes turned by mid-December of 1855 to Washington, where the Thirty-fourth Congress had gathered for its first session. It was the first Congress of a new party, the Republicans, and necessarily it was a Congress with many new faces.

In the House appeared a tall, spare, youngish man with bearded jaw, deep-set eyes, and determined expression, an attorney from a small county seat of central Ohio—John Sherman. He was an intensely practical man, the very type of a keen and somewhat chilly Yankee transplanted to the Middle West. At fourteen he had undertaken his first trading adventure; now at thirty-one he had acquired a modest competence, and he had recently written his brother William Tecumseh that "the spirit of the age is progressive and commercial." Having lately made a trip to the borders of Nebraska, he had views which commanded attention.[1] From South Bend, Ind., came a man ten years older and decidedly better known; Schuyler Colfax, long editor of the principal Whig journal in the northern part of his State, but now an ardent Republican. Two other newcomers were Anson Burlingame, who had been reared in Ohio and Michigan, but on graduating from Harvard Law School had taken up practise in Boston, and made his mark in Massachusetts politics; and Justin S. Morrill of Vermont, a tall, quiet, plain-mannered man with a background of storekeeping and farming, who liked to say that the escutcheon of his family was a blacksmith's hammer, but who combined sagacity and integrity in a fashion that was to give him an influential career. On the Democratic side, Cobb, Stephens, and others shook hands warmly with a famous newcomer, the short, whiskery Quitman.

The most striking of the new Senatorial figures was the rugged, sturdy "cobbler of Natick," Henry Wilson. No man there had been tempered in sterner fires of hardship. The son of an impoverished day-laborer, a "bound-out" lad who worked ten years for board, clothing, a month's schooling each winter, and a final quittance of six sheep and a yoke of oxen, he had educated himself

[1] John Sherman, *Recollections of Forty Years*, I, chs. 3–5; T. E. Burton, *John Sherman*, 8ff.

by incessant reading. Slowly he had struggled up the ladder—cobbler, petty shoe-manufacturer, schoolteacher, legislator, editor. A visit which he made in early life to Virginia for health implanted in him a loathing for slavery. He saw families parted at the auction block in Washington, and left that city (as he later said) "with the unalterable determination to give all that I had, and all that I hoped to have, of power, to the cause of emancipation in America."

Though not a man of Sumner's intellectual power, of Rufus Choate's penetration and wit, or of Everett's Ciceronian eloquence, Wilson brought the Senate virtues of a high type. He had a strong body capable of enormous labor, a stout heart which flinched at nothing, and a clear head. He was always in his place, he never neglected a duty, and when he took up a subject, he toiled until he had mastered it. Conscious of a defective education, he eschewed ornament in his speeches, giving all his attention to a straightforward statement of facts and ideas. Though he pursued with undeviating tenacity the two great objects of his life, the liberation of the slaves and the betterment of the workingman's lot, and though he never minced words, he was by no means intolerant. Whenever possible he spoke kindly of Southerners, expressing a belief that if encouraged and shown the true path, they would at no distant date get rid of slavery.[2] The other principal new Senator, Lyman Trumbull, was an able, calm, statesmanlike man, destined to prove in a dramatic impeachment trial his power to resist the fanatics of his party, and in a period of social turmoil his ability to accept radical new politico-economic ideas.

## [ I ]

The atmosphere of Washington, often intemperately partisan in the days of Whigs and Democrats, was rendered more feverish than ever by the appearance of the powerful new party which many Democratic politicians habitually represented as "abolitionist" and "disunionist." As one editor remarked, for months Chase, Seward, Sumner, Wilson, and other Republicans had now been held up in certain areas as monsters steeped in conspiracy. The national capital ought to have been a more reasonable place than the country at large. Instead, the disposition of members to collect in sectional boarding-house or hotel groups, the desire to speak lurid words for Buncombe County, the leadership of extremists in caucus gatherings, the trumpetings of the *Union, National Era,* and other radical journals, made the city a boiling caldron of party antagonisms. All the froth of the pot rose to the top in the Speakership contest which held the House deadlocked for two months.

2 For example, *Cong. Globe,* 33d Cong., 2d sess., 238. A biography of Wilson (the old volume by Nason and Russell being wholly inadequate) is much needed.

The initial fault could be laid at the Democratic door. The House membership was roughly classified as 108 Republican, 83 Democratic, and 43 Know-Nothing or American. Reasonable Democrats did not want to organize the House, for they would never be able to muster a majority behind any Democratic measure. The party might well have assented to a fairminded Republican. But the Saturday evening before Congress met a Democratic caucus adopted defiant resolutions, declaring that the recent elections had sustained both the Kansas-Nebraska Act and the doctrines of civil and religious liberty so violently assailed by the Know-Nothings, and that the Democratic members would keep their lines adamant against opponents of every description. The caucus then nominated for the Speakership William A. Richardson of Illinois, distinguished as a champion in carrying the Kansas-Nebraska Act through the House; a man highly offensive to all anti-Nebraska people, his very name anathema.

The idea of a moderate Speaker instantly perished. After first scattering their votes, and then fruitlessly trying to elect an old freesoil Whig of Ohio, Lewis D. Campbell, 105 Republicans concentrated (at the suggestion of a body of Northwestern members) upon Nathanial P. Banks of Massachusetts, who had shaken the dust of Democracy from his garments when the Kansas-Nebraska bill was introduced, and moved through Know-Nothingism into the Republican ranks. Naturally the Democrats detested him. Most Know-Nothings first fell in behind Humphrey Marshall, Representative from bloodstained Louisville, then turning to Henry M. Fuller. By the day before Christmas, when the sixty-eighth ballot was taken, Banks had 101 votes, Richardson 72, and Fuller 31, with eleven for minor figures.

Day after day the stupid, irritating procedure ground on with vote after vote, caucus after caucus, speech after speech. Strong personal as well as party feeling was aroused. The Republican majority was deeply hostile to half a dozen men elected on anti-Nebraska platforms who declined to support Banks. Newspapers in every section expressed growing indignation. The government, said the *National Intelligencer* in mid-January, had been brought to a point of virtual dissolution, where nothing but its innate strength maintained it.[3]

Much time was wasted in propounding strings of questions to the candidates, an exercise which inspired other members to "define their positions." Banks was asked by Barksdale of Mississippi whether he believed in the equality of the white and black races in the United States, and wished to promote that equality by legislation. He responded that it seemed to be the general law that the weaker of two juxtaposed races was absorbed or disappeared altogether. "Whether the black race . . . is equal to the white race, can only be determined

3 January 14, 1856.

by the absorption or disappearance of one or the other, and I propose to wait until the respective races can be properly subjected to this philosophical test before I give a decisive answer." This elicited roars of laughter. So did another member's satirical question whether each candidate believed in a future state, and if so, whether he thought it would be a free or a slave state. Pennington of New Jersey replied that there were two future states, one much hotter than the other, and it was a fair inference that this torrid land lay on the south side of the line and was a slave state.

It was to the House's credit that despite the prolonged friction no personal violence marred its sessions. One heated member from Arkansas, Albert Rust, did assault Horace Greeley, but that was outside the chamber. Even this episode had its humorous aspect. Rust, a six-footer of two hundred pounds, said that he approached Greeley not to attack him, but merely to expostulate regarding the *Tribune's* criticisms. But when he inquired of Greeley, "Would you resent an insult?" the editor rejoined, "I don't know, sir," in such a tone that it provoked the Congressman to strike him! [4] At times the House found relaxation from the strain in rowdy disorder. "Such a scene we have passed through you can hardly imagine," Justin S. Morrill wrote to his wife one January evening. "Mr. Cullen of Delaware, Mr. Bowie of Maryland, and Campbell of Kentucky have been very drunk and others a little drunk. We have kept good-natured, silly, and noisy." [5]

Finally, at the opening of February, the long struggle ended. A rule to elect the Speaker by plurality vote passed, whereupon Banks was chosen by 103 votes to 100 for Aiken of South Carolina. "Licked, by thunder!" yelled a Southern member. But a pleasant scene followed. Aiken claimed the privilege, which was his by House precedent, of escorting Banks to the Speaker's chair, and the chamber saw the gallant South Carolinian, owner of hundreds of slaves at his Jehossee Island plantation, march to the rostrum arm in arm with the politician sprung from the Waltham cotton-mills. Banks was soon to prove not only one of the most efficient, but one of the most impartial, of all Speakers; for he insisted that his post was purely executive and parliamentary, and was not to be used for partisan ends. Nevertheless, his elevation was regarded by Republicans as a signal victory—the greatest they had yet gained. Jubilation wreathed the faces of the majority members busy shaking hands and clapping each others' shoulders; while Waterloo sat on the countenances of the Democrats.

It was the first great victory, exclaimed the New York *Tribune*, obtained within the memory of living men by Freedom over Slavery.[6] Honest Joshua Giddings, who as the oldest member in unbroken service was deputed to admin-

4 N. Y. *Weekly Tribune*, February 2, 1856.
5 W. B. Parker, *Justin S. Morrill*, 63.
6 N. Y. *Weekly Tribune*, February 9, 1856.

ister the oath to Banks, murmured with heartfelt emotion: "I have attained the highest point of my ambition. *I am satisfied.*" [7]

## [ II ]

In one sense it was true, as the London *Daily News* remarked, that the speakership contest demonstrated the prosperous position of the republic; if an enemy had stood at the gates or a commercial crisis been raging, such delays would not have been endured; while Old World nations had the wolf constantly at the door, America could afford leisure and procrastination.[8] In another sense the government had no time to squander. The Kansas question filled exciting columns in every day's newspapers. The Senate met to find Wilson Shannon's nomination as governor laid before it—and hotly resisted. The House met to find two rivals each claiming admission as Territorial delegate: the frank, youthful, prepossessing John W. Whitfield, chosen the previous spring in that "regular" election which turned out to be so irregular, and the firmly-knit, middle-sized, grave-mannered Andrew H. Reeder, chosen by the Free-State settlers in the fall. Around Kansas most of the business of Congress in 1856 was plainly destined to revolve.

In view of the conflict between two rival governments, and the imminent danger of civil war, an efficient President could not have hesitated to take three steps: first, to maintain enough troops in the Territory to guarantee order; second, to bring about a careful investigation of the charges and countercharges in the area; and third, to see to the holding of a new election which should express the will of bona fide residents and no others. Unhappily, Pierce was neither efficient nor impartial. Everyone knew that he was sorely perplexed. It was said that, since Marcy refused to give any judgment, and since McClelland in the Interior Department leaned as notoriously to the Free-State side as Davis in the War Department did to the pro-slavery party, he was relying chiefly on Caleb Cushing's advice.[9] But the President seemed in no hurry to commit himself. His annual message, concerned chiefly with Central America, the Fugitive Slave Act, dangers to the Union, and theories of government, was brief and orphic in its paragraph on Kansas affairs. It asserted little beyond the truism that the people of a Territory must be protected in the right to determine their own institutions without interference on the part of citizens of any State.

Finally, in a special message of January 24, 1856, Pierce stated his conclusions

7 Julian, *Giddings*, 326. Hundred-gun salutes were fired in Maine, Massachusetts, and Illinois; Fred H. Harrington, "The First Northern Victory," *Journal of Southern History*, V, 186–205.

8 Quoted in *National Intelligencer*, January 26, 1856.

9 N. Y. *Weekly Tribune*, December 15, 1855.

and policy on Kansas. He denounced Governor Reeder for delay in reaching the Territory and holding elections; attacked the emigrant aid societies for designs and acts which had aroused intense irritation in Missouri, "whose domestic peace was thus the most directly endangered"; upheld the Shawnee Mission legislature on the ground that Reeder had certified its legality; endorsed its laws with the argument that a President had no right to ask whether a statute was wise or unwise, just or unjust—the only question was whether it was constitutional; and proposed that the Shawnee Mission legislature take steps to organize Kansas as a State by passing an act for the election of a constitutional convention. He declared that it was his duty to exert the whole power of the Federal Executive to support order in the Territory and enforce territorial legislation; and he characterized the Free-State movement, with the writing of the Topeka constitution and the election of Governor Robinson, as "of revolutionary character." If the movement led to organized resistance by force to the organic act or national government, it would be "treasonable insurrection."

Granting the President's assumptions regarding the legal position of the Shawnee Mission legislature and the validity of its laws, his conclusions were logical and proper. But what assumptions they were! Fully two-thirds of the votes polled for this legislature had been cast by Missourians, whose election-day invasion had been marked by violence, fraud, and general intimidation. Even the freesoil stronghold of Lawrence, known to be five to one against slavery, had been overwhelmed by these border forces, and had apparently given a large majority to a pro-slavery ticket. Pierce knew of the wholesale inquities of this election; he knew that when he wrote of "angry accusations that illegal votes had been polled abounding on all sides" he misrepresented the situation, for substantially all the wrongful acts had been committed on *one* side; [10] and he was well aware that Reeder's validation of a majority of the returns had been quickly followed by his emphatic and horrified repudiation of them. As for the laws which the President declared he would enforce, they included a statute making any kind of anti-slavery activity a crime, and another under which county officers for Kansas, including the sheriffs who executed this Draconian enactment, were appointed for six years in advance. Jefferson Davis and Cushing may not have guided Pierce's hand in writing this message, but if they had its language would not have read differently.

Pierce's message, in fact, went far toward giving the dubious acts of the

10 Pierce's old friend B. B. French later wrote his brother, as clerk of the House Committee on Claims, that he was daily at work examining a parcel of claims referred to that body to gain payment for damages. "There are about 500 of them. I have waded through about 100—and the evidence gives a minute history of how like a pack of infernal devils the border ruffians acted out there." Most claims referred to the later period of active civil war in Kansas, but the statement holds good of some "ruffians" from the start. October 28; French Papers.

Free-State Party in Kansas a justification which they had hitherto lacked. The gatherings at Big Springs and Topeka had followed a highly irregular course. Instead of contenting themselves with a dignified protest to the country, and an appeal to the national government for new and fair elections, these assemblages had taken intransigent and clearly extra-legal steps. Acting on the supposed precedent set by the people of Michigan and California when they applied for admission without a previous enabling act of Congress, the Free-State men had plunged ahead with their own Constitution and government. But in Michigan and California it was the whole people who had acted; in Kansas it was one party. In Michigan and California no revolt had been organized against authorities claiming to be duly constituted by the national government; in Kansas such a revolt was the essence of the situation. The unhappy freesoil settlers of Kansas seemed to many conservative sympathizers throughout the North to have been misled by the violent demagogue Jim Lane, the abolitionist-minded Robinson, and the politically ambitious Pomeroy. In Republican quarters there had certainly been too much disposition to make Kansas a tail to the party kite, and to magnify local abuses and disorders.

Nothing could have justified the extreme acts of the Topeka movement except clear evidence that President Pierce and the national government would furnish no redress; that the freesoil Kansans must strike hard for themselves, or be lost. Until the message of January 24th that justification was lacking. But now Pierce furnished it; he proved that he was so completely on the side of Atchison and Shawnee that no hope of justice could be placed in him. He demonstrated that the Free-State Party had been right when it dropped compromise and appeasement, and chose militancy.[11]

While from the South came a rumble of applause for the President's message, the governor of Ohio suddenly transfixed public attention by appearing in the lists as champion of free Kansas. In a special message to the legislature Chase

[11] A great deal of meaning may be read into the statement which a new governor was shortly to send Pierce: "Let us go back then to the origin of this Kansas difficulty and see what was the agitating cause, or causes, and let us candidly examine whether or not *our friends* were faultless. From the most reliable information I am satisfied that there was a settled determination in *high quarters* to make this a slave State *at all hazards*, that that policy was communicated to agents here, and that most of the public officers sent here were secured for its success. . . . This virulent spirit of dogged determination to *force* slavery into this Territory, has overshot its mark, and raised a storm, which nothing but an honest return to the beneficent provisions of our Organic Act can quell. Lecompte, Donaldson, Clarke, Woodson, *Calhoun*, and Isaacs, were prominent actors in this fearful tragedy, and willing tools to carry out this wicked policy. *They have, therefore, destroyed their public usefulness,* and their removal would be hailed with a tumult of joy by the entire population." John W. Geary, Lecompton, December 22, 1856, to Pierce; Pierce Papers. These words were written by a Democrat who, as he said, despised the abolitionist creed. The unfairness of Federal officeholders and lawlessness of Missouri invaders in Kansas did not justify the Topeka movement; the readiness of the Pierce Administration to uphold this unfairness and abet this lawlessness did.

capped a brief summary of events in the territory with a letter from Lane and Robinson dated January 21, 1856, asking for assistance. "We have authentic information," they wrote, "that an overwhelming force of the citizens of Missouri are organizing upon our border, amply supplied with artillery, for the avowed purpose of invading our territory, demolishing our towns, and butchering our unoffending Free-State citizens." What could Ohio do? Chase asked. It could express the sense of the people of Ohio in resolutions addressed to Congress; it could commend the cause of Kansas to the warm sympathy of the people; and it could urge her prompt admission with a freesoil Constitution. Appropriate resolutions were forthwith introduced. The fact that one State so promptly stood up against the President stirred a multitude of Northern hearts.[12]

[ III ]

Forthwith the debate in Congress sprang to life. It was stimulated by the action of the President in issuing a proclamation on February 11 warning both sides in Kansas to desist from violence, and placing Federal troops at Forts Leavenworth and Riley at the disposition of Governor Shannon—who, after a hard struggle, was confirmed. Colonels Sumner and Cooke were instructed to communicate with the President before taking any drastic steps, and a rumor that they had been authorized to arrest members of the Topeka Convention was denied. But many believed that Shannon would now act imperiously and that Pierce would support him.[13]

The dispute between Reeder and Whitfield as to the seat of the Kansas delegate gave the House an opportunity to intervene. The Committee on Elections demanded authority to send for persons and papers in the contest. Southern members earnestly opposed the proposal. As the debate proceeded it grew heated. Orr of South Carolina proposed a narrower course, which actually meant sending two Southern lawyers to Kansas. Dunn of Indiana suggested a much broader inquiry: that the Speaker should appoint three members "to inquire into and collect evidence in regard to the troubles in Kansas generally,

12 Governor Chase was soon to write Governor Grimes of Iowa urging prompt and joint action by the two States to protect freesoil settlers. Hart, *Chase*, 171, 172.
13 N. Y. *Weekly Tribune*, February 23, 1856. It must be borne in mind that Pierce was now held in general contempt. "I have been in Washington several times this winter," one of Buchanan's friends had written early in 1855, "for a few days each time, looking after our fee bill, etc. etc. Dined at the President's three times, in a very quiet manner, and each time was more and more charmed with the conversational powers of the President. He is personally very popular—but his Administration, I regret to say, is an utter and entire failure. . . . It is melancholy to hear the contemptuous manner he is personally alluded to by some of the most distinguished Senators and members of our party." January 29, 1855; Buchanan Papers.

and particularly in regard to any fraud or force attempted or practised in reference to any of the elections which have taken place in said Territory"; to investigate all acts of violence or public disturbance; and to take evidence, examine books and papers, and make other researches under power to cite obstructive persons to the House for contempt. President Pierce was requested to furnish military protection, if needed, to the committee. On March 19 the House boldly took the bit between its teeth. It seized upon Dunn's broad resolution and passed it by a vote of 101 to 92. "A triumph for free Kansas," "an glorious day's work," exclaimed freesoil observers. Their jubilance was justified, for this was the most constructive step Congress had yet taken on Kansas.[14]

Meanwhile, the Democratic majority in the Senate had been awaiting the return of Douglas to furnish them a resourceful leadership on the Kansas issue. For the first two months of the session ill health kept him continuously absent. But on March 12, as chairman of the Committee on Territories, he presented a report which thoroughly discussed the question. Once more he covered familiar terrain in reviewing the history of slavery and its constitutional position, and once more he argued at length for the Kansas-Nebraska bill. But he broke new ground in a violent attack on the Emigrant Aid Societies of the North, a denunciation of the Topeka Convention, and a threat that the military power of the Federal government would be used to maintain the existing territorial regime.

Douglas took the position that the legislature which President Pierce had recognized must at all costs be upheld as the embodiment of law, order, and legitimacy. Its acts were right and lawful; those who repudiated its laws were resisting both the proper territorial authority and the national government. Saying much of the activities of the Emigrant Aid Societies, he ignored the far more reprehensible interference of the Border Ruffians. Indeed, speaking that same day on his report, he characterized opposition to the existing legislature as treason and rebellion. "We understand that this is a movement for the purpose of producing a collision, with the hope that civil war may be the result if blood shall be shed in Kansas. Sir, we are ready to meet that issue. We stand upon the Constitution and the laws of the land. Our position is, the maintenance of the supremacy of the laws, and the putting down of violence, fraud, treason, and rebellion against the government."[15]

Three Senators joined Douglas in signing the majority report, while Collamer of Vermont stood alone in presenting a minority statement.[16] No document could have been more calmly resolute than his. He vigorously maintained the

14 N. Y. *Weekly Tribune*, March 22, 1856.
15 *Cong. Globe*, March 12, 1856; 34th Cong., 1st sess., p. 639. Sumner had just said that the issue "threatens to scatter from its folds civil war." *Ibid.*
16 Both reports, printed as Senate documents, were scattered broadcast, as were pamphlet editions of the speeches in the ensuing debates. Douglas's report appeared in German as well as in English. Milton, *Eve of Conflict*, 221.

right of all Americans who believed that Kansas should be freesoil to organize associations, and strive to promote free supremacy—nay, the duty of so acting; just as it was the right and duty of those who believed that Kansas should be slave territory to take similar lawful action. Men who did this were merely giving effect to their honest convictions of the public good. With equal firmness, he defended the very questionable Topeka movement. The freesoil men of Kansas had initiated it, he declared, because they saw no other means of righting an intolerable wrong, and their efforts to gain redress had so far been peaceful, constitutional, and entirely justifiable. Congress in his opinion ought to restore the Missouri Compromise; but if it would not do that, then it should annul all the acts of the existing legislature, and direct a reorganization of the government, with proper safeguards against illegal voting and violence.[17]

Douglas's reading of the majority report occupied two hours; Collamer's reading of the minority report one hour. They had no sooner finished than a vehement and mutually exasperating debate began. Sumner sprang up to say that the majority report smothered the true issue, while in Collamer's document it stood forth as a pillar of fire to guide the country. This issue was plain: the Emigrant Aid Company had used none but correct methods in Kansas, while the Border Ruffians had resorted to the grossest lawlessness. He must repel at once, he said, the attack of Douglas on the brave New England organization. "That company has done nothing for which it can be condemned under the laws and Constitution of the land. These it has not offended in letter or spirit; not in the slightest letter or remotest spirit. It is true, it has sent men to Kansas; and had it not a right to send them? It is true, I trust, that its agents love freedom and hate slavery. And have they not a right to do so? Their offense has this extent, and nothing more. Sir, to the whole arraignment of that Company, in the report of the Committee on Territories, I now for them plead 'Not Guilty!' and confidently appeal to the country for . . . honorable acquittal. . . ."

Douglas replied that the true issue was not between Northern legality and Border Ruffian illegality. The true issue, he said, was between outside interference and no outside interference in the affairs of Kansas. *All* intermeddling was a violation of the principles of the Kansas-Nebraska Act. "The minority report advocates foreign interference; we advocate self-government and non-interference. We are ready to meet this issue; and there will be no dodging." [18]

Unquestionably Sumner was right and Douglas was in the wrong. No reason

17 Collamer had previously taken steps to have the offensive territorial laws of Kansas printed by the government for public distribution; *Cong. Globe*, 34th Cong., 1st sess., 449.
18 *Idem*, 639. Debate was postponed for a week or more ·while members studied the reports. Meanwhile Butler and Seward discussed the question òf the population required in Kansas before admission; Butler demanding the Federal representation number, now over 90,000, Seward saying that the existing population (which he estimated at 25,000) was sufficient.

in law or equity existed why residents of slave States should not organize to promote their own type of migration to Kansas, and residents of free States a migration of freesoilers. The grand question of the destiny of Kansas did not affect its people alone. It was a matter of direct concern to Missourians and others that Kansas become a slave State; of direct concern to the Northwest and other areas that it become a free State. The real question was whether the methods used by outsiders were legal or illegal, and in view of the terms of the Kansas-Nebraska Act, the national government had a solemn responsibility to see that self-government by actual settlers was fully protected.

Yet Douglas stuck to his guns, and on March 20 made a long speech, heralded by much beating of Democratic tom-toms, to elaborate his position. His health was still precarious; he apologized for saying so much in one day on the ground that if he stopped, physical exhaustion would prevent him from rising again on the morrow. Some Southern Congressmen had taken the line that most allegations of border ruffian activity were false, and others grossly exaggerated. Representative Oliver of the Platte district in western Missouri protested that he did not *know* that a single Missourian had voted in Kansas, though some had gone over to guard the polls against abolitionist fraud and violence!

Douglas, however, admitted that fraud had occurred. He declared that it was committed under provocation; that Northern freesoilers had organized companies and poured in settlers to control Kansas, thus prompting the Missourians to send armed men across the boundary to seize Kansas voting-places. One wrong was in answer to the other, and the major blame attached to those "foreign" elements who began the contest. He further declared that the border ruffians frauds were much exaggerated in Collamer's report. It was perhaps true, he admitted, that seven of the eighteen election districts in Kansas had been carried by Missouri invasion, intimidation, and false voting, for so Reeder had certified; but the governor's acceptance of the result in the other eleven districts, which had chosen a majority both of House and Council, should be taken as final. If the election in these eleven districts was not entirely fair, then why did not the aggrieved voters file prompt complaints?—why did they not institute a contest when the legislature met?

Douglas's oratorical powers were now at their most effective pitch. Only forty-two years old this spring, he was at the height of his physical vigor. Dressed in black broadcloth and shining linen, his trim figure was full of vitality; there was nothing heavy in his thick chest, broad shoulders, and massive head, for he moved with vivacious quickness; he was one moment the picture of merry, convivial ease, the next the personification of forensic strength and power. Strongly knit, muscular, self-confident, he seemed built for combat. His lustrous eyes gleamed pugnaciously from beneath his high forehead, with the dark, scowling wrinkle set horizontally between them, and he threw his heavy brown locks back from his face with a defiant gesture. He marshalled his arguments as a general his battalions. Yet to every critical onlooker he seemed, as to Carl Schurz, rather a stalwart parliamentary pugilist than a commanding orator. Alert in retort, crafty in the manipulation of an argument, redoubtable and unscrupulous in attack, he seemed momentarily to sweep all opposition before him; yet he never quite convinced wary men, for his ideas lacked deep sincerity, and his manners had always a touch of the barroom. Mrs. Stowe was fascinated by the grace and force of his gestures, the clarity and melody of his voice; Greeley was impressed by his deliberate speech and air of latent power. But these judges agreed that he was a master of special pleading, deliberately confused his hearers, and made the most of quibbles and technicalities. He seemed dazzling—until men could think over his arguments.[19]

So it was in this speech. Those who could temporarily ignore his fallacies found his picture of an ideal sectional truce delightfully engaging. "When the time shall arrive," he asserted, "and I trust that it is near at hand, that the cardinal principle of self-government, non-intervention, and State equality shall be recognized as irrevocable rules of action, binding on all good citizens who regard, and are willing to obey, the Constitution as the supreme law of the land, there will be an end of the slavery controversy in Congress and between the different sections of the Union. The occupation of political agitators whose hopes of position and promotion depend upon their capacity to disturb the peace of the country will be gone. The controversy, if continued, will cease to be a national one—will dwindle into a mere local question, and will affect only those who, by their residence in the particular State or Territory, are interested in it, and have the exclusive right to control it." He emphasized the deep apprehensions which the Emigrant Aid Societies had created; and he drew a sharp contrast between the legal territorial legislature, so justly sustained by Pierce, and the "daring and defiant revolutionists" of Topeka, engaging in "rebellion" and "treason."

But Douglas's denunciation of the Emigrant Aid Society as "that vast moneyed corporation" was gross exaggeration; the society was poor. His assertion that its colonizing activities in Kansas were as improper as French or British intervention in Cuba, since every State in its domestic policy and internal concerns "stands in the relation of a foreign power to every other State," overlooked the facts that Kansas was not a State, and the private promotion of emigration was entirely legal and proper. His effort to place the law-abiding settler from the North, come to stay, upon the same footing

19  Clark E. Carr, *The Illini*, 164; Schurz, *Reminiscences*, II, 32, 33; N. Y. *Weekly Tribune*, March 29, 1856; N. Y. *Independent*, May 1, 1856.

as the Missouri intruder who outraged the Kansas ballot and then swiftly departed, was clearly disingenuous. And his statement that the governor had given certificates to legislators from eleven districts was a legal technicality; it did not touch the equities of the issue.

## [ IV ]

By the end of March two main legislative proposals respecting Kansas were before Congress and the people, Douglas sponsoring one, Seward the other. The first looked toward admission of Kansas whenever her population should reach 93,420, the apportionment number for a Representative in Congress. The second contemplated her immediate entry into the Union under the Topeka constitution. Since the House would never consent to Douglas's bill, and the Senate would certainly reject Seward's, neither marked an advance toward a solution. It was evident that a stubborn refusal on one hand to trust Pierce, his Territorial governor, or the bogus legislature, and a fixed determination on the other not to yield an inch to the "rebel" Topeka government, was almost certain to produce a deadlock—the imminent presidential campaign heightening the general disposition to appeal to prejudice.

Douglas's bill, which under normal circumstances would have been quite acceptable, had one fatal flaw. He proposed that a census be taken under direction of the governor; that when it showed the requisite population, the legislature should provide for the election of delegates to a constitutional convention; that voting for delegates be restricted to all white males over twenty-one, actual residents in the Territory for at least six months and the district for at least three months; and that each legislative district choose twice as many delegates as it was entitled to elect legislators.[20] The flaw was that this arrangement continued indefinitely the sway of a governor, legislature, and local officers detested by a great body of Free-State settlers, and enabled them to control all detailed arrangements for the convention. At the moment Kansas had probably not more than thirty thousand white settlers; nobody knew how long it would take to reach 93,420; and meanwhile the "tyranny" of Pierce, Shannon, and the old legislature, with the abomination of the Shawnee Mission laws, would persist. How fair would be the governor's census, and how well-guarded the election of delegates? Northern freesoilers snorted with angry derision when the bill was mentioned.

Seward's bill was even more objectionable. He proposed the immediate admission of Kansas under the Topeka constitution. This constitution was avowedly made by one party, excluding all dissenting elements, and written

20  *Cong. Globe,* 34th Cong., 1st sess., 693; March 20, 1856.

under every circumstance of haste and excitement. To impose it upon the whole people of Kansas would be outrageous. The fact was that partisanship stamped both bills. Douglas's speeches were partisan efforts, and the elaborate discourse which Seward pronounced on April 9th was rampantly partisan. Both Democrats and Republicans were lashing themselves into fury, and striving to imbue calm-minded observers with their own excitement.

The speech of Seward, much better than his bill, and indeed one of the most masterly of his career, was partly a stern rebuttal of all Pierce's arguments in his special message, and partly a harsh indictment of the Administration, the Missourians, and the pro-slavery forces generally for their injustices to Kansas.[21] An earnest, deliberate, impressive delivery added to the force of the address. In his defense of the Northern States and his arraignment of Pierce's course he attained a lofty eloquence. Whereas most of Collamer's speech had dealt with constitutional and historical phases of the subject, Seward treated rather the naked realities of recent months. He vindicated the right of Northern freesoilers to assist in colonizing Kansas, pointed to the clear evidence of Missouri border aggression before any settler sent by the emigrant aid organization had reached Kansas, and exposed the hollowness of Pierce's assertion that the Northern settlers had created fears of a relentless warfare upon Missouri slavery. "I confess my surprise that the sojourners used violent language; it seems unlike them. I confess my greater surprise that the borderers were disturbed so deeply by mere words; it seems unlike them." He then dealt in detail with the evidence that Missouri interferences had been much greater and more flagrant than the Administration admitted. The President was now defending usurpation and tyranny, said the Senator.

Sparing no epithets in his allegations of invasion, violence, and crime, all excused and glazed over by the Administration, Seward equally refused to mince words in his description of the fast-gathering storm. Though Pierce was supreme trustee for the Territory, he said, not property, nor liberty, nor life, was safe. "At this day, Kansas is becoming, more distinctly than before, the scene of a conflict of irreconcilable opinions, to be determined by brute force. No immigrant goes there unarmed, no citizen dwells there in safety unarmed; armed masses of men are proceeding into the Territory, from various parts of the United States, to complete the work of invasion and tyranny which he has thus begun, under circumstances of fraud and perfidy unworthy of the character of a ruler of a free people. . . . Whether, under the circumstances, it

21 Seward of course spoke repeatedly; but this speech, occupying twenty columns of the *Cong. Globe* (34th Cong. 1st sess., Appendix, 399ff) was his main effort. He made it clear that he would oppose the entry of another slave State at any time and under every circumstance. Various Southern States had made it plain that they would regard such debarment as ground for secession.

[the conflict] can be circumscribed within the limits of the Territory of Kansas, must be determined by statesmen, from their knowledge of the courses of civil commotions which have involved questions of moral right and conscientious duty, as well as balances of political power."

During April, May, and June nearly all other national business was set aside while both chambers dealt with the Kansas issues. A single day would sometimes bring more than a dozen Senators into the fray; for example, Hamlin, Hale, Harlan, Seward, and Trumbull on the side of free Kansas, and Mason, Butler, Hayward, Benjamin, Cass, Pugh, and Rusk on the opposing side. Lovers of peace like Crittenden and Clayton wrung their hands, making no concealment of their belief that many were exploiting the situation for personal aggrandizement and party advantage. Douglas distinguished himself by energetic forays, skilful use of minor points, and sharp personal attacks; once lashing out savagely at the elder Blair, who happened into the Senate chamber, as a good Democrat fallen into "Black Republicanism"—for that phrase was already familiar. He and his former friend Jim Lane exchanged the charge of "liar" over a question of the correct text of the Topeka constitution.[22] Others flung words as hot as petards. When Hale used the term "doughfaces," Toucey of Connecticut and Pugh of Ohio rose in resentment.[23] In the House, three men made brilliant debuts on the Kansas issue: Henry Winter Davis of Maryland, handsome and suave; Henry Waldron of Michigan, a quiet, self-possessed man of businesslike qualities; and Hiram Warner of Georgia, who had been judge of the State supreme court, and whose exposition of slavery arguments possessed a truly judicial balance. In the Senate, Geyer of Missouri used his special knowledge of border conditions in a really enlightening speech.[24]

Under the exhortations of press, pulpit, and politicians, public feeling on Kansas was steadily growing more intense. In the South expectations of victory had now been raised so high that most voters would regard defeat as proof that their section had been cheated. If Kansas comes in as a free State, a Georgia observer warned Alexander H. Stephens, the masses will turn in fury on their most sagacious leaders; for they "will take no test of reliability, soundness, and good policy except success." [25] He thought that any immediate decision in favor of the anti-slavery party in the Territory would mean the defeat of the Democratic Party in the national elections. Whenever a Northern speaker in Congress taunted the South with aggressions, or referred to her supposed

22  Washington correspondence dated April 14, 1856; N. Y. *Tribune*.
23  *Cong. Globe*, 34th Cong., 1st sess., Appendix, 592.
24  Of Davis we shall hear more; a Whig of handsome bearing and eloquent speech, he had gravitated into the Know-Nothing Party, and entered the House in 1855. At this time he was conservative; he was destined to grow radical. See the life by B. C. Steiner.
25  T. W. Thomas, February 25; *Toombs, Stephens, Cobb Corr.*, 361, 362.

inferiority, his words were certain to be telegraphed throughout the slave area, leaving a seared imprint behind them; while Southern editors lustily applauded the speeches in which such champions as Clay of Alabama and Benjamin of Louisiana defended their people. Representative Preston S. Brooks of South Carolina published in the Atchison *Squatter Sovereign* of March 25th a letter lamenting that his state had not imposed a tax of a dollar a head on slaves, and used the proceeds to transport emigrants to Kansas. He took the gravest view of the issue:

The admission of Kansas into the Union as a slave state is now a point of honor with the South. . . . It is my deliberate conviction that the fate of the South is to be decided with the Kansas issue. If Kansas becomes a hireling State, slave property will decline to half its present value in Missouri as soon as the fact is determined. Then abolitionism will become the prevailing sentiment. So with Arkansas; so with upper Texas.

Already talk of civil conflict was becoming common. Hale, catching up some indiscreet remark of Jones of Tennessee about war to the knife, and the knife to the hilt, retorted in still more regrettable terms. "Sir, Puritan blood has not always shrunk even from these encounters; and when the war has been proclaimed with the knife, and the knife to the hilt, the steel has sometimes glistened in their hands; and, when the battle was over, they were not always found second best." On another occasion Butler of South Carolina burst forth:[26]

God knows, as I have said, one drop of blood shed in civil strife in this country may not only dissolve this Union, but may do worse. Sir, I have such confidence in the good sense of the country that I believe republican institutions might survive the present Union. Really it is broken already; for the spirit which cherished it has been extinguished, and the very altars upon which we ought to worship have been profaned by false fires.

The North meanwhile rang with diatribes against the border ruffians, descriptions of "fresh outrages" in Kansas, and appeals for help to the hard-pressed Free-State men. Douglas was reported to have hurled at Sumner the angry threat: "We mean to subdue you, sir!"—and every possible change was rung on the remark.[27] This spring witnessed the publication in book form of Frederick Law Olmsted's wonderfully graphic and informative 700-page volume on *A Journey in the Seaboard Slave States*, first largely presented in letters

26 Hale in *Cong. Globe*, 34th Cong., 1st sess., 496; Butler, *idem*, 587.
27 Washington correspondence N. Y. *Tribune*, March 15, editorial March 20, 1856. Douglas did in fact say in his speech on his Kansas report that he and his party were ready to require submission to the laws and constituted authorities of Kansas; "to reduce to subjection those who resist them, and to punish rebellion and treason."

to the New York *Times;* and tens of thousands of readers hung entranced over its scenes, sometimes amused, sometimes sad, more often indignant. Spring found shipments of firearms going out to the Kansas settlers—part of them intercepted in Missouri and there confiscated. The business of furnishing Sharpe's rifles at $25 apiece to freesoil men, indeed, was growing apace. In February, Eli Thayer told a meeting at Worcester, Mass., that he was a man of peace, but that the price of peace was preparedness for war, and that he would buy ten rifles if Worcester citizens would make up the number to a hundred. Before he left the hall twenty-three had been subscribed for. A month later the *Tribune,* commenting on Douglas's speech, declared that what Kansas wanted was "the spirit of martyrdom and Sharpe's rifles." [28]

## [ V ]

It was quite true that as Seward said, armed bands were now wending their way toward Kansas—along with many more unarmed. As ice broke up on the Western rivers, the press teemed with announcements of companies small and large on their way to the new Territory. Emigration this year of '56 was expected to exceed all former records. Most colonists were more intent on taking goods, livestock, and furniture than firearms, but many carried fowling-pieces, old muskets, or "common country rifles."

Atchison had issued an appeal to the slave States to send out their young men, and to "let them come well armed!" The most important unit formed in the South was that under Colonel Jefferson Buford of Alabama. He had advertised for three hundred able-bodied recruits, willing to fight if necessary, and had engaged to spend $20,000 of his own funds, giving each man twenty acres of fertile land and a guarantee of support for a year. He actually sold his slaves to provide the money, while small contributions came in from many other sources. On April 7th the battalion, said to consist of about three hundred men, left Montgomery by boat. Before going, they marched to one of the churches, where a Methodist minister prayed for divine blessing, and a Baptist clergyman, presenting Buford with a Bible, said that money had been raised to give every emigrant the holy Book. It was expected that other recruits would join them at various landings on the Alabama River, at Mobile, and at New Orleans. [29]

28 N. Y. *Tribune,* March 19, 1856. Atchison, grumbling that the Missouri legislature had lacked the "moral courage" to reëlect him, had in a letter to A. R. Corbin on December 14, 1855, plainly threatened violent acts. He declared that he had been restraining his followers, but "when I do move in earnest there will be a noise louder than thunder," and that "before the moon shall fill her hours twelve times you shall hear more of me." Rutgers College MSS.

29 Montgomery *Journal,* April 7; *National Intelligencer,* April 12, 1856; W. L. Fleming, "The Buford Expedition to Kansas," *Am. Hist. Rev.,* VI, 38–48.

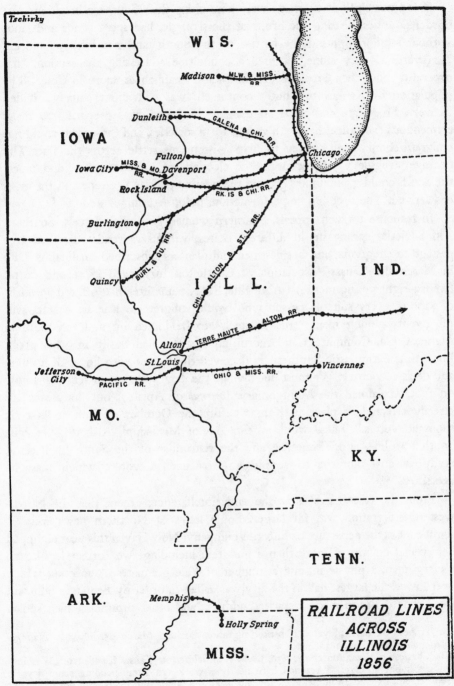

This shows main routes used to Kansas. Eastern connections are not indicated.

"Send us help!" Missourians were beseeching their Southern brethren. The border counties, bearing the brunt of the struggle, had spent funds and labor without stint in fighting the battles of the South, and not without success. "Lafayette County alone," argued a committee addressing the section, "has expended more than $100,000 in money and as much or more in time." The population of Kansas, this body continued, was still about equally divided between Free-State and Slave-State men; the North was preparing to make tremendous exertions; the South should form societies, and those who could not emigrate should send money to help Missourians settle across the line. The decisive struggle would occur in the elections of October, 1856, and unless the South could maintain her ground she would be lost. "We repeat it, the crisis has arrived. The time has come for action, bold, determined action." [30]

In response to such appeals, Southern women gave their jewels; Southern Aid Societies sprang up in different States; various railroads furnished free passage to emigrants; and businessmen and planters subscribed small sums. Late in March the Kansas Association of Charleston forwarded its second corps, twenty-eight young men. An Abbeville, S. C., committee had offered an outfit of $200 to every suitable person who would emigrate to Kansas. Atlanta sent off twenty young men, "true as steel," to be joined by a dozen more in Marietta, Ga. Committees and recruiting agents toiled busily in other areas. For a time enthusiastic Southerners deceived themselves with hopes of a quick and decisive victory. We must not divulge the details of the efficient plans now on foot, exclaimed the Montgomery *Journal* of April 7, but "measures are already effected to place in Kansas before the October election at least six thousand voters." These would stream out of Mississippi, Alabama, Georgia, South Carolina, and Tennessee; and the remainder of the South "will stand ready at any moment to supply any balance of voters which may be necessary." [31]

From the free States came the same intelligence, except that the Northwestern emigration was far larger. Some items of Northern news were as significant as the departure of Buford's company. New Haven this year equipped her special colony of more than a hundred, including two former legislators, a clergyman, a physician, and a number of Yale graduates. A meeting which overflowed the largest hall in the city was called to order by Benjamin Silliman; Dr. Leonard Bacon made a spirited address; and other prominent men spoke.

<hr />

30 Appeal of the Lafayette Kansas Emigration Society, March 25, 1856, in *National Intelligencer*, April 12, 1856.
31 Charleston *News*, March 27, 1856. J. W. Whitfield wrote Kansas friends from Washington December 4, 1855: "I reached here nearly a week ago after spending some days in Georgia, etc. I found an immense excitement in all the South, and if you can but hold your own hundreds will flock to Kansas." Daniel Woodson Papers, Kansas State Hist. Soc.

The junior class of Yale presented the leader with a richly mounted rifle inscribed *Ultima Ratio Liberarum;* while Henry Ward Beecher sent a letter notifying the gift of twenty-five Bibles and twenty-five Sharps rifles on behalf of his congregation. "There are times," he wrote, "when self-defence is a religious duty. If that duty was ever imperative it is now, and in Kansas." [32] A throng of citizens, after singing Whittier's "Song of the Kansas Emigrant," escorted about seventy of the company to the steamboat. Every man, it was said, had a rifle and revolver, and knew how to use these "persuaders." Beecher's remark that such weapons were a greater moral agency among border ruffians than the Scriptures gave currency to the phrase "Beecher's Bibles."

Another sign of the times was a vast assemblage at the Tabernacle in New York on April 29th, one of the most impressive meetings the city had ever seen. More than three thousand people jammed the building to listen to speeches by Benjamin F. Butler, William M. Evarts, Representative John A. Bingham of Ohio, Horace Greeley, and others. To see the conservative attorney D. D. Field on the same platform with John A. King, the still more conservative merchant Moses H. Grinnell seated beside William Cullen Bryant, the moderate Henry J. Raymond beside the fiery Robert Emmet, was a lesson in the momentous change which had overtaken metropolitan opinion. The list of vice-presidents and secretaries comprised some three-score of the most distinguished business and professional men of the city, representing its wealth, energy, and character. Resolutions pledging support to the Republican Party were unanimously adopted. "The variety of the components of the party," declared Curtis Noyes, himself a former Whig, "argues that all older differences are being merged in the new necessities of the times." [33] Throughout the North a crusading spirit was swiftly gaining depth and sweep.

[ VI ]

What did most to cast oil on the flames was the news from Kansas itself; by May not merely of passion and disturbance, but of collision trending toward open warfare. In midwinter, Siberian cold had shut down on the plains, keeping most people close within doors. The icy winds and heaped snowdrifts, causing intense suffering among a multitude of ill-housed settlers, seemed a lesson in the unsuitability of the land for slavery.

32 N. Y. *Tribune,* April 9, 1856; Paxton Hibben, *Henry Ward Beecher,* 159.
33 N. Y. *Weekly Tribune,* May 3, 1856; Foner, *Business and Slavery,* 103. The change in the position of New York businessmen, and notably merchants, in the years 1854-56, is one of the best demonstrations in our history of the fact that "economic motivation" becomes very flimsy indeed when the deeper convictions of intelligent men regarding justice and liberty are touched.

Yet even during these frigid weeks sporadic crimes occurred. The worst was the murder of a freesoil settler named E. P. Brown, who was waylaid near Leavenworth, fatally mangled with knives and a hatchet, and dumped in a dying condition at his cabin door with the words, "Here's Brown"—his wife losing her reason under the shock. An Illinoisan named Phillips, too, a believer in squatter sovereignty who had revolted against Missouri interferences, was foully murdered.[34] In a wild frontier area a few such crimes were inevitable. And as spring warmed the settlements into activity and ambition, tension rose to new heights. Armed settlers were pouring in from North and South, the heated exchanges in Congress were having their effect, and the Administration's denunciation of "rebellion" on one hand, the Northern avowals of a determination to wrench Kansas from the "grasp of slavery" on the other, encouraged militant attitudes.

One signal that a new chapter of conflict lay ahead was given on March 4 by the defiant meeting of the Free-State government at Topeka, complete with senators, representatives, and executive officers. Governor Robinson was of course there, tall, powerful, leonine-headed, awkwardly honest, and occasionally much tangled in his long sentences; so was Jim Lane, thin, hatchet-faced, and brunette, with beady, restless black eyes, and theatrically military mien, for he affected high boots, a red sash, a black cloak, and an officer's cap. Blaring his hostility, Sheriff Jones of Wakarusa War fame amused everybody by writing down the names of all the legislators as they took the oath. The two houses organized, Robinson delivered an inaugural address and sent the legislature a message, and debate began. The "governor" counselled the legislators to take no action in opposition to the national or Territorial authorities; but they did set up a joint committee to prepare a new code of laws for future adoption. All this provoked the ire of the South and the approval of most Republicans and freesoilers of the North. But news that the legislature had elected Reeder and Lane to the United States Senate was nowhere taken very seriously.[35]

Six weeks later the House investigating committee was arriving in Kansas. Speaker Banks had appointed Mordecai Oliver of Missouri, John Sherman, and William A. Howard of Michigan, who served as chairman. All three were

34 Brown was attacked by men half drunk; see the *Howard Report* (34th Cong., 1st sess., House Report 200), p. 981ff. For the murder of Phillips, see *Idem*, 963ff. Phillips, a modest, unassuming, studious young lawyer, was a friend of Senator Lyman Trumbull. He had gone to Kansas as a staunch believer in popular sovereignty. He had become outraged by the election frauds, and had given evidence on them to Reeder. As a result, on May 17, 1855, his house was attacked, and he fell pierced by a dozen balls. Previous to this he had been seized, his head was shaved, and he was tarred and feathered. "His wife was taken from Leavenworth," Trumbull told the Senate, "and the last I heard of her, she was in the lunatic asylum at Jacksonville, in the State of Illinois." *Cong. Globe*, March 17, 1858.

35 Long account in N. Y. *Weekly Tribune*, March 28, 1856. Lane is unsparingly denounced in Charles Robinson's *Kansas Conflict*.

capable men. Oliver, a Whig who had warmly favored the Nebraska bill, had been selected by the Democrats; Howard, who had been associated with Seward in an important legal case, was supposed to possess skill in examining witnesses and analyzing testimony. The best work was done by Sherman, who has left us a little sheaf of recollections. He emphasizes the rough frontier aspect of Kansas as he then saw it. Westport, the seat of the Santa Fé trade, full of mules, Indian ponies, prairie schooners, and whiskey-soaked drivers dressed in ten-gallon hats, flannel shirts, homespun trousers tucked in high boots, with plenty of knives and pistols, Lawrence, a neatly-planned free-state town still in embryo, with no building finished, not even the Free-State Hotel where Sherman and his wife slept; Lecompton, also just begun; and Topeka, a mere village.[36]

After a brief session at Lecompton, the committee held in Lawrence and Leavenworth a series of dramatic hearings. Sitting ten hours a day, they heard witness after witness give detailed evidence upon violence and fraud in the various elections, upon secret societies, upon the Wakarusa War, and upon the murder of freesoil settlers.[37] These statements aroused bitter feeling on both sides. For the first time responsible observers furnished graphic facts, with names, dates, places, and quoted speeches, upon the seizure of poll books, the driving of election judges from their seats, the deposit of hundreds of illegal ballots, and the intimidation of voters by shouts of "Cut his throat!" or "Tear his heart out!" Depositions were furnished by Reeder and Robinson on one side, Stringfellow and Shannon on the other. Some witnesses visibly trembled as they talked.

"I have been beaten and bruised because of my political opinions," said Edward Bourne of Atchison County, "and had to show my pistol to defend my life; and I think I am in danger now, when I tell what I do here. My wife has scarcely changed her clothes for the last six weeks, and a mob has threatened to come about my house and hang me if I did not leave in ten days, and called me an abolitionist, which I am not." [38]

As feeling rose, the pro-slavery press grew outrageous in its incitements to violence. The *Kansas Pioneer* called on Southerners to come with rifle, knife, and revolver to annihilate the abolitionists: "Send the scoundrels back to whence they came, or send them to hell, it matters not which. . . ." The Atchison *Squatter Sovereign* of May 8, chronicling an affray, cried for vengeance: "Blood for Blood! But for each drop spilled, we shall require one hundred fold! . . . Let us purge ourselves of all abolition emissaries . . . and give distinct notice that all who do not leave immediately for the East, *will leave for eternity!*

36 *Recollections of Forty Years*, I, ch. 5. The staff of the committee consisted of three clerks, three sergeants at arms, and one stenographer. They held their first session April 21.
37 34th Cong., 1st sess., House Report 200, a volume of 1206 pages.
38 *Idem*, 381.

## [ VII ]

In the midst of the hearings, the rough Judge Lecompte, jovial in ordinary aspect but fierce when aroused, offered a sudden diversion. Meeting with the grand jury near Lecompton, he charged them to indict all members of the Topeka government, both executive and legislative ("men who are dubbed governors . . . men who are dubbed all the various other dubs") as guilty of high treason, for resistance to the territorial laws was resistance to the authority of the United States. Even if the resistance were merely indirect, he instructed, through aid to combinations formed for opposing the laws, "then must you find bills for constructive treason." [39]

The jury forthwith found true bills against a number of men. One was "Governor" Robinson, who had just set out for the East, but was seized on a steamboat at Lexington, Mo., held for legal papers, and taken back to Lecompton. One was Lane. As for Reeder, who had accompanied the Congressional committee to Kansas and was giving it invaluable aid, a subpoena was issued requiring him to come to Lecompton to testify. Claiming the committee's protection and citing also his privileges as a contestant for the seat of delegate in Congress, he defied the Federal deputy-marshal to arrest him at his peril, a challenge that the officer did not accept. Lecompte's move for a prosecution of the Free-State leaders was obviously timed to distract attention from the committee's disclosures, while it seemed a natural result of Pierce's announced determination to deal forcibly with "insurrection." [40] The St. Louis correspondent of the New York *Tribune* believed that more drastic steps impended. "We are on the eve of great events," he wrote, asserting that the pro-slavery faction, alarmed at the prospect of a full exposure of their doings, were planning appropriate measures. "The fate of Kansas is sealed, unless the people of the North manifest a determination and a spirit that has never yet been manifested."

He was right as to the great events. On May 11 the Federal Marshal, J. B. Donaldson, issued a proclamation asserting that an attempt by a deputy-marshal to serve process on various persons (he later mentioned ex-Governor Reeder) in Lawrence had been violently resisted by a body of disorderly men, and that further resistance was certain—both statements being false. He therefore called upon law-abiding citizens of the Territory to appear at Lecompton in force to support him. This gave the slavery men precisely the opportunity they wanted; Lawrence was becoming an intolerable thorn in their flesh, and here was an opportunity to pluck it out. The grand jury had found indictments against two Lawrence newspapers, the *Herald of Freedom* and *Free Press*, for seditious

39  Atchison *Squatter Sovereign*, May 6, 13, 20; N. Y. *Tribune*, May 9, 1856.
40  See Pierce's proclamation of February 11, 1856.

language, and against the Free-State Hotel there as a parapeted and portholed fortress. Large bodies of armed men gathered at Lecompton in jubilant encampments. Tents whitened the ground; bugles shrilled and drums beat; officers drilled the infantry to charge, while troops of cavalry dashed over the hills. "All have determined to fight desperately in case of resistance," wrote one of them.[41]

On May 20, the valiant marshal ordered his motley array to concentrate just outside Lawrence. Before night they were in position, and next morning at dawn placed cannon to command the town while they awaited reinforcements. Additional forces straggled in during several hours, making a total array variously estimated at from five hundred to eight hundred men, with four six-pounder brass cannon. Part of the troops moved to a hill immediately overlooking the town, a group of eight under Deputy-Marshal W. P. Fain, who had recently arrived from Georgia, entered the main street, and the rest disposed themselves threateningly.

The next few days found Americans riveted to stories introduced by lurid shrieking headlines. "Startling News From Kansas—The War Actually Begun—Triumph of the Border Ruffians—Lawrence in Ruins—Several Persons Slaughtered—Freedom Bloodily Subdued," ran a typical set of freesoil captions. "Lawrence Taken—Glorious Triumph of the Law and Order Party Over Fanaticism in Kansas," proclaimed a slavery organ.[42]

What had happened was shocking enough without the exaggerations in which many Northern journals indulged. The marshal's force included the Lecompton Guards, the Doniphan Tigers, other units from eastern Kansas under Stringfellow and others, Buford's troop, and the Platte County Rifles under Atchison. The deputy-marshal, with a small posse, had no difficulty in arresting two offenders who were his special object. Free-State men did not intend to resist a Federal officer. Donaldson, Atchison, and various other leaders accepted the invitation of the proprietor of the Free-State Hotel to dine. The marshal then dissolved his posse, and Sheriff Jones of Douglas County took it over; a vindictive, blundering fool with a score of his own to settle, for to the great consternation of nearly all citizens of Lawrence, he had been wounded there the previous month by some person then unknown. He had a proprietary interest in a rival town not far from Lawrence. The slavery forces greeted him with deafening cheers.

Then, as a blood-red flag with a lone star in the center, emblazoned with "Southern Rights" on one side and "South Carolina" on the other, was raised above the *Herald of Freedom* office, the premises of that hated journal and of

41 Quoted in Lecompton *Union,* May 24, 1856.
42 N. Y. *Tribune,* May 28; Lecompton *Union,* May 24.

the *Free-State* were invaded; both presses were smashed and tossed into the river; and books and papers were destroyed. The excited mob thereupon planted three cannon near the hotel, fired some thirty shots in a vain effort to batter it to pieces, and tried to blow it up with a keg of gunpowder. Finally, after ransacking the rooms and seizing the stock of liquor, they burned it down. When the best hostelry in the Territory was a heap of ruins, they fired Governor Robinson's house and barn, destroying his furniture and library. Before setting out for home they also pillaged a number of shops and houses.[43]

Only one life was lost in the assault, and that by accident, while the damage was easily repaired. But this outrage upon fundamental civil rights, committed in the name of the law, with the partial connivance of the highest court in the Territory [44] and of the Federal Marshal, made a painful impression upon all thinking men. It was much to the credit of both Atchison and Buford that they had disapproved of the mob's work and tried to check it; but the majority had listened only to Jones.[45] The comment of various border newspapers was disgraceful. At last, exclaimed the Doniphan *Constitutionalist*, that notorious abolition hole Lawrence has been disciplined; the vile traitor Robinson has lost his house; the printing presses have been destroyed as nuisances; and all the work has been carried out with order and according to law!

Though few realized it at the moment, the retirement of the Jones-Atchison-Buford-Stringfellow army from Lawrence, covered with self-inflicted disgrace, was the heaviest defeat the pro-slavery faction in Kansas had yet met. There is no ruin like self-ruin. The people of Lawrence had wisely made no preparation to fight. On the contrary, a committee of safety appointed by a public meeting several days earlier had forbidden any resistance whatever, even advising men not to collect in knots in the streets, but to follow their proper employments. Several pieces of artillery, and according to one account, about a score of Sharps rifles, were surrendered to Sheriff Jones. The moral position of the Free-State men was perfect; that of the overwhelming force gathered to raid this little town of several hundred people, smashing, burning, and looting, was beyond redemption. Lecompte and Donaldson had not merely discredited themselves, but had cast a sardonic light upon the President's promise to uphold law and order, personified in this disreputable mob, against rebellion as per-

43 For full accounts, see Missouri *Democrat*, May 27; Independence, Mo., *Messenger*, May 24; N. Y. *Tribune*, May 28, 1856. Interesting correspondence by Governors Shannon and Geary bearing on the attack on Lawrence is printed in *Kansas State Hist. Colls.*, IV. For Jones's role, see Lawrence *Herald of Freedom*, October 31, 1857.

44 For a brief account of Judge Lecompte's subsequent defense, see Malin, *John Brown and the Legend of '56*, pp. 81, 82. Lecompte noted that the destruction of the hotel and newspaper press was no fault of the court's, for the court had taken no action respecting them.

45 Colonel Jackson of Georgia also opposed the burning of the hotel; Missouri *Democrat*, May 27, 1856.

sonified in the quiet, hardworking settlers of the Topeka government. It was significant that a Kentucky gentleman who had just reached Kansas, intending to bring in his slaves, beheld the pillaging with tears, and declared that he would at once return home as a duped man.[46]

And simultaneously, public opinion was electrified by a still more dramatic occurrence, which was to cast a black shadow down the succeeding years. At the same time that the Kansas struggle yielded these outrages on the plains, it produced a catastrophe in Washington.

## [ VIII ]

On May 19 and 20, before any inkling of the Lawrence occurrences reached Washington, Charles Sumner uttered in the Senate a protracted speech to which he subsequently gave the title of "The Crime Against Kansas"; a speech which, as he said, covered not only the crime, but "the apologies for the crime" and "the true remedy." The special repute of the speaker and the force of sectional tension made the occasion notable. Feeling was such that it had been reported for several days that he would speak well-armed.[47]

Sumner had now been in the Senate almost precisely five years. He had brought to his position a lofty devotion to principle, a fine sincerity, a wealth of learning, and a distinguished mastery of words; he brought to it also self-complacent egotism, coldness of heart, humorless pedantry, utter intolerance of contrary opinions, and a highly irritating assumption of superiority. Indeed, he was a remarkable combination of qualities good and bad.[48] A man of genuine cultivation, whose friendships embraced some of the most distinguished writers and scientists of Britain and America, he had done much to elevate the level and enrich the intellectual quality of Senate discussion. For all his egotism, he was essentially unselfish. His manners in social intercourse were a model of dignified courtesy, while his private life was without spot or blemish. Though his hatred of slavery and caste distinctions was as burning as that of the abolitionists, he creditably differed from them in two respects. One was his tolerance of the Constitution, which he interpreted as making freedom national, slavery sectional; the other was that while the Garrisonians looked at the slavery issue as purely moral, he regarded it as partly political. Neither, of course, thought of it as social or economic.

46 Leavenworth correspondence in N. Y. *Tribune*, May 22, 1856.
47 L. A. Gobright, *Recollections of Men and Things at Washington*, 150.
48 Gamaliel Bradford, *Union Portraits*, 233–261; James K. Hosmer, *The Lost Leaf*, 18–25; Julia Ward Howe, *Reminiscences 1819–1899*, pp. 171–182, are all revealing as to Sumner's personality. See also R. W. Emerson's sketch in *The Early Years of the Saturday Club, 1855–1870*, pp. 296–308. "There is a tradition at the Club," writes Emerson, "that he was dominant in conversation." Whittier's ode is well known.

Sumner's commanding figure, his noble head, his handsome features and frank look, made him appear every inch the statesman. To multitudes in the North he seemed an embodiment of all the virtues, and to much of New England in particular a great hero, representing everything that was best in the intellect and character of the section. The literary power of his best speeches had given them a wide currency in England, had obtained a large sale for a compilation recently issued by Ticknor & Fields, and had won the delighted applause of the freesoil press.[49]

Yet some of his basic attitudes, and certain of his ideas, were flawed with dangerous qualities. Ostentatiously looking upon all questions in a moral light, he regarded himself as an unerring exponent of moral law. The aim of legislation, in his opinion, was the realization of justice; justice meant the fullest development and most active exercise of the rights of man; and of all rights, freedom was the most essential and sacred. On this set of abstractions he reared, among other dogmas, and insistence upon the "unutterable woes and wrongs of slavery," and a demand for abolition that took no heed of obstacles. He had declared unremitting war on the basic Southern institution—"all that I am or may be, I freely offer to this cause."[50] He always exaggerated the national as opposed to the federal character of the government, paying scant attention to the rights of individual States—a bias that was to bear gnarled fruit in Reconstruction days.[51] No Republican inherited more of the centralizing tradition of the Federalists and Whigs. He had distinguished himself by the fierceness of his invective against Southern measures, terming the Fugitive Slave Act, for example, an "unutterable atrocity," a child of "usurpation, injustice, and cruelty." He equally distinguished himself by sharp personal attacks on Southern leaders, so that many fellow-Senators now refused to speak to him. By 1856 he was the best-hated man in the chamber. Not merely was he almost utterly humorless, but his taste was egregiously bad. The paintings he bought for a Boston museum were poor; many of the books he praised were poor; and his speeches contained much that was in wretched taste.[52] His arrogance and pride frequently made him cutting, and sometimes cruel.

A thrill of repugnance and apprehension must have run through half the Senate as Sumner intoned his first sentence: "Mr. President, you are now called to redress a great transaction." It was known that he had prepared himself

49  *Recent Speeches and Addresses.*
50  Speech on Fugitive Slave Act, *Works*, III, 66.
51  See the view of Sumner in Nevins, *Hamilton Fish, passim;* and the *Nation*, June 9, 1892.
52  The life by Miss Dawes (daughter of Senator H. L. Dawes) is especially severe upon his want of taste. When Sumner chose the seat just in front of the Whig Senator from Maryland, J. A. Pearce, the latter tried to remove to a different area. Pearce, September 15, 1855; Clayton Papers.

carefully. Douglas later said that he had "his speech written, printed, committed to memory, practised every night before the glass with a Negro boy to hold the candle and watch the gestures, and annoying the boarders in the neighboring rooms until they were forced to quit the house!" [53] It was also known that his studied preparation by no means ensured moderation of statement. But the worst anticipations of friends and enemies were surpassed by this particular speech. It reeked with emotion. Of fresh arguments and new facts upon Kansas it contained almost nothing; a few quotations from various newspapers, circulars, and speeches upon the Missouri incursions into Kansas were its sole contributions to knowledge. It was primarily a rhetorical exercise, and it is impossible to avoid the conclusion that Sumner was intent not upon convincing Senators or the general public of the justice of his position, but upon giving the intellectuals of the North, the reading public of Britain, and studious posterity an oration sufficiently chiselled and polished to compare with the great rhetorical productions of antiquity.

Cicero had denounced Verres and Catiline; Demosthenes had hurled the lances of his eloquence against Philip; and now Charles Sumner believed that he was arraigning the crime against Kansas in a similar literary masterpiece—was contemptuously embalming Douglas of Illinois and Butler of South Carolina in the amber of his discourse. Such is the only interpretation of the speech which makes its elaborate artificiality, its gemmings of simile, metaphor, historical allusion, and Miltonian quotation, and above all, its glowing intemperance of denunciation, understandable. At one point it amounted to a paraphrase of Demosthenes; at other points Sumner alluded to that orator, and to Cicero's excoriation of the looting of Sicily, in terms which clearly suggested an emulative effort. He had written Theodore Parker that he would deliver "the most thorough philippic" ever heard in a legislative chamber.[54] But the circumstances forbade that Democratic Senators should indulgently dismiss the speech as a schoolboy exercise; they had to take it with intense seriousness.

Sumner began by characterizing the treatment of Kansas as sacrilege, robbery, and tyrannical usurpation. "It is the rape of a virgin territory, compelling it to the hateful embrace of Slavery; and it may be clearly traced to a depraved longing for a new slave State, the hideous offspring of such a crime, in the hope of adding to the power of Slavery in the national government." He arraigned the 'Slave Power' for arrogantly corrupting public opinion and making officials, from President to border postmaster, its tools; and he pointed to it as the foulest of criminals, "heartless, grasping, and tyrannical." It had, he

53 *Cong. Globe,* 34th Cong., 1st sess., Appendix, 545.
54 Weiss, *Parker,* II, 179. The whole speech is in Sumner, *Works,* IV, 137-249; *Cong. Globe,* 34th Cong., 1st sess., Appendix, 529-544.

pedantically declared, "an audacity beyond that of Verres, a subtlety beyond that of Machiavel, a meanness beyond that of Bacon, and an ability beyond that of Hastings." Terming Senators Butler and Douglas the Don Quixote and Sancho Panza who had sallied forth in a crowning effort to defend the crime and criminal, he lashed them with insulting sentences. Butler, he said, "has chosen a mistress to whom he has made his vows, and who, though ugly to others, is always lovely to him; though polluted in the sight of the world, is chaste in his sight—I mean the harlot, Slavery. For her, his tongue is always profuse in words. . . . The frenzy of Don Quixote, in behalf of his wench, Dulcinea del Toboso, is all unsurpassed." As for Sancho Panza Douglas, he was the ready squire of Slavery, doing "all its humiliating offices"; in his recent labored address he had piled one mass of error upon another mass; he had arrogantly dreamed of subduing the North, but he would fail, for against him were arrayed nature and the human heart—"against him is God."

Continuing his imitation of classical models and growing heated with his own rhetoric, Sumner dwelt upon the transactions in Kansas. He had his characteristic phrases for the Missouri invaders. They were "murderous robbers"; "hirelings, picked from the drunken spew and vomit of an uneasy civilization"; men banded in secret lodges, who had "renewed the incredible atrocities of the Assassins and of the Thugs." The usurping legislature of Kansas, elected by these conspirators in their armed hordes, had passed an act to protect slavery which according to Sumner stood unparalleled in "its complex completeness of wickedness." He threw out a simile which always fascinated him, for he was to employ it a generation later against one of Grant's policies: "This act of thirteen sections is in itself a *Dance of Death.*" From denouncing "the Usurpation," he turned to assail the Administration which supported it. "Even now the black flag of the land pirates from Missouri waves at the mast-head; in their laws you hear the pirate yell, and see the flash of the pirate knife, while, incredible to relate! the President, gathering the Slave Power at his back, testifies a pirate sympathy." He defended the operations of the Emigrant Aid Society, entirely failing to bring out any new facts or ideas. He attacked the four apologies that he said were made for the Kansas crime— "the first is the Apology *Tyrannical;* the second the Apology *Imbecile;* the third. the Apology *Absurd;* the fourth, the Apology *Infamous.*" Finally, he outlined his idea of the true remedy, the passage of Seward's bill for the immediate admission of Kansas to the Union.

If Sumner, having finished his speech, had sat down—"Mr. President, an immense space has been traversed, and I now stand at the goal"—his worst offenses would not have been committed; but he could not dispense with a long rhetorical conclusion. From beginning to end its taste was deplorable. His rhetorical extravagances rose to pure rant in his closing sentences. But the most outrageous passages devoted an insulting phraseology to the States of South Carolina and Virginia, and to Senators Butler, Douglas, and Mason.

If the whole history of South Carolina were blotted out, the orator declared, civilization would lose less than it had already gained by the example of the freesoil men of Kansas. He spoke of its "shameful imbecility from Slavery, confessed throughout the Revolution." Turning to the patriarchal-looking Butler, whose kindly heart and exquisite graces of manner made him a general favorite—an accomplished gentleman, a conscientious legislator—he remarked that in a recent speech on Kansas the white-haired South Carolinian had "overflowed with rage," and that he had "with incoherent phrases, discharged the loose expectoration of his speech" upon the people of the Territory.[55] The Senator, he went on, touched nothing which he did not disfigure with error. "He shows an incapacity of accuracy, whether in stating the Constitution or in stating the law, whether in the details of statistics or the diversions of scholarship. He cannot open his mouth, but out there flies a blunder." Nor was this all; Sumner accused Butler of constant "deviation of truth." Douglas, he said, was one of those "mad spirits who would endanger and degrade the Republic, while they betray all the cherished sentiments of the Fathers and the spirit of the Constitution, in order to give new spread to slavery." Mason, he added, "represents that other Virginia, from which Washington and Jefferson now avert their faces, where human beings are bred as cattle for the shambles, and where a dungeon rewards the pious matron who teaches little children to relieve their bondage by reading the Book of Life." Finally, Sumner bade Congress "turn from that Slave Oligarchy which now controls the Republic, and refuse to be its tool," while he appealed from Congress to the people.

[ IX ]

The speech defeated its own ends, for its exaggerations and extravagances rendered much of it absurd, while its poverty of fact and logic robbed it of all real weight. But so great was Sumner's prestige, so quick was half the Northern press to applaud and enforce anything he said, that it was impossible to pass it over in silence.

No sooner had he sat down than Cass of Michigan, the Nestor of the Senate, rose to utter a weighty rebuke. He had listened, he said, with equal regret and surprise to the speech of the Massachusetts Senator. "Such a speech—the most un-American and unpatriotic that ever grated on the ears of the members of this high body—I hope never to hear again here or elsewhere." [56] Douglas followed him in a vein of hot anger. He could not forgive Sumner's utterances

55 A deliberate insinuation that Butler had been intoxicated; Cf. Beveridge, *Lincoln*, II, 342-345.
56 *Cong. Globe*, 34th Cong., 1st sess., Appendix, 544.

on the ground that it was the language of impulse. "The libels, the gross insults which we have heard today have been conned over, written with cool, deliberate malignity, repeated from night to night in order to catch the appropriate grace, and then he came here to spit forth that malignity upon men who differ from him—for that is their offense." But Douglas did not defend himself alone; he replied equally to the attacks upon Butler ("the venerable, the courteous, and the distinguished Senator from South Carolina") and upon Atchison ("a gentleman and an honest man, true and loyal to the Constitution"). Butler was away, while Atchison's term had ended. Both had been assailed in their absence in the most opprobrious terms. Butler had been accused of falsehood, and Atchison denounced as a Catiline. "Why these attacks on individuals by name, and two-thirds of the Senate collectively?" asked Douglas. "Is it the object to drive men here to dissolve social relations with political opponents? Is it to turn the Senate into a bear garden . . . ?"

Though the debates of the preceding weeks had been full of a rough give-and-take, no previous speeches justified the semi-hysterical outburst of Sumner. The speech by Butler which Sumner described as a loose and raging expectoration of phrases had in fact been moderate, devoid of offensive personalities, and couched in dignified language. It had contained no reference to Sumner himself. Butler, now almost sixty and separated by only a year from his grave, was a gentleman of the old South Carolina school, who had played a judicious and capable part in public life since his election to the legislature in 1824, and who had now sat in the Senate for nearly a decade. A graduate of South Carolina College, he maintained his scholarly interests by assiduous reading; a lawyer and former judge, he possessed uncommon legal erudition. In the heat of debate he always showed a chivalry of tone which made a marked impression. Rarely, said the Boston *Courier* at the time of his death, had any Senator "commanded such signal and general good will." [57] He was universally praised for his warm-hearted, frank, and genial qualities, which won him general affection.[58] His home at Stonelands, near Edgefield, S. C., where his mother had long presided (for he had lost two wives in rapid succession) had been a centre of hospitality. Though loyal to the interests of his State, he had consistently adopted moderate views, speaking for upland South Carolina rather than the coastal area, and opposing all movements for secession. It was characteristic of him that in 1854 he had generously complimented Sumner on a speech against the Kansas-Nebraska bill. If Sumner had attacked the universally esteemed Crittenden himself, he could not have given more general pain in the Senate and in Washington.

The rebukes to Sumner by Cass, Douglas, and Mason were just and warrant-

57 Quoted in *National Intelligencer*, June 4, 1857.
58 See the *Intelligencer*, June 4, for remarks on his "high intellectual attainments and manly qualities."

able, though Douglas adopted too much Sumner's own manner. But Sumner, hastening to retort, aggravated his original offense. He accused Douglas of indecent personalities, intemperance, and vulgarity. He should display more wisdom and candor! "Let the Senator bear these things in mind, and let him remember hereafter that the bowie knife and bludgeon are not the proper emblems of debate. Let him remember that the swagger of Bob Acres and the ferocity of the Malay cannot add dignity to this body." Referring to some of Douglas's charges, he said he would "brand them to his face as false." And he concluded with perhaps the most indecently offensive utterance made in Congress since John Randolph of Roanoke had quitted that body:

I say also to that Senator, and I wish him to bear it in mind, that no person with the upright form of man can be allowed—(hesitation).
Mr. Douglas. Say it.
Mr. Sumner. I will say it—no person with the upright form of man can be allowed, without violation of all decency, to switch out from his tongue the perpetual stench of offensive personality. Sir, this is not a proper weapon of debate, at least, on this floor. The noisome, squat, and nameless animal, to which I now refer, is not a proper model for an American Senator. Will the Senator from Illinois take notice?

Douglas retorted that he recognized the force of the illustration and would never imitate Sumner in that capacity. "Mr. President," rejoined Sumner, "again the Senator has switched his tongue, and again he fills the Senate with its offensive odor." [59]

Had the affair ended here, Sumner alone would have sustained damage from it. Unfortunately, Senator Butler's nephew, close neighbor, and devoted follower, Preston S. Brooks of Edgefield, now serving his second term in the House, resolved to avenge the insults to his kinsman. He had been an officer of the gallant Palmetto regiment which had formed its line on the beach at Vera Cruz, and six weeks later, had planted its battle-torn flag on the gates of Mexico City. Now he represented the Ninety-six District, the district of Harper, McDuffie, and Calhoun; names which alone dispelled the aspersions of Sumner upon South Carolina's fame. [60] The day after Sumner ended, Brooks told a friendly member of the House that he intended to call the Massachusetts Senator to account, and if he did not apologize, to chastise him.

59 Douglas's animosity toward Sumner was of several years' standing. "Last year," he had told the Senate on March 14, 1856, "when the Nebraska Bill was under consideration, the Senator from Massachusetts (Mr. Sumner) asked of me the courtesy to have it postponed a week, until he could examine the question. I afterward discovered that, previous to that time, he had written an exposition of the bill—a libel upon me—and sent it off under his own frank; and the postponement thus obtained by my courtesy was in order to take a week to circulate the libel."
60 Five of Brooks's relatives had fallen in the last battles in Mexico. Said John A. Quitman, who had reason to know: "Whether marching through the scorching sands of a

That night, according to his own story, the angry Congressman tossed feverishly on his bed. He had at first intended to accost Sumner in the Capitol passageways. Instead, on the 22nd he waited until the Senate adjourned in consequence of news of the death of a Representative from Missouri, entered the nearly empty Senate chamber, and approached the desk where Sumner was writing letters to catch an approaching mail. Sumner was so absorbed that he did not notice the Southerner until his name was uttered. He looked up to see a tall man standing directly over him, and to hear Brooks ejaculate: "I have read your speech twice over. It is a libel on South Carolina, and Mr. Butler, who is a friend of mine." Apparently he added a remark about Butler's age. With these words Brooks began raining a succession of blows with a gutta-percha cane on Sumner's bare head. The first stroke almost stunned Sumner, depriving him of sight. He strove instinctively to rise, and by a frenzied effort wrenched his desk from the floor, staggered forward, and collapsed some ten feet in front of it, as Representative Morgan of New York and others rushed to his assistance.

Brooks's intention had been merely to punish Sumner lightly. But he was betrayed by the intensity of his feelings into delivering such heavy blows that the Senator was dangerously injured. Toombs of Georgia, an approving witness of the attack, declared that the blows were very rapid, as hard as Brooks could strike, and very effective. Indeed, Brooks clearly intended to hit hard enough to render Sumner insensible, for he said later that he would have used a cowhide had he not feared that the powerful Senator would wrest it from his hand. Two men, Representatives Edmundson of Virginia and Keitt of South Carolina, had known of the anticipated assault, approved it, and along with perhaps fifteen or eighteen other persons, were present in the chamber when it occurred.[61]

---

tropical shore, or traversing the frosty mountain passes, he ever exhibited the serene, cheerful, and determined bearing of the soldier and gentleman." And Toombs of Georgia remarked: "Truth, sincerity, kindness, courage, and courtesy were stamped upon his moral nature. Though quick to resent an insult, he was generous, kind, and even gentle in his nature; and it gave him more pleasure to repair a wrong done by himself than to right one inflicted on him by another." *Cong. Globe*, January 29, 1857.

61 Gobright, *Recollections of Men and Things*, 150; N. Y. *Herald, Tribune, Times, Evening Post*, May 23, 1856. The chief source of material on the assault is the testimony taken by the House Committee (Reports, I, No. 182); and the testimony of witnesses before the District Circuit (Criminal) Court on July 9, 1856, given fully in the Washington press next day. H. Y. Leader of Philadelphia, testifying in court, said accurately that the cane was hollow and tapering, that it broke after five or six blows, and that Brooks kept on striking. He said also that several voices around the Senate exclaimed, "Hit him, Brooks, he deserves it." This witness declared that Senator Crittenden was the first to clutch Brooks; Senator Foster of Connecticut said that Morgan of New York was first to do so. Varying evidence was given on the question whether Brooks continued to strike after Sumner was down. Senator Pearce of Maryland was emphatic that he did not, and reported hearing Brooks exclaim: "I did not intend to kill him, but only to whip him." Brooks himself testified of the first blow that it was "but a tap, and intended to put him on his guard."

Though question was at once raised as to the real gravity of Sumner's injuries, there can be no doubt they were such as to incapacitate him for the next three and a half years. At first he seemed to improve, but a relapse brought on such serious symptoms—ulceration of the cuts, high fever, torturing pains in the head—that his physician forbade anyone to see him.[62] For a time erysipelas threatened. Gradually he recovered from his critical state, and was able to spend the summer of 1856 travelling to various places in search of health; but he had received such a heavy shock that sustained physical or mental effort was impossible.[63] He suffered from lassitude, insomnia, and grinding headaches, while his weak heart and uncertain gait crippled all activity. "My brain and whole nervous system," he wrote that autumn, "are jangled and subject to relapse." Not until February of 1857 was he able to return to his seat in the Senate, and then only for a single day to cast his vote on what he considered an important matter—the reduction of duties on raw materials. Describing that day, he wrote Theodore Parker: "After a short time the torment to my system became great and a cloud began to gather over my brain. I tottered out, and took to my bed. I long to speak but cannot."

## NEW YORK HERALD
## FRIDAY, MAY 23, 1856.

### THE LATEST NEWS.

#### BY MAGNETIC AND PRINTING TELEGRAPHS.

Assault on Senator Sumner in the Senate Chamber.

WASHINGTON, May 22, 1856.

About half past one, after the Senate adjourned, Col. Preston S. Brooks, M. C., of South Carolina, approached Senator Sumner, who was sitting in his seat, and said to him—

Mr. Sumner, I have read your speech against South Carolina, and have read it carefully, deliberately and dispassionately, in which you have libelled my State and slandered my white haired old relative, Senator Butler, who is absent, and I have come to punish you for it.

Col. Brooks then struck Senator Sumner with his cane some dozen blows over the head. Mr. Sumner at first showed fight, but was overpowered. Senator Crittenden and others interfered and separated them.

Mr. Keith, of South Carolina, did not interfere, only to keep persons off.

Senator Toombs declared that it was the proper place to have chastised Mr. Sumner.

The affair is regretted by all.

The stick used was gutta percha, about an inch in diameter, and hollow, which was broken up like a pipe-stem.

About a dozen Senators and many strangers happened to be in the chamber at the moment of the fight. Sumner, I learn, is badly whipped. The city is considerably excited, and crowds everywhere are discussing the last item. Sumner cried—"I'm most dead! oh! I'm most dead!" After Sumner fell between two desks, his own having been overturned, he lay bleeding, and cried out—"I am almost dead—almost dead!"

The Massachusetts legislature nevertheless reëlected him by all but unani-

---

62 Three physicians, Harvey Lindsly of Washington, Marshall S. Perry of Boston, and Casper Wistar of Philadelphia, writing Henry Wilson early that autumn, declared that the injuries were such as to incapacitate Sumner for the time being. Besides the external wounds, said Perry, he had suffered a severe shock. Dr. Wistar's explicit statement probably covers the case completely: "His condition awakened my solicitude, as it was difficult to determine whether he labored under functional or organic injury to the brain. It was evident the injuries he had originally received on the floor of the Senate had been aggravated by the peculiar condition of his nervous system at the time, a condition induced by severe mental exertion, and nervous tension from the loss of sleep for several consecutive nights, also by the peculiar susceptibility of his temperament, which is highly nervous." N. Y. *Tribune*, October 8, 1856. How much the injuries contributed to a nervous state which caused Hamilton Fish, R. H. Dana, Grant, and other observers later to believe Sumner touched with insanity, it is difficult to say. Sumner wrote S. G. Howe on June 27 in fierce indignation over the "gross calumny" that his prostration was simulated. Howe Papers, MHS.

63 Moorfield Storey, *Sumner*, 154ff.

mous action, and he took the oath of office. Then he sailed for Europe, where he spent the greater part of the years 1858–1859, travelling, seeing old English friends, visiting the American colony at Rome, and undergoing an extremely painful course of treatment at the hands of the famous Anglo-French specialist, Dr. Brown-Sequard. It was not until December, 1859, that, at last regarding himself as a well man—though now he suffered from recurrent attacks of angina pectoris—he was again permanently in his seat in Washington. That empty seat had spoken with rare eloquence.

## [ X ]

It was deeply disheartening to reasonable Americans to find that without conspicuous exception, Southern members of Senate and House attempted to justify and defend Brooks's course.[64] The provocation had indeed been great; but no provocation could excuse an act which assaulted not merely Sumner, but the dignity of the upper chamber, and the right of free parliamentary discussion. The Senate appointed a committee of inquiry which contained no Republican member. It reported, in dispassionate terms, that the body could not, for a breach of its privileges, arrest any member of the House, and could do nothing more than make complaint to the other chamber. A committee of investigation had meanwhile been appointed in the House, which heard witnesses, and brought in two reports. The Republican majority recommended that Brooks be expelled, and that the two Southern members who knew of his general intentions be censured; the Democratic minority merely declared that the House had no jurisdiction over the "alleged" assault, and that it was therefore improper to express any opinion upon it. In the end, the House failed to muster the two-thirds vote needed to expel Brooks, but did pass a resolution of censure. He forthwith resigned, returned to South Carolina, received an immediate reëlection, and within seven weeks was again in his wonted seat.

It was plain that the South, stirred from end to end by the excitement of the slavery contest, exulted in Brooks's act, or if it condemned his course, did so on grounds of expediency alone.[65] Sumner was a foul-mouthed poltroon, declared the Richmond *Examiner;* "when caned for cowardly vituperation, [he] falls to the floor an inanimate lump of incarnate cowardice." This "elegant and effectual caning" gave the Richmond *Whig* complete satisfaction. "The

64 A week after the affair, Representative Keitt of South Carolina wrote: "If the Northern men had stood up, the city would now float with blood. The fact is the feeling is wild and fierce. The Kansas fight has just occurred and the times are stirring. Everybody here feels as if we are upon a volcano." Quoted in Harold Schultz, *South Carolina and National Politics, 1852–60*, MS Dissertation, Duke University Library, p. 206.
65 Editors of the South were "virtually unanimous in approving Brooks"; *Idem*, p. 208.

only regret we feel is that Mr. Brooks did not employ a horsewhip or cowhide upon his slanderous back instead of a cane." The Petersburg *Intelligencer* was sorry that Brooks "dirtied his cane by laying it athwart the shoulders of the blackguard Sumner," not because the Senator did not deserve it, but because "the nasty scamp and his co-scamps will make capital for their foul cause out of the affair." [66] The Columbia *South Carolinian* rejoiced to note that a number of slaves had contributed money to buy an appropriate present for Brooks, "who has made the first *practical* issue for their preservation and protection in their rights and enjoyments as the happiest laborers on the face of the globe." [67] Even the Washington *Republic* lauded the caning. Various Southern groups, including students of the Universtiy of Virginia, gave Brooks handsome emblematic canes. Senator Butler warmly extolled him and expressed deep gratitude for his intervention.

It must be remembered that no Northerner, save perhaps William Lloyd Garrison, was more widely and deeply detested at the South than Sumner; and that his last speech seemed to those Southerners who read it a vulgar tirade of abuse and calumny that made the cane a fitting penalty. Moreover, the South had its own special code of manners and morals, which inclined it to pronounce such an act as Brooks's spirited, chivalrous, and fitting. Thus it was that a gentleman chastised an insulter of his people! [68]

But the North had a very different code, and it was more deeply aroused than by any event since the annexation of Texas. The Massachusetts Legislature hastened to pass resolutions condemning the assault as "a gross breach of Parliamentary privilege—a ruthless attack upon the liberty of speech—an outrage of the decencies of civilized life, and an indignity to the Commonwealth of Massachusetts." Indignation meetings were instantly held throughout the State. In Boston within a week two great gatherings took place. One was a spontaneous mass-meeting which heard speeches by James Freeman Clarke, Wendell Phillips, Theodore Parker, and others; the second a gathering in Faneuil Hall at which Governor Gardner presided, and resolutions were carried declaring that "we regard every blow inflicted upon our Senator as a blow aimed at us." Even more impressive was the huge New York meeting promptly held in the Tabernacle. Fully five thousand people, including most of the leading business and professional men of the city, jammed the old building. John A. Stevens, president of the Bank of Commerce, nominated George

66 Quoted in N. Y. *Weekly Tribune*, May 31, 1856.
67 Quoted by Representative Bingham, *Cong. Globe*, July 9, 1856.
68 What could be done with men like Sumner? asked the Washington *Sentinel* of May 27. "Nothing in this world but to cowhide bad manners *out* of him or good manners *into* him." These vulgar abolitionists, said the Richmond *Enquirer* of June 2, are getting above themselves. "They have grown saucy, and dare to be impudent to gentlemen!"

Griswold as chairman; William Cullen Bryant read the long and impressive list of vice-presidents; and ringing addresses were made by William M. Evarts, President Charles King of Columbia, Daniel Lord, Henry Ward Beecher, and others. Resolutions, passed with a shout, declared that "the general community of the Free States, by their public men and their public press," condemned and opposed every act and principle which "upholds violence as a means or mode of affecting political action or restraining personal freedom." The pulpits of the North and West resounded with forcible references to the assault. And Sumner's Crime Against Kansas speech, which might otherwise have been quickly forgotten, was selling in tens of thousands of copies as a thirty-two page pamphlet priced at $20 a thousand.[69]

"You can have little idea," wrote the conservative Robert C. Winthrop from Boston, "of the depth and intensity of the feeling which has been excited in New England. The concurrence of the Kansas horrors has wrought up the masses to a state of fearful desperation." Some people thought that a reckless leader could have raised an army to march upon Washington. Similar testimony was borne in New York by the eminent lawyer Daniel Lord. "The excitement here is very great. It swallows up all other party issues in this part of the country. There is but one mode to allay it.—Acting on the idea that the Senate report is right, bring in a law to punish any breach of privilege of either house which should also happen to be a breach of the peace, as a crime, by fine and imprisonment; without any privilege on behalf of any offender. If this could be done by Southern or Western men, it would spike many a gun which will tell with heavy effect upon, as I fear, the Union itself." [70] In Brooklyn, in Albany, in Worcester, in Lowell, in Jersey City, in dozens of other centers, outraged bodies of citizens passed resolutions and sent copies to the officers of Congress. Governor Metcalf of New Hampshire sent the legislature a message denouncing "the arrogant and aggressive demands" of the "slave power." [71]

69  The Northern press from May 24 to July 1 was full of records of these meetings. A significant incident is recorded by James Freeman Clarke in Memorial and Biog. Sketches, 434. Calling on Sumner in his Hancock Street house, Clarke found him with three men. He introduced one as John Brown of Osawatomie. "It was the first time I had ever seen John Brown. They were speaking of the assault by Preston Brooks, and Mr. Sumner said, 'The coat I had on at that time is hanging in that closet. Its collar is stiff with blood. You can see it, if you please, Captain.' John Brown arose, went to the closet, slowly opened the door, carefully took down the coat, and looked at it for a few minutes with the reverence with which a Roman Catholic regards the relics of a saint." To how many did Sumner exhibit his talismanic coat?

70  Winthrop June 3, Lord June 2; Crittenden Papers. Edward Everett, National Intelligencer, May 15, 1858, on the possible march to Washington.

71  George L. Stearns, wealthy lead-pipe manufacturer of Boston, was inspired by the assault to put all his energies and considerable funds into making Kansas a free State. In five months of 1856 he raised $48,000 for the Massachusetts State Kansas Association, while his wife obtained $20,000 to $30,000 worth of clothing and supplies. In January, 1857, Stearns was in conference in Boston with John Brown—by which hung a fateful tale. See

## [ XI ]

Looking at Kansas and the Senate Chamber, freesoilers of the North felt that the peaceful processes of American democracy were being supplanted by a régime of terror—that the most precious of Anglo-American political traditions were imperilled. William Cullen Bryant, editor of the *Evening Post*, saw in the assault no mere flash of Southern hotheadedness, but a new symptom of a widespread malady. "Violence reigns in the streets of Washington," he wrote; ". . . violence has now found its way into the Senate chamber. Violence lies in wait on all the navigable rivers and all the railways of Missouri, to obstruct those who pass from the free States into Kansas. Violence overhangs the frontiers of that Territory like a stormcloud charged with hail and lightning. Violence has carried election after election in that Territory. . . . In short, violence is the order of the day; the North is to be pushed to the wall by it, and this plot will succeed if the people of the free States are as apathetic as the slaveholders are insolent." [72] Edward Everett spoke of the assault as an instance of lawless violence unexampled in the annals of constitutional government. A host of Americans felt that if the nation moved further on this road, some Cromwellian figure would soon be sending a file of soldiers into the halls of the Capitol to take away the baubles which symbolized free parliamentary government.

The effect of Brooks's wild act upon the North was of course intensified by the news from Kansas. Men heard just before the assault, by telegraph from St. Louis, that Governor Robinson had been arrested, that large pro-slavery forces were mustering near Lawrence, and that an attack on that town was momentarily expected. They heard just after it of the "destruction" of Lawrence; to be exact, descriptions of the clubbing of Sumner were printed in many morning papers of May 23, while Kansas dispatches stating that Lawrence was destroyed reached Washington and other cities on May 24, and were confirmed with full details by the 26th. The Chicago *Tribune* on the last-named day issued an extra with descriptions by three men direct from Lawrence. On the vagueness of the early intelligence the freesoil newspapers pinned wild exaggerations. They declared that the heroic little city-state of the freesoilers, a very Athens of the prairies, had been "devastated and burned to ashes" by the Spartan Ruffians; that "a few bare and tottering chimneys, a

his testimony before the John Brown Committee, February 24, 1860; F. P. Stearns, *Life of . . . George Luther Stearns.* John D. Van Buren wrote Sumner June 10 that the assault "has changed me from a decided pro-slavery man into as decided a supporter of the Republican or Northern ticket. . . ." Sumner Papers.

72 Nevins, *Evening Post*, 253.

charred and blackened waste," marked the hallowed site; and that the only hope was that the inevitable slaughter had been limited.[73] And on the heels of these and other reports—reports that the "merciless" General Harney had been put in complete charge of troops in the Territory, that guerrilla bands were ranging the country, that a reign of terror existed—came news of the massacre committed on Pottawatomie Creek by John Brown.

73  N. Y. *Weekly Tribune,* May 29, 1856.

# *Onset of '56*

AS MAY ENDED IN 1856 is was clear that the Pierce Administration represented a collapse of American statesmanship, for which President and Congress
shared the responsibility. The primary task of statesmanship in this era was to
furnish a workable adjustment between the two sections, while offering strong
inducements to the Southern people to regard their labor system not as static
but evolutionary, and equal persuasions to the Northern people to assume a
helpful rather than scolding attitude. But the Pierce Administration had broken
down a very promising adjustment, and had accentuated the animosities between
free and slave States. It had then failed even in the comparatively simple task
of protecting representative institutions in Kansas. If Pierce had restored order,
had appointed a commission of imposing ability and impartiality to investigate
the situation, and had mobilized moderate opinion behind the creation of a new
and fairly elected Territorial régime, he would have done something to redeem
the errors of 1854. But on the record which he and his advisers had made, the
country was entitled to turn them out of office and look for men who would
act with elevation of temper and largeness of mind.

It was sad that a nation which had so many exigent tasks of internal
development should spend all its energies during this campaign year in a
barren debate upon slavery. It was sadder that the debate should be carried on
by bodies of such completely antipathetic views that it would tend to accentuate
rather than heal the sectional breach. The spectacle presented by the Old
World at the moment was singularly depressing. The Crimean War had just
ended after the butchery, mutilation, or destruction by disease of half a
million men. Producing a few heroic figures (the chief by all odds Florence
Nightingale), it had lifted to prominence many more who were decidedly
unheroic. While hardly weakening the despotism of St. Petersburg, it had
strengthened the barbaric tyranny of the Turk. Austria had its foot more firmly
than ever on the necks of Hungary and Venetia; the petty despots of the
German states bore their sway with unimpaired arrogance; Naples and Rome
lay under the most odious of governments; in France the unprincipled usurper

of the Napoleonic throne strutted more tyrannously than before. The American republic ought to have been the hope of oppressed men throughout the globe— and it was instead laying itself open to the scornful gibes of illiberal critics.

## [ I ]

Douglas was still so young that he could afford to wait for the great prize of American politics, and he was by no means so eager for a presidential nomination as his enemies assumed. He had told his friends the previous fall that he did not wish his name brought into the preliminary canvass. Neverthe-less, he unquestionably had his hopes. If his party had possessed the strength of its convictions, it should have chosen him. It was perhaps one of the great misfortunes of this period that it did not. Necessarily the party appealed to the country on the platform he had made. Throughout most of the North as of the South, Douglas's popular sovereignty doctrine was the basis on which the Democracy asked for votes. In critical Pennsylvania and New Jersey, said Senator Bigler after the contest ended, "the issues were met boldly and broadly. In the whole range of my observation and reading I cannot call to mind an instance where a public speaker or a Democratic newspaper demurred to the Democratic doctrine on the slavery question. . . . Indeed, it was the beauty and force of this broad doctrine that enabled the Democracy to with-stand the varied and potent elements of prejudice and passion employed on the other side." [1]

Thus using Douglas's principles, the party should have used their architect and defender, particularly as he was the most energetic, trenchant, and combative leader to be found in the organization. If elected, he would un-questionably have displayed his characteristic courage in attempting to make popular sovereignty work fairly and successfully, and in defending nationalism against disunion.

But "availability" was one of the curses of our governmental system; and for two main reasons Douglas was unavailable. As late as April, when he proved himself the party's doughtiest champion in repelling the assaults of Seward and Collamer, his friends' hopes had run high. But his chances suffered a heavy shock when May showed Kansas ablaze, and violence thrusting a mailed fist into the Senate chamber. So, it may be said, did the aspirations of Franklin Pierce, who had a far higher opinion of his record than anybody else. [2] Pierce had hoped that his championship of "law and order" as represented by

1 *Cong. Globe*, December 8, 1856.
2 Except his private secretary Sidney Webster, whose eulogistic account of the Ad-ministration, N. Y. *World*, January 31, 1892, was later issued in pamphlet form.

Lecompte, Shannon, and the titular legislature would prompt his party to renominate him; but his knight-errantry on behalf of a partisan government and tiltings against "treason" cost him dear when it became plain that they had encouraged desperate men to lawless courses. It is often popular to sow the wind, but the first breath of the whirlwind brings a revulsion.

The larger reason why Douglas was unavailable lay in his whole record since his return from Europe. Many Northern Democrats had gradually bowed to his principle, but they had not reconciled themselves to the manner in which he carried that principle into effect. If his Kansas-Nebraska proposal had been less sudden, if he had pushed it through Congress with less violence and more suasion, if he had lent himself less completely to Pierce's sweeping support of the Kansas régime and attack on the freesoil men as "traitors," he might have kept his following. But he had been altogether too dictatorial, partisan, and abusive; even Northern men who accepted his popular sovereignty ideas suspected him of being too dogmatic, bellicose, and brassily demagogic to make a safe President.[3]

No sooner had news of the attack on Lawrence and Brooks's assault filled the land than astute Democratic leaders began searching the horizon for a candidate unconnected with recent events. The argosies of Douglas and Pierce, scudding toward their goal, had grated keel on an unexpected reef. Nor was it necessary to search far for a brighter sail. When Buchanan, disappointed at not returning to the State Department, had taken his desk in the London legation, many friends had lamented that he was placed on the shelf. It proved a shelf safe out of harm's way. Any good Democrat could sweep the South; it was necessary to find a man who could win in the North. The vote of Pennsylvania, a closely-poised State where feeling was deeply offended by low tariffs and the Kansas disorders, had become especially important. Buchanan had kept his formal record straight by a letter penned late in 1855 to Slidell, declaring that the Missouri Compromise line was gone forever, and asserting that the only mode now left of quelling the reckless abolitionist spirit at the North was to adhere to the existing settlement without thought of wavering, and without regarding any storm raised against it.[4] But he had not gone any further. With his old friends Henry A. Wise in Virginia, Slidell in Lousiana, and August Belmont in New York laboring nimbly for him, he became steadily more confident of success. The organization of the Buchanan forces was far superior to that of the other groups, being both extensive and minute.

3  That interesting analysis of ante-bellum events by a Massachusetts Copperhead, George Lunt's *Origin of the Late War* (1866), p. 310, laments that the Democrats in 1856 made the same mistakes as the Whigs in 1852 in basing their nomination on expediency. W. L. G. Smith's *Life and Times of Lewis Cass* makes clear Cass's underlying distrust of Douglas.
4  *National Intelligencer*, August 8, 1856.

ORDEAL OF THE UNION

Douglas's primary strength lay in the West—in Illinois, Missouri, Iowa, Ohio, and Kentucky; Pierce's main fortresses were New England and the South. Early in the year hostile reports began to circulate that the Little Giant might not run at all. He had made himself "so peculiarly obnoxious to the freesoil sentiment of the North," chuckled the Richmond *Examiner*,[5] that his best advisers saw that, even if nominated, he could never win an electoral majority. His intimate friend and supporter, James W. Singleton of Quincy, Ill., indignantly denied this statement and announced that the Senator's name would be strongly urged at the Cincinnati Convention. But Douglas suffered a heavy blow in his own area this spring when Jesse D. Bright, the Senator who nominally represented Indiana but actually the Ohio River borderland, deserted him. For years the Indiana Democracy had been rent into two factions, one primarily freesoil under Joseph A. Wright, one predominantly conservative on slavery questions under Bright. The jealous Bright went into Buchanan's camp, and took Indiana's thirteen delegates with him; the widening of a breach destined to be momentous.

Both Pierce and Douglas fought tenaciously to the end, and each hoped that the other would get into trouble. "Pierce and Shannon seem determined to make a row in Kansas anyhow," wrote Douglas's lieutenant Sheahan, editor of the Chicago *Times*, on February 19.[6] "I wish they were both at Jericho. Pierce seems determined to get up a fight in which he is to be the champion. I think the Cincinnati Convention will nominate a man who will *settle the difficulty.*" When Sheahan's journal crossed swords with Pierce's organ the Washington *Union*, all government advertisements were forthwith withdrawn; proof to the editor of some conspiracy. Sheahan, after much quarreling with his partner Isaac Cook, bought out the latter—who of course went over to Buchanan's side, another desertion destined to have fateful results during the next Administration.[7] The city election in Chicago this spring meant much to Douglas's prestige. "The cry of the enemy is 'anti-Douglas,'" wrote Sheahan. "We will beat them on that cry. Wentworth is perfectly furious. His paper is awful in its impotent madness." This "Long John" Wentworth, the politician of uncouth height best remembered as Lincoln's friend, was editor of the *Demo-*

5 February 8, 1856.
6 N. Y. *Weekly Tribune*, February 27, 1858, describes this defection.
7 Cook was postmaster of Chicago, and hence amenable to Administration pressure. He had for some time been trying to force Douglas's staunch friend Sheahan out of the Chicago *Times* and instal an editor of his own. When he brought an injunction suit in April to stop the newspaper, E. R. Hooper sent a letter of protest to Douglas. "He now occupies about the same relation to the party that John Wentworth does—consults with no one—acts with no one—and abhors all who will not bow subconsciously to his dictation. Too long already have you endured the odium of an intimate association with him—too long have you suffered him to interpose his selfishness between you and those who would like to be your friends." April 10, 1856; Douglas Papers. The business manager, Cameron, wrote April 5 that either Cook must get out or he would. Cook finally sold out for $18,000.

*crat*, an anti-Nebraska daily. It was a joyous moment for the Douglasites when by a narrow majority they carried the election.

"The city last night and through today has been wild with enthusiasm," wrote an adherent. "Bonfires and illuminations by night, and processions, music, speeches, and guns by day, have made it a complete carnival." [8]

But the general current ran against the Senator, and in the end proved irresistible. Douglas was disappointed to find Michigan and most of Ohio against him. While his lieutenants hoped for much from New York city, that metropolis, like Philadelphia, inclined toward Buchanan. One friend suggested an ingenious scheme to set the Pierce and Buchanan men in New York State at each others' throats; holding out a hope that by judicious negotiations with various leaders, he might induce the "Hard" and "Soft" factions to unite on Douglas. But the difficulties were numerous, for Hardshells and Softshells detested each other, and to flirt with one was to alienate the other. Moreover, Governor Horatio Seymour seemed inclined to support the nomination of some Southern man (Andrew Johnson of Tennessee was mentioned) in the belief that he might himself be nominated for Vice-President. In the end the Hards, who hated the President, gave Buchanan seventeen delegates, while the Softs swung eighteen on the initial ballot to Pierce. [9]

Though Pierce had a large Southern following, and various State conventions from the Carolinas to Mississippi and Arkansas urged his renomination, his weakness was patent; other conventions, like Tennessee's, merely voted approval of his record without recommending his reëlection; and Virginia, Maryland, and Louisiana were hostile. It was clear that he had disappointed the country, and that many former admirers regarded him with contempt and aversion. His lack of principle was all too patent. Up to the Democratic convention he did all he could to placate the South; after it he was much firmer on the Kansas issue.

Perhaps the most scorching of numerous adverse judgments passed upon him this spring was that of his former secretary, B. B. French. This outspoken New Hampshire man, so recently a good Democrat, had always been treated well by the President, but had parted ways with him after the passage of the Kansas-Nebraska Act. Pierce, he wrote, "is in rather bad odor, and will stink worse yet before the 4th of next March. The Kansas outrages are all imputable to him, and if he is not called to answer for them here, 'In Hell they'll roast him like a herring.'" He quoted the chief justice of New Hampshire, who had remarked that Pierce had "the damndest black heart that ever was placed in mortal

8  February 24, March 5, 1856; Douglas Papers.
9  D. T. Disney, New York, February 25, March 1, and subsequent dates, proposed overtures to the Hards and Softs; Douglas Papers. See also Mitchell, *Horatio Seymour*, 178, 179; Alexander, *Political Hist. N. Y.*, II, 226.

bosom." Whoever may be elected, he exclaimed a little later, "we cannot get a poorer cuss than now disgraces the Presidential chair! Were he to come into my house, although I should probably treat him with the coldest kind of civility, my toe would feel a great inclination to perform the disagreeable duty of kicking him out!" [10]

The Warwick of the Buchanan movement was Slidell, who had now enjoyed his Senatorial seat for three years; a man moderate enough on those political issues which did not touch his expansionist hopes. He felt both personal and political reasons for disliking Douglas, the friend of his old rival Soulé, while he blamed Pierce for the failure of the designs upon Cuba and for a malfeasance prosecution against a friend. For Buchanan he had an old admiration, increased by the diplomat's share in the Ostend Manifesto. Coöperating with Bright, who aspired to make the Northwest a political fiefdom, with Henry A. Wise, and with Belmont and S. L. M. Barlow of New York, he laid astute plans to win the nomination for his favorite. In New Orleans he and Judah P. Benjamin conferred regularly; in New York a Buchanan "executive committee" held weekly meetings. A hard-working Pennsylvania group—Forney, Bigler, J. Glancy Jones, and others—lent their aid, as did James A. Bayard of Delaware.

Buchanan returned home to New York late in April to meet a public reception of the most cordial kind. Escorted by an aldermanic committee and cheered by the crowd, he proceeded up Broadway to the Everett House, where Mayor Fernando Wood, Senators Slidell and John B. Thompson of Kentucky, and Daniel Sickles greeted him. Refusing a public dinner, he went at once to Wheatland. By this time he was sure of the support of Pennsylvania, New Jersey, and Maryland, of the Hards of New York, and (after perhaps a complimentary vote to Cass) of Michigan.[11]

The great fear of Buchanan's managers was that Pierce and Douglas, uniting most of New England, the Northwest, and the Lower South, would combine against Buchanan. If they did, they could probably dictate the nomination. Dexterous friends saw to it that Buchanan emphatically restated his views on the Kansas question to a Pennsylvania committee, and that they were enforced in Congress by a speech from a Pennsylvania Representative, commending them to the South. Two weeks before the Cincinnati Convention began, Slidell,

10 B. B. French to H. F. French, May 29, July 15, 1856; French Papers. Douglas also had become outspoken in contempt of Pierce. Beverley Tucker wrote him concerning his "oft-repeated denunciation (not 'private' or to me alone) of General Pierce's Administration and of his *personal* bad faith. The latter you have illustrated by an anecdote, which has become widespread and general, and which I have heard told repeatedly." April 19, 1856; Douglas Papers.

11 L. M. Sears, *Slidell*, 122ff.; N. Y. *Herald, Tribune*, April 25, 1856; numerous letters in Buchanan Papers. Barlow was a man of wealth; so were Belmont and Bayard.

Announcing an Election Result, 1854: A painting by Caleb Bingham

Brooks Assaults Sumner: Two Contemporary Conceptions

Bright, and the wealthy W. W. Corcoran hired a spacious suite at the Burnet House for lavish entertainment of incoming delegates and other politicians. S. L. M. Barlow took a temporary home in the city, and as rumors of a Pierce-Douglas coalition thickened, Slidell gathered there a group of politicians hostile to both men. One of the plotters, Senator Bayard, was head of the committee on credentials, and when the New York Hards and Softs presented two contesting delegations, he helped see to it that the vote of that State was split equally between Buchanan and Douglas men. But Slidell stoutly declined to buy delegates for Buchanan by commitments which might later embarrass his chieftain. He showed a rare forbearance, for only two Southern States, Louisiana and Virginia, were cordial to Buchanan, while Northern adherents were scattered and ill-organized.[12]

The convention opened riotously on June 2 with an attempt by the irregular Benton delegation from Missouri to force an entrance to the hall. Bickerings over the status of this group, which was finally excluded, and over the New York feud, occupied most of two days. That part of the platform relating to domestic affairs, which included a strong endorsement of the Kansas-Nebraska Act, was voted unanimously. But the resolutions on foreign policy excited a little dissension. A declaration that "The time has come for the people of the United States to declare themselves in favor of free seas and progressive free trade throughout the world, and, by solemn manifestations, to place their moral influence at the side of their successful example," was carried 211 to 49. A plank which hinted strongly at the need of abrogating the Clayton-Bulwer Treaty was adopted 199 to 57.[13] The principal quarrel, however, was over the question of building a public road between the Atlantic and the Pacific. The resolution supporting this step was laid on the table by a vote of 138 to 120, with

12 Sears, *Slidell*, 122ff; Meade, *Judah P. Benjamin*, 105; Rhodes, II, 170. It should be said that at some points in the North, Buchanan workers were very active. D. A. Noble of Monroe, Mich., wrote Douglas on April 9: "The Buchanan organization throughout the State was much more enthusiastic and minute than I had any idea of, there has been great industry for months, quiet but persevering. But there is really and in truth no sentiment in it and not a particle of sympathy with Buchanan in the masses." Douglas Papers. E. C. West, writing from Wall Street in New York on April 8, spoke of the same careful preparation. "The gradual exposure all over the Union of a regular organization on the part of the Buchanan interests and the lack of a corresponding one upon the part of your friends places you in altogether the most respectable position. . . ." *Ibid.*

13 The platform planks upholding the Monroe Doctrine and American ascendency in the Caribbean excited much dissent. The Charleston *Mercury* of June 11 attacked these "extreme propositions" as being "in conformity with that wild and lawless spirit which seems destined to sweep over the country." It added: "The Monroe Doctrine, as now interpreted, is a pure figment of political demagogues and filibusters." The Missouri *Democrat's* correspondent wrote disgustedly from Cincinnati on June 4 that the South seemed trying to kill Buchanan off with a bad platform. Said the *National Intelligencer* of June 12: "We are glad to see the good sense of a portion of the Democratic press stepping in to rescue the country from the false position in which the extravagant assumptions of the Cincinnati platform would place it before the world."

California, Texas, Louisana, and the upper Mississippi Valley in favor of it, and the Atlantic States overwhelmingly adverse. California delegates showed illtemper over the defeat of the plank, for their hopes of a great national highway were running high. One Californian bitterly remarked that he did not believe that any fit nominee would feel bound by the vote.[14]

Four candidates were nominated in brief speeches: Buchanan, Pierce, Cass, and Douglas. The two-thirds rule of course prevailed. A first ballot gave Buchanan 135½ votes, Pierce 122½, Douglas 33, and Cass 5. Then Pierce gradually dropped back while Douglas forged up. On the final ballot of the day, the fourteenth, Buchanan had 152½ votes, Pierce 75, and Douglas 63. That night the Douglas men made frenzied efforts to induce Pierce's supporters to join them. As a result, on the first ballot next day Buchanan received 168½ votes, Douglas 118, and Pierce only 3—even New Hampshire now voting for Douglas.

As it became clear that a deadlock had developed between Buchanan and Douglas, angry emotions burst to the surface. They were intensified when the sixteenth ballot was taken without substantial change. Thereupon Preston of Kentucky, a friend of Douglas's, rose to say that as he and others had become convinced that the majority wished to nominate Buchanan, he would give way to W. A. Richardson of Illinois, Douglas's floor manager, who would read a letter. A profound hush fell on the assemblage. The letter, dated in Washington on June 4th, the day before the balloting began, breathed a spirit of rare generosity. Douglas wrote that since dispatches indicated that "an embittered state of feeling is being engendered in the convention," and since he was a thousandfold more anxious for the triumph of his principles than for personal elevation, he wished his followers to withdraw his name if that "will contribute to the harmony of our party or the success of our cause." In a subsequent telegram written at 9:30 P.M. on June 5, he had informed his managers that as Buchanan had a majority, he was entitled to the nomination.[15] Preston moved that Buchanan be declared chosen by acclamation, and the convention rose in uproarious applause.

In giving the votes of their States on the final or seventeenth ballot, chairman after chairman stated his delegation's views in a remarkable efflorescence of tributes to Douglas. The spokesman for Texas said that his State had supported first Pierce, then Douglas, "because they had been more actively engaged in the struggle which has of late convulsed every section of the country." Chairman

14 *Proceedings of the National Dem. Conv. Reported for Cincinnati Enquirer*, 1856.
15 All Douglas's dispatches went to W. A. Richardson, who made them public; *National Intelligencer*, June 10, 1856. Douglas might have felt that he could well afford to be magnanimous, for Buchanan was in his sixty-fifth year and hence unlikely to serve two terms; the track would be clear for the Illinoisan in 1860.

Avery of North Carolina recorded "our high appreciation of the eminent services rendered to his country by the author of the Kansas and Nebraska Bill." Harris of Missouri spoke of his deep admiration for the Illinoisan: "Mr. Douglas has endeared himself to the State of Missouri and the whole country, by manfully standing up for all the great principles of the Constitution, by justly interpreting and enforcing all its guarantees and powers, with a constancy and fidelity never surpassed by any statesman of the country." He particularly mentioned the Kansas-Nebraska Act. Gardner of Georgia remarked that when Pierce was put out of the running, his delegation felt bound to support Douglas, who had so manfully battled for great constitutional and conservative principles. Preston added Kentucky's tribute by referring to the crisis "when the genius of Douglas comprehended the danger that was looming in the immediate future, and when he provided for that danger by leading the forlorn hope in the Nebraska-Kansas bill." [16]

The South was grateful. The South had tried to repay Douglas for his services. It was by the votes of Northern Democrats that he was deprived of the nomination. And there were observers who thought he had missed it by a hair's-breadth; that, as the special correspondent of the New York *Tribune* wrote from Cincinnati, the combination against Buchanan failed only at the last minute, and then by the falling out of two or three votes. Had Massachusetts cast five votes for Douglas instead of three, he might have been nominated. "It was unmistakable," wrote an Illinois lieutenant, "that there was a deep under-current of feeling in your favor running through the entire convention, and had it not been for the eternal cry of 'availability,' 'Pennsylvania's last chance,' 'safe man,' 'prudent politic statesman,' 'can carry the doubtful Northern States,' and all such stuff, echoed and reechoed from ten thousand voices from the South, I firmly believe that you would have received the nomination." [17]

Buchanan's victorious managers, sparing no effort to spread balm among their opponents, made a grateful gesture toward Douglas by letting John C. Breckinridge of Kentucky be named for Vice-President; a favor especially asked by W. A. Richardson. Douglas himself continued to display the magnanimity which on occasion he could wear like a sparkling jewel. The party entered the canvass with unity and confidence, presenting its candidate as a man "conservative" both in domestic and foreign affairs. It was generally agreed that, as Horace Greeley admitted, he was the strongest leader that the Demo-

16 *Proceedings . . . Reported for Cincinnati Enquirer.* But many journals jeered at Douglas. He had been defeated, said the well-edited Warsaw, Ill., *Bulletin* of June 12, for two main reasons. One was that too much of the smoke of the Kansas conflict clung to his garments. The other was that he favored filibustering too much; for while the South wished to expand southward, it did not wish to do so at the risk of a war with Britain, which would cost Southerners their best markets.

17 Isaac R. Diller, June 10, 1856; Douglas Papers.

crats could have chosen. In his long career he had sometimes espoused doctrines quite unlike those he now supported; he had been in his day a protectionist, a slavery-restrictionist, an advocate of Federal internal improvements, and an opponent of filibustering. That he possessed great strength of character, elevation of spirit, or power of command, no one ever supposed. His salient qualities were discreet pliability, worldly prudence, and calculating discretion. To a delegation of Philadelphians which, headed by a brass band, made a Sunday excursion to his home, he declared that he would neither add to nor subtract from the Cincinnati platform by a single word, and that the Democracy had again demonstrated that it was "the true conservative party" of the nation.[18]

Conservatism was to be his watchword, and some might spell it timidity.

## [ II ]

On the morning of June 17, the doors of the Musical Fund Hall in Philadelphia swung open for the Republican National Convention, and delegates and spectators, two thousand in all, poured rapidly in. E. D. Morgan of New York, chairman of the national executive committee, mounted the platform and called the assemblage to order. "You are here today," he declared, "to give direction to a movement which is to decide whether the people of the United States are to be hereafter and forever chained to the present national policy of the extension of human slavery." Robert Emmet of New York, the temporary chairman, was supplanted that afternoon by Henry S. Lane of Indiana as permanent chairman. Speeches were made by both these men, by the radical Owen Lovejoy, by Caleb B. Smith of Ohio, and by Henry Wilson of Massachusetts. Thunderous cheers rolled through the hall when the names of David Wilmot (chosen head of the platform committee), Joshua Giddings, Preston King, and William H. Seward were mentioned. More than any other body since the convention system was born a quarter-century earlier, the gathering was animated by a spirit of crusading enthusiasm, an exalted fervor. Its officers boasted that in intelligence, intellectual and moral worth, and personal standing, no convention had ever stood higher and few had ever equalled it.[19]

18 N. Y. *Weekly Tribune*, June 14, 1856. Slidell continued to advise Douglas, urging him to propitiate F. J. Grund for his influence over German-Americans, and to win over Robert J. Walker, whose aid was indispensable. Sears, *Slidell*, 122ff.

19 W. E. Smith, *Blair Family in Politics*, I, 350–357; Julian, *Giddings*, 335, 336; Nevins, *Frémont, Pathmarker of the West*; Beveridge, *Lincoln*, II, 390ff. A call to Republicans had been sent out January 17, 1856, by the State chairmen in Ohio, Massachusetts, Pennsylvania, Vermont, and Wisconsin; and a preliminary convention met February 22 in Pittsburgh, with twenty-four States represented. It agreed upon resolutions written by Henry J. Raymond, and summoned the national convention for June 17. It was to consist of delegates from each State equal to twice the number of its Republicans in Congress, with one additional from every State. H. A. Smith, *Republican National Conventions*.

Actually it was a body strong in certain respects, weak in others. It was sectional in character, no Southern State sending any delegate, and but four of the border States, Delaware, Maryland, Virginia, and Kentucky, supplying a handful.[20] Some of its members held embarrassingly radical views, being not freesoilers but abolitionists. It gave room to territorial delegates from Kansas, Nebraska, and Minnesota, and the Kansans marched in to the roar of six enthusiastic cheers to find themselves heroes. There was a distressing lack of national chords and moderate overtones. But the gathering possessed eminent ability, for it included not a few men already distinguished—Francis P. Blair, Sr., Father Giddings, Preston King, Henry Wilson—and others who would become so: Zachariah Chandler, George Hoadly, Gideon Welles, and Rockwood Hoar. Its evangelistic spirit, its devotion to the highest ideals of democracy, its faith that a great movement for the liberation of America from tyrannous policies was under way, were inspiring to all beholders.

Cincinnati had witnessed an oldstyle political gathering, full of schemers, machine hacks, and barroom rowdies; the Philadelphia scene had a pristine freshness, a bright hopefulness, an evangelistic verve which made it wonderfully refreshing. Its debates throbbed with feeling—its speeches struck fire. Here were qualities which went back, somehow, to the Declaration of Independence, to the old bills of rights, to the passion of the English-speaking folk in bygone centuries for adventures in justice and freedom.[21]

Opponents of the Republican Party charged that it was an organization of but one idea, and its adherents gloried in the charge. The fact that it stood for opposition to slavery extension, and for little else, was emphasized by the platform which Wilmot reported on the second morning. A brief document of nine resolutions, it did not take ten minutes to recite. His strong voice threw out each plank with a defiant ring, and each was followed by a roar of applause. Five resolutions were devoted to the question of slavery in the Territories and and to Kansas, culminating in a demand for immediate admission of Kansas with her free Constitution. The sixth plank denounced the Ostend Manifesto; the seventh and eighth called for immediate construction, with government aid, of a railroad to the Pacific by "the most central and practical route"; and the ninth invited the coöperation of men of all parties, with a caveat against

---

20 All delegates who came were given seats (but not votes), and New York thus had ninety-six delegates, Pennsylvania eighty-one, Ohio sixty-nine, and some other States large groups.

21 For the revivalistic fervor of the convention, the reports in N. Y. *Tribune* and *Evening Post* are excellent; June 18–22, 1856. "The anniversary of Bunker Hill shall be the anniversary of the birth of Freedom," said Henry S. Lane on taking the chair. Speeches of "glowing enthusiasm" followed one another. Henry Wilson's tribute to Seward brought a deafening burst of applause. See George W. Julian, "The First Republican National Convention," *Am. Hist. Review*, IV, 313ff.

legislation impairing the securities of any group. Particularly tremendous were the cheers which greeted the characterization of the Ostend Circular as "the highwayman's plea that 'might makes right,'" and the declaration that it was the duty of Congress to prohibit in the Territories "those twin relics of barbarism—Polygamy and Slavery." Then the convention turned to the nomination of a candidate.

For months one name had been in the ascendency—that of the explorer John C. Frémont. During 1855 certain Democratic leaders, notably John B. Floyd and William Preston, had suggested to Frémont that he might be nominated by a combination of the Democratic Party and the Native Americans; but with the advice of his wife Jessie and Nathaniel P. Banks, he had rejected these approaches. They would in any event have come to nothing. But in Republican ranks the belief was strong that a young, bold, and determined party needed a young, bold, and determined candidate. His adventurous career, the dash, courage, and resourcefulness exhibited in his four different exploring expeditions, his connection with Thomas Hart Benton, who had made him a protégé after his romantic marriage with the brilliant Jessie Benton, his identification in California politics with freesoil ideas, and his friendship with numerous leading men East, West, and South, all commended him as a person likely to attract voters.[22]

As Buchanan was free from the Kansas-Nebraska taint, so Frémont was free from that taint of excessive radicalism on the slavery issue which made Seward and Chase dangerous as candidates. It was true that apart from brief service as Senator from California, he possessed no experience in politics. It was true that his career was sprinkled with incidents indicating that he lacked practical judgment, was deplorably erratic in his estimates of men, acted impulsively and egotistically, and wanted both tact and the stauncher traits of character. A certain hypersensitiveness in his relations with others, a tendency to stand too proudly upon his dignity, probably arose from his knowledge of his illegitimate birth, but was nevertheless unfortunate.[23] Yet it could not be denied that he was

22  Greeley knew Frémont well; and the *Tribune's* editorial plea to its 167,000 subscribers (June 19) attributed to the explorer "a singular force of character and a distinguished ability in every undertaking to which he has applied himself." The best summary of his contributions to science is in E. W. Gilbert's *Exploration of Western America, 1800–1850*, pp. 190, 199. "Frémont's surveys of the South Pass, the Great Salt Lake, the Humboldt River, and the Truckee Pass were all valuable additions to geographical knowledge, but there can be no doubt that his greatest scientific achievement was the discovery of the real nature of the Great Interior Basin of America." The fullest account of his Western achievements, F. S. Dellenbaugh's *Frémont and '49*, is frankly admiring.

23  W. M. Helm, Warrenton, Va., writing to Colonel Munford August 13, 1856, denies as slanderous the statement that the mother and father of Frémont were not legally married. "Mrs. Frémont was a daughter of Col. Thomas Whiting of Gloucester Co., Va. she was a sister of my wife's mother and I learn from my wife that after the death of Col. Whiting his widow married Major Saml Carey and that Mrs. Cary mother to Ann Beverley Whiting,

a man of quick intelligence; that he had made important contributions to American exploration, notably in the Great Basin; that even where he had traversed areas previously explored by others, his scientific depiction of the terrain in his successive reports had greatly enhanced public interest in the Far West, and stimulated a healthy emigration; that he had shown skill and intrepidity in overcoming difficulties; and that he possessed attractive personal qualities, making some of his intimates positive worshippers. He was sound on the Territorial question, but he had never uttered any statements which could alarm the South, while by birth and marriage he had valuable Southern connections.[24]

During the winter of 1855–56 Frémont had gained a long list of supporters. Banks and Henry Wilson were among the first to rally to his side, and Banks has some claim to be called the discoverer of Frémont as a presidential possibility. A California financier, Joseph Palmer of Palmer, Cook & Co., was active in his behalf. Banks, visiting several cities about Christmas, tried to convert John Bigelow of the *Evening Post* and Charles T. Congdon of the Boston *Atlas*, with former Representative Charles W. Upham of Salem, Mass. Bigelow found little difficulty in interesting his chief, William Cullen Bryant, in the explorer. Meanwhile, Frémont's powerful friend Francis P. Blair, with his son Frank P. Blair of St. Louis, took up the enterprise. Late in December, 1855, a conference met at Blair's Silver Spring estate to lay plans for a Republican convention, and it discussed Frémont's name. Apparently the members, who included Banks, Preston King, Sumner, and Chase, thought favorably of him; while a second conference, called in New York by John Bigelow early in 1856, found the elder Blair, E. D. Morgan, and other politicians convinced that he would make the best nominee. A vigorous organization was soon set up, with active full-time workers in both the East and Middle West. As spring opened, the St. Louis *Democrat*, Worcester *Spy*, New York *Evening Post*, and other journals were all quietly pressing the explorer. Bigelow reported that Thurlow Weed was satisfied to take him, "and if so, of course Seward is." [25]

There is little doubt that if Seward had desired the nomination, and his

---

used all her power to compel Ann to marry Major Pryor of Richmond on account of his supposed wealth that Miss Whiting was bitterly opposed to the match but yielded to her mother's importunities but wept and told her sister 'that death would be a relief to her rather than marry that old man (Pryor).' I learn the old major was disagreeable to her and she told him she would leave him and did so under the protection of Mr. Frémont. A divorce was obtained as soon as it conveniently could be and he married Miss Gray and she Mr. Frémont father of the Col." Henry A. Wise Papers. A different account in some particulars, with citations from contemporaneous newspapers, is given in Nevins's *Frémont, Pathmarker of the West*.

24  Kit Carson, who had served under Frémont, was one of his staunchest admirers.
25  Nevins, *Frémont*; John Bigelow, *Retrospections of an Active Life*, I, 142ff.; Margaret Clapp, *Forgotten First Citizen: John Bigelow*.

friends had made a determined fight for it, he could have borne off the prize. But Thurlow Weed believed that the chances of Republican success were too uncertain; Seward was himself at least half-convinced of this; and he was un-willing to stand on a platform which, he feared, would demand some modification of strong antagonism to nativist ideas.[26] Salmon P. Chase would have taken the nomination had it been freely presented him. But his radicalism, for like Seward, he had demanded the abolition of slavery in the District of Columbia and the repeal of the Fugitive Slave Act, made him seem undesirable; his consuming ambition and his religious mania repelled many; while his reputation outside Ohio was as yet limited. Representative Henry Waldron, a Michigan Republican, wrote late in April that "abolitionists from Pennsylvania admit to me that a candidate like Chase or Seward would not get one-fourth of the votes of the State."[27]

Still another person widely considered was John McLean of Ohio, associate justice of the Supreme Court, who was a favorite of many former Whigs, including Abraham Lincoln. The *National Intelligencer* thought him the logical candidate. But he was past seventy, an uninspiring, colorless figure; he had been quite as devious a self-seeker in politics as Buchanan; many ardent anti-slavery men regarded him as hopelessly undependable on the central issue of the campaign—"he has no sentiment of sympathy with the *principle of universal liberty*,"[28] wrote one; and the younger element among the Republicans turned away from him. McLean's principal support lay in Pennsylvania, Delaware, New Jersey, and Ohio, while some of his friends believed him popular among the Know-Nothings; but he failed to gain strength.

By the end of May Frémont was decidedly in the lead. The movement in the West for his nomination, wrote Samuel Bowles, was "going like a prairie fire"; and this statement was confirmed by the Chicago correspondent of the New York *Tribune*, who found him more popular in Illinois than any other Republican. "A sort of intrusive feeling pervades the people that he will be nominated and elected. The same sentiment is extending over Iowa and spreading into Wisconsin." James Gordon Bennett's *Herald* was supporting him in New York—and Bennett had remarkable skill in divining what the people

26 T. W. Barnes, *Thurlow Weed*, II, 245; Bancroft, *Seward*, I, 416–419.
27 April 26, 1856, to Charles S. May; May Papers, Detroit Public Library.
28 M. Scott, Warren, O., May 11, 1856; Wade Papers. McLean's friends were anxious to show that he had taken an early stand on the principle that Congress had no right to institute slavery in territory where it did not exist, and that such territory must remain free until the people therein should form a State government. On December 22, 1847, a long article expounding this view with many judicial decisions had been published in the *National Intelligencer*, and McLean was widely understood to be its author. It was now republished on the eve of the convention in the same paper, May 15, 1856. McLean was strong among the Methodists. But the abolitionists distrusted him, and Edmund Quincy wrote on June 21 that the proposal to name him had been monstrous; Quincy Papers.

wanted. The New York *Tribune* was leaning toward him. "I tell you Frémont is the man for us to beat with, and the only one," Charles A. Dana wrote to the Washington correspondent, Pike. "Besides he is the true metal, that I'll swear to, and more than that, if he is elected his Cabinet will be made up of our sort of men. With McLean we are all at sea, and besides he can't be elected. . . . I suspect our strong ticket is J. C. F., the Representative Man of Free Territory, and Charles Sumner, the Rep. of Free Speech." [29]

But as victory seemed about to fold its pinions and settle upon the Frémont standard, an embarrassing difficulty arose;[30] and to explain its nature, we must turn back to certain events earlier in the year.

[ III ]

From the beginning of 1856, it had been evident that out of the general confusion of parties and factions, the boiling mêlée of the previous twelve-month, a definite crystallization of new elements was emerging; for the presidential election demanded strong and comprehensive party organizations. In an off-year huge numbers of voters might be allowed to hesitate; in a close national contest, party managers would strive to whip them into line. If four parties continued to exist, plainly the Democrats, with their advantages in tradition, discipline, and nationwide strength, would romp to victory. The American political system never tolerates four strong parties; it never for long tolerates even three. In the North most Whigs were now entering the Republican Party, or stood in melancholy hesitation; in the South they joined the Democrats or Americans. But the picture must not be oversimplified, for the general reorganization involved a comprehensive *chassez-croisez*, many freesoil Democrats in the North joining the Republicans, and many anti-alien Democrats in the South clasping hands with the Americans. The great salient fact was that three parties were emerging out of four, the Whigs being steadily and inexorably eliminated—while the Americans had a precarious future.

On Monday evening, February 11, a select group of Whig leaders in Congress had met in a private room in Washington. They included Fessenden of Maine, Collamer, Foot, and Meacham of Vermont, Foster of Connecticut, Pearce of Maryland, Vinton, Schenck, and Ewing of Ohio, Bell of Tennessee, and Hamilton Fish of New York. The conclave, after waiting in vain for Reverdy Johnson, began to talk in the mournful tones of physicians consulting at a desperate bedside. Could the party they loved and revered be kept alive? Was it worth while to hold a national convention? Of the eleven men, ten still

29 June 11, 1856; Pike Papers.
30 Nevins, *Frémont*, 429.

termed themselves Whigs, Fessenden having openly joined the Republican Party. All eleven were what Fish called "strongly National Conservative." [31]

The gathering sadly reached the conclusion that the Whig Party was moribund. Fish, who had favored a convention, confessed that the unanimous adverse opinion of those present painfully impressed him with the impracticability of the attempt, "and I must add, almost forced upon me a conviction that the 'National Whig Party' no longer exists." In Vermont and Maine a fusion organization had swallowed up the great majority of oldtime Whigs, leaving a small remnant to join the Democrats or sulk at home. The Republicans were certain to sweep Maine at the next election. In Connecticut and New York the majority of Whigs had joined the Republicans, and while a conservative minority clung to their old allegiance, they were not sufficiently numerous to elect a separate ticket. A similar situation existed in Ohio. As for Maryland and Tennessee, there the American Party had absorbed most Whigs. Some conservative members had joined the Democrats; in Maryland the alliance had taken the name of Union Party, but it would obviously soon resume its Democratic livery. In most of the South a majority of Whigs seemed to be acting with the Americans, though many had refused to unite with the Know-Nothing Councils and repudiated the intolerance of the organization.

Three parties emerging out of four—and of these the Americans obviously possessing internal weaknesses which boded ill for their future. The principal defects of the American Party were its unrepresentative organization, which bred general discontent; the sharp division between Northern and Southern wings, the former objecting vehemently to the twelfth section of the Philadelphia platform adopted the previous summer, which in effect endorsed or accepted the Kansas-Nebraska Act; and its bigotry, for the eighth section of the same platform contained an anti-Catholic test. The twelfth section had been flatly repudiated by many freesoil groups, including the Pennsylvania State Council; the eighth section had been rejected by the Louisiana members and was disregarded by Know-Nothings in other Southern States.[32] In an attempt to heal the dissension over these two questions, the National Council of the American Order, composed of delegations from the various State Councils, had met in Philadelphia on February 18, just four days before the party nominating convention of some three hundred delegates assembled in the same city.

Confusion, anarchy, and rupture had marked the sessions both of Council and party. To begin with, all efforts of the Council to achieve harmony broke down. It sharply modified its old anti-Catholic stand, merely declaring that no

31 To Washington Hunt, February 13, 1856; Fish Papers.
32 *National Intelligencer*, February 21, 1856.

person should be elected to political office who recognized any allegiance or obligation to any political potentate or power, or who refused to regard the Federal or State Constitutions as paramount in the political sphere. This satisfied most members. But on the slavery question the Council's utterance, full of cloudy verbiage, retained a distinct popular-sovereignty flavor that was offensive to freesoilers and Calhounites alike. When it was agreed to rewrite the twelfth section, Boteler of Virginia made an excited speech declaring that the Northern party was composed of abolitionists, that it was a failure as a national body, and that the Council should adjourn *sine die*. The new plank used so many words to express a popular sovereignty intent that an Indiana delegate said that a President would be elected before the people found out what it meant. But several Ohioans asserted that it was a death-blow to the party in their State, others were equally hostile, and the final vote on the rewritten platform was 77 loud noes to 108 ayes.[33]

In the nominating convention the battle over a statement of principles was angrily renewed. Northern and Southern delegates all but flew at each other's throats. While various Southerners were determined to obtain a declaration of principles condemning the whole anti-slavery and anti-Nebraska propaganda, Northern members refused to permit anything of the sort. At times chaos possessed the hall, dozens of delegates yelling epithets and shaking their fists while others vainly shouted "Order!" Ex-Governor Call of Florida withdrew in a huff; the entire Delaware group threatened to follow him; and other slavery members seemed about to stamp out. Most Northerners wished to postpone a nomination until July, and 73 so voted, but the Southerners and a Northern minority insisted upon immediate action.

Finally the Council's platform was tacitly accepted, or at least not rejected, and the convention proceeded to ballot; the formal voting being by States, each with a voice equivalent to its Federal representation. Never has a presidential candidate been chosen in more irregular fashion. A single delegate in some instances was permitted to cast all the votes of his State. From the beginning Millard Fillmore was far in the lead. He was not a member of the party; he had never attended an American gathering; by no spoken or written word had he indicated a subscription to American tenets. Still abroad, he could not be consulted. But he was nominated by an overwhelming majority, while A. J. Donelson of Tennessee was named for second place. Essentially, these nominations were carried by the South in combination with New York, Pennsylvania, and Illinois.[34]

Neither the platform nor candidates had suited most Northern delegates.

33 N. Y. *Herald*, February 19, 20, 21, 1856; *National Intelligencer*, February 23.
34 N. Y. *Weekly Tribune*, March 1, 1856.

Seventy-one men, representing four New England States and part of Pennsylvania, with Ohio, Michigan, Wisconsin, and Illinois, immediately withdrew. They adopted a solemn protest, declaring the restoration of the Missouri Compromise line essential to redress an undeniable wrong, and asserting that they could never support a party which flouted Northern opinion on the subject. Though several Ohioans announced they would simply unite with the Republicans, a call was issued for a new nominating convention to be held in New York the following June. The ambition of most of the seceders was to join with the Republicans, but as co-equal allies, not as dependents. A preliminary Republican gathering had fixed, as we have seen, on June 17 for the party's first national convention at Philadelphia.

The seceding Americans chose a date just *before* that named by the Republicans! Obviously, their object was to bring pressure upon the Republicans to select a candidate suggested by or at least agreeable to them.[35]

The moment the American Convention broke into two parts, it had become clear that the real contest in 1856 would lie between the Democrats and Republicans. Fillmore, with the Southern Know-Nothings behind him, might possibly carry two or three border States, but he could not do more.[36] The American Party had failed to take any clear stand on principle. It had passed no explicit resolutions, adopted no platform, recognized no distinctive idea. Its candidate was a respectable mediocrity; a man who, for all his signal service in 1850, was without earnest convictions, personal force, or capacity for strong leadership. Fillmore had never counted for anything in American politics except the idea of sectional compromise, and since the day for easy compromise was gone, would now count for nothing whatever. His sole importance would lie in attracting enough conservative Whig votes in the North to weaken the Republicans. This was so plain that the New York *Tribune* had instantly placed its finger on the fact: "The action of the Philadelphia Convention is a manoeuvre of the New York Know-Nothing and Silver Gray politicians to damage the Republican Party and injure certain leading individuals therein." [37]

It was all the more important that the seceding wing of the Americans be induced to fall in behind the Republican nominee. Everybody knew this. The fact that the "North Americans" were to open their convention on June

35 South Carolina's American organization had dissolved to join the Democratic Party.
36 The division between North and South in the American Party was becoming very sharp. The party held its State convention in Tennessee at Nashville on February 12, and in Alabama at about the same time. Both gatherings condemned squatter sovereignty, denying the right of the people to act against slavery prior to the formation of a State constitution; both insisted upon the rights of the South. But when the Know-Nothings of Indiana held a meeting of their executive committee in Indianapolis, that body issued a manifesto (April 2) condemning the repeal of the Missouri Compromise, calling for its restoration, and declaring that if this were not done no more slave States should be admitted.
37 N. Y. *Tribune*, February 28, 1856.

12 made some preliminary understanding with them almost imperative. It was supposed that their favorite was McLean, and that they hoped to dictate his selection to both parties.

[ IV ]

Frémont's followers therefore seemed impaled on the horns of a dilemma. If the "North Americans" nominated McLean, and the Republicans accepted the same man, they had lost. If the Americans nominated McLean, and the Republicans chose Frémont, the two candidates would so divide the freesoil vote that victory would be impossible. Finally, if the Americans nominated Frémont, their action would prejudice him in the eyes of foreign-born voters, including the Germans of the Northwest, and might defeat him in the Republican Convention itself. "I cannot solve the problem," one of the Frémont workers wrote N. P. Banks; "it is out of my reach." Greeley, deeply worried, declared that "Our *real* trouble is the K. N. convention on the 12th." All good Republicans wished the American Party in Halifax. Frémont wrote a stiff letter, to be kept in reserve, declining the American nomination on any terms that might embarrass the Republicans; for voters, he declared, must rise above "all prejudices of birth and religion." [38]

But a simple way out was discovered by the astute Republican managers. They descended in force upon the American Convention; Thurlow Weed, Preston King, E. D. Morgan, and others joyously buttonholed the delegates; and if one observer can be believed, $30,000 was used to control the gathering. Their scheme was that the "North American" Party should nominate Banks for President and some good Whig for Vice-President, and that Banks should then withdraw in favor of Frémont as soon as the latter was nominated by the Republicans. Charles A. Dana misunderstood the scheme. "Banks has been arranging things in a quiet way," he wrote his *Tribune* associate J. S. Pike, "to sell us out at the Know-Nothing Convention tomorrow, so as to get himself nominated for President and force himself upon the Convention at Phila." [39] Happily, all went smoothly. On June 16 the "North Americans" nominated Banks and William F. Johnston of Pennsylvania (though a rump body chose Stockton of New Jersey and Kenneth Raynor of North Carolina), and then awaited the action of the Republicans.

This was not long in doubt. Some curious maneuvering preceded the initial Republican ballot. Judge McLean's friends first withdrew his name, and then re-presented him; Chase's friends definitely withdrew the Ohioan. An informal

38 Nevins, *Frémont*, 430.
39 June 11, 1856; Pike Papers.

ballot gave Frémont 359 votes, and McLean 196. A formal ballot followed, on which Frémont received all the votes except 37 from Pennsylvania and Ohio for McLean, and one from Pennsylvania for Seward.[40] Amid the usual scenes of enthusiasm—the band playing, the crowd yelling, handkerchiefs and hats tossing in air, a huge pennant inscribed "John C. Frémont for President" being drawn across the hall—the nomination was made unanimous. The convention then nominated William L. Dayton of New Jersey, a former Whig who was persona grata to the Americans, for Vice-President. This both Frémont and Thurlow Weed regarded as an error of the first magnitude. Pennsylvania would obviously be the principal battleground of the campaign, and Frémont believed that Simon Cameron, until lately a Democrat, but long an implacable foe of Buchanan, should have been selected.

The "North American" Party promptly but rather sulkily dropped Banks and substituted Frémont. For a time the question whether Dayton or Johnston should be the vice-presidential nominee remained undecided; but Dayton held his ground, and finally Johnston (after an interview with Frémont, in which he apparently received promises of preferment if Frémont were elected) gave way. The Republicans and "North Americans" thus united on the same men, and formed substantially one party.[41]

The campaign was well under way before the Whigs acted. In September a remnant of their party gathered in Baltimore, with delegates from twenty-one States; among them such respectable figures as Edward Bates of Missouri, Ex-Governor Washington Hunt of New York, Rives of Virginia, and Graham of North Carolina. Resolutions were adopted deploring sectional strife and attacking both the Republican and Democratic Parties for fostering it. Without committing itself to the principles of the Know-Nothings who had already nominated Fillmore, the Whigs declared that his election offered the best means of restoring peace to the nation, and endorsed A. J. Donelson for Vice-President. The gathering had been marked by unanimity if not by fervor; and it was evident that Fillmore would play no mean part in the contest.[42]

Speaking in practical terms, three tickets were now in the field: the Democratic under Buchanan, the Republican-"North American" under Frémont, and the Know-Nothing-Whig under Fillmore. Also speaking in practical terms, the battle lay essentially between Buchanan and Frémont—for while Fillmore might get a large minority vote, he could not win. The elements of the battle were simple. The free States had 176 electoral votes; the slave States had 120.

40 N. Y. *Weekly Tribune*, June 21, 1856.
41 Roy F. Nichols, "Some Problems of the First Republican Presidential Campaign," *Am. Hist. Rev.*, XXVIII, 492ff.
42 *National Intelligencer*, September 18, 19, 20, 1856; Nevins, *Fish*, 61, 62; *Reminiscences of James A. Hamilton*, 408ff.

It was evident that Frémont could never carry a single slave State. With 149 electoral votes required for success, he must obtain them all in the free States. This meant that if he lost 28 votes in this area he was defeated. Loss of New York alone would be fatal; so would the loss of Pennsylvania and any other free State; so would the loss of Illinois, Indiana, and New Jersey, and of various other combinations. The struggle was certain to rage with the greatest fierceness in Pennsylvania and Indiana, as the two most doubtful battlegrounds. As E. D. Morgan took charge of Frémont's campaign, and David A. Smalley of Vermont and C. L. Ward of Pennsylvania began organizing Buchanan's, they bent their gaze chiefly on these two States, with anxious secondary attention to New York and Illinois.

## [ V ]

The background of the presidential canvass was flaming Kansas and the reflection of its fires in the mirrors of Washington.[43] The capital could unhappily do nothing constructive for that Territory. Spurred to action by the enthusiasm of the Republican National Convention and the possibility that the new party might sweep the whole North, the Democratic leaders in Congress made a gallant effort. Douglas's bill for a constitutional convention in Kansas was taken up by Senator Toombs, who drafted a new measure which made large concessions to Northern feeling. It provided that five commissioners appointed by the President should take a census of the bona fide residents of Kansas, and oversee the registration of voters; that delegates to a constitutional convention should be chosen in November; and that the convention should assemble in December to draw up a framework of government.[44]

When debate began, moreover, various amendments were admitted to please the Republicans. Freesoil men driven from the Territory were given until

43 James Shields, Douglas's old colleague and supporter in the Senate, was now at Faribault, Minnesota Territory, where he witnessed the maltreatment of the freesoil settlers in Kansas with indignation. "My dear Douglas," he wrote, "I myself am a squatter now. I live amongst squatters. I know something of their conditions. They are building little cabins to shelter their families—cutting rails, making fences, and trying, mark I say trying, to live. I haul rails every day myself—I therefore speak with some experience on the subject. The 'idea' of a rebellion amongst us here now would be rather ludicrous—and yet the President seems to think there is a rebellion in Kansas. The poor squatters there are not better off I take it than here, and yet they are in rebellion and an army is to be sent against them. The seat of war is to be transferred from the Sioux to the squatters. Squatter Sovereignty is to be put under martial law—to have a bayonet at its throat. This is a sad commentary upon something. It took a world of mismanagement to turn poor harmless squatters who have fences to make and corn to raise and wives and children to feed into rebels to be kept down with ball and bayonet." Douglas Papers. He added: "I tell you frankly I don't like the army. More, were it attempted here I would resist to the death and so would every man of us."
44 *Cong. Globe*, 34th Cong., 1st sess., p. 1439.

October 1 to return and register; the more obnoxious Territorial laws were to be repealed.[45] Democratic leaders professed themselves ready, indeed, to make other reasonable changes desired by the opposition. When Republicans objected that Pierce would appoint unfit men as commissioners, Amos A. Lawrence talked with the President about the probable personnel of the body and reported that it would be satisfactory.

But the Republicans, conceding that the measure had many liberal features, were suspicious of Greeks bearing even the fairest gifts.[46] Hale remarked that there was much in the bill to approve, Seward admitted that it gave freedom an equal chance with slavery,[47] and others confessed that it had what the New York *Tribune* called some fair-seeming provisions. But to some extent because of partisanship, and much more largely because of fear that Pierce, the Pierce-appointed governor and commissioners, the local pro-slavery office-holders, and the "Border Ruffians" could not be trusted, the Republican House rejected the measure. It passed the Senate early in July, after a hard-hitting debate which lasted all night, 22 to 12. In the House it was hardly even considered. Douglas grew scornful. "All these gentlemen want," he said, "is to get up murder and bloodshed in Kansas for political effect. They do not mean that there shall be peace until after the presidential election. . . . Their capital for the presidential election is blood." [48] There was some truth in this ascription of political motives. A sound bill based on the Toombs measure could and should have been passed. At the same time, it was not the Republicans who had gotten up murder and bloodshed; and Douglas himself was primarily responsible for the deep mistrust that filled Republican breasts.

Kansas was left to its old controls—and by this time Kansas was in civil war. The attack on Lawrence had begun the conflict; John Brown's cold-blooded slaughter of five pro-slavery settlers on Pottawatomie Creek had immediately extended it. Of John Brown's background some special account is indispensable. His atrocious act cannot be understood without reference to his ancestry, his unhappy personal history, and the atmosphere of unrest and violence pervading the Kansas settlements.

A taint of insanity had marked Brown's family history; his mother and grandmother had died insane, while a maternal aunt and three maternal uncles suffered from the same malady. His father, a Connecticut Yankee and roving

45  *Idem,* Appendix, 795.
46  Lincoln's partner, W. W. Herndon had lately written of the opposition: "No tricks seem to be too low and no language too vulgar for the success of the 'nigger-driving,' I will not say Democracy–Despotism. Does it not seem that all virtue is lost in that section? Is Douglas lost to shame?" To Lyman Trumbull, April 24, 1856; Trumbull Papers. A collection of Herndon's many letters from this and similar sources would be a valuable work.
47  *Cong. Globe,* 34th Cong., 1st Sess., Appendix, 116, 768, 789.
48  Allen Johnson, *Douglas,* 304.

jack-of-all-trades, was an abolitionist, a devout church-goer, and a man of strong prejudices altogether. John Brown, brought up with little education, for he disliked school, followed his father in wandering widely, experimenting unsuccessfully with many vocations, and begetting a large family—by two wives he had twenty children.

Middle life found him a complete failure. His ventures in farming, tanning, land-speculation, sheep-growing, wool-brokerage, and what not all turned out badly; lawsuit had followed lawsuit; repeatedly he had been accused of dishonest practises, and once even of embezzlement; he could not even make a decent living for his family. He was never a hardworking farmer of steady habits. Instead, he was a restless trader, always looking for new deals, and with a visionary's belief that some spectacular transaction would yet make his fortune. Soon after Gerrit Smith furnished lands at North Elba, N. Y., for a community of Negroes, Brown decided to settle his family among them. This was in 1848. On his offer to take land, clear it, employ Negroes when possible, and "be a kind of father" to the blacks, Gerrit Smith gave him two farms on easy terms, an option on more land, and other benefits. But the Adirondack country was bleak and inhospitable, and he was soon back in Akron, O.[49]

Vague schemes of liberating the slaves had begun to possess his mind, for he was no less ardent an abolitionist than his father; and he made it clear, in organizing a Negro "League of Gileadites" to resist the Fugitive Slave Act, that he believed in the use of violence. Crops in Ohio were short, and the family again grew discontented. Five of his sons went to Kansas in the spring of 1855 to take up lands, primarily for their own betterment—though the cause of freedom may have counted for something; and late that summer he followed them with a wagon full of guns, ammunition, and general supplies. Among the weapons were a number of artillery sabres given by an Akron neighbor of Brown's. Of some money which he raised in the East he made no satisfactory accounting.

The attack on Lawrence found Brown fifty-six years of age, and older still in appearance. He was ignorant, narrow-minded, fanatically prejudiced on many issues, highly tenacious, a thoroughly selfish egotist, ready to commit acts that others would term unscrupulous and to justify them by devious psychological processes, and a man with a vein of hard cruelty. The corrosions of failure, ill-health, and fatigue had laid their mark upon him. His figure was bent, his hair graying; the Lawrence *Herald of Freedom* referred to him as

49  The revised edition of Oswald Garrison Villard's *John Brown* is the ablest biography, but it should be read in the light of the additional material and criticism in Malin's *John Brown and the Legend of '56*. Of the three parts of this book, one on the contemporary printed record, one on the growth of the John Brown legend, and one embodying a critique of John Brown and the Kansas Question, the last is the most important.

"an aged gentleman from Essex County, N. Y." Though the best evidence indicates that he had gone West to settle down peacefully, in the excited atmosphere of Kansas his mind, never well-balanced, became more and more warped. Some of his contemporaries there later wrote that in 1856 they knew him to be crazy.[50] A keen Yankee observer was presently to comment on the "little touch of insanity about his glittering gray-blue eyes." [51] He had a Hebraic sense that violent and even murderous deeds might be justified as acts of God's vengeance, visitations of the divine wrath. The Rev. S. L. Adair, at whose home near Osawatomie he often stayed, described him as "a man that had always been from his childhood impressed with the idea that God had raised him up on purpose to break the jaws of the wicked." [52]

When pro-slavery elements late in 1855 threatened Lawrence in the bloodless Wakarusa War, Brown had marched upon the scene as captain of a body of "Liberty Guards" recruited in his own Osawatomie district, a little unit with three lieutenants, eight non-coms, and eight privates. "I'll be one of ten men," he declared, "to go out and attack that Border Ruffian camp at night." The peaceful termination of the struggle apparently left him discontented. He read the inflammatory matter filling the Kansas press. He was pleased to receive a violent letter from Joshua Giddings, who wrote that the death of the first Kansas freesoiler at the hands of Pierce's myrmidons would bring every free State into action: "It will light up the fires of civil war throughout the North, and we shall stand or fall with you." [53] The early disorders of 1856, with the arrogant course of Sheriff Jones, Marshal Donaldson, and Judge Lecompte, fired Brown's temper. When word reached his part of Kansas that pro-slavery forces were again gathering against Lawrence, he spoke exultantly of buckling on his armor with the help of God. [54] The attack on Lawrence filled him with a feeling that immediate vengeance was required. The afternoon of May 23, two days after Lawrence was attacked, found him, four sons— Owen, Frederick, Salmon, and Oliver—and two other men, armed with pistols, rifles, and the two-edged sabres from the East, setting off to the Pottawatomie country on a special mission.

This mission was the murder of five helpless and unprepared pro-slavery settlers. John Brown's precise motive, beyond his general desire to wreak vengeance by a spectacular act, is uncertain. His son Salmon later stated that his father and several associates had decided that some retaliation on the border ruffians was needed "to cause a restraining fear" and "to prevent the utter

50  Villard, 184; Malin, 272.
51  *Letters and Recollections of John Murray Forbes*, I, 179.
52  Malin, 272.
53  Robert Penn Warren, *John Brown; The Making of a Martyr*, 137, 138; cf. Malin, 20.
54  Warren, *John Brown*, 130.

destruction of the whole community." Other apologists explained that five Free-State men had been killed the previous autumn and winter (actually there were six); that John Brown decided that a balance of lives must be struck; and that in accordance with his favorite maxim, that "without the shedding of blood there is no remission of sins," he set out to do God's will. What is certain is that on the night of May 24th, Brown and his fellows dragged five helpless victims from their rude cabins and shot or hacked them to death. One poor woman, frantically protesting, lost her husband and two sons. Whether Brown did or did not kill anybody with his own hands is debatable. Probably he did, and at any rate he took full responsibility for the murders. The crime, one of the blackest of this grim period, had no excuse save perhaps that of partial insanity, and remains a hideous blot upon the memory of a much-spotted man who later, when his determination to combat slavery carried him to still greater extremes, was exalted to the position of a martyr.

News of John Brown's "massacre" on Pottawatomie first reached the East in distorted form. It was necessary for the freesoilers to place the blame on the slavery men. The St. Louis *Democrat* of June 3 carried a mendacious story, attributed to a George N. Propper who had just arrived by steamer from Leavenworth, that five border ruffians had been just about to lynch a free-State man when a party secreted near by shot them all dead. The same day the New York *Tribune* printed the same report, forwarded by its Leavenworth correspondent. This gentleman, like the correspondent of the Chicago *Tribune*, was soon embroidering the tale in sensational fashion: [55]

Some seven or eight Pro-Slavery men on that creek had armed themselves last Friday, and gone to the house of a Free-State man, against whom they had some ill-will, and taken him prisoner. They took him off some distance and procured a rope and said they were going to hang him, meanwhile discussing the matter in a violent manner. While they were doing this, the alarm was raised, and eight Free-State neighbors of the man taken, armed themselves

55 The facts concerning the Pottawatomie massacre were long in coming to light, and national misunderstanding of them and of old Brown was general. John H. Gihon and other freesoil historians adopted the stock excuses of retaliation and preventive action to protect freesoil settlers; Gihon even invented "a sort of trial" (*Geary and Kansas*, 87). As late as 1878 Charles Robinson wrote: "I never had much doubt that Capt. Brown was the author of the blow at Pottawatomie, for the reason that he was the only man who comprehended the situation, and saw the absolute necessity of some such blow, and had the nerve to strike it." Then he got hold of the testimony which proved the total lack of necessity and the innocence of the victims. *Nation*, June 30, 1892. For the true heinousness of the crime see Malin, 560–592. But to understand Northern thought in the next few years on the subject, it must be remembered that it approximated the complacency of the footnote account in Nicolay and Hay's *Lincoln* (II, 191), which includes a strong suggestion that the massacre was excusable. Various charges have been made to blacken the names of the five murdered men. All of them have been disproved except, to be sure, the charge that the Doyles were illiterate—no high crime in America of that period. Malin, 480, 481.

thoroughly and found the party. A conflict ensued, in which five of the Pro-Slavery men were killed. The others then proceeded down the creek to the house of a wealthy old slave owner, who was supposed to have instigated the outrage, and taking him and his negroes in a cart they drove them back to Missouri. I give this for what it is worth; if true, it is the first aggressive act of the Free-State men, and is not to be wondered at.

But in Kansas the substantial truth was quickly known, and raised throughout the Territory a cry of horror. It was the first crime of its kind perpetrated on either side since the Kansas difficulties began. Heretofore threats of violence had been innumerable, weapons had been freely flourished, and a few isolated murders by irresponsible men had been committed, but no slaughter by an organized band had occurred. The wanton killing of five men and boys, under circumstances of cold-blooded cruelty, was without precedent, and seemed to break a practical truce. No Free-State man whatever had been slain in the southern part of the Territory. The massacre was doubly reprehensible in taking place at just the moment when the retirement of the pro-slavery army under Marshal Donaldson constituted a really impressive victory for the Free-State forces. Until John Brown struck, the general conduct of the freesoilers in Kansas had been unexceptionable, their moral if not legal case was perfect, and their outlook for the future was hopeful in the extreme. "Nothing remained," as Charles Robinson writes, "but to fill up the Territory with *bona fide* settlers, and to take possession of the government at the election of the legislature, when the day should arrive." But the crime of Pottawatomie gave the signal for guerrilla warfare.[56]

"WAR! WAR!" trumpeted the Westport, Mo., *Border Times* in its account of Brown's wild act published on May 27.

## [ VI ]

At once armed parties on both sides took the field. The settlers along Pottawatomie Creek, both freesoilers and pro-slavery men, held a meeting three days after the crime at which they condemned "the midnight assassins unknown" who had killed their neighbors, and adopted resolves which were forthwith printed: they would lay aside all political feelings, and act as men of common sense in opposing fanatics; they would discountenance all armed bands of men; and they would ferret out the authors of this crime and hand them over to the authorities for punishment. But it was too late to stop the wildfire.

News of the massacre ran from settlement to settlement, inflaming the

56 Robinson, *Kansas Conflict*, 265. "The sack of Lawrence on May 21 in the Kansas Valley, and the Pottawatomie massacre in the Marais des Cygnes valley opened in their respective regions the era of guerrilla warfare." Malin, 589.

border ruffians to the fiercest anger. The Westport *Border Times* issued an extra containing a lurid account of the murder of "eight pro-slavery men" on the Pottawatomie; and on the 28th the Leavenworth *Herald* reprinted the story with all its violent embellishments. An excited massmeeting in Leavenworth, with Stringfellow and General W. P. Richardson prominent, instantly decreed that all active Free-State men must quit Kansas soil.[57] Freesoilers, including witnesses about to appear before the Congressional investigating committee, were arrested in the streets. Threatening groups of armed men appeared at Westport, Atchison, and other border towns. Governor Robinson, held prisoner in the Shawnee House at Leavenworth, was in imminent danger of being lynched. Whitfield, the pro-slavery delegate to Congress, took command of some two hundred and fifty men, and on June 5th one of his scouting parties killed a freesoil settler named Cantrell. Henry Clay Pate, correspondent for the St. Louis *Missouri Republican* and pro-slavery resident, became captain of a body called Shannon's Sharp Shooters, recruited chiefly in Westport. He marched to Osawatomie in search of John Brown, burned and looted several buildings, and made two of Brown's sons prisoners. Then Brown turned the tables on him; collecting twenty-eight men, he surprised Pate's camp at dawn and captured the Missouri leader with twenty-three of his men.[58]

"Progress of the Civil War" was now a standing headline in many American newspapers. A three-hour engagement at Palmyra was reported, a pro-slavery attack on Franklin, another great gathering of border ruffians to assault Lawrence, and a rapid movement of bloodthirsty Missourians from the river area into Kansas. Free-State men, alarmed by the reports of invasion, left their farms to be tended by women and children while they drilled for defense. Between Osawatomie and Lawrence, they tilled the land in bands of five or ten, their arms within instant reach. Governor Shannon on June 4th issued a proclamation ordering all armed bands to disperse, warning aggressive parties outside the Territory not to enter it, and urging civil officers to protect persons and property. But the situation had deteriorated to a point which made proclamations worthless. When strangers met in Kansas that spring, wrote a traveller, they frequently approached each other pistol in hand, and the first salutation was "Free-State or pro-slave?" Sometimes the next sound was a pistol shot.[59]

---

57 Robinson, *Kansas Conflict*, 275ff.; Phillips, *Conquest of Kansas*, 318; N. Y. *Weekly Tribune*, May 28, 1856.
58 Spring, *Kansas*, 156; Sanborn, *John Brown*, 294–296; Gihon, *Geary*, 87, 88.
59 Redpath, *John Brown*, 103–108. An article in the St. Louis *Evening News* graphically describes the situation as the events at Lawrence and Pottawatomie intensified the hatred between freesoil and pro-slavery forces. Great numbers of the freesoil settlers in the northern part of Kansas, alarmed by the threats of their antagonists and expecting nothing but strife, broke up their households, allowed their farms to go to wreck and waste, and in bitterness of heart retired to the southern area of the Territory, where they organized

For some days the pro-slavery mob held control of Leavenworth. They made a list of nearly fifty business and professional men of Free-State sympathies, gave them three days to quit the Territory, and arrested nearly thirty. Many did flee the Territory; others took refuge in Lawrence. The special correspondent of the New York *Tribune* was hunted out of Leavenworth, and pursued across country. Hiding in the bushes, he repeatedly saw men with guns and bayonets searching for him, but finally gained Lawrence with his clothing in shreds. Osawatomie was attacked on June 7th by a band of Whitfield's men, who pillaged most of the houses, stole a number of horses, destroyed a newly opened printing establishment, and left several dead Free-State men behind them.[60] Some of Buford's hotheaded Southerners seized the sergeant-at-arms of the Congressional investigating committee, and held him prisoner until Representative Oliver intervened. Colonel Sumner had taken the field with a body of United States dragoons in an effort to restore order, but though he accomplished something in compelling the retirement of Whitfield's little army to their homes, he made no arrests, and his force was totally incapable of halting the guerrilla warfare that had fast overspread the land.

From every hand came reports of men killed and wounded, houses burned, horses stolen, and inoffensive settlers driven from their farms .Armed Missourians guarded all the approaches to Kansas, seized arms or other weapons shipped up the Missouri River, and required all river passengers to disclaim any freesoil leanings. "There is a reign of terror in Kansas," a Lawrence correspondent wrote the Chicago *Tribune*. "The prospects of freedom are gloomy. The Northern squatters are yielding to despair. Their only hope is in Northern resolution." [61]

But Northern resolution was equal to the test. All over the North, as news of the internecine struggle became more alarming, meetings were held, money was subscribed, and emigrants were encouraged to proceed west. The sack of Lawrence stimulated this activity more than all other occurrences combined.

---

armed companies. With their only line of communication eastward, the Missouri River, controlled by the enemy, they felt cut off from their friends in the Northern States. To a considerable extent they subsisted on wild game. Within a month, or by midsummer, the large body of Kansas settlers who had taken no active side with either Free-State or pro-slavery men, but had attended quietly to their own affairs and let politics alone, disappeared. They were compelled to align themselves with one side or another, and to take active measures with their parties. Roistering bands of lawless guerrillas, who used the plea that "civil war has begun" to kill or injure men, destroy property, and to pillage, began to devour the substance of the Territory. What six months earlier had been a fair and smiling land, offering the promise of abundant prosperity, became a scene of confusion and in some places of desolation. Quoted in N. Y. *Weekly Tribune*, June 21, 1856.
60 Lawrence correspondence in N. Y. *Tribune*, June 9, 1856.
61 Letter dated May 31, 1856.

Citizens of Chicago met in the courthouse on May 31 in an enthusiastic gathering addressed by James Lane, Isaac N. Arnold, Norman B. Judd, and others of prominence. It was announced that a hundred and twenty-five Chicagoans were ready to leave at once to settle in Kansas. Subscriptions were called for. Within a few minutes the sum pledged rose to $8,000. "Now," said Arnold, "make it $10,000." When it reached that sum the assemblage joined a popular singer in "The Star-Spangled Banner," and promptly made it $15,000.[62] Faneuil Hall had its gathering, with Senator Henry Wilson and Edward Everett Hale pleading for Kansas and denouncing the Administration for its course. At a Syracuse meeting a letter was read from Gerrit Smith proposing a national fund of a million, and offering to subscribe ten thousand dollars himself. Lively concourses of citizens met in Troy, Schenectady, Utica, Syracuse, Auburn, Rochester, Buffalo, and other New York cities, while the agitation extended far and wide throughout the Middle West.

Everywhere the same spirit was manifested. In New York city a massmeeting which filled the Tabernacle on the night of June 9th saw on the platform a young man and his wife, just driven out of Kansas, and an older man whose son had been killed there. They listened to a brief speech by Charles A. Dana, and heard Representative Samuel Galloway of Ohio declare: "The great question now before the people of this country is not the emancipation of the Negro, but the emancipation of the white man. The crisis has come. Here are two antagonistic powers about to come into collision—Freedom and Slavery. Which shall be the governing principle of our American institutions?"[63]

In the same heated terms, pro-slavery editors and agents were meanwhile appealing to the South to rally behind its sons beleaguered in the new Territory. The general outbreak of violence sent a wave of fleeing Missourians across the river to their old border homes. Most of them were peaceful and quiet citizens. They naturally blamed the freesoilers for their plight. Many of the men, depositing their wives and children in places of safety, caught up their firearms and returned to fight for their homes and household goods. Their stories, exaggerated with every repetition, spread throughout northwestern Missouri. "There is no use in disguising the fact," exclaimed the Independence *Messenger* of June 7, "that our border counties are upon the eve of emptying themselves into the Territory of Kansas and declaring a war of extermination against those abolition outlaws. The patience of our people is almost exhausted, and their powers of endurance well-nigh crushed under the accumulated and burning atrocities to which many of their friends and relations are subjected." Meetings were held and fierily addressed. To most slaveholding Missourians the Free-State

62 Chicago *Tribune,* June 1, 3, 1856.
63 N. Y. *Weekly Tribune,* June 14, 1856.

Party in Kansas was an organization of outlaws; its leaders were "abolitionists"; and the Northern sympathizers were "freedom-shriekers." [64]

To the Lower South, at the same time, went frantic appeals for men, money, and moral encouragement. A body of higher-law abolitionists, ran the theme, had put Kansas in flames by their wicked assumptions and provoking acts; their fanaticism must be repressed. Major Warren D. Wilkes returned to South Carolina in June as a plenipotentiary from fellow-settlers in Kansas to obtain assistance. The executive committee of the Kansas Association in Charleston gave wide currency to his appeal.[65] Our emigrants went out, he assured Carolinians, with no intention of fighting. They meant to take land, work hard, improve the country, and settle the issues at the fall election. But the Free-State Party refused to pay taxes or obey laws; they insulted and threatened Judge Cato; they tried to assassinate Sheriff Jones of Douglas County; they made violent speeches and passed incendiary resolutions; and they finally provoked open war. Now aid must be hurried to Kansas. Letters were sprinkled through the South, of which one from Platte City, Mo., perhaps by Atchison himself, may serve as example. "We have had a stirring time for the last few weeks," it declared. The slavery men had behaved valiantly. "My opinion is that the South will be stirred by the transactions of these few weeks, and will come up with men and money. The latter is particularly wanted to assist the men. In a few months, in my opinion, there will not be an abolitionist left in Kansas; they will be swept with a clean broom. Then the war will be carried elsewhere, if war we are to have." [66]

Naturally the great central issue of the presidential campaign was furnished by the conflict thus raging in Kansas. Newspaper readers all over the North tore open their journals to learn the latest news about "the progress of the civil war." Skirmish followed skirmish; the battle of Palmyra, the battle of Franklin, the battle of Osawatomie—for they were all termed battles. In some engagements Free-State men were the aggressors, in some pro-slavery men.

The attack on Franklin, for example, was begun by the freesoil forces or Rangers, as they called themselves. That hamlet, lying four and a half miles southeast of Lawrence, had more than once been used by the pro-slavery men as a rallying point. Early in June it was again a military station, some of Buford's Southern recruits, with various Missourians, drilling there and keeping in communication with fresh pro-slavery bands that entered the Territory. They had a brass six-pounder and a large quantity of ammunition and provisions. In their

64  See articles in Lexington, Mo., *Express*, and Jefferson, Mo., *Inquirer* for June, 1856.
65  Charleston *Mercury*, quoted in *National Intelligencer*, July 3, 1856.
66  This letter, dated May 27, 1856, was printed by the *Carolina Times* (Columbia, S. C.) as from "a distinguished gentleman of Platte City, Mo." Atchison was the most distinguished gentleman of Platte City. "We had no fighting, but it was owing to the cowardice, not the forbearance, of the abolitionists," ran the letter. Warsaw, Ill., *Bulletin*, July 3, 1858.

guardhouse they kept a freesoil prisoner. The Free-State Rangers determined to attack the place, and capture the cannon and ammunition. At three o'clock on the morning of the fourth, amid darkness thick as Erebus, a party invaded the town; brisk firing began; and at dawn the pro-slavery men retreated leaving their cannon behind. One pro-slavery man was killed and several injured. In this encounter the freesoilers were clearly censurable.[67]

But the much bloodier action called the battle of Osawatomie found their opponents in the rôle of attackers. A Missouri force under Atchison on August 29th moved into Kansas, and camped on Bull Creek fifteen miles north of Osawatomie. This place was known as the headquarters of "Old Brown," and no other freesoiler was hated so much. "General" John W. Reid with 250 or 300 men descended upon it at dawn on August 30th, shooting one of John Brown's sons dead as they entered the village. With about two-score followers, Brown took station among the trees and underbrush skirting the Marais des Cygnes, and for a time held the Missourians at bay. Then a charge put the defenders to headlong flight. Ten or twelve men were killed, and a number wounded, while the victorious invaders burned most of the town.[68]

The principal advantage of the pro-slavery party in Missouri and Kansas lay in their ability to obstruct the most direct avenues of communication. Even before the sack of Lawrence and the Pottawatomie massacre some travellers on the Missouri River boats had been threatened or turned back, and shipments of weapons seized. After these events Atchison and his confederates stopped at nothing. Steamers were searched, goods confiscated, and travellers peremptorily ordered to return. When the party of seventy-five freesoil settlers recruited at the great Chicago meeting of May 31 came up the Missouri, they were halted at Lexington and their Sharpe's rifles taken from them. At Leavenworth they were stopped again, and deprived of all their small arms. Finally they were sent back under guard to the Mississippi and landed near Alton, Ill., in a violent rainstorm. Throughout Illinois freesoil newspapers, enraged by the episode, printed violent editorials which the Eastern press echoed.[69] Northern emigrants who avoided the Missouri River boats and tried to cross Missouri by road were similarly intercepted. The Squatter Sovereign, declaring that mere stoppage was not enough, called for the hanging of two boatloads of emigrants.

As interferences grew, freesoil groups in the East proposed the outfitting of an armed steamboat to ascend the Missouri, and a united protest by Northern governors; but a simpler and more effective expedient was at hand.

Transit to Kansas was promptly opened by a flanking route through Iowa

67  Lawrence correspondence in N. Y. *Tribune*, June 5, 1856.
68  Spring, *Kansas*, 189–191.
69  Beveridge, *Lincoln*, II, 406.

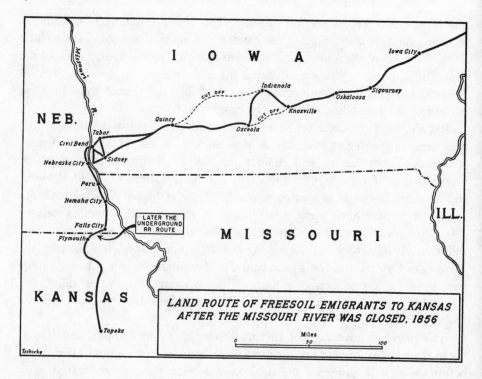

LAND ROUTE OF FREESOIL EMIGRANTS TO KANSAS
AFTER THE MISSOURI RIVER WAS CLOSED, 1856

and Nebraska. A committee appointed by Free-State settlers, meeting in mass-convention at Topeka, made the necessary arrangements for terminal facilities. On July 4 a circular announcing the establishment of the "Lane Trail" was issued in Iowa; local committees were organized there; and by the end of July companies from Massachusetts and four Middle Western States, including the undiscouraged Chicago emigrants, had reached Nebraska City, and to the number of nearly four hundred were rejoicing in the prospect of early arrival in Kansas. They were called the "Northern Army," and inasmuch as James Lane took over their command, martial action was by no means impossible. Governor Shannon, highly alarmed, called upon the Federal troops to intercept them. But Brigadier-General Persifor F. Smith, a judicious officer who had now succeeded Colonel Sumner, refused to be led into rash acts; and two representatives of the National Kansas Committee, Dr. S. G. Howe and Thaddeus Hyatt, reaching the encampment and finding it ill-clothed, ill-supplied, and nearly penniless, deposed the impetuous Lane. The "army," crossing the Kansas line in a thoroughly peaceful manner, merely established two new towns at Plymouth and Holton, strengthening the freesoil population elsewhere.

Other powerful parties followed the new overland route. As summer ended, James Redpath came in with 130 men. An expedition arrived under the leadership of a nineteen-year-old youth later famous, Preston B. Plumb.

Samuel C. Pomeroy and others came escorting a great force of six or seven hundred men, with three cannon and other implements of war—part of them furnished by the Iowa State Arsenal. Deputy Marshal Preston seized most of the arms, but the immigrants were permitted to swell the thickening ranks of the freesoil settlers.[70]

[ VI ]

The turmoil in Kansas rose to a climax in August and September. First the Free-State forces descended upon a heavily-built log cabin occupied by a force under Colonel H. T. Titus, the most active and hated "ruffian" in the Territory. After an exchange of shots in which three men were killed and eight wounded, the garrison of Fort Titus surrendered. They were taken to Lawrence, now boiling with military preparations. Governor Shannon hastily rode over, and though the mob at first seemed intent on killing him, brought about a peaceable agreement; Titus and his followers being released in exchange for the cannon captured in the sack of Lawrence, and for half a dozen prisoners taken after the attack on Franklin. Shannon returned to Lecompton quite unnerved, for he had seen many newcomers from Chicago and other points thirsting for battle. "We are threatened with utter extermination by a large body of free-state men," he wrote the departmental commander. ". . . I saw in that place at least eight hundred men who manifested a fixed purpose to destroy this town." On August 18th he penned his resignation. "I am unwilling to perform the duties of governor of this territory any longer," he informed Pierce.

The accession to power of the Territorial secretary, Daniel Woodson, who had always been a pro-slavery tool, delighted the Southern elements. Atchison and his associates had announced when Fort Titus fell that civil war was raging, and has issued a clarion call to all law-and-order men "who are not prepared to see their friends butchered" to rally instantly to the rescue. Acting-Governor Woodson abetted them by a proclamation on the 25th declaring the Territory in open insurrection, and urging all patriots to muster for the defense of the law. As the month ended Atchison's force moved into Kansas and camped on Bull Creek, fifteen miles north of Osawatomie.

70 See the MS by W. E. Connelley on the Lane Trail in the Lane Papers, Univ. of Kansas. An interesting feature of the summer was the restoration of the wrecked Lawrence newspaper, the *Herald of Freedom*. Editorials published far and wide in the North in June declared that the blow struck at freedom of the press in Kansas was a blow struck at its freedom everywhere. Conductors of the free newspapers of Chicago took the lead in the work of reviving the *Herald of Freedom*. The editor of that journal, G. W. Brown, was at the moment imprisoned in Kansas on a charge of treason. But the Chicago *Tribune* (Horace White, Joseph Medill), the *Democrat* (John Wentworth), the *Staats-Zeitung*, the *Democratic Press* (Scripps, Bross, and Spears), and the *Journal* (Wilson) organized a committee of five for the purpose. These were all anti-Nebraska sheets. They asked for subscriptions from the entire press of the North. Warsaw, Ill., *Bulletin*, June 12, 1856.

For a time it seemed that a series of pitched battles would take place. Woodson directed Colonel P. St. George Cooke to seize Topeka and disarm all its "insurrectionists," an order that Cooke (supported by General Smith) refused to execute. Instead, he did something far better. Two strong Free-State columns moved against Lecompton, the principal body under the fiery Lane appearing on the afternoon of September 5th. The terror-stricken inhabitants appealed to Cooke for protection, and the gallant colonel rode forth at the head of his dragoons. Haranguing the Free-State men, he convinced them that their expedition was needless, for Atchison's force were already retiring to Missouri, and all prisoners were about to be released.

"As I marched back over those beautiful hills, all crowned with moving troops and armed men," he wrote later, ". . . I rejoiced that I had stayed the madness of the hour, and prevented, on almost any terms, the fratricidal onslaught of countrymen and fellow-citizens." Thus was one menacing expedition halted. The freesoilers were somewhat mollified when five days later Governor Robinson was released on bail, this happy step having been effected by the personal intervention of Abbott and Amos A. Lawrence with President Pierce. But the stormclouds had no sooner been partially dissipated on one side than they lowered more thickly on the other. The pro-slavery forces under Atchison had retired across the Missouri boundary only to re-form their ranks, with a heavy reinforcement in equipment and numbers. The new army, more formidable than any which had preceded it, invaded the Territory early in October, and pushing on to Franklin, seemed on the point of effecting a complete conquest of Lawrence and Kansas. A fresh intervention was necessary.

It was supplied by a commanding new figure, John White Geary of Pennsylvania, whom Pierce had appointed governor and hurried to Kansas to rescue the situation—primarily in the interests of the nation as a whole, and secondarily of the Democratic presidential ticket.[71] He seemed precisely the virile, energetic, strong-minded man demanded by the crisis. Six feet five and a half inches tall, with a soldierly bearing, he was still in his middle thirties. Yet he had proved his quality in a variety of employments. Born in Pennsylvania and educated at Jefferson College, he had been attorney, civil engineer with the Allegheny Portage Railroad, a captain of volunteers in Mexico, where he commanded Chapultepec after its capture and attained the rank of colonel, first alcalde and later first mayor of San Francisco, and a prominent figure in early California

---

71 Geary was widely reported to have said that he was "carrying a Presidential candidate on his shoulders." It was true, for Northern sentiment was being deeply aroused. John H. Bryant, the poet's brother, had written Lyman Trumbull from Princeton, Ill.: "There is and can be no middle ground in the present state of our national politics. The South will suffer none and the North ought not to. This war must go on until Slavery or Freedom gains the unquestioned ascendency in the nation." March 24, 1856; Trumbull Papers.

politics. Possessing the habit of command, he knew how to manage men. Indeed, his self-confidence, optimism, and resourcefulness were such that he entered upon his task with something of elation. He had just declined the governorship of Utah, but the difficulties in Kansas gave him precisely the opportunity he desired. Though early in life he had spent some time in Kentucky, he favored free institutions and had helped to make California a free State. Now he meant to be prompt, decided, and impartial in all his measures. He at once perceived, as he later wrote, "that, in order to do any good, I must rise superior to all partisan considerations, and be in simple truth the governor of the entire people."

Pierce, moreover, now that he was out of politics, was taking a clearer view of his duty. Abbott Lawrence talked with him, and received assurances of his intention of seeing justice done in Kansas; assurances which Amos A. Lawrence at once transmitted to Charles Robinson.[72]

Geary, taking up his duties at Lecompton on September 11, immediately issued a proclamation dissolving the militia that Woodson had so unwisely called out, and summoning all irregular bands to disperse.[73] Actual settlers were to be enrolled as a new militia, subject to muster at short notice. This was an important step, for the existing militia had in great measure been composed of men from Missouri and other States, all of the pro-slavery party.

Then, together with Colonel Cooke, the governor intercepted the new Missouri army as it was bearing ominously down upon ill-defended Lawrence. The advance was halted while the governor, taken to headquarters at Franklin, parleyed with the pro-slavery leaders: Atchison, Whitfield, Titus, and others. He argued that violence was unnecessary, and that another sack of Lawrence would recoil upon pro-slavery heads, for it might ruin all Democratic chances, while they could trust him to see that the Free-State men were held in restraint. Atchison was satisfied, and once more the motley little army of Missourians and Southerners—2,500 men in all, horses and foot, with a six-pound battery— scattered to their homes. At the same time, Federal troops captured nearly ninety Free-State men who had just fought a pro-slavery band at Hickory Point, killing one border ruffian. These guerrilla troopers were committed to

---

72 See the sketch of Geary in W. C. Armor, *Lives of the Governors of Pa.;* J. H. Gihon, *Geary and Kansas;* A. A. Lawrence, September 16, 1856, Robinson Papers.

73 Geary's inaugural, delivered at Lecompton on September 11, was an admirable address. He pleaded with the people to bury the past in oblivion, and begin anew. "Men of the North, men of the South, of the East and the West in *Kansas,* you and you alone, have the remedy in your own hands. Will you not suspend fratricidal strife? Will you not cease to regard each other as enemies, and look upon one another as the children of a common mother, and come and reason together?" One sentence in the inaugural intimated that he thought some changes in the laws of the Territory desirable, and would take up that subject shortly. *National Intelligencer,* September 25, 1856.

jail without bail, and a number of them subsequently received penitentiary sentences.[74]

By these and other decisive acts, Geary restored temporary order in the Territory. The almost simultaneous arrest of fourteen Free-State troublemakers in Topeka, and the issuance of warrants for John H. Stringfellow and other pro-slavery agitators, convinced men that he was determined to execute even-handed justice. Freebooters and rowdies who had taken advantage of the general convulsion found it wise to retire to their lairs. The courts, stimulated by stern letters of rebuke which Geary addressed to the judges, began to evince more energy. It became evident to Chief Justice Lecompte, Indian Agent Clarke, and Marshal Donaldson that the governor bent a watchful eye upon their pro-slavery activities, and that his impartiality was backed by courage. Geary was presently able to spend twenty days in touring the now quiet Territory, and to report that the benign influences of peace dominated the situation. This was true. "Business is reviving," reported the Lecompton correspondent of the St. Louis *Republican* on September 26; "confidence is restored; men talk more kindly of each other; the axe, the saw, and the anvil are heard in their different vocations."

Democratic newspapers and campaign orators hastened to spread the news of Kansas pacification over the land, and Buchanan's candidacy immediately profited. Nevertheless, the Republicans maintained a thunder-roll of alarmist propaganda. Lydia Maria Child had hastily penned a novel, *The Kansas Emigrants*, which by October the New York *Weekly Tribune* was purveying to hundreds of thousand of readers all over the North and Northwest. The freesoil press made much of a remarkable article which Thomas H. Gladstone published in the London *Times* of October 11, detailing his experiences in Kansas, and giving a vivid depiction of the rowdy aspect, general ignorance and vulgarity, and violent behavior of the border ruffians. As a horrifying study of the rawest salient of the Missouri frontier, thrust into Kansas affairs, it produced a tremendous effect. Seward, meanwhile, was speaking on Kansas—as were hundreds of other Republicans. At Auburn, on October 21, he declared that "the Territory has been subjugated by slaveholders, and they, having usurped its sovereignty, are organizing a slave State there, which will offer for admission at the next session of Congress." It was a warning which profoundly impressed many Northerners.

Thus as Kansas still burned in the national consciousness, the presidential campaign entered on its final phase with the two chief parties apparently closely matched, and the result in genuine doubt.

74  Weston, Mo., *Reporter*, September 19; Independence, Mo., *Messenger*, September 20, 1856. The number of Federal troops in Kansas, as reported by the Secretary of War, rose to 980 for the fourth quarter of 1855, and to 1,086 for the first quarter of 1856. It then fell slightly, rising in the last quarter to 1,303.

# 14

## The Election of Buchanan

"IT IS DIFFICULT to sit still with such excitement in the air." So wrote Henry W. Longfellow, who had never before taken much interest in politics, at the beginning of the campaign of 1856. A young anti-slavery Virginian holding a pulpit in Washington had said in January that he was of no party; in July he preached a sermon declaring that voting was as solemn as prayer. "Henceforth," thundered this young man, Moncure D. Conway, "no freeman is ever going to be quiet." We are going to elect Frémont, are we not? demanded Lowell, newly returned from Europe, of his friend C. F. Briggs—adding that it would be the best event of his lifetime. "We shall begin to be a nation at last, I hope, instead of a clique, as hitherto—and a clique of gamblers, too." And John G. Whittier, whose militancy in high causes never failed, seeing more clearly than most the unescapable clash before the country, gave thanks that he lived in a time

> When Good and Evil, as for final strife,
> Close vast and dim on Armageddon's plain.[1]

As such utterances indicate, the presidential campaign, sluggish enough in the South where Buchanan's sweep was certain, was wild and stormy in the North. Three or four States there furnished the pivot of the contest. Frémont was certain to carry all New England, and almost certain of New York, Ohio, Michigan, Wisconsin, and Iowa. This left the decision resting primarily upon the States of Buchanan, Douglas, and Jesse Bright. The man who carried Pennsylvania and Indiana would be fairly certain to win the election. These two States, as it happened, would elect State officers in October. All eyes were therefore fastened upon them. In Indiana, a young attorney of Yankee lineage and brilliant talents, Oliver P. Morton, one of the many former Democrats who had revolted against the Kansas-Nebraska bill, had been nominated by a fusion of Republicans and Americans against the Democratic candidate Willard, and everybody knew that the contest would be close. In Pennsylvania the old radicals of

---

1 Samuel Longfellow, *Henry Wadsworth Longfellow*, II, 314; Conway, *Autobiography*, I, 239-241; Lowell, *Letters*, I, 274, 275.

David Wilmot stripe, the opportunists like Cameron, and the great central body of freesoilers like A. K. McClure, were striving to drag the State from the Democratic column. Illinois, too, was doubtful. Douglas had forced the nomination of his lieutenant Richardson for governor, and this proved a blunder; the anti-Nebraska nominee William H. Bissell was far stronger.[2]

## [ I ]

The Republicans, declaring that all Territories must be kept freesoil, gave their canvass a moral fervor hitherto unknown in American politics. The campaign of 1840, with its log cabins, hard cider, and rolling balls, had been riotously exuberant, but its enthusiasm had been untempered by ideas or ideals. Now an exalted purpose, a clear-cut set of national aims, lent strength to the ardor of the campaigners.

Millions of people North and West, after partially reconciling themselves to the Kansas-Nebraska Act, had been reawakened to intense resentment by the President's readiness to play the pro-slavery game in the Territory, the sack of Lawrence, and the Brooks-Sumner affair. They rallied against slavery in the Territories with spontaneous animation. Thousands of Wide-Awake companies, carrying banners and transparencies, sprang up from the Kennebec to the Mississippi. Fife-and-drum corps awoke sleepy towns to life. Frémont glee-clubs made the rafters of every theatre and concert-hall in the North ring. Editors issued newspapers flaming with exaggerated tales of the atrocities in Kansas and of the arrogance of the "Slave Power" in Washington. On Sundays, half the pastors of the North gave their sermons a Republican tinge. Once more "acres of men" gathered in the New England hills; mass-meetings enlivened every city from Portland to Dubuque; and in the prairie States long lines of buggies and spring-wagons raised the dust as farming-folk streamed to political picnics. So burning was the crusade that every man who could make a speech was enlisted. Never had such an array of speakers taken the stump. Even the austere Emerson and shy William Cullen Bryant were seen on the platform. In the East, Chase, Seward, Henry Wilson, Greeley, Banks, and Hale were among the prominent speakers, while in the West they included Giddings, Schuyler Colfax, Owen Lovejoy, and Lyman Trumbull. Carl Schurz was pressed into service addressing the Germans, and even youngsters like the journalist Whitelaw Reid were enlisted. Lincoln made some ninety speeches.[3]

Of all the picturesque and blood-stirring paraphernalia which had come to mark American political campaigns the Republicans made lavish use. Banners,

2  Allen Johnson, *Douglas*, 305, 306.
3  Nevins, *Frémont, Pathmarker of the West*, 441, 442; Beveridge, *Lincoln*, II, 296ff.; Schurz, *Reminiscences*, II, 68ff.

The Voice of Radical Freesoilers: W. H. SEWARD

A painting by Emanuel Leutze

Democratic Convention in Cincinnati, 1856

Millard Fillmore Cheered in New York, 1856

transparencies, and posters, pictures and cartoons, articles, pamphlets, and books, all were scattered broadcast. Some of the numerous special songs written celebrated Jessie Benton Frémont as ardently as her husband.[4] One set to the tune of Stephen Foster's "Camptown Races," describing the Pathfinder as a powerful mustang colt outstripping lame old Buchanan, swept the North. Campaign lives of Frémont, whose adventurous career was of great interest quite apart from politics, were distributed to bookstores and newsstands in huge quantities. The best, hurriedly compiled by the brilliant John Bigelow with assistance from Jessie Frémont, was issued by Derby Jackson of New York for a dollar, while another by a former Massachusetts Congressman, Charles W. Upham, was published by Ticknor & Fields. The *Tribune* sold a cheap but excellent pamphlet biography, written for Greeley by W. H. Bartlett, in large quantities. Whittier, Thomas Buchanan Read, and the Cary sisters penned campaign poetry for the party. The women of the North, stirred by the idealism of the Republican movement, emerged into political activity as never before.[5]

And yet the campaign differed sharply from previous appeals to mass enthusiasm, for one marked element in it was a sober intellectual note. The argument that the founders of the republic had hoped for and expected the ultimate extinction of slavery; that the Missouri Compromise had expressed this idealistic conviction of the fathers; that all the best hopes of the nation were bound up with the restriction of slavery to its existing domain until means could be found for its gradual abolition—this argument, which Lincoln was to develop at length during the next two years, was made the very heart of the appeal to Northern voters.

All over the North and Northwest, the impact of the Kansas news was still thrusting old Democratic leaders and newspapers into the Republican column. A. H. Reeder published a widely-circulated letter. For years, he wrote, he had striven to bring about Buchanan's nomination, and in 1848 and 1852 had helped elect district delegates pledged to him. But now he would unhesitatingly vote the Republican ticket. "I can see no reasonable hope of justice and sympathy for the people of Kansas in the success of the Democracy. In its ranks, and with the power to control its action, are found the border ruffians of Missouri and their accomplices of the South, who have trampled upon the Constitution and all the essential principles of our government, robbed Kansas of its civil liberty and right of suffrage, laid waste its territory with fire and sword, and repudiated even civilization itself." [6] Equally emphatic was George Bancroft, who had sat

4  John Raymond Howard, *Remembrance of Things Past*, 73-76.
5  Margaret Clapp, *John Bigelow*, covers his active part in the Frémont campaign.
6  N. Y. *Evening Post*, September 18, 1856.

in Polk's Cabinet and voted for Pierce in 1852. He wrote Marcy that the President's policy had been detestable. "Nothing could be more execrable than his purpose to enforce the enactments of the fraudulent legislature, which he called 'legitimate.' " The Democratic Party had fallen into a hopeless condition under "this bastard race that controls the organization, this unproductive hybrid got by southern arrogance upon northern subserviency." The Southern nullifiers had never been really democratic; they had always been the most aristocratic of parties. "This cruel attempt to conquer Kansas into slavery is the worst thing ever projected in our history." Personally he might wish Buchanan success, but he could never vote for the nullifying aristocracy that dominated the party.[7]

Many long-reluctant Whigs, discouraged by the death's-head aspect of their party, an uncoffined corpse, and attracted by the high moral principles avowed by the Republicans, followed their bolder brethren of 1854–55 into the new party. All spring and summer an impressive procession of these conservatives bade their adieux to the traditions of Clay and Webster. One was Abraham Lincoln, who took the plunge in May; his radical-minded partner, William H. Herndon, who had been speaking all over Illinois on the Kansas disorders, giving him a hearty shove from behind by signing his name (Lincoln was attending court elsewhere at the time) to a call for a Republican county convention.[8] Though Lincoln had favored McLean's nomination, he campaigned energetically for Frémont. In this he was encouraged by Lyman Trumbull, whose original impression that McLean would be the strongest candidate disappeared as he watched the mounting enthusiasm for the exploror. "I have never seen such a deepseated feeling among the people," he wrote Lincoln from Washington.[9] A young Marylander who had sat for the Eastern Shore Whigs in Congress, John W. Crisfield, was able to assert this summer that nearly every Whig of national reputation in the Free States was to be found with the Republicans. "In the House of Representatives are scarcely enough members from the free States who favor Mr. Fillmore's election to fill the Cabinet appointments; and if there is one member from those States in the Senate Mr. Fillmore could not name him."[10] The New York *Herald* announced that out of ninety-one anti-

7 Howe, *Bancroft*, II, 122–125. James Gordon Bennett's *Herald*, which liked to put a shilling on every horse, had been among the first journals to propose Frémont. It now espoused his cause with unwonted trenchancy, assailing Buchanan in terms which made that worthy wince. "Why," demanded the candidate, "am I so traduced and abused by this infamous knave Bennett? Have I no friends who will visit New York and punish him as he deserves? His ears should be taken off in the public streets!" Phila. *Press*, September 30.
8 R. H. Luthin, "Lincoln Becomes a Republican," *Pol. Science Quart.*, LIX, No. 3. Another convert was Hannibal Hamlin, who announced in the Senate that he must sever all connection with the Democratic Party which had so fully endorsed the disastrous Kansas Act. *Cong. Globe*, June 12, 1856.
9 July 5, 1856; Trumbull Papers.
10 Pvt. *Speech of John W. Crisfield*, 1856, Huntington Library.

Democratic journals which exchanged with it, seventy-eight were for Frémont, eleven for Fillmore, and two for Buchanan.[11]

The situation in New York was especially interesting. There the official Whig organization, with Seward at its head, had merged the previous autumn with the Republicans, their State conventions coalescing with every proof of hearty goodfellowship. It was a momentous event, for Seward thus took his place with and slightly above Chase and Sumner in a party triumvirate. A staunch conservative band under Washington Hunt, D. D. Barnard, and James A. Hamilton still termed themselves Whigs and gave in their allegiance to Fillmore.[12] But when the most influential of the waverers, Hamilton Fish, joined the new party, it was plain the revolution was complete. Fish thought Fillmore weak, and found the religious bigotry and racial exclusiveness of the American Party intolerable. Moreover, he believed that a direct and militant opposition to the Administration policies was imperative. Confronted with "outrage and brute force" in Washington, "violence, usurpation, and invasion in Kansas," it was necessary to stand fast. In external relations the Ostend manifesto and filibustering equally posed a governmental issue: "Shall peace and justice, or violence and outrage, be its policy?"[13] In a long argumentative letter to James A. Hamilton in September, Fish asserted that he would cast his vote for Frémont as the surest hope for a remedy of intolerable evils. Answering the charge that the Republicans were a sectional body, he remarked that he found the call of their convention national enough, and that if any part of the Union lacked representation in that body it was its own fault.

Fish's accession delighted the Republican leaders. Francis P. Blair assured Frémont that it was worth ten thousand votes. Thurlow Weed wrote that "it will prove more effective than anything we have had. It will set back the current which has been running all along for Fillmore."[14]

### [ II ]

Yet the Whig Party was still in the race. Although throughout New England the mass of the Whigs had deserted to the Republican standard, a group of Boston intellectuals and "cotton conservatives" shuddered at the idea of such a step: Rufus Choate, Edward Everett, Robert C. Winthrop, George S. Hillard, George T. Curtis, William Appleton, and others.[15] Back of them stood a hard core of party members in Massachusetts and Connecticut. They

11 *Idem.*
12 Among other prominent Whigs who clung to the party were Luther Bradish, F. A. Tallmadge, Samuel B. Ruggles, Henry Grinnell, and Hiram Ketchum, *National Intelligencer*, July 29, 1856.
13 Nevins, *Fish*, 60ff.
14 *National Intelligencer*, September 27, 1856; Nevins, *Fish*, 62.
15 Cf. Coleman, *Crittenden*, II, 130, 131.

felt the deepest concern for the fate of the Union. Choate had the courage of his honest conviction that it was better to endure a pro-slavery administration than to suffer secession and civil war; and like Henry Clay's son, James B. Clay, also a lifelong Whig, he pronounced emphatically for Buchanan. The eminent attorney had played but a minor part in public life since leaving the Senate in 1845. He had, however, been one of Webster's staunchest champions since the Seventh of March speech; he had made the finest address in the Whig Convention of 1852; and his influence (as his part in the Massachusetts Constitutional Convention of 1853 showed) was still great.[16]

Early in August, 1856, Choate addressed a letter to the Whig State Committee of Maine courageously defining his position. The first duty of Whigs, he asserted, "is to unite with some organization of our countrymen, to defeat and dissolve the new geographical party, calling itself Republican." It would be the maddest act of the times, he went on, to bring about the triumph of an organization "which knows one-half of America only to hate and dread it— from whose unconsecrated and revolutionary banner fifteen stars are erased or have fallen—in whose national anthem the old and endeared airs of Eutaw Springs and King's Mountain and Yorktown, and those, later, of New Orleans and Buena Vista and Chapultepec, breathe no more." It was not necessary to place the Republicans in power in order to keep slavery out of the Territories. No one believed that slavery would ever be possible in Utah, New Mexico, Minnesota, or any other Western area; it would be excluded from Kansas by action of the inhabitants as soon as calm was restored there. But what would be the result of giving the Republicans control of the government? [17]

To the fifteen States of the South that government will appear an alien government. It will appear worse. It will appear a hostile government. It will represent to their eyes a vast region of States organized upon anti-slavery, flushed by triumph, cheered onward by the voices of the pulpit, tribune, and press; its mission to inaugurate freedom and put down the oligarchy; its constitution the glittering and sounding generalities of natural right which make up the Declaration of Independence. And then and thus is the beginning of the end.

The warning was as forcible as it was courageous, though but few Northern Whigs were converted by it or by Choate's speeches on the theme. "I cannot go Buchanan and his platform," wrote Robert C. Winthrop.[18] Almost equally averse to Frémont, he, with Everett, Hillard, and the two Appletons, half-reluctantly supported Fillmore. They did not relish the American Party, but the feeble remnants of Whiggism seemed to them worth preserving.

16 C. M. Fuess, *Choate*, 201, 202.
17 S. G. Brown, *Rufus Choate*, 321-327.
18 *Memoir of Winthrop*, 186.

In the border States, despite the powerful drift to Democracy, a large body of influential Whig leaders still kept a numerous following loyal to their beloved organization. John Bell and John J. Crittenden had both opposed the Kansas-Nebraska Act, and both now felt that their dolorous prophecies with respect to that Pandora's box had been realized. Crittenden, holding to that middle path which in 1860–61 was to make him the nation's most powerful advocate of sectional compromise, supported Fillmore as a tried champion of conciliation. Bell took the same stand. Welcomed home to Nashville late in September, he made a three-hour speech to a large crowd scrutinizing the issues, and urging the importance of a large Southern vote for Fillmore.[19] William C. Rives of Virginia remained loyal to the Whig faith, while Clayton of Delaware was so deeply alarmed by the situation that he published a formal statement, saying that he did not feel at liberty to become an active partisan of any candidate, but would support any set of men that stood by the country.

Throughout the summer the *National Intelligencer*, yet staunch in the Whig cause, printed reports of "old-fashioned Whig meetings" in various parts of the Southern and border States. These gatherings were noteworthy for the vigor with which they condemned both the major candidates. In Wilkinson County, Miss., for example, a massmeeting not only attacked Frémont as a sectional nominee, but castigated Buchanan as "a man who has left a very equivocal record in many very important periods of his political life; who has had two sets of opinions upon almost all the leading questions of his time, and who now holds in all its ugliness the odious doctrine of squatter sovereignty, as it is understood by his party at the North; a doctrine denounced by Mr. Calhoun as the worst form of the Wilmot proviso; a doctrine hailed by Mr. Buchanan's friends as the most efficient form of the same proviso; a doctrine ever and only detestable to the South for its political absurdity, unconstitutionality, and injustice."[20] A Fillmore rally at Natchez on October 4th was described by the *Courier* of that city as the most enthusiastic political demonstration since 1840.[21]

In Missouri, Edward Bates predicted that if the Whigs would maintain their cadres intact, they would yet fill up to a full-strength army. "The nation cannot do without the Whig Party," he wrote. "Whether it constitutes a majority or a minority, it is still the balance wheel of the government; and without its steadying influences all other parts of the engine will jar and jolt until they are broken into fragments." He felt certain that the Americans and Republican

19 *National Intelligencer*, October 4, 1856.
20 Wilkinson *Whig*, September 20, 1856.
21 Quoted in *National Intelligencer*, October 11, 1856. The Whigs of Maryland and Virginia both held well-attended State conventions this summer; *National Intelligencer*, July 12, July 19, 1856. Clayton's rescript to the party is in the *Intelligencer*, September 13.

organizations would soon dissolve; and "if the Whig party will only keep itself organized and in battle array it will be the dominant party in the country before the end of the year 1857." [22] Nor were the Whigs without a strong remnant of their once-imposing array of newspapers. Besides the *Intelligencer*, they could count the New York *Commercial Advertiser*, the Baltimore *Patriot*, the Richmond *Whig*, the Norfolk *Herald*, and the Fayetteville *Observer*. These journals, together with a loyal group of party orators, strove to convince the rank and file that they might still exercise a profound influence in American affairs. At a Whig meeting in Washington on June 21, presided over by W. W. Seaton, Senator James C. Jones of Tennessee prophesied an immense Whig revival—but admitted that he might vote for Buchanan! [23]

All the Whig and Native American leaders, pleading for votes, emphasized the truly national character of their coalition and echoed the dark warnings of Rufus Choate. Late in June, Fillmore arrived in New York from Europe. Delegations from various cities were waiting to urge a national tour. A procession escorted him from the St. Nicholas Hotel to City Hall, where he was received with much cheering and a salute of cannon. Replying to a speech of welcome by Mayor Wood, he remarked: "You have been pleased to refer to the fact that my public life has been of a conservative character, and I regard this conservatism as the proudest principle I have been able to sustain. We have received from our fathers a Union and a Constitution above all price and value, and that man who cannot sacrifice anything for the support of both is unworthy of his country." At Albany he spoke more pointedly. The Republican Party, he said, was presenting candidates to be elected by one section only, but to rule over the whole Union. "Can they have the madness or folly to believe that our Southern brethren would submit to be governed by such a chief magistrate? . . . We are treading upon the brink of a volcano that is liable at any moment to break forth and overwhelm the nation." Repeatedly he referred to his success in 1850, with the aid of conservative Whigs and Democrats, in binding the nation together. The laws which finally restored peace to the agitated country "were the measures of the two great parties." While Fillmore accepted the tenets of the American Party as to a longer naturalization period and a preference for native-born in high office, he ran primarily upon a demand for moderate measures to save the Union. [24]

The great hope of the Whig-American alliance was that, by carrying New York and California in the North, Louisiana in the South, and Maryland,

---

22 Letter of May 2, 1856, to Marion County Whig Committee; *National Intelligencer*, June 24.
23 *National Intelligencer*, June 24.
24 N. Y. *Herald, Evening Post*, June 24, 25, 1856, for Fillmore's reception; *National Intelligencer*, June 28–July 6 for various speeches.

Kentucky, and Tennessee along the border, they could throw the election into the House. Late in October, Fillmore still believed this possible. In a letter to John P. Kennedy he declared it certain that Frémont could not be elected. "This is a great point gained, as it postpones the day of dissolution, and gives time, at least, for a 'sober second thought' which may save the country. But Buchanan is also a sectional candidate, in principle but not in form, and if he carries out the principles of the present Administration, the day of hostility and civil war is only postponed, not averted." [25] The one hope of saving the Union lay in giving the House the choice, which it would probably bestow upon himself.

## [ III ]

The Democrats, confident of victory, were superbly organized. National Chairman Smalley had ability, while the executive committee under Ward of Pennsylvania, and the committee on publicity and speakers under Representative C. J. Faulkner of Virginia toiled relentlessly. They had the assistance in Pennsylvania of men who felt that fortune or ruin hung on the result—Senator Bigler, Representative Glancy Jones, District Attorney J. C. Van Dyke, and that tireless knight of the pen, John W. Forney. Behind the serried ranks of politicians, moneyed men bore up the means of war. Corcoran in Washington, Glancy Jones and George Plitt (the State treasurer) in Philadelphia, and Slidell and Dan Sickles in New York knew how to reach sources of wealth. If the party was in danger of over-confidence, that menace was dispelled in September by the State election in Maine. The Republican candidate for governor, Hannibal Hamlin, raced to victory with about 70,000 votes as against 45,000 for his Democratic rival; and by an even larger margin the whole Republican Congressional ticket was returned. Instantly Slidell, Glancy Jones, Dan Sickles, and others were in Wall Street, raising sums unprecedented in American political history to make sure that Pennsylvania and Indiana were kept safe. Just how large they were no man knows. But contemporaneous evidence speaks of $70,000 for Pennsylvania, and half that much was probably contributed for Indiana. Corcoran meanwhile reached far into his own pocket. Long afterward it was stated that the postmaster of New York, a good-natured, sporty Tammany sachem named Isaac V. Fowler, was asked to help raise a total of $250,000 needed; that after some demur, he proposed to advance part of the money from postoffice funds if the party made it good after the election; and that he did so, but failed to receive restitution. It is certain that Fowler later defaulted

25 October 25, 1856; Kennedy Papers.

**for** a large sum, fled to Mexico, and in due time, the prosecution having been dismissed, returned home.

For propaganda, the Democrats poured forth a flood of tracts and pamphlets. Jeremiah Black, W. B. Reed, and Forney penned "Short Answers to Reckless Fabrications." Robert J. Walker issued "An Appeal for the Union." Wide circulation was given such publications as "Infidelity and Abolitionism: An Open Letter to the Friends of Religion, Morality, and the American Union." Michael V. Cluskey's *Democratic Handbook*, placed in the hands of speakers everywhere, attacked the Know-Nothings, appealed to old-line Whigs, and declared that the objects of the Black Republican leaders in 1856 were identical with those of the anti-war disunionists in 1812. It raised the hypothetical question of what the Republican Administration would do if, placed in power, it found the Supreme Court deciding that the Missouri Compromise was unconstitutional, and that no one could divest a man of his right to take slave property into a Territory. This was an interesting foreshadowing of the Dred Scott decision.

Aggressiveness was the keynote of the Democratic campaign, the leaders devoting most of their time and energy to attacks upon the Republican nominee. They had no difficulty in proving that Frémont was (in the same sense as Hamilton) of illegitimate birth; but that was not his fault, and the fact did him little if any injury. In the face of complete evidence that he was an Episcopalian, they bruited far and wide a report that he was christened a Catholic, had been married by a Catholic priest, had erected a cross in the West, and so on; and these stories did him material harm in the Northwest, both in keeping men in the American ranks who might have joined the Republicans, and in cooling the ardor of many supporters who feared that the tales possessed some substance. Catholics, on the other hand, tended to support Buchanan because the Northern Know-Nothings were arrayed behind Frémont. When Thurlow Weed and others urged the candidate to make a public statement on his religion, he very properly refused on the ground that he would make no concession to religious fanaticism.[26]

Other accusations concerned Frémont's military record in California, and his supposed connection with the much-hated San Francisco banking house of Palmer, Cook & Co. But Buchanan himself had testified, in a British judicial inquiry into certain suits against the explorer in 1852, that his military service in California had been "very valuable; he bore a more conspicuous part in the conquest of California than any other man." His sole relation with Palmer, Cook seems to have been that, like many others, he borrowed money from the

26 One of Frémont's supporters, Sperry of Connecticut, declared in the American Convention in New York on June 14 that he had driven Romanism out of California, substituting Protestantism. *National Intelligencer*, June 17, 1856.

firm. Numerous Californians defended his character, the former American consul at Monterey, Thomas O. Larkin, testifying: "I consider Mr. Frémont a just, correct, and moral man, abstemious, bold and persevering." Half a dozen newspapers, including the courageous sheet made famous by James King of William, the San Francisco *Bulletin*, took his side. But the charges were

## FOR
# SALT RIVER!
### DIRECT!!

**THE FAST SAILING STEAMER**

# BLACK REPUBLICAN!
### Capt. J. C. FREMONT, "No. 1,"

Has her Freight on board, and will have quick dispatch on

### NOVEMBER 4TH, 1856.

The following is a list of the Officers and Crew for the voyage:

| ENGINEERS: | MATE. |
|---|---|
| " FREE LOVE " GREELY, | " DU DAH " DAY. |
| "FOXY" RAYMOND. | |
| FIREMEN. | STEWARDS. |
| "HOLY RIFLE" BEECHER, | "SAUNEY" BENNETT, |
| FRED DOUGLASS. | " LET THE UNION SLIDE " BANKS. |
| PURSERS. | CHAMBERMAID. |
| KANSAS WAR COMMITTEE. | MRS. " BLEEDING KANSAS." |

Courtesy of the New York Historical Society.

damaging, particularly in those California circles where old rancors born of the rough-handed American conquest survived.[27]

Under the circumstances, it was natural that many Democrats should make energetic use of the threat of secession. Nothing else could do so much to induce both moderate and timid men to vote the Democratic ticket. Leading party journals, including the Washington *Union*, Richmond *Enquirer*, and Charleston *Mercury*, predicted that Frémont's election would herald an immediate dissolution of the Union. Even at a Democratic meeting in Philadelphia on September

27 Nevins, *Frémont*, 445ff.; Larkin Papers, Bancroft Library, under date August 2, 1856. Frémont ultimately polled about 20,000 votes in California. No other candidate running on Republican principles had ever polled more than 5,000; and few Californians believed that any other Republican nominee this year would have polled more than 10,000. N. Y. *Weekly Tribune*, January 7, 1856.

17 to celebrate the anniversary of the Constitution, disunion mottoes were displayed, disunion sentiments expressed, and disunion resolutions adopted. Menacing voices from South Carolina, which for twenty years had muttered of disunion, were of course numerous. Preston Brooks, addressing a meeting at Ninety-Six, said that if Frémont were elected it would be the duty of the South not merely to break up the Union but to "lay the strong arm of Southern freemen upon the treasury and archives of the government." [28] A similar clamor rose from some other areas. Senator Mason declared that a Republican victory would leave only one course open—"immediate, absolute, eternal separation." Senator Slidell asserted that if Frémont won, "the Union cannot and ought not to be preserved." [29] The Richmond *Enquirer* threatened John Minor Botts with lynching as a traitor because he defended the idea of an indissoluble Union. A Southern gentleman heard Howell Cobb of Georgia and Judge Stuart of Maryland declare emphatically that if the Republicans triumphed, secession would follow immediately.[30] A correspondent of the London *Daily News*, travelling in the South this summer, found men everywhere talking of civil war as in imminent possibility.[31]

Many of these overheated threats were obviously the outburst of a passionate hour, and the very intemperance of some stamped them as irresponsible rant. "We have got to hating everything with the prefix *free*," roared one Virginia editor, "from free negroes up and down through the whole catalogue—*free farms, free labor, free society, free will, free thinking, free children, and free schools*—all belonging to the same brood of damnable *isms*. But the worst of all these abominations is the modern system of *free schools*. . . . We abominate the system *because* the schools are free." A South Carolina journal remarked that the North was a diseased section: "The great evil of Northern *free* society is that it is burdened with a *servile class of mechanics and laborers*, unfit for self-government, and yet clothed with the attributes and powers of citizens."

And some Northerners were no less guilty than Southerners. James S. Pike printed a "disunion shriek" in the New York *Tribune* that aroused much protest. George W. Julian, making a political address, gloried in the fact that Republicans were a sectional party. "It is not alone a fight between the North and the South; it is a fight between freedom and slavery; between God and

28  N. Y. *Evening Post*, October 9, 1856.
29  Sears, *Slidell*, 122ff.
30  T. Turner to Hamilton Fish, September, 1856; Fish Papers.
31  Correspondence dated Selma, Ala., November 18, 1856. Andrew Johnson told the Senate later that "in 1856 I had seen a spirit and feeling manifested in the country that I had never seen before, which convinced me clearly and conclusively what the abolition agitation would eventuate in when it was pressed to its final ultimatum." It would end, he said, in disunion and a war of races. *Cong. Globe*, March 27, 1860.

the devil; between heaven and hell." Representative Anson Burlingame boasted that after Republican triumph and doughface extermination, "then, if the slave Senate will not give way, we will grind it between the upper and nether millstones of our power." Even the venerable Josiah Quincy hailed the prospective day when the free States, possessing the bulk of the nation's wisdom, talent, and virtues, would take full possession of the government. As for veteran abolitionists, they were of course jubilant in the hope of early disunion. Wendell Phillips, quarreling with the Republicans because they did not go far enough, admitted that they had one great virtue—they excluded all Southerners. "The first crack in the iceberg is visible; you will yet hear it go with a crash through the center." [32]

Just how great the danger was it is impossible to say. The *National Intelligencer* asserted its faith, as the campaign drew to a close, that the various trumpetings were political hysteria and represented no fundamental sentiment.[33] Senator Jesse D. Bright told a Michigan audience that the idea of disruption was ridiculous; neither Congress nor all the outside politicians could break up the confederacy. But other observers were genuinely worried. Jefferson Davis said that the triumph of a purely sectional party was itself secession, and he meant it.[34] President Pierce took the same view, calling the Republican Party "disunionists." [35] It was plain that with great piles of inflammables scattered about, reckless men were willing to touch a match to them. Washington Hunt predicted that on the morrow of a Republican victory, impetuous Southerners would probably make a rush to seize Kansas and hold it at all hazards.[36] Henry A. Wise was telling Virginians that it would be folly to await a warlike step. The hoisting of the "Black Republican flag in the hands of an adventurer . . . while the arms of civil war are already clashing" was itself to be regarded as "an overt act." [37]

Various prominent Northerners, on the other hand, thought the South needed a good trouncing. One exploded in July: "I hope and pray that Frémont may be elected. I think that with his energy and force of will he would straighten things out at once, and lick the South into good behavior, if they rebel. . . . Our people are ready for any sort of a fight. There has never before been anything like it. I think we could send an army from New Hampshire that would whip South Carolina, and set all her niggers free. New Hampshire will go for Frémont two to one, I should think, by present signs." [38]

32  All these quotations in *National Intelligencer*, October 21, 1856.
33  *Idem.*
34  Rainwater, *Mississippi*, 37, 38; McElroy, *Davis*, I, 170, 171.
35  To William Butterfield, September 24, 1856; Pierce Papers.
36  *National Intelligencer*, October 18, 1856.
37  Nevins, *Frémont*, 451.
38  H. F. French to B. B. French, Exeter, N. H., July 20, 1856; French Papers.

It was reassuring, however, to find that the best Southern elements pronounced against rash courses. When Wise of Virginia invited other Southern governors to meet at Raleigh, N. C., to concert a policy to be followed if Frémont were elected, it was plain that he hoped to organize for resistance. Herschel V. Johnson declined on the ground that he had no authority to act, and that Georgia had laid down a policy in accepting the Compromise of 1850 from which he believed she should not depart unless Congress should pass some law in contravention of the Compromise.[39] The Memphis *Inquirer*, denouncing the inflammatory utterances of the *Appeal*, emphasized its readiness to submit to the Constitution and the laws. "Moreover, when we do counsel resistance, we shall be for fighting the battle *in* the Union. Disunion will be the death-knell of the entire republic. Anarchy, civil war, servile war, military despotism, *must* follow in their order." [40] Frémont himself always believed that his important family connections in the Southern and border States—for his mother sprang from an old Virginia family, the Beverleys, while his wife was related to the Prestons, McDowells, and Randolphs—would have helped avert a breach. He gave much thought to a plan for the gradual emancipation of the slaves with Federal compensation, discussing it with Jeremiah S. Black.[41]

## [ IV ]

A remarkable and creditable part was played in the campaign by the veteran Thomas Hart Benton, a man increasingly distinguished in his later years for independence, breadth of view, and piquancy of utterance. He held abolitionists and slavery-extensionists in equal contempt, inveighing against every movement, from whatever side, toward disunion. Nominated for governor of Missouri by the anti-Atchison wing of the Democratic Party, he accepted in the face of certain defeat so that he might better voice his convictions. He believed, of course, neither in the new Northern doctrine of squatter sovereignty, nor the extreme Southern doctrine that the Constitution carried slavery into every Territory. "I believe in the old doctrine, that the Territories are the property of the United States and under the guardianship of Congress, and subject to such laws as Congress chooses to provide for them (or to permit them to make for themselves) until they become States. . . ." The slavery agitation was the greatest curse that could befall the Union; "and that curse is now upon us, and brought upon us designedly and for the worst of purposes." [42]

Bitterly denouncing the Kansas-Nebraska Act, assailing the theories of

39  Johnson, *Autobiography*, 133; P. S. Flippin, *H. V. Johnson*, 78, 79.
40  Quoted in *National Intelligencer*, October 14, 1856.
41  Nevins, *Frémont*, 458.
42  Letter of May to nominating committee; St. Louis *Democrat*, May 22, 1856.

Douglas on the one hand and Calhoun on the other, Benton nevertheless supported Buchanan—despite a personal feud which for six years had kept them from speaking to each other—as the best hope for peace. For forty days he canvassed Missouri, bringing his campaign to a climax in a tremendous speech in St. Louis on November 3rd.[43] For Fillmore he expressed high esteem, while he pronounced his son-in-law Frémont almost as dear as his own children. "There was nothing which a father could do for a son which I have not done to carry him through his undertakings, and to uphold him in the severe trials to which he has been subjected." But he knew so much of the difficulties of the presidency that he did not wish a near connection to undergo its severities, while he could not support a sectional ticket. He had realized a year earlier than the general public that Frémont would be the Republican candidate; and "I told him at once that I not only could not support him, but that I would oppose him." Buchanan he praised as a man of peace, a safe man, who would give the country tranquillity; and he appealed to the audience to support the Democratic ticket. No Republican candidate for governor appeared in Missouri; Trusten Polk was nominated by the pro-slavery Democrats, and elected over Robert C. Ewing of the American Party.

Little part was played in the campaign by issues secondary to slavery. The homestead question, to be sure, attracted some attention. Various Republican speakers pressed the issue, while Representative L. O. Branch of North Carolina made a fiery speech in the House against it on August 2, as "a most gigantic scheme of confiscation and agrarianism," and a first step "toward introducing communism and socialism." [44] These were harsh words; most Southerners would have frankly confessed that they opposed free homesteads because rapid settlement of the West would completely break down their veto power in the Senate. In California the Pacific Railroad question was much discussed. Frémont in the midst of the campaign published a letter stating that "from the day when my connection with the army was dissolved, I have considered my life consecrated to the construction of this Pacific Railroad," that he had no doubt of its constitutionality, and that pending its completion, every other facility of communication should be established. Buchanan was equally for building the road, and believed it constitutional. The tariff issue also received casual attention, the Republicans emphasizing it in industrial areas although their platform said nothing about it; for Buchanan had made an indiscreet speech in 1840 suggesting that to preserve a low tariff, American wages should be adjusted to those of Europe—whence the nickname "Ten Cent Jimmy." Dismissal of the British minister, Crampton, as a result of a dispute over enlistment activities on Ameri-

43  St. Louis *Leader*, November 4, 1856.
44  Letters of L. O. Branch, *N. Ca. Hist. Rev.*, 1933, X, 48.

can soil, meanwhile unquestionably won the Democrats some votes among the Anglophobes.[45]

The Democratic Party suffered throughout the Northwest, and especially in Michigan (where its chances were slight anyhow), from Pierce's recent veto of the appropriation for removing impediments to Great Lakes navigation at the St. Clair Flats. Every Democrat, exclaimed the Detroit *Free Press*, organ of Cass's followers, would feel mortification and indignation. "We thank God that President Pierce's term of office is drawing to a close."[46] But in general, Kansas and the slavery issue monopolized the thought of the country. This was true in Michigan itself, where Robert McClelland, Secretary of the Interior, joined Cass in an active canvass, but found people "infatuated."[47]

It was noteworthy that neither Buchanan nor Frémont played an active rôle in the campaign, though both conferred constantly with party leaders. Except for a visit to Bedford Springs, Pa., Buchanan remained quietly at Wheatland, his plain, commodious two-story dwelling of brick, shaded by tall forest trees, about a mile from Lancaster. Here the influx of politicians was so heavy that he complained of the pressure. John V. L. Pruyn of New York was one of many who drove out from town, stepped inside the colonnaded portico, and joined the groups chatting with Buchanan in the library which occupied one wing. He found the nominee with Slidell at his elbow, pleasant, sociable, and talkative; and remaining to tea, heard talk ranging from election prospects to the makeup of Polk's Cabinet.[48] Buchanan's retinue at Wheatland consisted only of his niece Harriet Lane, his secretary William V. McKean, a housekeeper, a female servant, and a small boy. The door was open to all callers, and sometimes on bright Sundays Buchanan walked with a group to the Presbyterian Church, where he was a pewholder. To him all other questions in the canvass were slight compared with the appalling issue of union or disunion. He believed with all his heart that Republican victory would mean immediate and inevitable secession—and he more than half indicated that he thought it would be justified.[49] But he made no public appearance until he spoke to some friends and neighbors just after the State elections, for he had cautiously decided to present no issues beyond the platform.

Frémont also kept mainly to his house at 56 West Ninth Street in New York, where the Blairs, John Bigelow, and some old California friends were special intimates. He greeted the curious people who thronged to the door,

45 On the tariff, see C. M. Myers, "Rise of the Republican Party in Pa.," MS dissertation, Univ. of Pittsburgh. For a full treatment of British relations see volume III of this work.
46 Quoted in Warsaw, Ill., *Bulletin*, June 12, 1856.
47 Secretary McClelland's Letter-Book, November 8, 10, 1856.
48 Pruyn Diary, September 12, 1856; N. Y. State Archives.
49 Curtis, *Buchanan*, II, 179–183. Forney in *Anecdotes of Public Men*, II, 237–241, gives a sketch of the campaign in Pennsylvania, saying "we had a tough fight" to elect Buchanan.

made brief speeches to delegations, and maintained a wide correspondence. "My nerves seem to preserve their usual tranquillity," he wrote Frank Blair; and Gideon Welles records that he showed an exemplary modesty, dignity, and reserve. But his contributions to the Republican cause certainly showed no force or imagination, while by some obscure personal act he gravely offended the elder Blair and his wife. Some of his Western advisers, moreover, were plausible, slippery men whom Welles and Bigelow distrusted at sight.

The fervor of the campaign in both the main parties had its alarming as well as captivating features. Among the Republicans, it showed that North and West were rallying against slavery extension with a new ardor. Events in Washington and Kansas had gradually aroused in millions a resentment which suddenly found expression. The late summer saw an endless succession of uproarious Frémont rallies, particularly in the Middle West: a demonstration of 50,000 people at Indianapolis, of 30,000 at Kalamazoo, of 25,000 at Massilon, O., and of as many more at Beloit, Wis. Lincoln spoke to a State Fair crowd at Alton estimated at 35,000 people, while Lyman Trumbull reviewed in Jacksonville (an old New England settlement) a procession a mile and a quarter long. The bellowing of cannon, the sonorous strains of a dozen brass bands, the lively chants of glee clubs; the exhilarating spectacle of platoon after platoon of brightly uniformed men, hundreds of banners and transparencies swaying above their columns; the pageantry of caparisoned floats rolling down the streets, each with its bevy of young women—all this gave the canvass a zest theretofore unknown in our politics. It was the first in which great torchlight processions turned the streets of cities into rivers of fire. On every corner, in every hall, could be heard the shouts of haranguing speakers. Breezes of the Aroostook, the Mohawk, the Wabash, lifted streamers swung across village streets: "We Follow the Pathfinder"; "We Are Buck-Hunting"; "No More Rule of Nigger-Drivers"; "Kansas Will Be Free." Lithographs of Frémont blazed by the hundred thousand in campaign headquarters, shops, and houses. Everywhere, in speeches and newspapers, rang the slogan: "Free Speech, Free Press, Free Soil, Free Men, Frémont and Victory."

It was exhilarating; but it had its dark side in constant appeals to prejudice against Southerners, animosity against fifteen States of the Union.

In parts of Dixie, meanwhile, raged a similar fever. J. W. DuBose describes the "great protracted political meeting" held near Uniontown, Ala., a typical gathering. Speaking was kept up for two days and nights. Thousands of people, drawn from Mobile, Huntsville, and all the intermediate towns and plantations, sat on rough pine benches lining the hillside, while black coachmen tied their horses in the grove and stood around the margin listening. After Senator C. C. Clay and other spellbinders spoke, Yancey was brought forward for the great final oration of three hours. His manner, writes DuBose, was all his own, "the delivery alternating between a conversational tone, common with gentlemen in the social circle, passing quickly to oratory that would lift men to their feet in uproar." As he finished his peroration, thousands were excitedly standing, hats clouded the skies, and yells rent the air. It was for Southern Rights no less than Buchanan he spoke, and every period carried its implication of hostility to Northern aggression. Nor did the fact that rumors of Negro unrest and insurrection ran over the South this year diminish the responsiveness to sectional incitements. The slave area was safe for Buchanan, and half the speeches made there had another purpose than inculcation of party loyalty.

While in the critical Northern States the Democrats could rely on that superior organization already noted, the Republicans had no such advantage. Their party was too new to have established a firm machinery. Unavoidably, the Frémont campaign had to be handed over to amateurs. To be sure, Thurlow Weed possessed ample experience, but it was chiefly in wire-pulling, while he was less prominent than the grave merchant E. D. Morgan, the journalist John Bigelow, and such other novices as Frank Blair and Isaac Sherman. A Republican journal, the Ashtabula *Sentinel*, later spoke of utter mismanagement by "as sublime a set of asses as the sun ever shown upon." In Pennsylvania, Anson Burlingame failed to appear at one much-advertised meeting. But the chief deficiency of the Republicans was in experienced money-raisers. While Slidell, Corcoran, and other Democrats were winning a decisive victory in what was called "the Wall Street War," Morgan was wringing his hands in despair.

"What can we do?" Greeley implored Colfax. "Give us some leader who *can* raise funds. We need terribly to send speakers and documents through New Jersey and Pennsylvania. . . . If I had control of $3,000, I would let loose speakers and documents on Pennsylvania that would make 5,000 votes difference." [50] In the final crisis Chase and Truman Smith joined Simon Cameron in Philadelphia to attempt to obtain funds; Morgan and others besought money from their Manhattan friends; a meeting of the true men of Boston was called. The Morgan papers contain a long list of givers, but their aggregate contribution was small. Another Republican disadvantage lay in the necessity of combating the solid army of Democratic officeholders. After some initial frigidity, the Administration used all its influence through the patronage. When McClelland hurried to Michigan to campaign, he neglected to ask Pierce's permission; but the President later told the Secretary that he only regretted he had not given more time. [51]

Throughout the North the Democrats were lavish in promises that Buchanan

50  July 18, 1856; Greeley-Colfax Corr. See also E. D. Morgan, October 22, 27, 1856; Welles Papers.
51  McClelland Letter-Book, October, day illegible.

would not interfere against the freesoil forces in Kansas. Many adherents explicitly asserted that his election would mean another free State. In Pennsylvania, Ohio, Indiana, and Illinois Democrats paraded under banners inscribed "Buchanan, Breckinridge, and Free Kansas." John Sherman saw Democratic streamers in his State flaunting the motto, "Kansas will bleed no longer." The Pittsburgh *Post* assured western Pennsylvania that Democratic victory would bring Kansas in forthwith—free. Republicans of course pleaded that their triumph alone would guarantee safety to the harried Territory. Reeder, touring the North, was received with eager curiosity. He described the plundering of Lawrence, the malfeasance of Shannon, Lecompte, and Atchison, and his own escape from the perilous region. Kansas, said he, was a sink of barbarism, its people groaning under oppressions worse than those visited on Russian serfs; for they were politically slaves, with no semblance of self-government left.[52]

### [V]

As the campaign closed, all eyes were focussed on the doubtful States, and particularly Pennsylvania and Indiana. "The political cauldron is certainly at the boiling point," wrote a Philadelphia observer on October 4, "and is bubbling and foaming in the most exciting manner in this city, and . . . all over the State." The Republicans had reason to bestir themselves desperately, for while Buchanan would still have a good chance if the State election went against him, Frémont would not. In his own State Buchanan was personally more popular than the lesser candidates. After all, Pennsylvania had never had a President! Moreover, while the Republicans and "North Americans" had combined on a unified State ticket, they failed to do so on a slate of presidential electors. The State elections in Pennsylvania and Indiana, taking place on October 14, would powerfully affect the national voting on November 4.

A week before election day the excitement in the Keystone State surpassed that of Jacksonian times. "Politics! Politics! Nothing but politics!" wrote one journalist. "Flags across the streets meet the eye in every direction; music in open carriages, with placards to announce political gatherings; ward meetings and mass meetings and committee meetings every day and every night, and, as it appears to me, at every hour in the day and night; and discussions and estimates and guesses at the result, with all the other accessories of the highest political excitement, are all you hear in this city." Passion for Frémont and freesoil principles, loyalty to Buchanan, were being whipped into a frenzy.[53]

Thurlow Weed, Preston King, Henry Wilson, Reeder, and other prominent

52 Pvt, *The Election and the Candidates*, Huntington Library.
53 *National Intelligencer*, October 9, 11, 1856.

Republicans reinforced such Pennsylvanians as Wilmot and Thaddeus Stevens on the stump. On the Democratic side, Reverdy Johnson, Josiah Randall, William E. Preston, and John Hickman were active, while Howell Cobb, genial, magnetic, and tolerant, produced a great impression with his demands for "fair play in Kansas." The Democrats spent money lavishly, their total expenditures in Pennsylvania later being estimated at $500,000. Remember, wrote Slidell to Buchanan at the end of September, "that every dollar contributed for Pennsylvania would economize ten for New York." John W. Forney and others came to New York, demanded large sums from merchants in the Southern trade, and used the money for speakers, handbills, public meetings, and above all, a general and liberal system of newspaper advertising, which helped win over some editors and soothed the asperities of others. August Belmont was reported to have given $50,000 for his friend Buchanan, and other Wall Street figures $100,000 more.[54] The Republicans, however, remained sadly pinched for funds. Early promises of money, speakers, and other aids were never fulfilled. New York city, according to Greeley, did not contribute one-tenth as much to the Republican chest as it did to either the Democratic or Know-Nothing, though the New York Republicans were mainly responsible for the campaign in Pennsylvania and New Jersey. "Each state is utterly miserable, so far as money is concerned." [55]

All that Chairman Morgan could do was to raise money in small driblets. By September 30 he had obtained $8,000 for Pennsylvania, and a week later almost $15,000. Then a bill for $8,000 came in from one of his workers; and this with other demands, he wrote, "will use up what we have collected and keep us busy hereafter." [56] A frenzied last minute drive apparently brought in promises of $80,000 more, but of this $70,000 was to be paid only if and when Frémont won! The Pennsylvania national committeeman, Charles Gibbons of Philadelphia, somehow failed to do effective work; and H. B. Stanton, commissioned to bring a cohort of speakers into the Keystone State, failed to get really first-rate men.[57]

54  Forney, *Anecdotes*, II, 239; *National Intelligencer*, October 11, 1856; Sears, *Slidell*, 122.
55  Pike, *First Blows of the Civil War*, 346; Going, *David Wilmot*, 493.
56  Morgan Papers, N. Y. State Archives; Morgan to Gideon Welles, September 30, October 8, 1856, Welles Papers.
57  Simon Cameron later wrote Thurlow Weed: "From the first I had little hopes of Penn. I saw the error committed in placing the movement in the hands of ignorant and conceited men. The Whigs of this State cannot control a campaign; and they would not permit Democrats to advise or help them. In the northern and western parts of the state, where they moved under a separate local organization, they made a different result from us of the coast. I believe if you and I had met in July and consulted on the campaign it could have been carried. . . . In our county of Dauphin we doubled our Oct. majority by sending agents to call at every house, and to see every voter, in every district. In the next fight we must pursue this system throughout the state. Big meetings and fine speeches do no good, with our slow Governor." November 9, 1856; Weed Papers, Univ. of Rochester

The final campaign meetings in critical States revealed a veritable fever of party feeling. In Lancaster, thirty thousand people congregated on October 8 to watch a gay procession and listen to speakers from innumerable stands; "the whole city was alive with excitement." In Philadelphia next day all three parties held massmeetings, the Republicans in Independence Square, the Fillmoreites in Central Square, and the Democrats at Second and Dock Streets. Meanwhile, Wall Street on two afternoons was choked with men to hear first N. P. Banks, and then John B. Floyd. A Democratic rally at Poughkeepsie brought a dozen loaded steamboats up the river, and while sour Republicans estimated the crowd at ten thousand, enthusiastic "Buchaneers" put it at a hundred thousand![58]

Election day in Pennsylvania dawned raw and drizzling, a fact which relieved observers who had feared a clash between riotous crowds. The streets of the principal cities were jammed that night with crowds eager to hear the news. Within two days it was certain that the Democratic State ticket was elected— but fuller returns showed that its majority fell short of three thousand.[59] A change of half this number would have elected the Republican-"North American" slate. Yet the vote was decisive, for all last-minute efforts to bring about a coalition of Frémont and Fillmore men on a slate of electors, pledged to divide their vote in the electoral college in proportion to the popular vote cast, failed; and since the Republicans and Americans combined had not carried the state ticket in the October election, it was plain that the Republicans alone would never be able to carry the national ticket in November.

Some Frémont men attributed the defeat to treachery on the part of the Fillmore men. "They feared absorption by the Republican Party, and their leaders, looking more to self than to the great question of liberty involved, basely sold themselves," wrote one, pointing to the fact that the old Whig-Know-Nothing strongholds in the southern part of the State had given the Democrats their narrow lead.[60] Frémont himself thought that if his wishes had been followed in the nomination of Simon Cameron for vice-president, and the creation early in the campaign of a strong organization to prevent Democratic corruption of the voters, his party would have triumphed. It was certainly true that the Republican organization was poor. A friend of Gideon Welles declared that the main factors in the unhappy result were (1) the large vote of the Fillmore men for the Democratic ticket; (2) the influence of the charge that

Library. Weed replied that "our organization in your State was sadly neglected," that "we had feeble men in Philadelphia," and that "With three or four exceptions the members of Congress were shamefully remiss in sending documents during the session." November 12; Cameron Papers.

58 *National Intelligencer*, October 2, 11, 1856.
59 Nevins, *Frémont*, 454; Stanwood, *Hist. Presidential Elections*, ch. 19; N. Y. *Weekly Tribune*, October 16, 23, 1856.
60 W. V. Pettit, Philadelphia, October 21; Welles Papers.

Frémont was a Catholic; (3) the abstention of two-thirds of the foreign-born voters of Philadelphia, including Germans and Welsh, from the polls; (4) the rôle of the liquor question; and (5) the fact that in two counties alone 1,400 Fillmoreites remained at home and did not vote, being persuaded by their friends to wait until November. Frauds also played an important part.

Indeed, Forney virtually confessed the use of fraudulent methods to Buchanan. Writing of the last-minute registrations in Pennsylvania, he assured the candidate that the results had been glorious. "We have naturalized a vast mass of men, and assessed many of the native-born citizens. . . . The Opposition are appalled. They cry fraud. Our most experienced men say *all is well*." In numerous Pennsylvania cities the Democrats unquestionably 'colonized' large groups of floaters. The Pittsburgh *Gazette* declared that on election day scores of ragged outcasts, all utter strangers, presented tax-receipts and cast their ballots. The State as a whole, it alleged, had been canvassed and the number of needed voters computed; money had been sent into cities and towns to line up ballots; and the result in Philadelphia was then kept back until it was seen just what margin was needed. Additional evidence was turned up the following February when the Philadelphia Court of Common Pleas held a clerk for issuing fraudulent naturalization papers. During the trial the clerk admitted that he had helped print 2,700 naturalizations for the Democrats, and that unnaturalized foreigners voted by using them. The leading Democratic nominees had won by margins ranging from 2,362 to 3,207; they had a close call at best. Had the vote been honestly cast and counted, declares the most careful student of the Pennsylvania election, the union ticket would have won.[61]

Another very important element was simply the fear of conservative Pennsylvanians, particularly in and about Philadelphia, that a Republican victory would produce an upheaval costly to peace and business prosperity. A Whig correspondent wrote the *National Intelligencer* from Philadelphia:[62]

The late election has fully confirmed the extreme weakness of the Frémont party in the city and county of Philadelphia. . . . There was no fusion in the office of prothonotary but each of the three parties had its own separate candidate. The Republican was a good nomination in every way, and also a very popular man, who was almost unanimously supported by the entire bar, who voted and worked for him, and yet . . . he received only about 8,000 votes, while the American candidate had upwards of 26,000 and the Democratic upwards of 33,000. Of the 8,000 votes probably, under the circumstances mentioned above, not more than 5,000 to 6,000 were Republican, which is about the real strength of that party in the city, where 68,000 votes were polled.

61  W. M. Chase, October 21, Welles Papers; Forney, October 3, Buchanan Papers; Pittsburgh *Gazette*, October 20, 21, 1856, February 13, 14, 1857; Myers, *op. cit.*, 131ff.
62  *National Intelligencer*, October 21, 1856.

THE ELECTION OF BUCHANAN

This is an item for the consideration of our Southern hot-headed friends who talk of disunion in case Fremont had been successful, as here they see they would wish to drive out of the Union and separate from 60,000 voters true to the South, because they had 8,000 anti-Southerners among them.

Indiana went Democratic the same day as Pennsylvania, Willard receiving 117,981 votes as against 112,139 cast for Oliver P. Morton. Here much more explicitly than in Pennsylvania charges of sweeping frauds followed the election. It was declared that the Democrats made unblushing use of repeaters in some counties; that along the Wabash invaders from neighboring Illinois voted on the Kansas plan; and above all, that thousands of railroad construction workers, with no residence in the State, cast ballots everywhere they held temporary jobs. These migratory hands were nearly all Irish on the Democratic side. Figures were cited—in De Kalb County, a hundred and fifty freshly-arrived Irish had voted; in Whitley County more than a hundred; in Noble County the same number, and so on. Altogether, it was alleged that frauds which more than covered Willard's majority had been established in various areas.[63]

Before these State elections, such Republicans as young Rutherford B. Hayes had been filled with confidence; afterwards they were heartsick. "The majorities are small—very small—but they discourage our side."[64] Democratic rejoicing spouted up in a great wave. This, the leaders said, settles the question. And Fillmore men who had been organizing to make a powerful effort in the border areas and Louisiana now dropped the hopeless tasks, many of them climbing aboard the Democratic bandwagon.

Yet Republican leaders determined to fight stubbornly on. Additional funds were raised in Boston, New York, and Philadelphia for the final Pennsylvania battle. By the 27th a number of party chieftains, including Cameron and Truman Smith, were hard at work with such sums as could be scraped up, including a "contingent fund" of $50,000 that would be paid only if Frémont were elected.[65] But Chairman Morgan was pessimistic. For one reason, he found that "the rabid Fillmores are pushing *their* own ticket in desperation or to elect Buchanan." For another, "our friends are more disappointed than it is pleasant to talk about with results both in Pennsylvania and Indiana. The latter gets worse as we get more of it. . . ." Nevertheless, "the battle is to be fought to the

63  Indianapolis *Journal*, October 22, 1856; W. H. English in *Cong. Globe*, December 17, 1856. Edmund Ruffin of Virginia later wrote in his Diary of the frauds in the Keystone State: "I have heard from Fisher and it was repeated today that enormous sums of money were spent in Pennsylvania from New York and a good deal from the Democrats of New England, to buy votes in Pennsylvania which turned the vote of that State. The victory over Frémont and Abolitionism, if thus gained, is worth less than I had formerly estimated."
64  C. R. Williams, *Life of Hayes*, I, 105–107.
65  E. D. Morgan to Gideon Welles, October 27; Welles Papers.

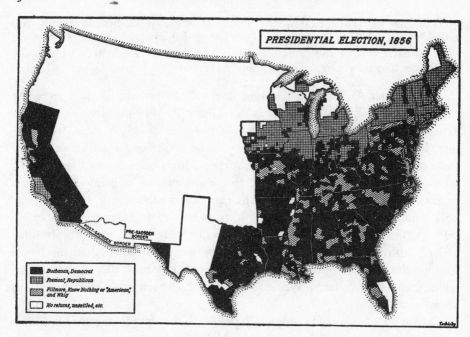

last ditch with all the power we can bring to it. Stranger things have happened than that Frémont should be our next President. I am confident that but for Americanism victory would be certain." [66] The stubborn impracticability of the Fillmore men indeed made Pennsylvania safe for Buchanan; for they rejected three or four methods proposed by the Frémont State Committee, their ultimatum being that their electoral ticket must be taken without any pledge.

Election day was uneventful save in New Orleans and Baltimore, where ill-feeling between the Democrats and Americans resulted in disgraceful rioting.[67] Ballot boxes were heavily stuffed by the nativists in New Orleans, while in Baltimore fighting with muskets, pistols, clubs, and knives resulted in heavy casualties. When the votes were counted, it appeared that Buchanan had carried nineteen States, Frémont eleven, and Fillmore one; that Buchanan had 174 electoral votes, Frémont 114, and Fillmore 8. The combined popular vote of Frémont and Fillmore was materially in excess of that for Buchanan, who was thus (unlike Pierce) a minority President; Buchanan receiving 1,838,169 votes, Frémont 1,341,364, and Fillmore 874,534. Though Frémont had carried New York, his vote outside the metropolis being prodigious, and had swept Ohio, Michigan, Wisconsin, and Iowa as well as all the New England States, he lost not only

66 October 22, 1856; Welles Papers.
67 *National Intelligencer*, November 6, 1856.

Pennsylvania and New Jersey, but Indiana, Illinois, and California. The result in Illinois was particularly interesting. The four northern Congressional districts gave Frémont a very large majority, but the five southern districts furnished Buchanan a still wider margin, thus turning the scale for the Democratic ticket by more than nine thousand votes. As the northern part of the State was increasing in population much more rapidly than the southern, the future political complexion of Illinois seemed clear—a fact of which it behooved Douglas to take notice.[68] In Pennsylvania and Indiana the combined Frémont-Fillmore vote very nearly equalled that for Buchanan, and in New Jersey surpassed it.

[ VI ]

On the whole, the Whig votes cast for Buchanan and Fillmore had done most to turn the tide in the election: votes which represented a conservative Union-saving and business-saving sentiment, and which clearly proved that the nation wanted peace. The "scare" over the disunionist threats of Southern leaders had proved something near a decisive force in the campaign. Among the lesser factors were the weak Republican organization; Buchanan's obvious superiority in experience over Frémont; the success of Geary and others in a temporary pacification of Kansas; and the widespread belief that Buchanan would really deal fairly with freesoil settlers in the West.

Much disputation took place over the rôle of the foreign vote in the election. It would seem that despite heavy Irish assistance to Buchanan in New York and Indiana, the Republicans profited most from the alien-born voters. German and Scandinavian citizens in the West had generally reprobated the Kansas-Nebraska bill, and if the Know-Nothing movement had temporarily cooled their anti-Democratic ardor, on the subsidence of that party they had generally turned to the Republicans.[69] One shrewd student of the election results, analyzing them county by county, concluded that in Ohio, Wisconsin, Illinois, and Iowa the Republicans had received from one-half to two-thirds of the naturalized vote, and would not have carried these States but for the alien-born. In Indiana they enlisted but one-third of the naturalized voters, for the State plat-

68 See the exhaustive letter by T. L. H. (doubtless Thomas L. Harris, the Democrat who had succeeded to Lincoln's Congressional seat in 1849) on the Illinois election in *National Intelligencer*, January 6, 1857.
69 The worry of the Republicans lest Know-Nothingism counteract the anti-slavery feeling of the Germans is well illustrated by a letter which C. H. Ray of the Chicago *Tribune* sent Trumbull early this year. "It is of the utmost importance that, in the approaching State Convention of the Anti-Nebraska men of Illinois, there should be some distinct ground assumed on which the 20,000 anti-slavery German voters of the State can stand, or we shall lose them in a body. They will go over to the enemy, and we are beaten. What can be done?" They must promise to let the naturalization laws alone. March 30; Trumbull Papers.

form favored a Maine law and used Know-Nothing sentiments—and so they lost Indiana. But the Germans in particular liked Republican principles, and admired Frémont, who was known to sympathize with immigrants, was a correspondent of Humboldt, and had made a German member of his exploring expeditions, Preuss, nationally famous.[70]

It was clear that the election carried no approval of Administration policy in Kansas. It was clear also that it marked the practical demise of the American Party. It was clear, finally, that it left the Republicans in a strong position; and the result in Illinois, Michigan, and New Hampshire came fairly close to being a repudiation of Douglas, Cass, and Pierce by their home constituencies. Above all, the election showed that the country wished peace, a quiet acceptance of the existing laws upon slavery, and a careful regard for the Union. But would peace indeed be safeguarded—would the Union be watchfully maintained? There were grounds for deep uneasiness on the subject.

For one reason, many Democrats showed an exultation that amounted to arrogance. We have won, was their view; we hold the Presidency, the Senate, and the Supreme Court; we have been vindicated. Events of the autumn were to show how inflated an interpretation Franklin Pierce placed on the election.[71] Only one member of the Administration, honest Marcy, could retire with high esteem; he alone could hang his honors o'er his garden gate, "in life's cool evening satiate of applause." Yet the party leaders were full of strut.

Not least was this cocksure arrogance evident, unfortunately, among those Southern leaders who had been talking of disunion if Frémont won. Some of these men regretted that a more radical nominee than Buchanan had not been selected. The ticket does not suit me, nor any other Southern Rights man to whom I have talked in confidence, wrote C. C. Clay, Sr., of Alabama. "It is a ticket for the Union wing of the Southern Democracy, such as Houston, Cobb of Georgia, and *id genus omne*. Pierce was my choice above all men in the South, North, East, or West. If we could keep him in office for four years longer, the tariff would be brought down to a purely revenue standard, the Democratic party put upon the true constitutional anti-internal improvement platform, the backbone of abolition broken, or badly strained, and the Government fixed in the old republican tack." [72] These Southern radicals intended to press the new Administration hard.

Still another reason for uneasiness lay in the fact that, as Benton pointed out,

70 E. L. Pierce, *Important Statistics in Regard to the Foreign Vote in the Presidential Election,* 1857, pvt, Huntington Library.
71 Douglas had specially little reason to share this exultation. His oldest and most devoted lieutenant, W. A. Richardson, had been badly beaten for governor by Bissell.
72 Clay added that he saw party division ahead. "The tariff will not be reduced and the $80,000,000 annually collected will be spent in making rivers and harbors and railroads and canals in the North and Northwest." June 7, 1856; C. C. Clay Papers.

the quarrel over the true interpretation of popular sovereignty had grown deeper than ever. The vague general doctrine was now a strict party test. But did it mean that, as Cass and Douglas said, settlers in a Territory should at once shape their own institutions? Or did it mean, as Calhoun had argued, that the Constitution carried slavery into every Territory, and the settlers could not interfere until they drew up a State Constitution? Once more that grisly demand of many Southerners, positive protection for slavery in the Territories, had been raised. The Democratic convention in Alabama had declared for—[73] "the unqualified right of the people of the slaveholding States to the protection of their property in the States, in the Territories, and in the wilderness in which Territorial governments are as yet unorganized."

It was also ground for uneasiness that Buchanan had always been and still was excessively deferential to the South. For years he had maintained a closer friendship and correspondence with a Southern group, including Slidell, William R. King, Cave Johnson, and Henry A. Wise, than with any similar Northern body. In the Democratic Convention of 1852 he had almost achieved the nomination by an alliance of Pennsylvania and Southern delegates, not "polluted" (as a friend put it) by a single Yankee. He had written just after this convention that Pierce would do well if surrounded by proper men, who ought not to include a single Democrat of Boston views. "The South are entitled to very great influence with him, and I hope will assert their rights in a proper manner. I shall aid them all in my power." [74] During the campaign now just ended he had reassured Henry A. Wise as to his continued loyalty to the slaveholding area.

"For many years of my life," he declared, "I was engaged in advocating Southern rights in the Senate, and afterwards sustaining them on the stump, in conversation, and in the newspapers before the people of Pennsylvania. . . . A crisis has now arrived in the affairs of the Republic seriously endangering the Union. In fifteen States there can be no Frémont electoral ticket. The sectional party has been distinctly formed; and the battle of union or disunion must be fought by the Democratic party of the free States, after having heartily adopted the principles endorsed by the South on the subject of slavery. It promises to be a fierce struggle. I have embarked in it with all my heart and shall give a

73 "Alabama and the Charleston Convention of 1860," *Ala. Hist. Soc. Pubs.*, V, 246.
74 Buchanan Papers. An earlier clue to Buchanan's intense Southern sympathies is afforded by a letter of January 22, 1850, to C. L. Ward, dealing with the Wilmot Proviso. Why does the South justly resist it? he asked. "The answer is easy. The agitation of the question of slavery at the North has infected the slaves of the South and rendered the condition of their masters insecure. It has endangered the lives of helpless women and children and filled them with dreadful apprehensions. This agitation may be sport to demagogues at the North, but it may also be death to the people of the South. It must cease or the Union is in more imminent danger than it has ever been since the adoption of the federal Constitution." Buchanan Papers.

direction to it so far as this may be proper. . . ." [75] Buchanan was by nature a man easily made subservient to others. There was no question in which direction his subservience would now fall.

Finally, ample ground for uneasiness was presented by the mood of the Republicans. They were fiercely unchastened of spirit. And why not? They had all but won; a few thousand more votes in October in Pennsylvania and Indiana, and they might have swept Frémont into power in November. They had gained an astonishing victory in New England. That section gave Frémont more than 300,000 votes, while Buchanan and Fillmore combined got fewer than two hundred thousand. Of the sixteen free States, Buchanan had carried only five. In these sixteen states, Frémont's vote exceeded Buchanan's by well over a hundred thousand. Douglas had made boastful predictions of the Illinois result. Clashing with Trumbull in the Senate during 1855–56, he had said not once but repeatedly that in the approaching election Illinois would furnish a certain Democratic majority of thirty to forty thousand. Yet in the result the Republicans had elected the State ticket, while Frémont and Fillmore together held a majority of some twenty-eight thousand over Buchanan.

The three Northern States that had given Buchanan his victory, Pennsylvania, Illinois, and Indiana, were all moving inexorably toward the Republican column; and the prospect loomed up that in the next election the North would be solidly Republican, and could then carry the Presidency without a single Southern vote. Furness of Philadelphia wrote Sumner that the Republicans did not have a President, but they possessed something which was better—a whole section; and that they had suffered "a victorious defeat." [76] Such a party need stand no nonsense, and it would not.

75 See Auchampaugh, *Robert Tyler*, 109–113, for the Wise-Buchanan exchange.
76 November 9, 1856; Sumner Papers.

# 15

## Contrast of Cultures

JUDICIOUS Americans, turning the leaves of their newspapers, listening to street-corner orators, gazing at shop-window caricatures, picking up the pamphlets that littered the land, were grieved by the explosive denunciations that filled the air in the closing phases of the campaign of 1856; fusillades of canister with which each section peppered the other. Ordinarily the angry objurgations of the last bitter days of a presidential canvass are subject to a heavy discount, and October defiances turn into December handshakings. But this time the accusations and counter-charges denoted a searing passion of sectional hatred. It was not a quick fire of leaves and grass; it was a forest conflagration taking hold with sullen roar. The London *Times*, noting the painful impression which the campaign made upon British lovers of America, remarked that no sneering exponent of Old World ideas had ever written or said one tithe the evil against the citizens of the republic which they were now uttering against themselves.[1]

In the North such men as Henry Wilson had made the characterization of Southerners as "lords of the lash" familiar to everybody.[2] Sumner, welcomed back to Boston with imposing honors on November 3, talked of the satanic carnival that slaveholders planned in the Territories, predicted that Cuba would be seized and the slave trade reopened with all its crime, woe, and shame, and declared that the whole country was trodden down by a brutal, domineering despotism. Greeley's *Tribune*, seeking the origin of the barbarism it found stamped upon Kansas and Washington, found it in a fundamental Southern trait. "It is the spirit of Privilege, of Caste . . . that has instigated all these crimes, which the civilized world regards with every just abhorrence."[3]

Meanwhile, the New Orleans *Delta* was not content with hailing slavery as the most conservative element in republican institutions. "In the Northern States," it continued, "free society has proved a failure. It is rotten to the core."[4]

---

1 October 28, 1856.
2 See Wilson's Tabernacle speech, October 4, 1856.
3 October 30, 1856.
4 Quoted in N. Y. *Weekly Tribune*, November 8, 1856.

The Richmond *Enquirer* agreed that free society was "unnatural, immoral, un-christian," that its evils were in the long run "insufferable," and that it must give way to the slavery regime, "a social system as old as the world, universal as man." [5] Scores of Southern sheets were using language like the Muscogee (Ala.) *Herald*, which venomously remarked that Northern wage-earners and farmers were hardly fit to sit with the body-servant of a Southern gentleman. "Free society! We sicken at the name! What is it but a conglomeration of greasy mechanics, filthy operatives, smallfisted farmers, and moonstruck theorists?" [6]

## [ I ]

The general restoration of peace in Kansas, accompanied by the subsidence of campaign rhetoric, furnished a delusive gleam of hope that the Buchanan Administration would be ushered into office under harmonious auspices. Governor Geary, delighted that he had put an end to riot and bloodshed, appointed a day of general thanksgiving. The first issues of the revived *Herald of Freedom* gave an encouraging sketch of the situation, showing that property in Lawrence had maintained its value despite all the recent storms, that two substantial churches had been erected, that houses were going up, and that freesoil settlers continued to arrive in gratifying numbers. When an inoffensive Free-State citizen was slain, Judge Lecompte had the effrontery to let the murderer run free on bail, with Marshal Donaldson as surety. But Geary indignantly had him rearrested, a step which immensely enhanced the governor's moral prestige. It was further strengthened when he went on to suspend Lecompte, whose unjudicial attitude in the Kansas troubles had really grown insufferable, and forced Donaldson's resignation. Unawed by the governor's sudden attack, Lecompte issued a writ citing him to appear in court at Lecompton to answer for illegal interference with the judiciary.[7] But Geary, holding his ground, appealed to the President; and it was clear that if Pierce sustained him, a far better day was dawning in Kansas.

For a few happy weeks, in fact, Americans ceased to think of slavery, feuding settlers, and disunionist plots. They turned their attention to Cyrus W. Field's announcement that he had his cable almost ready to be laid. They bent a rather cynical eye upon Walker's struggle in Nicaragua against increasing odds, for Commodore Vanderbilt was egging on the other Central American states to drive out the invader.[8] They shuddered over the disaster to the French steamer *Lyonnais*, which smashed into a Yankee bark off Nantucket, and sank

5 Quoted in London *Times*, October 28, 1856.
6 *Ibid.*
7 Lawrence correspondence in N. Y. *Weekly Tribune*, December 6, 1856.
8 Greene, *The Filibuster*, 263ff.

with the loss of more than a hundred lives. They talked of the new books, including two entertaining volumes of Webster's private correspondence.

But the dream of continued peace was harshly shattered when, in the opening December days of the new session of Congress, the clerks of the two chambers stood up to read Franklin Pierce's last annual message. House attendance was unusually large, for a new compensation law had brought in many who might have delayed at home. Only one really important piece of public business was anticipated in the short session, an attempt by the Democrats to carry some measure, probably based on the Toombs Bill, for the admission of Kansas. It now seemed plain that with a freesoil majority among the settlers, no rough legislation to make Kansas a slave State would be tolerated by many Northern Democrats. Some way must be found to bring her in as a free State without utterly estranging the South, and the quicker this was done the better.[9] Few expected Pierce's message to refer to any highly controversial points. But to the amazement of all and the horror of many, he tore the bandages from the half-healed wounds of sectional passion, and threw salt into the raw and bleeding flesh.

The petulance of a small man, repudiated and sorely humiliated, breathed in every paragraph. Half of the message was devoted to an arrogant, rancorous, and excited arraignment of the Republican Party, couched in terms much better suited to a stump speech than a state document. The recent election, he said, was essentially a condemnation of mere geographical parties. The considered sense of the nation had rejected a movement fraught with incalculable mischief, which would never have gained ground but for sinister misrepresentations acting upon a fevered state of the public mind, induced by causes temporary in character, and (it was to be hoped) transient in influence.

Ordinarily, said Pierce, the American scheme of government allowed perfect liberty of discussion. But how this had been abused! Under shelter of such freedom, organizations had been formed which pretended only to seek exclusion of slavery from the Territories, but really wished to destroy it in the States. To gain their end, they undertook the odious task of undermining the government, and of calumniating with wild invective not only all slaveholders but all who rejected their assaults upon the Constitution. They knew well that emancipation could be obtained only at the cost of burning cities, ravaged fields, and slaughtered populations, in a wild complication of foreign, civil, and servile wars. Nevertheless, they were endeavoring to lead the country into precisely this furnace of strife; they were appealing to sectional prejudices, and teaching Americans to stand face to face as enemies. Extremes had begotten extremes. Violent attacks from the North had been answered by proud defiance from the

9  Cf. N. Y. *Tribune* editorial December 3, 1856.

South. Thus the country had reached the fell consummation now so pointedly rebuked, the attempt of a sectional movement to usurp control of the nation's government.

This abusive condemnation of a party which had just polled one and a quarter million votes exasperated the Republicans to fury, and opened the gates to a violent new debate. It was a political blunder so damaging to national concord that in literal truth it was worse than a crime.

It was not difficult for a Republican cohort, springing to their feet, to repel Pierce's accusations. They roundly denied that their party sought the abolition of slavery; no plank of the platform, no public meeting, no authorized spokesman, had called for abolition; and the majorities given the party in eleven States testified to a faith in its sincerity. What had really aroused the sectional agitation? It was the repeal of the Missouri Compromise. "Burning cities!" exclaimed John Sherman. "Why, sir, I know of none except Lawrence and Osawatomie. I know of no ravaged fields or slaughtered populations except on the plains of Kansas." Who had labored to deprive the Constitution and laws of their moral authority? The men who, abetted by Administration officers, had robbed settlers of their franchises, had committed murder and arson, had laid waste towns, and had invented the crime of constructive treason. And when had the indoctrination of Americans in mutual hatred begun? In Douglas's famous report, with a new lesson in every act of the President since that time.[10]

The worst effect of the message was that once more, the North and South, through their newspapers and Congressional champions, were assailing each other hammer and tongs. All the billingsgate of the campaign was brought into use again. Mason of Virginia declared that he regarded Garrisonian abolitionists and Black Republicans as equally obnoxious. Rusk of Texas described the Frémonters as a rapacious set of politicians determined to take possession of the patronage of the government, and trample underfoot the sacred compact binding the nation together. Joshua Giddings talked of the infamous crimes of slavery; of masters scourging their servants into submission, and of white men who subjected Negro women to their pollutions and then sold their own offspring. "I want the member from Ohio," rasped Bennett of Mississippi, "to draw the distinction between the slaveholder bringing his slave into subjection by the lash, and the Northerners bringing their poor people into subjection by starvation." [11]

A new apple of discord, moreover, was tossed into the field as the old year closed and 1857 began. Few ideas were more repugnant to most sober Americans than the reopening of the slave trade. The traffic had been so sternly condemned

10  *Cong. Globe,* December 8, 1856.
11  *Idem,* December 4, 5, 1856; N. Y. *Weekly Tribune,* December 6, 1856.

by the united voice of Christendom that a nation which reverted to it would seemingly place itself outside the pale of civilization. Some three years earlier the Charleston *Standard* had proposed the step; and although numerous Southern journals condemned the suggestion, and others treated it with silent disdain, the Richmond *Examiner* and Charleston *Mercury* indicated their acquiescence. After Buchanan's victory the *Standard* spiritedly reopened its crusade. It was joined by the New Orleans *Delta*, which advocated a double Southern policy: acquisition of Cuba, northeastern Mexico, and other territories, and importation of enough black men to let every Southerner acquire one or two, and take them wherever opportunity beckoned to enterprise.

Most astounding of all, Governor J. H. Adams of South Carolina in his annual message called for reviving the traffic. Thus alone, he argued, could the South regain its old equality of power, and let the blessings of slavery be properly diffused. To many Northerners there was a nightmarish ring about his statement that slavery "has exalted the white race itself to higher hopes and purposes, and it is perhaps of the most sacred obligation that we should give it the means of expansion, and that we should press it forward to a perpetuity of progress." [12]

The South, fearing Kansas lost, felt a menacing pressure from the North. The North, despite the refusal of the South Carolina legislature to endorse Adams's hardy proposal, felt that menacing new pressures were being loosed in the cotton domain. It was understood that Pierre Soulé, visiting Walker in Nicaragua, had helped persuade him to decree the establishment of slavery. Free-soil observers envisaged a fierce thrust for the conquest of the Caribbean crescent, accompanied by a demand for the licit or illicit revival of colonization from Africa to fill these areas. The early weeks of 1857 found sectional animosity burning as redly as ever. [13]

In little over a decade, what 'bitter change of fierce extremes, extremes by change more fierce'! Only thirteen years earlier a Southern President, with a Cabinet largely of Southern men, had journeyed to Boston to attend a national celebration of the completion of Bunker Hill monument, and hear Webster deliver one of his noblest orations to forty thousand people. In the course of that visit an eminent South Carolinian, Hugh Swinton Legaré, fell ill. He was deeply admired by many a Massachusetts man. Not because he was Attorney-General, but because he was an old friend, known from student days in Edinburgh, George Tickner took him into his house. Only forty-seven, Legaré expired in

12 Quotations from the *Standard* and *Delta* are in N. Y. *Weekly Tribune*, November 8, 1856; Adams's message, November 21, 1856, was printed in pamphlet form; T. D. Jervey, *The Slave Trade*, 114–116.

13 W. J. Carnathan, "The Proposal to Reopen the Slave Trade," *South Atlantic Quarterly*, XXV, 410–430; New York *Evening Post, Tribune*, December, 1856.

Ticknor's arms. Our city, wrote the Boston scholar, is filled with consternation and sorrow. "He was a man of genius, full of refinement and poetry, and one of the best scholars in the country; but, more than this, he was of a most warm and affectionate spirit." To this South Carolinian, continued Ticknor, the country with great unanimity was beginning to look as a future President, with a perfect confidence in his talents, his principles, and his honor.[14] But by 1857, what faith would citizens of Massachusetts place in the most brilliant South Carolinian, and what confidence would South Carolinians have in the ablest New Englander?

Obviously, the political events of these thirteen years had much to do with the change. The Liberty Party, Texas, the Mexican War, Wilmot, the Fugitive Slave Act, the Nebraska Bill, Ostend, had all widened the chasm. But the fundamental causes of the cleavage lay deeper. Different standards, ideas, aims, outlooks, ideals; a different color of life and throb of pulse; different glories and different shames; different precedents and traditions; different fears and elations, had come to characterize the two sections, which, in a word, were by this time lapped in two divergent cultures. Was the ultimate story to be that of England and Ireland, Holland and Belgium, separating because too much divided by sentiment, or were North and South, like Saxon and Scot, Gascon and Norman, after all to submerge their differences in a larger unity? Men in 1857 found this an urgent question.

## [ II ]

Culture is a word hard to define, and of course many of the highest manifestations of culture simply ignored sectional lines. Science, art, and the purer works of literature knew no North or South, or very little of either. The best achievements in these fields had a national quality, and touched a great many patriotic chords. At the very least, they lifted men's eyes above sectional quarrels, and gave the nation a common stock in which it could take pride.

Take science, for example, which with literature was one of the two fields in which Americans attained enough distinction to attract admiring notice from the Old World. It was national and even international in spirit. The American Philosophical Society had been founded in colonial days to give the savants of the continent an opportunity of pooling their energies; and our science had been cosmopolitan in tone ever since Alexander Garden had corresponded with Linnaeus, Franklin had been honored by French and British students, and Benjamin Thompson, Count Rumford, had left his footprints all over Europe. The American Association for the Advancement of Science, which after its found-

14 *Life, Letters, and Journals*, II, 212, 213.

ing in 1848 quickly rose to a preëminent position, was a younger sister of the British Association. Its annual meetings, which became a notable feature of American intellectual life, were national affairs, attracting scientists from Georgia to Maine, open to the public, and given generous space in the press.

As for the central arsenal of American science, the Smithsonian Institution, it was a national agency founded by a British benefaction. The country well remembered how the clipper *Mediator* had delivered in Philadelphia £104,960 in gold sovereigns as James Smithson's gift for the increase and diffusion of knowledge among men. Though some members of Congress stubbornly opposed acceptance of the gift, the enlightened opinions of John Quincy Adams and others had prevailed; and Joseph Henry, brought from Princeton in 1846 to be secretary, had made the Institution a powerful auxiliary to almost every department of American research.[15]

Scientific journals, which had gained a secure footing, were also thoroughly national in content and spirit. Since the elder Benjamin Silliman set up the *American Journal of Sciences and Arts* in 1818, its publication had never been interrupted. His vigorous editorship, bringing it many original papers of value, with incisive reviews of European books and news of scientific developments everywhere, took no note of States or regions. His son, Benjamin Silliman, Jr., and his son-in-law, James Dwight Dana, succeeding to the conduct of the magazine, maintained its standards. Another important journal, *Science*, which had sprung up in connection with the American Association, was equally catholic in tone. These periodicals and the monographs of learned societies made Europe familiar with the beadroll of notable American investigators—Joseph Henry, Matthew Fontaine Maury, Elisha Mitchell, Henry R. Schoolcraft, Asa Gray, and A. D. Bache, national figures all.[16]

Few men, until a time later than this, thought of Mitchell and Maury as Southerners, Schoolcraft and Henry as Northerners, for their work had no such connotations.[17] Maury's activities, which specially touched the imagination of Americans, enlisted a very general pride. The main reasons for the appeal of his work were that it could be popularly understood, that its utility to navigation and commerce commended it to all practical men, that his eminence at foreign gatherings gave him unusual prestige, and that, touching the great

15 The *Memorial of Joseph Henry*, published by Congressional order in 1880, contains much on Smithsonian history; cf. W. J. Rhees, *Smithson and His Bequest*; N. S. Shaler, *United States*, III, 1040–1041.

16 J. G. Crowther, *Famous American Men of Science*; E. S. Dana et al., *A Century of Science in America*.

17 The adjective pseudo-scientific would best characterize the work of the ethnologist Josiah C. Nott of Alabama, whose seven-hundred-page volume *Types of Mankind*, published in 1854 in collaboration with G. R. Gliddon, comforted Southerners with the absurd doctrine that each of the various races of man was a fixed type "permanent through all recorded time."

mysterious seas, his writings had a poetic quality. Nobody had better reason than Yankee shipmasters for remembering how he had conceived the idea that science would benefit if mariners entered in their logbooks accurate records of ocean currents, depths, and temperatures; how little by little he gathered the data he needed, comparing it with that taken from older logs; how finally he announced his first noteworthy discovery, an improved sailing route to Rio de Janeiro; and how a skipper who consented to try it reached the equator in twenty-four days instead of the usual forty-one. "Navigators now for the first time," he had written, "appeared to comprehend what it was that I wanted them to do, *and why*." His next service had been in shortening the voyage to California by directions that cut the time by weeks. Every informed citizen knew that he had been the central figure of a remarkable international conference which sat at Brussels in 1853, as war clouds lowered darkly over Europe; a conference which arranged for a systematic collection of facts about winds, currents, temperatures, and tides, for the benefit of commerce everywhere.[18]

And Maury's fascinating book of 1855, *Physical Geography of the Sea*, was a national achievement, making scientists as well as general public familiar with striking new generalizations. By a happy phrase he called the Gulf Stream a river in the ocean; a warm-water stream whose fountain was the Gulf of Mexico, whose mouth was in the Arctic, and whose banks and bottom were cold water; its speed greater than that of the Mississippi or Amazon, and the demarcation between it and the ocean clearly visible to the eye as far north as the Carolina coast. He remarked that it was not to be regarded merely as a three-thousand-mile current, but as a balance-wheel, a part of the grand mechanism by which the earth was adapted to the well-being of its inhabitants. And not the water-ocean alone, but the air-ocean as well, fell within Maury's view. Showered with honors by foreign governments, he was better pleased by the thanks of the honest seamen for the charts upon which he had indicated the usual time and place of storms, fogs, rains, and calms.[19]

Next to Maury in popular eminence, and equally a national and international figure, ranked that adopted American, Jean Louis Rodolphe Agassiz, who on accepting his chair in the Lawrence Scientific School had no difficulty in taking leadership in the study of natural history in the United States. A very true

18  For Maury's foreign fame see the article on him in *Revue des Deux Mondes*, March, 1858; Lord Wrottesley's speech in House of Lords, April 26, 1853; John W. Wayland, *Pathfinder of the Seas*, chs. 13, 14.

19  The *National Intelligencer*, July 17, 1855, has a long review. Humboldt in 1855 announced to Maury that the King of Prussia had given him the gold medal designed for useful scientific work; *National Intelligencer*, February 3, April 19, 1855. For similar honors from France see M. Vattemare's correspondence with Maury, *National Intelligencer*, March 8, 1856. Napoleon III exclaimed: "Is it possible that such a work could have been undertaken and executed by one man?"

American he quickly became. When in 1857 the French Minister of Public Instruction offered him a post at the Museum of Natural History, he replied that he "could not sever abruptly the ties which for a number of years I have been accustomed to consider as binding me for the remainder of my days to the United States." [20] His home in Cambridge, humming with industry and glowing with enthusiasm, was a center of inspiration for naturalists and scholars from all parts of the republic. Like Maury, he planned a work of ambitious pitch and scope, a ten-volume study which he announced in 1855 under the title of *Contributions to the Natural History of the United States*. His prospectus, widely reprinted in the press, created a flutter. For more than eight years, he wrote, he had been investigating those classes of the animal kingdom which American naturalists had least touched, the time had come to publish his most important results, and he needed subscriptions for the ten quarto volumes at twelve dollars each. "Every man in the country who has the means," R. C. Winthrop told the novelist Kennedy, "ought to subscribe for a copy"—and Agassiz did receive some two thousand five hundred orders. But only four volumes were ever completed. [21]

The nature of his self-defined duties made Joseph Henry's work at the Smithsonian as wide as the nation, and almost as wide as science itself. As much an organizer as investigator, he seemed intent on making the Institution the incubator of American scientific effort in unentered areas. Though his own experiments in electro-magnetism resulted in discoveries of high value for the magnetic telegraph and the future electric-power industry, he would be best remembered for inspiring the work of others. At the end of the first decade he recapitulated the Smithsonian's labors. It had published seventy-one pieces of original investigations filling eight large quarto volumes. It had set up laboratories in terrestrial magnetism and chemistry, had sponsored a regular winter series of popular lectures, and boasted of a growing library, a museum, and an art gallery of sorts. As secretary, Henry corresponded widely to make the Smithsonian a national clearing-house of scientific information. "It is regrettable," he wrote with dry humor, "that so many minds of power and originality in our country should, from defective scientific training, be suffered to diverge so widely from the narrow path which alone leads to real advance in positive knowledge. Providence, however, seems in some measure to vindicate the equality of its distributions by assigning to such a double measure of hope and self-esteem, which serves them instead of success and reputation." [22]

Henry had adopted what he called the system of active operations, by which

20 Letter to M. Rouland, September 25, 1857, in *National Intelligencer*, October 8, 1857.
21 Winthrop, June 20, 1855, in Kennedy Papers; Elizabeth Cary Agassiz, *Louis Agassiz, His Life and Correspondence*.
22 *Tenth Annual Report*, 1855.

he meant pioneering investigation along a broad front. He was adamant in rejecting the proposal frequently urged upon the trustees, that a large part of the income be devoted to spreading knowledge of some branch of the practical arts; and though he feared that the timidity of some associates might permit such encroachments, his own policy steadily gained favor. The variety of the Smithsonian's activities was remarkable. In a typical year (1852) it made a preliminary exploration of the Bad Lands, publishing a description of them; furnished scientific instruments and other aids to an astronomical and geographical expedition to Chile; published results of botanical searches in Texas, New Mexico, and California; issued an illustrated memoir on the sea-plants of the North American coast; collected and published the statistics of American libraries; brought out a volume on the Dakota language; directed attention to American antiquities; and printed a variety of scientific papers. This plan of "active operations" stimulated investigation in many fields, made the exploration and settlement of the West contributory to science, and gave intelligent direction to the government's previously chaotic scientific work.[23]

For Washington in these years was displaying a keen interest in varied types of scientific research, exploration being naturally the most prominent. This was the period of the two so-called United States-Grinnell Expeditions in search of Sir John Franklin's men and a possible open polar sea; enterprises supported partly by the nation, partly by Henry Grinnell, which enabled the young naval surgeon Elisha Kent Kane to lift himself to fame. Kane's modest, graphic account of his tireless labors and frightful hardships, *Arctic Explorations* (1856) "lay for a decade with the Bible on almost literally every parlor table in America." He died at thirty-seven in Havana; and his funeral journey was a national pageant, the body lying in state in New Orleans, Louisville, Columbus, and Baltimore before it reached his native Philadelphia.[24]

In the midst of the presidential campaign of 1856 the North Pacific Survey-

23 The Smithsonian in 1885 published two volumes of the *Scientific Writings of Joseph Henry;* but a modern biography is needed. Quarrels over the policy of the Smithsonian were continuous. Henry earnestly but unsuccessfully opposed putting $200,000 of funds into the "Norman castle" which housed the institution. An important group, well represented among the Regents, regarded the accumulation of a great scientific library as properly the main purpose of the Smithsonian. A so-called compromise was adopted by which the income was divided between the library and museum on one side, the research, publications, and lectures on the other. In 1855 the quarrel broke into the Congressional debates; see Meacham's speech in the House, March 3, 1855.

24 The biography of Kane by William Elder is the subject of an interesting four-column article in the N. Y. *Weekly Tribune* of January 30, 1858. See *National Intelligencer,* September 27, 1856, for an estimate of Kane. Said the House Library Committee in a report of April 16, 1856, on Kane's work in the Arctic and Wilkes's in the Antarctic: "By the noble fruits of these voyages to opposite points of the globe, our country takes rank at once among the learned nations of Europe in the high departments of distant scientific discovery."

ing and Exploring Expedition commanded by Captain John Rodgers returned to the United States. It had surveyed parts of the almost unknown Japanese coasts, had examined Behring Sea, had explored various Pacific archipelagoes, and had brought back rich collections of plants and animals. Its best historian, Lieutenant A. W. Habersham, published next year a volume on the cruise which was compared with Melville. "We did what I suppose no vessel ever did before," he wrote, "we sounded around the world." Maury and John P. Kennedy, Secretary of the Navy when it was outfitted, had helped lay its plans.[25] In another direction lay the before-mentioned Chilean Expedition of 1849–52 under Lieutenant J. M. Gillies of the navy, and the expedition of 1853–56 to the countries bordering on the River Plate.[26] At home the work of exploring and mapping the American domain went steadily on. The commissioners who in 1850–53 had to run the new boundary with Mexico covered nearly five thousand miles of rough terrain. John Russell Bartlett, who began as merchant and amateur scientist, and lived to become a noted librarian, produced two fat volumes of "incidents" of adventure encountered in Sonora, Chihuahua, and New Mexico.[27] In the middle fifties an exploring expedition sent by the War Department to the Upper Missouri visited the Sioux, Rees, Mandans, Gros Ventres, Crows, and other tribes, and brought back from the Yellowstone Valley and Black Hills large collections of minerals, fossils, and biological specimens. Its commander was assisted by a young geologist, F. V. Hayden, who would later gain fame in government employ.[28] Meanwhile, a survey of Lake Superior was being pushed, and included a detailed mapping of the shores as well as careful soundings.

When Congress directed the Secretary of War to collect materials illustrating the history, condition, and prospects of the Indians, the importance of assigning the indefatigable Henry R. Schoolcraft to the task was generally recognized. "Go where he will, whether it be among Sacs and Foxes, or Sioux or Winnebagoes," wrote one who knew him well, "and so long as the 'good medicine' chooses to remain his person is safe from attack and his property from peril, while every man among his entertainers is anxious to do most to propitiate and gratify the guest. . . . He can set a broken limb, extract a ball or splinter, bleed at the arm and prescribe in cases of slight sickness, or he can repair an Indian's gunlock, solder up his broken kettle, and teach him to do the

25 Tuckerman, *Kennedy*, 217ff.
26 The results of the La Plata expedition were embodied in a large octavo by Thomas J. Page, U.S.N., called *La Plata, the Argentine Confederation, and Paraguay*, issued by Harpers. The exposition had some political and commercial objects, while it made no inconsiderable additions to knowledge of the geography, natural history, and customs of Paraguay.
27 Appletons, 1853–54.
28 *National Intelligencer*, December 6, 1856.

same. . . . Honest, kind, simple, and truthful, he wins his way to the hearts of those blunt, hardy men." [29] In 1851 the government published the first of Schoolcraft's six volumes of *Historical and Statistical Information* on the Indians, a work interestingly illustrated by Captain Seth Eastman of the army. This was the crowning achievement of an adventurous writer who had made trip after trip into the Indian country for thirty-five years, had written book after book since his work on the Ozarks in 1819, and had lent an especially strong impulse to ethnological study in his two volumes of *Algic Researches* (1839). Though his "great national work" [30] had its shortcomings, it proved full of indispensable information.

Science, it is clear, would have had frugal fare without government patronage. Maury of the Naval Observatory, Henry of the Smithsonian, A. D. Bache as superintendent of the Coast Survey, Schoolcraft, and Kane all held government posts or enjoyed indispensable Federal assistance. Even Agassiz, whose first important scientific trip was on a Coast Guard steamer as guest of the government, received some important aids. Joseph LeConte, after Maury perhaps the most eminent of Southern scientists, supported himself by teaching first at the University of Georgia, and then at the College of South Carolina. Silliman and the chemist Wolcott Gibbs, Elisha Mitchell of botanical and geological fame, and Benjamin Peirce, the mathematician and astronomer, all found academic havens, though Peirce was also connected with the Coast Survey. But the vigorous Federal interest in science contributed to make it national (so far as it was not international) in spirit. Men who gathered for meetings of the American Association naturally felt themselves citizens of a realm of culture which could only be weakened by sectional division. At the tenth session held in Albany in 1856, for example, all the scientists just mentioned gathered to hear Peirce discuss mathematical problems, Henry the principles of acoustics, and Bache the formulation of tide tables; Mitchell shaking hands with Silliman, Gibbs with Maury, as fellows in the same grand labors.

[ III ]

The best of American art, too, had no offensive sectional coloration. Few people thought of North or South in viewing the sculptures of Crawford and Powers, or the painting of Henry Inman or Eastman Johnson. A great part of

29  This sketch, probably by W. W. Seaton, is in the *National Intelligencer* of April 1, 1854. Schoolcraft had served the government in various official relations with the Indians, had negotiated treaties with the Chippewa by which the United States gained title to great tracts, had founded a society for the study of the aborigines, and had projected an ambitious Indian encyclopaedia.

30  The phrase used by the *National Intelligencer*, April 1, 1854. Eastman, another enthusiastic ethnologist, had a long acquaintance with the Indian tribes.

the country's limited artistic energy, in fact, went into the celebration of themes that were distinctly national and patriotic.

If the republic had no painters of genius, it certainly had some of high talent. To the late eighteenth-century school of portraitists headed by Gilbert Stuart had succeeded a variety of groups; notably the poets of landscape, with Thomas Cole (who died in 1848), Asher B. Durand, and the panoramic but neatly accurate John F. Kensett at their head; a number of technically dexterous men showing strong English or Dutch influence, such as Chester Harding, Henry Inman, and that sympathetic painter of rural scenes, Eastman Johnson; and a dashing coterie who transferred to America the romanticism of Düsseldorf (an unfortunate influence), among them William Hart and Emanuel Leutze. An incisive genre school, relating anecdotes of native flavor, had also arisen. Year by year a good many interesting and competent canvases were being finished. In New York the annual displays of the National Academy of Design, of which S. F. B. Morse had been the principal founder, might show one of Frederick E. Church's overdramatized and distantly Turneresque canvases—his erupting "Cotopaxi" of 1854 struck a new note of the grandiose; or a graphic illustration of homely life by William S. Mount, such as "Turning the Grindstone" or "Bargaining for a Horse." Boston had painters who remembered the tradition of Copley, Philadelphia its men inspired by the remarkable Peale family, and Charleston a few artists proud of Washington Allston, of the less famous Charles Fraser, who among other achievements had given Thomas Sully his first lessons, and of the gifted school of miniaturists once ensconced in the little city.[31]

It could justly be said, of course, that the nation's roll of distinguished artists was brief, its stock of artistic treasures small, and its fund of taste still slight. No public art gallery of importance yet rose in any city. To be sure, certain societies which purchased and exhibited works of art could be found scattered along the coast. The Redwood Library in Newport and the Charleston Museum, both of colonial origin, had a number of respectable paintings, while the Boston Athenaeum, the New York Historical Society, the Pennsylvania Academy, and the Maryland Institute all placed canvases and sculptures on view. In New York the art dealer had found secure foothold, Goupil of Paris having set up a branch establishment in the forties, while the Düsseldorf Gallery offered examples of the German method of transferring legend and literature into picture-frames.[32] "The builders of houses begin to look for something to cover their walls," wrote Evert Duyckinck after attending a winter auction at high prices in 1852. At first they had bought European copies of old masters; "now, within a very

31 Charles H. Caffin, *The Story of American Painting*, 46-121; Eugen Neuhaus, *History and Ideals of American Art*, 82ff.
32 F. J. Mather, Jr., "Painting" in *The American Spirit in Art*, 16.

few years, a desire to possess the original works of modern, and latterly (greatly through the Art Union) of American works, has sprung up." [33] In Washington the banker W. W. Corcoran had acquired a large collection and in 1859 began the construction of the Corcoran Gallery. In Baltimore, Granville S. Oldfield, making repeated trips to Europe, had spent about $70,000 for some six hundred and fifty pieces which were worth far more when he sold them at auction in 1855.[34] August Belmont in New York helped set a fashion of art-collecting, his intelligent purchases extending to fine porcelains and textiles.

A special service was done the country by several connoisseurs who, though hardly endowed with long purses, used learning, discrimination, and experience in buying European treasures for transfer to their bare if shining land. In 1853 Thomas J. Bryan, whose activities were in Edith Wharton's mind when she wrote False Dawn, imported with other paintings a group of about thirty examples of early Italian masters, later (1867) presented to the New York Historical Society. Bryan, testifies Gabriel Manigault of Charleston, was regarded as the most expert buyer among Americans abroad. Though he had no high-priced paintings, "there were nevertheless among the several hundred which he exhibited in Broadway in 1853 after his return enough to give a good idea of the history of European art, and of the styles of the different schools." Manigault himself was a collector of taste and assiduity, whose enthusiasm for art was first fully awakened by a visit to the Louvre in 1847, and who found that the auction rooms of the Rue Drouet sold admirable pieces. Already the European picture trade had swollen into an important branch of business, rich Britons were buying lavishly, and fakes abounded; but he obtained a number of canvases which South Carolinians flocked to see.[35]

The prince of collectors, however, was James Jackson Jarves, the Boston-born son of a glass manufacturer who took up his residence in Florence in the fifties and used his considerable means to satisfy an inborn love of art. He began buying early Italian painting while interest in them was as yet not widespread, and when fine specimens could be picked up, often for low sums, in out-of-the-way places.

"My adventures in this pursuit," he later wrote, "were often curious and instructive. They involved an inquisition into the intricacies of numberless villas, palaces, convents, churches, and household dens, all over this portion of Italy; the employment of many agents to scent out my prey; many fatiguing journeyings; miles upon miles of wearisome staircases; dusty explorations of dark retreats; dirt, disappointment, fraud, lies, and money often fruitlessly spent;

33 MS Diary, December 16, 1852, NYPL. This sale was attended by Corcoran, the Van Buren brothers, and the shipbuilder Webb.
34 National Intelligencer, April 24, 1855.
35 See Manigault's undated paper of reminiscences in the Charleston Historical Society.

all compensated, however, by the gradual accumulation of a valuable gallery."
He found a fine Perugino, smoked and dirty, discarded in the lumber-room of
a famous convent; he discovered a splendid full-length portrait of a Spanish
grandee by Velasquez, cut from its frame and crusted with dirt, but underneath
in fine preservation, among the rubbish of a disorderly villa. Jarves's collection,
a total of 145 pictures, was brought over in 1860 to be exhibited in the new
marble gallery of the Institute of Fine Arts at 625 Broadway. It had been well
advertised by enthusiastic letters from Americans and Britons, including T. A.
Trollope, in the *Crayon*, since 1854 the country's leading art magazine; for
though it contained no great commanding masterpiece, it finely represented
three centuries of Tuscan painting. But popular interest in New York and
Boston proved slight, only a few men, notably Charles Eliot Norton, appreciat-
ing what the country had gained.[36]

But from the point of view of nationalism, the American spirit was best
expressed by the genre painters, reproductions of whose genial scenes were
scattered broadcast by such commercial organizations as the American Art
Union. A typical figure was George Caleb Bingham, whose work so capitally
illustrates some picturesque phases of American life. His was the commonplace
story of hard beginnings in an unfavorable setting: Virginia birth, the Missouri
frontier at eight, painting with home-made pigments, a struggle for study first
at the Pennsylvania Academy and then in Europe, and mature residence in Missouri. A keen interest in politics, viewed on its homely institutional side, animated much of his work. His first painting to achieve any reclame was "The
Jolly Flatboatmen," selected by the American Art Union in 1846 as its annual
engraving. A succession of spirited works followed: "Raftsmen Playing Cards,"
"Canvassing for a Vote," "Emigration of Daniel Boone," "County Elections,"
"Stump Speaking," and "Verdict of the People," all popular in the fifties.
Authentic study of manners, and the democratic spirit of the frontier, characterized his work. He knew firsthand the explorers, fur-traders, emigrants, river-
men, politicians, farmers, teamsters, and other figures that he presents, and while
his work was faulty in technique, it showed realism, humor, and a keen eye for
characteristic scenes.[37]

The public character of much of the sculpture of the time gave it greater
popular prominence than painting, and lent it no little influence in instilling
patriotic feeling. If frequency of mention in the press be a test, Americans took
a livelier interest in the work of Crawford, Powers, Joel T. Hart, Story, Palmer,
and Clark Mills than in any similar group of painters. These men made Italy

36 *Letters Relating to a Collection of Pictures Made by Mr. James Jackson Jarves*
(privately printed, 1859); and see Jarves's numerous books, especially *Art Thoughts: The
Experiences and Observations of an American Amateur in Europe.*
37 Albert Christ-Janer, *George Caleb Bingham of Missouri.*

their headquarters. In Story's letters, in Hawthorne's *Italian Notebooks*, and in the life of Crawford which Thomas Hicks wrote soon after that artist's death, we catch rich glimpses of the American colony in the Roman ilex shade or silhouetted against the tawny Arno. The castles, churches, and ancient and medieval masterpieces of sculpture; the romantic villas which American dollars stretched so far in hiring; the almond-eyed children, the cleanly-dressed girls crowned with white-peaked *tovaglia*, the peasants selling squash-seeds, fruit, and pigs stuffed whole; the bright-colored crowds of the cities; the eager talk with Britons, Frenchmen, and Germans—all this was an inspiration. Women crossed the ocean too. Harriet Hosmer, daughter of a country physician in Massachusetts, a small, quick, gifted girl who, burning with ambition, went to Rome in 1852 to work under the English sculptor John Gibson and became a great pet of the Brownings, was but the most eminent of a sisterhood who, in Henry James's words, settled upon the hills in a white, marmorean flock. As James adds, the odd phenomenon of their practically simultaneous appearance has its significance "in any study of the growth of birth and taste in the simmering society that produced them."[38]

Public demand and the public purse channeled much of the energy of the principal sculptors toward national themes and heroes; and people read eagerly of the progress of Hart, Crawford, and Erastus D. Palmer on their chosen subjects.

All three had risen by hard struggle. Born near Winchester, Ky., Hart had, like Lincoln, educated himself by reading at the evening fire; had become a stone-mason; and meeting the sculptor S. V. Clevenger in Lexington at the beginning of the forties, had taken fire from his fame. His career began when a few years later a patriotic women's organization in Richmond asked him to execute a life-sized marble statue of Henry Clay for $5,000; and when Louisville offered $10,000 and New Orleans $14,000 for monuments to the same statesman, he was able to take up residence in Florence.[39] Crawford as a boy in New York had taken drawing-lessons, worked with a wood-carver, and finally become an apprentice to the leading monument-makers of the city, toiling meanwhile on marble busts and studying at the National Academy of Design. Going to Italy, he had first done sculptural work at a laborer's wage, but by the fifties was one of the best-paid artists in the world. The beginning of the decade found him commissioned to produce a grand equestrian statue of Washington for Richmond, to furnish the marble pediment of the Senate in Washington, and to chisel the figure of "Armed Liberty" surmounting the Capitol dome. Palmer, of rural New York origin, who graduated from wood-carving and

38 Henry James, *W. W. Story*, I, 257.
39 See *National Intelligencer*, November 17, 1857, for the New Orleans commission.

carpentry into mosaic-cutting, and thence into sculpture, exhibited his first important work, the "Infant Ceres," in the 1850 showing of the National Academy, and similarly enjoyed a national fame in the days of Buchanan's presidency.

In a land where statuary was rare, the influence of the commemorative pieces which these men scattered over the country was tremendous. As Italian workmen labored in the Capitol grounds on Crawford's huge pedimental work, "The Past and Present of America," the press teemed with descriptions of it. America, with laurel wreath and arrows, stood proudly in the center; about her finely-draped figure were disposed the conquered redskin, the pioneer hunter, the settler with his axe, the soldier, merchant, mechanic, and teacher. While the separate figures had power, the group as a whole breathed the American qualities of confidence and idealism. When Crawford's bronze statue of Washington was brought up the James by a Dutch brig in 1857, Richmond greeted it with jubilation—though saddening news arrived by the same ship that the artist's eager strivings had been ended at forty-four by cancer of the brain. A great crowd assembled to watch the heavy bronze, cast in Munich, slowly brought ashore; the Armory Band played patriotic airs; and at a formal luncheon the governor and leading citizens exchanged toasts.[40] When Hart came back to America in 1859 for the unveiling of his Clay in Richmond, he was handsomely feted. And so the tale ran with other men. Even the failures had a certain influence. When Palmer in 1857 completed his model for a group that he vainly hoped would occupy the House pediment in Washington—the landing of the Pilgrims, with the venerable Brewster, praying with upturned face, the central figure—the press spread vivid descriptions of it over the country.[41]

Story, settling in the Barberini Palace, began in 1852 his statue of his eminent father, and three years later Bostonians poured into the Athenaeum to see the figure of the benignant jurist, seated on the bench in judicial gown, one hand holding a book and the other raised in characteristic gesture. Behind Story lay years of law practise in Boston and the publication of legal texts; before him stretched a long career as sculptor, poet, and miscellaneous writer. He conspicuously illustrated the growing tendency among Americans of means to turn from practical to artistic pursuits. Though he lacked genius, with its all-compelling call, though he had been eminently successful at the bar, where

40 Crawford's statues of Jefferson and Patrick Henry for his Washington monument had reached Richmond in 1855. They were at once set up on the west side of the capitol with a railing to hold back the crowds. "They are universally admired as the creations of genius," wrote George B. Munford to Crawford; August 30, 1855, Governors' Letterbooks, No. 26, pp. 301, 302. Virginia was training her own sculptor at the time, Edward Virginius Valentine, who by 1857 had made several portrait busts and next year went to Paris.
41 *National Intelligencer*, April 16, 1857.

his mother wished him to continue, and though he knew that his aesthetic work wanted intensity and high inspiration, he had long loved painting, modelling, and music, and boldly took his leap in the dark. His range was wide, and it was his "Cleopatra" that Hawthorne immortalized in *The Marble Faun*, but he was destined in due time to give the country dignified statues of such sons as John Marshall, Joseph Henry, and George Peabody. His friend the loquacious Hiram Powers, who could talk of everything—of his humble beginnings in Ohio as tavern boy, bill collector, clockmaker, and waxwork modeller, his later struggles in Washington, his Italian friends—had a busy studio in Florence through all these years. His international fame dated from the furor caused by his "Greek Slave" at the Crystal Palace Exhibition in London, but his best work was his long series of portrait busts of Jackson, Marshall, Webster, Calhoun, and others. His full-length statue of the orator placed before the Massachusetts State House in 1859 struck Hawthorne as "very grand, very Webster." [42]

A good part of the artistic effort of the country, in short, went toward creating a national mythology. Leutze's historical rhetoric had begun in the forties with "Columbus Before the Council at Salamanca," and he, S. F. B. Morse (as in his really magnificent picture of the House in session in Monroe's time in its old hall), Daniel Huntington, and others enlarged the work that Trumbull, by his Revolutionary canvases, had begun in creating mementos of the national past. Robert W. Weir was paid $8,000 by the government for his painting of "The Embarkation of the Pilgrims" to hang in the Capitol. "We are about producing in steel after a large painting by Huntington," wrote the publisher C. L. Derby to John P. Kennedy in 1860,[43] "a great national picture entitled 'Washington Irving and his Contemporaries.'" He wished to make sure that F. O. C. Darley, the engraver, furnished a really accurate likeness of Kennedy. His word "national" is worth noting. The steel engravings of J. C. Buttré, whose studio was in New York, became famous, and he specialized in portraits of American leaders. Public men were glad to encourage young sculptors with money and praise, as the Preston brothers encouraged Powers, and as Douglas helped young Leonard W. Volk—who returned from Europe in time to make studies of both Lincoln and Douglas, as he saw them in the debates of 1858. But the new American mythology was by no means wholly

---

42 Late in 1841 Edward Everett, sitting to Powers for a bust, heard him express a wish to execute a statue of a Grecian slave-girl carried captive to Constantinople. Four years later the work was creating a minor sensation in London, with everyone from Prince Albert down coming to see it; the major sensation came later. Frothingham, *Everett*, 182, 252. For an account of the orders which poured in on Powers, see the *National Intelligencer*, May 3, 1855. "Since Thorwaldsen's death," one traveller wrote, "no one hesitates to award him the highest rank in his art."

43 October 5, 1860; Kennedy Papers.

romantic. The realism that went into the genre painting of the day stripped the toga from Washington and gave him a Continental uniform.[44]

## [ IV ]

The theatre, too, was in a very real sense a nationalizing influence, for plays of patriotic theme were numerous, while theatrical productions, as given in all parts of the Union, tended to establish common standards of speech, dress, and manners. The chief events of the Revolution, from Bunker Hill to Yorktown, were celebrated in literally scores of plays; a dozen dramas dealt with the War of 1812; and the titles of such pieces as *The Yankee in Tripoli, The Siege of Monterey*, and *Oregon, or The Disputed Boundary*, speak for themselves. In many a play of contemporary social life a patriotic *motif* was sharply introduced. And the stage was always reaching out its hands to the masses, touching a vein of common emotion in Bowery roughs, Southern gentlemen, and frontier farmers. When at the close of the fifties Joe Jefferson reworked three old versions of *Rip Van Winkle* into an improved play, and gave his inimitable depiction of both the insouciant young Rip, tossing off his dram among his cronies, and the old Rip, returning to his village in beard, tatters, and wonderment, he touched a chord of true Americanism.

No view could be more mistaken than that which regards the theatre of this period in metropolitan terms. All the rising cities of the West had their theatres; no New York house was more admirably built or appointed than the famous St. Charles of New Orleans; and in all States touring performers of the most brilliant type were well known—the second and third Joseph Jefferson, Tyrone Power, George P. Farren and his wife, Edwin Forrest, the finely cultured Macready, and, a little later, John McCullough and Lawrence Barrett. The West produced its own capable actors; for example, Joshua Silsbee, who first appeared in a theatre at Natchez, and who portrayed rural types to perfection. Even California had a gleaming figure, the child-actress Lotta Crabtree,

---

44 When Clark Mills found from measurements that Jackson had been anything but a well-proportioned man, he wrote the Jackson Monument Committee in Washington for instructions. They replied that they wanted "Jackson, and nothing but Jackson"—and Colonels Haynes, Hampton, Gadsden, and other old comrades in arms found the likeness perfect. Charleston *Courier*, March 8, 1848. John A. Dix, serving on a committee to receive designs for a statue of Washington, was pleased by what he saw in the Italian studios. He had always thought togas a gross anachronism. "Crawford has boldly departed from this prevalent usage, and I think with complete success." To Peter Force, December 8, 1844; Dix Papers, N. Y. Hist. Soc. The country had thrilled responsively to Henry A. Wise's declaration in the House, when Horatio Greenough's statue of a half-nude Washington had been delivered at the Washington Navy-yard: "The man does not live, and never did live, who ever saw Washington without his shirt."

the chief prodigy among the troupers of the gold-coast, who in the later fifties became the pet and pride of her section.

Vivid sketches of the life of travelling performers of the time are to be found in the memoirs of Mrs. Anna Cora Mowatt, and the charmingly humorous autobiography of the youngest and greatest of the three Joseph Jeffersons. A steamboat frozen in at a wild point on the Ohio; stage journeys over frontier roads in bitter midwinter; outbreaks of epidemics; playing of parts when desperately ill to avoid disappointing an audience; ludicrous or tragic accidents—this is the stuff of Mrs. Mowatt's best chapters. Jefferson, after shaking up dusty rat-traps of theatres in Wilmington and Savannah, played Mobile with the lively Julia Dean for six dollars a week apiece. For this reward they changed their politics, their religion, and their costumes at the will of the stage-manager. As Catholics they massacred the Huguenots, and as Pilgrims bade sad adieux to England; they were brigands, gentle shepherds, and revolutionaries by turns. Jefferson tells of the innumerable mischances that befell hastily-mustered companies on improvised stages; the balcony scene in *Romeo and Juliet*, for example, enacted before an audience exploding with laughter because the cornerstone of the Veronese edifice was a box advertising thirty pounds of short sixes. Edwin Booth made his first great impression in America by performances in Baltimore and a tour of the South in 1856. And while prominent figures gave the profitable areas of the West and South an opportunity to see them, scores of minor road companies barnstormed through heat and cold in raw new States and Territories, following the paths that Sol Smith, the great central actor of the frontier stage, had blazed. For Smith, down to his retirement in 1853, had often played in hamlets where it seemed impossible to obtain a respectable audience. The people, as he writes, "seemed to come out of the woods." [45]

The stage, in short, was a living force not only in cities and towns, but in remote areas; it left its imprint on rural society as well as urban; Lincoln, a young lawyer in Springfield, according to Joe Jefferson, defended the elder Jeffersons against an exorbitant tax imposed by church folk, enabling their company to spend a season in entertaining and educating the legislature; and the "floating theatre" of the Chapman family, with like showboat ventures by imitators, reached river hamlets all the way from Pittsburgh to New Orleans. A considerable part of the fare given by roving troupes and stock companies was of high literary quality. The comedies of Goldsmith, Sheridan, and Colman were perennial favorites; historical American pieces were popular; and dramatizations of Dickens and Scott had tremendous vogue. Charlotte Cush-

45 Anna Cora Mowatt's *Autobiography of an Actress* was published in 1853; *The Autobiography of Joseph Jefferson* in 1889–90. See Sol Smith, *Theatrical Management in the West and South for Thirty Years.*

man, greatest of American actresses in these years, was renowned for her acting as Nancy Sykes in *Oliver Twist* ("a tigress," wrote the English actor George Vandenhoff, "with a touch, and but one, of woman's almost deadened nature, blotted and trampled underfoot by man's cruelty and sin"),[46] and as Meg Merrilies in *Guy Mannering*, darkly, luridly, picturesquely impressive. Home's *Douglas*, Kotzebue's *Pizarro*, and Lytton's *Lady of Lyons* delighted multitudes. But Shakespeare was the staple and backbone of the American stage, and Mark Twain was faithful to reality when he made his two drunken, thievish, dilapidated old actors, floating down the Mississippi, try to pass themselves off as pupils of Kean and Garrick in Shakespearean rôles.

Nothing better illustrated the public importance of the stage than the veritable worship accorded to Edwin Forrest, an idol about whom surged turbulent nationalist passions. Making his debut in his native Philadelphia at fourteen as Young Norval, he went west for training; and Sol Smith, seeing him in *The Soldier's Daughter* in Cincinnati, prophesied his future greatness. By 1848 he was established as foremost among those actors who tear a passion to tatters, and his energy, audacity, vanity, and bumptious patriotism had installed him in the hearts of plain Americans everywhere. Powerfully built, aggressive in temper, full of animal spirits, he had been equal to anything, whether wandering the wild border country, playing to fiercely applauding Bowery audiences, making two runs in London, or touring all the large American cities. He liked turbulent characters, using his stalwart physique, sonorous voice, and impetuous manner to make them at times thrillingly effective, at times pathetically cheap: Richard III, Macbeth, Spartacus, Pizarro, the Indian chief Metamora. Men either liked or disliked him tremendously. His fits of passion made enemies on every hand. Wayward and irresponsible, he turned his marital difficulties into a public scandal, and when he assaulted N. P. Willis in June, 1856, for defending Mrs. Forrest, laid himself open to widespread censure.

But to the crowd he was not only America's representative tragedian, but an embodiment of the national spirit; the same spirit that flowed into the oratory of Clay and Douglas, the manifestoes of Young America, and the poetry of Whitman. His visits to London were regarded as an American challenge to the motherland. On his second tour he brought himself into collision (1854) with Macready, the lord of the Shakespearean stage. Forrest, choosing without warrant to believe that Macready had inspired the adverse criticisms of John Forster and others, intimated that the English actor (a highminded gentleman) had joined in a conspiracy against him. Attending one of Macready's performances in Edinburgh, he took a front seat and at an opportune moment

---

46 Vandenhoff, *Leaves from an Actor's Notebook*.

hissed! As Joseph Jefferson put it: "The eagle of the American stage was in a frenzy; his plumage had been ruffled by the British lion. So giving that intolerant animal one tremendous peck, he spread his wings and sailed away." The sequel was the bloody Astor Place riot of May 10, 1847, when Macready's appearance in *Macbeth* was the signal for an outburst by New York rowdies and Anglophobes. A stormy section of the audience howled down Macready's lines, a still angrier crowd assaulted the door with clubs and stones, and when soldiers appeared, seventeen persons were killed and many wounded. Deplorable as the riot was, it showed that Americans regarded the stage and its principal personages with great seriousness.[47]

It cannot be denied that there was something peculiarly American in Forrest; in his dauntless pride, his vigor, his democracy, and his preference for rough-and-ready effects. He was best in portraying such elemental, strong-willed rebels as Spartacus and Coriolanus; and a critic has remarked that he was himself an elemental, driving personality in perhaps unconscious revolt against the tamely idealized classical drama. Something of the rude force of pioneer America appeared in the man, so that Bowery boys and rough-fisted westerners saw in him a natural antagonist of Old World elegance, cultivation, and caste. His worst side was shown in the Edinburgh affront to a great fellow-actor, and in the caning of innocent Willis. He revealed his best side in his genuine concern for an American drama. It was his offer of a prize of $500 which inspired the writing of the first successful drama on an Indian theme, John A. Stone's *Metamora, The Pride of the Wampanoags*, with a rôle full of the heroics that he loved. His special tastes did much to inspire the dramatic writings of James Montgomery Bird in the thirties, and of Robert T. Conrad, the Philadelphia author of *Jack Cade*. With George H. Miles, whose *De Soto* was produced in 1852, these men prepared the way for the most important of American dramatists in the period, George Henry Boker.[48]

Science, art, the stage, all had their nationalizing influences, and so of course did literature. It was Bryant who sang "The Song of Marion's Men," and Whitman who, in "Starting from Paumanok," identified himself equally with Pennsylvanian and Arkansian, with every part of his "far breath'd land! Arctic braced! Mexican breezed!" Of the messages of congratulation which Irving received on his life of Washington the most prized came from Charlottesville, Va., written by his old travelling companion William C. Preston. In his letters Longfellow might express strong party feeling, but his verse carried no note

---

47  Walter Prichard Eaton, *The Actor's Heritage*, 119ff., has an appreciative chapter on Macready; his own account of the riot is in his *Reminiscences and Diaries*, 586ff. Montrose J. Moses has treated *The Fabulous Forrest*.
48  Arthur Hobson Quinn, *The American Drama From the Beginning to the Civil War*, 337ff.

really discordant with his lines of 1849 on that Ship of State which bore the brightest promise of humanity:

> Our hearts, our hopes, our prayers, our tears,
> Our faith triumphant o'er our fears,
> Are all with thee,—are all with thee!

But powerful currents in American culture (using the word in a somewhat broader sense) bore in a divisive if not actually disruptive direction. Great sections of cultural life were particularistic in character, and other sections were on a plane where they were quickly affected by partisan and polemic influences. It was impossible for Americans to be always harking back to 1776; they had to be thinking of 1848 and 1856. Not much of the country's life could really be thought of in the generalized terms which Emerson used in *The American Scholar*. The Lowell who wrote on commanding abstractions like democracy was a good deal less interesting and impressive than Lowell paying tribute to Wendell Phillips, and reviewing Mexican War issues in the *Biglow Papers*. Audiences sauntered in respectable numbers to see *Blanche of Brandywine*, but they rushed in eager hordes to *Uncle Tom's Cabin*. From 1846 to 1861 the main precipitants in letters, journalism, political oratory, and popular art were no longer national—they were sectional.

## [ V ]

They were sectional because two distinct cultures, Northern and Southern, each shading off toward the West in newer and not dissimilar forms, but nevertheless on the whole sharply differentiated, had come into existence. In two areas the sectional characteristics were intensified. Van Wyck Brooks has spoken of the "peculiar flavor of that old New England culture, so dry, so crisp, so dogmatic, so irritating," [49] and though the word stimulating should be added, the qualifications are accurate. At the opposite pole was the culture of the Lower South, genial, elegant, so old-fashioned that it was sometimes antique, and though alert enough in political directions, otherwise largely sterile. Boston and Charleston were now preoccupied with sectional stereotypes and antipathies, and as Garrisonian abolitionism colored all the thought of one city, so Calhounian nullification tinged all the ideas of the other. As Whittier's "Expostulation" was an arraignment of Southern society and its cultural ideals, so Grayson's "The Hireling and the Slave" was an indictment of the Northern economic and social order. New England and the Lower South had become

49 *America's Coming of Age*, 73.

almost incapable of understanding each other, and the Potomac and Ohio separated areas of wide mutual incomprehension.

No one dominant fact explains the special characteristics of Southern culture, which was a complex result of intricate causes. The idea of white domination, which has been called the "central theme" of the section's life, was certainly of fundamental importance.[50] The race question set a ritual for the Southern people which was followed long after slavery was dead. Other students have varied the formula. They have said that Southern culture was stamped above all by a conservatism based upon class stratification and the absence of competitive struggle, engendering an aristocratic, leisurely ideal of life, with much pride of family, scope for learning, and attachment to outdoor pursuits. It is certainly true that agrarian traits marked the South. In contrast with the more and more urbanized, industrialized North, its life was rural—so rural that Augustus Baldwin Longstreet hesitated to accept the presidency of the College of South Carolina because he thought it unwise to subject students to the temptations of a metropolis like Columbia, with its six thousand people.[51] Southerners themselves liked to explain their special culture in terms of ideals. Instead of being restless, unstable, and ruthlessly progressive, they said, they put their surplus energy into the life of the mind, and cultivated the greatest of all arts, the art of living.

In this art of living the tournaments, dinners, and balls of Virginia, the fox-hunting of the Shenandoah, the race-week of Charleston, the theatres and carnivals of New Orleans, were less important than the peaceful pursuits of plantations where the owner (like Jefferson Davis) divided his time among business, politics, and study. The Southern ideal, according to this view, approximated closely to the ideals of eighteenth-century English life. It is easy to romanticize the old South, and a myth-making process which unduly minimizes the importance of middle-class elements and ignores the squalor of the disinherited has gained much too wide an acceptance. Nevertheless, the elements emphasized by Basil L. Gildersleeve—pride of State and lineage, love of classical erudition, courtesy, reverence for the traditions of a static order, ambition to cultivate the graces of existence—did throw a charm over rather limited groups.[52]

A distinctive economic and social pattern, which was basic, became inter-meshed with a specialized body of ideas and customs. The South, completely committed to agriculture, and in great degree to the plantation system; to a labor force which had to be kept ignorant and unenterprising; to a patriarchal

50  Ulrich B. Phillips, "The Central Theme of Southern History," *Am Hist. Rev.*, XXIV, 30ff.
51  Wade, *Longstreet*, 315, 316.
52  *The Creed of the Old South, 1865-1915.*

ideal of social organization; to such limited production of wealth that great bodies of illiterate, shambling, badly-nourished whites became accepted as natural; to a soil-and-labor exploitation which gave one or two classes the means of elegance, learning, and leadership; to the mental conservatism which is bred by isolation—this land had peculiar defects and special virtues. In the Revolutionary period the South had produced more citizens of the world and thinkers of international repute than any other section. Mount Vernon, Monticello, Gunston Hall, Montpelier, had thrown a long shadow across the map. By 1846 the South was more largely withdrawn from the general movement of Western civilization than any other sizable area peopled by an English-speaking stock. Even its code of ethics, its conscience, had been immobilized; by Jefferson's standards, had been moved backward.[53]

The South liked to think of itself as having a warmly human civilization while that of the North was bookish and mechanical. In Yankeeland the long, dreary winters, the business appurtenances of society, the hard drive of the towns, and (said Southerners) the absence of social sympathies, led to the incessant production of technological devices and books. Below the Potomac the open air, bland climate, and agreeable society tempted men to blither pursuits. Southerners read for personal enjoyment and cultivation; Northerners read to invent or write. "The best thing which could happen for the New England literary mind," wrote one observer, "would be the banishment of all books from the studies of her foremost men."[54] The South, according to her sons, fostered conversational talent, while her platform oratory stimulated political thought more forcibly than the newspaper articles of the North. Where was better talk to be heard than at the table of well-educated Virginia planters, or in Natchez drawing-rooms, or at Russell's bookshop on busy King Street in Charleston, where seats were placed for the literary men of the town— William Gilmore Simms, Paul H. Hayne, J. L. Petigru, William J. Grayson, Alfred Huger, Mitchell King, and others? The rural Southerner, going to church, lounging at the crossroads store, and attending muster, barbecues, and co't day, equally loved talk.[55] Visiting Northerners, it was agreed in Richmond and Mobile, never equalled the clear, bold, graceful expression of their hosts. And the topics on which Yankees conversed were inferior; however well-informed and earnest on business subjects, they were at a loss whenever abstract ideas came up.

It was another staple belief of Southerners that their conservatism was wise

53 In Book I of *The Mind of the South*, W. J. Cash discusses the origin and development of the special Southern psychology.
54 *North and South: Impressions of Northern Society Upon a Southerner* (pvt, 1853).
55 Guion G. Johnson, *A Social History of North Carolina 1800-1860*, engagingly sketches the comradely aspects of Southern rural life.

and healthy. The North was swept by the Kossuth craze, but the South stood by the old principle of non-intervention in foreign quarrels. The North was full of Millerism, Shakerism, Spiritualism, Mormonism, and what not; the South clung to its pure and ancient religion. Northern politics was flawed by fads, theories, and unpredictable innovations, but Southern voters held the principles of the fathers. While the Southerner was heartily philanthropic and generous, the Yankees strangely compounded charity with cant, and mercy with malevolence. So ran the generalizations, all open to endless unprofitable argument, but all advanced with a force which went far toward proving that the South *was* different.

### [ VI ]

It is necessary to pierce behind these rather meaningless generalizations to discrete matters of fact. Asked just where, in detail, the differences of the South lay, we can answer under numerous headings.

The white population of the South was far more largely Anglo-Saxon than that of the North, for despite its numerous Germans, its hundred thousand Irish folk by 1860, its French Huguenots, and others, it was one of the purest British stocks in the world. Its dominant attitudes, particularly as to the color line, were Anglo-Saxon.[56] Its life was not merely rural, but rural after a special pattern; for the section was dotted over with large holdings representing great capital values and employing large bodies of slaves. It was a land of simple dogmatism in religion; of Protestant solidarity, of people who believed every word of the Bible, and of faith frequently refreshed by emotional revivalism. Its churches provided an emphasis on broadly social values contrasting with the intellectualization of morals to be found in the North.[57] In the South the yoke of law and government rested more lightly upon the individual than in other sections. Counties, often sprawling in extent, were the chief units of local administration; the States followed the rule that the best government was the least government; and the nation was held at arm's length.

The South drew from its economic position a special set of tenets, naturally accepting Francis Wayland's condemnation of protection as a violation of morality and common sense.[58] With equal inevitability, it drew from its minority position in the political fabric another special set of doctrines. It was a country in which romantic and hedonistic impulses, born of the opulence

56  And remained so; David L. Cohn, *Saturday Review of Literature*, February 22, 1941.
57  Cason, 90° *in the Shade*, 66.
58  Mrs. McCord published in 1848, through Putnam's, a translation of Bastiat's *Sophism of the Protective Policy*, while another translation of the same work appeared in instalments in *Russell's Magazine*.

of nature, had freer rein than in the North. The phrases "the merry South," "the sunny South," connoted a great deal. Genuine gusto went into William Elliot's *Carolina Sports by Land and Water*, describing thrilling adventures with devil-fishes in Port Royal Sound, and with wildcats and bears in upland Carolina woods; real delight colored the portrayal of plantation festivities in Caroline H. Gilman's *Recollections of a Southern Matron*, a bit of reality thinly garbed in fiction. The remote quality attaching to much Southern life, which made some travellers feel they had dropped into another world, and the sharp contrast of races, added to the atmosphere of romance.

To a far greater degree than the North, the South was a land of class stratification and vestigial feudalism. Various explanations were given for this fact. One was later repeated by N. S. Shaler when he remarked that Southerners were descendants of that portion of the English who were least modernized, and who "still retained a large element of the feudal notion." [59] It is now known that no such distinction existed between Northern and Southern colonists, for honest middle-class folk, not feudal-minded cavaliers, made up the bulk of Virginia as of Massachusetts settlers.[60] Slavery, the large plantation, and the agrarian cast of life, with some traditional inheritances from colonial days, accounted for the class structure. "Slavery helped feudalism," correctly remarked a Southern writer,[61] "and feudalism helped slavery, and the Southern people were largely the outcome of the interaction of these two formative principles."

The great colonial plantations, established along the South Atlantic seaboard and in Louisiana in days when tobacco, rice, and sugar reigned without thought of a new monarch named cotton, had possessed much the atmosphere and influence of the English manors. Even North Carolina had its first families, the Winstons, Taylors, and Byrds of the Tidewater.[62] The planters enjoyed the social dignities and political leadership of the English squires. They revered the old order, dispensed hospitality, and benignly guided their inferiors in Sir Roger de Coverley style. As a rigorous code of personal honor was enforced by the duel rather than by law, and gentlefolk deemed themselves highly sensitive to slights, they developed a punctilious courtesy. Yet the ideal Southern gentleman seldom appeared in perfection; politeness, gallantry, and dignity had often to be reconciled with the sudden passion of a Preston Brooks, and, as James Branch Cabell has mentioned, a weakness for miscegenation.[63] A planter who entertained much, thought much of the good old times, and

59 "The Peculiarities of the South," *North American Review*, October, 1890.
60 T. J. Wertenbaker, *Patrician and Plebeian in Virginia*.
61 W. P. Trent, *William Gilmore Simms*, 31.
62 Cf. *It's a Far Cry*, by Robert W. Winston (1937).
63 Quoted in Edwin Mims, *The Advancing South*, 214.

handed down his home acres to his oldest son even when primogeniture was no more, naturally made much of family ties. Kinship was counted to remote cousinhood, the penniless spinster who bore the family name had a welcome place in the household, and summer visitings from State to State, across many hundreds of miles, were common. Family did much to knit the South together.

Yet class lines can easily be overemphasized, for they were subject to powerful solvents. The fact that many a poor farmer and rich planter looked back to a common ancestor was one; wealth in such instances usually bowed before relationship. The fact that all white men had a sense of solidarity as against the Negro, and as against the encroaching North, also tended to reduce class stratification. As sectional tensions increased, the political elite of the South were more and more drawn from non-aristocratic levels. It cannot too often be emphasized that such men as Yancey, Wigfall, Reagan, Jefferson Davis, and A. H. Stephens in no wise represented the old aristocracy. Among the wealthy planters a large place was always taken by the *nouveaux riches*, and in the South no less than the North the transition from poverty to opulence and back to poverty, three generations from shirtsleeves to shirtsleeves, was not uncommon. It should be said, too, that the egalitarian theories of Thomas Jefferson (despite all the uneasy effort by various leaders to prove them outworn) made a real impression on thoughtful Southerners.

As in the North the advancing frontier was an unquestionable force for democracy, in the South it at least modified the features of aristocracy. The opening of the old Southwest had furnished a field in which the ambitious, energetic, and able pushed rapidly to the front. Combining cheap land and labor, they built up rich estates. It was not the old Tidewater aristocracy which took possession of the wealth of the western reaches, but younger and more aggressive elements. Of course the new aristocracy modelled its social order broadly after the coastal pattern. But comparatively few of the patrician names of Virginia, Carolina, and Louisiana—not more than five hundred all told— figured in the new beadroll of gentility.[64] Many a rich planter, like the Hairstons, was conscious of his humble origin, felt best at home in associating with the commonalty, and was ready himself to work in the fields. Across the Mississippi in Texas and Arkansas the atmosphere grew more democratic still.

But taken as a section, stretching from the Atlantic to the Father of Waters and from the Ohio to the Gulf, the South had a life of far more aristocratic tone than the North.[65] Both the central weakness of the South, and the main

64  This is the estimate of W. J. Cash in *Mind of the South*, ch. 1; "maybe not more than half that figure."

65  The tenacity of caste in the South is illustrated in John Dollard's *Caste and Class in a Southern Town*. The parvenues of the Mississippi Valley whom Olmsted describes so caustically, and the Cotton Snobs assailed by Daniel R. Hundley in *Social Relations in Our Southern States* (1860), had aristocratic—and autocratic—traits hardly to be matched in any equally large group in the North.

flaw in American social homogeneity, lay in the want of a great predominant body of intelligent, independent, thoughtful, and educated farmers in the slave States to match the similar body at the North. The nation had always drawn most of its sturdy common sense and integrity of character from its farmers. A really strong Southern yeomanry could have clasped hands with Northern tillers of the soil. But the plantation system was inimical to any such body. Whether developing or declining, it wasted soil and toil, reduced the mass of blacks and whites to poverty, kept them in ignorance, and destroyed their hopes. It was not a preparation for the appearance of an independent, industrious farmer class, but a "preface to peasantry." It gave the South the "forgotten man" that Walter Hines Page described in his memorable address at Greensboro a generation later; men too poor, ignorant, and politician-beguiled to be discontented with their poverty, ignorance, and docility.[66]

With all its natural gaiety, simplicity, and love of olden ways the South combined a trait common in countries with unhappy institutions, like Spain, and in lands left behind by modern progress, like Ireland; the trait of uneasy defensiveness. At the beginning of the century most Southerners had believed that Virginia would keep her primacy among the States in wealth, population, and influence, that their whole section would grow faster than the chilly North, and that their grasp on the national tiller would be unshaken. That belief had withered before the Mexican War. Clear-eyed men realized that in nearly all material elements of civilization the North had far outstripped them; and they knew that slavery stood indicted not merely as a moral wrong, but as responsible for this painful lag in progress. In the Southern mind a defensive mechanism clicked into operation. Slavery? It was a blessing. The Negro? They best understood him. "Whatever defects may belong to our system, it certainly has the merit of preserving the Negro and improving his situation. Look at the moderating influences. Look their own advance in health, comfort, virtue, and numbers." [67] Progress? No sane man wanted the "calculating avarice" that, as Calhoun said, marked the factory owner driving his wage slaves.[68]

Hand in hand with this defensive attitude, as all observers noted, went a passionate Southern pride. The Charlestonian loved to descant on St. Michael's, the Society Library, the Broad Street Theatre, the statue of Pitt. If you hinted that his college was but an academy, he spoke of the hospital, the St. Cecilia Society, and the three newspapers. If a visitor suggested that the city needed a good market, men described the ample shipments that came down to every gentleman from his plantation.[69] An aristocratic society is always proud, and

66  Arthur F. Raper's *Preface to Peasantry* (1936) is an antidote for some of the agrarian doctrines expressed in Allen Tate and others, *I'll Take My Stand.*
67  *North and South: Impressions of Northern Society Upon a Southerner.*
68  Quoted by Van Wyck Brooks, *The World of Washington Irving,* 230.
69  Trent, *Simms,* 224.

we might trace far back into colonial times the Southern conviction of superiority to Northern and British shilling-grabbers. Many slaveholders liked to talk, at first confidentially but later in speeches frankly addressed to Northern ears, of the defects of shirtsleeves democracy, Yankee industrialism, and the vomit of European slums. More and more, this pride was related to that inferiority complex which is so often a mark of superior peoples set amid unfavorable environments. The pride of the ruling class was bulwarked by an intellectual factor, the influence of the old writers—Hobbes in government, Dryden in poetry, Clarendon in history—who regarded aristocracy as the best form of social control.

In none of its varied manifestations was sectional pride more dangerous than in its constant assertions of superior fighting power. "If it comes to blows between the North and the South," a Yankee heard William Gilmore Simms exclaim, "we shall crush you as I would crush an egg." John B. Gordon heard a judge remark that in the event of war, the South could "whip the Yankees with children's pop-guns." [70] The well-born Southerner was convinced that he was a man of far more spirit and resource than the Northern counter-jumper. Nothing struck William H. Russell more forcibly, in his travels over the South just before the Civil War, than the widespread conviction that the free States would never fight, or if they did would be quickly put in their places. [71] A later writer on "the fighting South" has ascribed its militancy to the old habit of living dangerously, and to a depth of conviction, a 'totality of purehearted affirmation' natural in a simple society. [72] Perhaps more important were the conditions of Southern life, with much hunting, general use of horses, and frequent marksmanship contests; the existence of two fine schools of war, the Virginia Military Institute at Lexington, and the South Carolina Military Academy or "Citadel" at Charleston; and the memory of Southern prowess in the Mexican War. [73] The leading officers, Scott, Taylor, Quitman, Twiggs, and Davis, were all Southrons—if one forgot Kearny or Worth. Indeed, in what war had not Southern commanders stood foremost?

[ VII ]

Had Southern and Northern ideals of education been alike they would have done much to erase sectional lines, but they differed sharply. Education for utility was steadily gaining ground in the North; education for character

70  *Reminiscences of the Civil War*, 7.
71  "A love of military display is very different indeed from a true soldierly spirit"; Russell, *North and South*, ch. 33.
72  John Temple Graves, *The Fighting South*.
73  Richard Taylor, *Destruction and Reconstruction*, 20.

and grace held sway in the South—and the scope of education was far from identical.

The relatively high development of colleges in the South, and the comparatively low provision of common schools, perfectly fitted a semi-aristocratic society sparsely scattered over an area which had all too little of a prosperous yeoman class. The Southern college was in general decently supported, decently staffed, and well attended. In 1860 Virginia had twenty-three colleges enrolling 2,824 students, as against New York's seventeen colleges listing 2,970 students; and Georgia's thirty-two colleges with 3,302 students nominally overshadowed the eight Massachusetts colleges with 1,733 registrants.[74] To raise the question of standards would have been risky, for all States had too much glass to afford stone-throwing. Virginia spent annually some fifty thousand more than Massachusetts on colleges, and a large proportion of her population were college-trained. In 1856 the enrolment of 558 at the University of Virginia was far above Harvard's roll of 361 students.[75] To be sure, some Southern institutions, such as the University of Georgia, Transylvania, William and Mary, and South Carolina College, were sadly deliquescent. But others were advancing, and one hopeful institution, Bishop Leonidas Polk's University of the South at Sewanee, Tenn., for which an endowment of $500,000 had been collected or pledged, was born in 1859.[76] The South boasted that it had not only established the first State universities, but had cherished the ideal of a college-trained leadership more fixedly than the North.

Higher education appeared at its Southern best in the great university which Jefferson had founded, and which by the middle fifties already counted sons— Robert Toombs, A. H. H. Stuart, Henry Winter Davis—of distinction. The six

74 *Eighth Census, Mortality and Misc. Statistics,* 505.
75 Clement Eaton, *Freedom of Thought in the Old South,* 196. W. E. Dodd declares that in 1850–60 "practically every college and university in the South doubled its attendance"; *Cotton Kingdom,* 111. But Professor Eaton's excellent treatment of the curse of Southern illiteracy is not to be ignored. The Harvard figure does not include the professional schools.
76 Polk had long cherished a plan for a great Southern university, for he believed that south of Virginia the section had no institution worthy of that name. He regarded the University of North Carolina and the University of Mississippi as hardly more than colleges, while other "universities" were simply high schools. He wished to set up an Oxford or Göttingen for the South. His plan was to obtain a great landed domain, erect stately buildings, draw a faculty of distinction from all parts of the world, and build up a community of intellectual eminence which would attract distinguished writers. Strong inducements were to be offered planters and other men of wealth to make their summer homes near the university, which he wished placed somewhere in the mountain region surrounding Chattanooga. The Episcopal Church should sponsor the university, and an endowment of not less than three millions should be collected. An organizational meeting was held July 4, 1857, on Lookout Mountain, with a procession in which a Revolutionary veteran bore the flag, a band playing spirited airs, and an oration by Bishop Otey. It was an auspicious start. Nobody could foresee that within a few years the mountain would be wreathed in cannon-smoke. *University of the South Papers,* I: W. M. Polk, *Leonidas Polk,* I, 219ff.

schools of the collegiate course (ancient languages, modern languages, mathematics, natural philosophy, chemistry, and moral philosophy) were each headed by a professor who received $3,000 a year, a house, and appurtenant privileges, and who occupied a position of dignity in Southern esteem. Schools of medicine, surgery, anatomy, and law completed the university. "The entire establishment," wrote a visitor in 1854, "is on a liberal and enlightened scale." He was impressed by the wide geographic range of the 466 students of that year, who came from seventeen States and the Federal District; by the evident culture of the faculty; by the scholarship system under which the University educated thirty-two students at public expense; and by the searching final examination of each candidate, partly oral and partly written, conducted by a faculty committee. He liked, too, the genial atmosphere; "in passing through these extended arcades on a warm sunny morning we found the young men emerging from their rooms and pursuing their studies in the open and shaded air." [77] Other observers praised the honor system. Even Harvard treated students as unruly boys, but Virginia made them self-respecting gentlemen under a discipline which inculcated principle.

Both North and South, colleges still made the ancient classics and mathematics the core of their curricula, still let learned teachers occupy whole settees rather than chairs (Longstreet at Mississippi, teaching rhetoric, evidences of Christianity, logic, political economy, and philosophy while serving as president more than equalled the versatile Nairne at Columbia), and still neglected science. In 1855 F. A. P. Barnard, then teaching mathematics at Mississippi, wrote a brochure on the improvement practicable in the nation's colleges. Describing the chief objects of education as discipline and intellectual development, he declared that the courses should first of all require enough of the disciplinary studies for a thorough intellectual training. Once this was secured, the curriculum could then be expanded to cover studies valuable as subjects of knowledge. But how could room be found for the sciences? In two ways, he answered; by raising the exactions for admission, or by increasing the length of the college year. He was in favor of both. But if such steps proved impossible, he would dispense with the utilitarian and scientific subjects and continue to stress classical discipline.[78]

This old-fashioned view remained largely dominant in both sections. The newer view that dead languages should be ruthlessly thrust aside for science, history, and government was forcibly asserted in the South by Maury, President Philip Lindsley of the University of Nashville, and T. S. Grimké of Charleston. Nor was science utterly neglected, as Virginia's courses in chemistry and natural

77  *National Intelligencer*, September 7, 1854.
78  *Improvements Practicable in American Colleges*, Hartford, 1856.

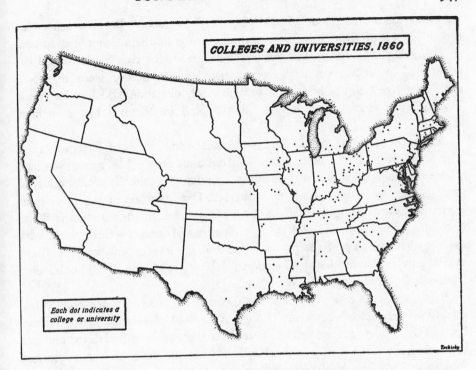

COLLEGES AND UNIVERSITIES, 1860

Each dot indicates a
college or university

philosophy proved. The University of North Carolina early in the fifties established professorships of civil engineering and agricultural chemistry.[79]

Secondary education, too, fared not too ill in the South. In both sections this was the era of the academy, a transitional type of school which was in general privately endowed but sometimes under semi-public control, and which offered a steadily broadening curriculum. The nation by 1850 had just over six thousand academies, of which the very respectable number of 2,640 were in the Southern States.[80] Estimates of the section's enrolment in these schools ran as high as two hundred thousand. One State, Kentucky, had passed a law to endow an academy in every county seat with six thousand acres of land; and numerous academies resulted, though the land was often sold before it gained real value. Of the nation's public high schools the South had only a

79 Of the 466 students at the University of Virginia in 1853-54, the books showed 220 studying chemistry and 106 natural philosophy. Students at North Carolina interested in civil engineering and agricultural chemistry could enter one or both courses at the end of the first senior term, with a view to remaining a year after obtaining the degree of B.A. President David L. Swain, a shrewd executive who rapidly built up the university, wrote Barnard that he favored meeting the demand for a practical education, for while Jefferson's conception of a university was admirable, south of Virginia "there is too little wealth and learned leisure in the country to afford the requisite patronage for such an institution." August 23, 1854; Swain Papers, N. C. Hist. Commission Library.

80 A. J. Inglis, *Principles of Secondary Education*, ch. 5.

handful—about thirty out of the 321 listed in 1860.[81] But the academies, practically all of them private institutions, many of them denomination-controlled, and most numerous in the piedmont areas (for rich lowlands and impoverished mountain country were equally uncongenial), were numerous enough to give a host of boys good grammar-school training. Such academies as Waddell's in South Carolina and Liberty Hall in Virginia had a national repute.[82]

Yet in the elementary field the broad humanitarian ideals of Jefferson failed. The South was for the most part a land without free public schools—a land where the poor man's son was likely to go untaught, and the workingman or small farmer to be ignorant if not illiterate. Here lay one of the great gulfs separating North from South. Said C. G. Memminger of the situation in South Carolina: "The mechanic and moving elements of society—those who work the actual machinery of the body politic and are its stay and support—these exhibit few of the results of education." [83] If this was true of Calhoun's own land, what was the situation elsewhere?

The question is easily answered. In Georgia by 1860 only one county had established a free school system. Though Arkansas had passed a general school law in 1843, it was estimated eleven years later that only one-fourth the children of school age were in any form of school. In Mississippi the cities were authorized to organize public school systems, but outside their limits little progress was made; for no local school tax could be laid without the consent of a majority of the heads of families. A public school system existed in Tennessee after 1830, and Andrew Johnson obtained a tax on both property and polls to support it, but it had little real vigor down to 1861. Alabama passed its first general law in 1854, but its system did not take firm root till twenty years later. Louisiana was proud that in 1851 about half her children were attending public schools. And so the story went. By far the best record was made by North Carolina, where the foundations of an elementary school system had been laid in 1839, and where after 1853 an able and devoted superintendent, Calvin H. Stowe—"the first campaigner for schools in the South"—labored to give it strength.[84]

The sharpest indictment of the general neglect of primary education came from Southerners themselves. W. H. Trescot, remarking that slavery was a great blessing, added that it had its inexorable requirements. Foremost among them was the elevation of free labor, for the white race must preserve its

81  Report U. S. Commr. of Ed., 1904, II, 1782ff.
82  R. S. Cotterill, The Old South, 283, 284.
83  Charleston Courier, January 12, 1857.
84  See summaries in Cubberley, Public Education in the U. S., 247-250; Charles W. Dabney, Universal Education in the South From the Beginnings to 1900.

superiority by making its work intellectual as well as manual; every white laborer should possess enough education to lift him high above the black.[85] Memminger bitterly indicted the charity schools of Charleston. Children avoided them as a badge of inferiority. When forced into them, they gave irregular attendance, learned without spirit, and left before they acquired the basic rudiments of knowledge. He confessed that when he saw the wretched buildings, and when he heard one youngster say that four plus four made four, and another state that the capital of England was Scotland, his heart sank.[86] Governor Henry A. Wise of Virginia passionately arraigned the school system of the Old Dominion. Pride, he wrote, "withholds thousands of our poor people from the *charity* of schools, even for the fifty-three days of time per annum, and for the pittance of the cost of $2.57 per capita for the fifty-three days of time; whilst a sound republican *community* of instruction among children of all classes would make all equally beneficiaries of public aid to education." Out of about 200,000 persons over seven and under twenty-one in the State, the middle fifties saw fewer than 42,000 getting "a morsel of mental food" at public cost.[87]

But while Northern education was steadily growing more democratic, the old Southern ideal remained aristocratic. Moncure D. Conway might protest that no real antipathy existed between slavery and free public education, and might argue that Virginia had an opportunity to set up the most perfect school system on earth. He was sharply contradicted by that Southern champion Ellwood Fisher, who declared that the conditions bred by slavery—the great size of agricultural units, sparsity of population, and so on—made schools of the Northern type impossible. "But Virginia has a system of oral instruction which compensates for her want of schools, and that is her social intercourse. The social intercourse of the South is probably much greater than that of any people that ever existed." [88] And a sharper opposition to public schools was often expressed, as by a friend of A. H. Stephens's whose letter indicated how much more education was needed: [89]

"You are aware that the people at the North are all *educated* by government, and where educated they expect to *live* upon government, either town, county, city, state, or national, and *they will do it. . . .* This idea of educating *everybody* is taking root in the South, our people are beginning to demand taxes for the education of the masses, there is to be no more ignorant after this generation

85 Quoted in "The Free School System of South Carolina," *Southern Quarterly Review*, November, 1856.
86 Charleston *Courier*, January 12, 1857.
87 Wise to D. W. A. Smith, December 9, 1856; Governors' Letter-Books.
88 Conway in *Addresses and Reprints*, 1–56; Fisher in *The North and the South*, pvt, 1849.
89 M. J. Crawford, April 8, 1860; Stephens Papers, LC.

according to the new philosophy, upon the idea that its easier to build school-houses than jails and colleges than state prisons, but there never was a greater error upon earth, we can build the latter much cheaper and they are decidedly more useful. . . .

"I am not sure but that you may educate two or three generations and about the third they will go crazy, as for instance in New England they are fanatical and foolish."

## [ VIII ]

If Southern reading differed markedly from that of the North, it was because it was confined to narrower, more aristocratic, and more old-fashioned circles. Fewer people bought books, and they kept less abreast of modern thought. Those with means sometimes formed large and select libraries (though even Simms's ten thousand volumes at his plantation Woodlands by no means challenged such collections as Everett's or Ticknor's), and the cultivated few probably read less ephemera and more standard works than the Northern public. The before-mentioned library of Muscoe Garnett, who shut up his Virginia house and went into the Civil War never to return, was a model collection in almost everything except contemporaneous politics, sociology, and economics. It contained a fine collection in the English classics, history ancient and modern, theology, Greek and Latin literature, and books in French, Italian, and other European languages. A shelf of dictionaries in various tongues affirmed the studious taste of Garnett, who was commencing Sanscrit when the bugles called him; and his heirs found a pile of the *Revue des Deux Mondes* the last numbers dating a few months after his death.[90] Such scholar-planters were the adornment of the South.

Even in a semi-frontier region like Texas literary taste could be austerely conservative. The diary of William Pitt Ballinger, an attorney in busy practise in Austin, reveals a strong taste for historical and political works. Among the books he read in 1860 were Brougham's address on his installation as chancellor of the University of Edinburgh, orations by Everett and G. T. Curtis, Hammond's discourse on Calhoun, a critique of Macaulay on Claverhouse, and Burke's *Reflections on the French Revolution*, which he pronounced a work of "wonderful genius." This was in addition to *The Marble Faun*, the *Tale of Two Cities,* and *The Mill on the Floss.* He subscribed to *Harper's Monthly* and kept abreast of political writing. "I have read the debates between Douglas and Lincoln all through with much interest," he notes after buying the book in St. Louis. "Douglas is far more practised, artful, and unscrupulous—Lincoln

90 Garnett Collection, University of Virginia. Dorfman, *Economic Mind*, II, 890–895.

is the fairer franker man of the two and improves greatly in the course of the debate." [91]

Even the rather stiff, dry R. M. T. Hunter was wont to say, "Books are a necessity to us," and he took his classics so seriously that he used to remark with emphasis: "I would not have written Macaulay's essay upon Chatham for an earldom." He read all the English historians from Clarendon and Hume to Milman and Carlyle; was familiar with Niebuhr and Mommsen; admired Prescott and Thiers; and was well versed in Thucydides, Diodorus, Polybius, and above all, his favorite Tacitus. Like most Southerners of culture, he had a warm reverence for the English giants—Shakespeare, Milton, Dryden, Johnson; he read and re-read Fielding and Smollett; but Scott was his favorite, and to the *Antiquary* he returned at intervals all his life with passionate delight. [92] His sister Martha Hunter has left a fragmentary diary for 1849–50 which describes her own wide reading. It embraced Neander, Macaulay, Thiers, Sir Humphrey Davy, Wiseman, and Mrs. Gaskell, with much in French and German. [93] Most cultivated Southerners read the British reviews. It is significant of the old-fashioned taste of the South that Longstreet, author, teacher, and president of two learned institutions, had a library rich in all the English classics "through Addison," and that he believed the New England writers too puerile for consideration. [94]

## [ IX ]

The cultivation of literature in the South was so sorely handicapped by social and economic factors that the effort to create a sectional literature terminated in total failure. The North summed up the reason for this failure in the word slavery. But a more complex explanation is required. The writers recognized that they worked in a highly unfavorable milieu. They needed one or several great cities, with capital and enterprise, where the attrition of intellects would sharpen the general mind; a larger middle-class, accustomed to buying books and magazines; and some prosperous, well-circulated periodicals. They needed at least one real publisher; not a printer or bookseller, but a firmly-established house like Harper's, Appleton's, or Little, Brown, issuing volumes week after week—ten or twenty a month—and therefore provided with facilities to advertise them, get them into a thousand bookstores, and sell them by mail. They needed the thousand bookshops. And finally, they needed a broader, stronger tradition of literary craftsmanship. [95]

91 Diary of W. P. Ballinger, Univ. of Texas Archives.
92 Unidentified MS memoir of Hunter in Va. State Library.
93 Hunter Papers, Univ. of Va.
94 Wade, *Longstreet*, 298ff.
95 Cf. "Literary Prospects of the South," *Russell's Magazine*, June, 1858.

Southern magazines operated under the same disabilities. The *Southern Review*, founded in 1828, published some able contributions by Legaré, Thomas Cooper, Stephen Elliott, and others, but perished within five years. The *Southern Literary Messenger*, begun in 1834, had two editors of ability, Poe and John R. Thompson. In quality it possibly compared with the *Knickerbocker* or *Graham's*, but not with the *Atlantic* or *Putnam's*. And whatever its quality, it made little appeal to Southerners themselves. The Charleston *Courier* remarked in 1849 that a copy was occasionally seen on the shelves of very literary gentlemen, but among the great mass of readers very rarely.[96] "I must say to you," wrote Thompson to C. R. Lanman in 1850, "that the highest rate of compensation that I allow for articles in the *Messenger* is $2 per page"— and most writers got seventy-five cents or a dollar.[97] By a brave effort in the spring of 1857, a little Charleston group launched *Russell's Magazine* as a rival to the *Atlantic*. The genial inspiration of Simms and his two literary disciples, Paul H. Hayne and Timrod, gave afflatus to the sails while the money of John Russell, proprietor of the well-known bookshop, helped keep it afloat. Though it contained the best interpretation of Southern thought and feeling, its life was to be short, and at no time did it come within sight of its scudding Northern antagonist.[98] The *Southern Quarterly Review* was printing three thousand copies in 1854, but it labored under heavy pecuniary embarrassments, and though its editor J. D. B. De Bow wrote that it represented "the last attempt to establish and build up Southern Literature,"[99] its influence was slight.

The trait which most heavily stamped Southern literature, whether in books or magazines, was its polemic or defensive quality. Literary expression in the

96 October 23, 1849. According to the *Courier*, in Montgomery, Ala., only one copy of the *Southern Quarterly Review* was being taken.

97 Many of Thompson's letters, scattered through various collections, are pathetic. He wrote Edwin De Leon in 1848 that only five copies went to Columbia, S. C., where De Leon was an active journalist. Could not De Leon obtain ten or fifteen new subscribers, keep the money, and in return write at the rate of one dollar a page? In 1851 he sent word that he was going south on a canvassing trip. "This step is most reluctantly taken and is assuredly disagreeable enough, but the *Messenger*, entre nous, is in dire need of accessions and it must be done. Surely, the Southern people will not suffer their only literary magazine to go down at the present juncture of affairs!" October 31, 1848, January 30, 1851; De Leon Papers, South Caroliniana Library.

Again, he wrote John P. Kennedy in 1860: "The *Messenger*, which I took in better days, has proved a dead loss to me—ever so much money actually sunk, and twelve years of early manhood spent unprofitably in maintaining it." He was then turning to newspaper work. March 25, 1860; Kennedy Papers.

98 Among other excellent articles, *Russell's Magazine* published during its brief career an extremely able criticism of Bancroft's history; a sound analysis of the character of Poe; Dr. Lieber's introductory lecture to his course on politics in Columbia College; and a valuable account of the rupture in 1830 between Jackson and Calhoun. Much of its matter was in defense of slavery. "The Dual Form of Labor" (October, 1859) is an exhaustive and skilful marshalling of all the justifications and palliations of the institution.

99 September 12, 1854; Claiborne Papers, Miss. Dept. Archives and Hist.

North showed sporadic sectional rancor; in the South this was a preoccupation which became painful. The section felt that with stormclouds lowering over it, every intellect was needed in the war for the defense of her institutions. Simms, finding his romances neglected, said goodbye to them and took up work instead that fostered Southern regard. From the moment of the Wilmot Proviso, his too-abundant literary productions fell into two channels, one of romantic dreams, the other of doctrinaire nightmares.[100] As much could be said for many another writer. With one pen Simms wrote his *Surrey*, and with the other assailed Lorenzo Sabine, a Yankee, for criticizing South Carolina's rôle in the Revolution. With one pen W. J. Grayson wrote his pleasant poetry, and with another a virulent article on "The Edinburgh Reviewer Reviewed." By 1859 Simms was exclaiming on behalf of all Southern writers: "We know but the South, and the South in danger!" [101]

## [ X ]

Altogether, South and North by 1857 were rapidly becoming separate peoples. The major Protestant denominations had broken in twain; one major party, the Whigs, had first split in half and then disappeared; press, pulpit, and education all showed a deepening cleavage. With every passing year, the fundamental assumptions, tastes, and cultural aims of the two sections became more divergent. As tension grew, militant elements on both sides resented the presence of "outsiders"; Southerners were exposed to insult at Northern resorts, while Yankees in the South were compelled to explain their business to a more and more suspicious population.

The Southerners loved the Union, for their forefathers had helped build it, and the gravestones of their patriot soldiers strewed the land. But they wanted a Union in which they could preserve their peculiar institutions, ancient customs, and well-loved ways of life and thought. They knew that all the main forces of modern society were pressing to create a more closely unified nation, and to make institutions homogeneous even if not absolutely uniform. Against this they recoiled; they wanted a hegemony, a loose confederacy, not a unified nation and a standardized civilization. They regarded the Union as an association of sovereign States and an alliance of regions that possessed national attributes. The North wishes to dictate to us on the slavery question, wrote Simms in 1852.[102] "But we are a people, *a nation*, with arms in our hands, and in sufficient

100 These are the phrases of W. P. Trent in his *Simms*, ch. 6.
101 *Op. cit.*, 249. As another evidence of the diversion of letters into political channels, note that in Wade's *Longstreet* the eighth chapter deals with "General Literary Effort in Georgia"; the twelfth with "Ecclesiastical Controversy Over Slavery."
102 Trent, *Simms*, 174; italics mine.

numbers to compel the respect of *other nations;* and we shall never submit the case to the judgment of *another people,* until they show themselves of superior virtue and intellect."

This schism in culture struck into the very substance of national life. Differences of thought, taste, and ideals gravely accentuated the misunderstandings caused by the basic economic and social differences; the differences between a free labor system and a slave labor system, between a semi-industrialized economy of high productiveness and an agrarian economy of low productiveness. An atmosphere was created in which emotions grew feverish; in which every episode became a crisis, every jar a shock.

The sands were running out. A few years more remained in which the national fabric might be reknit stronger than ever—if statesmanship were adequate to the task. But Congress had become an arena of constant sectional strife. Pierce had let the Presidency be drawn into the vortex of passion. And in the first weeks of 1857 brief warning items about the case of one Dred Scott began to appear in the press; a case on which the Supreme Court was soon to make a momentous pronouncement. Through the clash and clangor of the times men seemed to hear an ominous note of the future:

"So fierce you whirr and pound you drums—so shrill you bugles blow."

# *Index*

# INDEX

Accessory Transit Company, Central American commercial enterprise, friendly to William Walker, 407

Adams, Charles Francis, denounces Cushing's interference, 74; subscribes to stock in Massachusetts Emigrant Aid Society, 308

Adams, J. H., governor of South Carolina, proposes reopening of slave trade, 519

Adams, John Quincy, his views on Cuba, 347; advises acceptance of Smithson's gift, 521

Adams, Robert H., senator from Mississippi, supports Kansas-Nebraska Bill, 136, 144; complains of immigrant labor competition, 279

Affleck, Thomas, his influence in agrarian reform, 185; mentioned, 193

Agassiz, Jean Louis Rodolphe, scientist, on faculty of Lawrence Scientific School, leader in natural science, 522–523

Agriculture, development of, in America, 161 ff.

Aiken, William, representative in Congress from South Carolina and ex-governor, lavish receptions given by, 54–55; defeated for Speaker, 514

Alabama, legislature of, takes no stand on Kansas-Nebraska issue, 146; admitted as state of Union, rush of settlers to, 182

Alba, Duke of, insults Mrs. Soulé, fights duel with Pierre Soulé, 68

Albany *Argus*, supports Kansas-Nebraska Bill, 110

Albany Regency, coterie of New York Democratic leaders, mentioned, 15

Albany *Register*, advises on Whig policy, 321

Alexandria (Va.) *Gazette*, comments on Kansas-Nebraska Bill, 135

Allen, William, ex-senator from Ohio, opposes Kansas-Nebraska Bill, 147

Allston, Washington, art of, 527

Alton (Ill.) *Freie Blätter*, German language newspaper, champions murdered Lovejoy, 278

American Association for the Advancement of Science, founded, 520–521

*American Journal of Sciences and Arts*, established by Benjamin Silliman, 521

American party, see Know-Nothing party; meets in national convention, 399–400; absorbs Whig remnants, its bigotry, 466; split in, on sectional issues, 466–467; nominates Fillmore for president, Donelson for vice-president in 1856, 467; secedes from, to Republican party, 467–469; in campaign of 1856, 470 ff.; Know-Nothings in, 496; defeat of, in 1856 election, 512

American Protective Association, mentioned, 326

*American Railroad Journal*, quoted on growth of Chicago, 223

Andrew, John A., mentioned, 151

Andrews, Israel D., lobbyist for Canadian reciprocity treaty, 377

"Anti-Nebraska" movement, opposition to Missouri Compromise repeal contained in Douglas's Kansas-Nebraska Bill, 124 ff.; meetings held, 126–127; merchants, clergy, German-Americans join, 127–129

"Anti-Nebraska" party, see Republican party

A.P.A., see American Protective Association

"Appeal of the Independent Democrats in Congress to the People of the United States," document denouncing Kansas-Nebraska Bill, written by Chase, 111

Appleton, Nathan, unprogressive labor policy of, 299–300

Appleton, Tracy & Co., manufacturers of watches, 264

Appleton, William, remains loyal to Whig party, 491

Arkansas, rush of settlers to, 183

Armstrong, Robert J., becomes partner in Washington *Union*, 4; defeated for printer, 75

Arnold, Isaac N., Republican leader in Chicago, protests against Kansas outrages, 479

Art, appreciation and collecting of, in America, 526 ff.

Ashtabula (Ohio) *Journal*, criticizes conduct of Republican campaign in 1856, 504

Aspinwall, William H., aids in completing Ohio & Mississippi Railroad, 206